WESTERN CANON SERIES

The Western Canon's value is self-evident. Its status, however, has been under threat since the middle of the 20th century. Feminists, Marxists, intersectionalists, and others deny the Canon's existence by refusing to observe its traditional boundaries, throwing the borders open to invite all manner of second- and third-rate material. They intentionally misread the Canon, deconstructing it and looking for incoherence where men have only ever found genius.

Imperium Press' Western Canon series reclaims the Canon from the forces hostile to it. The series offers not only definitive versions of these works, but also supplementary material placing them at the centre of our aesthetic, intellectual, and spiritual life—where they belong.

THE EDDIC POET is traditionally held to be Sæmund the Wise, but the *Poetic Edda* is now thought to have been set to writing by a younger compatriot in the 13th century CE. Despite this late date, the material in the *Poetic Edda* has come down to us substantially intact from remarkably early times, with some of its structural and poetic features traceable perhaps as far back as 2,000 years earlier. it was discovered in 1643 in the *Codex Regius* by an Icelandic priest, and is, as Henry Adams Bellows puts it, "the original storehouse of Germanic mythology". Containing a wealth of mythological and legendary material, the *Poetic Edda* is one of the treasures of the ancient North, setting down the deeds of the gods and heroes of our Germanic past.

HENRY ADAMS BELLOWS was a polymath, founding member of the FCC, army colonel, poet, and academic. Born in Portland, Maine, in 1885, he was commissioned by the American-Scandinavian Foundation to produce a complete translation of the *Poetic Edda*. Published in 1923, it has remained a classic for serious Norse students ever since, given its extensive footnotes and heavy use of Germanic cognates.

POETIC EDDA

Translated into English alliterative verse by
HENRY ADAMS BELLOWS

Foreword by
THOMAS ROWSELL

Annotations by
TRISTAN POWERS

PERTH
IMPERIUM PRESS
2022

Published by Imperium Press

www.imperiumpress.org

First published by the American-Scandianvian Foundation, 1923

Map of Yggdrasil first published in
The Heroes of Asgard, 1907

Foreword © Thomas Rowsell, 2020
Annotations © Tristan Powers, 2022
The moral rights of the authors have been asserted
Used under license to Imperium Press

All rights are reserved. No part of this publication may be reproduced, stored in a retrieval system, or transmitted in any form or by any means, electronic, mechanical, photocopying, recording, or otherwise, without prior permission of Imperium Press. Enquiries concerning reproduction outside the scope of the above should be directed to Imperium Press.

First Edition

A catalogue record for this
book is available from the
National Library of Australia

ISBN 978-1-922602-63-3 Paperback
ISBN 978-1-922602-64-0 Hardcover
ISBN 978-1-922602-65-7 E-book

Imperium Press has no responsibility for the persistence or accuracy of URLs for external or third-party Internet websites referred to in this publication and does not guarantee that any content on such websites is, or will remain, accurate or appropriate.

CONTENTS

Foreword	xi
General Introduction	xix
Note on the Text	xxxi

Poetic Edda

Lays of the Gods

Voluspo	8
Hovamol	42
Vafthruthnismol	96
Grimnismol	120
Skirnismol	150
Harbarthsljoth	172
Hymiskvitha	196
Lokasenna	218
Thrymskvitha	252
Alvissmol	270
Baldrs draumar	288
Rigsthula	300
Hyndluljoth	322
Svipdagsmol	348

Lays of the Heroes

Volundarkvida	376
Helgakvitha Hjorvarthssonar	402
Helgakvitha Hundingsbana I	430
Helgakvitha Hundingsbana II	458
Fra Dautha Sinfjotla	490
Gripisspo	500

Reginsmol	524
Fafnismol	544
Sigrdrifumol	568
Brot af Sigurtharkvithu	594
Guthrunarkvitha I	608
Sigurtharkvitha en Skamma	624
Helreith Brynhildar	656
Drap Niflunga	666
Guthrunarkvitha en Forna	674
Guthrunarkvitha III	696
Oddrunargratr	706
Atlakvitha en Grönlenzka	724
Atlamol en Grönlenzku	748
Guthrunarhvot	790
Hamthesmol	806

APPENDICES

Genealogies	823
The Many Sons of Yngvi-Freyr	829
Bellows Introductions	835
Glossary of Obscure and Archaic Terms	881
Pronunciation Index	883

IMAGES

Die Nornen	ix
The Ride of the Valkyrs	xvii
Illustration of the World Tree Yggdrasil	xxxiii
The Giant with the Flaming Sword	7
Odin	41
A Mountain in Romsdal, Norway	95
The Wolves Pursuing Sol and Mani	119
Frey	149
Ægir	195
Loki and Sigyn	217
Thor and the Giants	251
The Elf-Dance	269
Jarl	299
The Swan-Maiden	375
A Foray	401
The Were-Wolves	429
A Viking Foray	457
The Death of Sinfjolti	489
The Rainbow Bridge	543
The Road to Valhalla	567
The Death of Siegfried	593

The Funeral Procession	607
Sigurd and Gunnar	623
Guthrun and Her Sons	695
Old Houses with Carved Posts	723
The Dises	747
The Three Norns	805
The Ride of the Valkyrs	821

Die Nornen
(Johannes Gehrts)

FOREWORD

Iceland can be seen as a literary refrigerator in which the most valuable works of the Germanic peoples have been preserved. Snorri Sturlusson's *Prose Edda*, a collection of old pagan myths written down by the Icelandic law-speaker and poet in the 13th century, over two centuries after the official conversion of Iceland from their traditional belief system to Christianity, was written as a sort of guide to help Christian poets. It was necessary for them to understand the complicated kennings and references to the old myths due to the conservative formulae of Icelandic poetry—which cannot be understood, let alone composed, without said knowledge. It was not written in order to preserve knowledge of the old "religion" as some may assume, but has been seen as a gift of providence in this regard, since without it so much of the Norse way of life would be even more of a mystery to us than it is today. This text was repeatedly copied out in new manuscripts over the 14th century and the most recent one is dated to around 1600. Admirers of the *Prose Edda* lamented the loss of the poetic works from which it was derived, until 1643 when the *Codex Regius* manuscript, also dated to the 13th century and likely penned by Snorri, was discovered in Iceland by Bishop Brynjólfur Sveinsson. It contained the *Eddic* poems about the Norse gods and myths that had been lost for so long and which have subsequently been published in many languages and editions usually under the title of the 'Elder Edda' or the 'Poetic Edda'. The particular translation of *Eddic* poetry you hold in your hands was written by the American businessman Henry Adams Bellows for The American-Scandinavian Foundation and was first published in 1923. Publications of the *Poetic Edda* often also include other poems which were not preserved in the *Codex Regius* manuscript, coming from sources such as the later *fornaldarsagas* "legendary sagas" and the tediously titled manuscript AM 748 I 4to. This translation includes, for example, *Baldrsdraumur*, which is absent in *Codex Regius* and can only be found in the *Arnamagnæan Codex*. *Eddic* poetry isn't defined by manuscript, but by subject; *Eddic* poems relate to the myths of gods and adjacent mythical beings, and are anonymously authored, while Skaldic poetry is about kings, battles and heroes and is usually attributed to a specific skald. The two types of poems overlap in style and themes, and many of each date to pagan times. Skaldic poetry is found in the Icelandic sagas but is really much older than they are, and not significantly distinct from that found in Beowulf, an Anglo-Saxon poem variously dated between the 7th and 9th centuries. The Anglo-Saxon 'scop' is almost exactly the same as the Norse 'skald' and in fact the figure of the courtly poet praising heroes and gods dates all the way back to the Proto-Indo-Europeans of Eastern Europe some 6,000 to 8,000 years ago.

The rediscovery of the *Codex Regius* manuscript in the 17th century caused a stir and it was sent to King Frederick III of Denmark, hence its name which means "Royal book". The following centuries saw increasing interest in Vikings and Norse culture and this interest was deeply interwoven with contemporary national identities in many countries from Iceland to Germany, and even America. Its significance must be understood in the context of the void it filled.

Since medieval times, Europeans north of the Alps suffered from a sense of inferiority brought about by the spread of Christianity. The official history of the world according to the church was supposed to be contained in the Bible and related Hebraic texts, and was also supplemented by surviving texts from Ancient Greece and Rome. The non-Semitic cultures that had surrounded the Roman Empire were preserved only through Roman accounts which are often disparaging and always biased. Coupling the Roman disdain for illiterate barbarians with the Hebrew hatred of polytheism, the emergent nations of Christianised Germanic (and Celtic and Slavic) Europe were naturally a bit embarrassed by their heritage. This inferiority complex is evident in Snorri's own attempts to explain the mythology in the *Prose Edda*; he adopts a popular Christian technique of euhemerism, claiming the gods were actually humans (more flattering than the alternative Christian explanation, which is that they were demons), and ascribes to them an Eastern origin, making use of clumsy folk etymology to equate the word Æsir with Asia. This gives the remote and comparatively irrelevant Icelandic nation a flattering origin in Troy, close to Constantinople, the centre of Christendom at the time. With this dubious genealogical claim, Snorri followed the medieval convention of other European scholars such as the Welshmen Nennius and Geoffrey of Monmouth, each of whom claimed the Ancient Britons descended from a group of errant Trojans led by Brutus after the Trojan war to the green and pleasant island. Not content with this fraudulent claim, they added an additional fabrication that connected Brutus to the Jews via a Hebrew named Javan. The French had been claiming a Trojan origin for their race since the seventh century, but this had been challenged in the ninth century by Freculf, Abbot of Fulda, who correctly traced the Franks, due to their Germanic language, to Scandinavia, the "womb of nations" whence ultimately sprang all Germanic peoples. It wasn't until the mid-16th century that intelligent Europeans finally abandoned the Trojan origin myth, while at the same time Ie Loyer's *The Ten Lost Tribes*, provided the first expression of the nonsense that Anglo-Saxon and other Germanic as well as Celtic cultures were direct descendants of the ancient Israelites. This pitiful attempt to appropriate the Christian prestige of the ancient Hebrews continued later in Scotland in a different form, which was based on the claim that when the Jews were expelled from England in 1290, many found refuge in Scotland, where they assimilated into the local population and infused their practices into the Scottish way of life. It is of course a fiction, but a powerful one which influenced Scottish nationalism, to the extent that 18th century opposition to unification with England was argued on the basis of England eating pork and black pudding and therefore not being Jewish enough! Not only did Scots abstain from pork for a period in the late 18th century but it was said that all the Jacobites after the battle of Culloden adopted the rite of circumcision—a peculiar custom surviving in the USA to this day.

All of this had been a way to cope with the painful accusation that the ancient Germanic and Celtic peoples had been naked barbarians with no culture of value. But it was an increasing antiquarian interest in ancient texts like the *Poetic Edda*, particularly in the 19th century, that redeemed our Northern ancestors. Historians, early archaeologists, folklorists and linguists finally managed to piece together what Christianity and the Roman Empire had destroyed—the rich heritage of the Northern peoples. The Nordic sagas and myths all helped to solidify a sense of Nordic-ness among the Scandinavian countries and the work of scholars like Jacob Grimm helped to connect this Norse heritage to a wider Germanic tradition including Germany, Holland and England. The National-Romantic movements were simultaneously a reaction against the increasingly urbanised and industrialised world of the 19th century while also a patriotic assertion of Teutonic identity.

Historically, nationalists of the 19th and 20th centuries have mainly been interested in the *Eddas* for non-religious reasons. It wasn't so much that they believed in the gods to whom these works referred, but rather that the gods became symbols through which narratives of national identity and belonging could be strengthened; inspiring collective pride in the nation, united in an ancient and distinctly Nordic (or more widely Germanic) identity. No doubt the poems and other ancient literature will continue to serve this purpose for centuries to come, but we must not forget the original religious context of these poems, if we are to appreciate them for what they really are. There was an attempt by some 19th and early 20th century theosophists to integrate Nordic religion into their bizarre new-age belief systems resulting in chimerical monstrosities like Irminism and Ariosophy—for which we can thank Madame Blavatsky, Guido von List and Karl Maria Wiligut. Many will claim that such eccentric beliefs were prevalent or even influential among the German National Socialists, but they certainly were not. The Nazis mainly used the religious imagery and mythology of the Norse peoples for a non-religious purpose, just as nationalists had for long before. There are also neo-pagans in our own times who seek to integrate an imagined Norse-world of feminist shield-maidens and tolerant transgender Vikings into their anachronistic and patently fake religion. Besides committed scholars of history, archaeology and comparative religion, the only people who seek to genuinely appreciate the spiritual worldview of the people for whom and by whom these poems were composed, are a small minority of devoted pagans, many of whom, perhaps not coincidentally, are politically of the right.

Those of us who look to these poems for insights into a true spiritual tradition need not always presume Christian contamination. Archaeological evidence has frequently proven the authenticity of the religion depicted in the *Eddas*. The description of Odin as a one-eyed god of the hanged certainly matches the one eyed hanged man carved in the 13th century Hegge stave church in Øystre Slidre municipality, Norway. While Odin's poetic associations with spears and ravens match the numerous archaeological examples of the "horned spear dancer/horned man" motif depicting a figure or face, sometimes with spears, who wears a headdress of two birds which appear to emanate from his head. This is an appropriate depiction of Odin's ravens since they are named Huginn ("thought") and Muninn ("memory").

Odin, from Proto-Germanic *Wōdanaz , was the patron of Germanic warrior bands. The Teutonic tradition of the *Männerbünde,* units of young raiders such as Vikings, derives from an Indo-European cultural tradition dating all the way back to the eneolithic Pontic-Caspian steppe. Odin himself has clear parallels in other Indo-European religions such as the Irish god *Lugh*, whose name likely derives from the same root which produced Gaulish *lougos* "raven", and who was associated with spears. Numerous scholars have also noted the parallels between the cult of Odin and the darker aspects of the *Shiva-Rudra* cult in India. Through Odin's strong-armed son, Thor, we see a clear reflection of the ancient Indo-European storm god *perk^{w}unos, who, like Thor, slew a vicious dragon with a bludgeoning weapon. The persistence of this prehistoric pagan myth was well explained by the Catholic author G. K. Chesterton when he wrote that fairy tales do not merely provoke fear of the dragon in the child, since this is an evil he can witness in the world himself; rather, they give him his first clear vision of the hero who can defeat the dragon. We are in need of such heroes now, more than ever, if we are to defeat the dragon of modernity.

THOMAS ROWSELL.

NOVEMBER 2020.

The Ride of the Valkyrs
(H. Hendrich)

GENERAL INTRODUCTION

There is scarcely any literary work of great importance which has been less readily available for the general reader, or even for the serious student of literature, than the *Poetic Edda*. Translations have been far from numerous, and only in Germany has the complete work of translation been done in the full light of recent scholarship. In English the only versions were long the conspicuously inadequate one made by Thorpe, and published about half a century ago, and the unsatisfactory prose translations in Vigfusson and Powell's *Corpus Poeticum Boreale*, reprinted in the Norrœna collection. An excellent translation of the poems dealing with the gods, in verse and with critical and explanatory notes, made by Olive Bray, was, however, published by the Viking Club of London in 1908. In French there exist only partial translations, chief among them being those made by Bergmann many years ago. Among the seven or eight German versions, those by the Brothers Grimm and by Karl Simrock, which had considerable historical importance because of their influence on nineteenth century German literature and art, and particularly on the work of Richard Wagner, have been largely superseded by Hugo Gering's admirable translation, published in 1892, and by the recent two volume rendering by Genzmer, with excellent notes by Andreas Heusler, 1914–1920. There are competent translations in both Norwegian and Swedish. The lack of any complete and adequately annotated English rendering in metrical form, based on a critical text, and profiting by the cumulative labors of such scholars as Mogk, Vigfusson, Finnur Jonsson, Grundtvig, Bugge, Gislason, Hildebrand, Lüning, Sweet, Niedner, Ettmüller, Müllenhoff, Edzardi, B. M. Olsen, Sievers, Sijmons, Detter, Heinzel, Falk, Neckel, Heusler, and Gering, has kept this extraordinary work practically out of the reach of those who have had neither time nor inclination to master the intricacies of the original Old Norse.

On the importance of the material contained in the *Poetic Edda* it is here needless to dwell at any length. We have inherited the Germanic traditions in our very speech, and the *Poetic Edda* is the original storehouse of Germanic mythology. It is, indeed, in many ways the greatest literary monument preserved to us out of the antiquity of the kindred races which we call Germanic. Moreover, it has a literary value altogether apart from its historical significance. The mythological poems include, in the *Voluspo*, one of the vastest conceptions of the creation and ultimate destruction of the world ever crystallized in literary form; in parts of the *Hovamol*, a collection of wise counsels that can bear comparison with most of the Biblical Book of Proverbs; in the *Lokasenna*, a comedy none the less full of vivid characterization because its humor is often broad; and in the *Thrymskvitha*, one of the finest ballads in the world. The hero poems give us, in its oldest and most vivid extant form, the story of Sigurth, Brynhild, and Atli, the Norse parallel to the German *Nibelungenlied*. The *Poetic Edda* is not only of great interest to the student of antiquity; it is a collection including some of the most remarkable poems which have been preserved to us from the period before the pen and the printing-press replaced the poet-singer and oral tradition. It is above all else the desire to make better known the dramatic force, the vivid and often tremendous imagery, and the superb conceptions embodied in these poems which has called forth the present translation.

WHAT IS THE POETIC EDDA?

Even if the poems of the so-called *Edda* were not so significant and intrinsically so valuable, the long series of scholarly struggles which have been going on over them for the better part of three centuries would in itself give them a peculiar interest. Their history is strangely mysterious. We do not know who composed them, or when or where they were composed; we are by no means sure who collected them or when he did so; finally, we are not absolutely certain as to what an "Edda" is, and the best guess at the meaning of the word renders its application to this collection of poems more or less misleading.

A brief review of the chief facts in the history of the *Poetic Edda* will explain why this uncertainty has persisted. Preserved in various manuscripts of the thirteenth and early fourteenth centuries is a prose work consisting of a very extensive collection of mythological stories, an explanation of the important figures and tropes of Norse poetic diction—the poetry of the Icelandic and Norwegian skalds was appallingly complex in this respect—and a treatise on metrics. This work, clearly a handbook for poets, was commonly known as the "Edda" of Snorri Sturluson, for at the head of the copy of it in the *Uppsalabok*, a manuscript written presumably some fifty or sixty years after Snorri's death, which was in 1241, we find: "This book is called Edda, which Snorri Sturluson composed." This work, well known as the *Prose Edda*, Snorri's *Edda* or the *Younger Edda*, has recently been made available to readers of English in the admirable translation by Arthur G. Brodeur, published by the American-Scandinavian Foundation in 1916.

Icelandic tradition, however, persisted in ascribing either this *Edda* or one resembling it to Snorri's much earlier compatriot, Sæmund the Wise (1056–1133). When, early in the seventeenth century, the learned Arngrimur Jonsson proved to everyone's satisfaction that Snorri and nobody else must have been responsible for the work in question, the next thing to determine was what, if anything, Sæmund had done of the same kind. The nature of Snorri's book gave a clue. In the mythological stories related a number of poems were quoted, and as these and other poems were to all appearances Snorri's chief sources of information, it was assumed that Sæmund must have written or compiled a verse *Edda*—whatever an "Edda" might be—on which Snorri's work was largely based.

So matters stood when, in 1643, Brynjolfur Sveinsson, Bishop of Skalholt, discovered a manuscript, clearly written as early as 1300, containing twenty-nine poems, complete or fragmentary, and some of them with the very lines and stanzas used by Snorri. Great was the joy of the scholars, for here, of course, must be at least a part of the long-sought Edda of Sæmund the Wise. Thus the good bishop promptly labeled his find, and as Sæmund's *Edda*, the *Elder Edda* or the *Poetic Edda* it has been known to this day.

This precious manuscript, now in the Royal Library in Copenhagen, and known as the *Codex Regius* (R2365), has been the basis for all published editions of the *Eddic* poems. A few poems of similar character found elsewhere have subsequently been added to the collection, until now most editions include, as in this translation, a total of thirty-four. A shorter manuscript now in the Arnamagnæan collection in Copenhagen (AM748), contains fragmentary or complete versions of six of the poems in the *Codex Regius*, and one other, *Baldrs Draumar*, not found in that collection. Four other poems (*Rigsthula*, *Hyndluljoth*, *Grougaldr* and *Fjolsvinnsmol*, the last two here combined under the title of *Svipdagsmol*), from various manuscripts, so closely resemble in subject-matter and style the poems in the *Codex Regius* that they have been included by most editors in the collection. Finally, Snorri's *Edda* contains one complete poem, the *Grottasongr*, which many editors have added to the poetic collection; it is, however, not included in this translation, as an admirable English version of it is available in Mr. Brodeur's rendering of Snorri's work.

From all this it is evident that the *Poetic Edda*, as we now know it, is no definite and plainly limited work, but rather a more or less haphazard collection of separate poems, dealing either with Norse mythology or with hero-cycles unrelated to the traditional history of greater Scandinavia or Iceland. How many other similar poems, now lost, may have existed in such collections as were current in Iceland in the later twelfth and thirteenth centuries we cannot know, though it is evident that some poems of this type are missing. We can say only that thirty-four poems have been preserved, twenty-nine of them in a single manuscript collection, which differ considerably in subject-matter and style from all the rest of extant Old Norse poetry, and these we group together as the *Poetic Edda*.

But what does the word "Edda" mean? Various guesses have been made. An early assumption was that the word somehow meant "Poetics," which fitted Snorri's treatise to a nicety, but which, in addition to the lack of philological evidence to support this interpretation, could by no stretch of scholarly subtlety be made appropriate to the collection of poems. Jacob Grimm ingeniously identified the word with the word "edda" used in one of the poems, the *Rigsthula*, where, rather conjecturally, it means "great-grandmother." The word exists in this sense nowhere else in Norse literature, and Grimm's suggestion of "Tales of a Grandmother," though at one time it found wide acceptance, was grotesquely inappropriate to either the prose or the verse work.

At last Eirikr Magnusson hit on what appears the likeliest solution of the puzzle: that "Edda" is simply the genitive form of the proper name "Oddi." Oddi was a settlement in the southwest of Iceland, certainly the home of Snorri Sturluson for many years, and, traditionally at least, also the home of Sæmund the Wise. That Snorri's work should have been called "The Book of Oddi" is altogether reasonable, for such a method of naming books was common—witness the "Book of the Flat Island" and other early manuscripts. That Sæmund may also have written or compiled another "Oddi-Book" is perfectly possible, and that tradition should have said he did so is entirely natural.

It is, however, an open question whether or not Sæmund had anything to do with making the collection, or any part of it, now known as the *Poetic Edda*, for of course the seventeenth-century assignment of the work to him is negligible. We can say only that he may have made some such compilation, for he was a diligent student of Icelandic tradition and history, and was famed throughout the North for his learning. But otherwise no trace of his works survives, and as he was educated in Paris, it is probable that he wrote rather in Latin than in the vernacular.

All that is reasonably certain is that by the middle or last of the twelfth century there existed in Iceland one or more written collections of Old

Norse mythological and heroic poems, that the *Codex Regius*, a copy made a hundred years or so later, represents at least a considerable part of one of these, and that the collection of thirty-four poems which we now know as the *Poetic* or *Elder Edda* is practically all that has come down to us of Old Norse poetry of this type. Anything more is largely guesswork, and both the name of the compiler and the meaning of the title "Edda" are conjectural.

THE ORIGIN OF THE EDDIC POEMS

There is even less agreement about the birthplace, authorship and date of the *Eddic* poems themselves than about the nature of the existing collection. Clearly the poems were the work of many different men, living in different periods; clearly, too, most of them existed in oral tradition for generations before they were first committed to writing. In general the mythological poems are strongly heathen in character, and as Christianity became generally accepted throughout Norway and Iceland early in the eleventh century, it is altogether likely that most of the poems dealing with the Norse gods antedate the year 1000. On the other hand, Hoffory, Finnur Jonsson and others have shown pretty conclusively from linguistic evidence that these poems cannot have assumed anything like their present form before the ninth century. As for the poems belonging to the hero cycles, one or two of them appear to be as late as 1100, but most of them clearly belong to the hundred years following 950. It is a fairly safe guess that the years between 900 and 1050 saw the majority of the *Eddic* poems put into shape, but it must be remembered that many changes took place during the long subsequent period of oral transmission, and also that many of the legends, both mythological and heroic, on which the poems were based, certainly existed in Norway, and quite possibly in verse form, long before the year 900. In considering such poems it is essential to forget the present mode of composition, whereby a poet at once fixes his thought and his style by means of writing, and to remember that for at least two centuries, and possibly much longer, the correct transmission of many of the *Eddic* poems depended solely on accurate hearing and retentive memory.

As to the origin of the legends on which the poems are based, the whole question, at least so far as the stories of the gods are concerned, is much too complex for discussion here. How much of the actual narrative material of the mythological lays is properly to be called Scandinavian is a matter for students of comparative mythology to guess at. The tales underlying the heroic lays are clearly of foreign origin: the Helgi story comes from Denmark, and that of Völund from Germany, as also the great mass of traditions centering around Sigurth (Siegfried), Brynhild, the sons of Gjuki, Atli (Attila), and Jormunrek (Ermanarich). The introductory notes to the various poems deal with the more important of these questions of origin.[1]

Of the men who composed these poems—"wrote" is obviously the wrong word—we know absolutely nothing, save that some of them must have been literary artists with a high degree of conscious skill. The *Eddic* poems are "folk-poetry"—whatever that may be—only in the sense that some of them strongly reflect racial feelings and beliefs; they are anything but crude or primitive in workmanship, and they show that not only the poets themselves, but also many of their hearers, must have made a careful study of the art of poetry.

Where the poems were composed is almost equally uncertain. The claims of Norway have been extensively advanced, but the great literary activity of Iceland after the settlement of the island by Norwegian emigrants late in the ninth century makes the theory of an Icelandic source for most of the poems plausible. The two Atli lays, with what authority we do not know, bear in the *Codex Regius* the superscription "the Greenland poem," and internal evidence indicates that this statement is correct. Certainly in one poem, the *Rigsthula*, and probably in several others, there are marks of Celtic influence. During a considerable part of the ninth and tenth centuries, Scandinavians were active in Ireland and in most of the western islands inhabited by branches of the Celtic race. Some scholars claim nearly all the *Eddic* poems for these "Western Isles," in sharp distinction from Iceland; their arguments are commented on in the introductory note to the *Rigsthula* [Appendix B]. However, as Iceland early came to be the true center of this Scandinavian island world, it may be said that most of the evidence concerning the birthplace of the *Eddic* poems in anything like their present form points in that direction, and certainly it was in Iceland that they were chiefly preserved.

THE EDDA AND OLD NORSE LITERATURE

Within the proper limits of an introduction it would be impossible to give any adequate summary of the history and literature with which the *Eddic* poems are indissolubly connected, but a mere mention of a few of the salient facts may be of some service to those who are unfamiliar with the subject. Old Norse literature covers approximately the period between

---

1 [ED. Bellows' original introductory notes have been moved to Appendix B on p. 835.]

850 and 1300. During the first part of that period occurred the great wanderings of the Scandinavian peoples, and particularly the Norwegians. A convenient date to remember is that of the sea-fight of Hafrsfjord, 872, when Harald the Fair-Haired broke the power of the independent Norwegian nobles, and made himself overlord of nearly all the country. Many of the defeated nobles fled overseas, where inviting refuges had been found for them by earlier wanderers and plunder-seeking raiders. This was the time of the inroads of the dreaded Northmen in France, and in 885 Hrolf Gangr (Rollo) laid siege to Paris itself. Many Norwegians went to Ireland, where their compatriots had already built Dublin, and where they remained in control of most of the island till Brian Boru shattered their power at the battle of Clontarf in 1014.

Of all the migrations, however, the most important were those to Iceland. Here grew up an active civilization, fostered by absolute independence and by remoteness from the wars which wracked Norway, yet kept from degenerating into provincialism by the roving life of the people, which brought them constantly in contact with the culture of the South. Christianity, introduced throughout the Norse world about the year 1000, brought with it the stability of learning, and the Icelanders became not only the makers but also the students and recorders of history.

The years between 875 and 1100 were the great spontaneous period of oral literature. Most of the military and political leaders were also poets, and they composed a mass of lyric poetry concerning the authorship of which we know a good deal, and much of which has been preserved. Narrative prose also flourished, for the Icelander had a passion for story-telling and story-hearing. After 1100 came the day of the writers. These sagamen collected the material that for generations had passed from mouth to mouth, and gave it permanent form in writing. The greatest bulk of what we now have of Old Norse literature—and the published part of it makes a formidable library—originated thus in the earlier period before the introduction of writing, and was put into final shape by the scholars, most of them Icelanders, of the hundred years following 1150.

After 1250 came a rapid and tragic decline. Iceland lost its independence, becoming a Norwegian province. Later Norway too fell under alien rule, a Swede ascending the Norwegian throne in 1320. Pestilence and famine laid waste the whole North; volcanic disturbances worked havoc in Iceland. Literature did not quite die, but it fell upon evil days; for the vigorous native narratives and heroic poems of the older period were substituted translations of French romances. The poets wrote mostly doggerel; the prose writers were devoid of national or racial inspiration.

The mass of literature thus collected and written down largely between 1150 and 1250 may be roughly divided into four groups. The greatest in volume is made up of the sagas: narratives mainly in prose, ranging all the way from authentic history of the Norwegian kings and the early Icelandic settlements to fairy-tales. Embodied in the sagas is found the material composing the second group: the skaldic poetry, a vast collection of songs of praise, triumph, love, lamentation, and so on, almost uniformly characterized by an appalling complexity of figurative language. There is no absolute line to be drawn between the poetry of the skalds and the poems of the *Edda*, which we may call the third group; but in addition to the remarkable artificiality of style which marks the skaldic poetry, and which is seldom found in the poems of the *Edda*, the skalds dealt almost exclusively with their own emotions, whereas the *Eddic* poems are quite impersonal. Finally, there is the fourth group, made up of didactic works, religious and legal treatises, and so on, studies which originated chiefly in the later period of learned activity.

PRESERVATION OF THE EDDIC POEMS

Most of the poems of the *Poetic Edda* have unquestionably reached us in rather bad shape. During the long period of oral transmission they suffered all sorts of interpolations, omissions and changes, and some of them, as they now stand, are a bewildering hodge-podge of little-related fragments. To some extent the diligent twelfth century compiler to whom we owe the *Codex Regius*—Sæmund or another—was himself doubtless responsible for the patchwork process, often supplemented by narrative prose notes of his own; but in the days before written records existed, it was easy to lose stanzas and longer passages from their context, and equally easy to interpolate them where they did not by any means belong. Some few of the poems, however, appear to be virtually complete and unified as we now have them.

Under such circumstances it is clear that the establishment of a satisfactory text is a matter of the utmost difficulty. As the basis for this translation I have used the text prepared by Karl Hildebrand (1876) and revised by Hugo Gering (1904). Textual emendation has, however, been so extensive in every edition of the *Edda*, and has depended so much on the theories of the editor, that I have also made extensive use of many other editions, notably those by Finnur Jonsson, Neckel, Sijmons, and Detter and Heinzel, together with numerous commentaries. The condition of the text in both the principal codices is such that no great reliance can be placed on the accuracy of the copyists, and frequently two editions will differ fundamentally as to their readings of a given passage or even of an entire poem. For this reason, and because guesswork necessarily plays so large a part in any edition or translation of the *Eddic* poems, I have risked overloading the pages with textual notes in order to show, as nearly as possible, the exact state of the original together with all the more significant emendations. I have done this particularly in the case of transpositions, many of which appear absolutely necessary, and in the indication of passages which appear to be interpolations.

THE VERSE-FORMS OF THE EDDIC POEMS

The many problems connected with the verse-forms found in the *Eddic* poems have been analyzed in great detail by Sievers, Neckel, and others. The three verse-forms exemplified in the poems need only a brief comment here, however, in order to make clear the method used in this translation. All of these forms group the lines normally in four-line stanzas. In the so-called Fornyrthislag ("Old Verse"), for convenience sometimes referred to in the notes as four-four measure, these lines have all the same structure, each line being sharply divided by a caesural pause into two half-lines, and each half-line having two accented syllables and two (sometimes three) unaccented ones. The two half-lines forming a complete line are bound together by the alliteration, or more properly initial-rhyme, of three (or two) of the accented syllables. The following is an example of the Fornyrthislag stanza, the accented syllables being in italics:

> *Vreiþr* vas *Vingþorr,*   es *vakna*þi
> ok *síns ham*ars   of *sakna*þi;
> *skegg* nam *hrista,*   *skǫr* nam *dý*ja,
> réþ *Jarþar burr*   *umb* at *þreifa*sk.

In the second form, the Ljothahattr ("Song Measure"), the first and third line of each stanza are as just described, but the second and fourth are shorter, have no caesural pause, have three accented syllables, and regularly two initial-rhymed accented syllables, for which reason I have occasionally referred to Ljothahattr as four-three measure. The following is an example:

> *Ar* skal *rísa*   sás *annars vill*
> *fé* eþa *fjǫr hafa;*
> *liggj*andi *ulfr*   sjaldan *láer* of *getr*
> né *sof*andi *maþr sigr.*

In the third and least commonly used form, the Malahattr ("Speech Measure"), a younger verse-form than either of the other two, each line of the four-line stanza is divided into two half-lines by a cæsural pause, each half-line having two accented syllables and three (sometimes four) unaccented ones; the initial rhyme is as in the Fornyrthislag. The following is an example:

> *Horsk* vas *hús*freyja,   *hug*þi at *mann*viti,
> *lag* heyrþi or*þ*a,   hvat á *laun máel*tu;
> *þá* vas *vant vit*ri,   *vil*di þeim *hjal*pa:
> skyldu of *sáe sig*la,   en *sjǫlf* né *kvams*kat.

A poem in Fornyrthislag is normally entitled -*kvitha* (*Thrymskvitha*, *Guthrunarkvitha*, etc.). which for convenience I have rendered as "lay," while a poem in Ljothahattr is entitled -*mol* (*Grimnismol, Skirnismol*, etc.), which I have rendered as "ballad." It is difficult to find any distinction other than metrical between the two terms, although it is clear that one originally existed.

Variations frequently appear in all three kinds of verse, and these I have attempted to indicate through the rhythm of the translation. In order to preserve so far as possible the effect of the *Eddic* verse, I have adhered, in making the English version, to certain of the fundamental rules governing the Norse line and stanza formations. The number of lines to each stanza conforms to what seems the best guess as to the original, and I have consistently retained the number of accented syllables. In translating from a highly inflected language into one depending largely on the use of subsidiary words, it has, however, been necessary to employ considerable freedom as to the number of unaccented syllables in a line. The initial-rhyme is generally confined to two accented syllables in each line. As in the original, all initial vowels are allowed to rhyme interchangeably, but I have disregarded the rule which lets certain groups of consonants rhyme only with themselves (e.g., I have allowed initial *s* or *st* to rhyme with *sk* or *sl*). In general, I have sought to preserve the effect of the original form whenever possible without an undue sacrifice of accuracy. For purposes of comparison, the translations of the three stanzas just given are here included:

Fornyrthislag:

> *Wild* was *Ving*thor   *when* he a*woke*,
> And *when* his *mighty*   *ham*mer he *missed*;
> He *shook* his *beard*,   his *hair* was *brist*ling,
> To *groping set* the *son* of *Jorth*.

Ljothahattr:

GENERAL INTRODUCTION xxix

He must *early* go *forth*   who *fain* the *blood*
Or the *goods* of an*oth*er would *get*;
The *wolf* that lies *id*le   shall *win* little *meat*.
Or the *sleep*ing *man* suc*cess*.

Malahattr:

Wise was the *woman*,   she *fain* would use *wis*dom,
She *saw* well what *meant*   all they *said* in *se*cret;
From her *heart* it was *hid*   how *help* she might *ren*der,
The *sea* they should *sail*,   while her*self* she should *go* not.

PROPER NAMES

The forms in which the proper names appear in this translation will undoubtedly perplex and annoy those who have become accustomed to one or another of the current methods of anglicising old Norse names. The nominative ending -r it has seemed best to omit after consonants, although it has been retained after vowels; in Baldr the final -r is a part of the stem and is of course retained. I have rendered the Norse þ by "th" throughout, instead of spasmodically by "d," as in many texts: e. ff., Othin instead of Odin.[2] For the Norse ø I have used its equivalent, "ö," e.g., Völund; for the ǫ I have used "o" and not "a," e.g., Voluspo, not Valuspa or Voluspa. To avoid confusion with accents the long vowel marks of the Icelandic are consistently omitted, as likewise in modern Icelandic proper names. The index at the end of the book indicates the pronunciation in each case.

CONCLUSION

That this translation may be of some value to those who can read the poems of the *Edda* in the original language I earnestly hope. Still more do I wish that it may lead a few who hitherto have given little thought to the Old Norse language and literature to master the tongue for themselves. But far above either of these I place the hope that this English version may give to some, who have known little of the ancient traditions of what is after all their own race, a clearer insight into the glories of that extraordinary past, and that I may through this medium be able to bring to others a small part of the delight which I myself have found in the poems of the

---

2 [This and other similar cases have been changed in this edition in order to conform with now-standard orthography.]

Poetic Edda.

NOTE ON THE TEXT

This edition of the *Poetic Edda* is substantially revised from the original Bellows translation of 1923. The Old Norse text used here is from Finnur Jónsson, the modern edition that best matches Bellows. Where Old Norse stanza numbers deviate from the English has been noted in the endnotes for each poem. Half lines in the Old Norse are indicated by a caesura to better allow facing text.

Bellows' translation has long been recognized as one of the most aesthetically faithful, rendering the *Poetic Edda* into readable English while staying as close as possible to the original meters of the poems. He often uses English words cognate to the original—his translation is the closest the reader will get to the original without learning Old Norse. However, the 1923 edition has also been recognized as somewhat flawed. In some cases, proper names were rendered in ways that will look alien to the modern reader (e.g., Odin = "Othin"). These have generally been changed to more familiar forms. Parentheses in the English have been removed unless they correspond to parentheses in the Old Norse edition. Acknowledgement must be made to Marion Ingham, whose work on Bellows' translation forms the basis of the prosodic emendations in this edition.

While Bellows had deep philological knowledge, more is known now than in his time about the conservative nature of Germanic poetry. 19th century scholarship often saw what is rough-hewn as evidence of interpolation and distortion, and this has caused him to systematically underestimate the age of these tales and to overestimate their corruption. As long as we bear this in mind, Bellows' introductions are still useful and have been collected in Appendix B, but the poems have been newly introduced by Tristan Powers who has provided an up-to-date view of Germanic scholarship. What's more, Powers' introductions to each poem are written from the perspective of a living practitioner of the Norse religion, giving us deeper insight into the worldview and religious spirit that animates them. Powers has updated Bellows' annotations where necessary, indicated in [square brackets]. He has also produced an appendix reconciling the inconsistencies between the Helgi and Sigurth lays, positing the heroic lineages as originating in Yngvi-Freyr rather than Odin, a point of difficulty usually glossed over by modern academics as a matter of scribal error or poetic interpolation.

This edition corrects the flaws and retains the strengths of the 1923 edition, and has brought it into line with current scholarship. The result is the definitive edition of the *Poetic Edda* both for serious students of Norse myth and legend, and for lovers of poetry.

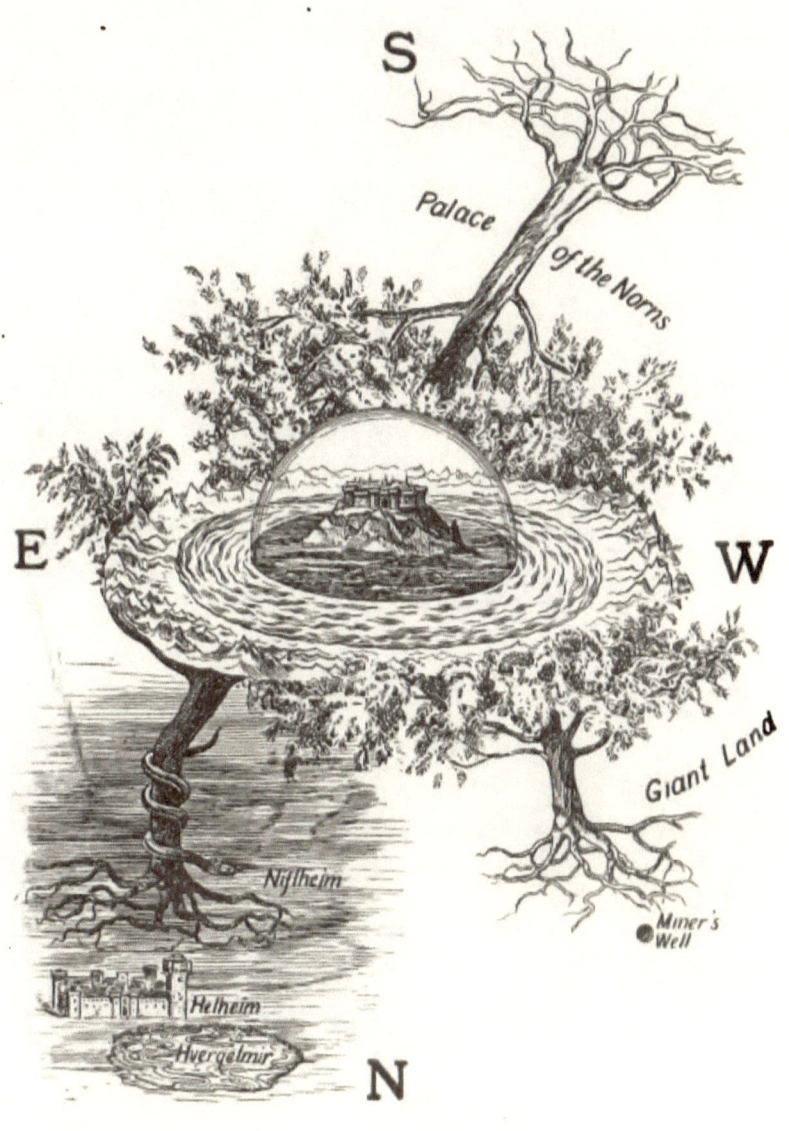

Illustration of the World Tree Yggdrasil,
its three roots, Asgard, and Bifrost

POETIC EDDA

VOLUSPO
THE SEERESS' PROPHECY

INTRODUCTION

The first poem—and often regarded as the most important—of the *Poetic Edda* is the *Völuspá* (or *Voluspo*, as Bellows transliterates it), primarily due to its length and subject matter. The *Voluspo* starts *in medias res* with the titular Volva (a witch, commonly understood here as a divinatory seeress) beginning to answer the God Odin and his questions concerning the history of the universe, the Gods, Jotnar and Man.

It quickly becomes obvious from her statements that the Volva is actually an enemy of the Gods, raised by the Jotnar and likely considering them close allies if not kin. She speaks with detachment about "The Sons of Bur" (i.e. the *Aesir*) as a separate tribe from herself, and it is commonly assumed that Odin, in his endless search for wisdom and knowledge, has utilized his skill with necromancy to raise the body of a dead and hostile witch to command it to speak to him of what she knows. The ending line of the poem, implying that she must sink back into the murky depths of the underworld, lends this interpretation credence.

Nevertheless, the Volva speaks from the beginning of her understanding of History, starting with the emptiness of Ginnungagap and the rule of the great primordial rime giant Ymir, whose story is given much more detail by Odin himself in the *Gylfaginning*. She speaks of the formation of the Earth, the Sun, and the Moon by the Gods and the construction of their home territories and political infrastructure. Of note here is that the Volva presents these primordial times as a golden age when the Gods lived in peace, able to sit at council among themselves and play at tables for fun with great golden gaming pieces, to build forges and temples and shrines. All of this changes when Three Giant Maidens from Jotunheim arrive and place upon them the bonds of fate, which ends this golden age and eventually dooms them to the events related by the Volva as predestined to occur. We know this fate today as *Ragnarök*—the fate of the Gods (sometimes confused as "Twilight of the Gods" through conflation with Wagner's *Götterdämmerung* and his *Ring Cycle*).

The *Voluspo* stands as one of the most detailed collections of metaphysical and cosmological information we possess about the history, chronology, and actions of the Gods. While many of the events spoken of are further detailed in other works, nothing within the *Eddas* comes close to the sheer scale of placing them all into their proper places. Not to be underestimated also is the poetic nature of the work and its early dating, assuring us that its contents were written by actual pagan practitioners before Christianization and lending further legitimacy to the successor works mentioning these events in further detail.

It cannot be said, however, that the *Voluspo* is totally free of interpolation, error, or addition. Fortunately, because of the strict metrical scale utilized we can easily determine where these issues are. It its generally considered that the 10–16th lines of *Voluspo*, collectively referred to as the *Dvergatal* (and immediately notable to the modern mind for being a roster of names made famous by one John Ronald Reuel Tolkien) are wholly or partially an interpolation not originally native to the poem due to the sudden break in the poetic meter and the seeming collection of scribal errors with repeated naming. Bellows' translation removes most of these scribal errors in an attempt to clean up the work, but a few instances can still be found.

Another stanza of considerable controversy relates to the 65th stanza and the lines:

> There comes on high, all power to hold,
> A mighty lord, all lands he rules.
> Rule he orders, and rights he fixes,
> Laws he ordains that ever shall live.

Traditionally giving rise to skepticism since it seemingly refers to the rise of a singular monolithic deity-ruler and the unmissable implications for Christianity, many academics consider this section to be of a later origin that has been added to an already completed work, probably for evangelical purposes. The first two lines of the work are included in this translation, but the latter two are not, as they are only found within the *Hauksbok* manuscript. It is worth noting that the original *Voluspo* contained in the *Codex Regius* completely lacks this stanza entirely. From both a matter of academic and historiological accuracy, and also of theological interpretation and rigor, we may rightfully ignore the stanza as an example of the infamous "Christian interpolations" that some have implied are hidden in all the poems.

Furthermore, a final bit of controversy is vested in the 66th stanza:

> From below the dragon dark comes forth,
> Nithhogg flying from Nithafjoll;
> The bodies of men on his wings he bears,
> The serpent bright: but now must I sink.

The general academic consensus holds that the first 3½ lines are seemingly out of place within the narrative, perhaps interpolated from their proper place around stanza 39 during the conflict of *Ragnarök* itself. It has been suggested that the lines might represent an attempt by the dragon Nithhoggr to arise once more at the final dawning of the golden age and then finally meeting his end, but if this is the case it would appear curiously glossed over, and we must favor the previous interpretation. Not all of the lines are out of place, however, and the last half line does remain as the traditional ending of the poem, with the grammatical gender of Old Norse making it obvious that the Volva herself sinks back to the underworld after her task for Odin is completed.

Of particular note is just how much of the information and names in the poem appear to be glossed over, as if they require no explanation to the listening audience, and this represents both a good example of its authenticity but also the deep knowledge and piety ascribed to the Norse peoples, such that the authorial *Skald* (Poet) believed his audience would surely understand the references and perhaps recall the various stories to which he is alluding. This tells us that the religious narrative our ancestors had access to was much broader and more complete than the one we see today, and had a homogenous agreement among peoples as to its composition.

The Giant with the Flaming Sword
(J. C. Dollman)

Hljóðs bið ek allar   helgar kindir,   1
meiri ok minni   mögu Heimdallar;
viltu, at ek, Valföðr!   vel framtelja
forn spjöll fíra,   þau er fremst um man.

Ek man jötna   ár um borna,   2
þá er forðum   mik fœdda höfðu;
níu man ek heima,   níu íviði,
mjötvið mœran   fyr mold neðan.

Ár var alda   þar er Ýmir bygði,   3
vara sandr né sær   né svalar unnir,
jörð fannsk æva   né upphiminn,
gap var ginnunga,   en gras hvergi.

Áðr Burs synir   bjöðum um ypðu,   4
þeir er Miðgarð   mœran skópu;
sól skein sunnan   á salar steina,
þá var grund gróin   grœnum lauki.

Sól varp sunnan,   sinni mána,   5
hendi inni hœgri   um himinjódyr;
sól þat ne vissi   hvar hon sali átti,
máni þat ne vissi   hvat hann megins átti,
stjörnur þat ne vissu   hvar þær staði áttu.

VOLUSPO

1. Hearing I ask from the holy races,
From Heimdall's sons, both high and low;
Thou wilt, Valfather, that well I relate
Old tales I remember of men long ago.

2. I remember yet the giants of yore,
Who gave me bread in the days gone by;
Nine worlds I knew, the nine in the tree
With mighty roots beneath the mold.

3. Of old was the age when Ymir lived;
Sea nor cool waves nor sand there were;
Earth had not been, nor heaven above,
But a yawning gap, and grass nowhere.

4. Then Bur's sons lifted the level land,
Mithgarth the mighty there they made;
The sun from the south warmed the stones of earth,
And green was the ground with growing leeks.

5. The sun, the sister of the moon, from the south
Her right hand cast over heaven's rim;
No knowledge she had where her home should be,
The moon knew not what might was his,
The stars knew not where their stations were.

Þá gengu regin öll   á rökstóla,   6
ginnheilug goð,   ok um þat gættusk;
nátt ok niðjum   nöfn um gáfu,
morgin hétu   ok miðjan dag,
undorn ok aptan,   árum at telja.

Hittusk æsir   á Iðavelli,   7
þeir er hörg ok hof   hátimbruðu,
afla lögðu,   auð smíðuðu,
tangir skópu   ok tól görðu.

Tefldu í túni,   teitir váru,   8
var þeim vettugis   vant ór gulli;
unz þrjár kvámu   þursa meyjar
ámátkar mjök   ór jötunheimum.

Þá gengu regin öll   á rökstóla,   9
ginnheilug goð,   ok um þat gættusk:
hverr skyldi dverga   drótt um skepja
ór brimi blóðgu   ok ór Bláins leggjum.

Þar var Móðsognir   mæztr um orðinn   10
dverga allra,   en Durinn annarr;
þeir mannlíkun   mörg um görðu
dvergar í jörðu,   sem Durinn sagði.

Nýi, Niði,   Norðri, Suðri,   11
Austri, Vestri,   Alþjófr, Dvalinn,
Nár ok Náinn,   Nípingr, Dáinn,
Bifurr, Bafurr,   Bömburr, Nori,
Ánn ok Ánarr,   Óinn, Mjöðvitnir.

Veggr ok Gandálfr,   Vindálfr, Þorinn,   12
Þrár ok Þráinn,   Þekkr, Litr ok Vitr,
Nýr ok Nýráðr,   nú hefi ek dverga,
Reginn ok Ráðsviðr,   rétt um talða.

Fili, Kili,   Fundinn, Nali,   13
Hepti, Vili,   Hanarr, Svíurr,
Billingr, Brúni,   Bildr ok Buri,
Frár, Hornbori,   Frægr ok Lóni,
Aurvangr, Jari,   Eikinskjaldi.

VOLUSPO

Then sought the gods their assembly-seats,   6
The holy ones, and council held;
Names then gave they to noon and twilight,
Morning they named, and the waning moon,
Night and evening, the years to number.

At Ithavoll met the mighty gods,   7
Shrines and temples they timbered high;
Forges they set, and they smithied ore,
Tongs they wrought, and tools they fashioned.

In their dwellings at peace they played at tables,   8
Of gold no lack did the gods then know—
Till thither came up giant-maids three,
Huge of might, out of Jotunheim.

Then sought the gods their assembly-seats,   9
The holy ones, and council held,
To find who should raise the race of dwarfs
Out of Brimir's blood and the legs of Blain.

There was Motsognir the mightiest made   10
Of all the dwarfs, and Durin next;
Many a likeness of men they made,
The dwarfs in the earth, as Durin said.

Nyi and Nithi, Northri and Suthri,   11
Austri and Vestri, Althjof, Dvalin,
Nar and Nain, Niping, Dain,
Bifur, Bofur, Bombur, Nori,
An and Onar, Ai, Mjothvitnir.

Vigg and Gandalf, Vindalf, Thrain,   12
Thekk and Thorin, Thror, Vit and Lit,
Nyr and Nyrath—now have I told—
Regin and Rathsvith—the list aright.

Fili, Kili, Fundin, Nali,   13
Heptifili, Hannar, Sviur,
Frar, Hornbori, Fræg and Loni,
Aurvang, Jari, Eikinskjaldi.

Mál er dverga   í Dvalins liði   14
ljóna kindum   til Lofars telja,
þeir er sóttu   frá salar steini
Aurvanga sjöt   til Jöruvalla.

Þar var Draupnir   ok Dólgþrasir,   15
Hár, Haugspori,   Hlévangr, Glóinn,
Dori, Ori,   Dúfr, Andvari,
Skirfir, Virfir,   Skafiðr, Ai.

Álfr ok Yngvi,   Eikinskjaldi,   16
Fjalarr ok Frosti,   Finnr ok Ginnarr;
þat man æ uppi,   meðan öld lifir,
langniðja tal   Lofars hafat.

Unz þrír kvámu   ór því liði   17
öflgir ok ástkir   æsir at húsi,
fundu á landi   lítt megandi
Ask ok Emblu   örlöglausa.

Önd þau ne áttu,   óð þau ne höfðu,   18
lá né læti   né litu góða;
önd gaf Óðinn,   óð gaf Hœnir,
lá gaf Lóðurr   ok litu góða.

Ask veit ek standa,   heitir Yggdrasill   19
hár baðmr, ausinn   hvíta auri;
þaðan koma döggvar   þærs í dala falla;
stendr æ yfir grœnn   Urðar brunni.

Þaðan koma meyjar   margs vitandi   20
þrjár, ór þeim sal   er und þolli stendr;
Urð hétu eina,   aðra Verðandi,
skáru á skíði,   Skuld ina þriðju;
þær lög lögðu,   þær líf kuru
alda börnum,   örlög seggja.

Þat man hon fólkvíg   fyrst í heimi,   21
er Gullveig   geirum studdu
ok í höll Hárs   hana brendu;
þrysvar brendu   þrysvar borna,
opt, ósjaldan,   þó hon enn lifir.

The race of the dwarfs in Dvalin's throng 14
Down to Lofar the list must I tell;
The rocks they left, and through wet lands
They sought a home in the fields of sand.

There were Draupnir and Dolgthrasir, 15
Hor, Haugspori, Hlevang, Gloin,
Dori, Ori, Duf, Andvari,
Skirfir, Virfir, Skafith, Ai.

Alf and Yngvi, Eikinskjaldi, 16
Fjalar and Frosti, Fith and Ginnar;
So for all time shall the tale be known,
The list of all the forbears of Lofar.

Then from the throng did three come forth, 17
From the home of the gods, the mighty and gracious;
Two without fate on the land they found,
Ask and Embla, empty of might.

Soul they had not, sense they had not, 18
Heat nor motion, nor goodly hue;
Soul gave Odin, sense gave Hönir,
Heat gave Lothur and goodly hue.

An ash I know, Yggdrasil its name, 19
With water white is the great tree wet;
Thence come the dews that fall in the dales,
Green by Urth's well does it ever grow.

Thence come the maidens mighty in wisdom, 20
Three from the dwelling down 'neath the tree;
Urth is one named, Verthandi the next—
On the wood they scored—and Skuld the third.
Laws they made there, and life allotted
To the sons of men, and set their fates.

The war I remember, the first in the world, 21
When the gods with spears had smitten Gollveig,
And in the hall of Hor had burned her—
Three times burned, and three times born,
Oft and again, yet ever she lives.

Heiði hana hétu,   hvars til húsa kom, 22
völu velspá,   vitti hon ganda,
seið hon hvars hon kunni,   seið hon hugleikin,
æ var hon angan   illrar brúðar.

Þá gengu regin öll   á rökstóla, 23
ginnheilug goð,   ok um þat gættusk:
hvárt skyldu æsir   afráð gjalda
eða skyldu goðin öll   gildi eiga.

Fleygði Óðinn   ok í fólk um skaut, 24
þat var enn fólkvíg   fyrst í heimi;
brotinn var borðveggr   borgar ása,
knáttu vanir vígská   völlu sporna.

Þá gengu regin öll   á rökstóla, 25
ginnheilug goð,   ok um þat gættusk:
hverr hefði lopt allt   lævi blandit
eða ætt jötuns   Óðs mey gefna.

Þórr einn þar vá   þrunginn móði, 26
hann sjaldan sitr   er hann slíkt um fregn;
á gengust eiðar,   orð ok sœri,
mál öll meginlig   er á meðal fóru.

Veit hon Heimdallar   hljóð um fólgit 27
undir heiðvönum   helgum baðmi;
á sér hon ausask   aurgum forsi
af veði Valföðrs.   Vituð ér enn eða hvat?

Ein sat hon úti,   þá er inn aldni kom 28
yggjungr ása   ok í augu leit.
Hvers fregnið mik?   Hví freistið mín?
Allt veit ek, Óðinn,   hvar þú auga falt,
í inum mæra   Mímisbrunni.
Drekkr mjöð Mímir   morgun hverjan
af veði Valföðrs.   Vituð ér enn—eða hvat?

Valði henni Herföðr   hringa ok men, 29
fekk spjöll spaklig   ok spá ganda,
sá hon vítt ok of vítt   of veröld hverja.

Heith they named her who sought their home,   22
The wide-seeing witch, in magic wise;
Minds she bewitched that were moved by her magic,
To evil women a joy she was.

On the host his spear did Odin hurl,   23
Then in the world did war first come;
The wall that girdled the gods was broken,
And the field by the warlike Wanes was trodden.

Then sought the gods their assembly-seats,   24
The holy ones, and council held,
Whether the gods should tribute give,
Or to all alike should worship belong.

Then sought the gods their assembly-seats,   25
The holy ones, and council held,
To find who with venom the air had filled,
Or had given Oth's bride to the giants' brood.

In swelling rage then rose up Thor—   26
Seldom he sits when he such things hears—
And the oaths were broken, the words and bonds,
The mighty pledges between them made.

I know of the horn of Heimdall, hidden   27
Under the high-reaching holy tree;
On it there pours from Valfather's pledge
A mighty stream: would you know yet more?

Alone I sat when the Old One sought me,   28
The terror of gods, and gazed in mine eyes:
"What hast thou to ask? why comest thou hither?
Odin, I know where thine eye is hidden."
I know where Odin's eye is hidden,
Deep in the wide-famed well of Mimir;
Mead from the pledge of Odin each morn
Does Mimir drink: would you know yet more?

Necklaces had I and rings from Heerfather,   29
Wise was my speech and my magic wisdom;
[...]
Widely I saw over all the worlds.

Sá hon valkyrjur   vítt of komnar,   30
görvar at ríða   til Goðþjóðar;
Skuld helt skildi,   en Skögul önnur,
Gunnr, Hildr, Göndul   ok Geirskögul.
Nú eru talðar   nönnur Herjans,
görvar at ríða   grund valkyrjur.

Ek sá Baldri,   blóðgum tívur,   31
Óðins barni,   örlög folgin;
stóð of vaxinn   völlum hæri
mjór ok mjök fagr   mistilteinn.

Varð af þeim meiði,   er mær sýndisk,   32
harmflaug hættlig,   Höðr nam skjóta;
Baldrs bróðir   var of borinn snemma,
sá nam Óðins sonr   einnættr vega.

Þó hann æva hendr   né höfuð kembði,   33
áðr á bál of bar   Baldrs andskota;
en Frigg of grét   í Fensölum
vá Valhallar.   Vituð ér enn—eða hvat?

Þá kná Váli   vígbönd snúa,   34
heldr váru harðgör   höft ór þörmum.

Haft sá hon liggja   und Hveralundi,   35
lægjarns líki   Loka áþekkjan;
þar sitr Sigyn   þeygi of sínum
ver vel glýjuð.   Vituð ér enn—eða hvat?

Á fellur austan   um eitrdala   36
söxum ok sverðum,   Slíðr heitir sú.

Stóð fyr norðan   á Niðavöllum   37
salr ór gulli   Sindra ættar;
en annarr stóð   á Ókólni
bjórsalr jötuns,   en sá Brimir heitir.

Sal sá hon standa   sólu fjarri   38
Náströndu á,   norðr horfa dyrr;
falla eitrdropar   inn um ljóra,
sá er undinn salr   orma hryggjum.

VOLUSPO 17

On all sides saw I Valkyries assemble, 30
Ready to ride to the ranks of the gods;
Skuld bore the shield, and Skogul rode next,
Guth, Hild, Gondul, and Geirskogul.
Of Herjan's maidens the list have ye heard,
Valkyries ready to ride o'er the earth.

I saw for Baldr, the bleeding god, 31
The son of Odin, his destiny set:
Famous and fair in the lofty fields,
Full grown in strength the mistletoe stood.

From the branch which seemed so slender and fair 32
Came a harmful shaft that Hoth should hurl;
But the brother of Baldr was born ere long,
And one night old fought Odin's son.

His hands he washed not, his hair he combed not, 33
Till he bore to the bale-blaze Baldr's foe.
But in Fensalir did Frigg weep sore
For Valhall's need: would you know yet more?

Then did Váli slaughter bonds twist: 34
Made farily grim were those fetters of guts.

One did I see in the wet woods bound, 35
A lover of ill, and to Loki like;
By his side does Sigyn sit, nor is glad
To see her mate: would you know yet more?

From the east there pours through poisoned vales 36
With swords and daggers the river Slith.
[...]
[...]

Northward a hall in Nithavellir 37
Of gold there rose for Sindri's race;
And in Okolnir another stood,
Where the giant Brimir his beer-hall had.

A hall I saw, far from the sun, 38
On Nastrond it stands, and the doors face north,
Venom drops through the smoke-vent down,
For around the walls do serpents wind.

Sá hon þar vaða   þunga strauma 39
menn meinsvara   ok morðvarga
ok þann er annars glepr   eyrarúnu;
þar saug Niðhöggr   nái framgengna,
sleit vargr vera.   Vituð ér enn—eða hvat?

Austr sat in aldna   í Járnviði 40
ok fæddi þar   Fenris kindir;
verðr af þeim öllum   einna nokkurr
tungls tjúgari   í trölls hami.

Fyllisk fjörvi   feigra manna, 41
rýðr ragna sjöt   rauðum dreyra;
svört verða sólskin   um sumur eftir,
veðr öll válynd.   Vituð ér enn—eða hvat?

Sat þar á haugi   ok sló hörpu 42
gýgjar hirðir,   glaðr Eggþér;
gól of hánum   í galgviði
fagrrauðr hani,   sá er Fjalarr heitir.

Gól of ásum   Gullinkambi, 43
sá vekr hölða   at Herjaföðrs;
en annarr gelr   fyr jörð neðan
sótrauðr hani   at sölum Heljar.

Geyr nú Garmr mjök   fyr Gnipahelli, 44
festr mun slitna,   en freki renna;
fjölð veit ek fræða,   fram sé ek lengra
um ragna rök   römm sigtíva.

Bræðr munu berjask   ok at bönum verðask, 45
munu systrungar   sifjum spilla;
hart er í heimi,   hórdómr mikill,
skeggöld, skalmöld,   skildir ro klofnir,
vindöld, vargöld,   áðr veröld steypisk;
mun engi maðr   öðrum þyrma.

Leika Míms synir,   en mjötuðr kyndisk 46
at inu galla   Gjallarhorni;
hátt blæss Heimdallr,   horn er á lofti,
mælir Óðinn   við Míms höfuð.

I saw there wading through rivers wild 39
Treacherous men and murderers too,
And workers of ill with the wives of men;
There Nithhogg sucked the blood of the slain,
And the wolf tore men; would you know yet more?

The giantess old in Ironwood sat, 40
In the east, and bore the brood of Fenrir;
Among these one in monster's guise
Was soon to steal the sun from the sky.

There feeds he full on the flesh of the dead, 41
And the home of the gods he reddens with gore;
Dark grows the sun, and in summer soon
Come mighty storms: would you know yet more?

On a hill there sat, and smote on his harp, 42
Eggther the joyous, the giants' warder;
Above him the cock in the bird-wood crowed,
Fair and red did Fjalar stand.

Then to the gods crowed Gollinkambi, 43
He wakes the heroes in Odin's hall;
And beneath the earth does another crow,
The rust-red bird at the bars of Hel.

Now Garm howls loud before Gnipahellir, 44
The fetters will burst, and the wolf run free;
Much do I know, and more can see
Of the fate of the gods, the mighty in fight.

Brothers shall fight and fell each other, 45
And sisters' sons shall kinship stain;
Hard is it on earth, with mighty whoredom;
Axe-time, sword-time, shields are sundered,
Wind-time, wolf-time, ere the world falls;
Nor ever shall men each other spare.

Fast move the sons of Mim, and fate 46
Is heard in the note of the Gjallarhorn;
Loud blows Heimdall, the horn is aloft,
In fear quake all who on Hel-roads are.

Skelfr Yggdrasils   askr standandi,   47
ymr it aldna tré,   en jötunn losnar;
hræðask allir   á helvegum
áðr Surtar þann   sefi of gleypir.

Hvat er með ásum?   Hvat er með alfum?   48
Gnýr allr Jötunheimr,   æsir ro á þingi,
stynja dvergar   fyr steindurum,
veggbergs vísir.   Vituð ér enn—eða hvat?

Geyr nú Garmr mjök   fyr Gnipahelli,   49
festr mun slitna   en freki renna;
fjölð veit ek fræða,   fram sé ek lengra
um ragna rök   römm sigtíva.

Hrymr ekr austan,   hefisk lind fyrir,   50
snýsk Jörmungandr   í jötunmóði;
ormr knýr unnir,   en ari hlakkar,
slítr nái niðfölr,   Naglfar losnar.

Kjóll ferr austan,   koma munu Múspells   51
of lög lýðir,   en Loki stýrir;
fara fíflmegir   með freka allir,
þeim er bróðir   Býleists í för.

Surtr ferr sunnan   með sviga lævi,   52
skínn af sverði   sól valtíva;
grjótbjörg gnata,   en gífr rata,
troða halir helveg,   en himinn klofnar.

Þá kemr Hlínar   harmr annarr fram,   53
er Óðinn ferr   við ulf vega,
en bani Belja   bjartr at Surti;
þá mun Friggjar   falla angan.

Geyr nú Garmr mjök   fyr Gnipahelli,   54
festr mun slitna,   en freki renna;
fjölð veit ek fræða,   fram sé ek lengra
um ragna rök   römm sigtíva

Þá kemr inn mikli   mögr Sigföður,   55
Víðarr, vega   at valdýri.
Lætr hann megi Hveðrungs   mundum standa
hjör til hjarta,   þá er hefnt föður.

Yggdrasil shakes, and shiver on high 47
The ancient limbs, and the giant is loose;
To the head of Mim does Odin give heed,
But the kinsman of Surt shall slay him soon.

How fare the gods? how fare the elves? 48
All Jotunheim groans, the gods are at council;
Loud roar the dwarfs by the doors of stone,
The masters of the rocks: would you know yet more?

Now Garm howls loud before Gnipahellir, 49
The fetters will burst, and the wolf run free
Much do I know, and more can see
Of the fate of the gods, the mighty in fight.

From the east comes Hrym with shield held high; 50
In giant-wrath does the serpent writhe;
O'er the waves he twists, and the tawny eagle
Gnaws corpses screaming; Naglfar is loose.

O'er the sea from the east there sails a ship 51
With the people of Muspell, at the helm stands Loki;
After the wolf do wild men follow,
And with them the brother of Byleist goes.

Surt fares from the south with the scourge of branches, 52
The sun of the battle-gods shone from his sword;
The crags are sundered, the giant-women sink,
The dead throng Hel-way, and heaven is cloven.

Now comes to Hlin yet another hurt, 53
When Odin fares to fight with the wolf,
And Beli's fair slayer seeks out Surt,
For there must fall the joy of Frigg.

Then comes Sigfather's mighty son, 54
Vithar, to fight with the foaming wolf;
In the giant's son does he thrust his sword
Full to the heart: his father is avenged.

Hither there comes the son of Hlothyn, 55
The bright snake gapes to heaven above;
[...]
Against the serpent goes Odin's son.

Þá kemr inn mæri   mögr Hlóðynjar,   56
gengr Óðins sonr   við orm vega,
drepr af móði   Miðgarðs véurr,
munu halir allir   heimstöð ryðja;
gengr fet níu   Fjörgynjar burr
neppr frá naðri   níðs ókvíðnum.

Sól tér sortna,   sígr fold í mar,   57
hverfa af himni   heiðar stjörnur;
geisar eimi   ok aldrnari,
leikr hár hiti   við himin sjalfan.

Geyr nú Garmr mjök   fyr Gnipahelli,   58
festr mun slitna   en freki renna;
fjölð veit ek fræða   fram sé ek lengra
um ragna rök   römm sigtíva

Sér hon upp koma   öðru sinni   59
jörð ór ægi   iðjagræna;
falla forsar,   flýgr örn yfir,
sá er á fjalli   fiska veiðir.

Finnask æsir   á Iðavelli   60
ok um moldþinur   máttkan dæma
ok minnask þar   á megindóma
ok á Fimbultýs   fornar rúnir.

Þar munu eftir   undrsamligar   61
gullnar töflur   í grasi finnask,
þærs í árdaga   áttar höfðu.

Munu ósánir   akrar vaxa,   62
böls mun alls batna,   Baldr mun koma;
búa þeir Höðr ok Baldr   Hrofts sigtoftir,
vé valtíva.   Vituð ér enn—eða hvat?

Þá kná Hænir   hlautvið kjósa   63
ok burir byggja   bræðra tveggja
vindheim víðan.   Vituð ér enn—eða hvat?

Sal sér hon standa   sólu fegra,   64
gulli þakðan   á Gimléi;
þar skulu dyggvar   dróttir byggja
ok um aldrdaga   yndis njóta.

In anger smites the warder of earth— 56
Forth from their homes must all men flee;
Nine paces fares the son of Fjorgyn,
And, slain by the serpent, fearless he sinks.

The sun turns black, earth sinks in the sea, 57
The hot stars down from heaven are whirled;
Fierce grows the steam and the life-feeding flame,
Till fire leaps high about heaven itself.

Now Garm howls loud before Gnipahellir, 58
The fetters will burst, and the wolf run free;
Much do I know, and more can see
Of the fate of the gods, the mighty in fight.

Now do I see the earth anew 59
Rise all green from the waves again;
The cataracts fall, and the eagle flies,
And fish he catches beneath the cliffs.

The gods in Ithavoll meet together, 60
Of the terrible girdler of earth they talk,
And the mighty past they call to mind,
And the ancient runes of the Ruler of Gods.

In wondrous beauty once again 61
Shall the golden tables stand mid the grass,
Which the gods had owned in the days of old,
[...]

Then fields unsowed bear ripened fruit, 62
All ills grow better, and Baldr comes back;
Baldr and Hoth dwell in Hropt's battle-hall,
And the mighty gods: would you know yet more?

Then Hönir wins the prophetic wand, 63
[...]
And the sons of the brothers of Tveggi abide
In Vindheim now: would you know yet more?

More fair than the sun, a hall I see, 64
Roofed with gold, on Gimle it stands;
There shall the righteous rulers dwell,
And happiness ever there shall they have.

Þá kemr inn ríki   at regindómi   65
öflugr ofan,   sá er öllu ræðr.

Þar kemr inn dimmi   dreki fljúgandi,   66
naðr fránn, neðan   frá Niðafjöllum;
berr sér í fjöðrum,   flýgr völl yfir,
Niðhöggr nái.   Nú mun hon sökkvask.

There comes on high, all power to hold,   65
A mighty lord, all lands he rules.
[...]
[...]

From below the dragon dark comes forth,   66
Nithhogg flying from Nithafjoll;
The bodies of men on his wings he bears,
The serpent bright: but now must I sink.

ENDNOTES

1. A few editors, following Bugge, in an effort to clarify the poem, place stanzas 22, 28 and 30 before stanzas 1–20, but the arrangement in both manuscripts, followed here, seems logical. In stanza 1 the Volva, or wise-woman, called upon by Odin, answers him and demands a hearing. Evidently she belongs to the race of the giants (cf. stanza 2), and thus speaks to Odin unwillingly, being compelled to do so by his magic power. *Holy*: omitted in *Regius*; the phrase "holy races" probably means little more than mankind in general. *Heimdall*: the watchman of the gods; cf. stanza 46 and note. Why mankind should be referred to as Heimdall's sons is uncertain, and the phrase has caused much perplexity. Heimdall seems to have had various attributes, and in the *Rigsthula*, wherein a certain Rig appears as the ancestor of the three great classes of men, a fourteenth century annotator identifies Rig with Heimdall, on what authority we do not know, for the Rig of the poem seems much more like Odin (cf. *Rigsthula*, introductory prose and note). *Valfather* ("Father of the Slain"): Odin, chief of the gods, so called because the slain warriors were brought to him at Valhall ("Hall of the Slain") by the Valkyries ("Choosers of the Slain").

2. *Nine worlds*: the worlds of the gods (Asgarth), of the Wanes (Vanaheim, cf. stanza 21 and note), of the elves (Alfheim), of men (Mithgarth), of the giants (Jotunheim), of fire (Muspellsheim, cf. stanza 47 and note), of the dark elves (Svartalfaheim), of the dead (Niflheim), and presumably of the dwarfs (perhaps Nithavellir, cf. stanza 37 and note, but the ninth world is uncertain). *The tree*: the world-ash Yggdrasil, symbolizing the universe; cf. *Grimnismol*, 29–35 and notes, wherein Yggdrasil is described at length.

3. *Ymir*: the giant out of whose body the gods made the world; cf. *Vafthruthnismol*, 21. In this stanza as quoted in Snorri's *Edda* the first line runs: "Of old was the age ere aught there was." *Yawning gap*: this phrase, "Ginnunga-gap," is sometimes used as a proper name.

4. *Bur's sons*: Odin, Vili, and Ve. Of Bur we know only that his wife was Bestla, daughter of Bolthorn; cf. *Hovamol*, 141. Vili and Ve are mentioned by name in the *Eddic* poems only in *Lokasenna*, 26. *Mithgarth* ("Middle Dwelling"): the world of men. *Leeks*: the leek was often used as the symbol of fine growth (cf. *Guthrunarkvitha* I, 17), and it was also supposed to have magic power (cf. *Sigrdrifumol*, 7).

5. Various editors have regarded this stanza as interpolated; Hoffory thinks it describes the northern summer night in which the sun does not set. Lines 3–5 are quoted by Snorri. In the manuscripts line 4 follows line 5. Regarding the sun and moon as daughter and son of Mundilferi, cf. *Vafthruthnismol*, 23 and note, and *Grimnismol*, 37 and note.

6. Possibly an interpolation, but there seems no strong reason for assuming this. Lines 1–2 are identical with lines 1–2 of stanza 9, and line 2 may have been inserted here from that later stanza.

7. *Ithavoll* ("Field of Deeds"?): mentioned only here and in stanza 60 as the meeting-place of the gods; it appears in no other connection.

8. *Tables*: [A reference to the Tafl family of games such as Hnefatafl, the game is a 1v1 strategic boardgame composted of figures representing soldiers in an army and requires a king to escape without being captured, and which was during the predominate board game during the viking age.] The exact nature of this game, and whether it more closely resembled chess or checkers, has been made the subject of a 400-page treatise, Willard Fiske's "Chess in Iceland." *Giant-maids*: perhaps the three great Norns, corresponding to the three fates; cf. stanza 20 and note. Possibly, however, something has been lost after this stanza, and the missing passage, replaced by the catalogue of the dwarfs (stanzas 9–16), may have explained the "giant-maids" otherwise than as Norns. In *Vafthruthnismol*, 49, the Norns (this time "three throngs" instead of simply "three") are spoken of as giant-maidens; *Fafnismol*, 13, indicates the existence of many lesser Norns, belonging to various races. *Jotunheim*: the world of the giants.

9. Here apparently begins the interpolated catalogue of the dwarfs, running through stanza 16; possibly, however, the interpolated section does not begin before stanza 11. Snorri quotes practically the entire section, the names appearing in a somewhat changed order. *Brimir* and *Blain*:

nothing is known of these two giants, and it has been suggested that both are names for Ymir (cf. stanza 3). Brimir, however, appears in stanza 37 in connection with the home of the dwarfs. Some editors treat the words as common rather than proper nouns, Brimir meaning 'the bloody moisture" and Blain being of uncertain significance.

10. Very few of the dwarfs named in this and the following stanzas are mentioned elsewhere. It is not clear why Durin should have been singled out as authority for the list. The occasional repetitions suggest that not all the stanzas of the catalogue came from the same source. Most of the names presumably had some definite significance, as Northri, Suthri, Austri, and Vestri ("North," "South," "East," and "West"), Althjof ("Mighty Thief"), Mjothvitnir ("Mead-Wolf"), Gandalf ("Magic Elf"), Vindalf ("Wind Elf"), Rathsvith ("Swift in Counsel"), Eikinskjaldi ("Oak Shield"), etc., but in many cases the interpretations are sheer guesswork.

12. The order of the lines in this and the succeeding four stanzas varies greatly in the manuscripts and editions, and the names likewise appear in many forms. *Regin*: probably not identical with Regin the son of Hreithmar, who plays an important part in the *Reginsmol* and *Fafnismol*, but cf. note on *Reginsmol*, introductory prose.

14. *Dvalin*: in Hovamol, 144, Dvalin seems to have given magic runes to the dwarfs, probably accounting for their skill in craftsmanship, while in *Fafnismol*, 13, he is mentioned as the father of some of the lesser Norns. The story that some of the dwarfs left the rocks and mountains to find a new home on the sands is mentioned, but unexplained, in Snorri's *Edda*; of *Lofar* we know only that he was descended from these wanderers.

15. *Andvari*: this dwarf appears prominently in the *Reginsmol*, which tells how the god Loki treacherously robbed him of his wealth; the curse which he laid on his treasure brought about the deaths of Sigurth, Gunnar, Atli, and many others.

17. Here the poem resumes its course after the interpolated section. Probably, however, something has been lost, for there is no apparent connection between the three giant-maids of stanza 8 and the three gods, Odin, Honir and Lothur, who in stanza 17 go forth to create man and woman. The word "three" in stanzas 8 and 17 very likely confused some early reciter, or perhaps the compiler himself. *Ask* and *Embla*: ash and elm; Snorri gives them simply as the names of the first man and woman, but says that the gods made this pair out of trees.

18. Hönir: little is known of this god, save that he occasionally appears in the poems in company with Odin and Loki, and that he survives the

destruction, assuming in the new age the gift of prophesy (cf. stanza 63). He was given by the gods as a hostage to the Wanes after their war, in exchange for Njorth (cf. stanza 21 and note). [Probably identical to either Vili or Vé. Lothur: Probably a byname of either of Odin's brothers Vili or Vé and reflecting their role in the creation of man alongside Odin, though scholarly opinions have varied between this, Freyr, or possibly even Loki and no consensus has been reached.] 19. *Yggdrasil:* cf. stanza 2 and note, and *Grimnismol,* 29–35 and notes. *Urth* ("The Past"): one of the three great Norns. The world-ash is kept green by being sprinkled with the marvelous healing water from her well.

20. *The maidens:* the three Norns; possibly this stanza should follow stanza 8. *Dwelling: Regius* has "sæ" (sea) instead of "sal" (hall, home), and many editors have followed this reading, although Snorri's prose paraphrase indicates "sal." *Urth, Verthandi* and *Skuld:* "Past," "Present" and "Future." *Wood,* etc.: the magic signs (runes) controlling the destinies of men were cut on pieces of wood. Lines 3–4 are probably interpolations from some other account of the Norns.

21. [This follows stanza 20 in Regius; in the Hauksbok version stanzas 25, 26, 27, 40 and 41 come between stanzas 20 and 21. Editors have attempted all sorts of rearrangements. The war: the first war was that between the gods and the Wanes. The two types of divinities were worshipped in common; hence the treaty which ended the war with the exchange of hostages. Chief among the Wanes were Njorth and his children, Freyr and Freyja and their extended family of whom we can surmise included the deities Nerthus (Jord), Dagr, Dellingr and Nott, all of whom became conspicuous among the gods. Beyond this we know little of the Wanes, who display an association with the Alfar and aspects of the natural world, most clearly that of the Sun. I remember: the manuscripts have "she remembers," but the Volva is apparently still speaking of her own memories, as in stanza 2. *Gollveig* ("Gold-Might"): apparently the first of the Wanes to come among the gods, her ill-treatment being the immediate cause of the war. Müllenhoff maintains that Gollveig is another name for Freyja which is most accepted academically, but Rydberg maintains that Gollveig is a byname for Heiðr and Aurboða, a claim which has not been taken up by mainstream academics. Lines 5–6, one or both of them probably interpolated, seem to symbolize the refining of gold by fire. *Hor* ("The High One"): Odin.]

22. *Heith* ("Shining One"?): a name often applied to wise-women and prophetesses. The application of this stanza to Gollveig is far from clear, though the reference may be to the magic and destructive power of gold. It is also possible that the stanza is an interpolation. Bugge maintains that

it applies to the Volva who is reciting the poem, and makes it the opening stanza, following it with stanzas 28 and 30, and then going on with stanzas 1 ff. The text of line 2 is obscure, and has been variously emended. [See citation 21 in connection with the theories of Rydberg as to her identity.]

23. This stanza and stanza 24 have been transposed from the order in the manuscripts, for the former describes the battle and the victory of the Wanes, after which the gods took council, debating whether to pay tribute to the victors, or to admit them, as was finally done, to equal rights of worship.

25. Possibly, as Finn Magnusen long ago suggested, there is something lost after stanza 24, but it was not the custom of the *Eddic* poets to supply transitions which their hearers could generally be counted on to understand. The story referred to in stanzas 25–26 (both quoted by Snorri) is that of the rebuilding of Asgarth after its destruction by the Wanes. The gods employed a giant as builder, who demanded as his reward the sun and moon, and the goddess Freyja for his wife. The gods, terrified by the rapid progress of the work, forced Loki, who had advised the bargain, to delay the giant by a trick, so that the work was not finished in the stipulated time (cf. *Grimnismol*, 44, note). The enraged giant then threatened the gods, whereupon Thor slew him. *Oth's bride*: Freyja; of Oth little is known beyond the fact that Snorri refers to him as a man who "went away on long journeys." [Much has been speculated regarding his identity, with most tying it to Odin himself. Rydberg offers a secondary interpretation relying primarily on the *Svipdagsmol* to contend that he is Svipdagr.]

26. *Thor*: the thunder-god, son of Odin and Jorth (Earth); cf. particularly *Harbarthsljoth* and *Thrymskvitha*, passim. *Oaths*, etc.: the gods, by violating their oaths to the giant who rebuilt Asgarth, aroused the undying hatred of the giants' race, and thus the giants were among their enemies in the final battle.

27. Here the Volva turns from her memories of the past to a statement of some of Odin's own secrets in his eternal search for knowledge (stanzas 27–29). Bugge puts this stanza after stanza 29. *The horn of Heimdall*: the Gjallarhorn ("Shrieking Horn"), with which Heimdall, watchman of the gods, will summon them to the last battle. Till that time the horn is buried under Yggdrasil. *Valfather's pledge*: Odin's eye, which he gave to the [Giant] Mimir (or Mim) in exchange for the latter's wisdom. It appears here and in stanza 29 as a drinking-vessel, from which Mimir drinks the magic mead, and from which he pours water on the ash Yggdrasil. Odin's

sacrifice of his eye in order to gain knowledge of his final doom is one of the series of disasters leading up to the destruction of the gods. There were several differing versions of the story of Odin's relations with Mimir; another one, quite incompatible with this, appears in stanza 47. In the manuscripts *I know* and *I see* appear as "she knows" and "she sees" (cf. note on 21).

28. The *Hauksbok* version omits all of stanzas 28–34, stanza 27 being there followed by stanzas 40 and 41. *Regius* indicates stanzas 28 and 29 as a single stanza. Bugge puts stanza 28 after stanza 22, as the second stanza of his reconstructed poem. The Volva here addresses Odin directly, intimating that, although he has not told her, she knows why he has come to her, and what he has already suffered in his search for knowledge regarding his doom. Her reiterated "would you know yet more?" seems to mean: "I have proved my wisdom by telling of the past and of your own secrets; is it your will that I tell likewise of the fate in store for you?" *The Old One*: Odin.

29. The first line, not in either manuscript, is a conjectural emendation based on Snorri's paraphrase. Bugge puts this stanza after stanza 20.

30. This is apparently the transitional stanza, in which the Volva, rewarded by Odin for her knowledge of the past (stanzas 1–29), is induced to proceed with her real prophecy (stanzas 31–66). Some editors turn the stanza into the third person, making it a narrative link. Bugge, on the other hand, puts it after stanza 28 as the third stanza of the poem. No lacuna is indicated in the manuscripts, and editors have attempted various emendations. *Heerfather* ("Father of the Host"): Odin.

31. *Valkyries*: these "Choosers of the Slain" (cf. stanza 1, note) bring the bravest warriors killed in battle to Valhall, in order to re-enforce the gods for their final struggle. They are also called "Wish-Maidens," as the fulfillers of Odin's wishes. The conception of the supernatural warrior-maiden was later interwoven with the South-Germanic tradition of the swan-maiden. A third complication developed when the originally quite human women of the hero-legends were endowed with the qualities of both Valkyries and swan-maidens, as in the cases of Brynhild (cf. *Gripisspo*, introductory note [Appendix B]), Svava (cf. *Helgakvitha Hjorvarthssonar*, prose after stanza 5 and note) and Sigrun (cf. *Helgakvitha Hundingsbana* 1, 17 and note). The list of names here given may be an interpolation; a quite different list is given in *Grimnismol*, 36. *Ranks of the gods*: some editors regard the word thus translated as a specific place name. *Herjan* ("Leader of Hosts"): Odin. It is worth noting that the name *Hild* ("Warrior") is the basis of Bryn-hild ("Warrior in MailCoat").

32. *Baldr*: The death of Baldr, the son of Odin and Frigg, was the first of the great disasters to the gods. The story is fully told by Snorri. Frigg had demanded of all created things, saving only the mistletoe, which she thought too [young] to be worth troubling about, an oath that they would not harm Baldr. Thus it came to be a sport for the gods to hurl weapons at Baldr, who, of course, was totally unharmed thereby. Loki, the trouble-maker, brought the mistletoe to Baldr's blind brother, Hoth, and guided his hand in hurling the twig. Baldr was slain, and grief came upon all the gods. Cf. *Baldrs Draumar*.

33. The lines in this and the following stanza have been combined in various ways by editors, lacunae having been freely conjectured, but the manuscript version seems clear enough. *The brother of Baldr*: Vali, whom Odin begot expressly to avenge Baldr's death. The day after his birth he fought and slew Hoth.

34. *Frigg*: Odin's wife. Some scholars have regarded her as a solar myth, calling her the sun-goddess, and pointing out that her home in *Fensalir* ("[the Fen-halls]") symbolizes the daily setting of the sun beneath the ocean horizon.

35. The translation here follows the *Regius* version. The *Hauksbok* has the same final two lines, but in place of the first pair has, "I know that Vali his brother gnawed, / With his bowels then was Loki bound." Many editors have followed this version of the whole stanza or have included these two lines, often marking them as doubtful, with the four from *Regius*. After the murder of Baldr, the gods took Loki and bound him to a rock with the bowels of his son Narfi, who had just been torn to pieces by Loki's other son, Vali. A serpent was fastened above Loki's head, and the venom fell upon his face. Loki's wife, *Sigyn*, sat by him with a basin to catch the venom, but whenever the basin was full, and she went away to empty it, then the venom fell on Loki again, till the earth shook with his struggles. "And there he lies bound till the end." Cf. *Lokasenna*, concluding prose.

36. Stanzas 36–39 describe the homes of the enemies of the gods: the giants (36), the dwarfs (37), and the dead in the land of the goddess Hel (38–39). The *Hauksbok* version omits stanzas 36 and 37. *Regius* unites 36 with 37, but most editors have assumed a lacuna. *Slith* ("the Fearful"): a river in the giants' home. The "swords and daggers" may represent the icy cold.

37. *Nithavellir* ("the Dark Fields"): a home of the dwarfs. Perhaps the word should be "Nithafjoll" ("the Dark Crags"). *Sindri*: the great worker

in gold among the dwarfs. *Okolnir* ("the Not Cold"): possibly a volcano. *Brimir*: the giant (possibly Ymir) out of whose blood, according to stanza 9, the dwarfs were made; the name here appears to mean simply the leader of the dwarfs.

38. Stanzas 38 and 39 follow stanza 43 in the *Hauksbok* version. Snorri quotes stanzas 38, 39, 40 and 41, though not consecutively. *Nastrond* ("Corpse-Strand"): the land of the dead, ruled by the goddess Hel. Here the wicked undergo tortures. *Smokevent*: the phrase gives a picture of the Icelandic house, with its opening in the roof serving instead of a chimney.

39. The stanza is almost certainly in corrupt form. The third line is presumably an interpolation, and is lacking in most of the late paper manuscripts. Some editors, however, have called lines 1–3 the remains of a full stanza, with the fourth line lacking, and lines 4–5 the remains of another. The stanza depicts the torments of the two worst classes of criminals known to Old Norse morality—oath-breakers and murderers. *Nithhogg* ("the Dread Biter"): the dragon that lies beneath the ash Yggdrasil and gnaws at its roots, thus symbolizing the destructive elements in the universe; cf. *Grimnismol*, 32, 35. *The wolf*: presumably the wolf Fenrir, one of the children of Loki and the giantess Angrbotha (the others being Mithgarthsorm and the goddess Hel), who was chained by the gods with the marvelous chain Gleipnir, fashioned by a dwarf "out of six things: the noise of a cat's step, the beards of women, the roots of mountains, the nerves of bears, the breath of fishes, and the spittle of birds." The chaining of Fenrir cost the god Tyr his right hand; cf. stanza 44.

40. The *Hauksbok* version inserts after stanza 39 the refrain-stanza (44), and puts stanzas 40 and 41 between 27 and 21. With this stanza begins the account of the final struggle itself. *The giantess*: her name is nowhere stated, and the only other reference to Ironwood is in *Grimnismol*, 39, in this same connection. The children of this giantess and the wolf Fenrir are the wolves Skoll and Hati, the first of whom steals the sun, the second the moon. Some scholars naturally see here an eclipse-myth.

41. In the third line many editors omit the comma after "sun," and put one after "soon," making the two lines run: "Dark grows the sun in summer soon, / Mighty storms — " etc. Either phenomenon in summer would be sufficiently striking.

42. In the *Hauksbok* version stanzas 42 and 43 stand between stanzas 44 and 38. *Eggther*: this giant, who seems to be the watchman of the giants, as Heimdall is that of the gods and Surt of the dwellers in the fire-world, is not mentioned elsewhere in the poems. *Fjalar*, the cock whose crowing

wakes the giants for the final struggle.

43. *Gollinkambi* ("Gold-Comb"): the cock who wakes the gods and heroes, as Fjalar does the giants. *The rust-red bird*: the name of this bird, who wakes the people of Hel's domain, is nowhere stated.

44. This is a refrain-stanza. In *Regius* it appears in full only at this point, but is repeated in abbreviated form before stanzas 50 and 59. In the *Hauksbok* version the full stanza comes first between stanzas 35 and 42, then, in abbreviated form, it occurs four times: before stanzas 45, 50, 55, and 59. In the *Hauksbok* line 3 runs: "Farther I see and more can say." *Garm*: the dog who guards the gates of Hel's kingdom; cf. *Baldrs Draumar*, 2 ff, and *Grimnismol*, 44. *Gniparhellir* ("the Cliff-Cave"): the entrance to the world of the dead. *The wolf*: Fenrir; cf. stanza 39 and note.

45. From this point on through stanza 57 the poem is quoted by Snorri, stanza 49 alone being omitted. There has been much discussion as to the status of stanza 45. Lines 4 and 5 look like an interpolation. After line 5 the *Hauksbok* has a line running: "The world resounds, the witch is flying." Editors have arranged these seven lines in various ways, with lacunae freely indicated. *Sisters' sons*: in all Germanic countries the relations between uncle and nephew were felt to be particularly close.

46. *Regius* combines the first three lines of this stanza with lines 3, 2, and 1 of stanza 47 as a single stanza. Line 4, not found in *Regius*, is introduced from the *Hauksbok* version, where it follows line 2 of stanza 47. *The sons of Mim*: the spirits of the water. On Mim (or Mimir) cf. stanza 27 and note. *Gjallarhorn*: the "Shrieking Horn" with which Heimdall, the watchman of the gods, calls them to the last battle.

47. In *Regius* lines 3, 2, and 1, in that order, follow stanza 46 without separation. Line 4 is not found in *Regius*, but is introduced from the *Hauksbok* version. *Yggdrasil*: cf. stanza 19 and note, and *Grimnismol*, 29–35. *The giant*: Fenrir. *The head of Mim*: various myths were current about Mimir. This stanza refers to the story that he was sent by the gods with Hönir as a hostage to the Wanes after their war (cf. stanza 21 and note), and that the Wanes cut off his head and returned it to the gods. Odin embalmed the head, and by magic gave it the power of speech, thus making Mimir's noted wisdom always available. Of course this story does not fit with that underlying the references to Mimir in stanzas 27 and 29. *The kinsman of Surt*: the wolf Fenrir, who slays Odin in the final struggle; cf. stanza 53. Surt is the giant who rules the fire-world, Muspellsheim; cf. stanza 52.

48. This stanza in *Regius* follows stanza 51; in the *Hauksbok* it stands, as

here, after 47. *Jotunheim*: the land of the giants.

49. Identical with stanza 44. In the manuscripts it is here abbreviated.

50. *Hrym*: the leader of the giants, who comes as the helmsman of the ship Naglfar (line 4). *The serpent*: Mithgarthsorm, one of the children of Loki and Angrbotha (cf. stanza 39, note). The serpent was cast into the sea, where he completely encircles the land; cf. especially *Hymiskvitha*, *passim*. *The eagle*: the giant Hræsvelg, who sits at the edge of heaven in the form of an eagle, and makes the winds with his wings; cf. *Vafthruthnismol*, 37, and *Skirnismol*, 27. *Naglfar*: the ship which was made out of dead men's nails to carry the giants to battle.

51. *North*: a guess; the manuscripts have "east," but there seems to be a confusion with stanza 50, line 1. *People of Hel*: the manuscripts have "people of Muspell," but these came over the bridge Bifrost (the rainbow), which broke beneath them, whereas the people of Hel came in a ship steered by Loki. *The wolf*: Fenrir. *The brother of Byleist*: Loki. Of Byleist (or Byleipt) no more is known.

52. *Surt*: the ruler of the fire-world. *The scourge of branches*: fire. This is one of the relatively rare instances in the *Eddic* poems of the type of poetic diction which characterizes the skaldic verse.

53. *Hlin*: apparently another name for Frigg, Odin's wife. After losing her son Baldr, she is fated now to see Odin slain by the wolf Fenrir. *Beli's slayer*: the god Freyr, who killed the giant Beli with his fist; cf. *Skirnismol*, 16 and note. On Freyr, who belonged to the race of the Wanes, and was the brother of Freyja, see especially *Skirnismol*, *passim*. *The joy of Frigg*: oossibly Odin or Freyr.

54. As quoted by Snorri the first line of this stanza runs: "Fares Odin's son to fight with the wolf." *Sigfather* ("Father of Victory"): Odin. His son, Vithar, is the silent god, famed chiefly for his great shield, and his strength, which is little less than Thor's. He survives the destruction. *The giant's son*: Fenrir.

55. This and the following stanza are clearly in bad shape. In *Regius* only lines 1 and 4 are found, combined with stanza 56 as a single stanza. Line 1 does not appear in the *Hauksbok* version, the stanza there beginning with line 2. Snorri, in quoting these two stanzas, omits 55, 2-4, and 56, 3, making a single stanza out of 55, 1, and 56, 4, 2, 1, in that order. Moreover, the *Hauksbok* manuscript at this point is practically illegible. The lacuna (line 3) is, of course, purely conjectural, and all sorts of arrangements of the lines have been attempted by editors. *Hlothyn*: another name

for Jorth ("Earth"), Thor's mother; his father was Odin. *The snake*: Mithgarthsorm; cf. stanza 50 and note. *Odin's son*: Thor. The fourth line in *Regius* reads "against the wolf," but if this line refers to Thor at all, and not to Vithar, the *Hauksbok* reading, "serpent," is correct.

56. *The warder of earth*: Thor. *The son of Fjorgyn*: again Thor, who, after slaying the serpent, is overcome by his venomous breath, and dies. Fjorgyn appears in both a masculine and a feminine form. In the masculine it is a name for Odin; in the feminine, as here and in *Harbarthsljoth*, 56, it apparently refers to Jorth.

57. With this stanza ends the account of the destruction.

58. Again the refrain-stanza (cf. stanza 44 and note), abbreviated in both manuscripts, as in the case of stanza 49. It is probably misplaced here.

59. Here begins the description of the new world which is to rise out of the wreck of the old one. It is on this passage that a few critics have sought to base their argument that the poem is later than the introduction of Christianity (*circa* 1000), but this theory has never seemed convincing (cf. introductory note [Appendix B]).

60. The third line of this stanza is not found in *Regius*. *Ithavoll*: cf. stanza 7 and note. *The girdler of earth*: Mithgarthsorm, who, lying in the sea, surrounded the land. *The Ruler of Gods*: Odin. The runes were both magic signs, generally carved on wood, and sung or spoken charms.

61. The *Hauksbok* version of the first two lines runs:

"The gods shall find there, wondrous fair,
The golden tables amid the grass."

No lacuna (line 4) is indicated in the manuscripts. *Golden tables*: cf. stanza 8 and note.

62. *Baldr*: cf. stanza 32 and note. Baldr and his brother, Hoth, who unwittingly slew him at Loki's instigation, return together, their union being a symbol of the new age of peace. *Hropt*: another name for Odin. His "battle-hall" is Valhall.

63. No lacuna (line 2) indicated in the manuscripts. Hönir: cf. stanza 18 and note. In this new age he has the gift of foretelling the future. *Tveggi* ("The Twofold"): another name for Odin. His brothers are Vili and Ve (cf. *Lokasenna*, 26, and note). Little is known of them, and nothing, beyond this reference, of their sons. *Vindheim* ("Home of the Wind"): a realm of the heavens inhabited by Alfar.

64. This stanza is quoted by Snorri. *Gimle*: Snorri makes this the name of the hall itself, while here it appears to refer to a mountain on which the hall stands. It is the home of the happy, as opposed to another hall, not here mentioned, for the dead. Snorri's description of this second hall is based on *Voluspo*, 38, which he quotes, and perhaps that stanza properly belongs after 64.

65. This stanza is not found in *Regius*, and is probably spurious. No lacuna is indicated in the *Hauksbok* version, but late paper manuscripts add two lines, running:

> "Rule he orders, and rights he fixes,
> Laws he ordains that ever shall live."

The name of this new ruler is nowhere given, and of course the suggestion of Christianity is unavoidable. It is not certain, however, that even this stanza refers to Christianity, and if it does, it may have been interpolated long after the rest of the poem was composed.

66. This stanza, which fits so badly with the preceding ones, may well have been interpolated. It has been suggested that the dragon, making a last attempt to rise, is destroyed, this event marking the end of evil in the world. But in both manuscripts the final half-line does not refer to the dragon, but, as the gender shows, to the Volva herself, who sinks into the earth; a sort of conclusion to the entire prophecy. Presumably the stanza (barring the last half-line, which was probably intended as the conclusion of the poem) belongs somewhere in the description of the great struggle. *Nithhogg*: the dragon at the roots of Yggdrasil; cf. stanza 39 and note. *Nithafjoll* ("the Dark Crags"); nowhere else mentioned. *Must I*: the manuscripts have "must she."

HOVAMOL
THE WORDS OF THE HIGH ONE

INTRODUCTION

The *Hovamol* represents perhaps the portion of the *Poetic Edda* most popular and accessible to the modern man, representing the words of advice from the God Odin about various matters ranging from guests, friendship, love, romance, courtship, ethical philosophy, introspection, and proper conduct. It is traditionally broken into five sections. The first is the *Gestaþáttr*, containing advice for guests, manners, and forthright conduct, and warnings as to the dangers in unknown places. The second section is "Odin's Love Quests" detailing his sometimes amusing and instructive escapades attempting to woo women, advising men as to the fickle minds of their would be targets and the troubles it may cause them if they are not clever about it. The third section comprises the *Loddfafnismol*, a gnomic collection of advice and wisdom about proper conduct, life and behavior addressed to "Loddfafnir"—the Stray Singer, and perhaps meant to be a stand-in for any wandering man. The fourth section comprises the *Rúnatal*, Odin's quest for the runes and his attainment of them after self-sacrifice. The last and final section comprises the *Ljothatal* detailing the eighteen charms Odin possesses and his skills in the magical craft of *Galdr*.

The *Hovamol* contains some of the most famous and striking of the poetic statements of the Norse people, with such standouts as the famous "cattle die, and kinsmen die" line showcasing the Norse tendency towards fatalism, but it varies from the imminently practical,

> The son of a king shall be silent and wise,

And bold in battle as well

to the rather amusing line:

> A witless man, when he meets with men,
> Had best in silence abide;
> For no one shall find that nothing he knows,
> If his mouth is not open too much.

The *Hovamol* might well have been just as popular among our ancestors as it is today, with several elements cropping up in other places, such as a line delivered in a sage account, and a portion quoted in *Hákonarmál*. The latter element allows us to firmly date the poem as being in existence by at least the year 961, due to the inclusion of the "cattle die, and kinsmen die" line by the poet Eyvindr skáldaspillir to remember the Norwegian king Hákon the Good after his death at the battle of Fitjar that year, and his reception into Valhalla.

Odin
(Sir E. Burne-Jones)

Gáttir allar   áðr gangi fram   1
um skoðask skyli,
um skyggnast skyli,
því at óvíst er at vita   hvar óvinir
sitja á fleti fyrir.

Gefendr heilir!   2
Gestr er inn kominn,
hvar skal sitja sjá?   Mjök er bráðr
sá er á bröndum skal   síns of freista frama.

Elds er þörf   þeims inn er kominn   3
ok á kné kalinn.
Matar ok váða   er manni þörf,
þeim er hefr um fjall farit.

Vatns er þörf   þeim er til   4
verðar kemr,   þerru ok þjóðlaðar,
góðs of æðis   ef sér geta mætti
orðs ok endrþögu.

Vits er þörf þeim er víða ratar;   5
dælt er heima hvat;
at augabragði verðr
sá er ekki kann ok með snotrum sitr.

HOVAMOL

Within the gates ere a man shall go,   1
  Full warily let him watch,
Full long let him look about him;
For little he knows where a foe may lurk,
  And sit in the seats within.

Hail to the giver! a guest has come;   2
Where shall the stranger sit?
Swift shall he be who, with swords shall try
The proof of his might to make.

Fire he needs who with frozen knees   3
Has come from the cold without;
Food and clothes must the farer have,
The man from the mountains come.

Water and towels and welcoming speech   4
Should he find who comes, to the feast;
If renown he would get, and again be greeted,
Wisely and well must he act.

Wits must he have who wanders wide,   5
But all is easy at home;
At the witless man the wise shall wink
When among such men he sits.

At hyggjandi sinni   skyli-t maðr hræsinn vera,   6
heldr gætinn at geði;   þá er horskr ok þögull
kemr heimisgarða til,   sjaldan verðr víti vörum,
því at óbrigðra vin   fær maðr aldregi
en mannvit mikit.

Inn vari gestr,   er til verðar kemr,   7
þunnu hljóði þegir,   eyrum hlýðir,
en augum skoðar;
svá nýsisk fróðra hverr fyrir.

Hinn er sæll,   er sér of getr   8
lof ok líknstafi;
ódælla er við þat,
er maðr eiga skal   annars brjóstum í.

Sá er sæll,   er sjalfr of á   9
lof ok vit, meðan lifir;
því at ill ráð
hefr maðr oft þegit   annars brjóstum ór.

Byrði betri   berr-at maðr brautu at   10
en sé mannvit mikit;   auði betra
þykkir þat í ókunnum stað;
slíkt er válaðs vera.

Byrði betri   11
berr-at maðr brautu at
en sé mannvit mikit;   vegnest verra
vegr-a hann velli at   en sé ofdrykkja öls.

Er-a svá gótt   12
sem gótt kveða
öl alda sona,   því at færa veit,
er fleira drekkr   síns til geðs gumi.

Óminnishegri heitir   13
sá er yfir ölðrum þrumir,
hann stelr geði guma;   þess fugls fjöðrum
ek fjötraðr vark   í garði Gunnlaðar.

Ölr ek varð,   14
varð ofrölvi
at ins fróða Fjalars;   því er ölðr bazt,
at aftr of heimtir   hverr sitt geð gumi.

6. A man shall not boast of his keenness of mind,
But keep it close in his breast;
To the silent and wise does ill come seldom
When he goes as guest to a house;
For a faster friend one never finds
Than wisdom tried and true.

7. The knowing guest who goes to the feast,
In silent attention sits;
With his ears he hears, with his eyes he watches,
Thus wary are wise men all.

8. Happy the one who wins for himself
Favor and praises fair;
Less safe by far is the wisdom found
That is hid in another's heart.

9. Happy the man who has while he lives
Wisdom and praise as well,
For evil counsel a man full oft
Has from another's heart.

10. A better burden may no man bear
For wanderings wide than wisdom;
It is better than wealth on unknown ways,
And in grief a refuge it gives.

11. A better burden may no man bear
For wanderings wide than wisdom;
Worse food for the journey he brings not afield
Than an over-drinking of ale.

12. Less good there lies than most believe
In ale for mortal men;
For the more he drinks the less does man
Of his mind the mastery hold.

13. Over beer the bird of forgetfulness broods,
And steals the minds of men;
With the heron's feathers fettered I lay
And in Gunnloth's house was held.

14. Drunk I was, I was dead-drunk,
When with Fjalar wise I was;
'Tis the best of drinking if back one brings
His wisdom with him home.

Þagalt ok hugalt 15
skyli þjóðans barn
ok vígdjarft vera;   glaðr ok reifr
skyli gumna hverr,   unz sinn bíðr bana.

Ósnjallr maðr   hyggsk munu ey lifa, 16
ef hann við víg varask;
en elli gefr   hánum engi frið,
þótt hánum geirar gefi.

Kópir afglapi   er til kynnis kemr, 17
þylsk hann um eða þrumir;
allt er senn, ef hann sylg of getr,
uppi er þá geð guma.

Sá einn veit   er víða ratar 18
ok hefr fjölð of farit,
hverju geði   stýrir gumna hverr,
sá er vitandi er vits.

Haldi-t maðr á keri, 19
drekki þó at hófi mjöð,
mæli þarft eða þegi,
ókynnis þess vár   þik engi maðr,
at þú gangir snemma at sofa.

Gráðugr halr,   nema geðs viti, 20
etr sér aldrtrega;
oft fær hlægis,   er með horskum kemr,
manni heimskum magi.

Hjarðir þat vitu,   nær þær heim skulu, 21
ok ganga þá af grasi;
en ósviðr maðr   kann ævagi
síns of mál maga.

Vesall maðr   ok illa skapi 22
hlær at hvívetna;
hittki hann veit,   er hann vita þyrfti,
at hann er-a vamma vanr.

Ósviðr maðr   vakir um allar nætr 23
ok hyggr at hvívetna;
þá er móðr,   er at morgni kemr,
allt er víl sem var.

The son of a king shall be silent and wise,   15
And bold in battle as well;
Bravely and gladly a man shall go,
Till the day of his death is come.

The sluggard believes he shall live forever,   16
If the fight he faces not;
But age shall not grant him the gift of peace,
Though spears may spare his life.

The fool is agape when he comes to the feast,   17
He stammers or else is still;
But soon if he gets a drink is it seen
What the mind of the man is like.

He alone is aware who has wandered wide,   18
And far abroad has fared,
How great a mind is guided by him
That wealth of wisdom has.

Shun not the mead, but drink in measure;   19
Speak to the point or be still;
For rudeness none shall rightly blame thee
If soon thy bed thou seekest.

The greedy man, if his mind be vague,   20
Will eat till sick he is;
The vulgar man, when among the wise,
To scorn by his belly is brought.

The herds know well when home they shall fare,   21
And then from the grass they go;
But the foolish man his belly's measure
Shall never know aright.

A paltry man and poor of mind   22
At all things ever mocks;
For never he knows, what he ought to know,
That he is not free from faults.

The witless man is awake all night,   23
Thinking of many things;
Care-worn he is when the morning comes,
And his woe is just as it was.

Ósnotr maðr   hyggr sér alla vera 24
viðhlæjendr vini;
hittki hann fiðr,   þótt þeir um hann fár lesi,
ef hann með snotrum sitr.

Ósnotr maðr   hyggr sér alla vera 25
viðhlæjendr vini;
þá þat finnr,   er at þingi kemr,
at hann á formælendr fáa.

Ósnotr maðr   þykkisk allt vita, 26
ef hann á sér í vá veru;
hittki hann veit,
hvat hann skal við kveða,
ef hans freista firar.

Ósnotr maðr,   er með aldir kemr, 27
þat er bazt, at hann þegi;
engi þat veit,   at hann ekki kann,
nema hann mæli til margt;
veit-a maðr,   hinn er vettki veit,
þótt hann mæli til margt.

Fróðr sá þykkisk,   er fregna kann 28
ok segja it sama;
eyvitu leyna   megu ýta synir,
því er gengr um guma.

Ærna mælir,   sá er æva þegir, 29
staðlausu stafi;
hraðmælt tunga,   nema haldendr eigi,
oft sér ógótt of gelr.

At augabragði skal-a   maðr annan hafa, 30
þótt til kynnis komi;
margr þá fróðr þykkisk,   ef hann freginn er-at
ok nái hann þurrfjallr þruma.

Fróðr þykkisk,   sá er flótta tekr, 31
gestr at gest hæðinn;
veit-a görla,   sá er of verði glissir,
þótt hann með grömum glami.

The foolish man for friends all those 24
Who laugh at him will hold;
When among the wise he marks it not
Though hatred of him they speak.

The foolish man for friends all those 25
Who laugh at him will hold;
But the truth when he comes to the council he learns,
That few in his favor will speak.

An ignorant man thinks that all he knows, 26
When he sits by himself in a corner;
But never what answer to make he knows,
When others with questions come.

A witless man, when he meets with men, 27
Had best in silence abide;
For no one shall find that nothing he knows,
If his mouth is not open too much.
But a man knows not, if nothing he knows,
When his mouth has been open too much.

Wise shall he seem who well can question, 28
And also answer well;
Nought is concealed that men may say
Among the sons of men.

Often he speaks who never is still 29
With words that win no faith;
The babbling tongue, if a bridle it find not,
Oft for itself sings ill.

In mockery no one a man shall hold, 30
Although he fare to the feast;
Wise seems one oft, if nought he is asked,
And safely he sits dry-skinned.

Wise a guest holds it to take to his heels, 31
When mock of another he makes;
But little he knows who laughs at the feast,
Though he mocks in the midst of his foes.

Gumnar margir   erusk gagnhollir,   32
en at virði vrekask;
aldar róg   þat mun æ vera,
órir gestr við gest.

Árliga verðar   skyli maðr oft fáa,   33
nema til kynnis komi:
str ok snópir,   lætr sem solginn sé
ok kann fregna at fáu.

Afhvarf mikit   er til ills vinar,   34
þótt á brautu búi,   en til góðs vinar
liggja gagnvegir,
þótt hann sé firr farinn.

Ganga skal,   skal-a gestr vera   35
ey í einum stað;
ljúfr verðr leiðr,   ef lengi sitr
annars fletjum á.

Bú er betra,   þótt lítit sé,   36
halr er heima hverr;
þótt tvær geitr eigi   ok taugreftan sal,
þat er þó betra en bæn.

Bú er betra,   þótt lítit sé,   37
halr er heima hverr;
blóðugt er hjarta,   þeim er biðja skal
sér í mál hvert matar.

Vápnum sínum   skal-a maðr velli á   38
feti ganga framar,
því at óvíst er at vita,
nær verðr á vegum úti   geirs of þörf guma.

Fannk-a ek mildan mann   eða svá matar góðan,   39
at væri-t þiggja þegit,
eða síns féar
svági glöggvan,   at leið sé laun, ef þægi.

Féar síns,   er fengit hefr,   40
skyli-t maðr þörf þola;
oft sparir leiðum,   þats hefr ljúfum hugat;
margt gengr verr en varir.

Friendly of mind are many men,   32
Till feasting they mock at their friends;
To mankind a bane must it ever be
When guests together strive.

Oft should one make an early meal,   33
Nor fasting come to the feast;
Else he sits and chews as if he would choke,
And little is able to ask.

Crooked and far is the road to a foe,   34
Though his house on the highway be;
But wide and straight is the way to a friend,
Though far away he fare.

Forth shall one go, nor stay as a guest   35
In a single spot forever;
Love becomes loathing if long one sits
By the hearth in another's home.

Better a house, though a hut it be,   36
A man is master at home;
A pair of goats and a patched-up roof
Are better far than begging.

Better a house, though a hut it be,   37
A man is master at home;
His heart is bleeding who needs must beg
When food he fain would have.

Away from his arms in the open field   38
A man should fare not a foot;
For never he knows when the need for a spear
Shall arise on the distant road.

If wealth a man has won for himself,   39
Let him never suffer in need;
Oft he saves for a foe what he plans for a friend,
For much goes worse than we wish.

None so free with gifts or food have I found   40
That gladly he took not a gift,
Nor one who so widely scattered his wealth
That of recompense hatred he had.

Vápnum ok váðum   skulu vinir gleðjask;   41
þat er á sjalfum sýnst;
viðrgefendr ok endrgefendr   erusk lengst vinir,
ef þat bíðr at verða vel.

Vin sínum   skal maðr vinr vera   42
ok gjalda gjöf við gjöf;
hlátr við hlátri   skyli hölðar taka
en lausung við lygi.

Vin sínum   skal maðr vinr vera,   43
þeim ok þess vin;
en óvinar síns   skyli engi maðr
vinar vinr vera.

Veiztu, ef þú vin átt,   þann er þú vel trúir,   44
ok vill þú af hánum gótt geta,
geði skaltu við þann blanda
ok gjöfum skipta,   fara at finna oft.

Ef þú átt annan,   þanns þú illa trúir,   45
vildu af hánum þó gótt geta,
fagrt skaltu við þann mæla   en flátt hyggja
ok gjalda lausung við lygi.

Það er enn of þann   er þú illa trúir   46
ok þér er grunr at hans geði,
hlæja skaltu við þeim   ok um hug mæla;
glík skulu gjöld gjöfum.

Ungr var ek forðum,   fór ek einn saman,   47
þá varð ek villr vega;
auðigr þóttumk,   er ek annan fann,
maðr er manns gaman.

Mildir, fræknir   menn bazt lifa,   48
sjaldan sút ala;
en ósnjallr maðr   uggir hotvetna,
sýtir æ glöggr við gjöfum.

Váðir mínar   gaf ek velli at   49
tveim trémönnum;
rekkar þat þóttusk,   er þeir rift höfðu;
neiss er nökkviðr halr.

Friends shall gladden each other with arms and garments,   41
As each for himself can see;
Gift-givers' friendships are longest found,
If fair their fates may be.

To his friend a man a friend shall prove,   42
And gifts with gifts requite;
But men shall mocking with mockery answer,
And fraud with falsehood meet.

To his friend a man a friend shall prove,   43
To him and the friend of his friend;
But never a man shall friendship make
With one of his foeman's friends.

If a friend thou hast whom thou fully wilt trust,   44
And good from him wouldst get,
Thy thoughts with his mingle, and gifts shalt thou make,
And fare to find him oft.

If another thou hast whom thou hardly wilt trust,   45
Yet good from him wouldst get,
Thou shalt speak him fair, but falsely think,
And fraud with falsehood requite.

So is it with him whom thou hardly wilt trust,   46
And whose mind thou mayst not know;
Laugh with him mayst thou, but speak not thy mind,
Like gifts to his shalt thou give.

Young was I once, and wandered alone,   47
And nought of the road I knew;
Rich did I feel when a comrade I found,
For man is man's delight.

The lives of the brave and noble are best,   48
Sorrows they seldom feed;
But the coward fear of all things feels,
And not gladly the niggard gives.

My garments once in a field I gave   49
To a pair of carven poles;
Heroes they seemed when clothes they had,
But the naked man is nought.

Hrörnar þöll,   sú er stendr þorpi á,   50
hlýr-at henni börkr né barr;
svá er maðr,   sá er manngi ann.
Hvat skal hann lengi lifa?

Eldi heitari   brennr með illum vinum   51
friðr fimm daga,
en þá sloknar,   er inn sétti kemr,
ok versnar allr vinskapr.

Mikit eitt   skal-a manni gefa;   52
oft kaupir sér í litlu lof,
með halfum hleif   ok með höllu keri
fekk ek mér félaga.

Lítilla sanda   lítilla sæva   53
lítil eru geð guma;
því allir menn   urðu-t jafnspakir;
half er öld hvar.

Meðalsnotr   skyli manna hverr;   54
æva til snotr sé;
þeim er fyrða   fegrst at lifa,
er vel margt vitu.

Meðalsnotr   skyli manna hverr,   55
æva til snotr sé;
því at snotrs manns hjarta
verðr sjaldan glatt,
ef sá er alsnotr, er á.

Meðalsnotr   skyli manna hverr,   56
æva til snotr sé;
örlög sín   viti engi fyrir,
þeim er sorgalausastr sefi.

Brandr af brandi   brenn, unz brunninn er,   57
funi kveikisk af funa;
maðr af manni   verðr at máli kuðr,
en til dælskr af dul.

Ár skal rísa,   sá er annars vill   58
fé eða fjör hafa;
sjaldan liggjandi ulfr
lær of getr   né sofandi maðr sigr.

On the hillside drear the fir-tree dies,   50
All bootless its needles and bark;
It is like a man whom no one loves—
Why should his life be long?

Hotter than fire between false friends   51
Does friendship five days burn;
When the sixth day comes the fire cools,
And ended is all the love.

No great thing needs a man to give,   52
Oft little will purchase praise;
With half a loaf and a half-filled cup
A friend full fast I made.

A little sand has a little sea,   53
And small are the minds of men;
Though all men are not equal in wisdom,
Yet half-wise only are all.

A measure of wisdom each man shall have,   54
But never too much let him know;
The fairest lives do those men live
Whose wisdom wide has grown.

A measure of wisdom each man shall have,   55
But never too much let him know;
For the wise man's heart is seldom happy,
If wisdom too great he has won.

A measure of wisdom each man shall have,   56
But never too much let him know;
Let no man the fate before him see,
For so is he freest from sorrow.

A brand from a brand is kindled and burned,   57
And fire from fire begotten;
And man by his speech is known to men,
And the stupid by their stillness.

He must early go forth who fain the blood   58
Or the goods of another would get;
The wolf that lies idle shall win little meat,
Or the sleeping man success.

Ár skal rísa,   sá er á yrkjendr fáa,   59
ok ganga síns verka á vit;
margt of dvelr,   þann er um morgin sefr,
hálfr er auðr und hvötum.

Þurra skíða   ok þakinna næfra,   60
þess kann maðr mjöt,   þess viðar,
er vinnask megi   mál ok misseri.

Þveginn ok mettr   61
ríði maðr þingi at,
þótt hann sé-t væddr til vel;
skúa ok bróka   skammisk engi maðr
né hests in heldr,   þótt hann hafi-t góðan

Snapir ok gnapir,   er til sævar kemr,   62
örn á aldinn mar;
svá er maðr,   er með mörgum kemr
ok á formælendr fáa.

Fregna ok segja   skal fróðra hverr,   63
sá er vill heitinn horskr;
einn vita   né annarr skal,
þjóð veit, ef þrír ro.

Ríki sitt   skyli ráðsnotra   64
hverr í hófi hafa;
þá hann þat finnr,   er með fræknum kemr
at engi er einna hvatastr.

[...]   65
[...]
orða þeira,   er maðr öðrum segir
oft hann gjöld of getr.

Mikilsti snemma   kom ek í marga staði,   66
en til síð í suma;
öl var drukkit,   sumt var ólagat,
sjaldan hittir leiðr í líð.

Hér ok hvar   myndi mér heim of boðit,   67
ef þyrftak at málungi mat,
eða tvau lær hengi   at ins tryggva vinar,
þars ek hafða eitt etit.

He must early go forth whose workers are few, 59
Himself his work to seek;
Much remains undone for the morning-sleeper,
For the swift is wealth half won.

Of seasoned shingles and strips of bark 60
For the thatch let one know his need,
And how much of wood he must have for a month,
Or in half a year he will use.

Washed and fed to the council fare, 61
But care not too much for thy clothes;
Let none be ashamed of his shoes and hose,
Less still of the steed he rides,
Though poor be the horse he has.

When the eagle comes to the ancient sea, 62
He snaps and hangs his head;
So is a man in the midst of a throng,
Who few to speak for him finds.

To question and answer must all be ready 63
Who wish to be known as wise;
Tell one thy thoughts, but beware of two—
All know what is known to three.

The man who is prudent a measured use 64
Of the might he has will make;
He finds when among the brave he fares
That the boldest he may not be.

[...] 65
[...]
Oft for the words that to others one speaks
He will get but an evil gift.

Too early to many a meeting I came, 66
And some too late have I sought;
The beer was all drunk, or not yet brewed;
Little the loathed man finds.

To their homes men would bid me hither and yon, 67
If at meal-time I needed no meat,
Or would hang two hams in my true friend's house,
Where only one I had eaten.

Eldr er beztr   með ýta sonum   68
ok sólar sýn,   heilyndi sitt,
ef maðr hafa náir,
án við löst at lifa.

Er-at maðr alls vesall,   69
þótt hann sé illa heill;
sumr er af sonum sæll,   sumr af frændum,
sumr af fé ærnu,   sumr af verkum vel.

Betra er lifðum   en sé ólifðum,   70
ey getr kvikr kú;
eld sá ek upp brenna   auðgum manni fyrir,
en úti var dauðr fyr durum.

Haltr ríðr hrossi,   hjörð rekr handar vanr,   71
daufr vegr ok dugir,
blindr er betri   en brenndr séi,
nýtr manngi nás.

Sonr er betri,   þótt sé síð of alinn   72
eftir genginn guma;
sjaldan bautarsteinar   standa brautu nær,
nema reisi niðr at nið.

Tveir ro eins herjar,   tunga er höfuðs bani;   73
er mér í heðin hvern   handar væni.

Nótt verðr feginn   sá er nesti trúir,   74
skammar ro skips ráar;
hverf er haustgríma;
fjölð of viðrir á fimm dögum
en meira á mánuði.

Veit-a hinn,   er vettki veit,   75
margr verðr af aurum api;
maðr er auðigr,   annar óauðigr,
skyli-t þann vítka váar.

Deyr fé,   deyja frændr,   76
deyr sjalfr it sama,
en orðstírr   deyr aldregi,
hveim er sér góðan getr.

Fire for men is the fairest gift,   68
And power to see the sun;
Health as well, if a man may have it,
And a life not stained with sin.

All wretched is no man, though never so sick;   69
Some from their sons have joy,
Some win it from kinsmen, and some from their wealth,
And some from worthy works.

It is better to live than to lie a corpse,   70
The live man catches the cow;
I saw flames rise for the rich man's pyre,
And before his door he lay dead.

The lame rides a horse, the handless is herdsman,   71
The deaf in battle is bold;
The blind man is better than one that is burned,
No good can come of a corpse.

A son is better, though late he be born,   72
And his father to death have fared;
Memory-stones seldom stand by the road
Save when kinsman honors his kin.

Two make a battle, the tongue slays the head;   73
In each furry coat a fist I look for.

He welcomes the night whose fare is enough,   74
Short are the yards of a ship,
Uneasy are autumn nights;
Full oft does the weather change in a week,
And more in a month's time.

A man knows not, if nothing he knows,   75
That gold oft apes begets;
One man is wealthy and one is poor,
Yet scorn for him none should know.

Among Fitjung's sons saw I well-stocked folds—   76
Now bear they the beggar's staff;
Wealth is as swift as a winking eye,
Of friends the falsest it is.

Deyr fé,   deyja frændr,   77
deyr sjalfr it sama,
ek veit einn,   at aldrei deyr:
dómr um dauðan hvern.

Fullar grindr   sá ek fyr Fitjungs sonum,   78
nú bera þeir vánar völ;
svá er auðr   sem augabragð,
hann er valtastr vina.

Ósnotr maðr,   79
ef eignask getr
fé eða fljóðs munuð,
metnaðr hánum þróask,
en mannvit aldregi,
fram gengr hann drjúgt í dul.

Þat er þá reynt,   er þú að rúnum spyrr   80
inum reginkunnum,   þeim er gerðu ginnregin
ok fáði fimbulþulr,   þá hefir hann bazt, ef hann þegir.

At kveldi skal dag leyfa,   81
konu, er brennd er,   mæki, er reyndr er,
mey, er gefin er,   ís, er yfir kemr,
öl, er drukkit er.

Í vindi skal við höggva,   82
veðri á sjó róa,   myrkri við man spjalla,
mörg eru dags augu;   á skip skal skriðar orka,
en á skjöld til hlífar,   mæki höggs,
en mey til kossa.

Við eld skal öl drekka,   83
en á ísi skríða,   magran mar kaupa,
en mæki saurgan,   heima hest feita,
en hund á búi.

Meyjar orðum   skyli manngi trúa   84
né því, er kveðr kona,   því at á hverfanda hvéli
váru þeim hjörtu sköpuð,   brigð í brjóst of lagið.

Brestanda boga,   brennanda loga,   85
gínanda ulfi,   galandi kráku,
rýtanda svíni,   rótlausum viði,
vaxanda vági,   vellanda katli,

Cattle die, and kinsmen die, 77
And so one dies one's self;
But a noble name will never die,
If good renown one gets.

Cattle die, and kinsmen die, 78
And so one dies one's self;
One thing now that never dies,
The fame of a dead man's deeds.

Certain is that which is sought from runes, 79
That the gods so great have made,
And the Master-Poet painted;
[...]
[...] of the race of gods:
Silence is safest and best.

An unwise man, if a maiden's love 80
Or wealth he chances to win,
His pride will wax, but his wisdom never,
Straight forward he fares in conceit.

Give praise to the day at evening, 81
to a woman on her pyre,
To a weapon which is tried, to a maid at wed lock,
To ice when it is crossed, to ale that is drunk.

When the gale blows hew wood, in fair winds seek the water; 82
Sport with maidens at dusk, for day's eyes are many;
From the ship seek swiftness, from the shield protection,
Cuts from the sword, from the maiden kisses.

By the fire drink ale, over ice go on skates; 83
Buy a steed that is lean, and a sword when tarnished,
The horse at home fatten, the hound in thy dwelling.

A man shall trust not the oath of a maid, 84
Nor the word a woman speaks;
For their hearts on a whirling wheel were fashioned,
And fickle their breasts were formed.

In a breaking bow or a burning flame, 85
A ravening wolf or a croaking raven,
In a grunting boar, a tree with roots broken,
In billowy seas or a bubbling kettle.

Fljúganda fleini,   fallandi báru,   86
ísi einnættum,   ormi hringlegnum,
brúðar beðmálum   eða brotnu sverði,
bjarnar leiki   eða barni konungs.

Sjúkum kalfi,   sjalfráða þræli,   87
völu vilmæli,   val nýfelldum.

Akri ársánum   trúi engi maðr   88
né til snemma syni,   veðr ræðr akri.
en vit syni;
hætt er þeira hvárt.

Bróðurbana sínum   þótt á brautu mæti,   89
húsi hálfbrunnu,   hesti alskjótum,
þá er jór ónýtr,   ef einn fótr brotnar,
verði-t maðr svá tryggr   at þessu trúi öllu.

Svá er friðr kvenna,   þeira er flátt hyggja,   90
sem aki jó óbryddum   á ísi hálum,
teitum, tvévetrum   ok sé tamr illa,
eða í byr óðum   beiti stjórnlausu,
eða skyli haltr henda   hrein í þáfjalli.

Bert ek nú mæli,   því at ek bæði veit,   91
brigðr er karla hugr konum;
þá vér fegrst mælum,   er vér flást hyggjum:
þat tælir horska hugi.

Fagrt skal mæla   ok fé bjóða,   92
sá er vill fljóðs ást fá,
líki leyfa   ins ljósa mans,
sá fær, er fríar.

Ástar firna skyli engi maðr   93
annan aldregi;
oft fá á horskan,   er á heimskan né fá,
lostfagrir litir.

Eyvitar firna   er maðr annan skal,   94
þess er um margan gengr guma;
heimska ór horskum   gerir hölða sonu
sá inn máttki munr.

In a flying arrow or falling waters,   86
In ice new formed or the serpent's folds,
In a bride's bed-speech or a broken sword,
In the sport of bears or in sons of kings,

In a calf that is sick or a stubborn thrall,   87
A flattering witch or a foe new slain.

In a brother's slayer, if thou meet him abroad,   88
In a half-burned house, in a horse full swift—
One leg is hurt and the horse is useless—
None had ever such faith as to trust in them all.

Hope not too surely for early harvest,   89
Nor trust too soon in thy son;
The field needs good weather, the son needs wisdom,
And oft is either denied.

The love of women fickle of will   90
Is like starting o'er ice with a steed unshod,
A two-year-old restive and little tamed,
Or steering a rudderless ship in a storm,
Or, lame, hunting reindeer on slippery rocks.

Clear now will I speak, for I know them both,   91
Men false to women are found;
When fairest we speak, then falsest we think,
Against wisdom we work with deceit.

Soft words shall he speak and wealth shall he offer   92
Who longs for a maiden's love,
And the beauty praise of the maiden bright;
He wins whose wooing is best.

Fault for loving let no man find   93
Ever with any other;
Oft the wise are fettered, where fools go free,
By beauty that breeds desire.

Fault with another let no man find   94
For what touches many a man;
Wise men oft into witless fools
Are made by mighty love.

Hugr einn þat veit,   er býr hjarta nær,   95
einn er hann sér of sefa;
öng er sótt verri   hveim snotrum manni
en sér engu at una.

Þat ek þá reynda,   er ek í reyri sat,   96
ok vættak míns munar;
hold ok hjarta   var mér in horska mær;
þeygi ek hana at heldr hefik.

Billings mey   ek fann beðjum á   97
sólhvíta sofa;
jarls ynði   þótti mér ekki vera
nema við þat lík at lifa.

"Auk nær aftni   skaltu, Óðinn, koma,   98
ef þú vilt þér mæla man;
allt eru ósköp,   nema einir viti
slíkan löst saman."

Aftr ek hvarf   ok unna þóttumk   99
vísum vilja frá;
hitt ek hugða,   at ek hafa mynda
geð hennar allt ok gaman.

Svá kom ek næst,   at in nýta var   100
vígdrótt öll of vakin   með brennandum ljósum
ok bornum viði,   svá var mér vílstígr of vitaðr.

Auk nær morgni,   er ek var enn of kominn,   101
þá var saldrótt of sofin;
grey eitt ek þá fann   innar góðu konu
bundit beðjum á.

Mörg er góð mær,   ef görva kannar,   102
hugbrigð við hali;
þá ek þat reynda,   er it ráðspaka
teygða ek á flærðir fljóð;
háðungar hverrar   leitaði mér it horska man,
ok hafða ek þess vettki vífs.

The head alone knows what dwells near the heart,   95
A man knows his mind alone;
No sickness is worse to one who is wise
Than to lack the longed-for joy.

This found I myself, when I sat in the reeds,   96
And long my love awaited;
As my life the maiden wise I loved,
Yet her I never had.

Billing's daughter I found on her bed,   97
In slumber bright as the sun;
Empty appeared an earl's estate
Without that form so fair.

"Odin, again at evening come,   98
If a woman thou wouldst win;
Evil it were if others than we
Should know of such a sin."

Away I hastened, hoping for joy,   99
And careless of counsel wise;
Well I believed that soon I should win
Measureless joy with the maid.

So came I next when night it was,   100
The warriors all were awake;
With burning lights and waving brands
I learned my luckess way.

At morning then, when once more I came,   101
And all were sleeping still,
A dog found in the fair one's place,
Bound there upon her bed.

Many fair maids, if a man but tries them,   102
False to a lover are found;
That did I learn when I longed to gain
With wiles the maiden wise;
Foul scorn was my meed from the crafty maid,
And nought from the woman I won.

Heima glaðr gumi   ok við gesti reifr,　　　　　　　103
sviðr skal um sig vera,   minnigr ok málugr,
ef hann vill margfróðr vera,
oft skal góðs geta;
fimbulfambi heitir,   sá er fátt kann segja,
þat er ósnotrs aðal.

Inn aldna jötun ek sótta,　　　　　　　　　　　　104
nú em ek aftr of kominn: fátt gat ek þegjandi þar;
mörgum orðum   mælta ek í minn frama
í Suttungs sölum.

Gunnlöð mér of gaf   gullnum stóli á　　　　　　105
drykk ins dýra mjaðar;
ill iðgjöld   lét ek hana eftir hafa
síns ins heila hugar,   síns ins svára sefa.

Rata munn　　　　　　　　　　　　　　　　　　106
létumk rúms of fá   ok um grjót gnaga;
yfir ok undir
stóðumk jötna vegir,
svá hætta ek höfði til.

Vel keypts litar   hefi ek vel notit,　　　　　　107
fás er fróðum vant,
því at Óðrerir
er nú upp kominn   á alda vés jaðar.

Ifi er mér á,   at ek væra enn kominn　　　　　108
jötna görðum ór,
ef ek Gunnlaðar né nytak,
innar góðu konu,
þeirar er lögðumk arm yfir.

Ins hindra dags   gengu hrímþursar　　　　　　109
Háva ráðs at fregna   Háva höllu í;
at Bölverki þeir spurðu,
ef hann væri með   böndum kominn
eða hefði hánum Suttungr of sóit.

Baugeið Óðinn,   hygg ek, at unnit hafi;　　　110
hvat skal hans tryggðum trúa?
Suttung svikinn   hann lét sumbli frá
ok grætta Gunnlöðu.

Though glad at home, and merry with guests,   103
A man shall be wary and wise;
The sage and shrewd, wide wisdom seeking,
Must see that his speech be fair;
A fool is he named who nought can say,
For such is the way of the witless.

I found the old giant, now back have I fared,   104
Small gain from silence I got;
Full many a word, my will to get,
I spoke in Suttung's hall.

The mouth of Rati made room for my passage,   105
And space in the stone he gnawed;
Above and below the giants' paths lay,
So rashly I risked my head.

Gunnloth gave on a golden stool   106
A drink of the marvelous mead;
A harsh reward did I let her have
For her heroic heart,
And her spirit troubled sore.

The well-earned beauty well I enjoyed,   107
Little the wise man lacks;
So Othrörir now has up been brought
To the midst of the men of earth.

Hardly, methinks, would I home have come,   108
And left the giants' land,
Had not Gunnloth helped me, the maiden good,
Whose arms about me had been.

The day that followed, the frost-giants came,   109
Some word of Hor to win,
And into the hall of Hor;
Of Bolverk they asked, were he back midst the gods,
Or had Suttung slain him there?

On his ring swore Odin the oath, methinks;   110
Who now his troth shall trust?
Suttung's betrayal he sought with drink,
And Gunnloth to grief he left.

Mál er at þylja   þular stóli á   111
Urðarbrunni at,   sá ek ok þagðak,
sá ek ok hugðak,
hlýdda ek á manna mál;
of rúnar heyrða ek dæma,
né of ráðum þögðu
Háva höllu at,   Háva höllu í,
heyrða ek segja svá:

Ráðumk þér, Loddfáfnir,   en þú ráð nemir—   112
njóta mundu, ef þú nemr,
þér munu góð, ef þú getr:
nótt þú rís-at   nema á njósn séir
eða þú leitir þér innan út staðar.

Ráðumk þér, Loddfáfnir,   en þú ráð nemir—   113
njóta mundu, ef þú nemr,
þér munu góð, ef þú getr:
fjölkunnigri konu   skal-at-tu í faðmi sofa,
svá at hon lyki þik liðum.

Hon svá gerir,   at þú gáir eigi   114
þings né þjóðans máls;
mat þú vill-at   né mannskis gaman,
ferr þú sorgafullr at sofa.

Ráðumk þér, Loddfáfnir,   115
en þú ráð nemir—
njóta mundu, ef þú nemr,   þér munu góð, ef þú getr:
annars konu   teygðu þér aldregi
eyrarúnu at.

Ráðumk þér, Loddfáfnir,   116
en þú ráð nemir—
njóta mundu, ef þú nemr,
þér munu góð, ef þú getr:
á fjalli eða firði,   ef þik fara tíðir,
fásktu at virði vel.

It is time to chant from the chanter's stool; 111
By the wells of Urth I was,
I saw and was silent, I saw and thought,
And heard the speech of Hor.
Of runes heard I words, nor were counsels wanting,
At the hall of Hor,
In the hall of Hor;
Such was the speech I heard.

I rede thee, Loddfafnir! and hear thou my rede— 112
Profit thou hast if thou hearest,
Great thy gain if thou learnest:
Rise not at night, save if news thou seekest,
Or fain to the outhouse wouldst fare.

I rede thee, Loddfafnir! and hear thou my rede— 113
Profit thou hast if thou hearest,
Great thy gain if thou learnest:
Beware of sleep on a witch's bosom,
Nor let her limbs ensnare thee.

Such is her might that thou hast no mind 114
For the council or meeting of men;
Meat thou hatest, joy thou hast not,
And sadly to slumber thou farest.

I rede thee, Loddfafnir! and hear thou my rede— 115
Profit thou hast if thou hearest,
Great thy gain if thou learnest:
Seek never to win the wife of another,
Or long for her secret love.

I rede thee, Loddfafnir! and hear thou my rede— 116
Profit thou hast if thou hearest,
Great thy gain if thou learnest:
If o'er mountains or gulfs thou fain wouldst go,
Look well to thy food for the way.

Ráðumk þér, Loddfáfnir, 117
en þú ráð nemir—
njóta mundu, ef þú nemr,   þér munu góð, ef þú getr:
illan mann   láttu aldregi
óhöpp at þér vita,
því at af illum manni   fær þú aldregi
gjöld ins góða hugar.

Ofarla bíta   ek sá einum hal 118
orð illrar konu;
fláráð tunga   varð hánum at fjörlagi
ok þeygi of sanna sök.

Ráðumk þér, Loddfáfnir,   en þú ráð nemir— 119
njóta mundu, ef þú nemr,
þér munu góð, ef þú getr:
veistu, ef þú vin átt,
þann er þú vel trúir,
far þú at finna oft,   því at hrísi vex
ok hávu grasi   vegr, er vættki treðr.

Ráðumk þér, Loddfáfnir,   en þú ráð nemir— 120
njóta mundu, ef þú nemr,
þér munu góð, ef þú getr:
góðan mann   teygðu þér at gamanrúnum
ok nem líknargaldr, meðan þú lifir.

Ráðumk þér, Loddfáfnir, 121
en þú ráð nemir—
njóta mundu, ef þú nemr,
þér munu góð, ef þú getr:
vin þínum   ver þú aldregi
fyrri at flaumslitum;
sorg etr hjarta,   ef þú segja né náir
einhverjum allan hug.

Ráðumk þér, Loddfáfnir,   en þú ráð nemir— 122
njóta mundu, ef þú nemr,
þér munu góð, ef þú getr:
orðum skipta   þú skalt aldregi
við ósvinna apa,
Því at af illum ma

HOVAMOL

I rede thee, Loddfafnir! and hear thou my rede— 117
Profit thou hast if thou hearest,
Great thy gain if thou learnest:
An evil man thou must not let
Bring aught of ill to thee;
For an evil man will never make
Reward for a worthy thought.

I saw a man who was wounded sore 118
By an evil woman's word;
A lying tongue his death-blow launched,
And no word of truth there was.

I rede thee, Loddfafnir! and hear thou my rede— 119
Profit thou hast if thou hearest,
Great thy gain if thou learnest:
If a friend thou hast whom thou fully wilt trust,
Then fare to find him oft;
For brambles grow and waving grass
On the rarely trodden road.

I rede thee, Loddfafnir! and hear thou my rede— 120
Profit thou hast if thou hearest,
Great thy gain if thou learnest:
A good man find to hold in friendship,
And give heed to his healing charms.

I rede thee, Loddfafnir! and hear thou my rede— 121
Profit thou hast if thou hearest,
Great thy gain if thou learnest:
Be never the first to break with thy friend
The bond that holds you both;
Care eats the heart if thou canst not speak
To another all thy thought.

I rede thee, Loddfafnir! and hear thou my rede— 122
Profit thou hast if thou hearest,
Great thy gain if thou learnest:
Exchange of words with a witless ape
Thou must not ever make.

nni mundu aldregi 123
góðs laun of geta,
en góðr maðr
mun þik gerva mega líknfastan at lofi.

Sifjum er þá blandat, hver er segja ræðr 124
einum allan hug;
allt er betra en sé brigðum at vera;
er-a sá vinr öðrum, er vilt eitt segir.

Ráðumk, þér Loddfáfnir, en þú ráð nemir— 125
njóta mundu, ef þú nemr, þér munu góð, ef þú getr:
þrimr orðum senna skal-at-tu þér við verra mann
oft inn betri bilar,
þá er inn verri vegr.

Ráðumk þér, Loddfáfnir, 126
en þú ráð nemir—
njóta mundu, ef þú nemr,
þér munu góð, ef þú getr:
skósmiðr þú verir né skeftismiðr,
nema þú sjalfum þér séir:
skór er skapaðr illa eða skaft sé rangt,
þá er þér böls beðit.

Ráðumk þér, Loddfáfnir, 127
en þú ráð nemir—
njóta mundu, ef þú nemr, þér munu góð, ef þú getr:
hvars þú böl kannt, kveð þú þér bölvi at
ok gef-at þínum fjándum frið.

Ráðumk þér, Loddfáfnir, en þú ráð nemir— 128
njóta mundu, ef þú nemr,
þér munu góð, ef þú getr:
illu feginn ver þú aldregi,
en lát þér at góðu getit.

Ráðumk þér, Loddfáfnir, en þú ráð nemir— 129
njóta mundu, ef þú nemr,
þér munu góð, ef þú getr:
upp líta skal-at-tu í orrustu,
gjalti glíkir verða gumna synir—
síðr þitt of heilli halir.

For never thou mayst from an evil man 123
A good requital get;
But a good man oft the greatest love
Through words of praise will win thee.

Mingled is love when a man can speak 124
To another all his thought;
Nought is so bad as false to be,
No friend speaks only fair.

I rede thee, Loddfafnir! and hear thou my rede— 125
Profit thou hast if thou hearest,
Great thy gain if thou learnest:
With a worse man speak not three words in dispute,
Ill fares the better oft
When the worse man wields a sword.

I rede thee, Loddfafnir! and hear thou my rede— 126
Profit thou hast if thou hearest,
Great thy gain if thou learnest:
A shoemaker be, or a maker of shafts,
For only thy single self;
If the shoe is ill made, or the shaft prove false,
Then evil of thee men think.

I rede thee, Loddfafnir! and hear thou my rede— 127
Profit thou hast if thou hearest,
Great thy gain if thou learnest:
If evil thou knowest, as evil proclaim it,
And make no friendship with foes.

I rede thee, Loddfafnir! and hear thou my rede, 128
Profit thou hast if thou hearest,
Great thy gain if thou learnest:
In evil never joy shalt thou know,
But glad the good shall make thee.

I rede thee, Loddfafnir! and hear thou my rede— 129
Profit thou hast if thou hearest,
Great thy gain if thou learnest:
Look not up when the battle is on—
Like madmen the sons of men become—
Lest men bewitch thy wits.

Ráðumk þér, Loddfáfnir,   en þú ráð nemir—   130
njóta mundu, ef þú nemr,
þér munu góð, ef þú getr:
ef þú vilt þér góða konu   kveðja at gamanrúnum
ok fá fögnuð af,   fögru skaltu heita
ok láta fast vera;
leiðisk manngi gótt, ef getr.

Ráðumk þér, Loddfáfnir,   en þú ráð nemir—   131
njóta mundu, ef þú nemr,
þér munu góð, ef þú getr:
varan bið ek þik vera   ok eigi ofvaran;
ver þú við öl varastr   ok við annars konu
ok við þat it þriðja,   at þjófar né leiki.

Ráðumk þér, Loddfáfnir,   en þú ráð nemir—   132
njóta mundu, ef þú nemr,
þér munu góð, ef þú getr:
at háði né hlátri   hafðu aldregi
gest né ganganda.

Oft vitu ógörla,   þeir er sitja inni fyrir,   133
hvers þeir ro kyns, er koma;
er-at maðr svá góðr   at galli né fylgi,
né svá illr, at einugi dugi.

Ráðumk þér, Loddfáfnir,   en þú ráð nemir—   134
njóta mundu, ef þú nemr,
þér munu góð, ef þú getr:
at hárum þul   hlæ þú aldregi,
oft er gótt,
þat er gamlir kveða;
oft ór skörpum belg   skilin orð koma
þeim er hangir með hám   ok skollir með skrám
ok váfir með vílmögum.

Ráðumk þér, Loddfáfnir,   en þú ráð nemir—   135
njóta mundu, ef þú nemr,
þér munu góð, ef þú getr:
gest þú né geyja   né á grind hrekir;
get þú váluðum vel.

I rede thee, Loddfafnir! and hear thou my rede— 130
Profit thou hast if thou hearest,
Great thy gain if thou learnest:
If thou fain wouldst win a woman's love,
And gladness get from her,
Fair be thy promise and well fulfilled;
None loathes what good he gets.

I rede thee, Loddfafnir! and hear thou my rede— 131
Profit thou hast if thou hearest,
Great thy gain if thou learnest:
I bid thee be wary, but be not fearful;
Beware most with ale or another's wife,
And third beware lest a thief outwit thee.

I rede thee, Loddfafnir! and hear thou my rede— 132
Profit thou hast if thou hearest,
Great thy gain if thou learnest:
Scorn or mocking ne'er shalt thou make
Of a guest or a journey-goer.

Oft scarcely he knows who sits in the house 133
What kind is the man who comes;
None so good is found that faults he has not,
Nor so wicked that nought he is worth.

I rede thee, Loddfafnir! and hear thou my rede— 134
Profit thou hast if thou hearest,
Great thy gain if thou learnest:
Scorn not ever the gray-haired singer,
Oft do the old speak good;
Oft from shrivelled skin come skillful counsels,
Though it hang with the hides,
And flap with the pelts,
And is blown with the bellies.

I rede thee, Loddfafnir! and hear thou my rede— 135
Profit thou hast if thou hearest,
Great thy gain if thou learnest:
Curse not thy guest, nor show him thy gate,
Deal well with a man in want.

Rammt er þat tré,   er ríða skal   136
öllum at upploki;
baug þú gef,   eða þat biðja mun
þér læs hvers á liðu.

Ráðumk þér, Loddfáfnir,   en þú ráð nemir—   137
njóta mundu, ef þú nemr,   þér munu góð, ef þú getr:
hvars þú öl drekkir,   kjós þér jarðar megin,
því at jörð tekr við ölðri,   en eldr við sóttum,
eik við abbindi,   ax við fjölkynngi,
höll við hýrógi,
heiftum skal mána kveðja,
beiti við bitsóttum,   en við bölvi rúnar,
fold skal við flóði taka.

Veit ek, at ek hekk   vindga meiði á   138
nætr allar níu,   geiri undaðr
ok gefinn Óðni,
sjalfr sjalfum mér,
á þeim meiði,   er manngi veit
hvers af rótum renn.

Við hleifi mik   139
sældu né við hornigi;
nýsta ek niðr,   nam ek upp rúnar,
æpandi nam,   fell ek aftr þaðan.

Fimbulljóð níu   140
nam ek af inum frægja syni   Bölþorns, Bestlu föður,
ok ek drykk of gat
ins dýra mjaðar,   ausinn Óðreri.

Þá nam ek frævask   ok fróðr vera   141
ok vaxa ok vel hafask,
orð mér af orði
orðs leitaði,   verk mér af verki
verks leitaði.

Rúnar munt þú finna   ok ráðna stafi,   142
mjök stóra stafi,   mjök stinna stafi,
er fáði fimbulþulr
ok gerðu ginnregin
ok reist hroftr rögna.

Strong is the beam that raised must be   136
To give an entrance to all;
Give it a ring, or grim will be
The wish it would work on thee.

I rede thee, Loddfafnir! and hear thou my rede—   137
Profit thou hast if thou hearest,
Great thy gain if thou learnest:
When ale thou drinkest seek might of earth,
For earth cures drink, and fire cures ills,
The oak cures tightness, the ear cures magic,
Rye cures rupture, the moon cures rage,
Grass cures the scab, and runes the sword-cut;
The field absorbs the flood.

I ween that I hung on the windy tree,   138
Hung there for nights full nine;
With the spear I was wounded, and offered I was
To Odin, myself to myself,
On the tree that none may ever know
What root beneath it runs.

None made me happy with loaf or horn,   139
And there below I looked;
I took up the runes, shrieking I took them,
And forthwith back I fell.

Nine mighty songs I got from the son   140
Of Bolthorn, Bestla's father;
And a drink I got of the goodly mead
Poured out from Othrörir.

Then began I to thrive, and wisdom to get,   141
I grew and well I was;
Each word led me on to another word,
Each deed to another deed.

Runes shalt thou find, and fateful signs,   142
That the king of singers colored,
And the mighty gods have made;
Full strong the signs, full mighty the signs
That the ruler of gods doth write.

Óðinn með ásum,   en fyr alfum Dáinn,   143
Dvalinn ok dvergum fyrir,
Ásviðr jötnum fyrir,
ek reist sjalfr sumar.

Veistu, hvé rísta skal?   Veistu, hvé ráða skal?   144
Veistu, hvé fáa skal?   Veistu, hvé freista skal?
Veistu, hvé biðja skal?   Veistu, hvé blóta skal?
Veistu, hvé senda skal?   Veistu, hvé sóa skal?

Betra er óbeðit   en sé ofblótit,   145
ey sér til gildis gjöf;
betra er ósent   en sé ofsóit.
Svá Þundr of reist   fyr þjóða rök,
þar hann upp of reis,   er hann aftr of kom.

Ljóð ek þau kann,   146
er kann-at þjóðans kona
ok mannskis mögr.
Hjalp heitir eitt,   en þat þér hjalpa mun
við sökum ok sorgum   ok sútum görvöllum.

Þat kann ek annat,   147
er þurfu ýta synir,
þeir er vilja læknar lifa.

Það kann ek þriðja: 148
ef mér verðr þörf mikil   hafts við mína heiftmögu,
eggjar ek deyfi   minna andskota,
bíta-t þeim vápn né velir.

Þat kann ek it fjórða: 149
ef mér fyrðar bera   bönd að boglimum,
svá ek gel,
at ek ganga má,
sprettr mér af fótum fjöturr,   en af höndum haft.

Þat kann ek it fimmta: 150
ef ek sé af fári skotinn   flein í folki vaða,
fýgr-a hann svá stinnt,
at ek stöðvig-a-k   ef ek hann sjónum of sék.

Odin for the gods, Dain for the elves,   143
And Dvalin for the dwarfs,
Alsvith for giants and all mankind,
And some myself I wrote.

Knowest how one shall write, knowest how one shall rede?   144
Knowest how one shall tint, knowest how one makes trial?
Knowest how one shall ask, knowest how one shall offer?
Knowest how one shall send, knowest how one shall sacrifice?

Better no prayer than too big an offering,   145
By thy getting measure thy gift;
Better is none than too big a sacrifice,
[...]
So Thund of old wrote ere man's race began,
Where he rose on high when home he came.

The songs I know that king's wives know not,   146
Nor men that are sons of men;
The first is called help, and help it can bring thee
In sorrow and pain and sickness.

A second I know, that men shall need   147
Who leechcraft long to use;
[...]
[...]

A third I know, if great is my need   148
Of fetters to hold my foe;
Blunt do I make mine enemy's blade,
Nor bites his sword or staff.

A fourth I know, if men shall fasten   149
Bonds on my bended legs;
So great is the charm that forth I may go,
The fetters spring from my feet,
Broken the bonds from my hands.

A fifth I know, if I see from afar   150
An arrow fly 'gainst the folk;
It flies not so swift that I stop it not,
If ever my eyes behold it.

Þat kann ek it sétta: 151
ef mik særir þegn á vrótum hrás viðar,
ok þann hal er mik heifta kveðr,
þann eta mein heldr en mik.

Þat kann ek it sjaunda: 152
ef ek sé hávan loga sal of sessmögum,
brennr-at svá breitt, at ek hánum bjargig-a-k;
þann kann ek galdr at gala.

Þat kann ek it átta, er öllum er 153
nytsamligt at nema:
hvars hatr vex með hildings sonum
þat má ek bæta brátt.

Þat kann ek it níunda: 154
ef mik nauðr of stendr at
bjarga fari mínu á floti,
vind ek kyrri vági á
ok svæfik allan sæ.

Þat kann ek it tíunda: 155
ef ek sé túnriður leika lofti á,
ek svá vinnk, at þær villar fara
sinna heimhama, sinna heimhuga.

Þat kann ek it ellifta: 156
ef ek skal til orrostu leiða langvini,
und randir ek gel,
en þeir með ríki fara
heilir hildar til, heilir hildi frá,
koma þeir heilir hvaðan.

Þat kann ek it tolfta: 157
ef ek sé á tré uppi
váfa virgilná,
svá ek ríst ok í rúnum fák,
at sá gengr gumi ok mælir við mik.

Þat kann ek it þrettánda: 158
ef ek skal þegn ungan verpa vatni á,
mun-at hann falla, þótt hann í folk komi,
hnígr-a sá halr fyr hjörum.

A sixth I know, if harm one seeks | 151
With a sapling's roots to send me;
The hero himself who wreaks his hate
Shall taste the ill ere I.

A seventh I know, if I see in flames | 152
The hall o'er my comrades' heads;
It burns not so wide that I will not quench it,
I know that song to sing.

An eighth I know, that is to all | 153
Of greatest good to learn;
When hatred grows among heroes' sons,
I soon can set it right.

A ninth I know, if need there comes | 154
To shelter my ship on the flood;
The wind I calm upon the waves,
And the sea I put to sleep.

A tenth I know, what time I see | 155
House-riders flying on high;
So can I work that wildly they go,
Showing their true shapes,
Hence to their own homes.

An eleventh I know, if needs I must lead | 156
To the fight my long-loved friends;
I sing in the shields, and in strength they go
Whole to the field of fight,
Whole from the field of fight,
And whole they come thence home.

A twelfth I know, if high on a tree | 157
I see a hanged man swing;
So do I write and color the runes
That forth he fares,
And to me talks.

A thirteenth I know, if a thane full young | 158
With water I sprinkle well;
He shall not fall, though he fares mid the host,
Nor sink beneath the swords.

Þat kann ek it fjögurtánda: 159
ef ek skal fyrða liði   telja tíva fyrir,
ása ok alfa   ek kann allra skil;
fár kann ósnotr svá.

Þat kann ek it fimmtánda 160
er gól Þjóðrerir   dvergr fyr Dellings durum:
afl gól hann ásum,   en alfum frama,
hyggju Hroftatý.

Þat kann ek it sextánda: 161
ef ek vil ins svinna mans
hafa geð allt ok gaman,   hugi ek hverfi
hvítarmri konu,   ok sný ek hennar öllum sefa.

Þat kann ek it sjautjánda 162
at mik mun seint firrask
it manunga man.
Ljóða þessa   mun þú, Loddfáfnir,
lengi vanr vera;
þó sé þér góð, ef þú getr,
nýt ef þú nemr,   þörf ef þú þiggr.

Þat kann ek it átjánda, 163
er ek æva kennik   mey né manns konu,
allt er betra, er einn of kann;
þat fylgir ljóða lokum—
nema þeiri einni,   er mik armi verr,
eða mín systir sé.

Nú eru Háva mál   kveðin Háva höllu í, 164
allþörf ýta sonum,   óþörf jötna sonum;
heill sá, er kvað,   heill sá, er kann,
njóti sá, er nam,   heilir, þeirs hlýddu.

A fourteenth I know, if fain I would name   159
To men the mighty gods;
All know I well of the gods and elves,
Few be the fools know this.

A fifteenth I know, that before the doors   160
Of Delling sang Thjothrörir the dwarf;
Might he sang for the gods, and glory for elves,
And wisdom for Hroptatyr wise.

A sixteenth I know, if I seek delight   161
To win from a maiden wise;
The mind I turn of the white-armed maid,
And thus change all her thoughts.

A seventeenth I know, so that seldom shall go   162
A maiden young from me;
Long these songs thou shalt, Loddfafnir,
Seek in vain to sing;
Yet good it were if thou mightest get them,
Well, if thou wouldst them learn,
Help, if thou hadst them.

An eighteenth I know, that ne'er will I tell   163
To maiden or wife of man—
The best is what none but one's self doth know,
So comes the end of the songs—
Save only to her in whose arms I lie,
Or who else my sister is.

Now are Hor's words spoken in the hall,   164
Kind for the kindred of men,
Cursed for the kindred of giants:
Hail to the speaker, and to him who learns!
Profit be his who has them!
Hail to them who hearken!

ENDNOTES

1. This stanza is quoted by Snorri, the second line being omitted in most of the *Prose Edda* manuscripts.[1]

2. Probably the first and second lines had originally nothing to do with the third and fourth, the last two not referring to host or guest, but to the general danger of backing one's views with the sword.

6. Lines 5 and 6 appear to have been added to the stanza.

12. Some editors have combined this stanza in various ways with the last two lines of stanza 11, as in the manuscript the first two lines of the latter are abbreviated, and, if they belong there at all, are presumably identical with the first two lines of stanza 10.

13. *The heron*: the bird of forgetfulness, referred to in line 1. *Gunnloth*: the daughter of the giant Suttung, from whom Odin won the mead of poetry. For this episode see stanzas 104–110.

14. *Fjalar*: apparently another name for Suttung. This stanza, and probably 13, seem to have been inserted as illustrative.

25. The first two lines are abbreviated in the manuscript, but are doubtless identical with the first two lines of stanza 24.

27. The last two lines were probably added as a commentary on lines 3

---

1 No corrections have been made to Bellows' annotations, but it should be noted that most of his references to prosodic interpolations or errors derive from an obsolete view of the schemes which was argued and accepted mostly after his time. His annotations have not been altered, as it would require substantial revision of many of them.
 For information on this issue, see the introduction to *Hamthismol* in this volume.

and 4.

36. The manuscript has "little" in place of "a hut" in line 1, but this involves an error in the initial-rhymes, and the emendation has been generally accepted.

37. Lines 1 and 2 are abbreviated in the manuscript, but are doubtless identical with the first two lines of stanza 36.

39. In the manuscript this stanza follows stanza 40.

40. The key-word in line 3 is missing in the manuscript, but editors have agreed in inserting a word meaning "generous."

41. In line 3 the manuscript adds "givers again" to "gift-givers."

55–56. The first pairs of lines are abbreviated in the manuscript.

61. The fifth line is probably a spurious addition.

62. This stanza follows stanza 63 in the manuscript, but there are marks therein indicating the transposition.

65. The manuscript indicates no lacuna (lines 1 and 2). Many editors have filled out the stanza with two lines from late paper manuscripts, the passage running:

"A man must be watchful and wary as well,
And fearful of trusting a friend."

70. The manuscript has "and a worthy life" in place of "than to lie a corpse" in line 1, but Rask suggested the emendation as early as 1818, and most editors have followed him.

73–74. These seven lines are obviously a jumble. The two lines of stanza 73 not only appear out of place, but the verse form is unlike that of the surrounding stanzas. In 74, the second line is clearly interpolated, and line 1 has little enough connection with lines 3, 4 and 5. It looks as though some compiler (or copyist) had inserted here various odds and ends for which he could find no better place.

75. The word "gold" in line 2 is more or less conjectural, the manuscript being obscure. The reading in line 4 is also doubtful.

76. in the manuscript this stanza follows 78, the order being: 77, 78, 76, 80, 79, 81. *Fitjung* ("the Nourisher"): Earth.

79. This stanza is certainly in bad shape, and probably out of place here. Its reference to runes as magic signs suggests that it properly belongs in some list of charms like the *Ljothatal* (stanzas 147–165). The stanza-form is so irregular as to show either that something has been lost or that there have been interpolations. The manuscript indicates no lacuna; Gering fills out the assumed gap as follows:

"Certain is that which is sought from runes, The runes—" etc.

81. With this stanza the verse-form, as indicated in the translation, abruptly changes to Malahattr. What has happened seems to have been something like this. Stanza 80 introduces the idea of man's love for woman. Consequently some reciter or compiler (or possibly even a copyist) took occasion to insert at this point certain stanzas concerning the ways of women. Thus stanza 80 would account for the introduction of stanzas 81 and 82, which, in turn, apparently drew stanza 83 in with them. Stanza 84 suggests the fickleness of women, and is immediately followed—again with a change of verse-form—by a list of things equally untrustworthy (stanzas 85–90). Then, after a few more stanzas on love in the regular measure of the *Hovamol* (stanza 91–95), is introduced, by way of illustration, Odin's story of his {footnote p. 46} adventure with Billing's daughter (stanzas 96–102). Some such process of growth, whatever its specific stages may have been, must be assumed to account for the curious chaos of the whole passage from stanza 81 to stanza 102.

84. Lines 3 and 4 are quoted in the *Fostbræthrasaga*.

85. Stanzas 85–88 and 90 are in Fornyrthislag, and clearly come from a different source from the rest of the *Hovamol*.

87. The stanza is doubtless incomplete. Some editors add from a late paper manuscript two lines running:

"In a light, clear sky or a laughing throng, In the bowl of a dog or a harlot's grief!"

89. This stanza follows stanza 89 in the manuscript. Many editors have changed the order, for while stanza 89 is pretty clearly an interpolation wherever it stands, it seriously interferes with the sense if it breaks in between 87 and 88.

96. Here begins the passage (stanzas 96–102) illustrating the falseness of woman by the story of Odin's unsuccessful love affair with Billing's daughter. Of this person we know nothing beyond what is here told, but the story needs little comment.

102. Rask adds at the beginning of this stanza two lines from a late paper manuscript, running:

"Few are so good that false they are never
To cheat the mind of a man."

He makes these two lines plus lines 1 and 2 a full stanza, and line 3, 4, 5, and 6 a second stanza.

103. With this stanza the subject changes abruptly, and apparently the virtues of fair speech, mentioned in the last three lines, account for the introduction, from what source cannot be known, of the story of Odin and the mead of song (stanzas 104–110).

104. The giant *Suttung* ("the old giant") possessed the magic mead, a draught of which conferred the gift of poetry. Odin, desiring to obtain it, changed himself into a snake, bored his way through a mountain into Suttung's home, made love to the giant's daughter, Gunnloth, and by her connivance drank up all the mead. Then he flew away in the form of an eagle, leaving Gunnloth to her fate. While with Suttung he assumed the name of Bolverk ("the Evil-Doer").

105. *Rati* ("the Traveller"): the gimlet with which Odin bored through the mountain to reach Suttung's home.

106. Probably either the fourth or the fifth line is a spurious addition.

107. *Othrörir*: here the name of the magic mead itself, whereas in stanza 141 it is the name of the vessel containing it. Odin had no intention of bestowing any of the precious mead upon men, but as he was flying over the earth, hotly pursued by Suttung, he spilled some of it out of his mouth, and in this way mankind also won the gift of poetry.

108. *Hor*: Odin ("the High One"). The frost-giants, Suttung's kinsmen, appear not to have suspected Odin of being identical with Bolverk, possibly because the oath referred to in stanza 110 was an oath made by Odin to Suttung that there was no such person as Bolverk among the gods. The giants, of course, fail to get from Odin the information they seek concerning Bolverk, but Odin is keenly conscious of having violated the most sacred of oaths, that sworn on his ring.

111. With this stanza begins the Loddfafnismol (stanzas 111–138). Loddfafnir is apparently a wandering singer, who, from his "chanter's stool," recites the verses which he claims to have received from Odin. *Wells of Urth*: cf. Voluspo, 19 and note. Urth ("the Past") is one of the

three Norns. This stanza is apparently in corrupt form, and editors have tried many experiments with it, both in rejecting lines as spurious and in rearranging the words and punctuation. It looks rather as though the first four lines formed a complete stanza, and the last four had crept in later. The phrase translated "the speech of Hor" is "Hova mol," later used as the title for the entire poem.

112. Lines 1–3 are the formula, repeated (abbreviated in the manuscript) in most of the stanzas, with which Odin prefaces his counsels to Loddfafnir, and throughout this section, except in stanzas 111 and 138, Loddfafnir represents himself as simply quoting Odin's words. The material is closely analogous to that contained in the first eighty stanzas of the poem. In some cases (e. g., stanzas 117, 119, 121, 126 and 130) the formula precedes a full four-line stanza instead of two (or three) lines.

129. Line 5 is apparently interpolated.

131. Lines 5–6 probably were inserted from a different poem.

133. Many editors reject the last two lines of this stanza as spurious, putting the first two lines at the end of the preceding stanza. Others, attaching lines 3 and 4 to stanza 132, insert as the first two lines of stanza 133 two lines from a late paper manuscript, running:

"Evil and good do men's sons ever
"Mingled bear in their breasts."

134. Presumably the last four lines have been added to this stanza, for the parallelism in the last three makes it probable that they belong together. The wrinkled skin of the old man is compared with the dried skins and bellies of animals kept for various purposes hanging in an Icelandic house.

136. This stanza suggests the dangers of too much hospitality. The beam (bolt) which is ever being raised to admit guests becomes weak thereby. It needs a ring to help it in keeping the door closed, and without the ability at times to ward off guests a man becomes the victim of his own generosity.

137. The list of "household remedies" in this stanza is doubtless interpolated. Their nature needs no comment here.

138. In the manuscript this stanza comes at the end of the entire poem, following stanza 165. Most recent editors have followed Müllenhoff in shifting it to this position, as it appears to conclude the passage introduced by the somewhat similar stanza 111.

139. With this stanza begins the most confusing part of the *Hovamol*: the group of eight stanzas leading up to the *Ljothatal*, or list of charms. Certain paper manuscripts have before this stanza a title: "Odin's Tale of the Runes." Apparently stanzas 139, 140 and 142 are fragments of an account of how Odin obtained the runes; 141 is erroneously inserted from some version of the magic mead story (cf. stanzas 104–110); and stanzas 143, 144, 145, and 146 are from miscellaneous sources, all, however, dealing with the general subject of runes. With stanza 147 a clearly continuous passage begins once more. *The windy tree*: the ash Yggdrasil (literally "the Horse of Odin," so called because of this story), on which Odin, in order to win the magic runes, hanged himself as an offering to himself, and wounded himself with his own spear. Lines 5 and 6 have presumably been borrowed from *Svipdagsmol*, 30.

140. This stanza, interrupting as it does the account of Odin's winning the runes, appears to be an interpolation. The meaning of the stanza is most obscure. Bolthorn was Odin's grandfather, and Bestla his mother. We do not know the name of the uncle here mentioned, but it has been suggested that this son of Bolthorn was Mimir (cf. *Voluspo*, 27 and note, and 47 and note). In any case, the nine magic songs which he learned from his uncle seem to have enabled him to win the magic mead (cf. stanzas 104–110). Concerning *Othrörir*, here used as the name of the vessel containing the mead, cf. stanza 107 and note.

142. This and the following stanza belong together, and in many editions appear as a single stanza. They presumably come from some lost poem on the authorship of the runes. Lines 2 and 3 follow line 4 in the manuscript; the transposition was suggested by Bugge. *The king of singers*: Odin. The magic signs (runes) were commonly carved in wood, then colored red.

143. *Dain* and *Dvalin*: dwarfs; cf. *Voluspo*, 14, and note. Dain, however, may here be one of the elves rather than the dwarf of that name. The two names also appear together in *Grimnismol*, 33, where they are applied to two of the four harts that nibble at the topmost twigs of Yggdrasil. *Alsvith* ("the All Wise") appears nowhere else as a giant's name. *Myself*: Odin. We have no further information concerning the list of those who wrote the runes for the various races, and these four lines seem like a confusion of names in the rather hazy mind of some reciter.

144. This Malahattr stanza appears to be a regular religious formula, concerned less with the runes which one "writes" and "tints" (cf. stanza 79) than with the prayers which one "asks" and the sacrifices which one "offers" and "sends." Its origin is wholly uncertain, but it is clearly an interpolation here. In the manuscript the phrase "knowest?" is abbreviated

after the first line.

145. This stanza as translated here follows the manuscript reading, except in assuming a gap between lines 3 and 5. In Vigfusson and Powell's *Corpus Poeticum Boreale* the first three lines have somehow been expanded into eight. The last two lines are almost certainly misplaced; Bugge suggests that they belong at the end of stanza 144. *Thund*: another name for Odin. *When home he came*: presumably after obtaining the runes as described in stanzas 139 and 140.

146. With this stanza begins the *Ljothatal*, or list of charms. The magic songs themselves are not given, but in each case the peculiar application of the charm is explained. The passage, which is certainly approximately complete as far as it goes, runs to the end of the poem. In the manuscript and in most editions line 4 falls into two half-lines, running:

"In sickness and pain and every sorrow."

147. *Second*, etc., appear in the manuscript as Roman numerals. The manuscript indicates no gap after line 2.

151. The sending of a root with runes written thereon was an excellent way of causing death. So died the Icelandic hero Grettir the Strong.

155. *House-riders*: witches, who ride by night on the roofs of houses, generally in the form of wild beasts. Possibly one of the last two lines is spurious.

156. The last line looks like an unwarranted addition, and line 4 may likewise be spurious.

157. Lines 4–5 are probably expanded from a single line.

158. The sprinkling of a child with water was an established custom long before Christianity brought its conception of baptism.

160. This stanza, according to Müllenhoff, was the original conclusion of the poem, the phrase "a fifteenth" being inserted only after stanzas 162–165 had crept in. *Delling*: a seldom mentioned god who married Not (Night). Their son was Dag (Day). *Thjothrörir*: not mentioned elsewhere. *Hroptatyr*: Odin.

162. Some editors have combined these two lines with stanza 164. Others have assumed that the gap follows the first half-line, making "so that from me" the end of the stanza.

163. This stanza is almost totally obscure. The third and fourth lines look like interpolations.

164. In the manuscript this stanza comes at the end of the entire poem, following stanza 163. Most recent editors have followed Müllenhoff in shifting it to this position, as it appears to conclude the passage introduced by the somewhat similar stanza 111.

VAFTHRUTHNISMOL
THE BALLAD OF VAFTHRUTHNIR

INTRODUCTION

The *Vafthruthnismol* represents the first poem in the vein of a riddle game held between two or more participants, to demonstrate their skill and wisdom for the audience. As such, it probably existed as a religious mnemonic tool by *Goði* (Priests) or *Skalds* (Poets) to learn and retain large amounts of cosmological information within a convenient narrative format. In a matter of speaking, the stories exist as a sort of encyclopedia of Germanic mythology. An interesting quandary arises, then, of how literally one is to take the events of the story in a religious sense, if they do indeed exist mostly as a mnemonic tool for instruction. The interpretation favored here is that the literal event must have been believed to have occurred (Odin travels to play a riddle game with the giant Vafthruthnir), but many of the questions therein are creatively repurposed for man's need. Perhaps the only real record of the event is the ending twist, which otherwise stands out as without purpose but which would be wholly within the character of Odin to ask. In any case, we may be assured that the various answers delivered between the pair are all themselves theologically accurate.

The *Vafthruthnismol* in particular is of famous origin, starting with a discussion between the Gods Odin and Frigg in which the latter holds the *jotun* Vafthruthnir and his wisdom in high repute, leading Odin to seek him out for a riddle game to put him to the test and presumably see if he may hold knowledge of value to the wandering God. This leads to Odin disguising himself and a series of riddle contests between the two ensue, ending in the famously controversial tactic of Odin asking his foe

"What spake Odin himself in the ears of his son, ere in the bale-fire he burned?"—a question to which only Odin would have the answer and which is, quite obviously, not a proper riddle at all.

Some readers may find this exchange somewhat familiar, for it also served as the basis and inspiration for Tolkien in the Hobbit, when Bilbo Baggins finds the One Ring in a cave and participates in a riddle contest with the malevolent Gollum, besting him by asking the question "what do I have in my pocket?" and revealing that he has stolen the Ring.

A Mountain in Romsdal, Norway

Óðinn kvað:
"Ráð þú mér nú, Frigg,
alls mik fara tíðir   at vitja Vafþrúðnis;
forvitni mikla   kveð ek mér á fornum stöfum
við þann inn alsvinna jötun."

Frigg kvað:
"Heima letja   ek mynda Herjaföðr
í görðum goða;
því at engi jötun   ek hugða jafnramman
sem Vafþrúðni vera."

Óðinn kvað:
"Fjölð ek fór,   fjölð ek freistaða,
fjölð ek reynda regin;
hitt vil ek vita,   hvé Vafþrúðnis
salakynni sé."

Frigg kvað:
"Heill þú farir!
heill þú aftr komir!
heill þú á sinnum sér!
æði þér dugi,   hvars þú skalt, Aldaföðr,
orðum mæla jötun.

VAFTHRUTHNISMOL

Odin spake: 1
"Counsel me, Frigg, for I long to fare,
And Vafthruthnir fain would find;
Fit wisdom old with the giant wise
Myself would I seek to match."

Frigg spake: 2
"Heerfather here at home would I keep,
Where the gods together dwell;
Amid all the giants an equal in might
To Vafthruthnir know I none."

Odin spake: 3
"Much have I fared, much have I found.
Much have I got from the gods;
And fain would I know how Vafthruthnir now
Lives in his lofty hall."

Frigg spake: 4
"Safe mayst thou go, safe come again,
And safe be the way thou wendest!
Father of men, let thy mind be keen
When speech with the giant thou seekest."

Fór þá Óðinn   at freista orðspeki   5
þess ins alsvinna jötuns;
at höllu hann kom,   ok átti Íms faðir;
inn gekk Yggr þegar.

Óðinn kvað: 6
"Heill þú nú, Vafþrúðnir,   nú em ek í höll kominn
á þik sjalfan sjá;
hitt vil ek fyrst vita,   ef þú fróðr sér
eða alsviðr jötunn."

Vafþrúðnir kvað: 7
"Hvat er þat manna   er í mínum sal
verpumk orði á?
Út þú né komir   órum höllum frá,
nema þú inn snotrari sér."

Óðinn kvað: 8
"Gagnráðr ek heiti,   nú emk af göngu kominn,
þyrstr til þinna sala;
laðar þurfi   hef ek lengi farit
ok þinna andfanga, jötunn."

Vafþrúðnir kvað: 9
"Hví þú þá, Gagnráðr,   mælisk af golfi fyr?
Far þú í sess í sal!
Þá skal freista,   hvárr fleira viti,
gestr eða inn gamli þulr."

Óðinn kvað: 10
"Óauðigr maðr,   er til auðigs kemr,
mæli þarft eða þegi;
ofrmælgi mikil,   hygg ek, at illa geti
hveim er við kaldrifjaðan kemr."

Vafþrúðnir kvað: 11
"Seg þú mér, Gagnráðr,   alls þú á golfi vill
þíns of freista frama,
hvé sá hestr heitir,
er hverjan dregr   dag of dróttmögu."

Óðinn kvað: 12
"Skinfaxi heitir,   er inn skíra dregr
dag of dróttmögu;
hesta beztr   þykkir hann með Hreiðgotum;
ey lýsir mön af mari."

The wisdom then of the giant wise 5
Forth did he fare to try;
He found the hall of the father of Im,
And in forthwith went Ygg.

Odin spake: 6
"Vafthruthnir, hail! to thy hall am I come,
For thyself I fain would see;
And first would I ask if wise thou art,
Or, giant, all wisdom hast won."

Vafthruthnir spake: 7
"Who is the man that speaks to me,
Here in my lofty hall?
Forth from our dwelling thou never shalt fare,
Unless wiser than I thou art."

Odin spake: 8
"Gagnrath they call me, and thirsty I come
From a journey hard to thy hall;
Welcome I look for, for long have I fared,
And gentle greeting, giant."

Vafthruthnir spake: 9
"Why standest thou there on the floor whilst thou speakest?
A seat shalt thou have in my hall;
Then soon shall we know whose knowledge is more,
The guest's or the sage's gray."

Odin spake: 10
"If a poor man reaches the home of the rich,
Let him wisely speak or be still;
For to him who speaks with the hard of heart
Will chattering ever work ill."

Vafthruthnir spake: 11
"Speak forth now, Gagnrath, if there from the floor
Thou wouldst thy wisdom make known:
What name has the steed that each morn anew
The day for mankind doth draw?"

Odin spake: 12
"Skinfaxi is he, the steed who for men
The glittering day doth draw;
The best of horses to heroes he seems,
And brightly his mane doth burn."

Vafþrúðnir kvað: 13
"Seg þú þat, Gagnráðr,   alls þú á golfi vill
þíns of freista frama,
hvé sá jór heitir,
er austan dregr   nótt of nýt regin."

Óðinn kvað: 14
"Hrímfaxi heitir,   er hverja dregr
nótt of nýt regin;
méldropa fellir hann   morgin hvern;
þaðan kemr dögg um dala."

Vafþrúðnir kvað: 15
Seg þú þat, Gagnráðr,   alls þú á golfi vill
þíns of freista frama,   hvé sú á heitir,
er deilir með jötna sonum
grund ok með goðum."

Óðinn kvað: 16
"Ífing heitir á,   er deilir með jötna sonum
grund ok með goðum;
opin renna   hon skal of aldrdaga;
verðr-at íss á á."

Vafþrúðnir kvað: 17
Seg þú þat, Gagnráðr,   alls þú á golfi vill
þíns of freista frama,   hvé sá völlr heitir,
er finnask vígi at Surtr
ok in svásu goð."

Óðinn kvað: 18
"Vígríðr heitir völlr,   er finnask vígi at
Surtr ok in svásu goð;
hundrað rasta   hann er á hverjan veg;
sá er þeim völlr vitaðr."

Vafþrúðnir kvað: 19
"Fróðr ertu nú, gestr,   far þú á bekk jötuns,
ok mælumk í sessi saman;
höfði veðja   vit skulum höllu í,
gestr, of geðspeki.

Vafthruthnir spake:
"Speak forth now, Gagnrath, if there from the floor
Thou wouldst thy wisdom make known:
What name has the steed that from East anew
Brings night for the noble gods?"

Odin spake:
"Hrimfaxi name they the steed that anew
Brings night for the noble gods;
Each morning foam from his bit there falls,
And thence come the dews in the dales."

Vafthruthnir spake:
"Speak forth now, Gagnrath, if there from the floor
Thou wouldst thy wisdom make known:
What name has the river that 'twixt the realms
Of the gods and the giants goes?"

Odin spoke:
"Ifing is the river that 'twixt the realms
Of the gods and the giants goes;
For all time ever open it flows,
No ice on the river there is."

Vafthruthnir spake:
"Speak forth now, Gagnrath, if there from the floor
Thou wouldst thy wisdom make known:
What name has the field where in fight shall meet
Surt and the gracious gods?"

Odin spake:
"Vigrith is the field where in fight shall meet
Surt and the gracious gods;
A hundred miles each way does it measure.
And so are its boundaries set."

Vafthruthnir spake:
"Wise art thou, guest! To my bench shalt thou go,
In our seats let us speak together;
Here in the hall our heads, O guest,
Shall we wager our wisdom upon."

Óðinn kvað: 20
"Seg þú þat it eina, ef þitt æði dugir
ok þú, Vafþrúðnir, vitir, hvaðan jörð of kom
eða upphiminn fyrst, inn fróði jötunn."

Vafþrúðnir kvað: 21
"Ór Ymis holdi var jörð of sköpuð,
en ór beinum björg, himinn ór hausi
ins hrímkalda jötuns,
en ór sveita sær."

Óðinn kvað: 22
"Seg þú þat annat, ef þitt æði dugir
ok þú, Vafþrúðnir, vitir,
hvaðan máni kom, sá er ferr menn yfir,
eða sól it sama."

Vafþrúðnir kvað: 23
"Mundilfari heitir, hann er mána faðir
ok svá Sólar it sama;
himin hverfa þau skulu hverjan dag
öldum at ártali."

Óðinn kvað: 24
"Seg þú þat it þriðja, alls þik svinnan kveða
ok þú, Vafþrúðnir, vitir, hvaðan dagr of kom,
sá er ferr drótt yfir, eða nótt með niðum."

Vafþrúðnir kvað: 25
"Dellingr heitir, hann er Dags faðir,
en Nótt var Nörvi borin;
ný ok nið skópu nýt regin
öldum at ártali."

Óðinn kvað: 26
"Seg þú þat it fjórða,
alls þik fróðan kveða, ok þú, Vafþrúðnir, vitir,
hvaðan vetr of kom eða varmt sumar
fyrst með fróð regin."

Vafþrúðnir kvað: 27
"Vindsvalr heitir, hann er Vetrar faðir,
en Svásuðr sumars."

Odin spake: 20
"First answer me well, if thy wisdom avails,
And thou knowest it, Vafthruthnir, now:
In earliest time whence came the earth,
Or the sky, thou giant sage?"

Vafthruthnir spake: 21
"Out of Ymir's flesh was fashioned the earth,
And the mountains were made of his bones;
The sky from the frost-cold giant's skull,
And the ocean out of his blood."

Odin spake: 22
"Next answer me well, if thy wisdom avails,
And thou knowest it, Vafthruthnir, now:
Whence came the moon, o'er the world of men
That fares, and the flaming sun?"

Vafthruthnir spake: 23
"Mundilferi is he who begat the moon,
And fathered the flaming sun;
The round of heaven each day they run,
To tell the time for men."

Odin spake: 24
"Third answer me well, if wise thou art called,
If thou knowest it, Vafthruthnir, now:
Whence came the day, o'er mankind that fares,
Or night with the narrowing moon?"

Vafthruthnir spake: 25
"The father of day is Delling called,
And the night was begotten by Nor;
Full moon and old by the gods were fashioned,
To tell the time for men."

Odin spake: 26
"Fourth answer me well, if wise thou art called,
If thou knowest it, Vafthruthnir, now:
Whence did winter come, or the summer warm,
First with the gracious gods?"

Vafthruthnir spake: 27
"Vindsval he was who was winter's father,
And Svosuth summer begat."

Óðinn kvað: 28
"Seg þú þat it fimmta,
alls þik fróðan kveða,
ok þú, Vafþrúðnir, vitir,
hverr ása ellztr   eða Ymis niðja
yrði í árdaga."

Vafþrúðnir kvað: 29
"Órófi vetra   áðr væri jörð of sköpuð,
þá var Bergelmir borinn,   Þrúðgelmir
var þess faðir,   en Aurgelmir afi."

Óðinn kvað: 30
"Seg þú þat it sétta,
alls þik svinnan kveða,   ok þú, Vafþrúðnir, vitir,
hvaðan Aurgelmir kom   með jötna sonum
fyrst, inn fróði jötunn."

Vafþrúðnir kvað: 31
"Ór Élivágum   stukku eitrdropar,
svá óx, unz varð jötunn;
þar eru órar ættir   komnar allar saman;
því er þat æ allt til atalt."

Óðinn kvað: 32
"Seg þú þat it sjaunda,
alls þik svinnan kveða,
ok þú, Vafþrúðnir, vitir,   hvé sá börn gat,
inn baldni jötunn,   er hann hafði-t gýgjar gaman."

Vafþrúðnir kvað: 33
"Undir hendi vaxa   kváðu hrímþursi
mey ok mög saman;
fótr við fæti   gat ins fróða jötuns
sexhöfðaðan son."

Óðinn kvað: 34
"Seg þú þat it átta,
alls þik svinnan kveða,
ok þú, Vafþrúðnir, vitir,   hvat þú fyrst of mant
eða fremst of veizt,   þú ert alsviðr, jötunn."

Odin spake: 28
"Fifth answer me well, if wise thou art called,
If thou knowest it, Vafthruthnir, now:
What giant first was fashioned of old,
And the eldest of Ymir's kin?"

Vafthruthnir spake: 29
"Winters unmeasured ere earth was made
Was the birth of Bergelmir;
Thruthgelmir's son was the giant strong,
And Aurgelmir's grandson of old."

Odin spake: 30
"Sixth answer me well, if wise thou art called,
If thou knowest it, Vafthruthnir, now:
Whence did Aurgelmir come with the giants' kin,
Long since, thou giant sage?"

Vafthruthnir spake: 31
"Down from Elivagar did venom drop,
And waxed till a giant it was;
And thence arose our giants' race,
And thus so fierce are we found."

Odin spake: 32
"Seventh answer me well, if wise thou art called,
If thou knowest it, Vafthruthnir, now:
How begat he children, the giant grim,
Who never a giantess knew?"

Vafthruthnir spake: 33
"They say 'neath the arms of the giant of ice
Grew man-child and maid together;
And foot with foot did the wise one fashion
A son that six heads bore."

Odin spake: 34
"Eighth answer me well, if wise thou art called,
If thou knowest it, Vafthruthnir, now:
What farthest back dost thou bear in mind?
For wide is thy wisdom, giant!"

Vafþrúðnir kvað: 35
Órófi vetra   áðr væri jörð of sköpuð,
þá var Bergelmir borinn;
þat ek fyrst of man,   er sá inn fróði jötunn
á var lúðr of lagiðr."

Óðinn kvað: 36
"Seg þú þat it níunda,   alls þik svinnan kveða,
ok þú, Vafþrúðnir, vitir,   hvaðan vindr of kemr,
svá at ferr vág yfir;
æ menn han sjalfan of sjá."

Vafþrúðnir kvað: 37
"Hræsvelgr heitir,   er sitr á himins enda,
jötunn í arnar ham;
af hans vængjum   kvæða vind koma
alla menn yfir."

Óðinn kvað: 38
"Seg þú þat it tíunda,   alls þú tíva rök
öll, Vafþrúðnir, vitir,   hvaðan Njörðr of kom
með ása sonum   hofum ok hörgum
hann ræðr hundmörgum—
ok varð-at hann ásum alinn."

Vafþrúðnir kvað: 39
"Í Vanaheimi   skópu hann vís regin
ok seldu at gíslingu goðum,   í aldar rök
hann mun aftr koma   heim með vísum vönum."

Óðinn kvað: 40
"Seg þú þat et ellifta,
hvar ýtar túnum í   höggvask hverjan dag;
val þeir kjósa   ok ríða vígi frá,
sitja meir of sáttir saman."

Vafþrúðnir kvað: 41
"Allir einherjar   Óðins túnum í
höggvask hverjan dag,   val þeir kjósa
ok ríða vígi frá,   sitja meirr of sáttir saman."

Vafthruthnir spake: 35
"Winters unmeasured ere earth was made
Was the birth of Bergelmir;
This first knew I well, when the giant wise
In a boat of old was borne."

Odin spake: 36
"Ninth answer me well, if wise thou art called
If thou knowest it, Vafthruthnir, now:
Whence comes the wind that fares o'er the waves
Yet never itself is seen?"

Vafthruthnir spake: 37
"In an eagle's guise at the end of heaven
Hræsvelg sits, they say;
And from his wings does the wind come forth
To move o'er the world of men."

Odin spake: 38
"Tenth answer me now, if thou knowest all
The fate that is fixed for the gods:
Whence came up Njorth to the kin of the gods—
Rich in temples and shrines he rules—
Though of gods he was never begot?"

Vafthruthnir spake: 39
"In the home of the Wanes did the wise ones create him,
And gave him as pledge to the gods;
At the fall of the world shall he fare once more
Home to the Wanes so wise."

Odin spake: 40
"Eleventh answer me well,
Who issue forth from the stronghold
To hack each other every day?
Slaughter they choose and ride to war
Sit the glorious ones in reconciliation together."

Vafthruthnir spake: 41
"The heroes all in Odin's hall
Each day to fight go forth;
They fell each other, and fare from the fight
All healed full soon to sit."

Óðinn kvað: 42
"Seg þú þat it tolfta, hví þú tíva rök
öll, Vafþrúðnir, vitir, frá jötna rúnum
ok allra goða segir þú it sannasta,
inn alsvinni jötunn."

Vafþrúðnir kvað: 43
"Frá jötna rúnum ok allra goða
ek kann segja satt, því at hvern hef ek
heim of komit;
níu kom ek heima fyr Niflhel neðan;
hinig deyja ór helju halir."

Óðinn kvað: 44
"Fjölð ek fór, fjölð ek freistaðak,
fjölð ek of reynda regin:
Hvat lifir manna, þá er inn mæra líðr
fimbulvetr með firum?"

Vafþrúðnir kvað: 45
"Líf ok Lífþrasir, en þau leynask munu
í holti Hoddmímis;
morgindöggvar þau sér at mat hafa,
en þaðan af aldir alask."

Óðinn kvað: 46
"Fjölð ek fór, fjölð ek freistaðak,
fjölð ek of reynda regin:
Hvaðan kemr sól á inn slétta himin,
er þessa hefr fenrir farit?"

Vafþrúðnir kvað: 47
"Eina dóttur berr alfröðull,
áðr hana fenrir fari;
sú skal ríða, þá er regin deyja,
móður brautir, mær."

Óðinn kvað: 48
"Fjölð ek fór, fjölð ek freistaðak,
fjölð ek of reynda regin:
Hverjar ro þær meyjar, er líða mar yfir,
fróðgeðjaðar fara?"

Odin spake: 42

"Twelfth answer me now how all thou knowest
Of the fate that is fixed for the gods;
Of the runes of the gods and the giants' race
The truth indeed dost thou tell,
And wide is thy wisdom, giant!"

Vafthruthnir spake: 43

"Of the runes of the gods and the giants' race
The truth indeed can I tell,
For to every world have I won;
To nine worlds came I, to Niflhel beneath,
The home where dead men dwell."

Odin spake: 44

"Much have I fared, much have I found,
Much have I got of the gods:
What shall live of mankind when at last there comes
The mighty winter to men?"

Vafthruthnir spake: 45

"In Hoddmimir's wood shall hide themselves
Lif and Lifthrasir then;
The morning dews for meat shall they have,
Such food shall men then find."

Odin spake: 46

"Much have I fared, much have I found,
Much have I got of the gods:
Whence comes the sun to the smooth sky back,
When Fenrir has snatched it forth?"

Vafthruthnir spake: 47

"A daughter bright Alfrothul bears
Ere Fenrir snatches her forth;
Her mother's paths shall the maiden tread
When the gods to death have gone."

Odin spake: 48

"Much have I fared, much have I found,
Much have I got of the gods:
What maidens are they, so wise of mind.
That forth o'er the sea shall fare?"

Vafþrúðnir kvað: 49
"Þríar þjóðár   falla þorp yfir
meyja Mögþrasis;
hamingjur einar   þær er í heimi eru,
þó þær með jötnum alask."

Óðinn kvað: 50
"Fjölð ek fór,   fjölð ek freistaðak,
fjölð ek of reynda regin:
Hverir ráða æsir   eignum goða,
þá er sloknar Surta logi?"

Vafþrúðnir kvað: 51
"Víðarr ok Váli   byggja vé goða,
þá er sloknar Surta logi,
Móði ok Magni   skulu Mjöllni hafa
Vingnis at vígþroti."

Óðinn kvað: 52
"Fjölð ek fór,   fjölð ek freistaðak,
fjölð ek of reynda regin;
Hvat verðr Óðni   at aldrlagi,
þá er of rjúfask regin?"

Vafþrúðnir kvað: 53
"Ulfr gleypa   mun Aldaföðr,
þess mun Víðarr vreka;
kalda kjafta   hann klyfja mun
vitnis vígi at."

Óðinn kvað: 54
"Fjölð ek fór,   fjölð ek freistaðak,
fjölð ek of reynda regin;
Hvat mælti Óðinn,   áðr á bál stigi,
sjalfr í eyra syni?"

Vafþrúðnir kvað: 55
"Ey manni þat veit,   hvat þú í árdaga
sagðir í eyra syni;
feigum munni   mælta ek mína forna stafi
ok of ragnarök.
Nú ek við Óðin   deildak mína orðspeki;
þú ert æ vísastr vera."

Vafthruthnir spake: 49
"O'er Mogthrasir's hill shall the maidens pass,
And three are their throngs that come;
They all shall protect the dwellers on earth,
Though they come of the giants' kin."

Odin spake: 50
"Much have I fared, much have I found,
Much have I got of the gods:
Who then shall rule the realm of the gods,
When the fires of Surt have sunk?"

Vafthruthnir spake: 51
"In the gods' home Vithar and Vali shall dwell,
When the fires of Surt have sunk;
Mothi and Magni shall Mjollnir have
When Vingnir falls in fight."

Odin spake: 52
"Much have I fared, much have I found,
Much have I got of the gods:
What shall bring the doom of death to Odin,
When the gods to destruction go?"

Vafthruthnir spake: 53
"The wolf shall fell the father of men,
And this shall Vithar avenge;
The terrible jaws shall he tear apart,
And so the wolf shall he slay."

Odin spake: 54
"Much have I fared, much have I found,
Much have I got from the gods:
What spake Odin himself in the ears of his son,
Ere in the bale-fire he burned?"

Vafthruthnir spake: 55
"No man can tell what in olden time
Thou spak'st in the ears of thy son;
With fated mouth the fall of the gods
And mine olden tales have I told;
With Odin in knowledge now have I striven,
And ever the wiser thou art."

ENDNOTES

1. The phrases "Odin spake," "Frigg spake," etc., appear in abbreviated form in both manuscripts. *Frigg*: Odin's wife; cf. *Voluspo*, 34 and note. *Vafthruthnir* ("the Mighty in Riddles"): nothing is known of this giant beyond what is told in this poem.

2. *Heerfather* ("Father of the Host"): Odin.

5. This single narrative stanza is presumably a later interpolation. *Im*: the name appears to be corrupt, but we know nothing of any son of Vafthruthnir. *Ygg* ("the Terrible"): Odin.

8. *Gagnrath* ("the Gain-Counsellor"): Odin on his travels always assumes a name other than his own.

10. This stanza sounds very much like many of those in the first part of the *Hovamol*, and may have been introduced here from some such source.

12. *Skinfaxi*: "Shining-Mane."

13. Here, and in general throughout the poem, the two-line introductory formulæ are abbreviated in the manuscripts.

14. *Hrimfaxi*: "Frosty-Mane."

16. *Ifing*: there is no other reference to this river, which never freezes, so that the giants cannot cross it.

17. *Surt*: the ruler of the fire-world (Muspellsheim), who comes to attack the gods in the last battle; cf. *Voluspo*, 52.

18. *Vigrith*: "the Field of Battle." Snorri quotes this stanza. *A hundred*

miles: a general phrase for a vast distance.

19. With this stanza Vafthruthnir, sufficiently impressed with his guest's wisdom to invite him to share his own seat, resigns the questioning to Odin.

20. The fragmentary version of this poem in the *Arnamagnæan Codex* begins in the middle of the first line of this stanza.

21. *Ymir*: the giant out of whose body the gods made the world; cf. *Voluspo*, 3 and note.

22. In this and in Odin's following questions, both manuscripts replace the words "next," "third," "fourth," etc., by Roman numerals.

23. Mundilferi ("the Turner"?): known only as the father of Mani (the Moon) and Sol (the Sun). [Note that, curiously enough for those most familiar with the mythological structure of classical Greece, Mani is the male and Sol the female, but this arrangement is the most common among Indo-European peoples in general and can be seen as far afield as the Hindu *Vedas*.] According to Snorri, Sol drove the horses of the sun, and Mani those of the moon, for the gods, indignant that they should have been given such imposing names, took them from their father to perform these tasks. Cf. *Grimnismol*, 37.

25. *Delling* ("the Dayspring"? Probably another form of the name, Dogling, meaning "Son of the Dew" is more correct): the husband of Not (Night); their son was Dag (Day); cf. *Hovamol*, 161. *Nor*: Snorri calls the father of Night Norvi or Narfi, and puts him among the giants. Lines 3–4: cf. *Voluspo*, 6.

27. Neither the *Regius* nor the *Arnamagnæan Codex* indicates a lacuna. Most editors have filled out the stanza with two lines from late paper manuscripts: "And both of these shall ever be, / Till the gods to destruction go." Bugge ingeniously paraphrases Snorri's prose: "Vindsval's father was Vosuth called, / And rough is all his race." *Vindsval*: "the Wind-Cold," also called Vindljoni, "the Wind-Man." *Svosuth*: "the Gentle."

28. *Ymir's kin*: the giants.

29. *Bergelmir*: when the gods slew Ymir in order to make the world out of his body, so much blood flowed from him that all the frost-giants were drowned except Bergelmir and his wife, who escaped in a boat; cf. stanza 35. Of *Thruthgelmir* ("the Mightily Burning") we know nothing, but Aurgelmir was the frost-giants' name for Ymir himself. Thus Ymir was

ENDNOTES 115

the first of the giants, and so Odin's question is answered.

31. Snorri quotes this stanza, and the last two lines are taken from his version, as both of the manuscripts omit them. *Elivagar* ("Stormy Waves"): Mogk suggests that this river may have been the Milky Way. At any rate, the venom carried in its waters froze into ice-banks over Ginnunga-gap (the "yawning gap" referred to in *Voluspo*, 3), and then dripped down to make the giant Ymir.

33. Snorri gives, without materially elaborating on it, the same account of how Ymir's son and daughter were born under his left arm, and how his feet together created a son. That this offspring should have had six heads is nothing out of the ordinary, for various giants had more than the normal number, and Hymir's mother is credited with a little matter of nine hundred heads; cf. *Hymiskvitha*, 8. Of the career of Ymir's six headed son we know nothing; he may have been the Thruthgelmir of stanza 29.

35. Snorri quotes this stanza. *Bergelmir*: on him and his boat cf. stanza 29 and note.

37. Snorri quotes this stanza. *Hræsvelg* ("the Corpse-Eater") on this giant in eagle's form cf. *Voluspo*, 50, and *Skirnismol*, 27.

38. With this stanza the question-formula changes, and Odin's questions from this point on concern more or less directly the great final struggle. Line 4 is presumably spurious. *Njorth*: on Njorth and the Wanes, who gave him as a hostage to the gods at the end of their war, cf. *Voluspo*, 21 and note.

40. In both manuscripts, apparently through the carelessness of some older copyist, stanzas 40 and 41 are run together: "Eleventh answer me well, what men in the home mightily battle each day? They fell each other, and fare from the fight all healed full soon to sit." Luckily Snorri quotes stanza 41 in full, and the translation is from his version.[1]

41. *The heroes*: those brought to Valhall by the Valkyries. After the day's fighting they are healed of their wounds and all feast together.

43. *Nine worlds*: cf. *Voluspo*, 2. *Niflhel*: "Dark-Hell."

44. *The mighty winter*: Before the final destruction three winters follow one another with no intervening summers.

---

1 This stanza has been edited to replace the empty gaps, all of the stanza after the opening "Eleventh answer me well" is taken from Bugge's edition as a literal translation by Dr. Marion Ingham.

45. Snorri quotes this stanza. *Hoddmimir's wood*: probably this is the ash-tree Yggdrasil, which is sometimes referred to as "Mimir's Tree," because Mimir waters it from his well; cf. *Voluspo*, 27 and note, and *Svipdagsmol*, 30 and note. Hoddmimir is presumably another name for Mimir. *Lif* ("Life") and *Lifthrasir* ("[Life's Lover]"?): nothing further is known of this pair, from whom the new race of men is to spring.

46. *Fenrir*: there appears to be a confusion between the wolf Fenrir (cf. *Voluspo*, 39 and note) and his son, the wolf Skoll, who steals the sun (cf. *Voluspo*, 40 and note).

47. Snorri quotes this stanza. *Alfrothul* ("the Elf-Beam") the sun.

49. *Mogthrasir* ("Desiring Sons"): not mentioned elsewhere in the Eddic poems, or by Snorri. *The maidens*: apparently Norns, like the "giant-maids" in *Voluspo*, 8. These Norns, however, are kindly to men.

50. *Surt*: cf. *Voluspo*, 52 and note.

51. *Vithar*: a son of Odin, who slays the wolf Fenrir; cf. *Voluspo*, 54 and note. *Vali*: the son whom Odin begot to avenge Baldr's death; cf. *Voluspo*, 33 and note. *Mothi* ("Wrath") and *Magni* ("Might"): the sons of the god Thor, who after his death inherit his famous hammer, *Mjollnir*. Concerning this hammer cf. especially *Thrymskvitha, passim. Vingnir* ("the Hurler"): Thor. Concerning his death cf. *Voluspo*, 56. This stanza is quoted by Snorri.

53. *The wolf*: Fenrir; cf. *Voluspo*, 53 and 54.

54. *His son*: Baldr. Bugge changes lines 3–4 to run: "What did Odin speak in the ear of Baldr, / When to the bale-fire they bore him?" For Baldr's death cf. *Voluspo*, 32 and note. The question is, of course, unanswerable save by Odin himself, and so the giant at last recognizes his guest.

55. *Fated*: in stanza 19 Vafthruthnir was rash enough to wager his head against his guest's on the outcome of the contest of wisdom, so he knows that his defeat means his death.

GRIMNISMOL
THE BALLAD OF GRIMNIR

INTRODUCTION

The *Grimnismol* opens with a prose introduction to set the stage and explain the context of the poem—a rather interesting and unusual feature, but one that is native to the original *Codex Regius* itself. Linguistic analysis of the prose introduction categorizes it as a late addition sometime in the 12–13th century, in contrast to the poem itself which bears hallmarks of an authentic 10th century work.

The stage is set by recounting past events regarding the sons of a king, Agnar and Geirroth, who are taken in by a poor peasant and his wife who raise them until they are fit to return to their father's kingdom. We are then told that this peasant couple is actually Odin and Frigg in disguise, and that each of the pair has taken to a specific one of the boys. Odin whispers secretly to Geirroth upon their leaving, presumably advising him of the tenuous situation he finds himself in, wherein only one of the boys may claim their father's kingly seat, and perhaps of the method by which he rids himself of his rival brother.

Another interesting narrative angle depicted here is that the prose introduction features an argument between the Gods about the character of the king Geirroth, and a bragging competition between them about the fates of each of their respective "sons" with Odin insinuating that Frigg's chosen Agnar is of low worth and character due to his living in cave coupled with a giantess (themselves enemies of the Gods), whereas Frigg maintains that Geirroth is so ungenerous as to torture guests who call upon him. Odin maintains that this statement is a great lie and the narrator seemingly confirms the truth of his stance, as does Frigg's later action in poisoning Geirroth against Odin by convincing him that the man might be a sorcerer of dark arts come to enchant him—a serious accusation for our ancestors, to whom such things were no laughing matter.

Fair arguments may be presented that the events of the prose narrative represent a distorted view of the gods, biased against them and presenting them as evil creatures who lie and falsely guide man. However, some of Odin's own names presented in the poetic section itself imply otherwise, with bynames like Bolverk (Evil Worker), Glapsviðr (Swift in Deceit) and Ygg (The Terrible One) lending credence to the narrative events as something our ancestors might legitimately have expected of such a deity. Commentary and discussion on how this may be rectified with a proper theological view of the Gods is beyond the scope of this introduction, but interested parties may wish to take the narrative presented to heart when discussing the Asagods and the Father of the Slain.

The Wolves Pursuing Sol and Mani
(J. C. Dollman)

FRÁ SONUM HRAUÐUNGS KONUNGS

Hrauðungr konungr átti tvá sonu. Hét annarr Agnarr, en annarr Geirröðr. Agnarr var tíu vetra, en Geirröðr átta vetra. Þeir reru tveir á báti með dorgar sínar at smáfiski. Vindr rak þá í haf út. Í náttmyrkri brutu þeir við land ok gengu upp, fundu kotbónda einn. Þar váru þeir um vetrinn. Kerling fóstraði Agnar, en karl fóstraði Geirröð ok kenndi honum ráð. At vári fekk karl þeim skip.

En er þau kerling leiddu þá til strandar, þá mælti karl einmæli við Geirröð.

Þeir fengu byr ok kómu til stöðva föður síns. Geirröðr var fram í skipi. Hann hljóp upp á land, en hratt út skipinu ok mælti: "Farðu nú, þar er smyl hafi þik." Skipit rak í haf út, en Geirröðr gekk upp til bæjar. Honum var þar vel fagnat, en faðir hans þá andaðr. Var þá Geirröðr til konungs tekinn ok varð maðr ágætr. Óðinn ok Frigg sátu í Hliðskjálfu ok sáu um heima alla. Óðinn mælti: "Sér þú Agnar, fóstra þinn, hvar hann elr börn við gýgi í hellinum, en Geirröðr, fóstri minn, er konungr ok sitr nú at landi?" Frigg segir: "Hann er matníðingr sá, at hann kvelr gesti sína, ef honum þykkja of margir koma."

Óðinn segir, at þat er in mesta lygi. Þau veðja um þetta mál. Frigg sendi eskimey sína Fullu til Geirröðar. Hon bað konung varast, at eigi fyrirgerði honum fjölkunnigr maðr, sá er þar var kominn í land, ok sagði þat mark á, at engi hundr var svá ólmr, at á hann mundi hlaupa.

En þat var inn mesti hégómi, at Geirröðr konungr væri eigi matgóðr, ok þó lætr hann handtaka þann mann, er eigi vildu hundar á ráða. Sá var

GRIMNISMOL

OF THE SONS OF KING HRAUTHUNG

King Hrauthung had two sons: one was called Agnar, and the other Geirröth. Agnar was ten winters old, and Geirröth eight. Once they both rowed in a boat with their fishing-gear to catch little fish; and the wind drove them out into the sea. In the darkness of the night they were wrecked on the shore; and going up, they found a poor peasant, with whom they stayed through the winter. The housewife took care of Agnar, and the peasant cared for Geirröth, and taught him wisdom. In the spring the peasant gave him a boat; and when the couple led them to the shore, the peasant spoke secretly with Geirröth. They had a fair wind, and came to their father's landing-place. Geirröth was forward in the boat; he leaped up on land, but pushed out the boat and said, "Go thou now where evil may have thee!" The boat drifted out to sea. Geirröth, however, went up to the house, and was well received, but his father was dead. Then Geirröth was made king, and became a renowned man.

Odin and Frigg sat in Hlithskjolf and looked over all the worlds. Odin said: "Seest thou Agnar, thy fosterling, how he begets children with a giantess in the cave? But Geirröth, my fosterling, is a king, and now rules over his land." Frigg said: "He is so miserly that he tortures his guests if he thinks that too many of them come to him." Odin replied that this was the greatest of lies; and they made a wager about this matter. Frigg sent her maidservant, Fulla, to Geirröth. She bade the king beware lest a magician who was come thither to his land should bewitch him, and told this sign concerning him, that no dog was so fierce as to leap at him. Now it

í feldi blám ok nefndist Grímnir og sagði ekki fleira frá sér, þótt hann væri at spurðr. Konungr lét hann pína til sagna ok setja milli elda tveggja, ok sat hann þar átta nætr.

Geirröðr konungr átti þá son tíu vetra gamlan, ok hét Agnarr eftir bróður hans. Agnarr gekk at Grímni ok gaf honum horn fullt at drekka ok sagði, at faðir hans gerði illa, er hann píndi þenna mann saklausan. Grímnir drakk af. Þá var eldrinn svá kominn, at feldrinn brann af Grímni. Hann kvað:

Heitr ertu, hripuðr, ok heldr til mikill; 1
göngumk firr, funi!
loði sviðnar, þótt ek á loft berak;
brennumk feldr fyr.

Átta nætr sat ek milli elda hér, 2
svá at mér manngi mat né bauð
nema einn Agnarr, er einn skal ráða,
Geirröðar sonr, Gotna landi.

Heill skaltu, Agnarr, alls þik heilan biðr 3
Veratýr vera;
eins drykkjar þú skalt aldrigi
betri gjöld geta.

Land er heilagt, er ek liggja sé 4
ásum ok alfum nær;
en í Þrúðheimi skal Þórr vera
unz of rjúfask regin.

Ýdalir heita, þar er Ullr hefir 5
sér of görva sali;
Alfheim Frey gáfu í árdaga
tívar at tannféi.

Bær er sá inn þriði, er blíð regin 6
silfri þökðu sali;
Valaskjalf heitir, er vélti sér
áss í árdaga.

Sökkvabekkr heitir inn fjórði, 7
en þar svalar knegu unnir yfir glymja;
þar þau Óðinn ok Sága drekka um alla daga
glöð ór gullnum kerum.

was a very great slander that King Geirröth was not hospitable; but nevertheless he had them take the man whom the dogs would not attack. He wore a dark-blue mantle and called himself Grimnir, but said no more about himself, though he was questioned. The king had him tortured to make him speak, and set him between two fires, and he sat there eight nights. King Geirröth had a son ten winters old, and called Agnar after his father's brother. Agnar went to Grimnir, and gave him a full horn to drink from, and said that the king did ill in letting him be tormented without cause. Grimnir drank from the horn; the fire had come so near that the mantle burned on Grimnir's back. He spake:

1. Hot art thou, fire! too fierce by far;
Get ye now gone, ye flames!
The mantle is burnt, though I bear it aloft,
And the fire scorches the fur.

2. 'Twixt the fires now eight nights have I sat,
And no man brought meat to me,
Save Agnar alone, and alone shall rule
Geirröth's son o'er the Goths.

3. Hail to thee, Agnar! for hailed thou art
By the voice of Veratyr;
For a single drink shalt thou never receive
A greater gift as reward.

4. The land is holy that lies hard by
The gods and the elves together;
And Thor shall ever in Thruthheim dwell,
Till the gods to destruction go.

5. Ydalir call they the place where Ull
A hall for himself hath set;
And Alfheim the gods to Freyr once gave
As a tooth-gift in ancient times.

6. A third home is there, with silver thatched
By the hands of the gracious gods:
Valaskjolf is it, in days of old
Set by a god for himself.

7. Sökkvabekk is the fourth, where cool waves flow,
And amid their murmur it stands;
There daily do Odin and Saga drink
In gladness from cups of gold.

Glaðsheimr heitir inn fimmti, 8
þars in gullbjarta   Valhöll víð of þrumir;
en þar Hroftr kýss   hverjan dag
vápndauða vera.

Mjök er auðkennt,   þeim er til Óðins koma 9
salkynni at séa;
sköftum er rann reft,   skjöldum er salr þakiðr,
brynjum um bekki strát.

Mjök er auðkennt,   þeir er til Óðins koma 10
salkynni at séa:
vargr hangir   fyr vestan dyrr,
ok drúpir örn yfir.

Þrymheimr heitir inn sétti,   er Þjazi bjó, 11
sá inn ámáttki jötunn;
en nú Skaði byggvir,   skír brúðr goða,
fornar tóftir föður.

Breiðablik eru in sjaundu,   en þar Baldr hefir 12
sér of gerva sali,   á því landi,
er ek liggja veit   fæsta feiknstafi.

Himinbjörg eru in áttu,   en þar Heimdall 13
kveða valda véum;
þar vörðr goða   drekkr í væru ranni
glaðr inn góða mjöð.

Fólkvangr er inn níundi,   en þar Freyja ræðr 14
sessa kostum í sal;
halfan val   hon kýss hverjan dag,
en halfan Óðinn á.

Glitnir er inn tíundi,   hann er gulli studdr 15
ok silfri þakðr it sama;
en þar Forseti   byggir flestan dag
ok svæfir allar sakir.

Nóatún eru in elliftu,   en þar Njörðr hefir, 16
sér of görva sali;
manna þengill   inn meins vani
hátimbruðum hörgi ræðr.

The fifth is Glathsheim, and gold-bright there 8
Stands Valhall stretching wide;
And there does Odin each day choose
The men who have fallen in fight.

Easy is it to know for him who to Odin 9
Comes and beholds the hall;
Its rafters are spears, with shields is it roofed,
On its benches are breastplates strewn.

Easy is it to know for him who to Odin 10
Comes and beholds the hall;
There hangs a wolf by the western door,
And o'er it an eagle hovers.

The sixth is Thrymheim, where Thjazi dwelt, 11
The giant of marvelous might;
Now Skathi abides, the god's fair bride,
In the home that her father had.

The seventh is Breithablik; Baldr has there 12
For himself a dwelling set,
In the land I know that lies so fair,
And from evil fate is free.

Himinbjorg is the eighth, and Heimdall there 13
O'er men holds sway, it is said;
In his well-built house does the warder of heaven
The good mead gladly drink.

The ninth is Folkvang, where Freyja decrees 14
Who shall have seats in the hall;
The half of the dead each day does she choose,
And half does Odin have.

The tenth is Glitnir; its pillars are gold, 15
And its roof with silver is set;
There most of his days does Forseti dwell,
And sets all strife at end.

The eleventh is Noatun; there has Njorth 16
For himself a dwelling set;
The sinless ruler of men there sits
In his temple timbered high.

Hrísi vex   ok háu grasi   17
Víðars land viði;
en þar mögr of læzt   af mars baki
frækn at hefna föður.

Andhrímnir   lætr í Eldhrímni   18
Sæhrímni soðinn,   fleska bezt;
en þat fáir vitu,
við hvat einherjar alask.

Gera ok Freka   seðr gunntamiðr   19
hróðigr Herjaföður;
en við vín eitt   vápngöfugr
Óðinn æ lifir.

Huginn ok Muninn   fljúga hverjan dag   20
Jörmungrund yfir;
óumk ek of Hugin,   at hann aftr né komi-t,
þó sjámk meir of Munin.

Þýtr Þund,   unir Þjóðvitnis   21
fiskr flóði í;
árstraumr þykkir   ofmikill
Valglaumni at vaða.

Valgrind heitir,   er stendr velli á   22
heilög fyr helgum dyrum;
forn er sú grind,   en þat fáir vitu,
hvé hon er í lás of lokin.

Fimm hundruð dura   ok umb fjórum tögum,   23
svá hygg ek á Valhöllu vera;
átta hundruð Einherja   ganga senn ór einum durum,
þá er þeir fara við vitni at vega.

Fimm hundruð golfa   ok umb fjórum tögum,   24
svá hygg ek Bilskirrni með bugum;
ranna þeira,   er ek reft vita,
míns veit ek mest magar.

Heiðrún heitir geit,   er stendr höllu á   25
ok bítr af Læraðs limum;
skapker fylla   hon skal ins skíra mjaðar;
kná-at sú veig vanask.

Filled with growing trees and high-standing grass   17
Is Vithi, Vithar's land;
But there did the son from his steed leap down,
When his father he fain would avenge.

In Eldhrimnir Andhrimnir cooks   18
Sæhrimnir's seething flesh—
The best of food, but few men know
On what fare the warriors feast.

Freki and Geri does Heerfather feed,   19
The far-famed fighter of old:
But on wine alone does the weapon-decked god,
Odin, forever live.

O'er Mithgarth Hugin and Munin both   20
Each day set forth to fly;
For Hugin I fear lest he come not home,
But for Munin my care is more.

Loud roars Thund, and Thjothvitnir's fish   21
Joyously fares in the flood;
Hard does it seem to the host of the slain
To wade the torrent wild.

There Valgrind stands, the sacred gate,   22
And behind are the holy doors;
Old is the gate, but few there are
Who can tell how it tightly is locked.

Five hundred doors and forty there are,   23
I ween, in Valhall's walls;
Eight hundred fighters through one door fare
When to war with the wolf they go.

Five hundred rooms and forty there are   24
I ween, in Bilskirnir built;
Of all the homes whose roofs I beheld,
My son's the greatest meseemed.

Heithrun is the goat who stands by Heerfather's hall,   25
And the branches of Lærath she bites;
The pitcher she fills with the fair, clear mead,
Ne'er fails the foaming drink.

Eikþyrnir heitir hjörtr,   er stendr höllu á   26
ok bítr af Læraðs limum;
en af hans hornum   drýpr í Hvergelmi,
þaðan eigu vötn öll vega.

Síð ok Víð,   Sækin ok Eikin,   27
Svöl ok Gunnþró,   Fjörm ok Fimbulþul,
Rín ok Rennandi,   Gipul ok Göpul,
Gömul ok Geirvimul,   þær hverfa um hodd goða,
Þyn ok Vín,   Þöll ok Höll,
Gráð ok Gunnþorin.

Vína heitir ein,   önnur Vegsvinn,   28
þriðja Þjóðnuma,   Nyt ok Nöt,
Nönn ok Hrönn,   Slíð ok Hríð,
Sylgr ok Ylgr,   Víð ok Ván,
Vönd ok Strönd,   Gjöll ok Leiftr,
þær falla gumnum nær,   er falla til Heljar heðan.

Körmt ok Örmt   ok Kerlaugar tvær,   29
þær skal Þórr vaða   dag hvern,
er hann dæma ferr   at aski Yggdrasils,
því at ásbrú   brenn öll loga,
heilög vötn hlóa.

Glaðr ok Gyllir,   Glær ok Skeiðbrimir,   30
Silfrintoppr ok Sinir,   Gísl ok Falhófnir,
Gulltoppr ok Léttfeti,   þeim ríða æsir jóm
dag hvern,   er þeir dæma fara
at aski Yggdrasils.

Þríar rætr   standa á þría vega   31
undan aski Yggdrasils;
Hel býr und einni,   annarri hrímþursar,
þriðju mennskir menn.

Ratatoskr heitir íkorni,   er renna skal   32
at aski Yggdrasils,   arnar orð
hann skal ofan bera   ok segja Niðhöggvi niðr.

Eikthyrnir is the hart who stands by Heerfather's hall   26
And the branches of Lærath he bites;
From his horns a stream into Hvergelmir drops,
Thence all the rivers run.

Sith and Vith, Sækin and Ækin,   27
Svol and Fimbulthul, Gunnthro, and Fjorm,
Rin and Rinnandi,
Gipul and Gopul, Gomul and Geirvimul,
That flow through the fields of the gods;
Thyn and Vin, Thol and Hol,
Groth and Gunnthorin.

Vino is one, Vegsvin another,   28
And Thjothnuma a third;
Nyt and Not, Non and Hron,
Slith and Hrith, Sylg and Ylg,
Vith and Von, Vond and Strond,
Gjol and Leipt, that go among men,
And hence they fall to Hel.

Kormt and Ormt and the Kerlaugs twain   29
Shall Thor each day wade through,
When dooms to give he forth shall go
To the ash-tree Yggdrasil;
For heaven's bridge burns all in flame,
And the sacred waters seethe.

Glath and Gyllir, Gler and Skeithbrimir,   30
Silfrintopp and Sinir,
Gisl and Falhofnir, Golltopp and Lettfeti,
On these steeds the gods shall go
When dooms to give each day they ride
To the ash-tree Yggdrasil.

Three roots there are that three ways run   31
'Neath the ash-tree Yggdrasil;
'Neath the first lives Hel, 'neath the second the frost-giants,
'Neath the last are the lands of men.

Ratatosk is the squirrel who there shall run   32
On the ash-tree Yggdrasil;
From above the words of the eagle he bears,
And tells them to Nithhogg beneath.

Hirtir eru ok fjórir, þeirs af hæfingar 33
gaghalsir gnaga:
Dáinn ok Dvalinn, Duneyrr ok Duraþrór.

Ormar fleiri liggja und aski Yggdrasils, 34
en þat of hyggi hverr ósviðra apa:
Góinn ok Móinn, þeir ro Grafvitnis synir,
Grábakr ok Grafvölluðr, Ófnir ok Sváfnir,
hygg ek, at æ skyli meiðs kvistu má.

Askr Yggdrasils drýgir erfiði 35
meira en menn um viti:
hjörtr bítr ofan, en á hliðu fúnar,
skerðir Niðhöggr neðan.

Hrist ok Mist vil ek, at mér horn beri, 36
Skeggjöld ok Skögul, Hildr ok Þrúðr,
Hlökk ok Herfjötur, Göll ok Geirönul,
Randgríðr ok Ráðgríðr ok Reginleif,
þær bera Einherjum öl.

Árvakr ok Alsviðr þeir skulu upp heðan 37
svangir sól draga;
en und þeira bógum fálu blíð regin,
æsir, ísarnkol.

Svalinn heitir, hann stendr sólu fyrir, 38
skjöldr, skínanda goði;
björg ok brim, ek veit, at brenna skulu,
ef hann fellr í frá.

Sköll heitir ulfr, er fylgir inu skírleita goði 39
til varna viðar, en annarr Hati,
hann er Hróðvitnis sonr, sá skal fyr heiða brúði himins.

Ór Ymis holdi var jörð of sköpuð, 40
en ór sveita sær, björg ór beinum,
baðmr ór hári, en ór hausi himinn.

Four harts there are, that the highest twigs 33
Nibble with necks bent back;
Dain and Dvalin [...]
Duneyr and Dyrathror.

More serpents there are beneath the ash 34
Than an unwise ape would think;
Goin and Moin, Grafvitnir's sons,
Grabak and Grafvolluth,
Ofnir and Svafnir shall ever, methinks,
Gnaw at the twigs of the tree.

Yggdrasil's ash great evil suffers, 35
Far more than men do know;
The hart bites its top, its trunk is rotting,
And Nithhogg gnaws beneath.

Hrist and Mist bring the horn at my will, 36
Skeggjold and Skogul;
Hild and Thruth, Hlok and Herfjotur,
Gol and Geironul,
Randgrith and Rathgrith and Reginleif
Beer to the warriors bring.

Arvak and Alsvith up shall drag 37
Weary the weight of the sun;
But an iron cool have the kindly gods
Of yore set under their yokes.

In front of the sun does Svalin stand, 38
The shield for the shining god;
Mountains and sea would be set in flames
If it fell from before the sun.

Skoll is the wolf that to Ironwood 39
Follows the glittering god,
And the son of Hrothvitnir, Hati, awaits
The burning bride of heaven.

Out of Ymir's flesh was fashioned the earth, 40
And the ocean out of his blood;
Of his bones the hills, of his hair the trees,
Of his skull the heavens high.

En ór hans brám   gerðu blíð regin 41
Miðgarð manna sonum,
en ór hans heila
váru þau in harðmóðgu
ský öll of sköpuð.

Ullar hylli   hefr ok allra goða 42
hverr er tekr fyrstr á funa,
því at opnir heimar
verða of ása sonum,   þá er hefja af hvera.

Ívalda synir   gengu í árdaga 43
Skíðblaðni at skapa,
skipa bezt,   skírum Frey,
nýtum Njarðar bur.

Askr Yggdrasils,   hann er æðstr viða, 44
en Skíðblaðnir skipa,   Óðinn ása,
en jóa Sleipnir,   Bilröst brúa,
en Bragi skalda,   Hábrók hauka,
en hunda Garmr.

Svipum hef ek nú yppt 45
fyr sigtíva sonum,
við þat skal vilbjörg vaka;
öllum ásum   þat skal inn koma
Ægis bekki á,   Ægis drekku at.

Hétumk Grímr,   hétumk Gangleri, 46
Herjann ok Hjalmberi,
Þekkr ok Þriði,
Þundr ok Uðr,   Herblindi ok Hár.

Saðr ok Svipall   ok Sanngetall, 47
Herteitr ok Hnikarr,
Bileygr, Báleygr,
Bölverkr, Fjölnir,   Grímr ok Grímnir,
Glapsviðr ok Fjölsviðr;

Síðhöttr, Síðskeggr, Sigföðr, Hnikuðr, 48
Alföðr, Valföðr, Atríðr ok Farmatýr;
einu nafni hétumk aldregi,
síz ek með folkum fór.

Mithgarth the gods from his eyebrows made,   41
And set for the sons of men;
And out of his brain the baleful clouds
They made to move on high.

His the favor of Ull and of all the gods   42
Who first in the flames will reach;
For the house can be seen by the sons of the gods
If the kettle aside were cast.

In days of old did Ivaldi's sons   43
Skithblathnir fashion fair,
The best of ships for the bright god Freyr,
The noble son of Njorth.

The best of trees must Yggdrasil be,   44
Skithblathnir best of boats;
Of all the gods is Odin the greatest,
And Sleipnir the best of steeds;
Bifrost of bridges, Bragi of skalds,
Hobrok of hawks, and Garm of hounds.

To the race of the gods my face have I raised,   45
And the wished-for aid have I waked;
For to all the gods has the message gone
That sit in Ægir's seats,
That drink within Ægir's doors.

Grim is my name, Gangleri am I,   46
Herjan and Hjalmberi,
Thekk and Thrithi, Thuth and Uth,
Helblindi and Hor;

Sath and Svipal and Sanngetal,   47
Herteit and Hnikar,
Bileyg, Baleyg, Bolverk, Fjolnir,
Grim and Grimnir, Glapsvith, Fjolsvith.

Sithhott, Sithskegg, Sigfather, Hnikuth,   48
Allfather, Valfather, Atrith, Farmatyr:
A single name have I never had
Since first among men I fared.

Grímni mik hétu   at Geirröðar,   49
en Jalk at Ásmundar,   en þá Kjalar,
er ek kjálka dró,   Þrór þingum at,
Viðurr at vígum,   Óski ok Ómi,
Jafnhár ok Biflindi,   Göndlir ok Hárbarðr með goðum.

Sviðurr ok Sviðrir   er ek hét at Sökkmímis,   50
ok dulðak þann inn aldna jötun,
þá er ek Miðvitnis vark   ins mæra burar
orðinn einbani.

Ölr ertu, Geirröðr,   hefr þú ofdrukkit;   51
miklu ertu hnugginn,   er þú ert mínu gengi,
öllum Einherjum   ok Óðins hylli.

Fjölð ek þér sagðak,   en þú fátt of mant;   52
of þik véla vinir;
mæki liggja   ek sé míns vinar
allan í dreyra drifinn.

Eggmóðan val   nú mun Yggr hafa,   53
þitt veit ek líf of liðit;
úfar ro dísir,   nú knáttu Óðin sjá,
nálgasktu mik, ef þú megir.

Óðinn ek nú heiti,   Yggr ek áðan hét,   54
hétumk Þundr fyr þat,   Vakr ok Skilfingr,
Váfuðr ok Hroftatýr,   Gautr ok Jalkr með goðum,
Ófnir ok Sváfnir,   er ek hygg, at orðnir sé
allir af einum mér.

Geirröðr konungr sat ok hafði sverð um kné sér ok brugðit til miðs. En er hann heyrði, at Óðinn var þar kominn, þá stóð hann upp ok vildi taka Óðin frá eldinum. Sverðit slapp ór hendi honum, ok vissu hjöltin niðr. Konungr drap fæti ok steypðist áfram, en sverðit stóð í gögnum hann, ok fekk hann bana. Óðinn hvarf þá, en Agnarr var þar konungr lengi síðan.

Grimnir they call me in Geirröth's hall,   49
With Asmund Jalk am I;
Kjalar I was when I went in a sledge,
At the council Thror am I called,
As Vithur I fare to the fight;
Oski, Biflindi, Jafnhor and Omi,
Gondlir and Harbarth midst gods.

I deceived the giant Sokkmimir old   50
As Svithur and Svithrir of yore;
Of Mithvitnir's son the slayer I was
When the famed one found his doom.

Drunk art thou, Geirröth, too much didst thou drink,   51
[...]
Much hast thou lost, for help no more
From me or my heroes thou hast.

Small heed didst thou take to all that I told,   52
And false were the words of thy friends;
For now the sword of my friend I see,
That waits all wet with blood.

Thy sword-pierced body shall Ygg have soon,   53
For thy life is ended at last;
The maids are hostile; now Odin behold!
Now come to me if thou canst!

Now am I Odin, Ygg was I once,   54
Ere that did they call me Thund;
Vak and Skilfing, Vofuth and Hroptatyr,
Gaut and Jalk midst the gods;
Ofnir and Svafnir, and all, methinks,
Are names for none but me.

King Geirröth sat and had his sword on his knee, half drawn from its sheath. But when he heard that Odin was come thither, then he rose up and sought to take Odin from the fire. The sword slipped from his hand, and fell with the hilt down. The king stumbled and fell forward, and the sword pierced him through, and slew him. Then Odin vanished, but Agnar long ruled there as king.

ENDNOTES

Prose. The texts of the two manuscripts differ in many minor details. *Hrauthung*: this mythical king is not mentioned elsewhere. *Geirröth*: the manuscripts spell his name in various ways. *Frigg*: Odin's wife. She and Odin nearly always disagreed in some such way as the one outlined in this story. *Hlithskjolf* ("Gate-Shelf"): Odin's [throne in Asgard], whence he can overlook all the nine worlds; cf. *Skirnismol*, introductory prose. *Grimnir*: "the Hooded One."

2. In the original lines 2 and 4 are both too long for the meter, and thus the true form of the stanza is doubtful. For line 4 both manuscripts have "the land of the Goths" instead of simply "the Goths." The word "Goths" apparently was applied indiscriminately to any South-Germanic people, including the Burgundians as well as the actual Goths, and thus here has no specific application; cf. *Gripisspo*, 35 and note.

3. *Veratyr* ("Lord of Men"): Odin. The "gift" which Agnar receives is Odin's mythological lore.

4. *Thruthheim* ("the Place of Might"): the place where Thor, the strongest of the gods, has his hall, Bilskirnir, described in stanza 24.

5. *Ydalir* ("Yew-Dales"): the home of Ull, the archer among the gods, a son of Thor's wife, Sif, by another marriage. The wood of the yew-tree was used for bows in the North just as it was long afterwards in England. *Alfheim*: the home of the elves. *Freyr*: cf. *Skirnismol*, introductory prose and note. *Tooth-gift*: the custom of making a present to a child when it cuts its first tooth is, according to Vigfusson, still in vogue in Iceland.

6. *Valaskjolf* ("the Shelf of the Slain"): Odin's home, in which is his

[throne], Hlithskjolf. Gering identifies this with Valhall, and as that is mentioned in stanza 8, he believes stanza 6 to be an interpolation.

7. *Sökkvabekk* ("the Sinking Stream"): of this spot and of Saga, who is said to live there, little is known. Saga may be an hypostasis of Frigg, but Snorri calls her a distinct goddess, and the name suggests some relation to history or story-telling.

8. *Glathsheim* ("the Place of Joy"): Odin's home, the greatest and most beautiful hall in the world. *Valhall* ("Hall of the Slain"): cf. *Voluspo*, 31 and note. Valhall is not only the hall whither the slain heroes are brought by the Valkyries, but also a favorite home of Odin.

10. The opening formula is abbreviated in both manuscripts. *A wolf*: probably the wolf and the eagle were carved figures above the door.

11. *Thrymheim* ("the Home of Clamor"): on this mountain the giant Thjazi built his home. The god, or rather Wane, Njorth (cf. *Voluspo*, 21, note) married Thjazi's daughter, Skathi. She wished to live in her father's hall among the mountains, while Njorth loved his home, Noatun, by the sea. They agreed to compromise by spending nine nights at Thrymheim and then three at Noatun, but neither could endure the surroundings of the other's home, so Skathi returned to Thrymheim, while Njorth stayed at Noatun. Snorri quotes stanzas 11–15.

12. *Breithablik* ("Wide-Shining"): the house in heaven, free from everything unclean, in which Baldr (cf. *Voluspo*, 32, note), the fairest and best of the gods, lived.

13. *Himinbjorg* ("Heaven's Cliffs"): the dwelling at the end of the bridge Bifrost (the rainbow), where Heimdall (cf. *Voluspo*, 27) keeps watch against the coming of the giants. In this stanza the two functions of Heimdall—as father of mankind (cf. *Voluspo*, 1 and note, and *Rigsthula*, introductory prose and note) and as warder of the gods—seem both to be mentioned, but the second line in the manuscripts is apparently in bad shape, and in the editions is more or less conjectural.

14. *Folkvang* ("Field of the Folk"): here is situated Freyja's hall, Sessrymnir ("Rich in Seats"). Freyja, the sister of Freyr, is the fairest of the goddesses, and the most kindly disposed to mankind. *Half of the dead*: Mogk has made it clear that Freyja represents a confusion between two originally distinct divinities: the wife of Odin (Frigg) and the northern goddess of love. This passage appears to have in mind her attributes as Odin's wife. Snorri has this same confusion, but there is no reason why the Freyja who was Freyr's sister should share the slain with Odin.

15. *Glitnir* ("the Shining"): the home of Forseti, a god of whom we know nothing beyond what Snorri tells us: "Forseti is the son of Baldr and Nanna, daughter of Nep. All those who come to him with hard cases to settle go away satisfied; he is the best judge among gods and men."

16. *Noatun* ("Ships'-Haven"): the home of Njorth, who calms the waves; cf. stanza 11 and *Voluspo*, 21.

17. *Vithi*: this land is not mentioned elsewhere. *Vithar* avenged his father, Odin, by slaying the wolf Fenrir.

18. Stanzas 18–20 appear also in Snorri's *Edda*. Very possibly they are an interpolation here. *Eldhrimnir* ("Sooty with Fire"): the great kettle in Valhall, wherein the gods' cook, *Andhrimnir* ("The Sooty-Faced") daily cooks the flesh of the boar *Sæhrimnir* ("The Blackened"). His flesh suffices for all the heroes there gathered, and each evening he becomes whole again, to be cooked the next morning.

19. *Freki* ("The Greedy") and *Geri* ("The Ravenous"): the two wolves who sit by Odin's side at the feast, and to whom he gives all the food set before him, since wine is food and drink alike for him. *Heerfather*: Odin.

20. *Mithgarth* ("The Middle Home"): the earth. *Hugin* ("Thought") and *Munin* ("Memory"): the two ravens who sit on Odin's shoulders, and fly forth daily to bring him news of the world.

21. *Thund* ("The Swollen" or "The Roaring"): the river surrounding Valhall. *Thjothvitnir's fish*: presumably the sun, which was caught by the wolf Skoll (cf. *Voluspo*, 40), Thjothvitnir meaning "the mighty wolf." Such a phrase, characteristic of all Skaldic poetry, is rather rare in the *Edda*. The last two lines refer to the attack on Valhall by the people of Hel; cf. *Voluspo*, 51.

22. *Valgrind* ("The Death-Gate"): the outer gate of Valhall; cf. *Sigurtharkvitha en skamma*, 68 and note.

23. This and the following stanza stand in reversed order in *Regius*. Snorri quotes stanza 23 as a proof of the vast size of Valhall. The last two lines refer to the final battle with Fenrir and the other enemies.

24. This stanza is almost certainly an interpolation, brought in through a confusion of the first two lines with those of stanza 23. Its description of Thor's house, Bilskirnir (cf. stanza 4 and note) has nothing to do with that of Valhall. Snorri quotes the stanza in his account of Thor.

25. The first line in the original is, as indicated in the translation, too

long, and various attempts to amend it have been made. *Heithrun*: the she-goat who lives on the twigs of the tree *Lærath* (presumably the ash Yggdrasil), and daily gives mead which, like the boar's flesh, suffices for all the heroes in Valhall. In Snorri's *Edda* Gangleri foolishly asks whether the heroes drink water, whereto Har replies, "Do you imagine that Odin invites kings and earls and other noble men, and then gives them water to drink?"

26. *Eikthyrnir* ("The Oak-Thorned," i.e., with antlers, "thorns," like an oak): this animal presumably represents the clouds. The first line, like that of stanza 25, is too long in the original. *Lærath*: cf. stanza 25, note. *Hvergelmir*: according to Snorri, this spring, "the Cauldron-Roaring," was in the midst of Niflheim, the world of darkness and the dead, beneath the third root of the ash Yggdrasil. Snorri gives a list of the rivers flowing thence nearly identical with the one in the poem.

27. The entire passage from stanza 27 through stanza 35 is confused. The whole thing may well be an interpolation. Bugge calls stanzas 27–30 an interpolation, and editors who have accepted the passage as a whole have rejected various lines. The spelling of the names of the rivers varies greatly in the manuscripts and editions. It is needless here to point out the many attempted emendations of this list. For a passage presenting similar problems, cf. *Voluspo*, 10–16. Snorri virtually quotes stanzas 27–28 in his prose, though not consecutively. The name *Rin*, in line 3, is identical with that for the River Rhine which appears frequently in the hero poems, but the similarity is doubtless purely accidental.

28. *Slith* may possibly be the same river as that mentioned in *Voluspo*, 36, as flowing through the giants' land. *Leipt*: in *Helgakvitha Hundingsbana II*, 29, this river is mentioned as one by which a solemn oath is sworn, and Gering points the parallel to the significance of the Styx among the Greeks. The other rivers here named are not mentioned elsewhere in the poems.

29. This stanza looks as though it originally had had nothing to do with the two preceding it. Snorri quotes it in his description of the three roots of Yggdrasil, and the three springs beneath them. "The third root of the ash stands in heaven and beneath this root is a spring which is very holy, and is called Urth's well." (Cf. *Voluspo*, 19) "There the gods have their judgment-seat, and thither they ride each day over Bifrost, which is also called the Gods' Bridge." Thor has to go on foot in the last days of the destruction, when the bridge is burning. Another interpretation, however, is that when Thor leaves the heavens (i.e., when a thunder-storm is over) the rainbow-bridge becomes hot in the sun. Nothing more is known of

the rivers named in this stanza. Lines 3–4 are almost certainly interpolated from stanza 30.

30. This stanza, again possibly an interpolation, is closely paraphrased by Snorri following the passage quoted in the previous note. *Glath* ("Joyous"): identified in the *Skaldskaparmal* with Skinfaxi, the horse of day; cf. *Vafthruthnismol*, 12. *Gyllir*: "Golden." *Gler*: "Shining." *Skeithbrimir*: "Swift-Going." *Silfrintopp*: "Silver-Topped." *Sinir*: "Sinewy." *Gisl*: the meaning is doubtful; Gering suggests "Gleaming." *Falhofnir*: "Hollow-Hoofed." *Golltopp* ("Gold-Topped"): this horse be longed to Heimdall (cf. *Voluspo*, I and 46). It is noteworthy that gold was one of the attributes of Heimdall's belongings, and, because his teeth were of gold, he was also called Gullintanni ("Gold-Toothed"). *Lettfeti*: "Light-Feet." Odin's eight footed horse, Sleipnir, is not mentioned in this list.

31. The first of these roots is the one referred to in stanza 26; the second in stanza 29 (cf. notes). Of the third root there is nothing noteworthy recorded. After this stanza it is more than possible that one has been lost, paraphrased in the prose of Snorri's *Edda* thus: "An eagle sits in the branches of the ash tree, and he is very wise; and between his eyes sits the hawk who is called Vethrfolnir."

32. *Ratatosk* ("The Swift-Tusked"): concerning this squirrel, the *Prose Edda* has to add only that he runs up and down the tree conveying the abusive language of the eagle (see note on stanza 31) and the dragon *Nithhogg* (cf. *Voluspo*, 39 and note) to each other. The hypothesis that Ratatosk "represents the undying hatred between the sustaining and the destroying elements—the gods and the giants," seems a trifle far-fetched.

33. Stanzas 33–34 may well be interpolated, and are certainly in bad shape in the Mss. Bugge points out that they are probably of later origin than those surrounding them. Snorri closely paraphrases stanza 33, but without elaboration, and nothing further is known of the four harts. It may be guessed, however, that they are a late multiplication of the single hart mentioned in stanza 26. Highest twigs: a guess; the Mss. words are baffling. Something has apparently been lost from lines 3–4, but there is no clue as to its nature.

34. Cf. note on previous stanza. Nothing further is known of any of the serpents here listed, and the meanings of many of the names are conjectural. Snorri quotes this stanza. Editors have altered it in various ways in an attempt to regularize the meter. *Goin* and *Moin*: meaning obscure. *Grafvitnir*: "The Gnawing Wolf." *Grabak*: "Gray-Back." *Grafvolluth*: "The Field Gnawer." *Ofnir* and *Svafnir* ("The Bewilderer" and "The

Sleep-Bringer"): it is noteworthy that in stanza 54 Odin gives himself these two names.

35. Snorri quotes this stanza, which concludes the passage, beginning with stanza 25, describing Yggdrasil. If we assume that stanzas 27–34 are later interpolations—possibly excepting 32—this section of the poem reads clearly enough.

36. Snorri quotes this list of the Valkyries, concerning whom cf. *Voluspo*, 31 and note, where a different list of names is given. *Hrist*: "Shaker." *Mist*: "Mist." *Skeggjold*: "Ax-Time." *Skogul*: "Raging" (?). *Hild*: "Warrior." *Thruth*: "Might." *Hlok*: "Shrieking." *Herfjotur*: "Host-Fetter." *Gol*: "Screaming." *Geironul*: "Spear-Bearer." *Randgrith*: "Shield-Bearer." *Rathgrith*: Gering guesses "Plan-Destroyer." *Reginleif*: "Gods'-Kin." Manuscripts and editions vary greatly in the spelling of these names, and hence in their significance.

37. Müllenhoff suspects stanzas 37–41 to have been interpolated, and Edzardi thinks they may have come from the *Vafthruthnismol*. Snorri closely paraphrases stanzas 37–39, and quotes 40–41. *Arvak* ("Early Waker") and *Alsvith* ("All Swift"): the horses of the sun, named also in *Sigrdrifumol*, 15. According to Snorri: "There was a man called Mundilfari, who had two children; they were so fair and lovely that he called his son Mani and his daughter Sol. The gods were angry at this presumption, and took the children and set them up in heaven; and they bade Sol drive the horses that drew the car of the sun which the gods had made to light the world from the sparks which flew out of Muspellsheim. The horses were called Alsvith and Arvak, and under their yokes the gods set two bellows to cool them, and in some songs these are called 'the cold iron.'

38. *Svalin* ("The Cooling"): the only other reference to this shield is in *Sigrdrifumol*, 15.

39. *Skoll* and *Hati*: the wolves that devour respectively the sun and moon. The latter is the son of Hrothvitnir ("The Mighty Wolf," i.e. Fenrir); cf. *Voluspo*, 40, and *Vafthruthnismol*, 46–47, in which Fenrir appears as the thief. *Ironwood*: a conjectural emendation of an obscure phrase; cf. *Voluspo*, 40.

40. This and the following stanza are quoted by Snorri. They seem to have come from a different source from the others of this poem; Edzardi suggests an older version of the *Vafthruthnismol*. This stanza is closely parallel to *Vafthruthnismol*, 21, which see, as also *Voluspo*, 3. Snorri, following this account, has a few details to add. The stones were made out of Ymir's teeth and such of his bones as were broken. Mithgarth was

a mountain-wall made out of Ymir's eyebrows, and set around the earth because of the enmity of the giants.

42. With this stanza Odin gets back to his immediate situation, bound as he is between two fires. He calls down a blessing on the man who will reach into the fire and pull aside the great kettle which, in Icelandic houses, hung directly under the smoke vent in the roof, and thus kept any one above from looking down into the interior. On *Ull*, the archer-god, cf. stanza 5 and note. He is specified here apparently for no better reason than that his name fits the initial-rhyme.

43. This and the following stanza are certainly interpolated, for they have nothing to do with the context, and stanza 45 continues the dramatic conclusion of the poem begun in stanza 42. This stanza is quoted by Snorri. *Ivaldi* ("The Mighty"): he is known only as the father of the craftsmen-dwarfs who made not only the ship Skithblathnir, but also Odin's spear Gungnir, and the golden hair for Thor's wife, Sif, after Loki had maliciously cut her own hair off. *Skithblathnir*: this ship ("Wooden-Bladed") always had a fair wind, whenever the sail was set; it could be folded up at will and put in the pocket. *Freyr*: concerning him and his father, see *Voluspo*, 21, note, and *Skirnismol*, introductory prose and note.

44. Snorri quotes this stanza. Like stanza 43 an almost certain interpolation, it was probably drawn in by the reference to Skithblathnir in the stanza interpolated earlier. It is presumably in faulty condition. One Ms. has after the fifth line half of a sixth—"Brimir of swords." *Yggdrasil*: cf. stanzas 25–35. *Skithblathnir*: cf. stanza 43, note. *Sleipnir*: Odin's eight-legged horse, one of Loki's numerous progeny, borne by him to the stallion Svathilfari. This stallion belonged to the giant who built a fortress for the gods, and came so near to finishing it, with Svathilfari's aid, as to make the gods fear he would win his promised reward—Freyja and the sun and moon. To delay the work, Loki turned himself into a mare, whereupon the stallion ran away, and the giant failed to complete his task within the stipulated time. *Bilrost*: probably another form of Bifrost (which Snorri has in his version of the stanza), on which cf. stanza 29. *Bragi*: the god of poetry. He is one of the later figures among the gods, and is mentioned only three times in the poems of the *Edda*. In Snorri's *Edda*, however, he is of great importance. His wife is Ithun, goddess of youth. *Hobrok*: nothing further is known of him. *Garm*: cf. *Voluspo*, 44.

45. With this stanza the narrative current of the poem is resumed. *Ægir*: the sea-god; cf. *Lokasenna*, introductory prose.

46. Concerning the condition of stanzas 46–50, quoted by Snorri, noth-

ing definite can be said. Lines and entire stanzas of this "catalogue" sort undoubtedly came and went with great freedom all through the period of oral transmission. Many of the names are not mentioned elsewhere, and often their significance is sheer guesswork. As in nearly every episode Odin appeared in disguise, the number of his names was necessarily almost limitless. *Grim*: "The Hooded." *Gangleri*: "The Wanderer." *Herjan*: "The Ruler." *Hjalmberi*: "The Helmet-Bearer." *Thekk*: "The Much-Loved." *Thrithi*: "The Third" (in Snorri's *Edda* the stories are all told in the form of answers to questions, the speakers being Har, Jafnhar and Thrithi. Just what this tripartite form of Odin signifies has been the source of endless debate.) *Thuth* and *Uth*: both names defy guesswork. *Helblindi*: "Hel-Blinder" (two manuscripts have Herblindi—"Host-Blinder"). *Hor*: "The High One."

47. *Sath*: "The Truthful." *Svipal*: "The Changing." *Sanngetal*: "The Truth-Teller." *Herteit*: "Glad of the Host." *Hnikar*: "The Overthrower." *Bileyg*: "The Shifty-Eyed." *Baleyg*: "The Flaming-Eyed." *Bolverk*: "Doer of Ill" (cf. *Hovamol*, 104 and note). *Fjolnir*: "The Many-Shaped." *Grimnir*: "The Hooded." *Glapswith*: "Swift in Deceit." *Fjolsvith*: "Wide of Wisdom."

48. *Sithhott*: "With Broad Hat." *Sithskegg*: "Long-Bearded." *Sigfather*: 'Father of Victory." *Hnikuth*: "Overthrower." *Valfather*: 'Father of the Slain." *Atrith*: "The Rider." *Farmatyr*: "Helper of Cargoes" (i.e., god of sailors).

49. Nothing is known of Asmund, of Odin's appearance as Jalk, or of the occasion when he "went in a sledge" as Kjalar ("Ruler of Keels"?). *Thror* and *Vithur* are also of uncertain meaning. *Oski*: "God of Wishes." *Biflindi*: the manuscripts vary widely in the form of this name. *Jafnhor*: "Equally High" (cf. note on stanza 46). *Omi*: "The Shouter." *Gondlir*: "Wand-Bearer." *Harbarth*: "Graybeard" (cf. *Harbarthsljoth*, introduction).

50. Nothing further is known of the episode here mentioned Sokkmimir is presumably Mithvitnir's son. Snorri quotes the names Svithur and Svithrir, but omits all the remainder of the stanza.

51. Again the poem returns to the direct action, Odin addressing the terrified Geirröth. The manuscripts show no lacuna. Some editors supply a second line from paper manuscripts: "Greatly by me art beguiled."

53. *Ygg*: Odin ("The Terrible"). *The maids*: the three Norns.

54. Possibly out of place, and probably more or less corrupt. *Thund*:

"The Thunderer." *Vak*: "The Wakeful." *Skilfing*: "The Shaker." *Vofuth*: "The Wanderer." *Hroptatyr*: "Crier of the Gods." *Gaut*: "Father." *Ofnir* and *Svafnir*: cf. stanza 34.

SKIRNISMOL
THE BALLAD OF SKIRNIR

INTRODUCTION

The *Skirnismol* is a unique work in that it is one of the few *Eddic* poems consisting almost entirely of dialogue between deities or their immediate associates, putting it into a class with the *Lokasenna* (with which, many believe, it may share an author) or the *Thrymskvitha*. Of particular note is that the focus of the story is upon the God Yngvi-Freyr and his household, rather than the normal poetic subjects of Odin, Thor, or other members of the *Aesir* proper.

Freyr was by all accounts one of the most actively worshiped and popular of the deities in Scandinavia and later Iceland, intimately connected to the royal authority in Sweden and then later to what would become the royal line of Norway, and archaeological examinations and the linguistic associations of place names confirm that he was extensively worshiped in both regions. It is, therefore, somewhat of a mystery that we do not possess a greater catalog of stories about the God. Allusions contained within the *Skirnismol* and other scattered references to Freyr (always grandiose and complimentary) hint at a much larger narrative role and function, and at a missing body of material covering his story.

As it stands, many of the statements made about Freyr and his household are somewhat vague and mysterious, open to different interpretations. The *Skirnismol* itself opens with a short prose introduction positioning the deity as sitting within Odin's high seat of Hlidskjalf, which is known to allow its occupant to see over all the worlds. We might wonder why Freyr was occupying the seat to begin with, and so brusquely refuses to leave when Odin demands it, being reduced to seeking out his father and companion for aid in convincing him. This has two main variant interpretations. The first posits that Freyr's lovesickness is a punishment for his pride in placing himself in Odin's seat and thus constituting a narrative where the chain of events unfolds, leading to his eventual death at *Ragnarök* sans his sword. The counter-interpretation presents the events as emblematic of a political struggle within Asgard itself, with Freyr (perhaps as a representative of the *Vanir* themselves) claiming royal authority as Odin's equal, with the latter unable to do anything about this but approach the matter diplomatically by appealing to his own kin. This perhaps reflects a larger cultic struggle between that of Odin and Freyr in the mortal sphere with the royal powers of Denmark and the continent preferring to trace themselves back to Odin and the royal powers of Scandinavia proper tracing themselves back to Freyr.

The main narrative point of view of the poem is that of Freyr's companion Skirnir, who appears in a role not dissimilar from that of a squire or page. There is some mystery regarding Skirnir's exact nature, as he is asked of his origin and replies "I am not of the elves, nor the offspring of gods, Nor of the wise Wanes," leaving many at a loss as to which people Skirnir may actually descend from. His mission extends to him seeking the bride Gerth, daughter of Gymir, for his lord and to end his lovesickness. Skirnir first attempts to woo her with gold and treasure, then moves to the threat of violence, and ultimately succeeds when he uses the threat of magic to give her a loathsome fate in which she would otherwise only be married to a three headed troll. Of rather interesting note here is also that Gerth, afterwards Freyr's wife, is also the origin of the later Yngling lineage of Swedish (and Norwegian) kings themselves, suggesting that the story, and its highly complimentary tone towards Freyr, may originate with one of these peoples.

Frey
(Jacques Reich)

Freyr, sonr Njarðar, hafði einn dag setzt í Hliðskjálf, ok sá um heima alla. Hann sá í Jötunheima ok sá þar mey fagra, þá er hon gekk frá skála föður síns til skemmu. Þar af fekk hann hugsóttir miklar. Skírnir hét skósveinn Freys. Njörðr bað hann kveðja Frey máls. Þá mælti Skaði:

"Rístu nú, Skírnir,   1
ok gakk skjótt at beiða
okkarn mála mög   ok þess at fregna,
hveim inn fróði sé   ofreiði afi."

Skírnir kvað: 2
"Illra orða   er mér ón at ykkrum syni,
ef ek geng at mæla við mög
ok þess at fregna,
hveim inn fróði sé
ofreiði afi."

"Segðu mér þat, Freyr,   folkvaldi goða,   3
ok ek vilja vita:
Hví þú einn sitr   endlanga sali,
minn dróttinn, um daga?"

SKIRNISMOL

Freyr, the son of Njorth, had sat one day in Hlithskjolf, and looked over all the worlds. He looked into Jotunheim, and saw there a fair maiden, as she went from her father's house to her bower. Forthwith he felt a mighty love-sickness. Skirnir was the name of Freyr's servant; Njorth bade him ask speech of Freyr. He said:

"Go now, Skirnir! and seek to gain
Speech from my son;
And answer to win, for whom the wise one
Is mightily moved."

1

Skirnir spake:
"Ill words do I now await from thy son,
If I seek to get speech with him,
And answer to win, for whom the wise one
Is mightily moved."

2

Skirnir spake:
"Speak prithee, Freyr, foremost of the gods,
For now I fain would know;
Why sittest thou here in the wide halls,
Days long, my prince, alone?"

3

Freyr kvað: 4
"Hví um segjak þér,   seggr inn ungi,
mikinn móðtrega?
Því at álfröðull   lýsir um alla daga
ok þeygi at mínum munum."

Skírnir kvað: 5
"Muni þína   hykk-a ek svá mikla vera,
at þú mér, seggr, né segir,
því at ungir saman   várum í árdaga,
vel mættim tveir trúask."

Freyr kvað: 6
"Í Gymis görðum   ek ganga sá
mér tíða mey;
armar lýstu,   en af þaðan
allt loft ok lögr."

"Mær er mér tíðari   en manna hveim 7
ungum í árdaga;
ása ok alfa   þat vill engi maðr
at vit samt séim."

Skírnir kvað: 8
"Mar gefðu mér þá
þann er mik um myrkvan beri
vísan vafrloga,   ok þat sverð,
er sjalft vegisk   við jötna ætt."

Freyr kvað: 9
"Mar ek þér þann gef,
er þik um myrkvan berr
vísan vafrloga,   ok þat sverð,
er sjalft mun vegask
ef sá er horskr, er hefr."

Skírnir mælti við hestinn: 10
"Myrkt er úti,
mál kveð ek okkr fara
úrig fjöll yfir,   þursa þjóð yfir;
báðir vit komumk,   eða okkr báða tekr
sá inn ámáttki jötunn."

Skírnir reið í Jötunheima til Gymisgarða. Þar váru hundar ólmir ok bundnir fyrir skíðgarðs hliði, þess er um sal Gerðar var. Hann reið at þar, er féhirðir sat á haugi, og kvaddi hann:

Freyr spake: 4
"How shall I tell thee, thou hero young,
Of all my grief so great?
Though every day the elfbeam dawns,
It lights my longing never."

Skirnir spake: 5
"Thy longings, methinks, are not so large
That thou mayst not tell them to me;
Since in days of yore we were young together,
We two might each other trust."

Freyr spake: 6
"From Gymir's house I beheld go forth
A maiden dear to me;
Her arms glittered, and from their gleam
Shone all the sea and sky."

"To me more dear than in days of old 7
Was ever maiden to man;
But no one of gods or elves will grant
That we both together should be."

Skirnir spake: 8
"Then give me the horse that goes through the dark
And magic flickering flames;
And the sword as well that fights of itself
Against the giants grim."

Freyr spake: 9
"The horse will I give thee that goes through the dark
And magic flickering flames,
And the sword as well that will fight of itself
If a worthy hero wields it."

Skirnir spake to the horse: 10
"Dark is it without, and I deem it time
To fare through the wild fells,
To fare through the giants' fastness;
We shall both come back, or us both together
The terrible giant will take."

Skirnir rode into Jotunheim to Gymir's house. There were fierce dogs bound before the gate of the fence which was around Gerth's hall. He rode to where a herdsman sat on a hill, and said:

"Segðu þat, hirðir,   er þú á haugi sitr   11
ok varðar alla vega:
Hvé ek at andspilli   komumk ins unga mans
fyr greyjum Gymis?"

Hirðir kvað: 12
"Hvárt ertu feigr,   eða ertu framgenginn?
[...]
Andspillis vanr   þú skalt æ vera
góðrar meyjar Gymis."

Skírnir kvað: 13
"Kostir ro betri   heldr en at klökkva sé,
hveim er fúss er fara;
einu dægri   mér var aldr of skapaðr
of allt líf of lagit."

Gerðr kvað: 14
"Hvat er þat hlym hlymja,   er ek heyri nú til
ossum rönnum í?
Jörð bifask,   en allir fyrir
skjalfa garðar Gymis."

Ambátt kvað: 15
"Maðr er hér úti,   stiginn af mars baki,
jó lætr til jarðar taka."
[...]

Gerðr kvað: 16
"Inn bið þú hann ganga   í okkarn sal
ok drekka inn mæra mjöð;
þó ek hitt óumk,   at hér úti sé
minn bróðurbani.

Hvat er þat alfa   né ása sona   17
né víssa vana?
Hví þú einn of komt   eikinn fúr yfir
ór salkynni at séa?"

Skírnir kvað: 18
"Emk-at ek alfa   né ása sona
né víssa vana;
þó ek einn of komk   eikinn fúr yfir
yðor salkynni at séa."

"Tell me, herdsman, sitting on the hill, 11
And watching all the ways,
How may I win a word with the maid
Past the hounds of Gymir here?"

The herdsman spake: 12
"Art thou doomed to die or already dead,
Thou horseman that ridest hither?
Barred from speech shalt thou ever be
With Gymir's daughter good."

Skirnir spake: 13
"Boldness is better than plaints can be
For him whose feet must fare;
To a destined day has mine age been doomed,
And my life's span thereto laid."

Gerth spake: 14
"What noise is that which now so loud
I hear within our house?
The ground shakes, and the home of Gymir
Around me trembles too."

The Serving-Maid spake: 15
"One stands without who has leapt from his steed,
And lets his horse loose to graze;"
[...]
[...]

Gerth spake: 16
"Bid the man come in, and drink good mead
Here within our hall;
Though this I fear, that there without
My brother's slayer stands."

"Art thou of the elves or the offspring of gods, 17
Or of the wise Wanes?
How camst thou alone through the leaping flame
Thus to behold our home?"

Skirnir spake: 18
"I am not of the elves, nor the offspring of gods,
Nor of the wise Wanes;
Though I came alone through the leaping flame
Thus to behold thy home."

"Epli ellifu   hér hef ek algullin,   19
þau mun ek þér, Gerðr, gefa,
frið at kaupa,   at þú þér Frey kveðir
óleiðastan lifa."

Gerðr kvað: 20
"Epli ellifu   ek þigg aldregi
at mannskis munum,   né vit Freyr,
meðan okkart fjör lifir,
byggjum bæði saman."

Skírnir kvað: 21
"Baug ek þér þá gef,   þann er brenndr var
með ungum Óðins syni;
átta eru jafnhöfðir,   er af drjúpa
ina níundu hverja nótt."

Gerðr kvað: 22
"Baug ek þikk-a-k,   þótt brenndr séi
með ungum Óðins syni;
er-a mér gulls vant   í görðum Gymis,
at deila fé föður."

Skírnir kvað: 23
"Sér þú þenna mæki, mær,   mjóvan, málfáan,
er ek hef í hendi hér?
Höfuð höggva   ek mun þér hálsi af,
nema þú mér sætt segir."

Gerðr kvað: 24
"Ánauð þola   ek vil aldregi
at mannskis munum;
þó ek hins get,   ef it Gymir finnizk,
vígs ótrauðir,   at ykkr vega tíði."

Skírnir kvað: 25
"Sér þú þenna mæki, mær,   mjóvan, málfáan,
er ek hef í hendi hér?
Fyr þessum eggjum   hnígr sá inn aldni jötunn,
verðr þinn feigr faðir.

Tamsvendi ek þik drep,   en ek þik temja mun,   26
mær, at mínum munum;
þar skaltu ganga,   er þik gumna synir
síðan æva séi.

"Eleven apples, all of gold,   19
Here will I give thee, Gerth,
To buy thy troth that Freyr shall be
Deemed to be dearest to you."

Gerth spake: 20
"I will not take at any man's wish
These eleven apples ever;
Nor shall Freyr and I one dwelling find
So long as we two live."

Skirnir spake: 21
"Then do I bring thee the ring that was burned
Of old with Odin's son;
From it do eight of like weight fall
On every ninth night."

Gerth spake: 22
"The ring I wish not, though burned it was
Of old with Odin's son;
In Gymir's home is no lack of gold
In the wealth my father wields."

Skirnir spake: 23
"Seest thou, maiden, this keen, bright sword
That I hold here in my hand?
Thy head from thy neck shall I straightway hew,
If thou wilt not do my will."

Gerth spake: 24
"For no man's sake will I ever suffer
To be thus moved by might;
But gladly, methinks, will Gymir seek
To fight if he finds thee here."

Skirnir spake: 25
"Seest thou, maiden, this keen, bright sword
That I hold here in my hand?
Before its blade the old giant bends—
Thy father is doomed to die."

"I strike thee, maid, with my magic staff,   26
To tame thee to work my will;
There shalt thou go where never again
The sons of men shall see thee."

Ara þúfu   á skaltu ár sitja 27
horfa heimi ór,   snugga heljar til;
matr né þér meir leiðr   en manna hveim
innfráni ormr með firum.

At undrsjónum þú verðir, 28
er þú út kemr;
á þik Hrímnir hari,   á þik hotvetna stari;
víðkunnari þú verðir   en vörðr með goðum,
gapi þú grindum frá.

Tópi ok ópi,   tjösull ok óþoli, 29
vaxi þér tár með trega;
sezk þú niðr,   en ek mun segja þér
sváran súsbreka   ok tvennan trega:

Tramar gneypa   þik skulu gerstan dag 30
jötna görðum í;
til hrímþursa hallar   þú skalt hverjan dag
kranga kostalaus,   kranga kostavön;
grát at gamni   skaltu í gögn hafa
ok leiða með tárum trega.

Með þursi þríhöfðuðum   þú skalt æ nara, 31
eða verlaus vera;
þitt geð grípi,   þik morn morni;
ver þú sem þistill,   sá er var þrunginn
í önn ofanverða.

Til holts ek gekk   ok til hrás viðar, 32
gambantein at geta,   gambantein ek gat.

Reiðr er þér Óðinn,   reiðr er þér Ásabragr, 33
þik skal Freyr fíask,   in firinilla mær,
en þú fengit hefr   gambanreiði goða.

Heyri jötnar,   heyri hrímþursar, 34
synir Suttungs,   sjalfir ásliðar,
hvé ek fyrbýð,   hvé ek fyrirbanna
manna glaum mani,   manna nyt mani.

"On the eagle's hill shalt thou ever sit,   27
And gaze on the gates of Hel;
More loathsome to thee than the light-hued snake
To men, shall thy meat become."

"Fearful to see, if thou comest forth,   28
Hrimnir will stand and stare,
Men will marvel at thee;
More famed shalt thou grow than the watchman of the
    gods!
Peer forth, then, from thy prison."

"Rage and longing, fetters and wrath,   29
Tears and torment are thine;
Where thou sittest down my doom is on thee
Of heavy heart
And double dole."

"In the giants' home shall vile things harm thee   30
Each day with evil deeds;
Grief shalt thou get instead of gladness,
And sorrow to suffer with tears."

"With three-headed giants thou shalt dwell ever,   31
Or never know a husband;
Let longing grip thee, let wasting waste thee—
Be like to the thistle that in the loft
Was cast and there was crushed."

"I go to the wood, and to the wet forest,   32
To win a magic wand;
[...]
I won a magic wand."

"Odin grows angry, angered is the best of the gods,   33
Freyr shall be thy foe,
Most evil maid, who the magic wrath
Of gods hast got for thyself."

"Give heed, frost-rulers, hear it, giants.   34
Sons of Suttung,
And gods, ye too,
How I forbid and how I ban
The meeting of men with the maid,
The joy of men with the maid."

Hrímgrímnir heitir þurs,   er þik hafa skal   35
fyr nágrindr neðan;
þar þér vílmegir   á viðarrótum
geitahland gefi;
æðri drykkju   fá þú aldregi,
mær, af þínum munum,
mær, at mínum munum.

Þurs ríst ek þér   ok þría stafi,   36
ergi ok æði ok óþola;
svá ek þat af ríst,   sem ek þat á reist,
ef gerask þarfar þess."

Gerðr kvað: 37
"Heill ver þú nú heldr, sveinn,
ok tak við hrímkálki
fullum forns mjaðar;
þó hafðak ek þat ætlat,
at myndak aldregi
unna vaningja vel."

Skírnir kvað: 38
"Öendi mín   vil ek öll vita,
áðr ek ríða heim heðan,
nær þú á þingi   munt inum þroska
nenna Njarðar syni."

Gerðr kvað: 39
"Barri heitir,   er vit bæði vitum,
lundr lognfara;
en eft nætr níu   þar mun Njarðar syni
Gerðr unna gamans."

Þá reið Skírnir heim. Freyr stóð úti ok kvaddi hann ok spurði tíðenda:

"Segðu mér þat, Skírnir,   áðr þú verpir söðli af mar   40
ok þú stígir feti framar:
Hvat þú árnaðir   í Jötunheima
þíns eða míns munar?"

"Hrimgrimnir is he, the giant who shall have thee | 35
In the depth by the doors of Hel;
To the frost-giants' halls each day shalt thou fare,
Crawling and craving in vain,
Crawling and having no hope."

"Base wretches there by the root of the tree | 36
Will hold for thee horns of filth;
A fairer drink shalt thou never find,
Maid, to meet thy wish,
Maid, to meet my wish."

"I write thee a charm and three runes therewith, | 37
Longing and madness and lust;
But what I have writ I may yet unwrite
If I find a need therefor."

Gerth spake: | 38
"Find welcome rather, and with it take
The frost-cup filled with mead;
Though I did not believe that I should so love
Ever one of the Wanes."

Skirnir spake: | 39
"My tidings all must I truly learn
Ere homeward hence I ride:
How soon thou wilt with the mighty son
Of Njorth a meeting make."

Gerth spake: | 40
"Barri there is, which we both know well,
A forest fair and still;
And nine nights hence to the son of Njorth
Will Gerth there grant delight."

Then Skirnir rode home. Freyr stood without, and spoke to him, and asked for tidings:

"Tell me, Skimir, ere thou take off the saddle, | 41
Or farest forward a step:
What hast thou done in the giants' dwelling
To make glad thee or me?"

Skírnir kvað: 41
"Barri heitir,   er vit báðir vitum,
lundr lognfara;
en eft nætr níu   þar mun Njarðar syni
Gerðr unna gamans."

Freyr kvað: 42
"Löng er nótt,   langar ro tvær,
hvé of þreyjak þrjár?
Oft mér mánaðr   minni þótti
en sjá half hýnótt."

Skirnir spoke: 42
"Barri there is, which we both know well,
A forest fair and still;
And nine nights hence to the son of Njorth
Will Gerth there grant delight."

Freyr spake: 43
"Long is one night, longer are two;
How then shall I bear three?
Often to me has a month seemed less
Than now half a night of desire."

ENDNOTES

Prose. Freyr: concerning his father, Njorth, and the race of the Wanes in general, cf. *Voluspo*, 21 and note. Snorri thus describes Njorth's family: "Njorth begat two children in Noatun; the son was named Freyr, and the daughter Freyja; they were fair of aspect and mighty. Freyr is the noblest of the gods; he rules over rain and sunshine, and therewith the fruitfulness of the earth; it is well to call upon him for plenty and welfare, for he rules over wealth for mankind. Freyja is the noblest of the goddesses. When she rides to the fight, she has one-half of the slain, and Odin has half. When she goes on a journey, she drives her two cats, and sits in a cart. Love-songs please her well, and it is good to call on her in love-matters." *Hlithskjolf*: Odin's [throne]; cf. *Grimnismol*, introductory prose. *He said*: both manuscripts have "Then Skathi said:" (Skathi was Njorth's wife), but Bugge's emendation, based on Snorri's version, is [possibly] correct.

1. *My son*: both manuscripts, and many editors, have "our son," which, of course, goes with the introduction of Skathi in the prose. As the stanza is clearly addressed to Skirnir, the change of pronouns seems justified. The same confusion occurs in stanza 2, where Skirnir in the manuscripts is made to speak of Freyr as "your son" (plural). The plural pronoun in the original involves a metrical error, which is corrected by the emendation.

4. *Elfbeam*: the sun, so called because its rays were fatal to elves and dwarfs; cf. *Alvissmol*, 35.

6. *Gymir*: a mountain-giant, husband of Aurbotha, and father of Gerth, fairest among women. This is all Snorri tells of him in his paraphrase of the story.

7. Snorri's paraphrase of the poem is sufficiently close so that his addition

of another sentence to Freyr's speech makes it probable that a stanza has dropped out between 7 and 8. This has been tentatively reconstructed, thus: "Hither to me shalt thou bring the maid, / And home shalt thou lead her here, / If her father wills it or wills it not, / And good reward shalt thou get." Finn Magnusen detected the probable omission of a stanza here as early as 1821.

8. *The sword*: Freyr's gift of his sword to Skirnir eventually proves fatal, for at the last battle, when Freyr is attacked by Beli, whom he kills bare-handed, and later when the fire-demon, Surt, slays him in turn, he is weaponless; cf. *Voluspo*, 53 and note. *Against the giants grim*: the condition of this line makes it seem like an error in copying, and it is possible that it should be identical with the fourth line of the next stanza.

10. Some editors reject line 3 as spurious.

12. Line 2 is in neither manuscript, and no gap is indicated. I have followed Grundtvig's conjectural emendation.

13. This stanza is almost exactly like many in the first part of the *Hovamol*, and may well have been a separate proverb. After this stanza the scene shifts to the interior of the house.

15. No gap indicated in either manuscript. Bugge and Niedner have attempted emendations, while Hildebrand suggests that the last two lines of stanza 14 are spurious, 14, 1–2, and 15 thus forming a single stanza, which seems doubtful.

16. *Brother's slayer*: perhaps the brother is Beli, slain by Freyr; the only other references are in *Voluspo*, 53, and in Snorri's paraphrase of the *Skirnismol*, which merely says that Freyr's gift of his sword to Skirnir "was the reason why he was weaponless when he met Beli, and he killed him bare-handed." Skirnir himself seems never to have killed anybody.

17. *Wise Wanes*: Cf. *Voluspo*, 21 and note.

18. The *Arnamagnæan Codex* omits this stanza.

19. *Apples*: the apple was the symbol of fruitfulness, and also of eternal youth. According to Snorri, the goddess Ithun had charge of the apples which the gods ate whenever they felt themselves growing old.

21. *Ring*: the ring Draupnir ("Dropper") was made by the dwarfs for Odin, who laid it on Baldr's pyre when the latter's corpse was burned (Cf. *Voluspo*, 32 and note, and *Baldrs Draumar*). Baldr, however, sent the ring back to Odin from hell. How Freyr obtained it is nowhere stated. And-

vari's ring (Andvaranaut) had a similar power of creating gold; cf. *Reginsmol*, prose after stanza 4 and note. Lines 3 and 4 of this stanza, and the first two of stanza 22, are missing in the *Arnamagnæan Codex*.

25. The first two lines are abbreviated in both manuscripts.

26. With this stanza, bribes and threats having failed, Skirnir begins a curse which, by the power of his magic staff, is to fall on Gerth if she refuses Freyr.

27. *Eagle's hill*: the hill at the end of heaven, and consequently overlooking hell, where the giant Hræsvelg sits "in an eagle's guise," and makes the winds with his wings; cf. *Vafthruthnismol*, 37, also *Voluspo*, 50. The second line is faulty in both manuscripts; Hildebrand's emendation corrects the error, but omits an effective touch; the manuscript line may be rendered "And look and hanker for hell." The *Arnamagnæan Codex* breaks off with the fourth line of this stanza.

28. *Hrimnir*: a frost-giant, mentioned elsewhere only in *Hyndluljoth*, 33. Line 3 is probably spurious. *Watchman of the gods*: Heimdall; cf. *Voluspo*, 46.

29. Three nouns of doubtful meaning, which I have rendered *rage*, *longing*, and *heart* respectively, make the precise force of this stanza obscure. Niedner and Sijmons mark the entire stanza as interpolated, and Jonsson rejects line 5.

30. In *Regius* and in nearly all the editions the first two lines of this stanza are followed by lines 3–5 of stanza 35. I have followed Niedner, Sijmons, and Gering. The two words here translated *vile things* are obscure; Gering renders the phrase simply "Kobolde."

31. The confusion noted as to the preceding stanza, and a metrical error in the third line, have led to various rearrangements and emendations; line 3 certainly looks like an interpolation. *Three-headed giants*: concerning giants with numerous heads, cf. *Vafthruthnismol*, 33, and *Hymiskvitha*, 8.

32. No gap indicated in the manuscript; Niedner makes the line here given as 4 the first half of line 3, and fills out the stanza thus: "with which I will tame you, / Maid, to work my will." The whole stanza seems to be either interpolated or out of place; it would fit better after stanza 25.

33. Jonsson marks this stanza as interpolated. The word translated *most evil* is another case of guesswork.

34. Most editors reject line 3 as spurious, and some also reject line 6.

Lines 2 and 3 may have been expanded out of a single line running approximately "Ye gods and Suttung's sons." *Suttung*: concerning this giant cf. *Hovamol*, 104 and note.

35. Most editors combine lines 1–2 with stanza 36 (either with the first two lines thereof or the whole stanza), as lines 3–5 stand in the manuscript after line 2 of stanza 30. *Hrimgrimnir* ("The Frost-Shrouded"): a giant not elsewhere mentioned. Line 5, as a repetition of line 4, is probably a later addition.

36. For the combination of this stanza with the preceding one, cf. note on stanza 35. The scribe clearly did not consider that the stanza began with line 1, as the first word thereof in the manuscript does not begin with a capital letter and has no period before it. The first word of line 3, however, is so marked. Line 5 may well be spurious.

37. Again the scribe seems to have been uncertain as to the stanza divisions. This time the first line is preceded by a period, but begins with a small letter. Many editors have made line 2 into two half-lines. *A charm*: literally, the rune Thurs (Þ); the runic letters all had magic attributes; cf. *Sigrdrifumol*, 6–7 and notes.

40. *Barri*: "The Leafy."

42. Abbreviated to initial letters in the manuscript.

43. The superscription is lacking in *Regius*. Snorri quotes this one stanza in his prose paraphrase, *Gylfaginning*, chapter 37. The two versions are substantially the same, except that Snorri makes the first line read, "Long is one night, long is the second."

HARBARTHSLJOTH
THE POEM OF HARBARTH

INTRODUCTION

The *Harbarthsljoth* is notable for two particular qualities. The first is the chaotic state of its transcription which switches between the *Malahattr* meter and one that matches no known Norse metrical meter whatsoever. Many have sought to explain or rewrite the poem to fix this problem to varying and largely unaccepted degrees of success, whereas others assume the poem's author was simply incompetent and unskilled, or that the poem might feature large amounts of rewritten material from a later date and thus serve questionably as an authentic piece of pre-Christian lore. One should be cautioned against the latter conclusion given the poems overwhelming cavalcade of information displaying a varied and indepth knowledge of Germanic lore and the histories and struggles of the characters involved, which would be incommensurate with a later Christian revision.

More recent scholars such as Carol Clover identify the poem as belonging to the genre of "Senna" or a flyting poem similar in respects to the *Mannjafnaðr*, but arranged in such a way as to represent a deliberate parody of the traditional structure on the part of Harbarth and the confusion and outrage of a noncomprehending Thor, which can account for the perceived flaws in the metrical scheme by way of deliberate comedy to a Norse listener. Other scholars such as Bax and Padmos challenge this interpretation and maintain that the contest is highly structured and organized, with the majority of the poem organized as a *Mannjafnaðr* interspersed with two Sennur, and that both participants readily understand the rules and structure of the format.

The second feature for which the poem is known is the scholarly dispute about the person of Harbarth himself, whose name means "Grey Beard". Early scholars such as F. W. Bergmann and Viktor Rydberg argue that Harbarth is none other than Loki in disguise, which accounts for Thor addressing him as you would a youth, his hostility and vindictiveness towards Thor, his general demeanor matching the character we see in the *Lokasenna*, and the supposition that many of his deeds alluded to bear more resemblance with Loki than they do Odin. More recent scholars such as Finnur Jónsson, Carol Clover, and Felix Niedner argue for the position of Harbarth as representing a disguised Odin for, among other things, his references to varied dalliances with giant women, knowledge gained from the dead, leading of warhosts and the unequal treatments delivered unto mortals therein, and rather convincingly, the fact that Odin records the name Harbarth as one of his own in the *Grimnismol* itself.

Þórr fór ór Austrvegi ok kom at sundi einu. Öðrum megin sundsins var ferjukarlinn með skipit. Þórr kallaði:

"Hverr er sá sveinn sveina,   er stendr fyr sundit handan?"   1

Ferjukarlinn kvað: 2
"Hverr er sá karl karla,   er kallar of váginn?"

Þórr kvað: 3
"Fer þú mik um sundit,   fæði ek þik á morgun;
meis hef ek á baki,   verðr-a matr in betri;
át ek í hvíld,   áðr ek heiman fór,
síldr ok hafra;
saðr em ek enn þess."

Ferjukarlinn kvað: 4
"Árligum verkum   hrósar þú, verðinum;
veizt-at-tu fyrir görla,   döpr eru þín heimkynni,
dauð, hygg ek, at þín móðir sé."

HARBARTHSLJOTH

Thor was on his way back from a journey in the East, and came to a sound; on the other side of the sound was a ferryman with a boat. Thor called out:

"Who is the fellow yonder, on the farther shore of the sound?" 1

The ferryman spake: 2
"What kind of a peasant is yon, that calls o'er the bay?"

Thor spake: 3
"Ferry me over the sound; I will feed thee therefor in the morning;
A basket I have on my back, and food therein, none better;
At leisure I ate, ere the house I left,
Of herrings and porridge, so plenty I had."

The ferryman spake: 4
"Of thy morning feats art thou proud, but the future thou knowest not wholly;
Doleful thine home-coming is: thy mother, me thinks, is dead."

Þórr kvað: 5
"Þat segir þú nú,   er hverjum þykkir
mest at vita,   at mín móðir dauð sé."

Ferjukarlinn kvað: 6
"Þeygi er sem þú   þrjú bú góð eigir;
berbeinn þú stendr   ok hefr brautinga gervi,
þatki, at þú hafir brækr þínar."

Þórr kvað: 7
"Stýrðu hingat eikjunni,   ek mun þér stöðna kenna,
eða hverr á skipit,   er þú heldr við landit?"

Ferjukarlinn kvað: 8
"Hildolfr sá heitir,   er mik halda bað,
rekkr inn ráðsvinni,   er býr í Ráðseyjarsundi;
bað-at hann hlennimenn flytja   eða hrossaþjófa,
góða eina   ok þá, er ek görva kunna;
segðu til nafns þíns,   ef þú vill um sundit fara!"

Þórr kvað: 9
"Segja mun ek til nafns míns,
þótt ek sekr séak,   ok til alls eðlis:
Ek em Óðins sonr,   Meila bróðir,
en Magna faðir,   þrúðvaldr goða,
við Þór knáttu hér dæma!
Hins vil ek nú spyrja,   hvat þú heitir."

Ferjukarlinn kvað: 10
"Hárbarðr ek heiti,   hylk um nafn sjaldan."

Þórr kvað: 11
"Hvat skaltu of nafn hylja,   nema þú sakar eigir?"

Hárbarðr kvað: 12
"En þótt ek sakar eiga,   þá mun ek forða fjörvi mínu
fyr slíkum sem þú ert,   nema ek feigr sé."

Þórr kvað: 13
"Harm ljótan   mér þykkir í því
at vaða um váginn til þín   ok væta ögur minn;
skylda ek launa   kögursveini þínum
kanginyrði,   ef ek kæmumk yfir sundit."

Thor spake: 5
"Now hast thou said what to each must seem
The mightiest grief, that my mother is dead."

The ferryman spake: 6
"Three good dwellings, methinks, thou hast not;
Barefoot thou standest, and wearest a beggar's dress;
Not even hose dost thou have."

Thor spake: 7
"Steer thou hither the boat; the landing here shall I show thee;
But whose the craft that thou keepest on the shore?"

The ferryman spake: 8
"Hildolf is he who bade me have it,
A hero wise; his home is at Rathsey's sound.
He bade me no robbers to steer, nor stealers of steeds,
But worthy men, and those whom well do I know.
Say now thy name, if over the sound thou wilt fare."

Thor spake: 9
"My name indeed shall I tell, though in danger I am,
And all my race; I am Odin's son,
Meili's brother, and Magni's father,
The strong one of the gods; with Thor now speech canst thou get.
And now would I know what name thou hast."

The ferryman spake: 10
"Harbarth am I, and seldom I hide my name."

Thor spake: 11
"Why shouldst thou hide thy name, if quarrel thou hast not?"

Harbarth spake: 12
"And though I had a quarrel, from such as thou art
Yet none the less my life would I guard,
Unless I be doomed to die."

Thor spake: 13
"Great trouble, methinks, would it be to come to thee,
To wade the waters across, and wet my middle;
Weakling, well shall I pay thy mocking words,
if across the sound I come."

Hárbarðr kvað: 14
"Hér mun ek standa   ok þín heðan bíða;
fannt-a þú mann in harðara   at Hrungni dauðan."

Þórr kvað: 15
"Hins viltu nú geta,   er vit Hrungnir deildum,
sá inn stórúðgi jötunn,   er ór steini var höfuðit á;
þó lét ek hann falla   ok fyrir hníga.
Hvat vanntu þá meðan, Hárbarðr?"

Hárbarðr kvað: 16
"Var ek með Fjölvari   fimm vetr alla
í ey þeiri,   er Algræn heitir;
vega vér þar knáttum   ok val fella,
margs at freista,   mans at kosta."

Þórr kvað: 17
"Hversu snúnuðu yðr konur yðrar?"

Hárbarðr kvað: 18
"Sparkar áttu vér konur,   ef oss at spökum yrði;
horskar áttu vér konur,   ef oss hollar væri;
þær ór sandi   síma undu,
ok ór dali djúpum
grund of grófu;
varð ek þeim einn öllum   efri at ráðum;
hvílda ek hjá þeim systrum sjau,
ok hafða ek geð þeira allt ok gaman.
Hvat vanntu þá meðan, Þórr?"

Þórr kvað: 19
"Ek drap Þjaza,   inn þrúðmóðga jötun,
upp ek varp augum   Alvalda sonar
á þann inn heiða himin;
þau eru merki mest   minna verka,
þau er allir menn síðan of séa.
Hvat vanntu þá meðan, Hárbarðr?"

Hárbarðr kvað: 20
"Miklar manvélar   ek hafða við myrkriður,
þá er ek vélta þær frá verum;
harðan jötun   ek hugða Hlébarð vera,
gaf hann mér gambantein,   en ek vélta hann ór viti."

Þórr kvað: 21
"Illum huga   launaðir þú þá góðar gjafar."

Harbarth spake: 14
"Here shall I stand and await thee here;
Thou hast found since Hrungnir died no fiercer man."

Thor spake: 15
"Fain art thou to tell how with Hrungnir I fought,
The haughty giant, whose head of stone was made;
And yet I felled him, and stretched him before me.
What, Harbarth, didst thou the while?"

Harbarth spake: 16
"Five full winters with Fjolvar was I,
And dwelt in the isle that is Algrön called;
There could we fight, and fell the slain,
Much could we seek, and maids could master."

Thor spake: 17
"How won ye success with your women?"

Harbarth spake: 18
"Lively women we had, if they wise for us were;
Wise were the women we had, if they kind for us were;
For ropes of sand they would seek to wind,
And the bottom to dig from the deepest dale.
Wiser than all in counsel I was,
And there I slept by the sisters seven,
And joy full great did I get from each.
What, Thor, didst thou the while?"

Thor spake: 19
"Thjazi I felled, the giant fierce,
And I hurled the eyes of Alvaldi's son
To the heavens hot above;
Of my deeds the mightiest marks are these,
That all men since can see.
What, Harbarth, didst thou the while?"

Harbarth spoke: 20
"Much love-craft I wrought with them who ride by night,
When I stole them by stealth from their husbands;
A giant hard was Hlebarth, methinks:
His wand he gave me as gift,
And I stole his wits away."

Thor spake: 21
"Thou didst repay good gifts with evil mind."

Hárbarðr kvað: 22
"Þat hefr eik, er af annarri skefr,
of sik er hverr í slíku.
Hvat vanntu þá meðan Þórr?"

Þórr kvað: 23
"Ek var austr ok jötna barðak
brúðir bölvísar, er til bjargs gengu;
mikil myndi ætt jötna, ef allir lifði
vætr myndi manna undir Miðgarði.
Hvat vanntu þá meðan, Hárbarðr?"

Hárbarðr kvað: 24
"Var ek á Vallandi ok vígum fylgdak,
atta ek jöfrum, en aldri sættak;
Óðinn á jarla, þá er í val falla,
en Þórr á þrælakyn."

Þórr kvað: 25
"Ójafnt skipta er þú myndir með ásum liði,
ef þú ættir vilgi mikils vald."

Hárbarðr kvað: 26
"Þórr á afl ærit, en ekki hjarta;
af hræðslu ok hugbleyði þér var í hanzka troðit,
ok þóttisk-a þú þá Þórr vera;
hvárki þú þá þorðir fyr hræðslu þinni
hnjósa né físa, svá at Fjalarr heyrði."

Þórr kvað: 27
"Hárbarðr inn ragi, ek mynda þik í hel drepa,
ef ek mætta seilask um sund."

Hárbarðr kvað: 28
"Hvat skyldir um sund seilask, er sakir ro alls engar?
Hvat vanntu þá, Þórr?"

Þórr kvað: 29
"Ek var austr ok ána varðak,
þá er mik sóttu þeir Svárangs synir;
grjóti þeir mik börðu, gagni urðu þeir þó lítt fegnir,
þó urðu þeir mik fyrri friðar at biðja.
Hvat vanntu þá meðan, Hárbarðr?"

Harbarth spake: 22
"The oak must have what it shaves from another;
In such things each for himself.
What, Thor, didst thou the while?"

Thor spake: 23
"Eastward I fared, of the giants I felled
Their ill-working women who went to the mountain;
And large were the giants' throng if all were alive;
No men would there be in Mithgarth more.
What, Harbarth, didst thou the while?"

Harbarth spake: 24
"In Valland I was, and wars I raised,
Princes I angered, and peace brought never;
The noble who fall in the fight hath Odin,
And Thor hath the race of the thralls."

Thor spake: 25
"Unequal gifts of men wouldst thou give to the gods,
If might too much thou shouldst have."

Harbarth spake: 26
"Thor has might enough, but never a heart;
For cowardly fear in a glove wast thou fain to crawl,
And there forgot thou wast Thor;
Afraid there thou wast, thy fear was such,
To fart or sneeze lest Fjalar should hear."

Thor spake: 27
"Thou womanish Harbarth, to hell would I smite thee straight,
Could mine arm reach over the sound."

Harbarth spake: 28
"Wherefore reach over the sound, since strife we have none?
What, Thor, didst thou do then?"

Thor spake: 29
"Eastward I was, and the river I guarded well,
Where the sons of Svarang sought me there;
Stones did they hurl; small joy did they have of winning;
Before me there to ask for peace did they fare.
What, Harbarth, didst thou the while?"

Hárbarðr kvað: 30
"Ek var austr   ok við einhverja dæmðak,
lék ek við ina línhvítu   ok launþing háðak;
gladdak ina gullbjörtu,   gamni mær unði."

Þórr kvað: 31
"Góð átt þú þér mankynni þar þá."

Hárbarðr kvað: 32
"Liðs þíns   væra ek þá þurfi, Þórr,
at ek helda þeiri inni línhvítu mey."

Þórr kvað: 33
"Ek munda þér þá þat veita,   ef ek viðr of kæmumk."

Hárbarðr kvað: 34
"Ek mynda þér þá trúa,   nema þú mik í tryggð véltir."

Þórr kvað: 35
"Emk-at ek sá hælbítr   sem húðskór forn á vár."

Hárbarðr kvað: 36
"Hvat vanntu þá meðan, Þórr?"

Þórr kvað: 37
"Brúðir berserkja   barðak í Hléseyju;
þær höfðu verst unnit,   vélta þjóð alla."

Hárbarðr kvað: 38
"Klæki vanntu þá, Þórr,   er þú á konum barðir."

Þórr kvað: 39
"Vargynjur þat váru,   en varla konur, skelldu skip mitt,
er ek skorðat hafðak,   ægðu mér járnlurki
en eltu Þjalfa.
Hvat vanntu meðan, Hárbarðr?"

Hárbarðr kvað: 40
"Ek vark í hernum,   er hingat gerðisk
gnæfa gunnfana,   geir at rjóða."

Þórr kvað: 41
"Þess viltu nú geta,   er þú fórt oss óljúfan at bjóða."

Harbarth spake: 30
"Eastward I was, and spake with a certain one,
I played with the linen-white maid, and met her by stealth;
I gladdened the gold-decked one, and she granted me joy."

Thor spake: 31
"Full fair was thy woman-finding."

Harbarth spake: 32
"Thy help did I need then, Thor, to hold the white maid fast."

Thor spake: 33
"Gladly, had I been there, my help to thee had been given."

Harbarth spake: 34
"I might have trusted thee then, didst thou not betray thy troth."

Thor spake: 35
"No heel-biter am I, in truth, like an old leather shoe in spring."

Harbarth spoke: 36
"What, Thor, didst thou the while?"

Thor spake: 37
"In Hlesey the brides of the Berserkers slew I;
Most evil they were, and all they betrayed."

Harbarth spake: 38
"Shame didst thou win, that women thou slewest, Thor."

Thor spake: 39
"She-wolves they were like, and women but little;
My ship, which well I had trimmed, did they shake;
With clubs of iron they threatened, and Thjalfi they drove off.
What, Harbarth, didst thou the while?"

Harbarth spake: 40
"In the host I was that hither fared,
The banners to raise, and the spear to redden."

Thor spake: 41
"Wilt thou now say that hatred thou soughtest to bring us?"

Hárbarðr kvað: 42
"Bæta skal þér þat þá   munda baugi,
sem jafnendr unnu,   þeir er okkr vilja sætta."

Þórr kvað: 43
"Hvar namtu þessi   in hnæfiligu orð,
er ek heyrða aldregi   in hnæfiligri?"

Hárbarðr kvað: 44
"Nam ek at mönnum   þeim inum aldrænum,
er búa í heimis skógum."

Þórr kvað: 45
"Þó gefr þú gott nafn dysjum,   er þú kallar þær heimis
   skóga."

Hárbarðr kvað: 46
"Svá dæmi ek of slíkt far."

Þórr kvað: 47
"Orðkringi þín   mun þér illa koma,
ef ek ræð á vág at vaða;
ulfi hæra   hygg ek þik æpa munu,
ef þú hlýtr af hamri högg."

Hárbarðr kvað: 48
"Sif á hó heima,   hans muntu fund vilja,
þann muntu þrek drýgja,   þat er þér skyldara."

Þórr kvað: 49
"Mælir þú at munns ráði,   svá at mér skyldi verst þykkja,
halr inn hugblauði,   hygg ek, at þú ljúgir."

Hárbarðr kvað: 50
"Satt hygg ek mik segja;
seinn ertu at för þinni,   langt myndir þú nú kominn, Þórr,
ef þú litum færir."

Þórr kvað: 51
"Hárbarðr inn ragi,   heldr hefr þú nú mik dvalðan."

Hárbarðr kvað: 52
"Ása-Þórs hugða ek   aldregi mundu
glepja féhirði farar."

Harbarth spake: 42
"A ring for thy hand shall make all right for thee,
As the judge decides who sets us two at peace."

Thor spake: 43
"Where foundest thou so foul and scornful a speech?
More foul a speech I never before have heard."

Harbarth spake: 44
"I learned it from men, the men so old,
Who dwell in the hills of home."

Thor spake: 45
"A name full good to heaps of stones thou givest
When thou callest them hills of home."

Harbarth spake: 46
"Of such things speak I so.

Thor spake: 47
"Ill for thee comes thy keenness of tongue,
If the water I choose to wade;
Louder, I ween, than a wolf thou cryest,
If a blow of my hammer thou hast.

Harbarth spake: 48
"Sif has a lover at home, and him shouldst thou meet;
More fitting it were on him to put forth thy strength."

Thor spake: 49
"Thy tongue still makes thee say what seems most ill to me,
Thou witless man! Thou liest, I ween."

Harbarth spake: 50
"Truth do I speak, but slow on thy way thou art;
Far hadst thou gone if now in the boat thou hadst fared."

Thor spake: 51
"Thou womanish Harbarth! here hast thou held me too
  long."

Harbarth spake: 52
"I thought not ever that Asathor would be hindered
By a ferryman thus from faring."

Þórr kvað: 53
"Ráð mun ek þér nú ráða;
ró þú hingat bátinum,   hættum hætingi,
hittu föður Magna."

Hárbarðr kvað: 54
"Farðu firr sundi,   þér skal fars synja."

Þórr kvað: 55
"Vísa þú mér nú leiðina,   alls þú vill mik eigi um váginn ferja."

Hárbarðr kvað: 56
"Lítit er at synja,   langt er at fara;
stund er til stokksins,   önnur til steinsins,
haltu svá til vinstra vegsins,   unz þú hittir Verland;
þar mun Fjörgyn   hitta Þór, son sinn,
ok mun hon kenna hánum áttunga brautir   til Óðins landa."

Þórr kvað: 57
"Mun ek taka þangat í dag?"

Hárbarðr kvað: 58
"Taka við víl ok erfiði,   at upprennandi sólu,
er ek get þána."

Þórr kvað: 59
"Skammt mun nú mál okkat,   alls þú mér skætingu einni svarar;
launa mun ek þér farsynjun,   ef vit finnumk í sinn annat."

Hárbarðr kvað: 60
"Far þú nú,   þars þik hafi allan gramir."

Thor spake: 53
"One counsel I bring thee now: row hither thy boat;
No more of scoffing; set Magni's father across."

Harbarth spake: 54
"From the sound go hence; the passage thou hast not."

Thor spake: 55
"The way now show me, since thou takest me not o'er the
  water."

Harbarth spake: 56
"To refuse it is little, to fare it is long;
A while to the stock, and a while to the stone;
Then the road to thy left, till Verland thou reachest;
And there shall Fjorgyn her son Thor find,
And the road of her children she shows him to Odin's
  realm."

Thor spake: 57
"May I come so far in a day?"

Harbarth spake: 58
"With toil and trouble perchance,
While the sun still shines, or so I think."

Thor spake: 59
"Short now shall be our speech, for thou speakest in
  mockery only;
The passage thou gavest me not I shall pay thee if ever we
  meet."

Harbarth spake: 60
"Get hence where every evil thing shall have thee!"

ENDNOTES

Prose. Harbarth ("Gray-Beard"): [Odin by popular academic consensus, though the identification as Loki by Rydberg stands as a secondary option]. On the nature of the prose notes found in the manuscripts, cf. *Grimnismol*, introduction. *Thor*: the journeys of the thunder-god were almost as numerous as those of Odin; cf. *Thrymskvitha* and *Hymiskvitha*. Like the Robin Hood of the British ballads, Thor was often temporarily worsted, but always managed to come out ahead in the end. His "Journey in the East" is presumably the famous episode, related in full by Snorri, in the course of which he encountered the giant Skrymir, and in the house of Utgartha-Loki lifted the cat which turned out to be Mithgarthsorm. The *Hymiskvitha* relates a further incident of this journey.

2. The superscriptions to the speeches are badly confused in the manuscripts, but editors have agreed fairly well as to where they belong.

3. From the fact that in *Regius* line 3 begins with a capital letter, it is possible that lines 3–4 constitute the ferryman's reply, with something lost before stanza 4.

4. *Thy mother*: Jorth (Earth).

5. Some editors assume a lacuna after this stanza.

6. *Three good dwellings*: this has been generally assumed to mean three separate establishments, but it may refer simply to the three parts of a single farm, the dwelling proper, the cattle barn and the storehouse; i.e., Thor is not even a respectable peasant.

8. *Hildolf* ("slaughtering wolf"): not elsewhere mentioned in the *Edda*.

Rathsey ("Isle of Counsel"): likewise not mentioned elsewhere.

9. *In danger*: Thor is "sekr," i.e., without the protection of any law, so long as he is in the territory of his enemies, the giants. *Meili*: a practically unknown son of Odin, mentioned here only in the *Edda*. *Magni*: son of Thor and the giantess Jarnsaxa; after Thor's fight with Hrungnir (cf. stanza 14, note) Magni, though but three days old, was the only one of the gods strong enough to lift the dead giant's foot from Thor's neck. After rescuing his father, Magni said to him: "There would have been little trouble, father, had I but come sooner; I think I should have sent this giant to hell with my fist if I had met him first." Magni and his brother, Mothi, inherit Thor's hammer.

12. This stanza is hopelessly confused as to form, but none of the editorial rearrangements have materially altered the meaning. *Doomed to die*: the word "feigr" occurs constantly in the Old Norse poems and sagas; the idea of an inevitable but unknown fate seems to have been practically universal throughout the pre-Christian period. On the concealment of names from enemies, cf. *Fafnismol*, prose after stanza 1.

13. This stanza, like the preceding one, is peculiarly chaotic in the manuscript, and has been variously emended.

14. *Hrungnir*: this giant rashly wagered his head that his horse, Gullfaxi, was swifter than Odin's Sleipnir. In the race, which Hrungnir lost, he managed to dash uninvited into the home of the gods, where he became very drunk. Thor ejected him, and accepted his challenge to a duel. Hrungnir, terrified, had a helper made for him in the form of a dummy giant nine miles high and three miles broad. Hrungnir himself had a three-horned heart of stone and a head of stone; his shield was of stone and his weapon was a grindstone. But Thjalfi, Thor's servant, told him the god would attack him out of the ground, wherefore Hrungnir laid down his shield and stood on it. The hammer Mjollnir shattered both the grindstone and Hrungnir's head, but part of the grindstone knocked Thor down, and the giant fell with his foot on Thor's neck (cf. note on stanza 9). Meanwhile Thjalfi dispatched the dummy giant without trouble.

16. *Fjolvar*: not elsewhere mentioned in the poems; perhaps the father of the "seven sisters" referred to in stanza 18. *Algrön*: "The All-Green": not mentioned elsewhere in the *Edda*.

17. Thor is always eager for stories of this sort; cf. stanzas 31 and 33.

19. Lines 1–2 are obscure, but apparently Harbarth means that the women were wise to give in to him cheerfully, resistance to his power being as

impossible as (lines 3–4) making ropes of sand or digging the bottoms out of the valleys. Nothing further is known of these unlucky "seven sisters."

19. *Thjazi*: this giant, by a trick, secured possession of the goddess Ithun and her apples (cf. *Skirnismol*, 19, note), and carried her off into Jotunheim. Loki, through whose fault she had been betrayed, was sent after her by the gods. He went in Freyja's "hawk's-dress" (cf. *Thrymskvitha*, 3), turned Ithun into a nut, and flew back with her. Thjazi, in the shape of an eagle, gave chase. But the gods kindled a fire which burnt the eagle's wings, and then they killed him. Snorri's prose version does not attribute this feat particularly to Thor. Thjazi's daughter was Skathi, whom the gods permitted to marry Njorth as a recompense for her father's death. *Alvaldi*: of him we know only that he was the father of Thjazi, Ithi and Gang, who divided his wealth, each taking a mouthful of gold. The name is variously spelled. It is not known which stars were called "Thjazi's Eyes." In the middle of line 4 begins the fragmentary version of the poem found in the *Arnamagnæan Codex*.

20. *Riders by night*: witches, who were supposed to ride on wolves in the dark. [Nothing further is known of this adventure but may reference the line (stanza 155) in the Havamal about Odin's ability to confound witches as they ride.]

22. *The oak, etc.*: this proverb is found elsewhere (e.g., *Grettissaga*) in approximately the same words. its force is much like our "to the victor belong the spoils."

23. Thor killed no women of the giants' race on the "journey to the East" so fully described by Snorri, his great giant-killing adventure being the one narrated in the *Thrymskvitha*.

24. *Valland*: this mythical place ("Land of Slaughter") is elsewhere mentioned, but not further characterised; cf. prose introduction to *Völundarkvitha*, and *Helreith Brynhildar*, 2. On the bringing of slain heroes to Odin, cf. *Voluspo*, 31 and note, and, for a somewhat different version, *Grimnismol*, 14. Nowhere else is it indicated that Thor has an asylum for dead [slaves].

26. The reference here is to one of the most familiar episodes in Thor's eastward journey. He and his companions came to a house in the forest, and went in to spend the night. Being disturbed by an earthquake and a terrific noise, they all crawled into a smaller room opening from the main one. In the morning, however, they discovered that the earthquake had been occasioned by the giant Skrymir's lying down near them, and the noise by his snoring. The house in which they had taken refuge was

his glove, the smaller room being the thumb. Skrymir was in fact Utgartha-Loki himself. That he is in this stanza called Fjalar (the name occurs also in *Hovamol*, 14) is probably due to a confusion of the names by which Utgartha-Loki went. Loki taunts Thor with this adventure in *Lokasenna*, 60 and 62, line 3 of this stanza being perhaps interpolated from *Lokasenna*, 60, 4.

29. *The river*: probably Ifing, which flows between the land of the gods and that of the giants; cf. *Vafthruthnismol*, 16. *Sons of Svarang*: presumably the giants; Svarang is not elsewhere mentioned in the poems, nor is there any other account of Thor's defense of the passage.

30. Odin's adventures of this sort were too numerous to make it possible to identify this particular person. *By stealth*: so the *Arnamagnæan Codex*; *Regius*, followed by several editors, has "long meeting with her."

35. *Heel-biter*: this effective parallel to our "back-biter" is not found elsewhere in Old Norse.

37. *Hlesey*: "the Island of the Sea-God" (Hler = Ægir), identified with the Danish island Läsö, in the Kattegat. It appears again, much out of place, in *Oddrunargratr*, 28. *Berserkers*: [a religious mannerbund order with totemic animal patrons (Bear, Wolf and Boar) characterized by their frenzied anger and bloodlust and sometimes the ability to shapechange into the animal of choice]; cf. *Hyndluljoth*, 23 and note. The women here mentioned are obviously of the [latter] type.

39. *Thjalfi*: Thor's servant; cf. note on stanza 14.

40. To what expedition this refers is unknown, but apparently Odin speaks of himself as allied to the foes of the gods.

41. *Hatred*: so *Regius*; the other manuscript has, apparently, "sickness."

42. Just what Odin means, or why his words should so have enraged Thor, is not evident, though he may imply that Thor is open to bribery. [Modern scholarship notes that there may perhaps be a ribald reference to the anus inferred and thus some kind of accusation of sexual perversity.] Perhaps a passage has dropped out before stanza 43.

44. Odin refers to the dead, from whom he seeks information through his magic power.

48. *Sif*: Thor's wife, the lover being presumably Loki; cf. *Lokasenna*, 54.

52. *Asathor*: Thor goes by various names in the poems: e.g., Vingthor,

Vingnir, Hlorrithi. Asathor[1] means "[The Mighty Thor]."

53. *Magni*: Thor's son; cf. stanza 9 and note.

56. *Line 2*: the phrases mean simply "a long way"; cf. "over stock and stone." *Verland*: the "Land of Men" to which Thor must come from the land of the giants. The *Arnamagnæan Codex* has "Valland" (cf. stanza 24 and note), but this is obviously an error. *Fjorgyn*: a feminine form of the same name, which belongs to Odin (cf. *Voluspo*, 56 and note); here it evidently means Jorth (Earth), Thor's mother. *The road*: the rainbow bridge, Bifrost; cf. *Grimnismol*, 29 and note.

58. *Line 2*: so *Regius*; the other manuscript has "ere sunrise."

60. The Arnamagnæan Codex clearly indicates Harbarth as the speaker of this line, but Regius has no superscription, and begins the line with a small letter not preceded by a period, thereby assigning it to Thor.

---

1 The title of the gods itself means "the mighty ones", cognate to *Asura* and *Ahura* in Indo-Iranian myth.

HYMISKVITHA
THE LAY OF HYMIR

INTRODUCTION

The *Hymiskvitha* is notorious for being an awkwardly composed poem with many scholars noting that it appears to be composed of three separate and disjointed poems welded together inexpertly. The first portion of the story appears as a sort of prelude to the *Lokasenna*, setting up the narrative of the doomed feast in Aegir's Hall by way of the recovery of a brewing vessel from the giant Hymir. The second recounts the narrative of Thor's fishing trip and attempt to catch the Midgard Serpent Jormundgandr before the events of *Ragnarök* and his own fated battle with the creature. The third portion of the poem appears to reference the story spoken of in *Gylfaginning*, in which Thor shares with a peasant family a meal of his own chariot-goats, where one of them mistakenly cracks the leg bone of Thor's goat, resulting in it being maimed after they are resurrected the next morning.

Even beyond the clumsy welding together of these different poems, several peculiarities appear in the narrative. One of the more perplexing is the poem's claim of the parentage of Tyr himself, who is described herein as being the son of the giant Hymir, despite otherwise being noted as the son of Odin and unsuspiciously counted among the other ranks of the *Aesir*. The poem does not note the reaction of Tyr at the end when Thor slaughters his father and his men after he leads an army in pursuit of them, which, given the normal cultural standards of kin loyalty, we would expect to be a rather large ordeal going forward if this relationship was indeed accurate. Perhaps what is meant here is that Tyr's relationship with Hymir is actually one of foster-fatherhood, a common practice among the Norse wherein a man, frequently of lesser status and means, takes care of the child of another in exchange for political and social considerations and remuneration. As the father-like relationship often leads to a friendliness between both houses afterwards, it was often used between enemies to repair relations, or even as a mandated settlement for a crime having been committed by one party against the other.

The second peculiarity here is the maiming of Thor's Goats, which the poem specifies is the work of Loki (somehow, despite him not being involved in the story thus far) and implies that it may have happened due to the battle with Hymir and his "many headed throng". Neither of these incidences conform with the tale recorded in *Gylfaggining* in which the children of a simple peasant family errantly break the leg at dinner to get at the marrow and Thor takes the children as his personal servants in reparation—a story that is related neither to the conflict with Hymir, nor a battle, nor could be blamed upon the wiles of Loki. Strangely, the poem itself seems to allude to the alternative story within its own narrative asking "But ye all have heard—for of them who have, the tales of the gods, who better can tell? What prize he won from the wilderness-dweller, who both his children gave him to boot."

The only explanation that could be rendered here is that the poem's author has made a mistake in setting down three separate existing poems together and created a connection where there should not be one, making the events of the poem altogether rather skeptical as to its legitimacy and accuracy. However, a point in its favor is that the second part of the poem, regarding the fishing expedition with Hymir, is one of the stories most commonly rendered upon runestones and artwork, the oldest of which can be reliably dated to the 8th century, making the story itself legitimately ancient and authentically pre-Christian in origin.

Ægir
(J. P. Molin)

Ár valtívar   veiðar námu
ok sumblsamir,   áðr saðir yrði,
hristu teina   ok á hlaut sáu;
fundu þeir at Ægis   ørkost hvera.   1

Sat bergbúi   barnteitr fyr
mjök glíkr megi   miskorblinda;
leit í augu   Yggs barn í þrá:
"Þú skalt ásum   oft sumbl gera."   2

Önn fekk jötni   orðbæginn halr,
hugði at hefndum   hann næst við goð,
bað hann Sifjar   ver sér færa hver,
"þanns ek öllum öl   yðr of heita."   3

Né þat máttu   mærir tívar
ok ginnregin   of geta hvergi,
unz af tryggðum   Týr Hlórriða
ástráð mikit   einum sagði: 4

"Býr fyr austan   Élivága
hundvíss Hymir   at himins enda;
á minn faðir   móðugr ketil,
rúmbrugðinn hver,   rastar djúpan."   5

HYMISKVITHA

Of old the gods made feast together, 1
And drink they sought ere sated they were;
Twigs they shook, and blood they tried:
Rich fare in Ægir's hall they found.

The mountain-dweller sat merry as boyhood, 2
But soon like a blinded man he seemed;
The son of Ygg gazed in his eyes:
"For the gods a feast shalt thou forthwith get."

The word-wielder toil for the giant worked, 3
And so revenge on the gods he sought;
He bade Sif's mate the kettle bring:
"Therein for ye all much ale shall I brew."

The far-famed ones could find it not, 4
And the holy gods could get it nowhere;
Till in truthful wise did Tyr speak forth,
And helpful counsel to Hlorrithi gave.

"There dwells to the east of Elivagar 5
Hymir the wise at the end of heaven;
A kettle my father fierce doth own,
A mighty vessel a mile in depth."

Þórr kvað: 6
"Veiztu ef þiggjum   þann lögvelli?"
Týr kvað:
"Ef, vinr, vélar   vit gervum til."

Fóru drjúgum   dag þann fram 7
Ásgarði frá,   unz til Egils kvámu;
hirði hann hafra   horngöfgasta;
hurfu at höllu,   er Hymir átti.

Mögr fann ömmu   mjök leiða sér, 8
hafði höfða   hundruð níu,
en önnur gekk   algullin fram
brúnhvít bera   bjórveig syni:

"Áttniðr jötna,   ek viljak ykkr 9
hugfulla tvá   und hvera setja;
er minn fríi   mörgu sinni
glöggr við gesti,   görr ills hugar."

En váskapaðr   varð síðbúinn 10
harðráðr Hymir   heim af veiðum,
gekk inn í sal,   glumðu jöklar,
var karls, en kom,   kinnskógr frörinn.

Frilla kvað: 11
"Ver þú heill, Hymir,
í hugum góðum,   nú er sonr kominn
til sala þinna,   sá er vit vættum
af vegi löngum;
fylgir hánum   hróðrs andskoti,
vinr verliða;
Véurr heitir sá.

Sé þú, hvar sitja   und salar gafli, 12
svá forða sér,   stendr súl fyrir."
Sundr stökk súla   fyr sjón jötuns,
en áðr í tvau   áss brotnaði.

Stukku átta,   en einn af þeim 13
hverr harðsleginn   heill af þolli;
fram gengu þeir,   en forn jötunn
sjónum leiddi   sinn andskota.

Thor spake: 6
"May we win, dost thou think, this whirler of water?"
Tyr spake:
"Aye, friend, we can, if cunning we are."

Forward that day with speed they fared, 7
From Asgarth came they to Egil's home;
The goats with horns bedecked he guarded;
Then they sped to the hall where Hymir dwelt.

The youth found his grandam, that greatly he loathed, 8
And full nine hundred heads she had;
But the other fair with gold came forth,
And the bright-browed one brought beer to her son.

"Kinsman of giants, beneath the kettle 9
Will I set ye both, ye heroes bold;
For many a time my dear-loved mate
To guests is wrathful and grim of mind."

Late to his home the misshapen Hymir, 10
The giant harsh, from his hunting came;
The icicles rattled as in he came,
For the fellow's chin-forest frozen was.

"Hail to thee, Hymir! good thoughts mayst thou have; 11
Here has thy son to thine hall now come;
For him have we waited, his way was long;
And with him fares the foeman of Hroth,
The friend of mankind, and Veur they call him.

"See where under the gable they sit! 12
Behind the beam do they hide themselves."
The beam at the glance of the giant broke,
And the mighty pillar in pieces fell.

Eight fell from the ledge, and one alone, 13
The hard-hammered kettle, of all was whole;
Forth came they then, and his foes he sought,
The giant old, and held with his eyes.

Sagði-t hánum   hugr vel þá,   14
er hann sá gýgjar græti
á golf kominn,   þar váru þjórar
þrír of teknir,   bað senn jötunn
sjóða ganga.

Hvern létu þeir   höfði skemmra   15
ok á seyði   síðan báru;
át Sifjar verr,   áðr sofa gengi,
einn með öllu   öxn tvá Hymis.

Þótti hárum   Hrungnis spjalla   16
verðr Hlórriða   vel fullmikill:
"Munum at aftni   öðrum verða
við veiðimat   vér þrír lifa."

Véurr kvaðzk vilja   á vág róa,   17
ef ballr jötunn   beitr gæfi.
Hymir kvað:
"Hverf þú til hjarðar,   ef þú hug trúir,
brjótr berg-Dana,   beitur sækja.

Þess vænti ek,   at þér myni-t   18
ögn af oxa   auðfeng vera."
Sveinn sýsliga   sveif til skógar,
þar er uxi stóð   alsvartr fyrir.

Braut af þjóri   þurs ráðbani   19
hátún ofan   horna tveggja.
Hymir kvað:
"Verk þykkja þín   verri miklu
kjóla valdi   en þú kyrr sitir."

Bað hlunngota   hafra dróttinn   20
áttrunn apa   útar færa,
en sá jötunn   sína talði
lítla fýsi   at róa lengra.

Dró meir Hymir   móðugr hvali   21
einn á öngli   upp senn tváa,
en aftr í skut   Óðni sifjaðr
Véurr við vélar   vað gerði sér.

Much sorrow his heart foretold when he saw
The giantess' foeman come forth on the floor;
Then of the steers did they bring in three;
Their flesh to boil did the giant bid.
  14

By a head was each the shorter hewed,
And the beasts to the fire straight they bore;
The husband of Sif, ere to sleep he went,
Alone two oxen of Hymir's ate.
  15

To the comrade hoary of Hrungnir then
Did Hlorrithi's meal full mighty seem;
"We should at evening next time
Of food from the hunt make our meal."
  16

[...]
Fain to row on the sea was Veur, he said,
If the giant bold would give him bait.
  17

Hymir spake:
"Go to the herd, if thou hast it in mind,
Thou slayer of giants, thy bait to seek;
For there thou soon mayst find, methinks,
Bait from the oxen easy to get."
  18

Swift to the wood the hero went,
Till before him an ox all black he found;
From the beast the slayer of giants broke
The fortress high of his double horns.
  19

Hymir spake:
"Thy works, methinks, are worse by far,
Thou steerer of ships, than when still thou sittest."
[...]
[...]
  20

The lord of the goats bade the ape-begotten
Farther to steer the steed of the rollers;
But the giant said that his will, forsooth,
Longer to row was little enough.
  21

Egndi á öngul,   sá er öldum bergr,   22
orms einbani   uxa höfði;
gein við agni,   sú er goð fía,
umgjörð neðan   allra landa.

Dró djarfliga   dáðrakkr Þórr   23
orm eitrfáan   upp at borði;
hamri kníði   háfjall skarar
ofljótt ofan   ulfs hnitbróður.

Hraungalkn hlumðu,   en hölkn þutu,   24
fór in forna   fold öll saman;
sökkðisk síðan   sá fiskr í mar.

Óteitr jötunn,   er aftr reru,   25
svá at ár Hymir   ekki mælti,
veifði hann ræði   veðrs annars til.

Hymir kvað: 26
"Mundu of vinna   verk halft við mik,
at þú heim hvali   haf til bæjar
eða flotbrúsa   festir okkarn."

Gekk Hlórriði,   greip á stafni   27
vatt með austri   upp lögfáki,
einn með árum   ok með austskotu
bar hann til bæjar   brimsvín jötuns
ok holtriða   hver í gegnum.

Ok enn jötunn   um afrendi,   28
þrágirni vanr,   við Þór sennti,
kvað-at mann ramman,   þótt róa kynni
kröfturligan,   nema kálk bryti.

En Hlórriði,   er at höndum kom,   29
brátt lét bresta   brattstein gleri;
sló hann sitjandi   súlur í gögnum;
báru þó heilan   fyr Hymi síðan.

Unz þat in fríða   frilla kenndi   30
ástráð mikit,   eitt er vissi:
"Drep við haus Hymis,   hann er harðari,
kostmóðs jötuns   kálki hverjum."

Two whales on his hook did the mighty Hymir 22
Soon pull up on a single cast;
In the stern the kinsman of Odin sat,
And Veur with cunning his cast prepared.

The warder of men, the worm's destroyer, 23
Fixed on his hook the head of the ox;
There gaped at the bait the foe of the gods,
The girdler of all the earth beneath.

The venomous serpent swiftly up 24
To the boat did Thor, the bold one, pull;
With his hammer the loathly hill of the hair
Of the brother of Fenrir he smote from above.

The monsters roared, and the rocks resounded, 25
And all the earth so old was shaken;
[...]
Then sank the fish in the sea forthwith.

[...] 26
Joyless as back they rowed was the giant;
Speechless did Hymir sit at the oars,
With the rudder he sought a second wind.

Hymir spake:
"The half of our toil wilt thou have with me, 27
And now make fast our goat of the flood;
Or home wilt thou bear the whales to the house,
Across the gorge of the wooded glen?"

Hlorrithi stood and the stem he gripped, 28
And the sea-horse with water awash he lifted;
Oars and bailer and all he bore
With the surf-swine home to the giant's house.

His might the giant again would match, 29
For stubborn he was, with the strength of Thor;
None truly strong, though stoutly he rowed,
Would he call save one who could break the cup.

Hlorrithi then, when the cup he held, 30
Struck with the glass the pillars of stone;
As he sat the posts in pieces he shattered,
Yet the glass to Hymir whole they brought.

Harðr reis á kné   hafra dróttinn,   31
færðisk allra   í ásmegin;
heill var karli   hjalmstofn ofan,
en vínferill   valr rifnaði.

"Mörg veit ek mæti   mér gengin frá,   32
er ek kálki sé   ór knéum hrundit;"
karl orð of kvað:
"knákat ek segja   aftr ævagi,
þú ert, ölðr, of heitt.

Þat er til kostar,   ef koma mættið   33
út ór óru   ölkjól hofi."
Týr leitaði   tysvar hræra;
stóð at hváru   hverr kyrr fyrir.

Faðir Móða   fekk á þremi   34
ok í gegnum steig   golf niðr í sal;
hóf sér á höfuð upp   hver Sifjar verr,
en á hælum   hringar skullu.

Fóru-t lengi,   áðr líta nam   35
aftr Óðins sonr   einu sinni;
sá hann ór hreysum   með Hymi austan
folkdrótt fara   fjölhöfðaða.

Hóf hann sér af herðum   36
hver standanda,   veifði hann Mjöllni
morðgjörnum fram,   ok hraunhvala
hann alla drap.

Fóru-t lengi,   áðr liggja nam   37
hafr Hlórriða   halfdauðr fyrir;
var skær skökuls   skakkr á beini,
en því inn lævísi   Loki of olli.

En ér heyrt hafið,   38
hverr kann of   þat goðmálugra
görr at skilja?
hver af hraunbúa   hann laun of fekk,
er hann bæði galt   börn sín fyrir.

Þróttöflugr kom   á þing goða   39
ok hafði hver,   þanns Hymir átti;
en véar hverjan   vel skulu drekka
ölðr at Ægis   eitt hörmeitið.

But the loved one fair of the giant found   31
A counsel true, and told her thought:
"Smite the skull of Hymir, heavy with food,
For harder it is than ever was glass."

The goats' mighty ruler then rose on his knee,   32
And with all the strength of a god he struck;
Whole was the fellow's helmet-stem,
But shattered the wine-cup rounded was.

Hymir spake: 33
"Fair is the treasure that from me is gone,
Since now the cup on my knees lies shattered;"
So spake the giant: "No more can I say
In days to be, 'Thou art brewed, mine ale.'

"Enough shall it be if out ye can bring   34
Forth from our house the kettle here."
Tyr then twice to move it tried,
But before him the kettle twice stood fast.

The father of Mothi the rim seized firm,   35
And before it stood on the floor below;
Up on his head Sif's husband raised it,
And about his heels the handles clattered.

Not long had they fared, ere backwards looked   36
The son of Odin, once more to see;
From their caves in the east beheld he coming
With Hymir the throng of the many-headed.

He stood and cast from his back the kettle,   37
And Mjollnir, the lover of murder, he wielded;
[...]
So all the whales of the waste he slew.

Not long had they fared ere one there lay   38
Of Hlorrithi's goats half-dead on the ground;
In his leg the pole-horse there was lame;
The deed the evil Loki had done.

But ye all have heard—for of them who have   39
The tales of the gods, who better can tell?
What prize he won from the wilderness-dweller,
Who both his children gave him to boot.

The mighty one came to the council of gods,   40
And the kettle he had that Hymir's was;
So gladly their ale the gods could drink
In Ægir's hall at the autumn-time.

ENDNOTES

1. *Twigs*: Vigfusson comments at some length on "the rite practised in the heathen age of inquiring into the future by dipping bunches of chips or twigs into the blood (of sacrifices) and shaking them." But the two operations may have been separate, the twigs being simply "divining-rods" marked with runes. In either case, the gods were seeking information by magic as to where they could find plenty to drink. *Ægir*: a giant who is also [associated with the sea]; little is known of him outside of what is told here and in the introductory prose to the *Lokasenna*, though Snorri has a brief account of him, giving his home as Hlesey (Läsö, cf. *Harbarthsljoth*, 37). *Grimnismol*, 45, has a reference to this same feast.

2. *Mountain-dweller*: the giant (Ægir). *Line 2*: the principal word in the original has defied interpretation, and any translation of the line must be largely guesswork. *Ygg*: Odin; his son is Thor. Some editors assume a gap after this stanza.

3. *Word-wielder*: Thor. *The giant*: Ægir. *Sif*: Thor's wife; cf. *Harbarthsljoth*, 48. *The kettle*: Kettles were used by the Germanic people as objects of religious ritual.

4. *Tyr*: the god of battle; his two great achievements were thrusting his hand into the mouth of the wolf Fenrir so that the gods might bind him, whereby he lost his hand (cf. *Voluspo*, 39, note), and his fight with the hound Garm in the last battle, in which they kill each other. *Hlorrithi*: Thor.

5. *Elivagar* ("Stormy Waves"): possibly the Milky Way; cf. *Vafthruthnismol*, 31, note. *Hymir*: this giant figures only in this episode. It is not clear why Tyr, who is elsewhere spoken of as a son of Odin, should here call

Hymir his father. Finnur Jonsson, in an attempt to get round this difficulty, deliberately changed the word "father" to "grandfather," but this does not help greatly.

6. Neither manuscript has any superscriptions, but most editors have supplied them as above. From this point through stanza 11 it the editors have varied considerably in grouping the lines into stanzas. The manuscripts indicate the third lines of stanzas 7, 8, 9, and 10 as beginning stanzas, but this makes more complications than the present arrangement. It is possible that, as Sijmons suggests, two lines have been lost after stanza 6.

7. *Egil*: possibly, though by no means certainly, the father of Thor's servant, Thjalfi, for, according to Snorri, Thor's first stop on this journey was at the house of a peasant whose children, Thjalfi and Roskva, he took into his service; cf. stanza 38, note. The *Arnamagnæan Codex* has "Ægir" instead of "Egil," but, aside from the fact that Thor had just left Ægir's house, the sea-god can hardly have been spoken of as a goat-herd.

8. *The youth*: Tyr, whose extraordinary grandmother is Hymir's mother. We know nothing further of her, or of *the other*, who is Hymir's wife and Tyr's mother. It may be guessed, however, that she belonged rather to the race of the gods than to that of the giants.

11. Two or three editors give this stanza a superscription ("The concubine spake," "The daughter spake"). Line 3 is commonly regarded as spurious. *The foeman of Hroth*: of course this means Thor, but nothing is known of any enemy of his by this name. Several editors have sought to make a single word meaning "the famous enemy" out of the phrase. Concerning Thor as the friend of man, particularly of the peasant class, cf. introduction to *Harbarthsljoth*. *Veur*: another name, of uncertain meaning, for Thor.

13. *Eight*: the giant's glance, besides breaking the beam, knocks down all the kettles with such violence that all but the one under which Thor and Tyr are hiding are broken.

14. Hymir's wrath does not permit him to ignore the duties of a host to his guests, always strongly insisted on.

15. Thor's appetite figures elsewhere; cf. *Thrymskvitha*, 24.

16. *The comrade of Hrungnir*: Hymir, presumably simply because both are giants; cf. *Harbarthsljoth*, 14 and note.[1]

---

[1] Bellows did not attempt to completely translate this stanza; the third and fourth line have been translated literally in this edition, where to "hunt" can also refer to fishing.

17. The manuscripts indicate no lacuna, and many editors unite stanza 17 with lines 1 and 2 of 18. Sijmons and Gering assume a gap after these two lines, but it seems more probable that the missing passage, if any, belonged before them, supplying the connection with the previous stanza.

18. The manuscripts have no superscription. Many editors combine lines 3 and 4 with lines 1 and 2 of stanza 19. In Snorri's extended paraphrase of the story, Hymir declines to go fishing with Thor on the ground that the latter is too small a person to be worth bothering about. "You would freeze," he says, "if you stayed out in mid-ocean as long as I generally do." *Bait* (line 4): the word literally means "chaff," hence any small bits; Hymir means that Thor should collect dung for bait.

19. Many editors combine lines 3 and 4 with stanza 20. *Fortress*, etc.: the ox's head; cf. introductory note concerning the diction of this poem [Appendix B]. Several editors assume a lacuna after stanza 19, but this seems unnecessary.

20. The manuscripts have no superscription. *Steerer of ships*: probably merely a reference to Thor's intention to go fishing. The lacuna after stanza 20 is assumed by most editors.

21. *Lord of the goats*: Thor, because of his goat-drawn chariot. *Ape-begotten*: Hymir; the word "api," rare until relatively late times in its literal sense, is fairly common with the meaning of "fool." Giants were generally assumed to be stupid. *Steed of the rollers*: a ship, because boats were pulled up on shore by means of rollers.

23. *Warder of men*: Thor; cf. stanza 11. *Worm's destroyer*: likewise Thor, who in the last battle slays, and is slain by, Mithgarthsorm; cf. *Voluspo*, 56. *The foe of the gods*: Mithgarthsorm, who lies in the sea, and surrounds the whole earth.

24. *Hill of the hair*: head—a thoroughly characteristic skaldic phrase. *Brother of Fenrir*: Mithgarthsorm was, like the wolf Fenrir and the goddess Hel, born to Loki and the giantess Angrbotha (cf. *Voluspo*, 39 and note), and I have translated this line accordingly; but the word used in the text has been guessed as meaning almost anything from "comrade" to "enemy."

25. No gap is indicated in the manuscripts, but that a line or more has been lost is highly probable. In Snorri's version, Thor pulls so hard on the line that he drives both his feet through the flooring of the boat, and

stands on bottom. When he pulls the serpent up, Hymir cuts the line with his bait-knife, which explains the serpent's escape. Thor, in a rage, knocks Hymir overboard with his hammer, and then wades ashore. The lines of stanzas 25 and 26 have been variously grouped.[2]

26. No gap is indicated in the manuscripts, but line 2 begins with a small letter. *A second wind*: another direction, i.e., he put about for the shore.

27. No superscription in the manuscripts. In its place Bugge supplies a line—"These words spake Hymir, the giant wise." The manuscripts reverse the order of lines 2 and 3, and in both of them line 4 stands after stanza 28. *Goat of the flood*: boat.

28. *Sea-horse*: boat. *Surf-swine*: the whales.

29. Snorri says nothing of this episode of Hymir's cup. The glass which cannot be broken appears in the folklore of various races.

31. *The loved one*: Hymir's wife and Tyr's mother; cf. stanza 8 and note. The idea that a giant's skull is harder than stone or anything else is characteristic of the later Norse folk-stories, and in one of the so-called "mythical sagas" we find a giant actually named Hard-Skull.

32. *Helmet-stem*: head.

33. The manuscripts have no superscription. Line 4 in the manuscripts is somewhat obscure, and Bugge, followed by some editors, suggests a reading which may be rendered (beginning with the second half of line 3): "No more can I speak / Ever again as I spoke of old."

35. *The father of Mothi* and *Sif's husband*: Thor.

36. *The many-headed*: The giants, although rarely designated as a race in this way, sometimes had two or more heads; cf. stanza 8, *Skirnismol*, 31 and *Vafthruthnismol*, 33. Hymir's mother is, however, the only many-headed giant actually to appear in the action of the poems.

37. No gap is indicated in the manuscripts. Some editors put the missing line as 2, some as 3, and some, leaving the present three lines together, add a fourth, and metrically incorrect, one from late paper manuscripts: "Who with Hymir followed after." *Whales of the waste*: giants.

38. According to Snorri, when Thor set out with Loki (not Tyr) for the giants' land, he stopped first at a peasant's house (cf. stanza 7 and note).

---

[2] It is at this stanza that Bellows' numbering scheme deviates from that of the Old Norse used in this edition.

There he proceeded to cook his own goats for supper. The peasant's son, Thjalfi, eager to get at the marrow, split one of the leg-bones with his knife. The next morning, when Thor was ready to proceed with his journey, he called the goats to life again, but one of them proved irretrievably lame. His wrath led the peasant to give him both his children as servants (cf. stanza 39). Snorri does not indicate that Loki was in any way to blame.

39. This deliberate introduction of the story-teller is exceedingly rare in the older poetry.

40. The translation of the last two lines is mostly guesswork, as the word rendered "gods" is uncertain, and the one rendered "at the autumn-time" is quite obscure.

LOKASENNA
LOKI'S WRANGLING

INTRODUCTION

The *Lokasenna* is one of the more interesting of the *Eddic* poems, partially due to the subject matter (Loki's various insults against the Gods), but also due to the fact that the poem itself alludes to a large number of mythological incidents, many of which we have no other records of, again implying that we lack a full view of the Nordic mythological structure, including many myths that might have been very popular and commonly known.

The poem connects in some way from the previous one of the *Hymiskvitha*, with the feast in Aegir's Hall now underway due to Thor and Tyr recovering the large drinking vessel from Hymir. Loki is angered by the praise heaped upon two of Aegir's servants for their skill at serving and kills them in jealousy, returning to the feast in what appears to be an extremely intoxicated state and demanding to be seated, calling upon an old sworn oath between himself and Odin.

This precipitates the exchange of a particularly vitriolic series of insults between Loki and all of the Gods present, accusing them all of various misdeeds or shameful histories and character, eventually culminating in Loki admitting his culpability in the death of Baldr, and Thor arriving and threatening to kill Loki if he does not silence himself. A prose explanation of the events afterward stands in agreement with the more detailed narrative in *Gylfaginning*, recording the Gods' capture and binding of Loki in penance for his crimes here.

As it is often misunderstood, we should note here that the poem reflects a take on the cultural tradition of Flyting—a type of ritualized insult duel popular among the Germanic people for entertainment and a show of wit, and one in which the usually violent and vengeful reaction to public insults is nonexistent and ignored according to the rules of the "game". The poem subverts this cultural expectation by presenting an extremely intoxicated Loki who is attempting to perform this ritual to a group of the Gods who are extremely reluctant if not outright hostile and refusing it. This leads to Loki's insults being less a show of comedic wit and rhetorical skill (which Odin explicitly points out to his opponent) and more one of malice and boorishness to which the Gods do not take kindly. Also of note here is that one cannot rely upon the accuracy of the insults levied upon the Gods, and there is no indication anywhere that most of these (especially the sexual ones levied against the Goddesses) are actually true and believed by our forefathers.

The poem itself shows some evidence of an origin in the Freyr-centered cult common through Sweden, Norway, and Iceland at the likely time of its composition in the mid to late 10th century, With statements resembling those in *Skirnismal* such as Njord saying: "The son did I have whom no man hates, and foremost of gods is found," and Tyr replying "Of the heroes brave is Freyr the best, here in the home of the gods, he harms not maids nor the wives of men, and the bound from their fetters he frees." Indeed, it is Freyr himself who subtly but ultimately makes the eventual threat to Loki regarding his binding, saying "By the mouth of the river the wolf remains, till the gods to destruction go; thou too shalt soon, if thy tongue is not stilled, be fettered, thou forger of ill." This is an example of what was probably to be understood as the famous oracular foresight of the Vanir.

Loki and Sigyn
(M. E. Winge)

Ægir, er öðru nafni hét Gymir, hann hafði búit ásum öl, þá er hann hafði fengit ketil inn mikla, sem nú er sagt. Til þeirar veizlu kom Óðinn ok Frigg, kona hans. Þórr kom eigi, því at hann var í austrvegi. Sif var þar, kona Þórs, Bragi ok Iðunn, kona hans. Týr var þar. Hann var einhendr, Fenrisúlfr sleit hönd af honum, þá er hann var bundinn. Þar var Njörðr ok kona hans Skaði, Freyr ok Freyja, Víðarr, son Óðins. Loki var þar ok þjónustumenn Freys, Byggvir ok Beyla. Margt var þar ása ok alfa. Ægir átti tvá þjónustumenn, Fimafengr ok Eldir. Þar var lýsigull haft fyrir elts ljós. Sjálft barst þar öl. Þar var griðastaðr mikill. Menn lofuðu mjök, hversu góðir þjónustumenn Ægis váru. Loki mátti eigi heyra þat, ok drap hann Fimafeng. Þá skóku æsir skjöldu sína ok æpðu at Loka ok eltu hann braut til skógar, en þeir fóru at drekka. Loki hvarf aftr ok hitti úti Eldi. Loki kvaddi hann:

"Segðu þat, Eldir, svá at þú einugi 1
feti gangir framar, hvat hér inni
hafa at ölmálum sigtíva synir."

LOKASENNA

Ægir, who was also called Gymir, had prepared ale for the gods, after he had got the mighty kettle, as now has been told. To this feast came Odin and Frigg, his wife. Thor came not, as he was on a journey in the East. Sif, Thor's wife, was there, and Brag, with Ithun, his wife. Tyr, who had but one hand, was there; the wolf Fenrir had bitten off his other hand when they had bound him. There were Njorth and Skathi his wife, Freyr and Freyja, and Vithar, the son of Odin. Loki was there, and Freyr's servants Byggvir and Beyla. Many were there of the gods and elves.

Ægir had two serving-men, Fimafeng and Eldir. Glittering gold they had in place of firelight; the ale came in of itself; and great was the peace. The guests praised much the ability of Ægir's serving-men. Loki might not endure that, and he slew Fimafeng. Then the gods shook their shields and howled at Loki and drove him away to the forest, and thereafter set to drinking again. Loki turned back, and outside he met Eldir. Loki spoke to him:

"Speak now, Eldir, for not one step   1
Farther shalt thou fare;
What ale-talk here do they have within,
The sons of the glorious gods?"

Eldir kvað: 2
"Of vápn sín dæma ok um vígrisni sína
sigtíva synir;
ása ok alfa er hér inni eru,
manngi er þér í orði vinr."

Loki kvað: 3
"Inn skal ganga Ægis hallir í
á þat sumbl at sjá;
jöll ok áfu færi ek ása sonum,
ok blend ek þeim svá meini mjöð."

Eldir kvað: 4
"Veiztu, ef þú inn gengr Ægis hallir í
á þat sumbl at sjá, hrópi ok rógi
ef þú eyss á holl regin,
á þér munu þau þerra þat."

Loki kvað: 5
"Veiztu þat, Eldir, ef vit einir skulum
sáryrðum sakask, auðigr verða
mun ek í andsvörum,
ef þú mælir til margt."

Síðan gekk Loki inn í höllina. En er þeir sá, er fyrir váru, hverr inn var
kominn, þögnuðu þeir allir.

Loki kvað: 6
"Þyrstr ek kom þessar hallar til,
Loftr, um langan veg ásu at biðja,
at mér einn gefi mæran drykk mjaðar.

Hví þegið ér svá, þrungin goð, 7
at þér mæla né meguð?
Sessa ok staði velið mér sumbli at
eða heitið mik heðan."

Bragi kvað: 8
"Sessa ok staði velja þér sumbli at
æsir aldregi, því at æsir vitu,
hveim þeir alda skulu gambansumbl of geta."

Eldir spake: 2
"Of their weapons they talk, and their might in war,
The sons of the glorious gods;
From the gods and elves who are gathered here
No friend in words shalt thou find."

Loki spake: 3
"In shall I go into Ægir's hall,
For the feast I fain would see;
Bale and hatred I bring to the gods,
And their mead with venom I mix."

Eldir spake: 4
"If in thou goest to Ægir's hall,
And fain the feast wouldst see,
And with slander and spite wouldst sprinkle the gods,
Think well lest they wipe it on thee."

Loki spake: 5
"Bethink thee, Eldir, if thou and I
Shall strive with spiteful speech;
Richer I grow in ready words
If thou speakest too much to me."

Then Loki went into the hall, but when they who were there saw who had entered, they were all silent.

Loki spake: 6
"Thirsty I come into this thine hall,
I, Lopt, from a journey long,
To ask of the gods that one should give
Fair mead for a drink to me.

"Why sit ye silent, swollen with pride, 7
Ye gods, and no answer give?
At your feast a place and a seat prepare me,
Or bid me forth to fare."

Bragi spake: 8
"A place and a seat will the gods prepare
No more in their midst for thee;
For the gods know well what men they wish
To find at their mighty feasts."

Loki kvað: 9
"Mantu þat, Óðinn, er vit í árdaga
blendum blóði saman?
Ölvi bergja lézktu eigi mundu,
nema okkr væri báðum borit."

Óðinn kvað: 10
"Rístu þá, Víðarr, ok lát ulfs föður
sitja sumbli at, síðr oss Loki
kveði lastastöfum Ægis höllu í."

Þá stóð Víðarr upp ok skenkði Loka. En áðr hann drykki, kvaddi hann ásuna:

"Heilir æsir, heilar ásynjur 11
ok öll ginnheilög goð
nema sá einn áss er innar sitr,
Bragi, bekkjum á."

Bragi kvað: 12
"Mar ok mæki
gef ek þér míns féar,
ok bætir þér svá baugi Bragi,
síðr þú ásum öfund of gjaldir,
grem þú eigi goð at þér."

Loki kvað: 13
"Jós ok armbauga mundu æ vera
beggja vanr, Bragi;
ása ok alfa, er hér inni eru,
þú ert við víg varastr
ok skjarrastr við skot."

Bragi kvað: 14
"Veit ek, ef fyr útan værak,
svá sem fyr innan emk,
Ægis höll of kominn,
höfuð þitt bæra ek í hendi mér;
lykak þér þat fyr lygi."

Loki spake: 9
"Remember, Odin, in olden days
That we both our blood have mixed;
Then didst thou promise no ale to pour,
Unless it were brought for us both."

Odin spake: 10
"Stand forth then, Vithar, and let the wolf's father
Find a seat at our feast;
Lest evil should Loki speak aloud
Here within Ægir's hall."

Then Vithar arose and poured drink for Loki; but before he drank he spoke to the gods:

"Hail to you, gods! ye goddesses, hail! 11
Hail to the holy throng!
Save for the god who yonder sits,
Bragi there on the bench."

Bragi spake: 12
"A horse and a sword from my hoard will I give,
And a ring gives Bragi to boot,
That hatred thou makst not among the gods;
So rouse not the great ones to wrath."

Loki spake: 13
"In horses and rings thou shalt never be rich,
Bragi, but both shalt thou lack;
Of the gods and elves here together met
Least brave in battle art thou,
And shyest thou art of the shot."

Bragi spake: 14
"Now were I without as I am within,
And here in Ægir's hall,
Thine head would I bear in mine hands away,
And pay thee the price of thy lies."

Loki kvað: 15
"Snjallr ertu í sessi,
skal-at-tu svá gera,
Bragi bekkskrautuðr;
vega þú gakk, ef þú vreiðr séir;
hyggsk vætr hvatr fyrir."

Iðunn kvað: 16
"Bið ek þik, Bragi, barna sifjar duga
ok allra óskmaga, at þú Loka
kveðir-a lastastöfum Ægis höllu í."

Loki kvað: 17
"Þegi þú, Iðunn, þik kveð ek allra kvenna
vergjarnasta vera, síztu arma þína
lagðir ítrþvegna um þinn bróðurbana."

Iðunn kvað: 18
"Loka ek kveðk-a lastastöfum
Ægis höllu í:
Braga ek kyrri bjórreifan;
vilk-at ek, at it vreiðir vegizk."

Gefjun kvað: 19
"Hví it æsir tveir skuluð inni hérv sáryrðum sakask?
Loftki þat veit, at hann leikinn er
ok hann fjörg öll fía."

Loki kvað: 20
"Þegi þú, Gefjun, þess mun ek nú geta,
er þik glapði at geði sveinn inn hvíti,
er þér sigli gaf ok þú lagðir lær yfir."

Óðinn kvað: 21
"Ærr ertu, Loki, ok örviti,
er þú fær þér Gefjun at gremi,
því at aldar örlög
hygg ek, at hon öll of viti
jafngörla sem ek."

Loki spake: 15
"In thy seat art thou bold, not so are thy deeds,
Bragi, adorner of benches!
Go out and fight if angered thou feelest,
No hero such forethought has."

Ithun spake: 16
"Well, prithee, Bragi, his kinship weigh,
Since chosen as wish-son he was;
And speak not to Loki such words of spite
Here within Ægir's hall."

Loki spake: 17
"Be silent, Ithun! thou art, I say,
Of women most lustful in love,
Since thou thy washed-bright arms didst wind
About thy brother's slayer."

Ithun spake: 18
"To Loki I speak not with spiteful words
Here within Ægir's hall;
And Bragi I calm, who is hot with beer,
For I wish not that fierce they should fight."

Gefjun spake: 19
"Why, ye gods twain, with bitter tongues
Raise hate among us here?
Loki is famed for his mockery foul,
And the dwellers in heaven he hates."

Loki spake: 20
"Be silent, Gefjun! for now shall I say
Who led thee to evil life;
The boy so fair gave a necklace bright,
And about him thy leg was laid."

Odin spake: 21
"Mad art thou, Loki, and little of wit,
The wrath of Gefjun to rouse;
For the fate that is set for all she sees,
Even as I, methinks."

Loki kvað: 22
"Þegi þú, Óðinn, þú kunnir aldregi
deila víg með verum;
oft þú gaft, þeim er þú gefa skyldir-a,
inum slævurum sigr."

Óðinn kvað: 23
"Veiztu, ef ek gaf, þeim er ek gefa né skylda,
inum slævurum, sigr, átta vetr
vartu fyr jörð neðan, kýr mólkandi ok kona,
ok hefr þú þar börn borit, ok hugða ek þat args aðal."

Loki kvað: 24
"En þik síða kóðu Sámseyu í,
ok draptu á vétt sem völur;
vitka líki fórtu verþjóð yfir,
ok hugða ek þat args aðal."

Frigg kvað: 25
"Örlögum ykkrum skylið aldregi
segja seggjum frá, hvat it æsir tveir
drýgðuð í árdaga;
firrisk æ forn rök firar."

Loki kvað: 26
"Þegi þú, Frigg, þú ert Fjörgyns mær
ok hefr æ vergjörn verit, er þá Véa ok Vilja
léztu þér, Viðris kvæn, báða i baðm of tekit."

Frigg kvað: 27
"Veiztu, ef ek inni ættak Ægis höllum i
Baldri líkan bur, út þú né kvæmir
frá ása sonum, ok væri þá at þér vreiðum vegit."

Loki kvað: 28
"Enn vill þú, Frigg, at ek fleiri telja
mína meinstafi:
ek því réð, er þú ríða sér-at
síðan Baldr at sölum."

Loki spake: 22
"Be silent, Odin! not justly thou settest
The fate of the fight among men;
Oft gavst thou to him who deserved not the gift,
To the baser, the battle's prize."

Odin spake: 23
"Though I gave to him who deserved not the gift,
To the baser, the battle's prize;
Winters eight wast thou under the earth,
Milking the cows as a maid,
Ay, and babes didst thou bear;
Unmanly thy soul must seem."

Loki spake: 24
"They say that with spells in Samsey once
Like witches with charms didst thou work;
And in witch's guise among men didst thou go;
Unmanly thy soul must seem."

Frigg spake: 25
"Of the deeds ye two of old have done
Ye should make no speech among men;
Whate'er ye have done in days gone by,
Old tales should ne'er be told."

Loki spake: 26
"Be silent, Frigg! thou art Fjorgyn's wife,
But ever lustful in love;
For Vili and Ve, thou wife of Vithrir,
Both in thy bosom have lain."

Frigg spake: 27
"If a son like Baldr were by me now,
Here within Ægir's hall,
From the sons of the gods thou shouldst go not forth
Till thy fierceness in fight were tried."

Loki spake: 28
"Thou wilt then, Frigg, that further I tell
Of the ill that now I know;
Mine is the blame that Baldr no more
Thou seest ride home to the hall."

Freyja kvað: 29
"Ærr ertu, Loki, er þú yðra telr
ljóta leiðstafi;
örlög Frigg, hygg ek, at öll viti,
þótt hon sjalfgi segi."

Loki kvað: 30
"Þegi þú, Freyja, þik kann ek fullgörva,
er-a þér vamma vant:
ása ok alfa, er hér inni eru,
hverr hefir þinn hór verit."

Freyja kvað: 31
"Flá er þér tunga, hygg ek, at þér fremr myni
ógótt of gala;
reiðir ro þér æsir ok ásynjur,
hryggr muntu heim fara."

Loki kvað: 32
"Þegi þú, Freyja, þú ert fordæða
ok meini blandin mjök, síz þik at bræðr þínum
stóðu blíð regin ok myndir þú þá, Freyja, frata."

Njörðr kvað: 33
"Þat er válítit, þótt sér varðir
vers fái, hós eða hvárs;
hitt er undr, er áss ragr er hér inn of kominn
ok hefir sá börn of borit."

Loki kvað: 34
"Þegi þú, Njörðr, þú vart austr heðan
gíls of sendr at goðum;
Hymis meyjar höfðu þik at hlandtrogi
ok þér i munn migu."

Njörðr kvað: 35
"Sú erumk líkn, er ek vark langt heðan
gísl of sendr at goðum, þá ek mög gat,
þann er mangi fíár, ok þykkir sá ása jaðarr."

Freyja spake:
"Mad art thou, Loki, that known thou makest
The wrong and shame thou hast wrought;
The fate of all does Frigg know well,
Though herself she says it not."

Loki spake:
"Be silent, Freyja! for fully I know thee,
Sinless thou art not thyself;
Of the gods and elves who are gathered here,
Each one as thy lover has lain."

Freyja spake:
"False is thy tongue, and soon shalt thou find
That it sings thee an evil song;
The gods are wroth, and the goddesses all,
And in grief shalt thou homeward go."

Loki spake:
"Be silent, Freyja! thou foulest witch,
And steeped full sore in sin;
In the arms of thy brother the bright gods caught thee
When Freyja her wind set free."

Njorth spake:
"Small ill does it work though a woman may have
A lord or a lover or both;
But a wonder it is that this womanish god
Comes hither, though babes he has borne."

Loki spake:
"Be silent, Njorth; thou wast eastward sent,
To the gods as a hostage given;
And the daughters of Hymir their privy had
When use did they make of thy mouth."

Njorth spake:
"Great was my gain, though long was I gone,
To the gods as a hostage given;
The son did I have whom no man hates,
And foremost of gods is found."

Loki kvað: 36
"Hættu nú, Njörðr, haf þú á hófi þik,
munk-a ek því leyna lengr:
við systur þinni gaztu slíkan mög,
ok er-a þó vánu verr."

Týr kvað: 37
"Freyr er beztr allra ballriða
ása görðum í;
mey hann né grætir né manns konu
ok leysir ór höftum hvern."

Loki kvað: 38
"Þegi þú, Týr, þú kunnir aldregi
bera tilt með tveim;
handar innar hægri mun ek hinnar geta,
er þér sleit Fenrir frá."

Týr kvað: 39
"Handar em ek vanr, en þú hróðrsvitnis,
böl er beggja þrá;
ulfgi hefir ok vel, er í böndum skal
bíða ragnarökrs."

Loki kvað: 40
"Þegi þú, Týr, þat varð þinni konu,
at hon átti mög við mér;
öln né penning hafðir þú þess aldregi
vanréttis, vesall."

Freyr kvað: 41
"Ulfr sé ek liggja árósi fyrir,
unz rjúfask regin; því mundu næst, nema þú nú þegir,
bundinn, bölvasmiðr."

Loki kvað: 42
"Gulli keypta léztu Gymis dóttur
ok seldir þitt svá sverð;
en er Múspells synir ríða Myrkvið yfir,
veizt-a þú þá, vesall, hvé þú vegr."

LOKASENNA

Loki spake: 36
"Give heed now, Njorth, nor boast too high,
No longer I hold it hid;
With thy sister hadst thou so fair a son,
Thus hadst thou no worse a hope."

Tyr spake: 37
"Of the heroes brave is Freyr the best
Here in the home of the gods;
He harms not maids nor the wives of men,
And the bound from their fetters he frees."

Loki spake: 38
"Be silent, Tyr! for between two men
Friendship thou ne'er couldst fashion;
Fain would I tell how Fenrir once
Thy right hand rent from thee."

Tyr spake: 39
"My hand do I lack, but Hrothvitnir thou,
And the loss brings longing to both;
Ill fares the wolf who shall ever await
In fetters the fall of the gods."

Loki spake: 40
"Be silent, Tyr! for a son with me
Thy wife once chanced to win;
Not a penny, methinks, wast thou paid for the wrong,
Nor wast righted an inch, poor wretch."

Freyr spake: 41
"By the mouth of the river the wolf remains
Till the gods to destruction go;
Thou too shalt soon, if thy tongue is not stilled,
Be fettered, thou forger of ill."

Loki spake: 42
"The daughter of Gymir with gold didst thou buy,
And sold thy sword to boot;
But when Muspell's sons through Myrkwood ride,
Thou shalt weaponless wait, poor wretch."

Byggvir kvað: 43
"Veiztu, ef ek eðli ættak sem Ingunar-Freyr
ok svá sælligt setr, mergi smæra
mölða ek þá meinkráku ok lemða alla í liðu."

Loki kvað: 44
"Hvat er þat it litla er ek þat löggra sék
ok snapvíst snapir?
At eyrum Freys mundu æ vera ok und kvernum klaka."

Byggvir kvað: 45
"Byggvir ek heiti, en mik bráðan kveða
goð öll ok gumar;
því em ek hér hróðugr, at drekka Hrofts megir
allir öl saman."

Loki kvað: 46
"Þegi þú, Byggvir, þú kunnir aldregi
deila með mönnum mat, ok þik í flets strái
finna né máttu, þá er vágu verar."

Heimdallr kvað: 47
"Ölr ertu, Loki, svá at þú ert örviti,
hví né lezk-a-ðu, Loki?
því at ofdrykkja veldr alda hveim,
er sína mælgi né man-at."

Loki kvað: 48
"Þegi þú, Heimdallr, þér var í árdaga
it ljóta líf of lagit;
örgu baki þú munt æ vera ok vaka vörðr goða."

Skaði kvað: 49
"Létt er þér, Loki;
mun-at-tu lengi svá leika lausum hala,
því at þik á hjörvi skulu ins hrímkalda magar
görnum binda goð."

Byggvir spake: 43
"Had I birth so famous as Ingunar-Freyr,
And sat in so lofty a seat,
I would crush to marrow this croaker of ill,
And beat all his body to bits."

Loki spake: 44
"What little creature goes crawling there,
Snuffling and snapping about?
At Freyr's ears ever wilt thou be found,
Or muttering hard at the mill."

Byggvir spake: 45
"Byggvir my name, and nimble am I,
As gods and men do grant;
And here am I proud that the children of Hropt
Together all drink ale."

Loki spake: 46
"Be silent, Byggvir! thou never couldst set
Their shares of the meat for men;
Hid in straw on the floor, they found thee not
When heroes were fain to fight."

Heimdall spake: 47
"Drunk art thou, Loki, and mad are thy deeds,
Why, Loki, leavst thou this not?
For drink beyond measure will lead all men
No thought of their tongues to take."

Loki spake: 48
"Be silent, Heimdall! in days long since
Was an evil fate for thee fixed;
With back held stiff must thou ever stand,
As warder of heaven to watch."

Skathi spake: 49
"Light art thou, Loki, but longer thou mayst not
In freedom flourish thy tail;
On the rocks the gods bind thee with bowels torn
Forth from thy frost-cold son."

Loki kvað: 50
"Veiztu, ef mik á hjörvi skulu ins hrímkalda magar
görnum binda goð, fyrstr ok efstr
var ek at fjörlagi, þars vér á Þjaza þrifum."

Skaði kvað: 51
"Veiztu, ef fyrstr ok efstr vartu at fjörlagi,
þá er ér á Þjaza þrifuð, frá mínum véum
ok vöngum skulu þér æ köld ráð koma."

Loki kvað: 52
"Léttari í málum vartu við Laufeyjar son,
þá er þú létz mér á beð þinn boðit;
getit verðr oss slíks, ef vér görva skulum
telja vömmin vár."

þá gekk Sif fram ok byrlaði Loka í hrímkálki mjöð ok mælti:

"Heill ver þú nú, Loki, ok tak við hrímkálki 53
fullum forns mjaðar, heldr þú hana eina
látir með ása sonum vammalausa vera."

Hann tók við horni ok drakk af:

"Ein þú værir, ef þú svá værir, 54
vör ok gröm at veri;
einn ek veit, svá at ek vita þykkjumk,
hór ok af Hlórriða, ok var þat sá inn lævísi Loki."

Beyla kvað: 55
"Fjöll öll skjalfa;
hygg ek á för vera heiman Hlórriða;
han ræðr ró, þeim er rægir hér
goð öll ok guma."

Loki spake: 50
"Though on rocks the gods bind me with bowels torn
Forth from my frost-cold son,
I was first and last at the deadly fight
There where Thjazi we caught."

Skathi spake: 51
"Wert thou first and last at the deadly fight
There where Thjazi was caught,
From my dwellings and fields shall ever come forth
A counsel cold for thee."

Loki spake: 52
"More lightly thou spakest with Laufey's son,
When thou badst me come to thy bed;
Such things must be known if now we two
Shall seek our sins to tell."

Then Sif came forward and poured mead for Loki in a crystal cup, and said:

"Hail too thee, Loki, and take thou here   53
The crystal cup of old mead;
For me at least, alone of the gods,
Blameless thou knowest to be."

He took the horn, and drank therefrom:

"Alone thou wert if truly thou wouldst   54
All men so shyly shun;
But one do I know full well, methinks,
Who had thee from Hlorrithi's arms—
Loki the crafty in lies."

Beyla spake: 55
"The mountains shake, and surely I think
From his home comes Hlorrithi now;
He will silence the man who is slandering here
Together both gods and men."

Loki kvað: 56
"Þegi þú, Beyla, þú ert Byggvis kvæn
ok meini blandinn mjök, ókynjan meira
kom-a med ása sonum;
öll ertu, deigja, dritin."

Þá kom Þórr at ok kvað:

"Þegi þú, rög vættr, þér skal minn þrúðhamarr, 57
Mjöllnir, mál fyrnema;
herðaklett drep ek þér halsi af,
ok verðr þá þínu fjörvi of farit."

Loki kvað: 58
"Jarðar burr er hér nú inn kominn,
hví þrasir þú svá, Þórr?
En þá þorir þú ekki, er þú skalt við ulfinn vega,
ok svelgr hann allan Sigföður."

Hann tók við horni ok drakk af:

Þórr kvað: 59
"Þegi þú, rög vættr, þér skal minn þrúðhamarr,
Mjöllnir, mál fyrnema;
upp ek þér verp ok á austrvega,
síðan þik manngi sér."

Loki kvað: 60
"Austrförum þínum skaltu aldregi
segja seggjum frá, síz í hanska þumlungi
hnúkðir þú einheri, ok þóttisk-a þú þá Þórr vera."

Þórr kvað: 61
"Þegi þú, rög vættr, þér skal minn þrúðhamarr,
Mjöllnir, mál fyrnema;
hendi inni hægri drep ek þik Hrungnis bana,
svá at þér brotnar beina hvat."

Loki spake: 56
"Be silent, Beyla! thou art Byggvir's wife,
And deep art thou steeped in sin;
A greater shame to the gods came ne'er,
Befouled thou art with thy filth."

Then came Thor forth, and spake:

"Unmanly one, cease, or the mighty hammer, 57
Mjollnir, shall close thy mouth;
Thy shoulder-cliff shall I cleave from thy neck,
And so shall thy life be lost."

Loki spake: 58
"Lo, in has come the son of Earth:
Why threaten so loudly, Thor?
Less fierce thou shalt go to fight with the wolf
When he swallows Sigfather up."

Thor spake: 59
"Unmanly one, cease, or the mighty hammer,
Mjollnir, shall close thy mouth;
I shall hurl thee up and out in the East,
Where men shall see thee no more."

Loki spake: 60
"That thou hast fared on the East-road forth
To men shouldst thou say no more;
In the thumb of a glove didst thou hide, thou great one,
And there forgot thou wast Thor."

Thor spake: 61
"Unmanly one, cease, or the mighty hammer,
Mjollnir, shall close thy mouth;
My right hand shall smite thee with Hrungnir's slayer,
Till all thy bones are broken."

Loki kvað: 62
"Lifa ætla ek mér langan aldr,
þóttú hætir hamri mér;
skarpar álar þóttu þér Skrýmis vera,
ok máttir-a þú þá nesti ná,
ok svalzt þú þá hungri heill."

Þórr kvað: 63
"Þegi þú, rög vættr, þér skal minn þrúðhamarr,
Mjöllnir, mál fyrnema;
Hrungnis bani mun þér í hel koma
fyr nágrindr neðan."

Loki kvað: 64
"Kvað ek fyr ásum, kvað ek fyr ása sonum,
þats mik hvatti hugr, en fyr þér einum
mun ek út ganga, því at ek veit, at þú vegr.

Öl gerðir þú, Ægir, en þú aldri munt 65
síðan sumbl of gera;
eiga þín öll, er hér inni er,
leiki yfir logi, ok brenni þér á baki."

En eftir þetta falst Loki í Fránangrsforsi í lax líki. Þar tóku æsir hann. Hann var bundinn með þörmum sonar síns, Vála, en Narfi, sonr hans, varð at vargi. Skaði tók eitrorm ok festi upp yfir annlit Loka. Draup þar ór eitr. Sigyn, kona Loka, sat þar ok helt munnlaug undir eitrið. En er munnlaugin var full, bar hon út eitrið, en meðan draup eitrit á Loka. Þá kippðist hann svá hart við, at þaðan af skalf jörð öll. Þat eru nú kallaðir landsskjálftar.

Loki spake: 62
"Along time still do I think to live,
Though thou threatenest thus with thy hammer;
Rough seemed the straps of Skrymir's wallet,
When thy meat thou mightest not get,
And faint from hunger didst feel."

Thor spake: 63
"Unmanly one, cease, or the mighty hammer,
Mjollnir, shall close thy mouth;
The slayer of Hrungnir shall send thee to hell,
And down to the gate of death."

Loki spake: 64
"I have said to the gods and the sons of the god,
The things that whetted my thoughts;
But before thee alone do I now go forth,
For thou fightest well, I ween."

"Ale hast thou brewed, but, Ægir, now 65
Such feasts shalt thou make no more;
O'er all that thou hast which is here within
Shall play the flickering flames,
And thy back shall be burnt with fire."

And after that Loki hid himself in Franang's waterfall in the guise of a salmon, and there the gods took him. He was bound with the bowels of his son Vali, but his son Narfi was changed to a wolf. Skathi took a poison-snake and fastened it up over Loki's face, and the poison dropped thereon. Sigyn, Loki's wife, sat there and held a shell under the poison, but when the shell was full she bore away the poison, and meanwhile the poison dropped on Loki. Then he struggled so hard that the whole earth shook therewith; and now that is called an earthquake.

ENDNOTES

Prose. Ægir: the [sea-giant]; Snorri gives Hler as another of his names, but he is not elsewhere called Gymir, which is the name of the giant, Gerth's father, in the *Skirnismol*. On Ægir cf. *Grimnismol*, 45, and *Hymiskvitha*, 1. *Frigg*: though Odin's wife is often mentioned, she plays only a minor part in the *Eddic* poems; cf. *Voluspo*, 34, *Vafthruthnismol*, 1, and *Grimnismol*, introductory prose. *Thor*: the compiler is apparently a trifle confused as to Thor's movements; the "Journey in the East" here mentioned cannot be the one described in the *Hymiskvitha*, nor yet the one narrated by Snorri, as Loki was with Thor throughout that expedition. He probably means no more than that Thor was off killing giants. *Sif*: concerning Thor's wife the chief incident is that Loki cut off her hair, and, at the command of the wrathful Thor, was compelled to have the dwarfs fashion her a new supply of hair out of gold; cf. *Harbarthsljoth*, 48. *Bragi*: the god of poetry; cf. *Grimnismol*, 44 and note. *Ithun*: the goddess of youth; cf. note on *Skirnismol*, 19. Ithun is not mentioned by name in any other of the *Eddic* poems, but Snorri tells in detail how the giant Thjazi stole her and her apples, explaining the reference in *Harbarthsljoth*, 19 (q. v.). *Tyr*: the god of battle; cf. *Hymiskvitha*, 4, and (concerning his dealings with the wolf Fenrir) *Voluspo*, 39, note. *Njorth*: the chief of the Wanes, and father of *Freyr* and *Freyja*; cf. (concerning the whole family) *Skirnismol*, introductory prose and note, also *Voluspo*, 21 and note. *Skathi*: Njorth's wife was the daughter of the giant Thjazi; cf. *Harbarthsljoth*, 19, note, and *Grimnismol*, 11. *Vithar*: the silent god, the son of Odin who avenged his father by slaying the wolf Fenrir; cf. *Voluspo*, 54, *Vafthruthnismol*, 51, and *Grimnismol*, 17. *Loki*: [erstwhile ally of the Gods and hence their enemy]; in addition to the many references to his career in the *Lokasenna*, cf. particularly *Voluspo*, 32 and 35, and notes. *Byggvir and Beyla*: not mentioned elsewhere in the poems; Freyr's conspicuous servant is Skirnir, hero of the *Skirnismol. Fimafeng* ("The Swift Handler") and *Eldir* ("The Man of the Fire"): mentioned only in connection with this incident. *Glittering gold*: Ægir's use of gold to light his hall, which was often thought of as under the sea, was responsible for the phrase "flame of the flood," and sundry kindred phrases, meaning "gold."

6. *Lopt*: another name for Loki; cf. *Hyndluljoth*, 43, and *Svipdagsmol*, 42.

7. In the manuscript this stanza begins with a small letter, and Heinzel unites it with stanza 6.

8. *Bragi*: cf. note on introductory prose. Why Loki taunts him with cowardice (stanzas 11, 13, 15) is not clear, for poetry, of which Bragi was the patron, was generally associated in the Norse mind with peculiar valor, and most of the skaldic poets were likewise noted fighters.

9. There exists no account of any incident in which Odin and Loki thus swore blood-brotherhood, but they were so often allied in enterprises that the idea is wholly reasonable. The common process of "mingling blood" was carried out quite literally, and the promise of which Loki speaks is characteristic of those which, in the sagas, often accompanied the ceremony; cf. *Brot af Sigurtharkvithu*, 18 and note.

10. In stanzas 10–31 the manuscript has nothing to indicate the identity of the several speakers, but these are uniformly clear enough through the context. *Vithar*: cf. note on introductory prose. *The wolf's father*: Loki; cf. *Voluspo*, 39 and note.

13. Sijmons makes one line of lines 4–5 by cutting out a part of each; Finnur Jonsson rejects 5 as spurious.

14. The text of line 4 is somewhat obscure, and has been variously emended, one often adopted suggestion making the line read, "Little is that for thy lies."

15. *Adorner of benches*: this epithet presumably implies that Bragi is not only slothful, but also effeminate, for a very similar word, "pride of the benches," means a bride.

16. *Ithun*: Bragi's wife; cf. note on introductory prose. The goddesses who, finding that their husbands are getting the worst of it, take up the cudgels with Loki, all find themselves confronted with [similar slanders]; cf. stanzas 26 (Frigg), 52 (Skathi) and 54 (Sif). Gefjun and Freyja are silenced in similar fashion. *Wish-son*: adopted son; Loki was the son of the

giant Farbauti and the giantess Laufey, and hence was not of the race of the gods, but had been virtually adopted by Odin, who subsequently had good reason to regret it.

17. We do not even know who Ithun's brother was, much less who slew him.

19. *Gefjun*: a goddess, not elsewhere mentioned in the poems, who, according to Snorri, was served by the women who died maidens. Beyond this nothing is known of her. Lines 3–4 in the manuscript are puzzling, and have been freely emended.

20. Nothing is known of the incident here mentioned. There is a good deal of confusion as to various of the gods and goddesses, and it has been suggested that Gefjun is really Frigg under another name, with a little of Freyja—whose attributes were frequently confused with Frigg's—thrown in. Certainly Odin's answer (stanza 21, lines 3–4) fits Frigg perfectly, for she shared his knowledge of the future, whereas it has no relation to anything known of Gefjun. As for the necklace (line 3), it may be the Brisings' necklace, which appears in the *Thrymskvitha* as Freyja's, but which, in some mythological writings, is assigned to Frigg.

21. Snorri quotes line 1; cf. note on stanza 29.

23. There is no other reference to Loki's having spent eight years underground, or to his cow-milking. On one occasion, however, he did bear offspring. A giant had undertaken to build the gods a fortress, his reward being Freyja and the sun and moon, provided the work was done by a given time. His sole helper was his horse, Svathilfari. The work being nearly done, and the gods fearing to lose Freyja and the sun and moon, Loki turned himself into a mare, and so effectually distracted Svathilfari from his task that shortly afterwards Loki gave birth to Odin's eight-legged horse, Sleipnir. In such contests of abuse a man was not infrequently taunted with having borne children; cf. *Helgakvitha Hundingsbana* I, 39–45. One or two of the last three lines may be spurious.

24. *Samsey*: perhaps the Danish island of Samsö. Odin was the god of magic, but there is no other reference to his ever having disguised himself as a witch.

25. Frigg: Odin's wife; cf. note to introductory prose.

24. *Samsey*: perhaps the Danish island of Samsö. Odin was the god of magic, but there is no other reference to his ever having disguised himself as a witch.

25. *Frigg*: Odin's wife; cf. note to introductory prose.

26. *Fjorgyn*: Odin; cf. *Voluspo*, 56 and note. *Vili and Ve*: Odin's brothers, who appear merely as, with Odin, the sons of Bur and Bestla; cf. *Voluspo*, 4. The *Ynglingasaga* says that, during one of Odin's protracted absences, his two brothers took Frigg as their mistress. *Vithrir*: another name for Odin.

27. On the death of Baldr, slain through Loki's cunning by the blind Hoth, cf. *Voluspo*, 32 and note.

29. *Freyja*: daughter of Njorth and sister of Freyr; cf. note on introductory prose. Snorri, in speaking of Frigg's knowledge of the future, makes a stanza out of *Lokasenna*, 21, 1; 47, 2; 29, 3-4, thus: "Mad art thou, Loki, and little of wit, / Why, Loki, leavst thou this not? / The fate of all does Frigg know well, / Though herself she says it not."

30. According to Snorri, Freyja was a model of fidelity to her husband, Oth, [and in *Thrysmkvitha* she is outraged at the suggestion that she may appear lustful or immodest].

32. Before each of stanzas 32-42 the manuscript indicates the speaker, through the initial letter of the name written in the margin. *Thy brother*: Freyr; there is no other indication that such a relation existed between these two, but they themselves were the product of such a union; cf. stanza 36 and note.

33. *Njorth*: father of Freyr and Freyja, and given by the Wanes as a hostage, in exchange for Hönir, at the close of the first war; cf. *Voluspo*, 21 and note, also *Skirnismol*, introductory prose and note. *Babes*: cf. stanza 23 and note. Bugge suggests that this clause may have been a late insertion.

34. *Daughters of Hymir*: we have no clue to who these were, though Hymir is doubtless the frost-giant of the Hymiskvitha (q.v.). Loki's point is that Njorth is not a god, but the product of an inferior race (the Wanes).

35. *The son*: Freyr.

36. *Thy sister*: the *Ynglingasaga* supports this story of Njorth's having had two children by his sister before he came among the gods. Snorri, on the other hand, specifically says that Freyr and Freyja were born after Njorth came to the gods.

37. *Tyr*: the god of battle; cf. notes on *Hymiskvitha*, 4, and *Voluspo*, 39. *Freyr*; concerning his noble qualities cf. *Skirnismol*, introductory prose

and note.

38. Snorri mentions Tyr's incompetence as a peacemaker. *Fenrir*: the wolf, Loki's son; cf. *Voluspo*, 39.

39. *Hrothvitnir* ("The Mighty Wolf"): Fenrir, who awaits in chains the final battle and death at the hands of Vithar. The manuscript has a metrical error in line 3, which has led to various emendations, all with much the same meaning.

40. *Thy wife*: there is no other reference to Tyr's wife, nor do we know who was the son in question.

41. *The mouth of the river*: according to Snorri, the chained Fenrir "roars horribly, and the slaver runs from his mouth, and makes the river called Vam; he lies there till the doom of the gods." Freyr's threat is actually carried out; cf. concluding prose.

42. *The daughter of Gymir*: Gerth, heroine of the *Skirnismol*, which gives the details of Freyr's loss of his sword. *Muspell's sons*: the name Muspell is not used elsewhere in the poems; Snorri uses it frequently, but only in this same phrase, "Muspell's sons." They are the dwellers in the fireworld, Muspellsheim, led by Surt against the gods in the last battle; cf. *Voluspo*, 47 and 52 and notes. *Myrkwood*: here the dark forest bounding the fire-world; in the *Atlakvitha* (stanza 3) the name is used of another boundary forest.

43. *Byggvir*: one of Freyr's two servants; cf. introductory prose. *Ingunar-Freyr*: the name is not used elsewhere in the poems, or by Snorri; it may be the genitive of a woman's name, Ingun, the unknown sister of Njorth who was Freyr's mother (cf. stanza 36), or a corruption of the name Ingw, used for Freyr (Fro) in old German mythology.

44. Beginning with this stanza, the names of the speakers are lacking in the manuscript. *The mill*: i.e., at slaves' tasks.

45. Nothing further is known of either Byggvir's swiftness or his cowardice. *Hropt*: Odin.

47. *Heimdall*: besides being the watchman of the gods (cf. *Voluspo*, 27), he appears also as the god of light (cf. *Thrymskvitha*, 14), and possibly also as a complex cultural deity in the *Rigsthula*. He was a son of Odin, born of nine sisters; cf. *Hyndluljoth*, 37–40. In the last battle he and Loki slay one another. Line 2 is quoted by Snorri; cf. stanza 29, note.

49. *Skathi*: the wife of Njorth, and daughter of the giant Thjazi, concern-

ing whose death cf. *Harbarthsljoth*, 19, note. *Bowels*, etc.: according to the prose note at the end of the *Lokasenna*, the gods bound Loki with the bowels of his son Vali, and changed his other son, Narfi, into a wolf. Snorri turns the story about, Vali being the wolf, who tears his brother to pieces, the gods then using Narfi's intestines to bind Loki. Narfi—and presumably Vali—were the sons of Loki and his wife, Sigyn. They appear only in this episode, though Narfi (or Nari) is named by Snorri in his list of Loki's children. Cf. concluding prose, and note.

52. *Laufey's son*: Loki; not much is known of his parents beyond their names. His father was the giant Farbauti, his mother Laufey, sometimes called Nal. There is an elaborate but far-fetched hypothesis explaining these three on the basis of a nature-myth. 'There is no other reference to such a relation between Skathi and Loki as he here suggests.

53. *Sif*: Thor's wife; cf. *Harbarthsljoth*, 48, where her infidelity is again mentioned. The manuscript omits the proper name from the preceding prose, and a few editors have, obviously in error, attributed the speech to Beyla.

54. *Hlorrithi*: Thor. Line 5 is probably spurious.

55. *Beyla*: Freyr's servant, wife of Byggvir; cf. introductory prose and note.

57. *Mjollnir*: concerning Thor's famous hammer see particularly *Thrymskvitha*, 1 and note. *Shoulder-cliff*: head; concerning the use of such diction in the *Edda*, cf. introductory note to *Hymiskvitha* [Appendix B]. The manuscript indicates line 3 as the beginning of a stanza, but this is apparently a scribal error.

58. *Son of Earth*: Thor, son of Odin and Jorth (Earth). The manuscript omits the word "son," but all editors have agreed in supplying it. *The wolf*: Fenrir, Loki's son, who slays Odin (*Sigfather*: "Father of Victory") in the final battle. Thor, according to Snorri and to the *Voluspo*, 56, fights with Mithgarthsorm and not with Fenrir, who is killed by Vithar.

59. Lines 1–2 are abbreviated in the manuscript, as also in stanzas 61 and 63.

60. Loki's taunt that Thor hid in the thumb of Skrymir's glove is similar to that of Odin, *Harbarthsljoth*, 26, in the note to which the story is outlined. Line 4 is identical with line 3 of *Harbarthsljoth*, 26.

61. *Hrungnir's slayer*: the hammer; the story of how Thor slew this

stone-headed giant is indicated in *Harbarthsljoth*, 14–15, and outlined in the note to stanza 14 of that poem.

62. On the day following the adventure of the glove, Thor, Loki and Thor's servants proceed on their way in company with Skrymir, who puts all their food in his wallet. At evening Skrymir goes to sleep, and Thor tries to get at the food, but cannot loosen the straps of the wallet. In a rage he smites Skrymir three times on the head with his hammer, but the giant—[who was merely an illusion]—is totally undisturbed. Line 5 may well be spurious.

65. *The flames*: the fire that consumes the world on the last day; cf. *Voluspo*, 57. Line 5 may be spurious.

Prose: Snorri tells the same story, with minor differences, but makes it the consequence of Loki's part in the slaying of Baldr, which undoubtedly represents the correct tradition. The compiler of the poems either was confused or thought the incident was useful as indicating what finally happened to Loki. Possibly he did not mean to imply that Loki's fate was brought upon him by his abuse of the gods, but simply tried to round out the story. *Franang*: "Gleaming Water." *Vali and Narfi*: cf. stanza 49 and note. *Sigyn*: cf. *Voluspo*, 35, the only other place where she is mentioned in the poems. Snorri omits the naive note about earthquakes, his narrative ending with the words, "And there he lies till the destruction of the gods."

THRYMSKVITHA
THE LAY OF THRYM

INTRODUCTION

The *Thrymskvitha* is found only in *Codex Regius* but is nevertheless one of the most historically popular of the *Eddic* poems, not only in the modern day in light of its narrative skill and panache, but also in the medieval and early modern period when it was the topic of several popular songs and ballads in Iceland, the Faroe Islands, and Scandinavia itself up to the 19th century.

The actual dating of the *Thrymskvitha* is subject to scholarly dispute. Early acceptance of a composition around the year 900 has given way to more modern examination by scholars such as Jakobsen and Hallberg who have argued for a very late post-Christian origin, with Jacobsen even offering Snorri himself as the author due to the poem's stylistic and verbal similarities to older *Eddic* poems, suggesting that they may have been deliberately studied and copied in its creation, but also due to the comedic portrayal of the Gods presented, the composition of which many scholars consider to be unlikely during a period of authentic religious piety.

Another possible author is the same individual who wrote *Skirnismol*, *Baldrsdraumar* and the *Lokasenna*. This particular explanation may go some way toward explaining some of the textual inconsistencies we see between the portrayal of Freya as utterly indignant to sexual immorality and social shame versus the portrayal of her as sexually promiscuous, which may showcase a differing view of the Goddess within the context of a cultic group centered around her brother, and which seems rather unlikely if the author was a Christian intent on ridiculing the Gods. Likewise, archaeological finds from Iceland such as the Eyrarland Statue (dated to the year 1000), believed to represent Thor finally receiving his hammer from a seated position at the wedding feast and grasping it with both hands, imply a latest date for at least part of the story's events within the Norse mythological tradition.

Many of the comedic and narrative elements of the story require a cultural familiarity with the Norse tradition of laws and behavior, in particular the status of *ragr* or its grammatical variant *argr*, meaning "unmanly, cowardly, homosexual" and constituting the highest degree of insult and accusation among the Nordic peoples, which Thor uses when he exclaims: "Mik munu æsir *argan* kalla"—rendered by Bellows as "Me would the gods *unmanly* call"—and his humorous inability to properly disguise himself as a woman, with his virility and masculinity being perfectly obvious despite his clothing and attempted demeanor. This is counterpoised by the person of Loki dressed as "Freya's" female maid, who presents no such issues in gender swapping and refers to himself casually using the neuter plural form of the numeral two, *tvau*, in an obvious reference to his own neuter position in regards to proper Norse gender roles and behavior.

Of particular interest are the familiar renditions of Thor's excuses to the giant Thrymr while at the wedding to explain his inconsistent appearance, being the origin of the early modern folk story of *Little Red Riding Hood* and the big bad wolf's comedic excuses for why he obviously does not resemble Red's grandmother, again showcasing the continuing popularity and influence of the poem within the spheres of northern Europe.

Thor and the Giants
(M. E. Winge)

Vreiðr var þá Vingþórr   er hann vaknaði   1
ok síns hamars   of saknaði,
skegg nam at hrista,   skör nam at dýja,
réð Jarðar burr   um at þreifask.

Ok hann þat orða   alls fyrst of kvað: 2
"Heyrðu nú, Loki,   hvat ek nú mæli
er eigi veit   jarðar hvergi
né upphimins:
áss er stolinn hamri!"

Gengu þeir fagra   Freyju túna,   3
ok hann þat orða   alls fyrst of kvað:
"Muntu mér, Freyja,   fjaðrhams léa,
ef ek minn hamar   mættak hitta?"

Freyja kvað: 4
"Þó munda ek gefa þér   þótt ór gulli væri,
ok þó selja,   at væri ór silfri."

Fló þá Loki,   fjaðrhamr dunði,   5
unz fyr útan kom   ása garða
ok fyr innan kom   jötna heima.

THRYMSKVITHA

Wild was Vingthor when he awoke, 1
And when his mighty hammer he missed;
He shook his beard, his hair was bristling,
As the son of Jorth about him sought.

Hear now the speech that first he spake: 2
"Harken, Loki, and heed my words,
Nowhere on earth is it known to man,
Nor in heaven above: our hammer is stolen."

To the dwelling fair of Freyja went they, 3
Hear now the speech that first he spake:
"Wilt thou, Freyja, thy feather-dress lend me,
That so my hammer I may seek?"

Freyja spake: 4
"Thine should it be though of silver bright,
And I would give it though 'twere of gold."
Then Loki flew, and the feather-dress whirred,
Till he left behind him the home of the gods,
And reached at last the realm of the giants.

Thrym sat on a mound, the giants' master, 5
Leashes of gold he laid for his dogs,
And stroked and smoothed the manes of his steeds.

Þrymr sat á haugi,   þursa dróttinn,   6
greyjum sínum   gullbönd sneri
ok mörum sínum   mön jafnaði.

Þrymr kvað: 7
"Hvat er með ásum?   Hvat er með alfum?
Hví ertu einn kominn   í Jötunheima?"
Loki kvað:
"Illt er með ásum,   illt er með alfum;
hefr þú Hlórriða   hamar of folginn?"

Þrymr kvað: 8
"Ek hef Hlórriða   hamar of folginn
átta röstum   fyr jörð neðan;
hann engi maðr   aftr of heimtir,
nema færi mér   Freyju at kvæn."

Fló þá Loki,   fjaðrhamr dunði,   9
unz fyr útan kom   jötna heima
ok fyr innan   kom ása garða.
Mætti hann Þór   miðra garða,
ok þat hann orða   alls fyrst of kvað:

"Hefr þú erendi   sem erfiði?   10
Segðu á lofti   löng tíðendi,
oft sitjanda   sögur of fallask
ok liggjandi   lygi of bellir."

Loki kvað: 11
"Hef ek erfiði   ok erendi;
Þrymr hefr þinn hamar,   þursa dróttinn;
hann engi maðr   aftr of heimtir,
nema hánum færi   Freyju at kván.

Ganga þeir fagra   Freyju at hitta,   12
ok hann þat orða   alls fyrst of kvað:
"Bittu þik, Freyja,   brúðar líni;
vit skulum aka tvau   í Jötunheima."

Reið varð þá Freyja   ok fnasaði,   13
allr ása salr   undir bifðisk,
stökk þat it mikla   men Brísinga:
"Mik veiztu verða   vergjarnasta,
ef ek ek með þér   í Jötunheima."

Thrym spake: 6
"How fare the gods, how fare the elves?
Why comst thou alone to the giants' land?"

Loki spake:
"Ill fare the gods, ill fare the elves!
Hast thou hidden Hlorrithi's hammer?"

Thrym spake: 7
"I have hidden Hlorrithi's hammer,
Eight miles down deep in the earth;
And back again shall no man bring it
If Freyja I win not to be my wife."

Then Loki flew, and the feather-dress whirred, 8
Till he left behind him the home of the giants,
And reached at last the realm of the gods.
There in the courtyard Thor he met:
Hear now the speech that first he spake:

"Hast thou found tidings as well as trouble? 9
Thy news in the air shalt thou utter now;
Oft doth the sitter his story forget,
And lies he speaks who lays himself down."

Loki spake: 10
"Trouble I have, and tidings as well:
Thrym, king of the giants, keeps thy hammer,
And back again shall no man bring it
If Freyja he wins not to be his wife."

Freyja the fair then went they to find 11
Hear now the speech that first he spake:
"Bind on, Freyja, the bridal veil,
For we two must haste to the giants' home."

Wrathful was Freyja, and fiercely she snorted, 12
And the dwelling great of the gods was shaken,
And burst was the mighty Brisings' necklace:
"Most lustful indeed should I look to all
If I journeyed with thee to the giants' home."

Then were the gods together met, 13
And the goddesses came and council held,
And the far-famed ones a plan would find,
How they might Hlorrithi's hammer win.

Senn váru æsir   allir á þingi   14
ok ásynjur   allar á máli,
ok um þat réðu   ríkir tívar
hvé þeir Hlórriða   hamar of sætti.

Þá kvað þat Heimdallr,   hvítastr ása,   15
vissi hann vel fram   sem vanir aðrir:
"Bindum vér Þór þá   brúðar líni,
hafi hann it mikla   men Brísinga.

Látum und hánum   hrynja lukla   16
ok kvenváðir   um kné falla,
en á brjósti   breiða steina
ok hagliga   um höfuð typpum."

Þá kvað þat Þór,   þrúðugr áss: 17
"Mik munu æsir   argan kalla,
ef ek bindask læt   brúðar líni!"

Þá kvað þat Loki   Laufeyjar sonr: 18
"Þegi þú, Þórr,   þeira orða.
Þegar munu jötnar   Ásgarð búa,
nema þú þinn hamar   þér of heimtir."

Bundu þeir Þór þá   brúðar líni   19
ok inu mikla   meni Brísinga,
létu und hánum   hrynja lukla
ok kvenváðir   um kné falla,
en á brjósti   breiða steina,
ok hagliga   um höfuð typpðu.

Þá kvað Loki   Laufeyjar sonr: 20
"Mun ek ok með þér   ambótt vera,
vit skulum aka tvær   í Jötunheima."

Senn váru hafrar   heim of reknir,   21
skyndir at sköklum,   skyldu vel renna;
björg brotnuðu,   brann jörð loga,
ók Óðins sonr   í Jötunheima.

Þá kvað þat Þrymr,   þursa dróttinn: 22
"Standið upp, jötnar,   ok stráið bekki,
nú færa mér   Freyju at kván
Njarðar dóttur   ór Nóatúnum.

Then Heimdall spake, whitest of the gods,   14
Like the Wanes he knew the future well:
"Bind we on Thor the bridal veil,
Let him bear the mighty Brisings' necklace;

"Keys around him let there rattle,   15
And down to his knees hang woman's dress;
With gems full broad upon his breast,
And a pretty cap to crown his head."

Then Thor the mighty his answer made: 16
"Me would the gods unmanly call
If I let bind the bridal veil."

Then Loki spake, the son of Laufey: 17
"Be silent, Thor, and speak not thus;
Else will the giants in Asgarth dwell
If thy hammer is brought not home to thee."

Then bound they on Thor the bridal veil,   18
And next the mighty Brisings' necklace.

Keys around him let they rattle,   19
And down to his knees hung woman's dress;
With gems full broad upon his breast,
And a pretty cap to crown his head.

Then Loki spake, the son of Laufey: 20
"As thy maid-servant thither I go with thee;
We two shall haste to the giants' home."

Then home the goats to the hall were driven,   21
They wrenched at the halters, swift were they to run;
The mountains burst, earth burned with fire,
And Odin's son sought Jotunheim.

Then loud spake Thrym, the giants' leader: 22
"Bestir ye, giants, put straw on the benches;
Now Freyja they bring to be my bride,
The daughter of Njorth out of Noatun.

Ganga hér at garði   gullhyrnðar kýr,   23
öxn alsvartir   jötni at gamni;
fjölð á ek meiðma,   fjölð á ek menja,
einnar mér Freyju   ávant þykkir."

Var þar at kveldi   of komit snemma   24
ok fyr jötna   öl fram borit;
einn át oxa,   átta laxa,
krásir allar,   þær er konur skyldu,
drakk Sifjar verr   sáld þrjú mjaðar.

Þá kvat þat Þrymr,   þursa dróttinn: 25
"Hvar sáttu brúðir   bíta hvassara?
Sák-a ek brúðir   bíta breiðara,
né inn meira mjöð   mey of drekka."

Sat in alsnotra   ambótt fyrir,   26
er orð of fann   við jötuns máli:
"Át vætr Freyja   átta nóttum,
svá var hon óðfús   í Jötunheima."

Laut und línu,   lysti at kyssa,   27
en hann útan stökk   endlangan sal:
"Hví eru öndótt   augu Freyju?
Þykki mér ór augum   eldr of brenna."

Sat in alsnotra   ambótt fyrir,   28
er orð of fann   við jötuns máli:
"Svaf vætr Freyja   átta nóttum,
svá var hon óðfús   í Jötunheima."

Inn kom in arma   jötna systir,   29
hin er brúðféar   biðja þorði:
"Láttu þér af höndum   hringa rauða,
ef þú öðlask vill   ástir mínar,
ástir mínar,   alla hylli.

Þá kvað þat Þrymr,   þursa dróttinn: 30
"Berið inn hamar   brúði at vígja,
lekkið Mjöllni   í meyjar kné,
vígið okkr saman   Várar hendi."

Hló Hlórriða   hugr í brjósti,   31
er harðhugaðr   hamar of þekkði;
Þrym drap hann fyrstan,   þursa dróttin,
ok ætt jötuns   alla lamði.

"Gold-horned cattle go to my stables, 23
Jet-black oxen, the giant's joy;
Many my gems, and many my jewels,
Freyja alone did I lack, methinks."

Early it was to evening come, 24
And forth was borne the beer for the giants;
Thor alone ate an ox, and eight salmon,
All the dainties as well that were set for the women;
And drank Sif's mate three tuns of mead.

Then loud spake Thrym, the giants' leader: 25
"Who ever saw bride more keenly bite?
I ne'er saw bride with a broader bite,
Nor a maiden who drank more mead than this!"

Hard by there sat the serving-maid wise, 26
So well she answered the giant's words:
"From food has Freyja eight nights fasted,
So hot was her longing for Jotunheim."

Thrym looked 'neath the veil, for he longed to kiss, 27
But back he leaped the length of the hall:
"Why are so fearful the eyes of Freyja?
Fire, methinks, from her eyes burns forth."

Hard by there sat the serving-maid wise, 28
So well she answered the giant's words:
"No sleep has Freyja for eight nights found,
So hot was her longing for Jotunheim."

Soon came the giant's luckless sister, 29
Who feared not to ask the bridal fee:
"From thy hands the rings of red gold take,
If thou wouldst win my willing love,
My willing love and welcome glad."

Then loud spake Thrym, the giants' leader: 30
"Bring in the hammer to hallow the bride;
On the maiden's knees let Mjollnir lie,
That us both the band of Vor may bless."

The heart in the breast of Hlorrithi laughed 31
When the hard-souled one his hammer beheld;
First Thrym, the king of the giants, he killed,
Then all the folk of the giants he felled.

Drap hann ina öldnu   jötna systur, 32
hin er brúðféar   of beðit hafði;
hon skell of hlaut   fyr skillinga,
en högg hamars   fyr hringa fjölð.

Svá kom Óðins sonr   endr at hamri. 33

The giant's sister old he slew, 32
She who had begged the bridal fee;
A stroke she got in the shilling's stead,
And for many rings the might of the hammer.

And so his hammer got Odin's son. 33

ENDNOTES

1. *Vingthor* ("Thor the Hurler"): another name for Thor, equivalent to Vingnir (*Vafthruthnismol*, 51). Concerning Thor and his hammer, Mjollnir, cf. *Hymiskvitha, Lokasenna,* and *Harbarthsljoth, passim. Jorth*: Earth, Thor's mother, Odin being his father.

2. *Loki*: cf. *Lokasenna, passim.*

3. *Freyja*: Njorth's daughter, and sister of Freyr; cf. *Lokasenna*, introductory prose and note, also *Skirnismol*, introductory prose. Freyja's house was Sessrymnir ("Rich in Seats") built in Folkvang ("Field of the Folk"); cf. *Grimnismol*, 14. *Feather-dress*: this flying equipment of Freyja's is also used in the story of Thjazi, wherein Loki again borrows the "hawk's dress" of Freyja, this time to rescue Ithun; cf. *Harbarthsljoth*, 19 and note.

4. The manuscript and most editions have lines 1–2 in inverse order. Several editors assume a lacuna before line 1, making a stanza out of the two conjectural lines (Bugge actually supplies them) and lines 1–2 of stanza 4. Thus they either make a separate stanza out of lines 3–5 or unite them in a six-line stanza with 5. The manuscript punctuation and capitalization—not wholly trustworthy guides—indicate the stanza divisions as in this translation.

6. *Line 1*: cf. *Voluspo*, 48, 1. The manuscript does not indicate Loki as the speaker of lines 3–4. *Hlorrithi*: Thor.

7. No superscription in the manuscript. Vigfusson made up and inserted lines like "Then spake Loki the son of Laufey" whenever he thought they would be useful.

9. The manuscript marks line 2, instead of line 1, as the beginning of a stanza, which has caused editors some confusion in grouping the lines of stanzas 8 and 9.

10. No superscription in the manuscript.

12. Many editors have rejected either line 2 or line 3. Vigfusson inserts one of his own lines before line 4. *Brisings' necklace*: a marvelous necklace fashioned by the dwarfs, here called Brisings (i.e., "Twiners"); cf. *Lokasenna*, 20 and note.

13. Lines 1–3 are identical with *Baldrs Draumar*, 1, 1–3.

14. *Heimdall*: the phrase "whitest of the gods" suggests that Heimdall [was particularly fair or held a particularly holy status, white being the color of piety], as well as being the watchman. His wisdom was probably connected with his sleepless watching over all the worlds; cf. *Lokasenna*, 47 and note. On the Wanes cf. *Voluspo*, 21 and note.

16. Possibly a line has been lost from this stanza.

17. *Laufey*: Loki's mother, cf. *Lokasenna*, 52 and note.

18–19. The manuscript abbreviates all six lines, giving only the initial letters of the words. The stanza division is thus arbitrary; some editors have made one stanza of the six lines, others have combined the last two lines of stanza 19 with stanza 20. It is possible that a couple of lines have been lost.

21. *Goats*: Thor's wagon was always drawn by goats; cf. *Hymiskvitha*, 38 and note. *Jotunheim*: the world of the giants.

22. *Njorth*: cf. *Voluspo*, 21, and *Grimnismol*, 11 and 16. *Noatun* ("Ships'-Haven"): Njorth's home, where his wife, Skathi, found it impossible to stay; cf. *Grimnismol*, 11 and note.

24. Grundtvig thinks this is all that is left of two stanzas describing Thor's supper. Some editors reject line 4. in line 3 the manuscript has "he," the reference being, of course, to Thor, on whose appetite cf. *Hymiskvitha*, 15. *Sif*: Thor's wife; cf. *Lokasenna*, note to introductory prose and stanza 53.

27. For clearness I have inserted Thrym's name in place of the pronoun of the original. *Fire*: the noun is lacking in the manuscript; most editors have inserted it, however, following a late paper manuscript.

28. In the manuscript the whole stanza is abbreviated to initial letters, except for "sleep," "Freyja," and "found."

29. *Luckless*: so the manuscript, but many editors have altered the word "arma" to "aldna," meaning "old," to correspond with line 1 of stanza 32. Line 5 may well be spurious.

30. Hallow: [Thor's hammer was used to bless religious rituals, especially weddings, and may have been a common priestly ritual tool. See also the *Saga of Haakon the Good* and its usage of the "sign of the Hammer". The symbol appears in the form of the swastika (or fylfot) in archaeological findings across the Germanic world, associated with good fortune. In Snorri's story of Thor's resuscitation of his cooked goat (cf. *Hymiskvitha*, 38, note) the god "hallows" the goat with his hammer.] Vor: the goddess of vows, particularly between men and women; Snorri lists a number of little-known goddesses similar to Vor, all of them apparently little more than names for Frigg.

33. Some editors reject this line, which, from a dramatic standpoint, is certainly a pity. In the manuscript it begins with a capital letter, like the opening of a new stanza.

ALVISSMOL
THE BALLAD OF ALVIS

INTRODUCTION

The *Alvissmol* is a poem only found within the *Codex Regius* and representative of the genre of wisdom verse, featuring a question-and-answer scheme, this time revolving around the unlikely candidate of Thor and his opponent Alviss (All-Wise), a dwarf who has been promised the hand of Thor's daughter in marriage by the rest of the Gods, and towards whom Thor is incredibly hostile and generally outraged. This is in reference to the fact that Thor is, in various stories, inimical to the race of the Dwarves and frequently murders them comically, such as by kicking them into the bale-fire of Baldr as he passes by.

Thor subjects Alviss to thirteen questions about various cosmological objects or places such as the name of the sky, the name of the sun and moon, the wind and rain, etc., with Alviss recounting the names of each according to the various races of the *Aesir*, *Vanir*, Elves, Dwarves, *Jotnar*, and Men. This continues until the thirteenth question when Thor reveals in triumph that he has tricked Alviss into standing about as the dawning sun rises and turn him to stone, killing him—this being a racial weakness of the Dwarves and the reason why they live underground.

The dating for the poem is subject to intense scholarly disagreement with some early scholars like Finnur Jónsson placing it as a 10th century Norwegian poem, but most modern scholars arguing for it as one of the youngest poems of the late 12th or 13th century on the basis of it serving as a mnemonic encyclopedia for *kennings* (poetic bynames used in Germanic poetry, such as calling a ship "Oar-steed") rather than serving as an actual narrative event. Arguments for a younger origin are based on the narrative perhaps serving as the origin of Thor's racial enmity with the Dwarves, with a much older and continuing reference to a riddle game leading to someone being turned to stone, such as the giantess in *Helgakvitha Hjorvarthssonar*, which is almost a 1:1 reflection of that in *Alvissmol*, or the similar incident featuring the troll-woman in *Grettis Saga*—clearly this is a common motif in Norse thought.

The Elf-Dance
(N. J. O. Blommér)

Alvíss kvað:
"Bekki breiða, nú skal brúðr með mér
heim í sinni snúask;
hratat um mægi mun hverjum þykkja,
heima skal-at hvíld nema."

Þórr kvað:
"Hvat er þat fíra?
Hví ertu svá fölr um nasar?
Vartu í nótt með ná?
Þursa líki þykki mér á þér vera;
ert-at-tu til brúðar borinn."

Alvíss kvað:
"Alvíss ek heiti, bý ek fyr jörð neðan,
á ek undir steini stað;
vagna vers ek em á vit kominn;
bregði engi föstu heiti fíra."

Þórr kvað:
"Ek mun bregða því at ek brúðar á
flest of ráð sem faðir;
vark-a ek heima, þá er þér heitit var,
at sá einn, er gjöf er, með goðum."

1

2

3

4

ALVISSMOL

Alvis spake: 1
"Now shall the bride my benches adorn,
And homeward haste forthwith;
Eager for wedlock to all shall I seem,
Nor at home shall they rob me of rest."

Thor spake: 2
"What, pray, art thou? Why so pale round the nose?
By the dead hast thou lain of late?
To a giant like dost thou look, methinks;
Thou wast not born for the bride."

Alvis spake: 3
"Alvis am I, and under the earth
My home 'neath the rocks I have;
With the wagon-guider a word do I seek,
Let the gods their bond not break."

Thor spake: 4
"Break it shall I, for over the bride
Her father has foremost right;
At home was I not when the promise thou hadst,
And I give her alone of the gods."

Alvíss kvað:　　　　　　　　　　　　　　　　　　　　5
"Hvat er þat rekka,　　er í ráðum telsk
fljóðs ins fagrglóa?
Fjarrafleina　　þik munu fáir kunna;
hverr hefr þik baugum borit?"

Þórr kvað:　　　　　　　　　　　　　　　　　　　　6
"Vingþórr ek heiti,　　ek hef víða ratat,
sonr em ek Síðgrana;
at ósátt minni skal-at-tu　　þat it unga man hafa
ok þat gjaforð geta."

Alvíss kvað:　　　　　　　　　　　　　　　　　　　　7
"Sáttir þínar　　er ek vil snemma hafa
ok þat gjaforð geta;
eiga vilja　　heldr en án vera
þat it mjallhvíta man."

Þórr kvað:　　　　　　　　　　　　　　　　　　　　8
"Meyjar ástum　　mun-a þér verða,
vísi gestr, of varit,　　ef þú ór heimi kannt
hverjum at segja　　allt þat, er ek vil vita."

"Segðu mér þat, Alvíss,　　öll of rök fira　　　　　9
vörumk, dvergr, at vitir:
hvé sú jörð heitir,　　er liggr fyr alda sonum
heimi hverjum í?"

Alvíss kvað:　　　　　　　　　　　　　　　　　　　　10
"Jörð heitir með mönnum,　　en með ásum fold,
kalla vega vanir,　　ígræn jötnar,
alfar gróandi,　　kalla aur uppregin."

Þórr kvað:　　　　　　　　　　　　　　　　　　　　11
"Segðu mér þat, Alvíss,　　öll of rök fira
vörumk, dvergr, at vitir:
hvé sá himinn heitir,　　erakendi,
heimi hverjum í?"

Alvíss kvað:　　　　　　　　　　　　　　　　　　　　12
"Himinn heitir með mönnum,　　en hlýrnir með goðum,
kalla vindófni vanir,　　uppheim jötnar,
alfar fagraræfr,　　dvergar drjúpansal."

Alvis spake: 5
"What hero claims such right to hold
O'er the bride that shines so bright?
Not many will know thee, thou wandering man!
Who was bought with rings to bear thee?"

Thor spake: 6
"Vingthor, the wanderer wide, am I,
And I am Sithgrani's son;
Against my will shalt thou get the maid,
And win the marriage word."

Alvis spake: 7
"Thy good-will now shall I quickly get,
And win the marriage word;
I long to have, and I would not lack,
This snow-white maid for mine."

Thor spake: 8
"The love of the maid I may not keep thee
From winning, thou guest so wise,
If of every world thou canst tell me all
That now I wish to know."

"Answer me, Alvis! thou knowest all, 9
Dwarf, of the doom of men:
What call they the earth, that lies before all,
In each and every world?"

Alvis spake: 10
"'Earth' to men, 'Field' to the gods it is,
'The Ways' is it called by the Wanes;
'Ever Green' by the giants, 'The Grower' by elves,
'The Moist' by the holy ones high."

Thor spake: 11
"Answer me, Alvis! thou knowest all,
Dwarf, of the doom of men:
What call they the heaven, beheld of the high one,
In each and every world?"

Alvis spake: 12
"'Heaven' men call it, 'The Height' the gods,
The Wanes 'The Weaver of Winds';
Giants 'The Up-World,' elves 'The Fair-Roof,'
The dwarfs 'The Dripping Hall.'"

Þórr kvað: 13
"Segðu mér þat, Avlíss,   öll of rök fira
vörumk, dvergr, at vitir:
hversu máni heitir,   sá er menn séa,
heimi hverjum í?"

Alvíss kvað: 14
"Máni heitir með mönnum,   en mylinn með goðum,
kalla hverfanda hvél helju í,   skyndi jötnar,
en skin dvergar,   kalla alfar ártala."

Þórr kvað: 15
"Segðu mér þat, Alvíss,   öll of rök fira
vörumk, dvergr, at vitir:
hvé sú sól heitir,   er séa alda synir,
heimi hverjum í?"

Alvíss kvað: 16
"Sól heitir með mönnum,   en sunna með goðum,
kalla dvergar Dvalins leika,   eygló jötnar,
alfar fagrahvél,   alskír ása synir."

Þórr kvað: 17
"Segðu mér þat, Alvíss,   öll of rök fira
vörumk, dvergr, at vitir:
hvé þau ský heita,   er skúrum blandask,
heimi hverjum í?"

Alvíss kvað: 18
"Ský heita með mönnum,   en skúrván með goðum,
kalla vindflot vanir,   úrván jötnar,
alfar veðrmegin,   kalla í helju hjalm hulíðs."

Þórr kvað: 19
"Segðu mér þat, Alvíss,   öll of rök fira
vörumk, dvergr, at vitir:
hvé sá vindr heitir,   er víðast ferr,
heimi hverjum í?"

Thor spake: 13
"Answer me, Alvis! thou knowest all,
Dwarf, of the doom of men:
What call they the moon, that men behold,
In each and every world?"

Alvis spake: 14
"'Moon' with men, 'Flame' the gods among,
'The Wheel' in the house of hell;
'The Goer' the giants, 'The Gleamer' the dwarfs,
The elves 'The Teller of Time.'"

Thor spake: 15
"Answer me, Alvis! thou knowest all,
Dwarf, of the doom of men:
What call they the sun, that all men see,
In each and every world?"

Alvis spake: 16
"Men call it 'Sun,' gods 'Orb of the Sun,'
'The Deceiver of Dvalin' the dwarfs;
The giants 'The Ever-Bright,' elves 'Fair Wheel,'
'All-Glowing' the sons of the gods."

Thor spake: 17
"Answer me, Alvis! thou knowest all,
Dwarf, of the doom of men:
What call they the clouds, that keep the rains,
In each and every world?"

Alvis spake: 18
"'Clouds' men name them, 'Rain-Hope' gods call them,
The Wanes call them 'Kites of the Wind';
'Water-Hope' giants, 'Weather-Might' elves,
'The Helmet of Secrets' in hell."

Thor spake: 19
"Answer me, Alvis! thou knowest all,
Dwarf, of the doom of men:
What call they the wind, that widest fares,
In each and every world?"

Alvíss kvað: 20
"Vindr heitir með mönnum,　en váfuðr með goðum,
kalla gneggjuð ginnregin,　æpi jötnar,
alfar dynfara,　kalla í helju hviðuð."

Þórr kvað: 21
"Segðu mér þat, Alvíss,　öll of rök fira
vörumk, dvergr, at vitir:
hvé þat logn heitir,　er liggja skal,
heimi hverjum í?"

Alvíss kvað: 22
"Logn heitir með mönnum,　en lægi með goðum,
kalla vindlot vanir,　ofhlý jötnar,
alfar dagsefa,　kalla dvergar dags veru."

Þórr kvað: 23
"Segðu mér þat, Alvíss,　öll of rök fira
vörumk, dvergr, at vitir:
hvé sá marr heitir,　er menn róa,
heimi hverjum í?"

Alvíss kvað: 24
"Sær heitir með mönnum,　en sílægja með goðum,
kalla vág vanir,　álheim jötnar,
alfar lagastaf,　kalla dvergar djúpan mar."

Þórr kvað: 25
"Segðu mér þat, Alvíss,　öll of rök fira
vörumk, dvergr, at vitir:
hvé sá eldr heitir,　er brennr fyr alda sonum,
heimi hverjum í?"

Alvíss kvað: 26
"Eldr heitir með mönnum,　en með ásum funi,
kalla vág vanir,　frekan jötnar,
en forbrenni dvergar,　kalla í helju hröðuð."

Alvis spake: 20

"'Wind' do men call it, the gods 'The Waverer,'
'The Neigher' the holy ones high;
'The Wailer' the giants, 'Roaring Wender' the elves,
In hell 'The Blustering Blast.'"

Thor spake: 21

"Answer me, Alvis! thou knowest all
Dwarf, of the doom of men:
What call they the calm, that quiet lies,
In each and every world?"

Alvis spake: 22

"'Calm' men call it, 'The Quiet' the gods,
The Wanes 'The Hush of the Winds';
'The Sultry' the giants, elves 'Day's Stillness,'
The dwarfs 'The Shelter of Day.'"

Thor spake: 23

"Answer me, Alvis! thou knowest all,
Dwarf, of the doom of men:
What call they the sea, whereon men sail,
In each and every world?"

Alvis spake: 24

"'Sea' men call it, gods 'The Smooth-Lying,'
'The Wave' is it called by the Wanes;
'Eel-Home' the giants, 'Drink-Stuff' the elves,
For the dwarfs its name is 'The Deep.'"

Thor spake: 25

"Answer me, Alvis! thou knowest all,
Dwarf, of the doom of men:
What call they the fire, that flames for men,
In each of all the worlds?"

Alvis spake: 26

"'Fire' men call it, and 'Flame' the gods,
By the Wanes is it 'Wildfire' called;
'The Biter' by giants, 'The Burner' by dwarfs,
'The Swift' in the house of hell."

278   POETIC EDDA

Þórr kvað: 27
"Segðu mér þat, Alvíss,   öll of rök fira
vörumk, dvergr, at vitir:
hvé viðr heitir,   er vex fyr alda sonum,
heimi hverjum í?"

Alvíss kvað: 28
"Viðr heitir með mönnum,   en vallarfax með goðum,
kalla hlíðþang halir,   eldi jötnar
alfar fagrlima,   kalla vönd vanir."

Þórr kvað: 29
"Segðu mér þat, Alvíss,   öll of rök fira
vörumk, dvergr, at vitir,   hvé sú nótt heitir,
in Nörvi kennda,   heimi hverjum í?"

Alvíss kvað: 30
"Nótt heitir með mönnum,   en njól með goðum,
kalla grímu ginnregin,   óljós jötnar,
alfar svefngaman,   kalla dvergar draumnjörun."

Þórr kvað: 31
"Segðu mér þat, Alvíss,   öll of rök fira
vörumk, dvergr, at vitir:
hvé þat sáð heitir,   er sá alda synir,
heimi hverjum í?"

Alvíss kvað: 32
"Bygg heitir með mönnum,   en barr með goðum,
kalla vöxt vanir,   æti jötnar,
alfar lagastaf,   kalla í helju hnipin."

Þórr kvað: 33
"Segðu mér þat, Alvíss,   öll of rök fira
vörumk, dvergr, at vitir:
hvé þat öl heitir,   er drekka alda synir,
heimi hverjum í?"

Thor spake: 27
"Answer me, Alvis! thou knowest all,
Dwarf, of the doom of men:
What call they the wood, that grows for mankind,
In each and every world?"

Alvis spake: 28
"Men call it 'The Wood,' gods 'The Mane of the Field,'
'Seaweed of Hills' in hell;
'Flame-Food' the giants, 'Fair-Limbed' the elves,
'The Wand' is it called by the Wanes."

Thor spake: 29
"Answer me, Alvis! thou knowest all,
Dwarf, of the doom of men:
What call they the night, the daughter of Nor,
In each and every world?"

Alvis spake: 30
"'Night' men call it, 'Darkness' gods name it,
'The Hood' the holy ones high;
The giants 'The Lightless,' the elves 'Sleep's joy,'
The dwarfs 'The Weaver of Dreams.'"

Thor spake: 31
"Answer me, Alvis! thou knowest all,
Dwarf, of the doom of men:
What call they the seed, that is sown by men,
In each and every world?"

Alvis spake: 32
"Men call it 'Grain,' and 'Corn' the gods,
'Growth' in the world of the Wanes;
'The Eaten' by giants, 'Drink-Stuff' by elves,
In hell 'The Slender Stem.'"

Thor spake: 33
"Answer me, Alvis! thou knowest all,
Dwarf, of the doom of men:
What call they the ale, that is quaffed of men,
In each and every world?"

Alvíss kvað: 34
"Öl heitir með mönnum,   en með ásum bjórr,
kalla veig vanir,   hreinalög jötnar,
en í helju mjöð,   kalla sumbl Suttungs synir."

Þórr kvað: 35
"Í einu brjósti   ek sák aldrigi
fleiri forna stafi;
miklum tálum   kveð ek tældan þik:
Uppi ertu, dvergr,   of dagaðr, nú skínn sól í sali."

Alvis spake: 34
"'Ale' among men, 'Beer' the gods among,
In the world of the Wanes 'The Foaming';
'Bright Draught' with giants, 'Mead' with dwellers in hell,
The 'Feast-Draught' with Suttung's sons."

Thor spake: 35
"In a single breast I never have seen
More wealth of wisdom old;
But with treacherous wiles must I now betray thee:
The day has caught thee, dwarf!
Now the sun shines here in the hall."

ENDNOTES

1. *Alvis* ("All-Knowing"): a dwarf, not elsewhere mentioned. The manuscript nowhere indicates the speakers' names. The bride in question is Thor's daughter; Thruth ("Might") is the only daughter of his whose name is recorded, and she does not appear elsewhere in the poems. Her mother was Sif, Thor's wife, whereas the god's sons were born of a giantess. *Benches*: cf. *Lokasenna*, 15 and note.

2. The dwarfs, living beyond the reach of the sun, which was fatal to them (cf. stanzas 16 and 35), were necessarily pale. Line 3 is, of course, ironical. [An alternative interpretation would see the Dwarfs as not wholly pale but black except for the uppermost of their extremities (cf. *Gylfaginning* where Snorri describes them as the opposite of the Light Elves and black as pitch) such as the nose. Line 2 then refers to them as resembling corpses rotting, with line 3 a statement about their monstrosity.]

3. *Wagon-guider*: Thor, who travels habitually on his goat drawn wagon. Bugge changes "Vagna vets" to "Vapna verþs," rendering the line "I am come to seek the cost of the weapons." In either case, Alvis does not as yet recognize Thor.

4. Apparently the gods promised Thor's daughter in marriage to Alvis during her father's absence, perhaps as a reward for some craftsmanship of his (cf. Bugge's suggestion as to stanza 3). The text of line 4 is most uncertain.

5. *Hero*: ironically spoken; Alvis takes Thor for a tramp, the god's uncouth appearance often leading to such mistakes; cf. *Harbarthsljoth*, 6. Line 4 is a trifle uncertain; some editors alter the wording to read "What worthless woman bore thee?"

284   POETIC EDDA

6. *Vingthor* ("Thor the Hurler"): cf. *Thrymskvitha*, 1. *Sithgrani* ("Long-Beard"): Odin.

8. *Every world*: concerning the nine worlds, cf. *Voluspo*, 2 and note. Many editors follow this stanza with one spoken by Alvis, found in late paper manuscripts, as follows:

> "Ask then, Vingthor, since eager thou art
> The lore of the dwarf to learn;
> Oft have I fared in the nine worlds all,
> And wide is my wisdom of each."

10. *Men*, etc.: nothing could more clearly indicate the author's mythological inaccuracy than his confusion of the inhabitants of the nine worlds. Men (dwellers in Mithgarth) appear in each of Alvis's thirteen answers; so do the gods (Asgarth) and the giants (Jotunheim). The elves (Alfheim) appear in eleven answers, the Wanes (Vanaheim) in nine, and the dwarfs (who occupied no special world, unless one identifies them with the dark elves of Svartalfaheim) in seven. The dwellers "in hell" appear in six stanzas; the phrase probably refers to the world of the dead, though Mogk thinks it may mean the dwarfs. In stanzas where the gods are already listed appear names elsewhere applied only to them—"holy ones," "sons of the gods" and "high ones,"—as if these names meant beings of a separate race. "Men" appears twice in the same stanza, and so do the giants, if one assumes that they are "the sons of Suttung." Altogether it is useless to pay much attention to the mythology of Alvis's replies.

11. Lines 1, 2, and 4 of Thor's questions are regularly abbreviated in the manuscript. *Beheld*, etc.: the word in the manuscript is almost certainly an error, and all kinds of guesses have been made to rectify it. All that can be said is that it means "beheld of" or "known to" somebody.

14. *Flame*: a doubtful word; Vigfusson suggests that it properly means a "mock sun." *Wheel*: the manuscript adds the adjective "whirling," to the destruction of the metre; cf. *Hovamol*, 84, 3.

16. *Deceiver of Dvalin*: Dvalin was one of the foremost dwarfs; cf. *Voluspo*, 14, *Fafnismol*, 13, and *Hovamol*, 144. The sun "deceives" him because, like the other dwarfs living under ground, he cannot live in its light, and always fears lest sunrise may catch him unaware. The sun's rays have power to turn the dwarfs into stone, and the giantess Hrimgerth meets a similar fate (cf. *Helgakvitha Hjorvarthssonar*, 30). Alvis suffers in the same way; cf. stanza 35.

20. Snorri quotes this stanza in the *Skaldskaparmal*. *Waverer*: the word

is uncertain, the *Prose Edda* manuscripts giving it in various forms. *Blustering Blast*: two *Prose Edda* manuscripts give a totally different word, meaning "The Pounder."

22. *Hush*, etc.: the manuscript, by inserting an additional letter, makes the word practically identical with that translated "Kite" in stanza 18. Most editors have agreed as to the emendation.

24. *Drink-Stuff*: Gering translates the word thus; I doubt it, but can suggest nothing better.

26. *Wildfire*: the word may mean any one of various things, including "Wave," which is not unlikely.

28. *In hell*: the word simply means "men," and it is only a guess, though a generally accepted one, that here it refers to the dead.

29. *Nor*: presumably the giant whom Snorri calls Norvi or Narfi, father of Not (Night) and grandfather of Dag (Day). cf. *Vafthruthnismol*, 25.

30. Snorri quotes this stanza in the *Skaldskaparmal*. The various *Prose Edda* manuscripts differ considerably in naming the gods, the giants, etc. *Lightless*: some manuscripts have "The Unsorrowing."

32. *Grain*: the two words translated "grain" and "corn" apparently both meant primarily barley, and thence grain in general, the first being the commoner term of the two. *Drink-Stuff*: the word is identical with the one used, and commented on, in stanza 24, and again I have followed Gering's interpretation for want of a better one. If his guess is correct, the reference here is evidently to grain as the material from which beer and other drinks are brewed.

34. *Suttung's sons*: these ought to be the giants, but the giants are specifically mentioned in line 3. The phrase "Suttung's sons" occurs in *Skirnismol*, 34, clearly meaning the giants. Concerning Suttung as the possessor of the mead of poetry, cf. *Hovamol*, 104.

35. Concerning the inability of the dwarfs to endure sunlight, which turns them into stone, cf. stanza 16 and note. Line 5 may be spurious.

BALDRS DRAUMAR
BALDR'S DREAMS

INTRODUCTION

Baldrsdraumar is the first of the poems presented in this collection that is not found within the original *Codex Regius* and is found only in the *Arnamagnæn Codex* and various other works where it is sometimes listed as "*Vegtamskvitha*"—*The Lay of Vegtam*, a word meaning "wanderer" and herein used by Odin as a covert identity.

Scholars have for many years asserted that there may be a connection between the author of this poem, *Thrymskvitha*, *Skirnirsmal*, and *Lokasenna* on the basis of a similarity in style of metrical prose and common wordings and phrases. Likewise, an argument has been established for a connection between it and the author of *Voluspo* itself, given the shared motif of Odin raising a Volva from the dead to recount her knowledge of events, and indeed the entire narrative appears to be a more detailed version of that given in *Voluspo* itself. Assuming a common authorship between this poem and the former three, it is interesting to note that, whatever the reason, archaeological place names in Sweden and Norway featuring Baldr are closely linked to, and commonly found within, areas connected to the aforementioned Freyr cult, which would support the contention that they share an origin.

Modern and older scholars are largely in agreement that the story originates linguistically from the early to mid 10th century and was probably composed in Iceland from recent Norwegian immigrants, aligning broadly with the speculative origins described above.

Senn váru æsir   allir á þingi   1
ok ásynjur   allar á máli,
ok um þat réðu   ríkir tívar,
hví væri Baldri   ballir draumar.

Upp reis Óðinn,   alda gautr,   2
ok hann á Sleipni   söðul of lagði;
reið hann niðr þaðan   niflheljar til;
mætti hann hvelpi,   þeim er ór helju kom.

Sá var blóðugr   um brjóst framan   3
ok galdrs föður   gól of lengi;
fram reið Óðinn,   foldvegr dunði;
hann kom at hávu   Heljar ranni.

Þá reið Óðinn   fyrir austan dyrr,   4
þar er hann vissi   völu leiði;
nam hann vittugri   valgaldr kveða,
unz nauðig reis,   nás orð of kvað:

"Hvat er manna þat   mér ókunnra,   5
er mér hefir aukit   erfitt sinni?
Var ek snivin snævi   ok slegin regni
ok drifin döggu,   dauð var ek lengi."

BALDRS DRAUMAR

Once were the gods together met, 1
And the goddesses came and council held,
And the far-famed ones the truth would find,
Why baleful dreams to Baldr had come.

Then Odin rose, the enchanter old, 2
And the saddle he laid on Sleipnir's back;
Thence rode he down to Niflhel deep,
And the hound he met that came from hell.

Bloody he was on his breast before, 3
At the father of magic he howled from afar;
Forward rode Odin, the earth resounded
Till the house so high of Hel he reached.

Then Odin rode to the eastern door, 4
There, he knew well, was the wise-woman's grave;
Magic he spoke and mighty charms,
Till spell-bound she rose, and in death she spoke:

"What is the man, to me unknown, 5
That has made me travel the troublous road?
I was snowed on with snow, and smitten with rain,
And drenched with dew; long was I dead."

Óðinn kvað: 6
"Vegtamr ek heiti, sonr em ek Valtams;
segðu mér ór helju, ek mun ór heimi:
Hveim eru bekkir baugum sánir,
flet fagrlig flóuð gulli?"

Völva kvað: 7
"Hér stendr Baldri of brugginn mjöðr,
skírar veigar, liggr skjöldr yfir,
en ásmegir í ofvæni;
nauðug sagðak, nú mun ek þegja."

Óðinn kvað: 8
"Þegj-at-tu, völva, þik vil ek fregna,
unz alkunna, vil ek enn vita:
Hverr mun Baldri at bana verða
ok Óðins son aldri ræna?"

Völva kvað: 9
"Höðr berr hávan hróðrbaðm þinig,
hann mun Baldri at bana verða
ok Óðins son aldri ræna;
nauðug sagðak, nú mun ek þegja."

Óðinn kvað: 10
"Þegj-at-tu, völva, þik vil ek fregna,
unz alkunna, vil ek enn vita:
Hverr mun heift Heði hefnt of vinna
eða Baldrs bana á bál vega?"

Völva kvað: 11
"Rindr berr Vála í vestrsölum,
sá mun Óðins sonr einnættr vega:
hönd of þvær né höfuð kembir,
áðr á bál of berr Baldrs andskota;
nauðug sagðak, nú mun ek þegja."

Óðinn kvað: 12
"Þegj-at-tu, völva, þik vil ek fregna,
unz alkunna, vil ek enn vita:
Hverjar ro þær meyjar, er at muni gráta
ok á himin verpa halsa skautum?"

Odin spake: 6
"Vegtam my name, I am Valtam's son;
Speak thou of hell, for of heaven I know:
For whom are the benches bright with rings,
And the platforms gay bedecked with gold?"

The Wise-Woman spake: 7
"Here for Baldr the mead is brewed,
The shining drink, and a shield lies o'er it;
But their hope is gone from the mighty gods.
Unwilling I spake, and now would be still."

Odin spake: 8
"Wise-woman, cease not! I seek from thee
All to know that I fain would ask:
Who shall the bane of Baldr become,
And steal the life from Odin's son?"

The Wise-Woman spake: 9
"Hoth thither bears the far-famed branch,
He shall the bane of Baldr become,
And steal the life from Odin's son.
Unwilling I spake, and now would be still."

Odin spake: 10
"Wise-woman, cease not! I seek from thee
All to know that I fain would ask:
Who shall vengeance win for the evil work,
Or bring to the flames the slayer of Baldr?"

The Wise-Woman spake: 11
"Rind bears Vali in Vestrsalir,
And one night old fights Odin's son;
His hands he shall wash not, his hair he shall comb not,
Till the slayer of Baldr he brings to the flames.
Unwilling I spake, and now would be still."

Odin spake: 12
"Wise-woman, cease not! I seek from thee
All to know that I fain would ask:
What maidens are they who then shall weep,
And toss to the sky the yards of the sails?"

Völva kvað: 13
"Ert-at-tu Vegtamr,   sem ek hugða,
heldr ertu Óðinn,   aldinn gautr."

Óðinn kvað:
"Ert-at-tu völva   né vís kona,
heldr ertu þriggja   þursa móðir."

Völva kvað: 14
"Heim ríð þú, Óðinn,   ok ver hróðigr,
svá komir manna   meir aftr á vit,
er lauss Loki   líðr ór böndum
ok ragna rök   rjúfendr koma."

The Wise-Woman spake: 13
"Vegtam thou art not, as erstwhile I thought;
Odin thou art, the enchanter old."

Odin spake:
"No wise-woman art thou, nor wisdom hast;
Of giants three the mother art thou."

The Wise-Woman spake: 14
"Home ride, Odin, be ever proud;
For no one of men shall seek me more
Till Loki wanders loose from his bonds,
And to the last strife the destroyers come."

ENDNOTES

1. Lines 1–3 are identical with *Thrymskvitha*, 13, 1–3. *Baldr*: concerning this best and noblest of the gods, the son of Odin and Frigg, who comes again among the survivors after the final battle, cf. *Voluspo*, 32 and 62, and notes. He is almost never mentioned anywhere except in connection with the story of his death, though Snorri has one short passage praising his virtue and beauty. After stanza 1 two old editions, and one later one, insert four stanzas from late paper manuscripts.

2. *Sleipnir*: Odin's eight-legged horse, the son of Loki and the stallion Svathilfari; cf. *Lokasenna*, 23, and *Grimnismol*, 44, and notes. *Niflhel*: the murky ("nifl") dwelling of Hel, goddess of the dead. *The hound*: Garm; cf. *Voluspo*, 44.

3. *Father of magic*: Odin appears constantly as the god of magic. *Hel*: offspring of Loki and the giantess Angrbotha, as were the wolf Fenrir and Mithgarthsorm. She ruled the world of the unhappy dead, either those who had led evil lives or, according to another tradition, those who had not died in battle. The manuscript marks line 3 as the beginning of a stanza, and thus the editions vary in their grouping of the lines of this and the succeeding stanzas.

6. The manuscript has no superscriptions indicating the speakers. *Vegtam* ("The Wanderer"): Odin, as usual, conceals his identity, calling himself the son of Valtam ("The Fighter"). In this instance he has unusual need to do so, for as the wise-woman belongs apparently to the race of the giants, she would be unwilling to answer a god's questions. *Heaven*: the word used includes all the upper worlds, in contrast to hell. *Benches*, etc.: the adornment of the benches and raised platforms, or elevated parts of the house, was a regular part of the preparation for a feast of welcome. The

text of the two last lines is somewhat uncertain.

7. Grundtvig, followed by, Edzardi, thinks a line has been lost between lines 3 and 4.

9. Concerning the blind Hoth, who, at Loki's instigation, cast the fatal mistletoe at Baldr, cf. *Voluspo*, 32–33 and notes. In the manuscript the last line is abbreviated, as also in stanza 11.

10. In the manuscript lines 1–2 are abbreviated, as also in stanza 12.

11. *Rind*: mentioned by Snorri as one of the goddesses. Concerning her son Vali, begotten by Odin for the express purpose of avenging Baldr's death, and his slaying of Hoth the day after his birth, cf. *Voluspo*, 33–34, where the lines of this stanza appear practically verbatim. *Vestrsalir* ("The Western Hall"): not elsewhere mentioned in the poems.

12. The manuscript marks the third line as the beginning of a stanza; something may have been lost. Lines 3–4 are thoroughly obscure. According to Bugge the maidens who are to weep for Baldr are the daughters of the sea-god Ægir, the waves, whose grief will be so tempestuous that they will toss the ships up to the very sky. "Yards of the sails" is a doubtfully accurate rendering; the two words, at any rate in later Norse nautical speech, meant respectively the "tack" and the "sheet" of the square sail.

13. Possibly two separate stanzas. *Enchanter*: the meaning of the original word is most uncertain.

14. Concerning Loki's escape and his relation to the destruction of the gods, cf. *Voluspo*, 35 and 51, and notes. While the wise-woman probably means only that she will never speak again till the end of the world, it has been suggested, and is certainly possible, that she intends to give Loki her counsel, thus revenging herself on Odin.

RIGSTHULA
THE LAY OF RIG

INTRODUCTION

The *Rigsthula* is both simultaneously one of the most controversial and important of the poems generally afforded the *Eddic* status, although it is not found within the *Codex Regius* or the *Arnamagnæn Codex*—it is only found at the very end of the *Codex Wormianus*, attached as a loose sheaf and whose ending is sadly missing. Many scholars both ancient and modern have speculated that the poem shows signs that the author was not Icelandic (given the poem's sheer social differences with those of Medieval Iceland) and was familiar with the culture of the western isles of Ireland and Scotland, if not himself a Norse-Gael, especially due to the inclusion of the word *Rig* which seems taken from the Old Irish term for king and not the Norse term *Konugr*. Because of these issues, some have questioned the legitimacy and authenticity of the poem itself, or at least its common acceptance throughout the Norse world.

An application of comparative mythology and a familiarity with the broader field of Indo-European studies suggests a much different reception, with the myth as presented aligning quite strikingly with what we know to be a common IE caste system. A historical enigma troubling many scholars is the clear connection the poem must have to the mythic references nearly a millennium earlier by Tacitus regarding the three Sons of Mannus, an earthly born God, who gives rise paternally to the entirety of the Germanic people. This reference is thereby strengthened by the fact that Hindu mythology records a similar "Manu" who is described as the progenitor of Man, a culture hero responsible for the formulation of religious devotional laws and rituals including the much more famous

Hindu caste system, which also follows the general color schema set forth in *Rigsthula* of Black(-Yellow)-Red-White. Although apparently speaking of the same function and process, the nature of the connection between Tacitus' Mannus and the later Norse Rig is unclear despite clearly being connected, and it is possible that one or more of these stories have been conflated with other similar stories either from Tacitus' original recollection in *Germania* or over time, resulting in the later Norse poem.

Linguistic issues revolving around the adoption of the word *Rig* itself are the subject of scholarly dispute, with many feeling it is a direct late Norse adoption of an Irish word, whereas another argument holds that the word is simply the result of an originally identical root word (the Proto-Germanic word *Rīks*, meaning king, being derived from the Proto-Celtic term *Rīxs*) developing into similar forms in descendant lexical cognates (Norse *Rig* vs. Irish *Ri[g]*). Regardless of the history of the term itself, there can be no doubt that the story is extremely ancient and perhaps one of the original formative myths of the IE peoples.

A second controversy relates to the ultimate personage of Rig himself. A separate sheet of paper attached to the original manuscript noting in prose that Rig is identical to Heimdall, has come under skepticism from many modern academics who see the actions, behavior, and cultural meaning of Rig hewing much more closely to that of Odin. The former argument is largely contingent on the opening lines of *Voluspo* speaking of "Heimdall's sons, both high and low", which, if the association is accurate, appears to be a direct reference to the narrative of *Rigsthula*; the latter argument for the identification with Odin derives from his much more prominent place in the lore and society of the Norse, in particular his associations with wanderings, sexual escapades, wisdom, warfare, and runelore.

Jarl
(Albert Edelfelt)

Svá segja menn í fornum sögum, at einnhverr af ásum, sá er Heimdallr hét, fór ferðar sinnar ok fram með sjóvarströndu nökkurri, kom at einum húsabæ ok nefndist Rígr. Eftir þeiri sögu er kvæði þetta:

Ár kváðu ganga   grænar brautir   1
öflgan ok aldinn   ás kunnigan,
ramman ok röskvan   Ríg stíganda.

Gekk hann meir at þat   miðrar brautar;   2
kom hann at húsi,   hurð var á gætti;
inn nam at ganga,   eldr var á golfi;
hjón sátu þar   hár at arni,
Ái ok Edda,   aldinfalda.

Rígr kunni þeim   ráð at segja;   3
meir settisk hann   miðra fletja,
en á hlið hvára   hjón salkynna.

Þá tók Edda   ökkvinn hleif,   4
þungan ok þykkvan,   þrunginn sáðum;
bar hon meir at þat   miðra skutla,
soð var í bolla,   setti á bjóð;
var kalfr soðinn   krása beztr.

RIGSTHULA

They tell in old stories that one of the gods, whose name was Heimdall, went on his way along a certain seashore, and came to a dwelling, where he called himself Rig. According to these stories is the following poem:

Men say there went by ways so green 1
Of old the god, the aged and wise,
Mighty and strong did Rig go striding.
[...]

Forward he went on the midmost way, 2
He came to a dwelling, a door on its posts;
In did he fare, on the floor was a fire,
Two hoary ones by the hearth there sat,
Ai and Edda, in olden dress.

Rig knew well wise words to speak, 3
Soon in the midst of the room he sat,
And on either side the others were.

A loaf of bread did Edda bring, 4
Heavy and thick and swollen with husks;
Forth on the table she set the fare,
And broth for the meal in a bowl there was.
Calf's flesh boiled was the best of the dainties.

Rígr kunni þeim   ráð at segja;   5
reis hann upp þaðan,   réðsk at sofna;
meir lagðisk hann   miðrar rekkju,
en á hlið hvára   hjón salkynna.

Þar var hann at þat   þríar nætr saman,   6
gekk hann meir at þat   miðrar brautar;
liðu meir at þat   mánuðr níu.

Jóð ól Edda   jósu vatni,   7
hörvi svartan,   hétu Þræl.

Hann nam at vaxa   ok vel dafna;   8
var þar á höndum   hrokkit skinn,
kropnir knúar,   fingr digrir,
fúlligt andlit,   lotr hryggr,
langir hælar.

Nam han meir at þat   magns of kosta,   9
bast at binda,   byrðar gerva;
bar hann heim at þat   hrís gerstan dag.

Þar kom at garði   gengilbeina,   10
aurr var á iljum,   armr sólbrunninn,
niðrbjúgt er nef,   nefndisk Þír.

Miðra fletja   meir settisk hon;   11
sat hjá henni   sonr húss;
ræddu ok rýndu,   rekkju gerðu
Þræll ok Þír   þrungin dægr.

Börn ólu þau,   12
bjuggu ok unðu,
hygg ek at héti   Hreimr ok Fjósnir,
Klúrr ok Kleggi,   Kefsir, Fúlnir,
Drumbr, Digraldi,   Dröttr ok Hösvir.
Lútr ok Leggjaldi;
lögðu garða,   akra töddu,
unnu at svínum,   geita gættu,
grófu torf.

Dætr váru þær   Drumba ok Kumba,   13
Ökkvinkalfa   ok Arinnefja,
Ysja ok Ambátt,   Eikintjasna,
Tötrughypja   ok Trönubeina.
Þaðan eru komnar   þræla ættir.

Rig knew well wise words to speak, 5
Thence did he rise, made ready to sleep;
Soon in the bed himself did he lay,
And on either side the others were.

Thus was he there for three nights long, 6
Then forward he went on the midmost way,
And so nine months were soon passed by.

A son bore Edda, with water they sprinkled him, 7
With a cloth his hair so black they covered;
Thræll they named him, [...]

The skin was wrinkled and rough on his hands, 8
Knotted his knuckles, [...]
Thick his fingers, and ugly his face,
Twisted his back, and big his heels.

He began to grow, and to gain in strength, 9
Soon of his might good use he made;
With bast he bound, and burdens carried,
Home bore faggots the whole day long.

One came to their home, crooked her legs, 10
Stained were her feet, and sunburned her arms,
Flat was her nose; her name was Thir.

Soon in the midst of the room she sat, 11
By her side there sat the son of the house;
They whispered both, and the bed made ready,
Thræll and Thir, till the day was through.

Children they had, they lived and were happy, 12
Fjosnir and Klur they were called, methinks,
Hreim and Kleggi, Kefsir, Fulnir,
Drumb, Digraldi, Drott and Leggjaldi,
Lut and Hosvir; the house they cared for,
Ground they dunged, and swine they guarded,
Goats they tended, and turf they dug.

Daughters had they, Drumba and Kumba, 13
Ökkvinkalfa, Arinnefla,
Ysja and Ambott, Eikintjasna,
Totrughypja and Tronubeina;
And thence has risen the race of thralls.

Gekk Rígr at þat   réttar brautir,   14
kom hann at höllu,   hurð var á skíði,
inn nam at ganga,   eldr var á golfi,
hjón sátu þar,   heldu á sýslu.

Maðr teglði þar   meið til rifjar;   15
var skegg skapat,   skör var fyrir enni,
skyrtu þröngva,   skokkr var á golfi.

Sat þar kona,   sveigði rokk,   16
breiddi faðm,   bjó til váðar;
sveigr var á höfði,   smokkr var á bringu,
dúkr var á halsi,   dvergar á öxlum.
Afi ok Amma   áttu hús.

Rígr kunni þeim   ráð at segja;   17
meir settisk hann   miðra fletja,
en á hlið hvára   hjón salkynna.

Þá tók Amma   [...]   18
var kalfr soðinn   krása beztr.

Rígr kunni þeim   ráð at segja   19
reis frá borði,   réð at sofna;
meir lagðisk hann   miðrar rekkju,
en á hlið hvára   hjón salkynna.

Þar var hann at þat   þríar nætr saman;   20
liðu meir at þat   mánuðr níu.

Jóð ól Amma   jósu vatni,   21
kölluðu Karl,   kona sveip rifti,
rauðan ok rjóðan,   riðuðu augu.

Hann nam at vaxa   ok vel dafna,   22
öxn nam at temja,   arðr at gerva,
hús at timbra   ok hlöður smíða,
karta at gerva   ok keyra plóg.

Heim óku þá   hanginluklu,   23
geitakyrtlu,   giftu Karli;
Snör heitir sú,   settisk und rifti;
bjuggu hjón,   bauga deildu,
breiddu blæjur   ok bú gerðu.

Forward went Rig, his road was straight,   14
To a hall he came, and a door there hung;
In did he fare, on the floor was a fire:
Afi and Amma owned the house.

There sat the twain, and worked at their tasks: 15
The man hewed wood for the weaver's beam;
His beard was trimmed, o'er his brow a curl,
His clothes fitted close; in the corner a chest.

The woman sat and the distaff wielded,   16
At the weaving with arms outstretched she worked;
On her head was a band, on her breast a smock;
On her shoulders a kerchief with clasps there was.

Rig knew well wise words to speak,   17
Soon in the midst of the room he sat,
And on either side the others were.

Then took Amma [...]   18
The vessels full with the fare she set,
Calf's flesh boiled was the best of the dainties.

Rig knew well wise words to speak,   19
He rose from the board, made ready to sleep;
Soon in the bed himself did he lay,
And on either side the others were.

Thus was he there for three nights long,   20
Then forward he went on the midmost way,
And so nine months were soon passed by.

A son bore Amma, with water they sprinkled him,   21
Karl they named him; in a cloth she wrapped him,
He was ruddy of face, and flashing his eyes.

He began to grow, and to gain in strength,   22
Oxen he ruled, and plows made ready,
Houses he built, and barns he fashioned,
Carts he made, and the plow he managed.

Home did they bring the bride for Karl,   23
In goatskins clad, and keys she bore;
Snör was her name, 'neath the veil she sat;
A home they made ready, and rings exchanged,
The bed they decked, and a dwelling made.

Börn ólu þau,   bjuggu ok unðu,   24
hét Halr ok Drengr,   Hölðr, Þegn ok Smiðr,
Breiðr, Bóndi,   Bundinskeggi,
Búi ok Boddi,   Brattskeggr ok Seggr.

Enn hétu svá   öðrum nöfnum,   25
Snót, Brúðr, Svanni,   Svarri, Sprakki,
Fljóð, Sprund ok Víf,   Feima, Ristill.
Þaðan eru komnar   karla ættir.

Gekk Rígr þaðan   réttar brautir;   26
kom hann at sal,   suðr horfðu dyrr,
var hurð hnigin,   hringr var í gætti.

Gekk hann inn at þat,   golf var stráat;   27
sátu hjón,   sáusk í augu,
Faðir ok Móðir,   fingrum at leika.

Sat húsgumi   ok sneri streng,   28
alm of bendi,   örvar skefti;
en húskona   hugði at örmum,
strauk of rifti,   sterti ermar.

Keisti fald,   kinga var á bringu,   29
síðar slæður,   serk bláfáan;
brún bjartari,   brjóst ljósara,
hals hvítari   hreinni mjöllu.

Rígr kunni þeim   ráð at segja;   30
meir settisk hann   miðra fletja,
en á hlið hvára   hjón salkynna.

Þá tók Móðir   merkðan dúk,   31
hvítan af hörvi,   hulði bjóð,
hon tók at þat   hleifa þunna,
hvíta af hveiti,   ok hulði dúk.

Framm setti hon   fulla skutla,   32
silfri varða, á bjóð,   fáin fleski
ok fugla steikða,   vín var í könnu,
varðir kálkar;
drukku ok dæmðu,   dagr var á sinnum.

Sons they had, they lived and were happy: 24
Hal and Dreng, Holth, Thegn and Smith,
Breith and Bondi, Bundinskeggi,
Bui and Boddi, Brattskegg and Segg.

Daughters they had, and their names are here: 25
Snot, Bruth, Svanni, Svarri, Sprakki,
Fljoth, Sprund and Vif, Feima, Ristil:
And thence has risen the yeomen's race.

Thence went Rig, his road was straight, 26
A hall he saw, the doors faced south;
The portal stood wide, on the posts was a ring,
Then in he fared; the floor was strewn.

Within two gazed in each other's eyes, 27
Fathir and Mothir, and played with their fingers;
There sat the house-lord, wound strings for the bow,
Shafts he fashioned, and bows he shaped.

The lady sat, at her arms she looked, 28
She smoothed the cloth, and fitted the sleeves;
Gay was her cap, on her breast were clasps,
Broad was her train, of blue was her gown,
Her brows were bright, her breast was shining,
Whiter her neck than new-fallen snow.

Rig knew well wise words to speak, 29
Soon in the midst of the room he sat,
And on either side the others were.

Then Mothir brought a broidered cloth, 30
Of linen bright, and the board she covered;
And then she took the loaves so thin,
And laid them, white from the wheat, on the cloth.

Then forth she brought the vessels full, 31
With silver covered, and set before them,
Meat all browned, and well-cooked birds;
In the pitcher was wine, of plate were the cups,
So drank they and talked till the day was gone.

Rígr kunni þeim   ráð at segja;   33
reis hann at þat,   rekkju gerði.
Þar var hann at þat   þríar nætr saman;
gekk hann meir at þat   miðrar brautar;
liðu meir at þat   mánuðr níu.

Svein ól Móðir,   silki vafði,   34
jósu vatni,   Jarl létu heita;
bleikt var hár,   bjartir vangar,
ötul váru augu   sem yrmlingi.

Upp óx þar   Jarl á fletjum;   35
lind nam at skelfa,   leggja strengi,
alm at beygja,   örvar skefta,
flein at fleygja,   frökkur dýja,
hestum ríða,   hundum verpa,
sverðum bregða,   sund at fremja.

Kom þar ór runni   Rígr gangandi,   36
Rígr gangandi,   rúnar kendi;
sitt gaf heiti,   son kveðsk eiga;
þann bað hann eignask   óðalvöllu,
óðalvöllu,   aldnar byggðir.

Reið hann meir þaðan   myrkvan við,   37
hélug fjöll,   unz at höllu kom;
skaft nam at dýja,   skelfði lind,
hesti hleypði   ok hjörvi brá;
víg nam at vekja,   völl nam at rjóða,
val nam at fella,   vá til landa.

Réð hann einn at þat   átján búum,   38
auð nam skipta,   öllum veita
meiðmar ok mösma,   mara svangrifja,
hringum hreytti,   hjó sundr baug.

Óku ærir   úrgar brautir,   39
kómu at höllu,   þar er Hersir bjó;
mey átti hann   mjófingraða,
hvíta ok horska,   hétu Erna.

Báðu hennar   ok heim óku,   40
giftu Jarli,   gekk hon und líni;
saman bjuggu þau   ok sér unðu,
ættir jóku   ok aldrs nutu.

Rig knew well wise words to speak, 32
Soon did he rise, made ready to sleep;
So in the bed himself did he lay,
And on either side the others were.

Thus was he there for three nights long, 33
Then forward he went on the midmost way,
And so nine months were soon passed by.

A son had Mothir, in silk they wrapped him, 34
With water they sprinkled him, Jarl he was;
Blond was his hair, and bright his cheeks,
Grim as a snake's were his glowing eyes.

To grow in the house did Jarl begin, 35
Shields he brandished, and bow-strings wound,
Bows he shot, and shafts he fashioned,
Arrows he loosened, and lances wielded,
Horses he rode, and hounds unleashed,
Swords he handled, and sounds he swam.

Straight from the grove came striding Rig, 36
Rig came striding, and runes he taught him;
By his name he called him, as son he claimed him,
And bade him hold his heritage wide,
His heritage wide, the ancient homes.

[...] 37
Forward he rode through the forest dark,
O'er the frosty crags, till a hall he found.

His spear he shook, his shield he brandished, 38
His horse he spurred, with his sword he hewed;
Wars he raised, and reddened the field,
Warriors slew he, and land he won.

Eighteen halls ere long did he hold, 39
Wealth did he get, and gave to all,
Stones and jewels and slim-flanked steeds,
Rings he offered, and arm-rings shared.

His messengers went by the ways so wet, 40
And came to the hall where Hersir dwelt;
His daughter was fair and slender-fingered,
Erna the wise the maiden was.

Burr var inn ellsti,   en Barn annat,   41
Jóð ok Aðal,   Arfi, Mögr,
Niðr ok Niðjungr,   námu leika,
Sonr ok Sveinn,   sund ok tafl,
Kundr hét enn,   Konr var inn yngsti

Upp óxu þar   Jarli bornir,   42
hesta tömðu,   hlífar bendu,
skeyti skófu,   skelfðu aska.

En Konr ungr   kunni rúnar,   43
ævinrúnar   ok aldrrúnar;
meir kunni hann   mönnum bjarga,
eggjar deyfa,   ægi lægja.

Klök nam fugla,   kyrra elda,   44
sefa of svefja,   sorgir lægja,
afl ok eljun   átta manna.

Hann við Ríg jarl   rúnar deildi,   45
brögðum beitti   ok betr kunni;
þá öðlaðisk   ok þá eiga gat
Rígr at heita,   rúnar kunna.

Reið Konr ungr   kjörr ok skóga,   46
kolfi fleygði,   kyrrði fugla.

Þá kvað þat kráka,   sat kvisti ein: 47
„Hvat skaltu, Konr ungr,   kyrra fugla?
Heldr mætti ér   hestum ríða,
hjörvi bregða   ok her fella.

Á Danr ok Danpr   dýrar hallir,   48
æðra óðal   en ér hafið;
þeir kunnu vel   kjóli at ríða,
egg at kenna,   undir rjúfa."

Brún bjartari,   brjóst ljósara,   49
hals hvítari   hreinni mjöllu.

Bjuggu hjón,   bauga deildu.   50

Her hand they sought, and home they brought her,   41
Wedded to Jarl the veil she wore;
Together they dwelt, their joy was great,
Children they had, and happy they lived.

Bur was the eldest, and Barn the next,   42
Joth and Athal, Arfi, Mog,
Nith and Svein, soon they began,
Sun and Nithjung, to play and swim;
Kund was one, and the youngest Kon.

Soon grew up the sons of Jarl,   43
Beasts they tamed, and bucklers rounded,
Shafts they fashioned, and spears they shook.

But Kon the Young learned runes to use,   44
Runes everlasting, the runes of life;
Soon could he well the warriors shield,
Dull the swordblade, and still the seas.

Bird-chatter learned he, flames could he lessen,   45
Minds could quiet, and sorrows calm;
[...]
The might and strength of twice four men.

With Rig-Jarl soon the runes he shared,   46
More crafty he was, and greater his wisdom;
The right he sought, and soon he won it,
Rig to be called, and runes to know.

Young Kon rode forth through forest and grove,   47
Shafts let loose, and birds he lured;
There spake a crow on a bough that sat:
"Why lurest thou, Kon, the birds to come?"

"'Twere better forth on thy steed to fare,   48
[...] and the host to slay.

"The halls of Dan and Danp are noble,   49
Greater their wealth than thou hast gained;
Good are they at guiding the keel,
Trying of weapons, and giving of wounds."

ENDNOTES

Prose. It would be interesting to know how much the annotator meant by the phrase *old stories*. Was he familiar with the tradition in forms other than that of the poem? If so, his introductory note was scanty, for, outside of identifying *Rig* as *Heimdall*, he provides no information not found in the poem. Probably he meant simply to refer to the poem itself as a relic of antiquity, and the identification of Rig as Heimdall may well have been an attempt at constructive criticism of his own. The note was presumably written somewhere about 1300, or even later, and there is no reason for crediting the annotator with any considerable knowledge of mythology. There is little to favor the identification of Rig with Heimdall, the watchman of the gods, beyond a few rather vague passages in the other poems. Thus in *Voluspo*, 1, the Volva asks hearing "from Heimdall's sons both high and low"; in *Grimnismol*, 13, there is a very doubtful line which may mean that Heimdall "o'er men holds sway, it is said," and in "the Short Voluspo" (*Hyndluljoth*, 40) he is called "the kinsman of men." On the other hand, everything in the *Rigsthula*, including the phrase "the aged and wise" in stanza 1, and the references to runes in stanzas 36, 44, and 46, fits Odin exceedingly well. It seems probable that the annotator was wrong, and that Rig is Odin, and not Heimdall. *Rig*: almost certainly based on the Old Irish word for "king," "ri" or "rig."

1. No gap is indicated, but editors have generally assumed one. Some editors, however, add line 1 of stanza 2 to stanza 1.

2. Most editions make line 5 a part of the stanza, as here, but some indicate it as the sole remnant of one or more stanzas descriptive of Ai and Edda, just as Afi and Amma, Fathir and Mothir, are later described. *Ai and Edda*: Great-Grandfather and Great-Grandmother; the latter name

was responsible for Jakob Grimm's famous guess at the meaning of the word "Edda" as applied to the whole collection (cf. Introduction).

3. A line may have been lost from this stanza.

4. Line 5 has generally been rejected as spurious.

5. The manuscript has lines 1–2 in inverse order, but marks the word "Rig" as the beginning of a stanza.

6. The manuscript does not indicate that these lines form a separate stanza, and as only one line and a fragment of another are left of stanza 7, the editions have grouped the lines in all sorts of ways, with, of course, various conjectures as to where lines may have been lost.

7. After line 1 the manuscript has only four words: "cloth," "black," "named," and "Thræll." No gap is anywhere indicated. Editors have pieced out the passage in various ways. *Water*, etc.: concerning the custom of sprinkling water on children, which long antedated the introduction of Christianity, cf. *Hovamol*, 159 and note. *Black*: dark hair, among the blond Scandinavians, was the mark of a foreigner, hence of a slave. *Thræll*: Thrall or Slave.

8. In the manuscript line 1 of stanza 9 stands before stanza 8, neither line being capitalized as the beginning of a stanza. I have followed Bugge's rearrangement. The manuscript indicates no gap in line 2, but nearly all editors have assumed one, Grundtvig supplying "and rough his nails."

9. The manuscript marks line 2 as the beginning of a stanza.

10. A line may well have dropped out, but the manuscript is too uncertain as to the stanza-divisions to make any guess safe. *Crooked*: the word in the original is obscure. *Stained*: literally, "water was on her soles." *Thir*: "Serving-Woman."

12. There is some confusion as to the arrangement of the lines and division into stanzas of 12 and 13. The names mean: *Fjosnir*, "Cattle-Man"; *Klur*, "The Coarse"; *Hreim*, "The Shouter"; *Kleggi*, "The Horse-Fly"; *Kefsir*, "Concubine-Keeper"; *Fulnir*, "The Stinking"; *Drumb*, "The Log"; *Digraldi*, "The Fat"; *Drott*, "The Sluggard"; *Leggjaldi*, "The Big-Legged"; *Lut*, "The Bent"; *Hosvir*, "The Grey."

13. The names mean: *Drumba*, "The Log"; *Kumba*, "The Stumpy"; *Ökkvinkalfa*, "Fat-Legged"; *Arinnefja*, "Homely Nosed"; *Ysja*, "The Noisy"; *Ambott*, "The Servant"; *Eikintjasna*, "The Oaken Peg" (?); *Totrughypja*, "Clothed in Rags"; *Tronubeina*, "Crane-Legged."

14. In the manuscript line 4 stands after line 4 of stanza 16, but several editors have rearranged the lines, as here. *Afi and Amma*: Grandfather and Grandmother.

15. There is considerable confusion among the editors as to where this stanza begins and ends.

16. The manuscript marks line 3 as the beginning of a stanza.

17. The manuscript jumps from stanza 17, line 1, to stanza 19, line 2. Bugge points out that the copyist's eye was presumably led astray by the fact that 17, 1, and 19, 1, were identical. Lines 2-3 of 17 are supplied from stanzas 3 and 29.

18. I have followed Bugge's conjectural construction of the missing stanza, taking lines 2 and 3 from stanzas 31 and 4.

19. The manuscript marks line 2 as the beginning of a stanza.

20. The manuscript omits line 2, supplied by analogy with stanza 6.

21. Most editors assume a lacuna, after either line 2 or line 3. Sijmons assumes, on the analogy of stanza 8, that a complete stanza describing *Karl* ("Yeoman") has been lost between stanzas 21 and 22.

22. No line Indicated in the manuscript as beginning a stanza. *Cart*: the word in the original, "kartr," is one of the clear signs of the Celtic influence noted in the introduction.

23. *Bring*: the word literally means "drove in a wagon"—a mark of the bride's social status. *Snör*: "Daughter-in-Law." Bugge, followed by several editors, maintains that line 4 was wrongly interpolated here from a missing stanza describing the marriage of Kon.

24. No line indicated in the manuscript as beginning a stanza. The names mean: *Hal*, "Man"; *Dreng*, "The Strong"; *Holth*, "The Holder of Land"; *Thegn*, "Freeman"; *Smith*, "Craftsman"; *Breith*, "The Broad-Shouldered"; *Bondi*, "Yeoman"; *Bundinskeggi*, "With Beard Bound" (i.e., not allowed to hang unkempt); *Bui*, "Dwelling-Owner"; *Boddi*, "Farm-Holder"; *Brattskegg*, "With Beard Carried High"; *Segg*, "Man."

25. No line indicated in the manuscript as beginning a stanza. The names mean: *Snot*, "Worthy Woman"; *Bruth*, "Bride"; *Svanni*, "The Slender"; *Svarri*, "The Proud"; *Sprakki*, "The Fair"; *Fljoth*, "Woman" (?); *Sprund*, "The Proud"; *Vif*, "Wife"; *Feima*, "The Bashful"; *Ristil*, "The Graceful."

26. Many editors make a stanza out of line 4 and lines 1–2 of the following stanza. *Strewn*: with fresh straw in preparation for a feast; cf. *Thrymskvitha*, 22.

27. *Fathir and Mothir*: Father and Mother. Perhaps lines 3–4 should form a stanza with 28, 1–3.

28. Bugge thinks lines 5–6, like 23, 4, got in here from the lost stanzas describing Kon's bride and his marriage.

31. The manuscript of lines 1–3 is obviously defective, as there are too many words for two lines, and not enough for the full three. The meaning, however, is clearly very much as indicated in the translation. Gering's emendation, which I have followed, consists simply in shifting "set before them" from the first line to the second—where the manuscript has no verb—and supplying the verb "brought" in line 1. The various editions contain all sorts of suggestions.

32. The manuscript begins both line 1 and line 2 with a capital preceded by a period, which has led to all sorts of strange stanza-combinations and guesses at lost lines in the various editions. The confusion includes stanza 33, wherein no line is marked in the manuscript as beginning a stanza.

34. *Jarl*: "Nobly-Born."

35. Various lines have been regarded as interpolations, 3 and 6 being most often thus rejected.

36. Lines 1, 2, and 5 all begin with capitals preceded by periods, a fact which, taken in conjunction with the obviously defective state of the following stanza, has led to all sorts of conjectural emendations. The exact significance of Rig's giving his own name to Jarl (cf. stanza 46), and thus recognizing him, potentially at least, as a king, depends on the conditions under which the poem was composed (cf. Introductory Note [Appendix B]). The whole stanza, particularly the reference to the teaching of magic (runes), fits Odin far better than Heimdall.

37. Something—one or two lines, or a longer passage—has clearly been lost, describing the beginning of Jarl's journey. Yet many editors, relying on the manuscript punctuation, make 37 and 38 into a single stanza.[1]

39. The manuscript marks both lines 1 and 2 as beginning stanzas.

---

[1] It is at this stanza that Bellows' numbering scheme deviates from that of the Old Norse used in this edition, due to the lacuna he mentions.

40. *Hersir*: "Lord"; the hersir was, in the early days before the establishment of a kingdom in Norway, the local chief, and hence the highest recognized authority. During and after the time of Harald the Fair-Haired the name lost something of its distinction, the hersir coming to take rank below the jarl. *Erna*: "The Capable."

42. The names mean: *Bur*, "Son"; *Barn*, "Child"; *Joth*, "Child"; *Athal*, "Offspring"; *Arfi*, "Heir"; *Mog*, "Son"; *Nith*, "Descendant"; *Svein*, "Boy"; *Sun*, "Son"; *Nithjung*, "Descend ant"; *Kund*, "Kinsman"; *Kon*, "Son" (of noble birth). Concerning the use made of this last name, see note on stanza 44. It is curious that there is no list of the daughters of Jarl and Erna, and accordingly Vigfusson inserts here the names listed in stanza 25. Grundtvig rearranges the lines of stanzas 42 and 43.

44. The manuscript indicates no line as beginning a stanza. *Kon the Young*: a remarkable bit of fanciful etymology; the phrase is "Konr ungr," which could readily be contracted into "Konungr," the regular word meaning "king." The "kon" part is actually not far out, but the second syllable of "konungr" has nothing to do with "ungr" meaning "young." *Runes*: a long list of just such magic charms, dulling swordblades, quenching flames, and so on, is given in *Hovamol*, 147–163.

45. The manuscript indicates no line as beginning a stanza. *Minds*: possibly "seas," the word being doubtful. Most editors assume the gap as indicated.

46. The manuscript indicates no line as beginning a stanza. *Rig-Jarl*: Kon's father; cf. stanza 36.

47. This stanza has often been combined with 48, either as a whole or in part. *Crow*: birds frequently play the part of mentor in Norse literature; cf., for example, *Helgakvitha Hundingsbana* I, 5, and *Fafnismol*, 32.

48. This fragment is not indicated as a separate stanza in the manuscript. Perhaps half a line has disappeared, or, as seems more likely, the gap includes two lines and a half. Sijmons actually constructs these lines, largely on the basis of stanzas 35 and 38, Bugge fills in the half-line lacuna as indicated above with "The sword to wield."

49. *Dan and Danp*: These names are largely responsible for the theory that the Rigsthula was composed in Denmark. According to the Latin epitome of the *Skjöldungasaga* by Arngrimur Jonsson, "Rig (Rigus) was a man not the least among the great ones of his time. He married the daughter of a certain Danp, lord of Danpsted, whose name was Dana; and later, having won the royal title for his province, left as his heir his

son by Dana, called Dan or Danum, all of whose subjects were called Danes." This may or may not be conclusive, and it is a great pity that the manuscript breaks off abruptly at this stanza.

HYNDLULJOTH
THE POEM OF HYNDLA

INTRODUCTION

The *Hyndluljoth* is another of the works featured neither in the original *Codex Regius* or in the *Arnamagnæn Codex*, and only to be found in the *Flateyjarbok* of Iceland. The poem itself is preserved in very rough shape and appears to be an example of two distinct poems inexpertly welded together, with the *Hyndluljoth* proper accounting for the majority of the poem and featuring a list of genealogical information and references to heroic sagas and older stories from the continent, and the inclusion of the "*Short Voluspo*" inserted—somewhat flippantly—into the middle of the narrative.

Regardless, the *Hyndluljoth* proper bears the hallmarks of an intensely Icelandic fascination with their own genealogical history and the desire to make it known that they descended from the noblest lineages of Scandinavia and not, as was a common slander of the time, from escaped slaves and lowborn Norse-Gael Vikings. This desire of the Icelandic aristocracy can also be seen in the *Íslendingabók*, which goes out of its way to trace each of the prominent men of each region's lineage back to continental gentry and in some cases outright royalty.

The poem features the Goddess Freya and her favorite mortal lover Ottar, and their attempt to produce a full and complete listing of his ancestry due to his bet with a neighbor over who had the greatest lineage with the entirety of his inheritance at stake (this again being an intensely Icelandic situation). Freya transforms Ottar into a boar which she rides to meet with the *Volva* Hyndla who recounts to Freya his ancestry, linking him not only as kin to some of the mightiest and most famous of Nordic heroes but also to all of the prominent royal houses of Scandinavia, and even explicitly to the Gods themselves. This feature goes a long way to dispute the common academic consensus that the people of Iceland existed within an openly egalitarian framework rejecting the social hierarchies of the continent, but this counter-narrative shows that Iceland possessed a noble aristocratic class that prided itself intensely on their own lineage and connections with myth and fable, with Freya making this statement explicit saying: "Now let us down from our saddles leap, and talk of the race of the heroes twain; the men who were born of the gods above".

Freyja kvað: 1
"Vaki mær meyja, vaki mín vina,
Hyndla systir, er í helli býr;
nú er rökkr rökkra, ríða vit skulum
til Valhallar ok til vés heilags.

Biðjum Herjaföðr í hugum sitja, 2
hann geldr ok gefr gull verðungu;
gaf hann Hermóði hjalm ok brynju,
en Sigmundi sverð at þiggja.

Gefr hann sigr sumum, en sumum aura, 3
mælsku mörgum ok mannvit firum;
byri gefr hann brögnum, en brag skaldum,
gefr hann mannsemi mörgum rekki.

Þórr mun hon blóta, þess mun hon biðja, 4
at hann æ við þik einart láti;
þó er hánum ótítt við jötuns brúðir.

Nú taktu ulf þinn einn af stalli, 5
lát hann renna með runa mínum."

HYNDLULJOTH

Freyja spake:
"Maiden, awake! wake thee, my friend, 1
My sister Hyndla, in thy hollow cave!
Already comes darkness, and ride must we
To Valhall to seek the sacred hall."

"The favor of Heerfather seek we to find, 2
To his followers gold he gladly gives;
To Hermoth gave he helm and mail-coat,
And to Sigmund he gave a sword as gift."

"Triumph to some, and treasure to others, 3
To many wisdom and skill in words,
Fair winds to the sailor, to the singer his art,
And a manly heart to many a hero."

"Thor shall I honor, and this shall I ask, 4
That his favor true mayst thou ever find;
[...]
Though little the brides of the giants he loves."

"From the stall now one of thy wolves lead forth, 5
And along with my boar shalt thou let him run;
For slow my boar goes on the road of the gods,
And I would not weary my worthy steed."

Hyndla kvað: 6
"Seinn er göltr þinn   goðveg troða,
vilk-at ek mar minn   mætan hlæða.
Flá ertu, Freyja,   er þú freistar mín,
vísar þú augum   á oss þannig,
er þú hefir ver þinn   í valsinni
Óttar unga   Innsteins bur."

Freyja kvað: 7
"Dulin ertu, Hyndla,   draums ætlak þér,
er þú kveðr ver minn   í valsinni,
þar er göltr glóar   Gullinbursti,
Hildisvíni,   er mér hagir gerðu,
dvergar tveir,   Dáinn ok Nabbi.

Senn vit ór söðlum   sitja vit skulum 8
ok um jöfra   ættir dæma,
gumna þeira,   er frá goðum kvámu.

Þeir hafa veðjat   Vala malmi 9
Óttarr ungi   ok Angantýr;
skylt er at veita,   svá at skati inn ungi
föðurleifð hafi   eftir frændr sína.

Hörg hann mér gerði   hlaðinn steinum, 10
nú er grjót þat   at gleri orðit;
rauð hann í nýju   nauta blóði;
æ trúði Óttarr   á ásynjur."

Freyja kvað: 11
"Nú láttu forna   niðja talða
ok upp bornar   ættir manna:
Hvat ek Skjöldunga,   hvat ek Skilfinga,
hvat er Öðlinga,   hvat er Ylfinga,
hvat er höldborit,   hvat er hersborit
mest manna val   und Miðgarði?"

Hyndla kvað: 12
"Þú ert, Óttarr,   borinn Innsteini,
en Innsteinn var   Alfi inum gamla,
Alfr var Ulfi,   Ulfr Sæfara,
en Sæfari   Svan inum rauða.

Hyndla spake: 6
"Falsely thou askest me, Freyja, to go,
For so in the glance of thine eyes I see;
On the way of the slain thy lover goes with thee.
Ottar the young, the son of Instein."

Freyja spake: 7
"Wild dreams, methinks, are thine when thou sayest
My lover is with me on the way of the slain;
There shines the boar with bristles of gold,
Hildisvini, he who was made
By Dain and Nabbi, the cunning dwarfs."

"Now let us down from our saddles leap, 8
And talk of the race of the heroes twain;
The men who were born of the gods above,
[...]"

"A wager have made in the foreign metal 9
Ottar the young and Angantyr;
We must guard, for the hero young to have,
His father's wealth, the fruits of his race."

"For me a shrine of stones he made, 10
And now to glass the rock has grown;
Oft with the blood of beasts was it red;
In the goddesses ever did Ottar trust."

"Tell to me now the ancient names, 11
And the races of all that were born of old:
Who are of the Skjoldungs, who of the Skilfings,
Who of the Othlings, who of the Ylfings,
Who are the free-born, who are the high-born,
The noblest of men that in Mithgarth dwell?"

Hyndla spake: 12
"Thou art, Ottar, the son of Instein,
And Instein the son of Alf the Old,
Alf of Ulf, Ulf of Sæfari,
And Sæfari's father was Svan the Red."

Móður átti faðir þinn   menjum göfga,   13
hygg ek, at hon héti   Hlédís gyðja;
Fróði var faðir þeirar,   en Fríund móðir;
öll þótti ætt sú   með yfirmönnum.

Auði var áðr   öflgastr manna,   14
Halfdan fyrri   hæstr Skjöldunga;
fræg váru folkvíg,   þau er framir gerðu,
hvarfla þóttu hans verk   með himins skautum.

Eflðisk hann við Eymund   æðstan manna,   15
en hann vá Sigtrygg   með svölum eggjum,
eiga gekk Almveig,   æðsta kvinna,
ólu þau ok áttu   átján sonu."

Hyndla kvað: 16
"Þaðan eru Skjöldungar,   þaðan Skilfingar,
þaðan Öðlingar,   þaðan Ynglingar,
þaðan höldborit,   þaðan hersborit,
mest manna val   und Miðgarði;
allt er þat ætt þín,   Óttarr heimski.

Var Hildigunnr   hennar móðir,   17
Sváfu barn   ok sækonungs;
allt er þat ætt þín,   Óttarr heimski.
Varðar, at viti svá.   Viltu enn lengra?

Dagr átti Þóru   drengja móður,   18
ólusk í ætt þar   æðstir kappar:
Fraðmarr ok Gyrðr   ok Frekar báðir,
Ámr ok Jösurmarr,   Alfr inn gamli.
Varðar, at viti svá.   Viltu enn lengra?

Ketill hét vinr þeira,   Klypps arfþegi,   19
var hann móðurfaðir   móður þinnar;
þar var Fróði   fyrr en Kári,
inn eldri var   Alfr of getinn.

Nanna var næst þar   Nökkva dóttir,   20
var mögr hennar   mágr þíns föður;
fyrnð er sú mægð,   fram tel ek lengra;
kunna ek báða   Brodd ok Hörvi;
allt er þat ætt þín,   Óttarr heimski."

"Thy mother, bright with bracelets fair, 13
Hight, methinks, the priestess Hledis;
Frothi her father, and Friaut her mother;
Her race of the mightiest men must seem."

"Of old the noblest of all was Ali, 14
Before him Halfdan, foremost of Skjoldungs;
Famed were the battles the hero fought,
To the corners of heaven his deeds were carried."

"Strengthened by Eymund, the strongest of men, 15
Sigtrygg he slew with the ice-cold sword;
His bride was Almveig, the best of women,
And eighteen boys did Almveig bear him."

"Hence come the Skjoldungs, hence the Skilfings, 16
Hence the Othlings, hence the Ynglings,
Hence come the free-born, hence the high-born,
The noblest of men that in Mithgarth dwell:
And all are thy kinsmen, Ottar, thou fool!

"Hildigun then her mother hight, 17
The daughter of Svava and Sækonung;
And all are thy kinsmen, Ottar, thou fool!
It is much to know, wilt thou hear yet more?"

"The mate of Dag was a mother of heroes, 18
Thora, who bore him the bravest of fighters,
Frathmar and Gyrth and the Frekis twain,
Am and Jofurmar, Alf the Old;
It is much to know, wilt thou hear yet more?"

"Her husband was Ketil, the heir of Klypp, 19
He was of thy mother the mother's-father;
Before the days of Kari was Frothi,
And horn of Hild was Hoalf then."

"Next was Nanna, daughter of Nokkvi, 20
Thy father's kinsman her son became;
Old is the line, and longer still,
And all are thy kinsmen, Ottar, thou fool!"

Hyndla kvað: 21
"Ísolfr ok Ásolfr Ölmóðs synir
ok Skúrhildar Skekkils dóttur;
skaltu til telja skatna margra;
allt er þat ætt þín, Óttarr heimski.

Gunnarr balkr, Grímr arðskafi, 22
járnskjöldr Þórir, Ulfr gínandi.

Hervarðr, Hjörvarðr, Hrani, Angantýr, 23
Búi ok Brámi, Barri ok Reifnir,
Tindr ok Tyrfingr, ok tveir Haddingjar;
allt er þat ætt þín, Óttarr heimski.

Austr í Bolm váru bornir 24
Arngríms synir ok Eyfuru,
brökun var berserkja, böl margs konar,
um lönd ok um lög sem logi færi;
allt er þat ætt þín, Óttarr heimski.

Kunnak báða Brodd ok Hörvi; 25
váru þeir í hirð Hrolfs ins gamla.
Allir bornir frá Jörmunreki,
Sigurðar mági, —hlýð þú sögu minni—
folkum grimms, þess er Fáfni vá."

Hyndla kvað: 26
Sá var vísir frá Völsungi
ok Hjördís frá Hrauðungi,
en Fylimi frá Öðlingum;
allt er þat ætt þín, Óttarr heimski.

Gunnarr ok Högni, Gjúka arfar, 27
ok it sama Guðrún, systir þeira;
eigi var Gutþormr Gjúka ættar,
þó var hann bróðir beggja þeira;
allt er þat ætt þín, Óttarr heimski.

Haraldr hilditönn borinn Hræreki 28
slöngvanbauga, sonr var hann Auðar,
Auðr djúpúðga Ívars dóttir,
en Ráðbarðr var Randvers faðir;
þeir váru gumnar goðum signaðir;
allt er þat ætt þín, Óttarr heimski."
[...]

"Isolf and Osolf, the sons of Olmoth, 21
Whose wife was Skurhild, the daughter of Skekkil,
Count them among the heroes mighty,
And all are thy kinsmen, Ottar, thou fool!"

"Gunnar the Bulwark, Grim the Hardy, 22
Thorir the Iron-shield, Ulf the Gaper,
Brodd and Hörvir both did I know;
In the household they were of Hrolf the Old."

"Hervarth, Hjorvarth, Hrani, Angantyr, 23
Bui and Brami, Barri and Reifnir,
Tind and Tyrfing, the Haddings twain,
And all are thy kinsmen, Ottar, thou fool!"

"Eastward in Bolm were born of old 24
The sons of Arngrim and Eyfura;
With berserk-tumult and baleful deed
Like fire o'er land and sea they fared,
And all are thy kinsmen, Ottar, thou fool!"

"The sons of Jormunrek all of yore 25
To the gods in death were as offerings given;
He was kinsman of Sigurth—hear well what I say—
The foe of hosts, and Fafnir's slayer."

"From Volsung's seed was the hero sprung, 26
And Hjordis was born of Hrauthung's race,
And Eylimi from the Othlings came,
And all are thy kinsmen, Ottar, thou fool!"

"Gunnar and Hogni, the heirs of Gjuki, 27
And Guthrun as well, who their sister was;
But Gotthorm was not of Gjuki's race,
Although the brother of both he was:
And all are thy kinsmen, Ottar, thou fool!"

"Of Hvethna's sons was Haki the best, 28
And Hjorvarth the father of Hvethna was;
[...]"

"Harald Battle-tooth of Auth was born, 29
Hrörek the Ring-giver her husband was;
Auth the Deep-minded was Ivar's daughter,
But Rathbarth the father of Randver was:
And all are thy kinsmen, Ottar, thou fool!"

Völuspo in skamma

Váru ellifu   æsir talðir,   29
Baldr er hné,   við banaþúfu;
þess lézk Váli   verðr at hefna,
síns of bróður   sló hann handbana.

Var Baldrs faðir   Burs arfþegi,   30
Freyr átti Gerði,   hon var Gymis dóttir,
jötna ættar,   ok Aurboðu;
þó var Þjazi,   þeira frændi,
skrautgjarn jötunn,   hans var Skaði dóttir.

Margt segjum þér   ok munum fleira;   31
vörumk, at viti svá.   Viltu enn lengra?

Haki var Hveðnu   hóti beztr sona,   32
en Hveðnu var   Hjörvarðr faðir;
Heiðr ok Hrossþjófr   Hrímnis kindar.

Eru völur allar   frá Viðolfi,   33
vitkar allir   frá Vilmeiði,
seiðberendr   frá Svarthöfða,
jötnar allir   frá Ymi komnir.

Margt segjum þér   ok munum fleira;   34
vörumk, at viti svá.   Viltu enn lengra?

Varð einn borin   í árdaga   35
rammaukinn mjök   rögna kindar;
níu báru þann   naddgöfgan mann
jötna meyjar   við jarðar þröm.

Hann Gjalp of bar,   hann Greip of bar,   36
bar hann Eistla   ok Eyrgjafa,
hann bar Ulfrún   ok Angeyja,
Imdr ok Atla   ok Járnsaxa.

Sá var aukinn   jarðar megni,   37
svalköldum sæ   ok sónardreyra.

Margt segjum þér   ok munum fleira;   38
vörumk, at viti svá.   Viltu enn lengra?

Fragment of "The Short Voluspo"

Eleven in number the gods were known, When Baldr o'er the hill of death was bowed; And this to avenge was Vali swift. When his brother's slayer soon he slew.	30
The father of Baldr was the heir of Bur, [...] Freyr's wife was Gerth, the daughter of Gymir, Of the giants' brood, and Aurbotha bore her; To these as well was Thjazi kin, The dark-loving giant; his daughter was Skathi.	31
Much have I told thee, and further will tell; There is much that I know; wilt thou hear yet more?	32
Heith and Hrossthjof, the children of Hrimnir. Of Hvethna's sons Haki was best by a bit, by Hjorvarth was Hvethna's father.	33
The sybils arose from Vitholf's race, From Vilmeith all the seers are, And the workers of charms are Svarthofthi's children, And from Ymir sprang the giants all.	34
Much have I told thee, and further will tell; There is much that I know; wilt thou hear yet more?	35
One there was born in the bygone days, Of the race of the gods, and great was his might; Nine giant women, at the world's edge, Once bore the man so mighty in arms.	36
Gjolp there bore him, Greip there bore him, Eistla bore him, and Eyrgjafa, Ulfrun bore him, and Angeyja, Imth and Atla, and Jarnsaxa.	37
Strong was he made with the strength of earth, With the ice-cold sea, and the blood of swine.	38
Much have I told thee, and further will tell; There is much that I know; wilt thou hear yet more?	39

Ól ulf Loki   við Angrboðu,   39
en Sleipni gat   við Svaðilfara;
eitt þótti skass   allra feiknast,
þat var bróður frá   Býleists komit.

Loki át hjarta   lindi brenndu,   40
fann hann halfsviðinn   hugstein konu;
varð Loftr kviðugr   af konu illri;
þaðan er á foldu flagð   hvert komit.

Haf gengr hríðum   við himin sjalfan,   41
líðr lönd yfir,   en loft bilar;
þaðan koma snjóvar   ok snarir vindar;
þá er í ráði,   at rögn of þrjóti.

Varð einn borinn   öllum meiri,   42
sá var aukinn   jarðar megni;
þann kveða stilli   stórúðgastan
sif sifjaðan   sjötum görvöllum.

Þá kemr annarr   enn máttkari,   43
þó þori ek eigi   þann at nefna;
fáir séa nú   fram of lengra
en Óðinn mun   ulfi mæta.

Freyja kvað: 44
"Ber þú minnisöl   mínum gesti,
svá hann öll muni   orð at tína
þessar ræðu   á þriðja morgni,
þá er þeir Angantýr   ættir rekja."

Hyndla kvað: 45
"Snúðu braut heðan,   sofa lystir mik,
fær þú fátt af mér   fríðra kosta;
hleypr þú, Óðs vina,   úti á náttum,
sem með höfrum   Heiðrún fari.

Rannt at Óði   ey þreyjandi,   46
skutusk þér fleiri   und fyrirskyrtu;
hleypr þú, Óðs vina,   úti á náttum,
sem með höfrum   Heiðrún fari."

The wolf did Loki with Angrbotha win,
And Sleipnir bore he to Svathilfari;
The worst of marvels seemed the one
That sprang from the brother of Byleist then.
  40

A heart ate Loki, in the embers it lay,
And half-cooked found he the woman's heart;
With child from the woman Lopt soon was,
And thence among men came the monsters all.
  41

The sea, storm-driven, seeks heaven itself,
O'er the earth it flows, the air grows sterile;
Then follow the snows and the furious winds,
For the gods are doomed, and the end is death.
  42

One there was born, the best of all,
And strong was he made with the strength of earth;
The proudest is called the kinsman of men
Of the rulers all throughout the world.
  43

Then comes another, a greater than all,
Though never I dare his name to speak;
Few are they now that farther can see
Than the moment when Odin shall meet the wolf.
  44

———⦅⦆———

Freyja spake:
"To my boar now bring the memory-beer,
So that all thy words, that well thou hast spoken,
The third morn hence he may hold in mind,
When their races Ottar and Angantyr tell."
  45

Hyndla spake:
"Hence shalt thou fare, for fain would I sleep,
From me thou gettest few favors good;
My noble one, out in the night thou leapest
As Heithrun goes the goats among."
  46

"To Oth didst thou run, who loved thee ever,
And many under thy apron have crawled;
My noble one, out in the night thou leapest,
As Heithrun goes the goats among."
  47

Freyja kvað: 47
"Ek slæ eldi   of íviðju,
svá at þú eigi kemsk   á braut heðan."

Hyndla kvað: 48
"Hyr sé ek brenna,   en hauðr loga,
verða flestir   fjörlausn þola;
ber þú Óttari   bjór at hendi
eitri blandinn mjök,   illu heilli."

Freyja kvað: 49
"Orðheill þín   skal engu ráða,
þóttú, brúðr jötuns,   bölvi heitir;
hann skal drekka   dýrar veigar;
bið ek Óttari   öll goð duga."

Freyja spake: 48
"Around the giantess flames shall I raise,
So that forth unburned thou mayst not fare."

Hyndla spake: 49
"Flames I see burning, the earth is on fire,
And each for his life the price must lose;
Bring then to Ottar the draught of beer,
Of venom full for an evil fate."

Freyja spake: 50
"Thine evil words shall work no ill,
Though, giantess, bitter thy baleful threats;
A drink full fair shall Ottar find,
If of all the gods the favor I get."

ENDNOTES

1. *Freyja*: The names of the speakers do not appear in the manuscripts. On Freyja cf. *Voluspo*, 21 and note; *Skirnismol*, introductory prose and note; *Lokasenna*, introductory prose and note. As stanzas 9–10 show, Ottar has made a wager of his entire inheritance with Angantyr regarding the relative loftiness of their ancestry, and by rich offerings has induced Freyja to assist him in establishing his genealogy. Freyja, having turned Ottar for purposes of disguise into a boar, calls on the giantess *Hyndla* ("She-Dog") to aid her. Hyndla does not appear elsewhere in the poems.

2. *Heerfather*: Odin; cf. *Voluspo*, 30. *Hermoth*: mentioned in the *Prose Edda* as a son of Odin who is sent to Hel to ask for the return of the slain Baldr. *Sigmund*: according to the *Volsungasaga* Sigmund was the son of Volsung, and hence Odin's great-great-grandson (note that Wagner eliminates all the intervening generations by the simple expedient of using Volsung's name as one of Odin's many appellations). Sigmund alone was able to draw from the tree the sword which a mysterious stranger (Odin, of course) had thrust into it (compare the first act of Wagner's *Die Walküre*).

3. Sijmons suggests that this stanza may be an interpolation.

4. No lacuna after line 2 is indicated in the manuscript. Editors have attempted various experiments in rearranging this and the following stanza.

5. Some editors, following Simrock, assign this whole stanza to Hyndla; others assign to her lines 3–4. Giving the entire stanza to Freyja makes better sense than any other arrangement, but is dependent on changing the manuscript's "thy" in line 3 to "my", as suggested by Bugge. The boar on which Freyja rides ("my worthy steed") is, of course, Ottar.

6. Hyndla detects Ottar, and accuses Freyja of having her lover with her. Unless Ottar is identical with Oth (cf. *Voluspo*, 25 and note), which seems most unlikely, there is no other reference to this love affair. *The way of the slain*: the road to Valhall.

7. Various experiments have been made in condensing the stanza into four lines, or in combining it with stanza 8. *Hildisvini* ("Battle-Swine"): perhaps Freyja refers to the boar with golden bristles given, according to Snorri, to her brother Freyr by the dwarfs. *Dain*: a dwarf; cf. *Voluspo*, 11. *Nabbi*: a dwarf nowhere else mentioned.

8. The first line is obviously corrupt in the manuscript, and has been variously emended. The general assumption is that in the interval between stanzas 7 and 8 Freyja and Hyndla have arrived at Valhall. No lacuna is indicated in the manuscript.

9. *Foreign metal*: gold. The word *valr*, meaning "foreign," and akin to "Welsh," is interesting in this connection, and some editors interpret it frankly as "Celtic," i.e., Irish, but the root of the name is much older than this suggests. Cf. the continental Proto-Germanic *Walhaz, meaning "foreigner", and applied to Romans, Celts, and Slavs.

10. *To glass*: i.e., the constant fires on the altar have fused the stone into glass. Glass beads, etc., were of very early use, though the use of glass for windows probably did not begin in Iceland much before 1200.

11. Possibly two stanzas, or perhaps one with interpolations. The manuscript omits the first half of line 4, here filled out from stanza 16, line 2. *Skjoldungs*: the descendants of Skjold, a mythical king who was Odin's son and the ancestor of the Danish kings; cf. *Snorri's Edda, Skaldskaparmal*, 43. *Skilfings*: mentioned by Snorri as descendants of King Skelfir, a mythical ruler in "the East." In *Grimnismol*, 54, the name Skilfing appears as one of Odin's many appellations. *Othlings*: Snorri derives this race from Authi, the son of Halfdan the Old (cf. stanza 14). *Ylfings*: some editors have changed this to "Ynglings," as in stanza 16, referring to the descendants of Yng or Yngvi, another son of Halfdan, but the reference may be to the same mythical family to which Helgi Hundingsbane belonged (cf. *Helgakvitha Hundingsbana* 1, 5).

12. *Instein*: mentioned in the *Halfssaga* as one of the warriors of King Half of Horthaland (the so-called Halfsrekkar). The others mentioned in this stanza appear in one of the later mythical accounts of the settlement of Norway.

14. Stanzas 14–16 are clearly interpolated, as Friaut (stanza 13, line 3) is

the daughter of Hildigun (stanza 17, line 1). *Halfdan* the Old, a mythical king of Denmark, called by Snorri "the most famous of all kings," of whom it was foretold that "for three hundred years there should be no woman and no man in his line who was not of great repute." After the slaying of Sigtrygg he married Almveig (or Alvig), daughter of King Eymund of Holmgarth (i.e., Russia), who bore him eighteen sons, nine at one birth. These nine were all slain, but the other nine were traditionally the ancestors of the most famous families in Northern hero lore.

16. Compare stanza 11. All or part of this stanza may be interpolated.

17. *Hildigun* (or Hildiguth): with this the poem returns to Ottar's direct ancestry, Hildigun being Friaut's mother. *Line 4*: cf. the refrain-line in the *Voluspo* (stanzas 27, 29, etc.).

18. Another interpolation, as Ketil (stanza 19, line 1) is the husband of Hildigun (stanza 17). *Dag*: one of Halfdan's sons, and ancestor of the Döglings. Line 5 may be a late addition.

19. *Ketil*: the semi-mythical Ketil Hortha-Kari, from whom various Icelandic families traced their descent. *Hoalf*: probably King Half of Horthaland, hero of the *Halfssaga*, and son of Hjorleif and Hild (cf. stanza 12, note).

20. *Nanna*: the manuscript has "Manna." Of Nanna and her father, Nokkvi, we know nothing, but apparently Nanna's son married a sister of Instein, Ottar's father.

21. *Olmoth*: one of the sons of Ketil Hortha-Kari. *Line 4*: here, and generally hereafter when it appears in the poem, this refrain-line is abbreviated in the manuscript to the word "all."

22. An isolated stanza, which some editors place after stanza 24, others combining lines 1–2 with the fragmentary stanza 23 In the manuscript lines 3–4 stand after stanza 24, where they fail to connect clearly with anything. *Hrolf the Old*: probably King Hrolf Gautreksson of Gautland, in the saga relating to whom (*Fornaldar sögur* III, 57 ff.) appear the names of Thorir the Iron-shield and Grim Thorkelsson.

23. Stanzas 23 and 24 name the twelve Berserkers, the sons of Arngrim and Eyfura, the story of whom is told in the *Hervararsaga* and the *Orvar-Oddssaga*. Saxo Grammaticus tells of the battle between them and Hjalmar and Orvar-Odd. Line 1 does not appear in the manuscript, but is added from the list of names given in the sagas. The Berserkers were wild warriors, distinguished above all by the fits of frenzy to which they were

subject in battle; during these fits they howled like wild beasts, foamed at the mouth, and gnawed the iron rims of their shields. At such times they were proof against steel or fire, but when the fever abated they were weak. The etymology of the word *berserk* is disputed; probably, however, it means "bear-shirt."

24. The manuscript omits the first half of line 1, here supplied from the *Orvar-Oddssaga*. *Bolm*: probably the island of Bolmsö, in the Swedish province of Smaland. In the manuscript and in most editions stanza 24 is followed by lines 3-4 of stanza 22. Some editors reject line 5 as spurious.

25. In the manuscript line 1 stands after line 4 of stanza 29. Probably a stanza enumerating Jormunrek's sons has been lost. Many editors combine lines 3-4 of stanza 22 and lines 2-4 of stanza 25 into one stanza. *Jormunrek*: the historical Ermanarich, king of the Goths, who died about 376. According to Norse tradition, in which Jormunrek played a large part, he slew his own sons (cf. *Guthrunarhvot* and *Hamthesmol*). In the saga Jormunrek married Sigurth's daughter, Svanhild. Stanzas 25-27 connect Ottar's descent with the whole Volsung-Sigurth-Jormunrek-Gjuki genealogy. The story of *Sigurth* is the basis for most of the heroic poems of the *Edda*, of the famous *Volsungasaga*, and, in Germany, of the *Nibelungenlied*. On his battle with the dragon *Fafnir* cf. *Fafnismol*.

26. *Volsung*: Sigurth's grandfather and Odin's great-grand son. *Hjordis*: daughter of King Eylimi, wife of Sigmund and mother of Sigurth. *Othlings*: cf. stanza 11.

27. *Gunnar*, *Hogni*, and *Guthrun*: the three children of the Burgundian king *Gjuki* and his wife Grimhild (Kriemhild); Guthrun was Sigurth's wife. *Gotthorm*, the third brother, who killed Sigurth at Brynhild's behest, was Grimhild's son, and thus a step-son of Gjuki. These four play an important part in the heroic cycle of *Eddic* poems. Cf. *Gripisspo*, introductory note [Appendix B].

28. In the manuscript and in many editions these two lines stand between stanzas 33 and 34. The change here made follows Bugge. The manuscript indicates no gap between stanzas 27 and 29. *Hvethna*: wife of King Halfdan of Denmark.[1]

29. The manuscript and many editions include line 1 of stanza 25 after line 4 of stanza 29. The story of *Harald Battle-tooth* is told in detail by Saxo Grammaticus. Harald's father was *Hrörek*, king of Denmark; his mother

---

[1] It is at this stanza that Bellows' numbering scheme deviates from that of the Old Norse used in this edition, due to his following the Bugge edition.

was *Auth*, daughter of *Ivar*, king of Sweden. After Ivar had treacherously destroyed Hrörek, Auth fled with Harald to Russia, where she married King *Rathbarth*. Harald's warlike career in Norway, and his death on the Bravalla-field at the hands of his nephew, Sigurth Ring, son of *Randver* and grandson of Rathbarth and Auth, were favorite saga themes.

30. At this point begins the fragmentary and interpolated "short *Voluspo*" identified by Snorri. The manuscript gives no indication of the break in the poem's continuity. *Eleven*: there are various references to the "twelve" gods (including Baldr); Snorri (*Gylfaginning*, 20–33) lists the following twelve in addition to Odin: Thor, Baldr, Njorth, Freyr, Tyr, Bragi, Heimdall, Hoth, Vithar, Vali, Ull and Forseti; he adds Loki as of doubtful divinity. *Baldr* and *Vali*: cf. *Voluspo*, 32–33.

31. The fragmentary stanzas 31–34 have been regrouped in various ways, and with many conjectures as to omissions, none of which are indicated in the manuscript. The order here is as in the manuscript, except that lines 1–2 of stanza 28 have been transposed from after line 2 of stanza 33. *Bur's heir*: Odin; cf. *Voluspo*, 4. *Freyr, Gerth, Gymir*: cf. *Skirnismol*. *Aurbotha*: a giantess, mother of Gerth. *Thjazi* and *Skathi*: cf. *Lokasenna*, 49, and *Harbarthsljoth*, 19.[2]

32. Cf. *Voluspo*, 44 and 27.

33. *Heith* ("Witch") and *Hrossthjof* ("Horse-thief"): the only other reference to the giant *Hrimnir* (*Skirnismol*, 28) makes no mention of his children.[3]

34. This stanza is quoted by Snorri (*Gylfaginning*, 5). Of *Vitholf* ("Forest Wolf"), *Vilmeith* ("Wish-Tree") and *Svarthoftli* ("Black Head") nothing further is known. *Ymir*: cf. *Voluspo*, 3.

36. According to Snorri (*Gylfaginning*, 27) Heimdall was the son of Odin and of nine sisters. As Heimdall was the watchman of the gods, this has given rise to much "solar myth" discussion. The names of his nine giantess mothers are frequently said to denote attributes of the sea.

37. The names of Heimdall's mothers may be rendered "Yelper," "Griper," "Foamer," "Sand-Strewer," "She-Wolf," "Sorrow-Whelmer," "Dusk," "Fury," and "Iron-Sword."

---

2 This stanza was originally stanzas 31 and 32 in the original Bellows edition—they have been combined here to match the Old Norse. From this point on, the stanza numbering in the original Bellows edition will disagree from the present edition.
3 The final two lines of this stanza have been taken from the Hollander translation, as Bellows did not translate them.

38. It has been suggested that these lines were interpolated from *Guthrunarkvitha* II, 22. Some editors add the refrain of stanza 36. *Swine's blood*: to Heimdall's strength drawn from earth and sea was added that derived from sacrifice.

40. Probably a lacuna before this stanza. Regarding the *wolf* Fenrir, born of Loki and the giantess *Angrbotha*, cf. *Voluspo*, 39 and note. *Sleipnir*: Odin's eight-legged horse, born of the stallion *Svathilfari* and of Loki in the guise of a mare (cf. *Grimnismol*, 44). *The worst*: doubtless referring to Mithgarthsorm, another child of Loki. *The brother of Byleist*: Loki; cf. *Voluspo*, 51.

41. Nothing further is known of the myth here referred to, wherein Loki (Lopt) eats the cooked heart of a woman and thus himself gives birth to a monster. The reference is not likely to be to the serpent, as, according to Snorri (*Gylfaginning*, 34), the wolf, the serpent, and Hel were all the children of Loki and Angrbotha.

43. Regarding Heimdall's kinship to the three great classes of men, cf. *Rigsthula*, introductory note [Appendix B], wherein the apparent confusion of his attributes with those of Odin is discussed.[4]

42. Probably an omission, perhaps of considerable length, before this stanza. For the description of the destruction of the world, cf. *Voluspo*, 57.

44. Cf. *Voluspo*, 65, where the possible reference to Christianity is noted. With this stanza the fragmentary "short *Voluspo*" ends, and the dialogue between Freyja and Hyndla continues.

45. Freyja now admits the identity of her boar as Ottar, who with the help of the "memory-beer" is to recall the entire genealogy he has just heard, and thus win his wager with Angantyr.

46. *Heithrun*: the she-goat that stands by Valhall (cf. *Grimnismol*, 25), the name being here used simply of she-goats in general, in caustic comment on Freyja's morals. Of these Loki entertained a similar view; cf. *Lokasenna*, 30.

47. *Oth*: cf. stanza 6 and note, and *Voluspo*, 25 and note. Lines 3–4, abbreviated in the manuscript, are very likely repeated here by mistake.

48. The manuscript repeats once again lines 3–4 of stanza 47 as the last

---

[4] In the original Bellows edition, this stanza comes before stanza 39. It has been moved back in the present edition to agree with the Old Norse.

two lines of this stanza. It seems probable that two lines have been lost, to the effect that Freyja will burn the giantess alive "If swiftly now thou dost not seek, / And hither bring the memory-beer."

SVIPDAGSMOL
THE BALLAD OF SVIPDAG

INTRODUCTION

The *Svipdagsmol* is the last of the poems not found in either of the principal codices that make up the standard material for the *Poetic Edda*, and can be said to be wholly unique in two respects.

Firstly, the work is composed of two wholly separate poems which remained as such until the 19th century, and which, through scholarly work, by general agreement now represent a single cohesive narrative thread. The poems of *Grougaldr* (The Spell of Groa) and *Fjolsvinnsmol* (The Ballad of Fjolsvith) are now well accepted as being originally conjoined material, with *Fjolsvinnsmol* directly following the narrative of *Grougaldr*. Whether these narratives were originally conjoined by means of a prose narrative explanation or missing poetic accompaniment is not known.

Secondly, the poems constituting the *Svipdagsmol* are unanimously accepted as being of an extremely late origin even when compared with the youngest poems generally assigned to the *Eddas*. They only feature in paper manuscripts dating no earlier than the 17th century, they contain a large number of kennings and poetic allusions, and they feature a literary tone and theme that is reminiscent of the later chivalric works of the continent with a hero (knight) setting off on a quest for the love of a princess, a narrative theme that is wholly absent and alien to the authentic Norse tradition. Even beyond those factors, the poem contains many basic theological errors that strongly suggest that the author was not particularly educated about mythology and knew only the rudiments, or was otherwise wholly unconcerned with accuracy and assumes his audience to be similarly uncaring.

Examples of these errors include the person of Fjolsvith himself, who despite transparently being the God Odin (Fjolsvith being one of his recorded names in *Grimnismol*) attempts to pass himself off as a frost giant named Vindkaldr (Wind Cold) despite these beings serving as the mortal enemies of the Gods. He is also accompanied by his hounds Geri and Gifr (the names of Odin's wolves are, in fact, Geri and Freki). Moreover, Fjolsvith's narrative role is to guard the castle imprisoning Mengloth (almost always identified as the Goddess Freya) with him ultimately giving her hand in marriage to Svipdagr. It strains the bounds of credulity that Odin, chief of the *Aesir*, would trouble himself to personally guard a castle, and it is incomprehensible that Odin would even have the authority to give Freya's hand away in marriage to begin with. No mention is made of Freya's twin brother Freyr, nor her father Njord, who, logic would dictate, would have much to say about the most eligible and prestigious of the Goddesses, the desire of all *Jotnar*, marrying a random mortal hero.

All things considered, we must accept that the poem's narrative is not a truly authentic depiction of pre-Christian religious beliefs, nor something that our ancestors believed to be a legitimate theological event, but rather the work of a late medieval poet intent on producing a romance saga for entertainment long after the figures had ceased to hold any cultural relevance to his audience.

I. Grógaldr

Sonr kvað:
"Vaki þú, Gróa,   vaki þú, góð kona,
vek ek þik dauðra dura,   ef þú þat mant,
at þú þinn mög bæðir   til kumbldysjar koma."

Gróa kvað:
"Hvat er nú annt   mínum eingasyni,
hverju ertu nú bölvi borinn,
er þú þá móður kallar,
er til moldar er komin
ok ór ljóðheimum liðin?"

Sonr kvað:
"Ljótu leikborði   skaut fyr mik in lævísa kona,
sú er faðmaði minn föður;
þar bað hon mik koma,   er kvæmtki veit,
móti Menglöðu."

Gróa kvað:
"Löng er för,   langir ro farvegar,
langir ro manna munir,   ef þat verðr,
at þú þinn vilja bíðr,
ok skeikar þá Skuld at sköpum."

SVIPDAGSMOL

I. Groa's Spell

Svipdag spake: 1
"Wake thee, Groa! wake, mother good!
At the doors of the dead I call thee;
Thy son, bethink thee, thou badst to seek
Thy help at the hill of death."

Groa spake: 2
"What evil vexes mine only son,
What baleful fate hast thou found,
That thou callest thy mother, who lies in the mould,
And the world of the living has left?"

Svipdag spake: 3
"The woman false whom my father embraced
Has brought me a baleful game;
For she bade me go forth where none may fare,
And Menglöth the maid to seek."

Groa spake: 4
"Long is the way, long must thou wander,
But long is love as well;
Thou mayst find, perchance, what thou fain wouldst have,
If the fates their favor will give."

Sonr kvað: 5
"Galdra þú mér gal, þá er góðir eru,
bjarg þú, móðir, megi;
á vegum allr hygg ek, at ek verða muna,
þykkjumk ek til ungr afi."

Gróa kvað: 6
"Þann gel ek þér fyrstan,
þann kveða fjölnýtan, þann gól Rindi Rani,
at þú of öxl skjótir, því er þér atalt þykkir;
sjalfr leið þú sjalfan þik.

Þann gel ek þér annan, ef þú árna skalt 7
viljalauss á vegum, Urðar lokur
haldi þér öllum megum, er þú á sinnum sér.

Þann gel ek þér inn þriðja, ef þér þjóðáar 8
falla at fjörlotum, Horn ok Ruðr
snúisk til heljar meðan, en þverri æ fyr þér.

Þann gel ek þér inn fjórða, ef þik fjándr standa 9
görvir á galgvegi, hugr þeim hverfi
til handa þér, ok snúisk þeim til sátta sefi.

Þann gel ek þér inn fimmta, ef þér fjöturr verðr 10
borinn at boglimum, leysigaldr læt ek
þér fyr legg of kveðinn, ok stökkr þá láss af limum,
en af fótum fjöturr."

Gróa kvað: 11
"Þann gel ek þér inn sétta,
ef þú á sjó kemr meira en menn viti,
logn ok lögr gangi þér í lúðr saman
ok léi þér æ friðdrjúgrar farar.

Þann gel ek þér inn sjaunda, 12
ef þik sækja kemr frost á fjalli háu,
hræva kulði megi-t þínu holdi fara,
ok haldisk æ lík at liðum.

Svipdag spake:
"Charms full good then chant to me, mother,
And seek thy son to guard;
For death do I fear on the way I shall fare,
And in years am I young, methinks."

Groa spake:
"Then first I will chant thee the charm oft-tried,
That Rani taught to Rind;
From the shoulder whate'er mislikes thee shake,
For helper thyself shalt thou have."

"Then next I will chant thee, if needs thou must travel,
And wander a purposeless way:
The bolts of Urth shall on every side
Be thy guards on the road thou goest."

"Then third I will chant thee, if threatening streams
The danger of death shall bring:
Yet to Hel shall turn both Horn and Ruth,
And before thee the waters shall fail."

"Then fourth I will chant thee, if come thy foes
On the gallows-way against thee:
Into thine hands shall their hearts be given,
And peace shall the warriors wish."

"Then fifth I will chant thee, if fetters perchance
Shall bind thy bending limbs:
O'er thy thighs do I chant a loosening-charm,
And the lock is burst from the limbs,
And the fetters fall from the feet."

"Then sixth I will chant thee, if storms on the sea
Have might unknown to man:
Yet never shall wind or wave do harm,
And calm is the course of thy boat."

"Then seventh I chant thee, if frost shall seek
To kill thee on lofty crags:
The fatal cold shall not grip thy flesh,
And whole thy body shall be."

Þann gel ek þér inn átta, 13
ef þik úti nemr   nótt á niflvegi,
at því firr megi   þér til meins gera
kristin dauð kona.

Þann gel ek þér inn níunda, 14
ef þú við inn naddgöfga   orðum skiptir jötun,
máls ok mannvits   sé þér á minni ok hjarta
gnóga of gefit.

Far þú nú æva,   þar er forað þykkir, 15
ok standi-t þér mein fyr munum;
á jarðföstum steini   stóð ek innan dura,
meðan ek þér galdra gól.

Móður orð   ber þú, mögr, heðan 16
ok lát þér í brjósti búa;
iðgnóga heill   skaltu of aldr hafa,
meðan þú mín orð of mant."

II. Fjölsvinnsmál

Útan garða   hann sá upp of koma 17
þursa þjóðar sjöt:
"Hvat er þat flagða,   er stendr fyr forgörðum
ok hvarflar um hættan loga?

Hvers þú leitar,   eða hvers þú á leitum ert, 18
eða hvat viltu, vinlaus, vita?
Úrgar brautir   árnaðu aftr heðan;
átt-at-tu hér, verndar vanr, veru."

Kómumaðr kvað: 19
"Hvat er þat flagða,   er stendr fyr forgarði
ok býðr-at líðöndum löð?
Sæmðarorðalauss   hefir þú, seggr, of lifat,
ok haltu heim heðan!"

"Then eighth will I chant thee, if ever by night   13
Thou shalt wander on murky ways:
Yet never the curse of a Christian woman
From the dead shall do thee harm."

"Then ninth will I chant thee, if needs thou must strive   14
With a warlike giant in words:
Thy heart good store of wit shall have,
And thy mouth of words full wise."

"Now fare on the way where danger waits,   15
Let evils not lessen thy love!
I have stood at the door of the earth-fixed stones,
The while I chanted thee charms."

"Bear hence, my son, what thy mother hath said,   16
And let it live in thy breast;
Thine ever shall be the best of fortune,
So long as my words shall last."

II. *The Lay of Fjolsvith*

Before the house he beheld one coming   17
To the home of the giants high.
Svipdag spake:
"What giant is here, in front of the house,
And around him fires are flaming?"

Fjolsvith spake: 18
"What seekest thou here? for what is thy search?
What, friendless one, fain wouldst thou know?
By the ways so wet must thou wander hence,
For, weakling, no home hast thou here."

Svipdag spake: 19
"What giant is here, in front of the house,
To the wayfarer welcome denying?"
Fjolsvith spake:
"Greeting full fair thou never shalt find,
So hence shalt thou get thee home."

Borgarvörðr kvað: 20
"Fjölsviðr ek heiti,   en ek á fróðan sefa,
þeygi em ek míns mildr matar;
innan garða   þú kemr hér aldregi,
ok dríf þú nú, vargr, at vegi!"

Kómumaðr kvað: 21
"Augna gamans   fýsir aftr at fá,
hvars hann getr svást at sjá;
garðar glóa   mér þykkja of gullna sali;
hér mynda ek eðli una."

Fjölsviðr kvað: 22
"Segðu mér, hverjum   ertu, sveinn, of borinn,
eða hverra ertu manna mögr?"

Kómumaðr kvað:
"Vindkaldr ek heiti,   Várkaldr hét minn faðir,
þess var Fjölkaldr faðir.

Segðu mér þat, Fjölsviðr,   er ek fregna mun 23
ok ek vilja vita:
Hverr hér ræðr   ok ríki hefir
eign ok auðsölum?"

Fjölsviðr kvað: 24
"Menglöð of heitir,   en hana móðir of gat
við Svafrþorins syni;
hon hér ræðr   ok ríki hefir
eign ok auðsölum."

Vindkaldr kvað: 25
"Segðu mér þat, Fjölsviðr,   er ek þik fregna mun
ok ek vilja vita:
Hvat sú grind heitir,   er með goðum sá-at
menn it meira forað?"

Fjölsviðr kvað: 26
"Þrymgjöll hon heitir,   en hana þrír gerðu
Sólblinda synir;
fjöturr fastr   verðr við faranda hvern
er hana hefr frá hliði."

"Fjolsvith am I, and wise am I found, 20
But miserly am I with meat;
Thou never shalt enter within the house,
Go forth like a wolf on thy way!"

Svipdag spake: 21
"Few from the joy of their eyes will go forth,
When the sight of their loves they seek;
Full bright are the gates of the golden hall,
And a home shall I here enjoy."

Fjolsvith spake: 22
"Tell me now, fellow, what father thou hast,
And the kindred of whom thou camst."

Svipdag spake:
"Vindkald am I, and Varkald's son,
And Fjolkald his father was."

"Now answer me, Fjolsvith, the question I ask, 23
For now the truth would I know:
Who is it that holds and has for his own
The rule of the hall so rich?"

Fjolsvith spake: 24
"Mengloth is she, her mother bore her
To the son of Svafrthorin;
She is it that holds and has for her own
The rule of the hall so rich."

Svipdag spake: 25
"Now answer me, Fjolsvith, the question I ask,
For now the truth would I know:
What call they the gate? for among the gods
Ne'er saw man so grim a sight."

Fjolsvith spake: 26
"Thrymgjol they call it; 'twas made by the three,
The sons of Solblindi;
And fast as a fetter the farer it holds,
Whoever shall lift the latch."

Vindkaldr kvað: 27
"Segðu mér þat, Fjölsviðr,   er ek þik fregna mun
ok ek vilja vita:
Hvat sá garðr heitir,   er með goðum sá-at
menn it meira forað?"

Fjölsviðr kvað: 28
"Gastrópnir heitir,   en ek hann görfan hefk
ór Leirbrimis limum;
svá hefik studdan,   at hann standa mun,
æ meðan öld lifir."

Vindkaldr kvað: 29
"Segðu mér þat, Fjölsviðr,   er ek þik fregna mun
ok ek vilja vita:
Hvat þeir garmar heita,   er gífrari hefik
enga fyrr í löndum lítit?"

Fjölsviðr kvað: 30
"Gífr heitir annarr,   en Geri annarr,
ef þú vilt þat vita;
varðir ellifu,   er þeir varða,
unz rjúfask regin."

Vindkaldr kvað: 31
"Segðu mér þat, Fjölsviðr,   er ek þik fregna mun
ok ek vilja vita,   hvárt sé manna nökkut,
þat er megi inn koma,   meðan sókndjarfir sofa."

Fjölsviðr kvað: 32
"Missvefni mikit var þeim   mjök of lagit,
síðan þeim var varzla vituð;   annarr of nætr sefr,
en annarr of daga,   ok kemsk þá vætr, ef þá kom."

Vindkaldr kvað: 33
"Segðu mér þat, Fjölsviðr,   er ek þik fregna mun
ok ek vilja vita,   hvárt sé matar nökkut,
þat er menn hafi,   ok hlaupi inn, meðan þeir eta."

Svipdag spake: 27
"Now answer me, Fjolsvith, the question I ask,
For now the truth would I know:
What call they the house? for no man beheld
'Mongst the gods so grim a sight."

Fjolsvith spake: 28
"Gastropnir is it, of old I made it
From the limbs of Leirbrimir;
I braced it so strongly that fast it shall stand
So long as the world shall last."

Svipdag spake: 29
"Now answer me, Fjolsvith, the question I ask,
For now the truth would I know:
What call they the hounds, that before the house
So fierce and angry are?"

Fjolsvith spake: 30
"Gif call they one, and Geri the other,
If now the truth thou wouldst know;
Great they are, and their might will grow,
Till the gods to death are doomed."

Svipdag spake: 31
"Now answer me, Fjolsvith, the question I ask,
For now the truth would I know:
May no man hope the house to enter,
While the hungry hounds are sleeping?"

Fjolsvith spake: 32
"Together they sleep not, for so was it fixed
When the guard to them was given;
One sleeps by night, the next by day,
So no man may enter ever."

Svipdag spake: 33
"Now answer me, Fjolsvith, the question I ask,
For now the truth would I know:
Is there no meat that men may give them,
And leap within while they eat?"

Fjölsviðr kvað: 34
"Vegnbráðir tvær   liggja í Viðópnis liðum,
ef þú vilt þat vita,   þat eitt er svá matar,
at þeim menn of gefi,   ok hlaupi inn, meðan þeir eta."

Vindkaldr kvað: 35
"Segðu mér þat, Fjölsviðr,   er ek þik fregna mun
ok ek vilja vita: Hvat þat barr heitir,
er breiðask um   lönd öll limar?"

Fjölsviðr kvað: 36
"Mímameiðr hann heitir,   en þat manngi veit,
af hverjum rótum renn;   við þat hann fellr,
er fæstan varir,   flær-at hann eld né járn."

Vindkaldr kvað: 37
"Segðu mér þat,   Fjölsviðr, er ek þik fregna mun
ok ek vilja vita:
Hvat af móði verðr   þess ins mæra viðar,
er hann flær-rat eld né járn?"

Fjölsviðr kvað: 38
"Út af hans aldni   skal á eld bera
fyr kelisjúkar konur;
útar hverfa   þats þær innar skyli,
sá er hann með mönnum mjötuðr."

Vindkaldr kvað: 39
"Segðu mér þat, Fjölsviðr,   er ek þik fregna mun
ok ek vilja vita:
Hvat sá hani heitir,   er sitr í inum háva viði,
allr hann við gull glóir?"

Fjölsviðr kvað: 40
"Víðópnir hann heitir,   en hann stendr veðrglasir
á meiðs kvistum Míma;
einum ekka   þryngr hann érófsaman
Surtr Sinmöru."

Fjolsvith spake: 34
"Two wing-joints there be in Vithofnir's body,
If now the truth thou wouldst know;
That alone is the meat that men may give them,
And leap within while they eat."

Svipdag spake: 35
"Now answer me, Fjolsvith, the question I ask,
For now the truth would I know:
What call they the tree that casts abroad
Its limbs o'er every land?"

Fjolsvith spake: 36
"Mimameith its name, and no man knows
What root beneath it runs;
And few can guess what shall fell the tree,
For fire nor iron shall fell it."

Svipdag spake: 37
"Now answer me, Fjolsvith, the question I ask,
For now the truth would I know:
What grows from the seed of the tree so great,
That fire nor iron shall fell?"

Fjolsvith spake: 38
"Women, sick with child, shall seek
Its fruit to the flames to bear;
Then out shall come what within was hid,
And so is it mighty with men."

Svipdag spake: 39
"Now answer me, Fjolsvith, the question I ask,
For now the truth would I know:
What cock is he on the highest bough,
That glitters all with gold?"

Fjolsvith spake: 40
"Vithofnir his name, and now he shines
Like lightning on Mimameith's limbs;
And great is the trouble with which he grieves
Both Surt and Sinmora."

Vindkaldr kvað: 41
"Segðu mér þat, Fjölsviðr,   er ek þik fregna mun
ok ek vilja vita:
hvárt sé vápna nökkut,   þat er knegi Viðópnir fyrir
hníga á Heljar sjöt?"

Fjölsviðr kvað: 42
"Lævateinn heitir hann,   en hann gerði Loftr rúnum
fyr nágrindr neðan;
í segjárnskeri   liggr hann hjá Sinmöru,
ok halda njarðlásar níu."

Vindkaldr kvað: 43
"Segðu mér þat, Fjölsviðr,   er ek þik fregna mun
ok ek vilja vita:
hvárt aftr kemr,   sá er eftir ferr
ok vill þann tein taka."

Fjölsviðr kvað: 44
"Aftr mun koma,   sá er eftir ferr
ok vill þann tein taka,   ef þat færir,
er fáir eigu,   Eiri örglasis."

Vindkaldr kvað: 45
"Segðu mér þat, Fjölsviðr,   er ek þik fregna mun
ok ek vilja vita:
hvárt sé mæta nökkut,   þat er menn hafi
ok verðr því in fölva gýgr fegin."

Fjölsviðr kvað: 46
"Ljósan léa   skaltu í lúðr bera,
þann er liggr   í Viðópnis völum,
Sinmöru at selja,   áðr hon söm telisk
vápn til vígs at ljá."

Vindkaldr kvað: 47
"Segðu mér þat, Fjölsviðr,   er ek þik fregna mun
ok ek vilja vita:
Hvat sá salr heitir,   er slunginn er
vísum vafrloga?"

Svipdag spake: 41
"Now answer me, Fjolsvith, the question I ask,
For now the truth would I know:
What weapon can send Vithofnir to seek
The house of Hel below?"

Fjolsvith spake: 42
"Lævatein is there, that Lopt with runes
Once made by the doors of death;
In Lægjarn's chest by Sinmora lies it,
And nine locks fasten it firm."

Svipdag spake: 43
"Now answer me, Fjolsvith, the question I ask,
For now the truth would I know:
May a man come thence, who thither goes,
And tries the sword to take?"

Fjolsvith spake: 44
"Thence may he come who thither goes,
And tries the sword to take,
If with him he carries what few can win,
To give to the goddess of gold."

Svipdag spake: 45
"Now answer me, Fjolsvith, the question I ask,
For now the truth would I know:
What treasure is there that men may take
To rejoice the giantess pale?"

Fjolsvith spake: 46
"The sickle bright in thy wallet bear,
Mid Vithofnir's feathers found;
To Sinmora give it, and then shall she grant
That the weapon by thee be won."

Svipdag spake: 47
"Now answer me, Fjolsvith, the question I ask,
For now the truth would I know:
What call they the hall, encompassed here
With flickering magic flames?"

Fjölsviðr kvað: 48
"Hyrr hann heitir, en hann lengi mun
á brodds oddi bifask;
auðranns þess munu um aldr hafa
frétt eina fírar."

Vindkaldr kvað: 49
"Segðu mér þat, Fjölsviðr, er ek þik fregna mun
ok ek vilja vita:
Hverr þat gerði, er ek fyr garð sák
innan, ásmaga?"

Fjölsviðr kvað: 50
"Uni ok Íri, Óri ok Bári,
Varr ok Vegdrasill;
Dóri ok Úri, Dellingr, Atvarðr,
Líðskjalfr, Loki."

Vindkaldr kvað: 51
"Segðu mér þat, Fjölsviðr, er ek þik fregna mun
ok ek vilja vita:
Hvat þat bjarg heitir, er ek sé brúði á
þjóðmæra þruma?"

Fjölsviðr kvað: 52
"Lyfjaberg þat heitir, en þat hefir lengi verit
sjúkum ok sárum gaman;
heil verðr hver, þótt hafi árs sótt,
ef þat klífr, kona."

Vindkaldr kvað: 53
"Segðu mér þat, Fjölsviðr, er ek þik fregna mun
ok ek vilja vita:
Hvat þær meyjar heita, er fyr Menglaðar knjám
sitja sáttar saman?"

Fjölsviðr kvað: 54
"Hlíf heitir, önnur Hlífþrasa,
þriðja Þjóðvarta, Björt ok Blíð,
Blíðr, Fríð, Eir ok Aurboða."

Fjolsvith spake: 48
"Lyr is it called, and long it shall
On the tip of a spear-point tremble;
Of the noble house mankind has heard,
But more has it never known."

Svipdag spake: 49
"Now answer me, Fjolsvith, the question I ask,
For now the truth would I know:
What one of the gods has made so great
The hall I behold within?"

Fjolsvith spake: 50
"Uni and Iri, Bari and Jari,
Var and Vegdrasil,
Dori and Ori, Delling, and there
Was Loki, the fear of the folk."

Svipdag spake: 51
"Now answer me, Fjolsvith, the question I ask,
For now the truth would I know:
What call they the mountain on which the maid
Is lying so lovely to see?"

Fjolsvith spake: 52
"Lyfjaberg is it, and long shall it be
A joy to the sick and the sore;
For well shall grow each woman who climbs it,
Though sick full long she has lain."

Svipdag spake: 53
"Now answer me, Fjolsvith, the question I ask,
For now the truth would I know:
What maidens are they that at Mengloth's knees
Are sitting so gladly together?"

Fjolsvith spake: 54
"Hlif is one named, Hlifthrasa another,
Thjothvara call they the third;
Bjort and Bleik, Blith and Frith,
Eir and Aurbotha."

Vindkaldr kvað: 55
"Segðu mér þat, Fjölsviðr,   er ek þik fregna mun
ok ek vilja vita:
Hvárt þær bjarga,   þeim er blóta þær,
ef gerask þarfar þess?"

Fjölsviðr kvað: 56
"Bjarga svinnar,   hvar er menn blóta þær
á stallhelgum stað;
eigi svá hátt forað   kemr at hölða sonum,
hvern þær ór nauðum nema."

Vindkaldr kvað: 57
"Segðu mér þat, Fjölsviðr,   er ek þik fregna mun
ok ek vilja vita,   hvárt sé manna nökkut,
er knegi á Menglaðar   svásum armi sofa?"

Fjölsviðr kvað: 58
"Vætr er þat manna,   er knegi á Menglaðar
svásum armi sofa,   nema Svipdagr einn,
hánum var sú in sólbjarta   brúðr at kván of kveðin."

Vindkaldr kvað: 59
"Hrittu á hurðir,   láttu hlið rúm,
hér máttu Svipdag sjá;
en þó vita far,   ef vilja myni
Menglöð mitt gaman."

Fjölsviðr kvað: 60
"Heyr þú, Menglöð,   hér er maðr kominn,
gakk þú á gest sjá;
hundar fagna,   hús hefir upp lokizk,
hygg ek, at Svipdagr sé."

Menglöð kvað: 61
"Horskir hrafnar   skulu þér á hám galga
slíta sjónir ór,   ef þú þat lýgr,
at hér sé langt kominn   mögr til minna sala."

Menglöð kvað: 62
"Hvaðan þú fórt,   hvaðan þú för gerðir,
hvé þik hétu hjú?
At ætt ok nafni   skal ek jartegn vita,
ef ek var þér kván of kveðin."

Svipdag spake: 55
"Now answer me, Fjolsvith, the question I ask,
For now the truth would I know:
Aid bring they to all who offerings give,
If need be found therefor?"

Fjolsvith spake: 56
"Soon aid they all who offerings give
On the holy altars high;
And if danger they see for the sons of men,
Then each from ill do they guard."

Svipdag spake: 57
"Now answer me, Fjolsvith, the question I ask,
For now the truth would I know:
Lives there the man who in Mengloth's arms
So fair may seek to sleep?"

Fjolsvith spake: 58
"No man there is who in Mengloth's arms
So fair may seek to sleep,
Save Svipdag alone, for the sun-bright maid
Is destined his bride to be."

Svipdag spake: 59
"Fling back the gates! make the gateway wide!
Here mayst thou Svipdag see!
Hence get thee to find if gladness soon
Mengloth to me will give."

Fjolsvith spake: 60
"Hearken, Mengloth, a man is come;
Go thou the guest to see!
The hounds are fawning, the house bursts open,
Svipdag, methinks, is there."

Mengloth spake: 61
"On the gallows high shall hungry ravens
Soon thine eyes pluck out,
If thou liest in saying that here at last
The hero is come to my hall."

"Whence camest thou hither? how camest thou here? 62
What name do thy kinsmen call thee?
Thy race and thy name as a sign must I know,
That thy bride I am destined to be."

Svipdagr kvað: 63
"Svipdagr ek heiti,   Sólbjartr hét minn faðir,
þaðan rákumk vindkalda vegu;
Urðar orði   kveðr engi maðr,
þótt þat sé við löst lagit."

Menglöð kvað: 64
"Vel þú nú kominn,   hefik minn vilja beðit,
fylgja skal kveðju koss;
forkunnar sýn   mun flestan glaða,
hvars hefir við annan ást.

Lengi ek sat   ljúfu bergi á, 65
beið ek þín dægr ok daga;
nú þat varð,   er ek vætt hefi,
at þú ert kominn, mögr, til minna sala.

Þrár hafðar   er ek hefi til þíns gamans, 66
en þú til míns munar;
nú er þat satt,   er vit slíta skulum
ævi ok aldr saman."

Svipdag spake: 63
"Svipdag am I, and Solbjart's son;
Thence came I by wind-cold ways;
With the words of Urth shall no man war,
Though unearned her gifts be given."

Mengloth spake: 64
"Welcome thou art, for long have I waited;
The welcoming kiss shalt thou win!
For two who love is the longed-for meeting
The greatest gladness of all."

"Long have I sat on Lyfjaberg here, 65
Awaiting thee day by day;
And now I have what I ever hoped,
For here thou art come to my hall."

"Alike we yearned; I longed for thee, 66
And thou for my love hast longed;
But now henceforth together we know
Our lives to the end we shall live."

ENDNOTES

1. *Svipdag* ("Swift Day"): the names of the speakers are lacking in the manuscripts.[1]

3. *The woman*: Svipdag's stepmother, who is responsible for his search for Mengloth ("Necklace-Glad"). This name has suggested that Mengloth is really Frigg, possessor of the famous Brisings' necklace, or else Freyja (cf. *Lokasenna*, 20, note).[2]

6. For this catalogue of charms (stanzas 6-14) cf. the *Ljothatal* (*Hovamol*, 147-165). *Rani* and *Rind*: the manuscripts, have these words in inverse relation; I have followed Neckel's emendation. Rind was the giantess who became the mother of Vali, Odin's son, the one-night-old avenger of Baldr (cf. *Voluspo*, 33-34, and *Baldrs Draumar*, 11 and note). Rani is presumably Odin, who, according to a skaldic poem, won Rind by magic.

7. *Urth*: one of the three Norns, or Fates; cf. *Voluspo*, 20.

8. *Horn* and *Ruth*: these two rivers, here used merely to symbolize all dangerous streams, are not included in the catalogue of rivers given in *Grimnismol*, 27-29, for which reason some editors have changed the names to Hron and Hrith.

10. This stanza is a close parallel to *Hovamol*, 150, and the fifth line may well be an interpolation from line 4 of that stanza.

13. *A dead Christian woman*: this passage has distressed many editors,

---

1 Bellows is using the name *Svipdag* whereas the Old Norse uses the term 'the son'. As Bellows notes, the manuscripts do not have any indication of who is speaking.
2 Bellows has made an error in that Frigg is not the possessor of Brisingamen; this is Freyja.

who have sought to emend the text so as to make it mean simply "a dead witch." The fact seems to be, however, that this particular charm was composed at a time when Christians were regarded by all conservative pagans as emissaries of darkness. A dead woman's curse would naturally be more potent, whether she was Christian or otherwise, than a living one's. Presumably this charm is much older than the poem in which it here stands.

16. At this point Groa's song ends, and Svipdag, thus fortified, goes to seek Mengloth. All the link that is needed between the poems is approximately this: "Then Svipdag searched long for Mengloth, and at last he came to a great house set all about with flames. And before the house there was a giant."

17. Most editors have here begun a new series of stanza numbers, but if the *Grougaldr* and the *Fjolsvinnsmol* are to be considered. as a single poem, it seems more reasonable to continue the stanza numbers consecutively. Bugge thinks a stanza has been lost before 17, including Fjolsvith's name, so that the "he" in line 1 might have something to refer to. However, just such a prose link as I have suggested in the note on stanza 16 would serve the purpose. Editors have suggested various rearrangements in the lines of stanzas 17–19. The substance, however, is clear enough. The giant *Fjolsvith* ("Much-Wise"), the warder of the house in which Mengloth dwells, sees Svipdag coming and stops him with the customary threats. The assignment of the speeches in stanzas 17–20, in the absence of any indications in the manuscripts, is more or less guesswork.

[19. The manuscript does not indicate who the speakers are or which of them says what. Bellows disagrees with the editor of the Old Norse at various points, such as in the second half of this stanza. No changes have been made to Bellows' text in these cases, but it causes his translation to not completely match the Old Norse text. For the same reason, the Old Norse calls Svipdag by different names: at first simply "the arriving man."]

22. *Vindkald* ("Wind-Cold"), *Varkald* ("Cold of Early Spring') and *Fjolkald* ("Much Cold"): Svipdag apparently seeks to persuade Fjolsvith that he belongs to the frost giants.

24. *Svafrthorin*: who he was, or what his name means, or who his son was, are all unknown.

26. *Thrymgjol* ("Loud-Clanging"): this gate, like the gate of the dead, shuts so fast as to trap those who attempt to use it (cf. *Sigurtharkvitha en skamma*, 68 and note). It was made by the dwarfs, sons of *Solblin-*

di ("Sun-Blinded"), the traditional craftsmen, who could not endure the light of day .

28. *Gastropnir*: "Guest-Crusher." *Leirbrimir's* ("Clay-Giant's") *limbs*: a poetic circumlocution for "clay"; cf. the description of the making of earth from the body of the giant Ymir, *Vafthruthnismol*, 21.

[29. The Bellows translation has been changed to match the Old Norse; Bellows has moved the six stanzas regarding Yggdrasil to cause the translation to not match the Old Norse manuscript. The last two lines have been variously emended.]

30. *Mimameith* ("Mimir's Tree"): the ash Yggdrasil, that overshadows the whole world. The well of Mimir was situated at its base; cf. *Voluspo*, 27–29.

32. Gering suggests that two stanzas have been lost between stanzas 15 and 16, but the giant's answer fits the question quite well enough. The fruit of Yggdrasil, when cooked, is here assumed to have the power of assuring safe childbirth.

34. *Vithofnir* ("Tree-Snake"): apparently identical with either the cock Gollinkambi (cf. *Voluspo*, 43) or Fjalar (cf. *Voluspo*, 42), the former of which wakes the gods to battle, and the latter the giants. *Surt*: the giant mentioned in *Voluspo*, 52, as ruler of the fire-world; here used to represent the giants in general, who are constantly in terror of the cock's eternal watchfulness. *Sinmora*: presumably Surt's wife, the giantess who possesses the weapon by which alone the cock Vithofnir may be slain.

35. The last two lines have been variously amended.

36. *Gif* and *Geri*: both names signify "Greedy." The first part of line 3 is conjectural; the manuscripts indicate the word "eleven," which clearly fails to make sense.

42. *Lævetein* ("Wounding Wand"): the manuscripts differ as to the form of this name. The suggestion that the reference is to the mistletoe with which Baldr was killed seems hardly reasonable. *Lopt*: Loki. *Lægjarn* ("Lover of Ill"): Loki; cf. *Voluspo*, 35, where the term appears as an adjective applied to Loki. This is Falk's emendation for the manuscripts' "Sægjarn," meaning "Sea Lover." *Sinmora*: cf. stanza 34.

44. *Goddess of gold*: poetic circumlocution for "woman," here meaning Sinmora.

46. *Sickle*: i.e., tail feather. With this the circle of impossibilities is com-

pleted. To get past the dogs, they must be fed with the wing-joints of the cock Vithofnir; the cock can be killed only with the sword in Sinmora's possession, and Sinmora will give up the sword only in return for the tail feather of the cock.

48. *Lyr* ("Heat-Holding"): just what the spear-point reference means is not altogether clear. Presumably it refers to the way in which the glowing brightness of the lofty hall makes it seem to quiver and turn in the air, but the tradition, never baffled by physical laws, may have actually balanced the whole building on a single point to add to the difficulties of entrance.

50. *Loki*, the one god named, was the builder of the hall, with the aid of the nine dwarfs. *Jari, Dori,* and *Ori* appear in the *Voluspo* catalogue of the dwarfs (stanzas 13 and 15); *Delling* appears in *Hovamol*, 161, and *Vafthruthnismol*, 25, in the latter case, however, the name quite possibly referring to someone else. The other dwarfs' names do not appear elsewhere. The manuscripts differ as to the forms of many of these names.

52. *Lyfjaberg* ("Hill of Healing"): the manuscripts vary as to this name; I have followed Bugge's suggestion. This stanza implies that Mengloth is a goddess of healing, and hence, perhaps, an hypostasis of Frigg, as already intimated by her name (cf. stanza 3, note). In stanza 54 Eir appears as one of Mengloth's handmaidens, and Eir, according to Snorri (*Gylfaginning*, 35) is herself the Norse Hygeia. Compare this stanza with stanza 22.

54. The manuscripts and editions show many variations in these names. They may be approximately rendered thus: Helper, Help-Breather, Folk-Guardian, Shining, White, Blithe, Peaceful, Kindly (?), and Gold-Giver.

55. One of the manuscripts omits stanzas 55 and 56.

56. The first line is based on a conjectural emendation.

63. *Solbjart* ("Sun-Bright"): not elsewhere mentioned. *The words of Urth*: i.e., the decrees of fate; cf. stanza 7.

65. Lyfjaberg cf. stanza 52 and note.

VOLUNDARKVITHA
THE LAY OF VOLUND

INTRODUCTION

The *Volundarkvitha* is the first of the *Lays of the Heroes* in the *Poetic Edda*, with the original manuscripts to be found in both the *Codex Regius* and the *Arnamagnæan Codex*, though the former is in terrible condition and the better preserved *Arnamagnæan* version only contains a portion of the opening prose introduction and nothing of the actual contents. As such, accurate reconstruction of the poem has been difficult. This situation is not helped by the fact that Volund the Smith, or his continental equivalent Weyland, is the subject of numerous folk lays and stories of questionable authenticity and authority and is prone to conflicting narrative details even among what is unquestionably the same "story", such that there exist multiple traditions even as to his origin and nature, with these ranging from portraying him as a God, an elf, a dwarf (or a *Svartalfar*, if such are recorded differently), or a man.

The narrative in this poem consists of Volund's maiming by King Nithuth and his subsequent revenge. The story appears in all respects to have been composed within the pre-Christian period, with the dramatic events of the story and its strikingly alien morality reflecting the cultural motifs and expectations of the time. The prose introduction alluding to a series of connected stories about Volund, which were accounted as "Old Tales" and with which the poet expected his audience to be familiar, are further evidence of the tales' connection to pre-Christian tradition. This seemingly authentic beginning faces many other problems, however, such as the person of Volund appearing in a stereotypically euhemerized format as a son of the king of Finland (the cultural depiction of Finns as eldritch sorcerers being common, with Volund's original non-human origin glossed over as merely uncanny foreignness) and his rival being a King of Sweden who surely did not actually exist and probably was not intended to be presented as factual, with his very name being a play on the Old Norse term *nithing*, someone guilty of moral and religious crimes, somewhat between a "sinner" and a "coward".

Many scholars both ancient and modern have suggested an origin for this story outside of Scandinavia, possibly from England or perhaps continental Germany. We tentatively favor this view given the euhemerized origin, but note that many of the arguments used to support it can instead serve as evidence that there once existed a continuous pan-Germanic cultural, literary, and religious tradition. This view is sadly neglected by many scholars in favor of a vestigial doubt that our ancestors' faith could be any more more than mean and rural local superstition. It is likely that the original Volund was a prince of the *Svartalfar* with a sizable cultic following that conflated him, practically speaking, with the *Goðin* proper, and which was well known among all three principal Germanic groups. The ancient connection made by Tacitus, in his seminal *Germania*, between the Angles and Saxons within the bounds of the purported *Ingaevones* folk group alongside that of Denmark and into coastal Sweden, supports the likelihood of an ancient religious and cultural exchange, not *between* different peoples but *within* what is fundamentally the same group.

In either case, and regardless of the origins of the story proper, modern readers must understand this instance of heroic poetry to fall most clearly within the category of "Fairy Tale Saga" and to be of questionable religious canonicity. It was most likely written and intended for the purposes of entertainment and should be regarded as such, even though many of its characters and allusions possibly refer to that which was canonically regarded as true.

The Swan-Maiden
(Gertrude Demain Hammond, R.I.)

Níðuðr hét konungr í Svíþjóð. Hann átti tvá sonu ok eina dóttur. Hon hét Böðvildr. Bræðr váru þrír, synir Finnakonungs. Hét einn Slagfiðr, annarr Egill, þriði Völundr. Þeir skriðu ok veiddu dýr. Þeir kómu í Úlfdali ok gerðu sér þar hús. Þar er vatn, er heitir Úlfsjár. Snemma of morgin fundu þeir á vatnsströndu konur þrjár, ok spunnu lín. Þar váru hjá þeim álftarhamir þeira. Þat váru valkyrjur. Þar váru tvær dætr Hlöðvés konungs, Hlaðguðr svanhvít ok Hervör alvitr, in þriðja var Ölrún Kjársdóttir af Vallandi. Þeir höfðu þær heim til skála með sér. Fekk Egill Ölrúnar, en Slagfiðr Svanhvítrar, en Völundr Alvitrar. Þau bjuggu sjau vetr. Þá flugu þær at vitja víga ok kómu eigi aftr. Þá skreið Egill at leita Ölrúnar, en Slagfiðr leitaði Svanhvítrar, en Völundr sat í Úlfdölum. Hann var hagastr maðr, svá at menn viti, í fornum sögum. Níðuðr konungr lét hann höndum taka, svá sem hér er um kveðit:

Meyjar flugu sunnan   myrkvið í gögnum,   1
Alvitr unga,   örlög drýgja;
þær á sævarströnd   settusk at hvílask
drósir suðrænar,   dýrt lín spunnu.

VOLUNDARKVIDA

There was a king in Sweden named Nithuth. He had two sons and one daughter; her name was Bothvild. There were three brothers, sons of a king of the Finns: one was called Slagfith, another Egil, the third Völund. They went on snowshoes and hunted wild beasts. They came into Ulfdalir and there they built themselves a house; there was a lake there which is called Ulfsjar. Early one morning they found on the shore of the lake three women, who were spinning flax. Near them were their swan garments, for they were Valkyries. Two of them were daughters of King Hlothver, Hlathguth the Swan-White and Hervor the All-Wise, and the third was Olrun, daughter of Kjar from Valland. These did they bring home to their hall with them. Egil took Olrun, and Slagfith Swan-White, and Völund All-Wise. There they dwelt seven winters; but then they flew away to find battles, and came back no more. Then Egil set forth on his snowshoes to follow Olrun, and Slagfith followed Swan White, but Völund stayed in Ulfdalir. He was a most skillful man, as men know from old tales. King Nithuth had him taken by force, as the poem here tells.

Maids from the south through Myrkwood flew,   1
Fair and young, their fate to follow;
On the shore of the sea to rest them they sat,
The maids of the south, and flax they spun.

Ein nam þeira   Egil at verja, 2
fögr mær fira,   faðmi ljósum;
önnur var Svanhvít,   svanfjaðrar dró,
en in þriðja   þeira systir
varði hvítan   hals Völundar.

Sátu síðan sjau   vetr at þat, 3
en inn átta   allan þráðu,
en inn níunda   nauðr of skilði;
meyjar fýstusk   á myrkvan við,
Alvitr unga,   örlög drýgja.

Kom þar af veiði   veðreygr skyti, 4
Völundr, líðandi   um langan veg,
Slagfiðr ok Egill,   sali fundu auða,
gengu út ok inn   ok um sáusk;
austur skreið Egill   at Ölrúnu,
en suðr Slagfiðr   at Svanhvítu.

En einn Völundr   sat í Ulfdölum, 5
hann sló gull rautt   við gim fastan,
lukði hann alla   lind baugum vel;
svá beið hann   sinnar ljóssar
kvánar, ef hánum   koma gerði.

Þat spyrr Níðuðr,   Níára dróttinn, 6
at einn Völundr   sat í Ulfdölum;
nóttum fóru seggir,   neglðar váru brynjur,
skildir bliku þeira   við inn skarða mána.

Stigu ór söðlum   at salar gafli, 7
gengu inn þaðan   endlangan sal;
sáu þeir á bast   bauga dregna,
sjau hundruð allra,   er sá seggr átti.

Og þeir af tóku   ok þeir á létu, 8
fyr einn útan,   er þeir af létu.
Kom þar af veiði   veðreygr skyti,
Völundr, líðandi   um langan veg.

Gekk hann brúnni   beru hold steikja, 9
ár brann hrísi   allþurr fura,
viðr inn vindþurri,   fyr Völundi.

[...] 2
Hlathguth and Hervor, Hlothver's children,
And Olrun the Wise Kjar's daughter was.

[...] 3
One in her arms took Egil then
To her bosom white, the woman fair.

Swan-White second, swan-feathers she wore, 4
[...]
And her arms the third of the sisters threw
Next round Völund's neck so white.

There did they sit for seven winters, 5
In the eighth at last came their longing again,
And in the ninth did need divide them.
The maidens yearned for the murky wood,
The fair young maids, their fate to follow.

Völund home from his hunting came, 6
From a weary way, the weather-wise bowman,
Slagfith and Egil the hall found empty,
Out and in went they, everywhere seeking.

East fared Egil after Olrun, 7
And Slagfith south to seek for Swan-White;
Völund alone in Ulfdalir lay,
[...]

Red gold he fashioned with fairest gems, 8
And rings he strung on ropes of bast;
So for his wife he waited long,
If the fair one home might come to him.

This Nithuth learned, the lord of the Njars, 9
That Völund alone in Ulfdalir lay;
By night went his men, their mail-coats were studded,
Their shields in the waning moonlight shone.

Sat á berfjalli,   bauga talði,   10
alfa ljóði,   eins saknaði;
hugði hann, at hefði   Hlöðvés dóttir,
Alvitr unga,   væri hon aftr komin.

Sat hann svá lengi,   at hann sofnaði,   11
ok hann vaknaði   viljalauss;
vissi sér á höndum   höfgar nauðir,
en á fótum   fjötur of spenntan.

Völundr kvað: 12
"Hverir ro jöfrar,   þeir er á lögðu
besti bör síma   ok mik bundu?"

Kallaði nú Níðuðr   Níara dróttinn: 13
"Hvar gaztu, Völundr,   vísi alfa,
vára aura   í Ulfdölum?"

Völundr kvað: 14
"Gull var þar eigi   á Grana leiðu,
fjarri hugða ek várt land   fjöllum Rínar;
man ek, at vér meiri   mæti áttum,
er vér heil hjú   heima várum.

Hlaðguðr ok Hervör   borin var Hlöðvé   15
kunn var Ölrún   Kíárs dóttir."

Völundr kvað: 16
Úti stóð kunnig   kván Níðaðar,
hon inn of gekk   endlangan sal,
stóð á golfi,   stillti röddu:
"Er-a sá nú hýrr,   er ór holti ferr."

Níðuðr konungr gaf dóttur sinni, Böðvildi gullhring þann, er hann tók af bastinu at Völundar, en hann sjálfr bar sverðit, er Völundr átti. En dróttning kvað:

"Ámun eru augu   ormi þeim inum frána,   17
tenn hánum teygjask,   er hánum er tét sverð
ok hann Böðvildar   baug of þekkir;
sníðið ér hann   sina magni
ok setið hann síðan   í Sævarstöð."

Svá var gert, at skornar váru sinar í knésfótum, ok settr í hólm einn, er þar var fyrir landi, er hét Sævarstaðr. Þar smíðaði hann konungi alls kyns

From their saddles the gable wall they sought,   10
And in they went at the end of the hall;
Rings they saw there on ropes of bast,
Seven hundred the hero had.

Off they took them, but all they left   11
Save one alone which they bore away.
[...]
[...]

Völund home from his hunting came,   12
From a weary way, the weather-wise bowman;
A brown bear's flesh would he roast with fire;
Soon the wood so dry was burning well,
The wind-dried wood that Völund's was.

On the bearskin he rested, and counted the rings,   13
The master of elves, but one he missed;
That Hlothver's daughter had it he thought,
And the all-wise maid had come once more.

So long he sat that he fell asleep,   14
His waking empty of gladness was;
Heavy chains he saw on his hands,
And fetters bound his feet together.

Völund spake: 15
"What men are they who thus have laid
Ropes of bast to bind me now?"
Then Nithuth called, the lord of the Njars:
"How gottest thou, Völund, greatest of elves,
These treasures of ours in Ulfdalir?"

Völund spake: 16
"The gold was not on Grani's way,
Far, methinks, is our realm from the hills of the Rhine;
I mind me that treasures more we had
When happy together at home we were."

Without stood the wife of Nithuth wise,   17
And in she came from the end of the hall;
On the floor she stood, and softly spoke:
"Not kind does he look who comes from the wood."

King Nithuth gave to his daughter Bothvild the gold ring that he had taken from the bast rope in Völund's house, and he himself wore the sword

görsimar. Engi maðr þorði at fara til hans nema konungr einn.

"Skínn Níðaði   sverð á linda, 18
þat er ek hvessta,   sem ek hagast kunna
ok ek herðak,   sem mér hægst þótti;
sá er mér fránn mækir   æ fjarri borinn,
sékk-a ek þann Völundi   til smiðju borinn.

Nú berr Böðvildr   brúðar minnar 19
bíðk-a ek þess bót,
bauga rauða."

Sat hann, né hann svaf, ávallt 20
ok hann sló hamri;
vél gerði hann heldr   hvatt Níðaði.
Drifu ungir tveir   á dýr séa
synir Níðaðar,   í Sævarstöð.

Kómu þeir til kistu,   kröfðu lukla, 21
opin var illúð   er þeir í sáu;
fjölð var þar menja,   er þeim mögum sýndisk
at væri gull rautt   ok görsimar.

Völundr kvað: 22
"Komið einir tveir,   komið annars dags;
ykkr læt ek þat gull   of gefit verða;
segið-a meyjum   né salþjóðum,
manni engum,   at it mik fyndið."

Snemma kallaði   seggr annan, 23
bróðir á bróður:
"Göngum baug séa!"
Kómu til kistu,   kröfðu lukla,
opin var illúð,   er þeir í litu.

that Völund had had. The queen spake:

"The glow of his eyes is like gleaming snakes, 18
His teeth he gnashes if now is shown
The sword, or Bothvild's ring he sees;
Let them straightway cut his sinews of strength,
And set him then in Sævarstath."

So was it done: the sinews in his knee-joints were cut, and he was set in an island which was near the mainland, and was called Sævarstath. There he smithied for the king all kinds of precious things. No man dared to go to him, save only the king himself. Völund spake:

"At Nithuth's girdle gleams the sword 19
That I sharpened keen with cunningest craft,
And hardened the steel with highest skill;
The bright blade far forever is borne,
Nor back shall I see it borne to my smithy;
Now Bothvild gets the golden ring
That was once my bride's, ne'er well shall it be."

He sat, nor slept, and smote with his hammer, 20
Fast for Nithuth wonders he fashioned;
Two boys did go in his door to gaze,
Nithuth's sons, into Sævarstath.

They came to the chest, and they craved the keys, 21
The evil was open when in they looked;
To the boys it seemed that gems they saw,
Gold in plenty and precious stones.

Völund spake: 22
"Come ye alone, the next day come,
Gold to you both shall then be given;
Tell not the maids or the men of the hall,
To no one say that me you have sought."

[...] 23
Early did brother to brother call:
"Swift let us go the rings to see."

Sneið af höfuð   húna þeira   24
ok und fen fjöturs   fætr of lagði;
en þær skálar,   er und skörum váru,
sveip hann útan silfri,   seldi Níðaði.

En ór augum   jarknasteina   25
sendi hann kunnigri   konu Níðaðar,
en ór tönnum   tveggja þeira
sló hann brjóstkringlur   sendi Böðvildi.

Þá nam Böðvildr   baugi at hrósa   26
[...]
bar hann Völundi,   er brotit hafði:
"Þorig-a ek at segja   nema þér einum."

Völundr kvað: 27
"Ek bæti svá   brest á gulli
at feðr þínum   fegri þykkir
ok mæðr þinni   miklu betri
ok sjalfri þér   at sama hófi."

Bar hann hana bjóri,   því at hann betr kunni   28
svá at hon í sessi   of sofnaði.
"Nú hef ek hefnt   harma minna
allra nema einna   íviðgjarna."

"Vel ek," kvað Völundr,   "verða ek á fitjum   29
þeim er mik Níðaðar   námu rekkar."
Hlæjandi Völundr   hófsk at lofti,
grátandi Böðvildr   gekk ór eyju,
tregði för friðils   ok föður reiði.

Úti stendr kunnig   kván Níðaðar,   30
ok hon inn of gekk   endlangan sal,
en hann á salgarð   settisk at hvílask:
"Vakir þú, Níðuðr   Níara dróttinn?"

Níðuðr kvað: 31
"Vaki ek ávallt   viljalauss,
sofna ek minnst   síz mína sonu dauða;
kell mik í höfuð,   köld eru mér ráð þín,
vilnumk ek þess nú,   at ek við Völund dæma.

Seg þú mér þat, Völundr,   vísi alfa,   32
af heilum hvat varð   húnum mínum."
Völundr kvað:

They came to the chest, and they craved the keys, 24
The evil was open when in they looked;
He smote off their heads, and their feet he hid
Under the sooty straps of the bellows.

Their skulls, once hid by their hair, he took, 25
Set them in silver and sent them to Nithuth;
Gems full fair from their eyes he fashioned,
To Nithuth's wife so wise he gave them.

And from the teeth of the twain he wrought 26
A brooch for the breast, to Bothvild he sent it;
[...]

Bothvild then of her ring did boast, 27
[...]
[...] "The ring I have broken,
I dare not say it save to thee."

Völund spake: 28
"I shall weld the break in the gold so well
That fairer than ever thy father shall find it,
And better much thy mother shall think it,
And thou no worse than ever it was."

Beer he brought, he was better in cunning, 29
Until in her seat full soon she slept.

Völund spake:
"Now vengeance I have for all my hurts,
Save one alone, on the evil woman."

[...] 30
[...]
Quoth Völund: "Would that well were the sinews
Maimed in my feet by Nithuth's men."

Laughing Völund rose aloft, 31
Weeping Bothvild went from the isle,
For her lover's flight and her father's wrath.

Without stood the wife of Nithuth wise, 32
And in she came from the end of the hall;
But he by the wall in weariness sat:
"Wakest thou, Nithuth, lord of the Njars?"

"Eiða skaltu mér áðr   alla vinna, 33
at skips borði   ok at skjaldar rönd,
at mars bægi   ok at mækis egg,
at þú kvelj-at   kván Völundar
né brúði minni   at bana verðir,
þótt vér kván eigim,   þá er ér kunnið,
eða jóð eigim   innan hallar.

Gakk þú til smiðju,   þeirar er þú gerðir, 34
þar fiðr þú belgi   blóði stokkna;
sneið ek af höfuð   húna þinna,
ok und fen fjöturs   fætr of lagðak.

En þær skálar,   er und skörum váru, 35
sveip ek útan silfri,   selda ek Níðaði;
en ór augum   jarknasteina
senda ek kunnigri   kván Níðaðar.

En úr tönnum   tveggja þeira 36
sló ek brjóstkringlur,   senda ek Böðvildi;
nú gengr Böðvildr   barni aukin,
eingadóttir   ykkur beggja."

Níðuðr kvað: 37
"Mæltir-a þú þat mál,   er mik meir tregi,
né ek þik vilja, Völundr,   verr of níta;
er-at svá maðr hár,   at þik af hesti taki,
né svá öflugr,   at þik neðan skjóti,
þar er þú skollir   við ský uppi."

Hlæjandi Völundr   hófsk at lofti, 38
en ókátr Níðuðr   sat þá eftir.

Níðuðr kvað: 39
"Upp rístu, Þakkráðr,   þræll minn inn bezti,
bið þú Böðvildi,   meyna bráhvítu,
ganga fagrvarið   við föður ræða.

Er þat satt, Böðvildr,   er sögðu mér: 40
Sátuð it Völundr   saman í holmi?"

Nithuth spake: 33
"Always I wake, and ever joyless,
Little I sleep since my sons were slain;
Cold is my head, cold was thy counsel,
One thing, with Völund to speak, I wish."

[...] 34
"Answer me, Völund, greatest of elves,
What happed with my boys that hale once were?"

Völund spake: 35
"First shalt thou all the oaths now swear,
By the rail of ship, and the rim of shield,
By the shoulder of steed, and the edge of sword,
That to Völund's wife thou wilt work no ill,
Nor yet my bride to her death wilt bring,
Though a wife I should have that well thou knowest,
And a child I should have within thy hall."

"Seek the smithy that thou didst set, 36
Thou shalt find the bellows sprinkled with blood;
I smote off the heads of both thy sons,
And their feet 'neath the sooty straps I hid."

"Their skulls, once hid by their hair, I took, 37
Set them in silver and sent them to Nithuth;
Gems full fair from their eyes I fashioned,
To Nithuth's wife so wise I gave them."

"And from the teeth of the twain I wrought 38
A brooch for the breast, to Bothvild I gave it;
Now big with child does Bothvild go,
The only daughter ye two had ever."

Nithuth spake: 39
"Never spakest thou word that worse could hurt me,
Nor that made me, Völund, more bitter for vengeance;
There is no man so high from thy horse to take thee,
Or so doughty an archer as down to shoot thee,
While high in the clouds thy course thou takest."

Laughing Völund rose aloft, 40
But left in sadness Nithuth sat.
[...]

Böðvildr kvað:
"Satt er þat, Níðuðr, er sagði þér:
Sátum vit Völundr saman í holmi
eina ögurstund, æva skyldi;
ek vætr hánum vinna kunnak,
ek vætr hánum vinna máttak."

41

Then spake Nithuth, lord of the Njars: 41
"Rise up, Thakkrath, best of my thralls,
Bid Bothvild come, the bright-browed maid,
Bedecked so fair, with her father to speak."

[...] 42
[...]
"Is it true, Bothvild, that which was told me;
Once in the isle with Völund wert thou?"

Bothvild spake: 43
"True is it, Nithuth, that which was told thee,
Once in the isle with Völund was I,
An hour of lust, alas it should be!
Nought was my might with such a man,
Nor from his strength could I save myself."

ENDNOTES

Prose. Nithuth ("Bitter Hater"): here identified as a king of Sweden, is in the poem (stanzas 9, 15 and 32) called lord of the Njars, which may refer to the people of the Swedish district of Nerike. In any case, the scene of the story has moved from Saxon lands into the Northeast. The first and last sentences of the introduction refer to the second part of the poem; the rest of it concerns the swan-maidens episode. *Bothvild* ("Warlike Maid"): Völund's victim in the latter part of the poem. *King of the Finns*: this notion, clearly later than the poem, which calls Völund an elf, may perhaps be ascribed to the annotator who composed the prose introduction. The Finns, meaning the dwellers in Lapland, were generally credited with magic powers. *Egil* appears in the *Thithrekssaga* as Völund's brother, but *Slagfith* is not elsewhere mentioned. *Ulfdalir* ("Wolf-Dale"), *Ulfsjar* ("Wolf-Sea"), *Valland* ("Slaughter-Land"): mythical, places without historical identification. *Valkyries*: cf. *Voluspo*, 31 and note; there is nothing in the poem to identify the three swan maidens as Valkyries except one obscure word in line 2 of stanza 1 and again in line 5 of stanza 5, which may mean, as Gering translates it, "helmed," or else "fair and wise." I suspect that the annotator, anxious to give the Saxon legend as much northern local color as possible, was mistaken in his mythology, and that the poet never conceived of his swan-maidens as Valkyries at all. However, this identification of swan-maidens with Valkyries was not uncommon; cf. *Helreith Brynhildar*, 7. The three maidens' names, *Hlathguth*, *Hervor*, and *Olrun*, do not appear in the lists of Valkyries. *King Hlothver*: this name suggests the southern origin of the story, as it is the northern form of Ludwig; the name appears again in *Guthrunarkvitha* II, 26, and that of *Kjar* is found in *Atlakvitha*, 7, both of these poems being based on German stories. It is worth noting that the composer of this introductory note seems to have had little or no information beyond what was actually contained in the poem as it has come down to us; he refers to the "old stories" about Völund, but either he was unfamiliar with them in detail or else he thought it needless to make use of them. His note simply puts in clear and connected form what the verse tells somewhat obscurely; his only additions are making Nithuth a king of Sweden and Völund's father a king of the Finns, supplying the name Ulfsjar for the lake, identifying the swan-maidens as Valkyries, and giving Kjar a home in Valland.

1. The manuscript indicates line 3 as the beginning of a stanza; two lines may have been lost before or after lines 1–2, and two more, or even six, with the additional stanza describing the theft of the swan-garments, after line 4. *Myrkwood*: [a partly mythologized forest, home to supernatural dangers, most probably a reference to the great Eurasian Hercynian Forest which once covered the continent from southern France to the Baltic, and which no longer exists in a contiguous form due to progressive deforestation]; cf. *Lokasenna*, 42.[1]

2. In the manuscript these two lines stand after stanza 16; editors have tried to fit them into various places, but the prose indicates that they belong here, with a gap assumed.

3. In the manuscript these two lines follow stanza 1, with no gap indicated, and the first line marked as the beginning of a stanza. Many editors have combined them with stanza 4.[2]

4. No lacuna indicated in the manuscript; one editor fills the stanza out with a second line running: "Then to her breast Slagfith embraced."

5. Line 3 looks like an interpolation, but line 5, identical with line 2 of stanza 1, may be the superfluous one.

6. The phrase "Völund home from a weary way" is an emendation of Bugge's, accepted by many editors. Some of those who do not include it reject line 4, and combine the remainder of the stanza with all or part of stanza 7.

7. The manuscript marks the second, and not the first, line as the beginning of a stanza. Some editors combine lines 2–3 with all or part of stanza 8. No gap is indicated in the manuscript, but many editors have assumed one, some of them accepting Bugge's suggested "Till back the maiden bright should come."

---

1 Bellows' numbering diverges significantly from the Old Norse throughout this poem, and will be annotated here in the respective stanzas. Bellows stanzas 1/2 = Old Norse stanza 1.
2 Bellows stanzas 3/4 = Old Norse stanza 2.

8. No line in this stanza is indicated in the manuscript as beginning a new stanza; editors have tried all sorts of experiments in regrouping the lines into stanzas with those of stanzas 7 and 9. In line 3 the word *long* is sheer guesswork, as the line in the manuscript contains a metrical error.

9. Some editors combine the first two lines with parts of stanza 8, and the last two with the first half of stanza 10. *Njars*: [refers to the people of the modern Swedish province of Nerike; the name is an unusual linguistic relic related to the English term "narrow" and refers to the narrow inlets that characterize the region.]

10. Some editors combine lines 3-4 with the fragmentary stanza 11.

11. No gap indicated in the manuscript; some editors combine these lines with lines 3-4 of stanza to, while others combine them with the first two lines of stanza 12. The one ring which Nithuth's men steal is given to Bothvild, and proves the cause of her undoing.

12. The manuscript indicates line 3, and not line 1, as the beginning of a stanza, which has given rise to a large amount of conjectural rearrangement. Line 2 of the original is identical with the phrase added by Bugge in stanza 6. Line 5 may be spurious, or lines 4-5 may have been expanded out of a single line running "The wind-dried wood for Völund burned well."

13. *Elves*: the poem here identifies Völund as belonging to the race of the elves. *Hlothver's daughter*: Hervor; many editors treat the adjective "all-wise" here as a proper name.

15. In this poem the manuscript indicates the speakers. Some editors make lines 1-2 into a separate stanza, linking lines 3-5 (or 4-5) with stanza 16. Line 3 is very possibly spurious, a mere expansion of "Nithuth spake." Nithuth, of course, has come with his men to capture Völund, and now charges him with having stolen his treasure.[3]

16. The manuscript definitely assigns this stanza to Völund, but many editors give the first two lines to Nithuth. In the manuscript stanza 16 is followed by the two lines of stanza 2, and many editions make of lines 3-4 of stanza 16 and stanza 2 a single speech by Völund. *Grani's way*: Grani was Sigurth's horse, on which he rode to slay Fafnir and win Andvari's hoard; this and the reference to the *Rhine* as the home of wealth betray the southern source of the story. If lines 1-2 belong to Völund, they mean that Nithuth got his wealth in the Rhine country, and that Völund's hoard

---

[3] Bellows stanza 15 = Old Norse stanzas 14/15.

has nothing to do with it; if the speaker is Nithuth, they mean that Völund presumably has not killed a dragon, and that he is far from the wealth of the Rhine, so that he must have stolen his treasure from Nithuth himself.

17. Line 1 is lacking in the manuscript, lines 2-4 following immediately after the two lines here given as stanza 2. Line 1, borrowed from line 1 of stanza 32, is placed here by many editors, following Bugge's suggestion. Certainly it is Nithuth's wife who utters line 4. *Who comes from the wood*: Völund, noted as a hunter. Gering assumes that with the entrance of Nithuth's wife the scene has changed from Völund's house to Nithuth's, but I cannot see that this is necessary.

Prose. The annotator inserted this note rather clumsily in the midst of the speech of Nithuth's wife.

18. In the manuscript lines 2-3 stand before line 1; many editors have made the transposition here indicated. Some editors reject line 3 as spurious. *Sævarstath*: "Sea-Stead."

19. This stanza is obviously in bad shape. Vigfusson makes two stanzas of it by adding a first line: "Then did Völund speak, sagest of elves." Editors have rejected various lines, and some have regrouped the last lines with the first two of stanza 20. The elimination of the passages in parenthesis produces a four-line stanza which is metrically correct, but it has little more than guesswork to support it.[4]

20. The editions vary radically in combining the lines of this stanza with those of stanzas 19 and 21, particularly as the manuscript indicates the third line as the beginning of a stanza. The meaning, however, remains unchanged.

21. Several editions make one stanza out of lines 1-4 of stanza 20 and lines 1-2 of stanza 21, and another out of the next four lines. *The evil was open*: i.e., the gold in the chest was destined to be their undoing.

22. The manuscript indicates line 3 as the beginning of a stanza, and several editors have adopted this grouping. In the *Thithrekssaga* Völund sends the boys away with instructions not to come back until just after a fall of snow, and then to approach his dwelling walking backward. The boys do this, and when, after he has killed them, Völund is questioned regarding them, he points to the tracks in the snow as evidence that they had left his house.

---

[4] Bellows stanza 19 = Old Norse stanzas 18/19.

23. No gap indicated in the manuscript. Some editors assume it, as here; some group the lines with lines 3-4 of stanza 22, and some with lines 1-2 of stanza 24.[5]

24. Some editions begin a new stanza with line 3.

25. The manuscript indicates line 3 as the beginning of a stanza, and many editors have adopted this grouping.

26. These two lines have been grouped in various ways, either with lines 3-4 of stanza 25 or with the fragmentary stanza 27. No gap is indicated in the manuscript, but the loss of something is so obvious that practically all editors have noted it, although they have differed as to the number of lines lost.

27. No gap indicated in the manuscript; the line and a half might be filled out (partly with the aid of late paper manuscripts) thus: "But soon it broke, and swiftly to Völund / She bore it and said—"

29. The manuscript does not name Völund as the speaker before line 3; Vigfusson again inserts his convenient line, "Then Völund spake, sagest of elves." A few editions combine lines 3-4 with the two lines of stanza 30.

30. No gap indicated in the manuscript; some editors combine the two lines with lines 3-4 of stanza 29, and many with the three lines of stanza 31.[6]

31. Something has probably been lost before this stanza, explaining how Völund made himself wings, as otherwise, owing to his lameness, he could not leave the island. The *Thithrekssaga* tells the story of how Völund's brother, Egil, shot birds and gave him the feathers, out of which he made a feather-garment. This break in the narrative illustrates the lack of knowledge apparently possessed by the compiler who was responsible for the prose notes; had he known the story told in the Thithrekssaga, it is hardly conceivable that he would have failed to indicate the necessary connecting link at this point. Some editors reject line 3 as spurious. The manuscript does not indicate any lacuna.

32. The manuscript indicates line 4 as the beginning of a stanza, and many editors have followed this arrangement.

33. The manuscript does not name the speaker. It indicates line 3 as the beginning of a new stanza. Vigfusson adds before line 1, "Then spake

---

5 Bellows stanzas 23/24 = Old Norse stanza 23.
6 Bellows stanzas 30/31 = Old Norse stanza 29.

Nithuth, lord of the Njars."

34. No gap indicated in the manuscript, but it seems clear that something has been lost. Some editors combine these two lines with lines 3-4 of stanza 33. Völund is now flying over Nithuth's hall.

35. The manuscript does not name the speaker; Vigfusson again makes two full stanzas with the line, "Then did Völund speak, sagest of elves." Some editors begin a new stanza with line 4, while others reject as interpolations lines 2-3 or 5-7. *Völund's wife*: the reference is to Bothvild, as Völund wishes to have his vengeance fall more heavily on her father than on her.

36. Lines 3-4 are nearly identical with lines 3-4 of stanza 24.

37. Identical, except for the pronouns, with stanza 25.

38. Lines 1-2: cf. stanza 26.

39. The manuscript does not name the speaker. Either line 4 or line 5 may be an interpolation; two editions reject lines 3-5, combining lines 1-2 with stanza 40. In the *Thithrekssaga* Nithuth actually compels Egil, Völund's brother, to shoot at Völund. The latter has concealed a bladder full of blood under his left arm, and when his brother's arrow pierces this, Nithuth assumes that his enemy has been killed. This episode likewise appears among the scenes from Völund's career rudely carved on an ancient casket of ivory, bearing an Anglo-Saxon inscription in runic letters, which has been preserved.

40. Line 1: cf. stanza 31. The manuscript indicates no lacuna.

41. The first line is a conjectural addition. *Thakkrath* is probably the northern form of the Middle High German name Dancrat.

42. The manuscript indicates no gap, but indicates line 3 as the beginning of a stanza; Vigfusson's added "Then Nithuth spake, lord of the Njars" seems plausible enough.

43. The manuscript does not name the speaker. Different editors have rejected one or another of the last three lines, and as the manuscript indicates line 4 as the beginning of a new stanza, the loss of two or three lines has likewise been suggested. According to the *Thithrekssaga*, the son of Völund and Bothvild was Vithga, or Witege, one of the heroes of Dietrich of Bern.

HELGAKVITHA HJORVARTHSSONAR
THE LAY OF HELGI THE SON OF HJORVARTH

INTRODUCTION

The *Helgakvitha Hjorvarthssonar*, or the *Lay of Helgi Hjorvarthsson*, is the first of the famous *Helgi Lays*, heroic sagas about ostensibly the same individual and his Valkyrie lover reincarnated twice over and destined to share in his fate, connected to each other over multiple lifetimes. The narrative of these poems is dazzlingly complex, each filled with dozens of characters and events conveyed in a manner particularly alien and disorienting to the casual modern reader. Nevertheless, the stories represent some of the most popular of the heroic lays of our forefathers, outdone by perhaps only the *Volsunga Saga* of Sigurth Dragonslayer and *The Saga of Hervör and Heidrek*.

All three sagas feature much conceptual and narrative overlap, leading many to conclude that there might be several degrees of mutual conflation between them as the stories wound their way across the continent and into Scandinavia proper. It is not irresponsible to say that if we take the stories at face value as recounting real, material historical events, then all of the characters and protagonists must have been within one or two degrees of each other's social circles at the time; such is the closeness of the events and time period depicted.

One of the more famous and puzzling quandaries is in regard to the possible conflations between the Sigurth narrative and that of the *Helgakvitha*. Both feature a talking bird who dispenses information about events (though in *Helgakvitha* the mechanism by which the protagonist can understand said bird is not mentioned, whereas this forms a critical narrative point in the *Sigurth Lay*) and both feature a hero who falls in love with a Valkyrie and their turbulent love life. Both narratives also feature a character named Atli, though ostensibly they are entirely different persons, with the *Volsung's* Atli being the historical Atilla the Hun and the *Helgakvitha* Atli being perhaps merely named after this famous individual.

Another interesting issue present within the narrative is the nature of the reincarnation used to tie the various incarnations of Helgi and his fated wife together, and the extremely convoluted connections regarding these, which we will here attempt to simplify in easily comprehensible terms.[1] In this first lay, Helgi is the son of Hjorvarth and marries Svava, the daughter of King Eylimi.[2] The first Helgi is reincarnated as Helgi Hundingsbane, the son of Sigmund and half-brother of Sigurth Dragonslayer, and Svava is reborn as Sigrun, daughter of Hogni the King of Östergötland. This Helgi and Sigrun are again reborn finally as Helgi Haddingjaskati (Lord of the Haddings) and Kara the daughter of King Halfdan of Denmark.

These connections appear fairly clear once laid out, but pose an issue with how reincarnation functions among the Germanic peoples in all other recorded instances, namely that it only occurs among the male line and never otherwise features the reincarnation of women. Possible familial connections between Hjorvarth and Sigmund, such that their sons might reincarnate as the same individual, are never explicitly stated in the narrative and the only familial connection that is mentioned is through Sigmund and Hjorvarth's wives both being daughters of King Eylimi. Both former Helgis also have no stated familial connection to Helgi of the Haddings (perhaps a reference to the Vandal noble clan of the Hasdingi), and his wife Kara is likewise seemingly unconnected to the previous lineages, though it is not wholly out of line to suggest that there was once an intention to depict all of these lines as ultimately agnatic cousins. Many scholars have suggested that the narrative of reincarnation is a *post facto* narrative tool used to connect otherwise unrelated stories, though this is promulgated mostly by an unawareness of the extent of the reincarnation doctrine within the Germanic peoples—such a narrative occurrence is not as unlikely and alien as it first appears. The serial reincarnation of Svava/Sigrun/Kara (female reincarnation being otherwise unattested) is perhaps attributable to their status as Valkyries and not mortal women to begin

---

1 The issue of Helgi's genealogy is further treated in Appendix A, see p.827.
2 Eylimi has another daughter Hjordis, who is the mother of Sigurth. It is not clear how a mortal King should give birth to Valkyries—those psychopomp *Disir* who serve Odin as his choosers of the Slain and who ferry the best of men back to Valhalla—and the narrative does not stop to speak about the matter.

with.

All these things considered, we must treat the heroic lay of Helgi Hjorvarthsson as a work combining assumed historical events with some amount of "poetic license" added to it over time. The work cannot be seen as fundamentally scriptural and reflecting notions of religious canon and truth, but it is likely that most of our ancestors would have broadly believed the events to have occurred.

A Foray
(A. Malmström)

I. Frá Hjörvarði ok Sigrlinn

Hjörvarðr hét konungr. Hann átti fjórar konur. Ein hét Álfhildr. Son þeira hét Heðinn. Önnur hét Særeiðr. Þeira son hét Humlungr. In þriðja hét Sinrjóð. Þeira son hét Hymlingr. Hjörvarðr konungr hafði þess heit strengt at eiga þá konu, er hann vissi vænsta. Hann spurði, at Sváfnir konungr átti dóttur allra fegrsta. Sú hét Sigrlinn. Iðmundr hét jarl hans. Atli var hans son, er fór at biðja Sigrlinnar til handa konungi. Hann dvalðist vetrlangt með Sváfni konungi. Fránmarr hét þar jarl, fóstri Sigrlinnar. Dóttir hans hét Álof. Jarlinn réð, at meyjar var synjat, ok fór Atli heim.

Atli jarls son stóð einn dag við lund nökkurn, en fugl sat í limunum uppi yfir hánum ok hafði heyrt til, at hans menn kölluðu vænstar konur þær, er Hjörvarðr átti. Fuglinn kvakaði, en Atli hlýddi, hvat hann sagði. Hann kvað:

HELGAKVITHA
HJORVARTHSSONAR

I. Of Hjorvarth and Sigrlin

Hjorvarth was the name of a king, who had four wives: one was called Alfhild, and their son was named Hethin; the second was called Særeith, and their son was named Humlung; the third was called Sinrjoth, and their son was named Hymling. King Hjorvarth had made a great vow to have as wife whatsoever woman he knew was fairest. He learned that King Svafnir had a daughter fairer than all others, whose name was Sigrlin. Ithmund was the name of one of his jarls; he had a son called Atli, who went to woo Sigrlin on behalf of the king. He dwelt the winter long with King Svafnir. There was a jarl called Franmar, Sigrlin's foster-father; his daughter was named Alof. The jarl told him that the maiden's hand was denied, and Atli went home.

Atli, the jarl's son, stood one day in a certain wood; a bird sat in the branches up over him, and it had heard that his men called Hjorvarth's wives the fairest of women. The bird twittered, and Atli hearkened to what it spoke. It said:

"Sáttu Sigrlinn   Sváfnis dóttur,   1
mey ina fegrstu   í munarheimi?
Þó hagligar   Hjörvarðs konur
gumnum þykkja   at Glasislundi."

Atli kvað: 2
"Mundu við Atla   Iðmundar son,
fugl fróðhugaðr,   fleira mæla?"
Fuglinn kvað:
"Mun ek, ef mik buðlungr   blóta vildi
ok kýs ek þats vil   ór konungs garði."

Atli kvað: 3
"Kjós-at-tu Hjörvarð   né hans sonu
né inar fögru   fylkis brúðir,
eigi brúðir þær,   er buðlungr á;
kaupum vel saman,   þat er vina kynni."

Fuglinn kvað: 4
"Hof mun ek kjósa,   hörga marga,
gullhyrnðar kýr   frá grams búi,
ef hánum Sigrlinn   sefr á armi
ok ónauðig   jöfri fylgir."

Þetta var, áðr Atli færi, en er hann kom heim ok konungr spurði hann tíðenda, hann kvað:

"Höfum erfiði   ok ekki örindi,   5
mara þraut óra   á meginfjalli,
urðum síðan   Sæmorn vaða,
þá var oss synjat   Sváfnis dóttur,
hringum gæddrar,   er vér hafa vildum."

Konungr bað, at þeir skyldu fara annat sinn. Fór hann sjálfr. En er þeir kómu upp á fjall, ok sá á Sváfaland landsbruna ok jóreyki stóra. Reið konungr af fjallinu fram í landit ok tók náttból við á eina. Atli helt vörð ok fór yfir ána. Hann fann eitt hús. Fugl mikill sat á húsinu ok gætti, ok var sofnaðr. Atli skaut spjóti fuglinn til bana, en í húsinu fann hann Sigrlinn konungs dóttur ok Álofu jarls dóttur ok hafði þær báðar braut með sér. Fránmarr jarl hafði hamazt í arnar líki ok varit þær fyrir hernum með fjölkynngi. Hróðmarr hét konungr, biðill Sigrlinnar. Hann drap Sváfakonung ok hafði rænt ok brent landit. Hjörvarðr konungr fekk Sigrlinnar, en Atli Álofar.

"Sawest thou Sigrlin, Svafnir's daughter,   1
The fairest maid in her home-land found?
Though Hjorvath's wives by men are held
Goodly to see in Glasir's wood."

Atli spake: 2
"Now with Atli, Ithmund's son,
Wilt thou say more, thou bird so wise?"

The bird spake:
"I may if the prince an offering makes,
And I have what I will from the house of the king."

Atli spake: 3
"Choose not Hjorvath, nor sons of his,
Nor the wives so fair of the famous chief;
Ask not the brides that the prince's are;
Fair let us deal in friendly wise."

The bird spake: 4
"A fane will I ask, and altars many,
Gold-horned cattle the prince shall give me,
If Sigrlin yet shall sleep in his arms,
Or free of will the hero shall follow."

This was before Atli went on his journey; but when he came home, and the king asked his tidings, he said:

Trouble we had, but tidings none,   5
Our horses failed in the mountains high,
The waters of Sæmorn we needs must wade;
Svafnir's daughter, with rings bedecked,
She whom we sought, was still denied us."

The king bade that they should go another time, and he went with them himself. But when they came up on the mountain, they saw Svavaland burning and mighty dust-clouds from many steeds. The king rode from the mountain forward into the land, and made a night's stay hard by a stream. Atli kept watch and went over the stream; he found there a house. A great bird sat on the housetop to guard it, but he was asleep. Atli hurled his spear at the bird and slew it, and in the house he found Sigrlin the king's daughter and Alof the jarl's daughter, and he brought them both thence with him. Jarl Franmar had changed himself into the likeness of an eagle, and guarded them from the enemy host by magic. Hrothmar was

II.

Hjörvarðr ok Sigrlinn áttu son mikinn ok vænan. Hann var þögull. Ekki nafn festist við hann. Hann sat á haugi. Hann sá ríða valkyrjur níu ok var ein göfugligust. Hon kvað:

"Síð muntu, Helgi,   hringum ráða, 6
ríkr rógapaldr,   né Röðulsvöllum,
örn gól árla,   ef þú æ þegir,
þótt þú harðan hug,   hilmir, gjaldir."

Helgi kvað: 7
"Hvat lætr þú fylgja   Helga nafni,
brúðr bjartlituð,   alls þú bjóða ræðr?
Hygg þú fyr öllum   atkvæðum vel.
Þigg ek eigi þat,   nema ek þik hafa."

Valkyrja kvað: 8
"Sverð veit ek liggja   í Sigarsholmi
fjórum færi   en fimm tögu;
eitt er þeira   öllum betra
vígnesta böl   ok varit gulli.

Hringr er í hjalti,   hugr er í miðju, 9
ógn er í oddi   þeim er eiga getr;
liggr með eggju   ormr dreyrfáiðr,
en á valböstu   verpr naðr hala."

Eylimi hét konungr. Dóttir hans var Sváfa. Hon var valkyrja ok reið loft ok lög. Hon gaf Helga nafn þetta ok hlífði hánum oft síðan í orrostum. Helgi kvað:

"Ert-at-tu, Hjörvarðr   heilráðr konungr, 10
folks oddviti,   þótt þú frægr séir;
léztu eld eta   jöfra byggðir,
en þeir angr við þik   ekki gerðu.

the name of a king, a wooer of Sigrlin; he slew the king of Svavaland and had plundered and burned his land. King Hjorvarth took Sigrlin, and Atli took Alof.

II.

Hjorvarth and Sigrlin had a son, mighty and of noble stature; he was a silent man, and no name stuck fast to him. He sat on a hill, and saw nine Valkyries riding; one of them was the fairest of all. She spake:

"Late wilt thou, Helgi, have hoard of rings,   6
Thou battle-tree fierce, or of shining fields,
The eagle screams soon, if never thou speakest,
Though, hero, hard thy heart may cry."

Helgi spake: 7
"What gift shall I have with Helgi's name,
Glorious maid, for the giving is thine?
All thy words shall I think on well,
But I want them not if I win not thee."

The Valkyrie spake: 8
"Swords I know lying in Sigarsholm,
Fifty there are save only four;
One there is that is best of all,
The shield-destroyer, with gold it shines."

"In the hilt is fame, in the haft is courage,   9
In the point is fear, for its owner's foes;
On the blade there lies a blood-flecked snake,
And a serpent's tail round the flat is twisted."

Eylimi was the name of a king, whose daughter was Svava; she was a Valkyrie, and rode air and sea. She gave Helgi this name, and shielded him oft thereafter in battle. Helgi spake:

Hjorvarth, king, unwholesome thy counsels,   10
Though famed thou art in leading the folk,
Letting fire the homes of heroes eat,
Who evil deed had never done thee."

En Hróðmarr skal   hringum ráða,   11
þeim er áttu   órir niðjar;
sá sésk fylkir   fæst at lífi,
hyggsk aldauða   arfi at ráða."

III.

Hjörvarðr svarar, at hann mundi fá lið Helga, ef hann vill hefna móðurföður síns. Þá sótti Helgi sverðit, er Sváfa vísaði hánum til. Þá fór hann ok Atli ok felldu Hróðmar ok unnu mörg þrekvirki. Hann drap Hata jötun, er hann sat á bergi nökkuru. Helgi ok Atli lágu skipum í Hatafirði. Atli helt vörð inn fyrra hluta nætrinnar. Hrímgerðr Hatadóttir kvað:

[Hrímgerðarmál]

"Hverir ro hölðar   í Hatafirði?   12
Skjöldum er tjaldat á skipum;
fræknliga látið,   fátt hygg ek yðr séask,
kennið mér nafn konungs."

Atli kvað: 13
"Helgi hann heitir,   en þú hvergi mátt
vinna grand grami;
járnborgir ro   of öðlings flota;
knegu-t oss fálur fara."

Hrímgerðr kvað: 14
"Hvé þik heitir,   halr inn ámáttki,
hvé þik kalla konir?
Fylkir þér trúir,   er þik í fögrum lætr
beits stafni búa."

Atli kvað: 15
"Atli ek heiti,   atall skal ek þér vera,
mjök em ek gífrum gramastr;
úrgan stafn   ek hefi oft búit
ok kvalðar kveldriður.

"Yet Hrothmar still the hoard doth hold, 11
The wealth that once our kinsmen wielded;
Full seldom care the king disturbs,
Heir to dead men he deems himself."

Hjorvarth answered that he would give Helgi a following if he fain would avenge his mother's father. Then Helgi got the sword that Svava had told him of. So he went, and Atli with him, and they slew Hrothmar, and they did many great deeds.

III.

He slew the giant Hati, whom he found sitting on a certain mountain. Helgi and Atli lay with their ships in Hatafjord. Atli kept watch during the first part of the night. Hrimgerth, Hati's daughter, spake:

"Who are the heroes in Hatafjord? 12
The ships are covered with shields;
Bravely ye look, and little ye fear,
The name of the king would I know."

Atli spake: 13
"Helgi his name, and never thou mayst
Harm to the hero bring;
With iron is fitted the prince's fleet,
Nor can witches work us ill."

Hrimgerth spake: 14
"Who now, thou mighty man, art thou?
By what name art thou known to men?
He trusts thee well, the prince who wills
That thou stand at the stem of his ship."

Atli spake: 15
"Atli am I, and ill shalt thou find me,
Great hate for witches I have;
Oft have I been in the dripping bows,
And to dusk-riders death have brought."

Atli kvað: 16
Hvé þú heitir,   hála nágráðug?
Nefndu þinn, fála, föður;
níu röstum   er þú skyldi neðar vera
ok vaxi þér á baðmi barr."

Hrímgerðr kvað: 17
"Hrímgerðr ek heiti,   Hati hét minn faðir,
þann vissa ek ámáttkastan jötun;
margar brúðir   hann lét frá búi teknar,
unz hann Helgi hjó."

Atli kvað: 18
"Þú vart, hála,   fyr hildings skipum
ok látt í fjarðar mynni fyrir;
ræsis rekka   er þú vildir Rán gefa,
ef þér kæmi-t í þverst þvari."

Hrímgerðr kvað: 19
"Duliðr ertu nú, Atli,   draums kveð ek þér vera,
síga lætr þú brýnn fyr bráar;
móðir mín   lá fyrir mildings skipum;
ek drekkða Hlövarðs sonum í hafi.

Gneggja myndir þú, Atli,   ef þú geldr né værir, 20
brettir sinn Hrímgerðr hala;
aftarla hjarta,   hygg ek, at þitt, Atli, sé,
þótt hafir reina rödd."

Atli kvað: 21
"Reini mun þér ek þykkja   ef þú reyna knátt,
ok stíga ek á land af legi,
öll muntu lemjask, ef mér er alhugat,
ok sveigja þinn, Hrímgerðr, hala."

Hrímgerðr kvað: 22
"Atli, gakk þú á land,   ef afli treystisk,
ok hittumk í vík Varins;
rifja rétti   er þú munt, rekkr, fáa,
ef þú mér í krummur kemr."

Atli kvað: 23
"Munk-a ek ganga,   áðr gumnar vakna
ok halda of vísa vörð;
er-a mér örvænt,   nær óru kemr
skass upp undir skipi."

"Corpse-hungry giantess, how art thou called? 16
Say, witch, who thy father was!
Nine miles deeper down mayst thou sink,
And a tree grow tall on thy bosom."

Hrimgerth spake: 17
"Hrimgerth am I, my father was Hati,
Of giants the most in might;
Many a woman he won from her home,
Ere Helgi hewed him down."

Atli spake: 18
"Witch, in front of the ship thou wast,
And lay before the fjord;
To Ron wouldst have given the ruler's men,
If a spear had not stuck in thy flesh."

Hrimgerth spake: 19
"Dull art thou, Atli, thou dreamest, methinks,
The lids lie over thine eyes;
By the leader's ships my mother lay,
Hlothvarth's sons on the sea I slew."

"Thou wouldst neigh, Atli, but gelded thou art, 20
See, Hrimgerth hoists her tail;
In thy hinder end is thy heart, methinks,
Though thy speech is a stallion's cry."

Atli spake: 21
"A stallion I seem if thou seekest to try me,
And I leap to land from the sea;
I shall smite thee to bits, if so I will,
And heavy sinks Hrimgerth's tail."

Hrimgerth spake: 22
"Go ashore then, Atli, if sure of thy might,
Let us come to Varin's cove;
Straight shall thy rounded ribs be made
If thou comest within my claws."

Atli spake: 23
"I will not go till the warriors wake,
Again their chief to guard;
I should wonder not, foul witch, if up
From beneath our keel thou shouldst come."

Hrímgerðr kvað: 24
"Vaki þú, Helgi,   ok bæt við Hrímgerði,
er þú lézt höggvinn Hata;
eina nótt   kná hon hjá jöfri sofa,
þá hefr hon bölva bætr."

Helgi kvað: 25
"Loðinn heitir, er þik skal eiga,
leið ertu mannkyni,   sá býr í Þolleyju þurs,
hundvíss jötunn,   hraunbúa verstr,
sá er þér makligr maðr."

Hrímgerðr kvað: 26
"Hina vildu heldr, Helgi,   er réð hafnir skoða
fyrri nótt með firum;
marggullin mær   mér þótti afli bera;
hér sté hon land af legi   ok festi svá yðvarn flota;
hon ein því veldr,   er ek eigi mák
buðlungs mönnum bana."

Helgi kvað: 27
"Heyr nú, Hrímgerðr,   ef ek bæti harma þér,
segðu görr grami:
Var sú ein vættr,   er barg öðlings skipum,
eða fóru þær fleiri saman?"

Hrímgerðr kvað: 28
"Þrennar níundir meyja,   þó reið ein fyrir
hvít und hjalmi mær;
marir hristusk,   stóð af mönum þeira
dögg í djúpa dali,   hagl í háva viðu;
þaðan kemr með öldum ár,   allt var mér þat leitt,
er ek leitk."

Helgi kvað: 29
"Austr líttu nú, Hrímgerðr,   ef þik lostna hefr
Helgi helstöfum;
á landi ok á vatni   borgit er lofðungs flota
ok siklings mönnum it sama."

HELGAKVITHA HJORVARTHSSONAR

Hrimgerth spake: 24
"Awake now, Helgi, and Hrimgerth requite,
That Hati to death thou didst hew;
If a single night she can sleep by the prince,
Then requited are all her ills."

Helgi spake: 25
"'Tis Lothin shall have thee, thou'rt loathsome to men,
His home in Tholley he has;
Of the wild-dwellers worst is the giant wise,
He is meet as a mate for thee."

Hrimgerth spake: 26
"More thou lovest her who scanned the harbor,
Last night among the men;
The gold-decked maid bore magic, methinks,
When the land from the sea she sought,
And fast she kept your fleet;
She alone is to blame that I may not bring
Death to the monarch's men."

Helgi spake: 27
"Hrimgerth, mark, if thy hurts I requite,
Tell now the truth to the king;
Was there one who the ships of the warrior warded,
Or did many together go?"

Hrimgerth spake: 28
"Thrice nine there were, but one rode first,
A helmed maid white of hue;
Their horses quivered, there came from their manes
Dew in the dales so deep,
Hail on the woods so high,
Thence men their harvest have,
But ill was the sight I saw."

Atli spake: 29
"Look eastward, Hrimgerth, for Helgi has struck thee
Down with the runes of death;
Safe in harbor floats the prince's fleet,
And safe are the monarch's men."

Atli kvað: 30
"Dagr er nú, Hrímgerðr,　　en þik dvalða hefr
Atli til aldrlaga;
hafnarmark　　þykkir hlægligt vera,
þars þú í steins líki stendr."

IV.

Helgi konungr var allmikill hermaðr. Hann kom til Eylima konungs ok
bað Sváfu dóttur hans. Þau Helgi ok Sváfa veittust várar ok unnust furðu
mikit. Sváfa var heima með feðr sínum, en Helgi í hernaði. Var Sváfa
valkyrja enn sem fyrr.
　　Heðinn var heima með föður sínum, Hjörvarði konungi, í Nóregi.
Heðinn fór einn saman heim ór skógi jólaaftan ok fann trollkonu. Sú reið
vargi ok hafði orma at taumum ok bauð fylgð sína Heðni. "Nei," sagði
hann. Hon sagði: "Þess skaltu gjalda at bragarfulli." Um kveldit óru heit-
strengingar. Var fram leiddr sónargöltr. Lögðu menn þar á hendr sínar
ok strengðu menn þá heit at bragarfulli. Heðinn strengði heit til Sváfu
Eylimadóttur, unnustu Helga, bróður síns, ok iðraðisk svá mjök, at hann
gekk á braut villistígu suðr á lönd ok fann Helga bróður sinn. Helgi kvað:

"Kom þú heill, Heðinn,　　hvat kanntu segja 31
nýra spjalla　　ór Nóregi?
Hví er þér, stillir,　　stökkt ór landi
ok ert einn kominn　　oss at finna?"

Heðinn kvað: 32
"Erumk-a, stillir,　　stökkt ór landi,
mik hefr miklu glæpr　　meiri sóttan:
Ek hefi körna　　ina konungbornu
brúði þína　　at bagarfulli."

Helgi kvað: 33
"Sakask eigi þú,　　sönn munu verða
ölmál, Heðinn,　　okkur beggja.
Mér hefir stillir　　stefnt til eyrar,
þriggja nátta　　skylak þar koma;
if er mér á því,　　at ek aftr koma;
þá má at góðu　　gerask slíkt, ef skal."

Helgi spake: 30
"It is day, Hrimgerth, for Atli held thee
Till now thy life thou must lose;
As a harbor mark men shall mock at thee,
Where in stone thou shalt ever stand."

IV.

King Helgi was a mighty warrior. He came to King Eylimi and sought the hand of his daughter, Svava. Then Helgi and Svava exchanged vows, and greatly they loved each other. Svava was at home with her father, while Helgi was in the field; Svava was still a Valkyrie as before.

Hethin was at home with his father, King Hjorvarth, in Norway. Hethin was coming home alone from the forest one Yule-eve, and found a troll-woman; she rode on a wolf, and had snakes in place of a bridle. She asked Hethin for his company. "Nay," said he. She said, "Thou shalt pay for this at the king's toast." That evening the great vows were taken; the sacred boar was brought in, the men laid their hands thereon, and took their vows at the king's toast. Hethin vowed that he would have Svava, Eylimi's daughter, the beloved of his brother Helgi; then such great grief seized him that he went forth on wild paths southward over the land, and found Helgi, his brother. Helgi said:

"Welcome, Hethin! what hast thou to tell 31
Of tidings new that from Norway come?
Wherefore didst leave thy land, O prince,
And fared alone to find us here?"

Hethin spake: 32
"A deed more evil I have done
Than, brother mine, thou e'er canst mend;
For I have chosen the child of the king,
Thy bride, for mine at the monarch's toast."

Helgi spake: 33
"Grieve not, Hethin, for true shall hold
The words we both by the beer have sworn;
To the isle a warrior wills that I go,
There shall I come the third night hence;
And doubtful must be my coming back,
So may all be well, if fate so wills."

Heðinn kvað: 34
"Sagðir þú, Helgi,   at Heðinn væri
góðs verðr frá þér   ok gjafa stórra;
þér er sæmra   sverð at rjóða,
en frið gefa   fjándum þínum."

Þat kvað Helgi, því at hann grunaði um feigð sína ok þat, at fylgjur hans höfðu vitjat Heðins, þá er hann sá konuna ríða varginum. Álfr hét konungr, son Hróðmars, er Helga hafði völl haslaðan á Sigarsvelli á þriggja nátta fresti. Þá kvað Helgi:

"Reið á vargi,   er rökvit var, 35
fljóð eitt, er Heðinn   fylgju beiddi;
hón vissi þat,   at veginn myndi
Sigrlinnar sonr   á Sigarsvöllum."

Þar var orrosta mikil, ok fekk þar Helgi banasár.

Sendi Helgi   Sigar at ríða 36
eftir Eylima   eingadóttur;
"Bið bráðliga   búna verða,
ef hon vill finna   fylki kvikvan."

Sigarr kvað: 37
"Mik hefr Helgi   hingat sendan
við þik, Sváfa,   sjalfa at mæla;
þik kvaðsk hilmir   hitta vilja,
áðr ítrborinn   öndu týndi."

Sváfa kvað: 38
"Hvat varð Helga   Hjörvarðs syni?
Mér er harðliga   harma leitat,
ef hann sær of lék   eða sverð of beit,
þeim skal ek gumna   grand of vinna."

Sigarr kvað: 39
"Fell hér í morgun   at Frekasteini,
buðlungr, sá er var,   baztr und sólu;
Alfr mun sigri   öllum ráða,
þótt þetta sinn   þörfgi væri."

Hethin spake: 34
"Thou saidst once, Helgi, that Hethin was
A friend full good, and gifts didst give him;
More seemly it were thy sword to redden,
Than friendship thus to thy foe to give."

Helgi spoke thus because he foresaw his death, for his following-spirits had met Hethin when he saw the woman riding on the wolf. Alf was the name of a king, the son of Hrothmar, who had marked out a battle-place with Helgi at Sigarsvoll after a stay of three nights. Then Helgi spake:

"On a wolf there rode, when dusk it was, 35
A woman who fain would have him follow;
Well she knew that now would fall
Sigrlin's son at Sigarsvoll."

There was a great battle, and there Helgi got a mortal wound.

Sigar riding did Helgi send 36
To seek out Eylimi's only daughter:
"Bid her swiftly ready to be,
If her lover alive she would find."

Sigar spake: 37
"Hither now has Helgi sent me,
With thee, Svava, thyself to speak;
The hero said he fain would see thee
Ere life the nobly born should leave."

Svava spake: 38
"What chanced with Helgi, Hjorvarth's son?
Hard to me is harm now come;
If the sea smote him, or sword bit him,
Ill shall I bring to all his foes."

Sigar spake: 39
"In the morn he fell at Frekastein,
The king who was noblest beneath the sun;
Alf has the joy of victory all,
Though need therefor is never his."

Helgi kvað: 40
"Heil vertu, Sváfa, hug skaltu deila,
sjá mun í heimi hinztr fundr vera;
téa buðlungi blæða undir,
mér hefir hjörr komit hjarta it næsta."

Helgi kvað: 41
Bið ek þik, Sváfa, —brúðr grát-at-tu—
ef þú vill mínu máli hlýða,
at þú Heðni hvílu gervir
ok jöfur ungan ástum leiðir."

Sváfa kvað: 42
"Mælt hafða ek þat í munarheimi,
þá er mér Helgi hringa valði,
myndig-a ek lostig at liðinn fylki
jöfur ókunnan armi verja."

Heðinn kvað: 43
"Kysstu mik, Sváfa, kem ek eigi áðr
Rogheims á vit né Röðulsfjalla,
áðr ek hefnt hefik Hjörvarðs sonar,
þess er buðlungr var beztr und sólu."

Helgi ok Sváfa, er sagt, at væri endrborin.

Helgi spake: 40
"Hail to thee, Svava! thy sorrow rule,
Our meeting last in life is this;
Hard the wounds of the hero bleed,
And close to my heart the sword has come."

"I bid thee, Svava, weep not, bride, 41
If thou wilt hearken to these my words,
The bed for Hethin have thou ready,
And yield thy love to the hero young."

Svava spake: 42
"A vow I had in my dear-loved home,
When Helgi sought with rings to have me,
That not of my will, if the warrior died,
Would I fold in my arms a man unfamed."

Hethin spake: 43
"Kiss me, Svava, I come not back,
Rogheim to see, or Rothulsfjoll,
Till vengeance I have for the son of Hjorvarth,
The king who was noblest beneath the sun."

Of Helgi and Svava it is said that they were born again.

ENDNOTES

Prose: In the manuscript the sub-title, "Of Hjorvarth and Sigrlin," stands as the title for the whole poem, though it clearly applies only to the first five stanzas. Most editions employ the title here given. Hjorvarth: the name is a not uncommon one; there are two men of that name mentioned in the mythical heroic genealogies of the *Hyndluljoth* (stanzas 23 and 28), and Hjorvarth appears in *Helgakvitha Hundingsbana I* (stanza 14) and *II* (prose after stanza 12) as a son of Hunding. This particular Hjorvarth is called by the annotator, but not directly so in the verse, a king of Norway. The name means "Sword-Guardian." Four wives: polygamy, while very infrequent, appears occasionally in the Norse sagas. Alfhild: "Elf-Warrior." Hethin: "Fur-Clothed"(?) Særeith: "Sea-Rider." Sinrjoth: "Ever-Red." The fourth wife, not here named, may be Sigrlin. It has been suggested that Særeith and Sinrjoth may be northern and southern forms of the same name, as also Humlung and Hymling, their sons. Svafnir: the annotator calls him king of Svavaland, apparently a place on the mainland which could be reached from Norway either by land or by sea. Sigrlin: "The Conquering Serpent." Atli: Norse form of the Gothic Attila (Etzel). Alof: perhaps a feminine form of Olaf. A bird: compare the counsel given by the birds to Sigurth after the slaying of Fafnir (*Fafnismol*, stanzas 32–38). This is one of the many curious resemblances between the Helgi and the Sigurth stories.

1. *Glasir's wood*: Snorri in the *Skaldskaparmal* quotes a half stanza to the effect that "Glasir stands with golden leaves before Odin's hall," and calls it "the fairest wood among gods and men." The phrase as used here seems to mean little.

4. The bird's demands would indicate that it is in reality one of the gods.

Gold-horned cattle: cf. *Thrymskvitha*, 23. There are other references to gilding the horns of cattle, particularly for sacrificial purposes.

Prose: The annotator contradicts himself here, as he had already stated that Atli was on his way home.

5. Possibly the remains of two stanzas, or perhaps a line has been added. *Sæmorn*: this river is nowhere else mentioned.

Prose. Sigrlin and Alof, protected by the latter's father, Franmar, have fled before the ravaging army of Sigrlin's rejected suitor, Hrothmar. The beginning of a new section (II) is indicated in the manuscript only by the unusually large capital letter with which "Hjorvarth" begins. *No name*, etc.: this probably means that Helgi had always been so silent that he would answer to no name, with the result that he had none. *Valkyries*: cf. *Voluspo*, 31 and note. The annotator insists here and in the prose after stanza 9 that Svava was a Valkyrie, but there is nothing in the verse to prove it, or, indeed, to identify the Svava of the last section of the poem with the person who gave Helgi his name. In the *Volsungasaga* Sigmund himself names his son Helgi, and gives him a sword, following *Helgakvitha Hundingsbana* I.

6. *Battle-free*: poetic phrase for "warrior." *Shining fields*: the words in the manuscript may form a proper name, Rothulsvoll, having this meaning.

7. *Gift*: not only was it customary to give gifts with the naming of a child, but the practice frequently obtained when a permanent epithet was added to the name of an adult.

8. *Sigarsholm* ("Isle of Sigar"): a place not identified, but probably related to the Sigarsvoll where Helgi was slain (stanza 35).

9. The sword is carved with magic runes and with snakes. *Fame*: the original word is uncertain.

Prose. Eylimi: this name is another link with the Sigurth story, as it is likewise the name of the father of Sigurth's mother, Hjordis.

10. With this stanza begins a new episode, that of Helgi's victory over King Hrothmar, who had killed his mother's father (cf. prose after stanza 5). It has been suggested, in consequence, that stanzas 10–11 may be a separate fragment. The verse tells nothing of the battle, merely giving Helgi's reproaches to his father for having left Svafnir's death and the burning of Svavaland unavenged.

Prose. The manuscript does not indicate any break, but the episode which forms the basis of the *Hrimgertharmol* (stanzas 12–30) clearly begins with the slaying of the giant Hati ("The Hateful"). *Hatafjord*: "Hati's Fjord." *Hrimgerth*: "Frost Shrouded" (?).

13. *Iron*: the keels of Norse ships were sometimes fitted with iron "shoes" at bow and stern, but it is not certain that this practice much antedated the year 1000, and thus this line has raised some question as to the antiquity of this stanza, if not of the entire *Hrimgertharmol*, which may have been composed as late as the eleventh century.

15. The manuscript does not indicate the speaker. The pun on "Atli" and "atall" (meaning "ill") is untranslatable.

17. The manuscript does not indicate the speaker.

18. From this point to the end the manuscript does not indicate the speakers. *Ron*: wife of the sea-god Ægir, who draws drowning men into the sea with her net. There is no other reference to the wounding of Hrimgerth.

19. Apparently both Hrimgerth and her mother, Hati's wife, had sought to destroy Helgi's ships, and had actually killed some of his companions, the sons of *Hlothvarth*, concerning whom nothing more is known. Many editors assume that a stanza containing a speech by Atli has been lost after stanza 19.

20. Apparently Hrimgerth has assumed the form of a mare.

22. *Varin's cove*: the name of Varin appears twice in place names in *Helgakvitha Hundingsbana I* (stanzas 27 and 39). The sagas mention a mythical King Varin who lived at Skorustrond in Rogaland (Norway).

25. Of the giant *Lothin* ("The Shaggy") and his home in *Tholley* ("Pine Island") nothing is known. Cf. *Skirnismol*, 35.

26. Something is clearly wrong with this stanza, and the manuscript indicates line 6 as the beginning of a new one. Perhaps a line (between lines 4 and 5) has been lost, or perhaps the lines in parenthesis are interpolations. Hrimgerth here refers to Svava, or to the protectress with whom the annotator has identified her, as having saved Helgi and his ships from the vengeance of the giantesses. In the original line 1 includes Helgi's name, which makes it metrically incorrect.

28. Again something is clearly wrong, and the last three lines look like interpolations, though some editors have tried to reconstruct two full stanzas. The passage suggests the identification of the Valkyries with the clouds.

29. Some editions give this speech to Helgi. *Eastward*: Atli and Helgi have held Hrimgerth in talk till sunrise, and the sun's rays turn her into stone. But dwarfs rather than giants were the victims of sunlight; cf. *Alvissmol*, stanzas 16 and 35.

30. Most editions give this stanza to Atli. With this the *Hrimgertharmol* ends, and after the next prose passage the meter reverts to that of the earlier sections.

Prose. The manuscript does not indicate a new section of the poem. *Eylimi*: cf. note on prose after stanza 9. *Valkyrie*: here, as before, the annotator has apparently nothing but his own imagination on which to base his statement. Svava in the ensuing stanzas certainly does not behave like a Valkyrie. *Norway*: the annotator doubtless based this statement on the reference to Norway in line 2 of stanza 31. *Yule-eve*: the Yule feast, marking the new year, was a great event in the heathen North. It was a time of feasting and merrymaking, vows ("New Year's resolutions"), ghosts and witches; the spirits had their greatest power on Yule-eve. *The king's toast*: vows made at the passing of the king's cup at the Yule feast were particularly sacred. *Sacred boar*: a boar consecrated to Freyr, an integral part of the Yule rites. Hethin's vow, which is, of course, the vengeance of the troll-woman, is too sacred to be broken, but he immediately realizes the horror of his oath.

31. *From Norway*: Bugge uses this phrase as evidence that the poem was composed in one of the Icelandic settlements of the western islands, but as the annotator himself seems to have thought that Hethin came to Helgi by land ("on wild paths southward"), this argument does not appear to have much weight.

32. The second line is conjectural; a line has clearly been lost from this stanza, and various emendations have been suggested.

33. Perhaps this is the remnant of two stanzas, or perhaps two lines (probably the ones in parenthesis) have been interpolated. *The isle*: duels were commonly fought on islands, probably to guard against treacherous interference, whence the usual name for a duel was "isle-going." A duel was generally fought three days after the challenge. Reckoning the lapse of time by nights instead of days was a common practice throughout the German and Scandinavian peoples.

Prose. Some editors place all or part of this prose passage after stanza 35. *Following-spirits*: the "fylgja" was a female guardian spirit whose appearance generally betokened death. The belief was common throughout the North, and has come down to recent times in Scottish and Irish folk-lore. Individuals and sometimes whole families had these following-spirits, but it was most unusual for a person to have more than one of them. *Alf*: son of the Hrothmar who killed Helgi's grandfather, and who was in turn later killed by Helgi. *Sigarsvoll* ("Sigar's Field"): cf. stanza 8 and note; the Sigar in question may be the man who appears as Helgi's messenger in stanzas 36–39.

36. *Sigar* ("The Victorious"): cf. the foregoing note.

39. *Frekastein* ("Wolf-Crag"): the name appears several times in the Helgi lays applied to battlefields; cf. *Helgakvitha Hundingsbana* I, 46 and 55, and II, 18 and 24. *Need*: i.e., Alf deserves no credit for the victory, which was due to the troll woman's magic.

41. One or two editors ascribe this stanza to Hethin.

43. A few editions make the extraordinary blunder of ascribing this speech to the dying Helgi. The point, of course, is that Hethin will satisfy Svava's vow by becoming famous as the slayer of Alf. *Rogheim* ("Rome of Battle") and *Rothulsfjoll* ("Sun-Mountain"): nowhere else mentioned; Hethin means simply that he will not come back to Svava till he has won fame.

Prose. Regarding this extraordinary bit see the prose note at the end of *Helgakvitha Hundingsbana II*. Gering thinks the reborn Helgi Hjorvarthsson was Helgi Hundingsbane, while Svava, according to the annotator himself, became Sigrun. The point seems to be simply that there were so many Helgi stories current, and the hero died in so many irreconcilable ways, that tradition had to have him born over again, not once only but several times, to accommodate his many deaths, and to avoid splitting him up into several Helgis. Needless to say, the poems themselves know nothing of this rebirth, and we owe the suggestion entirely to the annotator, who probably got it from current tradition.

HELGAKVITHA HUNDINGSBANA I
THE FIRST LAY OF HELGI HUNDINGSBANE

INTRODUCTION

The *First Lay of Helgi Hundsingsbane* is directly connected narratively to the previous story of Helgi, son of Hjorvarth, and as such I will not restate the various quandaries and intricacies of this connected narrative. Suffice it to say that this particular poem is accounted as being of a very late origination, based on the plethora of skaldic motifs and kennings and the extensive use of narrative poetry, which was not something native to the Germanic epic tradition and thus can be used to safely date the poem to some time after the year 1000. Although the poem's author appears to have compiled it fairly late, the contents and story are likely to be far older and we simply have received a newly written version of a very old and popular tale.

There is a great scholarly dispute about the origins and intentions of the poem's character, with one school of thought that would have them occurring in Denmark and Helgi thus being a member of the Royal house of the Ylfings, and a separate tradition seeing the characters and locations as centered in either Frankia or Sweden and descended questionably from either the Volsungs line or that of the Ynglings, which is a matter of much larger dispute between various narratives.

The poem itself features a substantial number of cleverly designed kennings that, without a very solid grasp of Norse culture and mythological associations, would be nigh unreadable to the modern man unless translated with attendant commentary, and to which no quality of translation can do justice without doing so. It is for this reason that we face a stark reality: that the true character of the Norse epics and lays is best grasped through the original language of the Skalds that composed them.

The nature and character of Helgi Hundingsbane is that of a hero in the ancient mold, in many respects not unlike that of Egil Skallagrimsson in the later Icelandic family sagas. Helgi is a hero predicated wholly on the righteous cause of vengeance and murderous retribution with a forthright finality and assurance that would leave adherents to modern cultural mores quite cold in response. The hero shows no signs of humanism, nor any idea of the compassion and forgiveness that characterize Christian Europe. In many ways, Helgi has more in common with the archaic heroes of Achilles or Odysseus or the heroic fighters of the *Ramayana* than he does with the knights and kings that characterize continental Europe post-Charlemagne. To truly understand the motivation and character of the ancient heroes we must realize that everything they think and believe lies in stark contrast to that of modernity. I will quote *Culture of the Teutons* regarding the matter of vengeance in the Germanic mindset:

> [The Teuton] has but one view of man; man asserting himself, maintaining his honour, as he calls it. All that moves within a man must be twisted round until it becomes associated with honour, before he can grasp it; and all his passion is thrust back and held, until it finds its way out in that one direction. This simplicity of character shows in his poetry, which is at heart nothing but lays and tales of great avengers, because revenge is the supreme act that concentrates his inner life and forces it out in the light.
>
> His poems of vengeance are always intensely human, because revenge to him is not an empty repetition of a wrong done, but a spiritual self-assertion, a manifestation of strength and value; and thus the anguish of an affront or the triumph of victory is able to open up the sealed depths of his mind and suffuse his words with passion and tenderness.[1]

---

1 Vilhelm Grönbech, *Culture Of The Teutons*, 1931, p. 9.

The Were-Wolves
(J. C. Dollman)

Hér hefr upp kvæði frá Helga Hundingsbana ok þeira Höðbrodds:

Ár var alda,   þat er arar gullu,   1
hnigu heilög vötn   af Himinfjöllum;
þá hafði Helga   inn hugumstóra
Borghildr borit   í Brálundi.

Nótt varð í bæ,   nornir kómu,   2
þær er öðlingi   aldr of skópu;
þann báðu fylki   frægstan verða
ok buðlunga   beztan þykkja.

Sneru þær af afli   örlögþáttu,   3
þá er borgir braut   í Brálundi;
þær of greiddu   gullin símu
ok und mánasal   miðjan festu.

Þær austr ok vestr   enda fálu,   4
þar átti lofðungr   land á milli;
brá nift Nera   á norðrvega
einni festi,   ey bað hon halda.

HELGAKVITHA HUNDINGSBANA I

Here begins the poem of Helgi Hundingsbane and that of Hodbrodd:

In olden days, when eagles screamed,   1
And holy streams from heaven's crags fell,
Was Helgi then, the hero-hearted,
Borghild's son, in Bralund born.

'Twas night in the dwelling, and Norns there came,   2
Who shaped the life of the lofty one;
They bade him most famed of fighters all
And best of princes ever to be.

Mightily wove they the web of fate,   3
While Bralund's towns were trembling all;
And there the golden threads they wove,
And in the moon's hall fast they made them.

East and west the ends they hid,   4
In the middle the hero should have his land;
And Neri's kinswoman northward cast
A chain, and bade it firm ever to be.

Eitt var at angri   Ylfinga nið 5
ok þeiri meyju,   er munúð fæddi;
hrafn kvað at hrafni,   sat á hám meiði
andvanr átu: "ek veit nökkut.

Stendr í brynju   burr Sigmundar 6
dægrs eins gamall,   nú er dagr kominn;
hvessir augu   sem hildingar,
sá er varga vinr,   vit skulum teitir."

Drótt þótti sá   döglingr vera, 7
kváðu með gumnum   góð ár komin;
sjalfr gekk vísi   ór vígþrimu
ungum færa   ítrlauk grami.

Gaf hann Helga nafn   ok Hringstaði, 8
Sólfjöll, Snæfjöll   ok Sigarsvöllu,
Hringstöð, Hátún   ok Himinvanga,
blóðorm búinn   bræðr Sinfjötla.

Þá nam at vaxa   fyr vina brjósti 9
almr ítrborinn   ynðis ljóma;
hann galt ok gaf   gull verðungu,
sparði eigi hilmir   hodd blóðrækinn.

Skammt lét vísi   vígs at bíða; 10
þá er fylkir var   fimmtán vetra,
ok hann harðan lét   Hunding veginn
þann er lengi réð   löndum ok þegnum.

Kvöddu síðan   Sigmundar bur 11
auðs ok hringa   Hundings synir,
því at þeir áttu   jöfri at gjalda
fjárnám mikit   ok föður dauða.

Lét-at buðlungr   bótir uppi 12
né niðja in heldr   nefgjöld fáa;
ván kvað hann mundu   veðrs ins mikla
grára geira   ok gremi Óðins.

Fara hildingar   hjörstefnu til, 13
þeirar er lögðu   at Logafjöllum;
sleit Fróða frið   fjánda á milli;
fara Viðris grey   valgjörn of ey.

Once sorrow had the Ylfings' son, 5
And grief the bride who the loved one had borne.
[...]
Quoth raven to raven, on treetop resting,
Seeking for food, "There is something I know."

"In mail-coat stands the son of Sigmund, 6
A half-day old; now day is here;
His eyes flash sharp as the heroes' are,
He is friend of the wolves; full glad are we."

The warrior throng a ruler thought him, 7
Good times, they said, mankind should see;
The king himself from battle-press came,
To give the prince a leek full proud.

Helgi he named him, and Hringstathir gave him, 8
Solfjoll, Snæfjoll, and Sigarsvoll,
Hringstoth, Hotun, and Himinvangar,
And a blood-snake bedecked to Sinfjotli's brother.

Mighty he grew in the midst of his friends, 9
The fair-born elm, in fortune's glow;
To his comrades gold he gladly gave,
The hero spared not the blood-flecked hoard.

Short time for war the chieftain waited, 10
When fifteen winters old he was;
Hunding he slew, the hardy wight
Who long had ruled o'er lands and men.

Of Sigmund's son then next they sought 11
Hoard and rings, the sons of Hunding;
They bade the prince requital pay
For booty stolen and father slain.

The prince let not their prayers avail, 12
Nor gold for their dead did the kinsmen get;
Waiting, he said, was a mighty storm
Of lances gray and Odin's grimness.

The warriors forth to the battle went, 13
The field they chose at Logafjoll;
Frothi's peace midst foes they broke,
Through the isle went hungrily Vithrir's hounds.

Settisk vísi,   þá er vegit hafði   14
Alf ok Eyjólf,   und arasteini,
Hjörvarð ok Hávarð,   Hundings sonu;
farit hafði hann allri   ætt geirmímis.

Þá brá ljóma   af Logafjöllum,   15
en af þeim ljómum   leiftrir kómu,
[...]
hávar und hjalmum   á Himinvanga,
brynjur váru þeira   blóði stokknar,
en af geirum   geislar stóðu.

Frá árliga   ór úlfíði   16
döglingr at því   dísir suðrænar,
ef þær vildi heim   með hildingum
þá nótt fara;   þrymr var alma.

En af hesti   Högna dóttir,   17
líddi randa rym,   ræsi sagði:
"Hygg ek, at vér eigim   aðrar sýslur
en með baugbrota   bjór at drekka.

Hefir minn faðir   meyju sinni   18
grimmum heitit   Granmars syni,
en ek hef, Helgi,   Höðbrodd kveðinn
konung óneisan   sem kattar son.

Þó kemr fylkir   fára nátta,   19
nema þú hánum vísir   valstefnu til
eða mey nemir   frá mildingi."

Helgi kvað: 20
"Uggi eigi þú   Ísungs bana;
fyrr mun dolga dynr,   nema ek dauðr séak."

Helgi kvað: 21
Sendi áru   allvaldr þaðan
of land ok um lög   leiðar at biðja,
iðgnógan   Ógnar ljóma
brögnum bjóða   ok burum þeira.

The king then sat, when he had slain 14
Eyjolf and Alf, 'neath the eagle-stone;
Hjorvarth and Hovarth, Hunding's sons,
The kin of the spear-wielder, all had he killed.

Then glittered light from Logafjoll, 15
And from the light the flashes leaped;
[...]
High under helms on heaven's field;
Their byrnies all with blood were red,
And from their spears the sparks flew forth.

Early then in wolf-wood asked 16
The mighty king of the southern maid,
If with the hero home would she
Come that night; the weapons clashed.

Down from her horse sprang Hogni's daughter, 17
The shields were still, and spake to the hero:
"Other tasks are ours, methinks,
Than drinking beer with the breaker of rings."

"My father has pledged his daughter fair 18
As bride to Granmar's son so grim;
But, Helgi, I once Hothbrodd called
As fine a king as the son of a cat."

"Yet the hero will come a few nights hence, 19
[...]
Unless thou dost bid him the battle-ground seek,
Or takest the maid from the warrior mighty."

Helgi spake: 20
"Fear him not, though Isung he felled,
First must our courage keen be tried,
Before unwilling thou fare with the knave;
Weapons will clash, if to death I come not."

Messengers sent the mighty one then, 21
By land and by sea, a host to seek,
Store of wealth of the water's gleam,
And men to summon, and sons of men.

"Biðið skjótliga   til skipa ganga
ok ór Brandeyju   búna verða."
Þaðan beið þengill,   unz þingat kómu
halir hundmargir   ór Heðinseyju.

22

Ok þar af ströndum   ór Stafnsnesi
beit her út skriðu   ok búin gulli;
spurði Helgi   Hjörleif at því:
"hefir þú kannaða   koni óneisa?"

23

En ungr konungr   öðrum sagði,
seint kvað at telja   af Trönueyri
langhöfðuð skip   und líðöndum,
þau er í Örvasund   útan fóru.

24

"Tolf hundruð   tryggra manna;
þó er í Hátúnum   halfu fleira
víglið konungs;   ván erum rómu."

25

Helgi kvað:
Svá brá stýrir   stafntjöldum af,
at mildinga   mengi vakði,
ok döglingar   dagsbrún séa
ok siklingar   sneru upp við tré
vefnistingum   á Varinsfirði.

26

Varð ára ymr   ok járna glymr,
brast rönd við rönd,   reru víkingar;
eisandi gekk   und öðlingum
lofðungs floti   löndum fjarri.

27

Svá var at heyra,   er saman kómu
kolgu systir   ok kilir langir,
sem björg eða brim   brotna myndi.

28

Draga bað Helgi   há segl ofar,
varð-at hrönnum   höfn þingloga,
þá er ógurlig   Ægis dóttir
stagstjórnmörum   steypa vildi.

29

En þeim sjalfum   Sigrún ofan
folkdjörf of barg   ok fari þeira;
snerisk ramliga   Rán ór hendi
gjalfrdýr konungs   at Gnipalundi.

30

"Bid them straightway seek the ships, 22
And off Brandey ready to be!"
There the chief waited till thither were come
Men by hundreds from Hethinsey."

Soon off Stafnsnes stood the ships, 23
Fair they glided and gay with gold;
Then Helgi spake to Hjorleif asking:
"Hast thou counted the gallant host?"

The young king answered the other then: 24
"Long were it to tell from Tronueyr
The long-stemmed ships with warriors laden
That come from without into Orvasund."

[...] 25
"There are hundreds twelve of trusty men,
But in Hotun lies the host of the king,
Greater by half; I have hope of battle."

The ship's-tents soon the chieftain struck, 26
And waked the throng of warriors all;
The heroes the red of dawn beheld;
And on the masts the gallant men
Made fast the sails in Varinsfjord.

There was beat of oars and clash of iron, 27
Shield smote shield as the ships'-folk rowed;
Swiftly went the warrior-laden
Fleet of the ruler forth from the land.

So did it sound, when together the sisters 28
Of Kolga struck with the keels full long,
As if cliffs were broken with beating surf,
[...]

Helgi bade higher hoist the sails, 29
Nor did the ships'-folk shun the waves,
Though dreadfully did Ægir's daughters
Seek the steeds of the sea to sink.

But from above did Sigrun brave 30
Aid the men and all their faring;
Mightily came from the claws of Rán
The leader's sea-beast off Gnipalund.

Helgi kvað: 31
Sat þar um aftan   í Unavágum,
flaust fagrbúin   fljóta knáttu;
en þeir sjalfir   frá Svarinshaugi
með hermðar hug   her könnuðu.

Frá góðborinn   Goðmundr at því: 32
"Hverr er landreki,   sá er liði stýrir
ok hann feiknalið   færir at landi?"

Sinfjötli kvað   slöng upp við rá   33
rauðum skildi,   rönd var ór gulli;
þar var sundvörðr,   sá er svara kunni
ok við öðlinga   orðum skipta:

"Segðu þat í aftan,   er svínum gefr   34
ok tíkr yðrar   teygir at solli,
at sé Ylfingar   austan komnir
gunnar gjarnir   fyr Gnipalundi.

Þar mun Höðbroddr   Helga finna   35
flugtrauðan gram   í flota miðjum,
sá er oft hefir   örnu sadda,
meðan þú á kvernum   kystir þýjar."

Guðmundr kvað: 36
"Fátt mantu, fylkir,   fornra spjalla,
er þú öðlingum   ósönnu bregðr;
þú hefir etnar   ulfa krásir
ok bræðr þínum   at bana orðit,
oft sár sogin   með svölum munni,
hefr í hreysi   hvarleiðr skriðit."

Sinfjötli kvað: 37
"Þú vart völva   í Varinseyju,
skollvís kona,   bartu skrök saman;
kvaztu engi mann   eiga vilja,
segg brynjaðan,   nema Sinfjötla.

Þú vart, in skæða,   skass, valkyrja,   38
ötul, ámátlig   at Alföður;
mundu einherjar   allir berjask,
svevís kona,   of sakar þínar.

At evening there in Unavagar　　　　　　　　　　31
Floated the fleet bedecked full fair;
But they who saw from Svarin's hill,
Bitter at heart the host beheld.

Then Gothmund asked, goodly of birth,　　　　32
[...]
"Who is the monarch who guides the host,
And to the land the warriors leads?"

Sinfjotli answered, and up on an oar　　　　　33
Raised a shield all red with golden rim;
A sea-sentry was he, skilled to speak,
And in words with princes well to strive.

"Say tonight when you feed the swine,　　　　34
And send your bitches to seek their swill,
That out of the East have the Ylfings come,
Greedy for battle, to Gnipalund."

"There will Hothbrodd Helgi find,　　　　　　35
In the midst of the fleet, and flight he scorns;
Often has he the eagles gorged,
Whilst thou at the quern wert slave-girls kissing."

Gothmund spake:　　　　　　　　　　　　　　36
"Hero, the ancient sayings heed,
And bring not lies to the nobly born.
[...]
[...]
"Thou hast eaten the entrails of wolves,
And of thy brothers the slayer been;
Oft wounds to suck thy cold mouth sought,
And loathed in rocky dens didst lurk."

Sinfjotli spake:　　　　　　　　　　　　　　37
"A witch in Varin's isle thou wast,
A woman false, and lies didst fashion;
Of the mail-clad heroes thou wouldst have
No other, thou saidst, save Sinfjotli only."

"A Valkyrie wast thou, loathly Witch,　　　　38
Evil and base, in Allfather's home;
The warriors all must ever fight,
Woman subtle, for sake of thee."

Níu áttu vit á nesi Ságu 39
ulfa alna, ek var einn faðir þeira."

Guðmundr kvað: 40
"Faðir var-at-tu fenrisulfa
öllum ellri, svá at ek muna,
síz þik geldu fyr Gnipalundi
þursa meyjar á Þórsnesi.

Guðmundr kvað: 41
Stjúpr vartu Siggeirs, látt und stöðum heima,
vargljóðum vanr á viðum úti;
kómu þér ógögn öll at hendi,
þá er bræðr þínum brjóst raufaðir;
gerðir þik frægjan af firinverkum."

Sinfjötli kvað: 42
"Þú vart brúðr Grana á Brávelli,
gullbitluð vart gör til rásar;
hafða ek þér móðri marg skeið riðit
svangri und söðli, simul, forbergis."

Guðmundr kvað: 43
"Sveinn þóttir þú siðlauss vera,
þá er þú Gullnis geitr molkaðir,
en í annat sinn Imðar dóttir
tötrughypja.
Vill þú tölu lengri?"

Sinfjötli kvað: 44
"Fyrr vilda ek at Frekasteini
hrafna seðja á hræum þínum
en tíkr yðrar teygja at solli
eða gefa göltum;
deili gröm við þik."

Helgi kvað: 45
"Væri ykkr, Sinfjötli, Sæmra miklu
gunni at heyja ok glaða örnu,
en sé ónýtum orðum at bregðask,
þótt hringbrotar heiftir deili.

"[...]   39
[...]
Nine did we in Sogunes
Of wolf-cubs have; I their father was."

Gothmund spake: 40
"Thou didst not father Fenrir's-wolves,
Though older thou art than all I know;
For they gelded thee in Gnipalund,
The giant-women at Thorsnes once."

"Under houses the stepson of Siggeir lay,   41
Fain of the wolf's cry out in the woods;
Evil came then all to thy hands,
When thy brothers' breasts thou didst redden,
Fame didst thou win for foulest deeds."

"In Bravoll wast thou Grani's bride,   42
Golden-bitted and ready to gallop;
I rode thee many a mile, and down
Didst sink, thou giantess, under the saddle."

Sinfjotli spake: 43
"A brainless fellow didst seem to be,
When once for Gollnir goats didst milk,
And another time when as Imth's daughter
In rags thou wentest; wilt longer wrangle?"

Gothmund spake: 44
"Sooner would I at Frekastein
Feed the ravens with flesh of thine
Than send your bitches to seek their swill,
Or feed the swine; may the fiends take you!"

Helgi spake: 45
"Better, Sinfjotli, thee 'twould beseem
Battle to give and eagles to gladden,
Than vain and empty words to utter,
Though ring-breakers oft in speech do wrangle."

Helgi kvað:
"Þykkja-t mér góðir Granmars synir,
þó dugir siklingum satt at mæla;
þeir hafa markat á Móinsheimum,
at hug hafa hjörum at bregða."

46

Þeir af ríki renna létu
Svipuð ok Sveggjuð Sólheima til
dala döggótta, dökkvar hlíðir;
skalf Mistar marr hvar er megir fóru.

47

Mættu þeir tyggja í túnhliði,
sögðu stríðliga stilli kómu;
úti stóð Höðbroddr hjalmi faldinn,
hugði hann jóreið ættar sinnar:
"Hví er hermðar litr á Hniflungum?"

48

Guðmundr kvað:
"Snúask hér at sandi snævgir kjólar,
rakka-hirtir ok ráar langar,
skildir margir, skafnar árar,
göfugt lið gylfa, glaðir Ylfingar.

49

Ganga fimmtán folk upp á land,
þó er í Sogn út sjau þúsundir;
liggja hér í grindum fyr Gnipalundi
brimdýr blásvört ok búin gulli;
þar er miklu mest mengi þeira;
mun-a nú Helgi hjörþing dvala."

50

Höðbroddr kvað:
"Renni rökn bitluð til Reginþinga,
en Sporvitnir at Sparinsheiði,
Mélnir ok Mýlnir til Myrkviðar;
látið engi mann eftir sitja,
þeira er benlogum bregða kunni.

51

Bjóðið ér Högna ok Hrings sonum,
Atla ok Yngva, Alf inum gamla,
þeir ró gjarnir gunni at heyja;
látum Völsunga viðrnám fáa."

52

"Good I find not the sons of Granmar,　　　　　　46
But for heroes 'tis seemly the truth to speak;
At Moinsheimar proved the men
That hearts for the wielding of swords they had."

Mightily then they made to run　　　　　　　　47
Sviputh and Sveggjuth to Solheimar;
By dewy dales and chasms dark,
Mist's horse shook where the men went by;
The king they found at his courtyard gate,
And told him the foeman fierce was come.

Forth stood Hothbrodd, helmed for battle,　　　48
Watched the riding of his warriors;
[...]
"Why are the Hniflungs white with fear?"

Gothmund spake:　　　　　　　　　　　　49
"Swift keels lie hard by the land,
Mast'ring harts and mighty yards,
Wealth of shields and well-planed oars;
The king's fair host, the Ylfings haughty;
Fifteen bands to land have fared,
But out in Sogn are seven thousand."

"At anchor lying off Gnipalund　　　　　　　　50
Are fire-beasts black, all fitted with gold;
There wait most of the foeman's men,
Nor will Helgi long the battle delay."

Hothbrodd spake:　　　　　　　　　　　　51
"Bid the horses run to the Reginthing,
Melnir and Mylnir to Myrkwood now,
And Sporvitnir to Sparinsheith;
Let no man seek henceforth to sit
Who the flame of wounds knows well to wield."

"Summon Hogni, the sons of Hring,　　　　　　52
Atli and Yngvi and Alf the Old;
Glad they are of battle ever;
Against the Volsungs let us go."

Svipr einn var þat,   er saman kómu 53
fölvir oddar   at Frekasteini;
ey var Helgi   Hundings bani
fyrstr í fólki,   þar er firar börðusk,
æstr á ímu,   alltrauðr flugar;
sá hafði hilmir   hart móðakarn.

Kómu þar ór himni   hjalmvítr ofan, 54
óx geira gnýr,   þær er grami hlífðu;
þá kvað þat Sigrún,   sárvitr fluga
át hálu skær   af hugins barri:

"Heill skaltu, vísi,   virða njóta, 55
áttstafr Yngva,   ok una lífi,
er þú fellt hefir   inn flugartrauða
jöfur, þann er olli   ægis dauða.

Ok þér, buðlungr,   samir bæði vel 56
rauðir baugar   ok in ríkja mær;
heill skaltu, buðlungr,   bæði njóta
Högna dóttur   ok Hringstaða,
sigrs ok landa.
Þá er sókn lokit."

Swift as a storm there smote together 53
The flashing blades at Frekastein;
Ever was Helgi, Hunding's slayer,
First in the throng where warriors fought;
Fierce in battle, slow to fly,
Hard the heart of the hero was.

From heaven there came the maidens helmed, 54
The weapon-clang grew, who watched o'er the king;
Spake Sigrun fair, the wound-givers flew,
And the horse of the giantess raven's-food had:

"Hail to thee, hero! full happy with men, 55
Offspring of Yngvi, shalt ever live,
For thou the fearless foe hast slain
Who to many the dread of death had brought."

"Warrior, well for thyself hast won 56
Red rings bright and the noble bride;
Both now, warrior, thine shall be,
Hogni's daughter and Hringstathir,
Wealth and triumph; the battle wanes."

ENDNOTES

1. The manuscript contains the superscription: "Here begins the lay of Helgi Hundingbane and h. (Hothbrodd?) The lay of the Volsungs."[1] *Eagles*, etc.: the screaming of eagles and water pouring from heaven were portents of the birth of a hero. *Borghild*: Sigmund's first wife; *Bralund* was her home, not Sigmund's.

2. *Norns*: cf. *Voluspo*, 20 and note. Here it is the Norns who preside over Helgi's early destiny, and not a Valkyrie, as in *Helgakvitha Hjorvarthssonar*.

3. Line 2 is largely guesswork, the manuscript being obscure. *Moon's hall*: the sky.

4. *East*, etc.: the Norris give Helgi fame in the East, West, and North; in the North his renown is particularly to endure. This suggests that the poet was aware of the spread of the Helgi story over many lands. *Neri's kinswoman*: evidently one of the Norns, but nothing further is known of Neri, and the word may not be a proper name at all.

5. The manuscript indicates no gap, but it looks as though something had been lost after line 2. *Ylfings' son*: Sigmund is evidently meant, though calling him an Ylfing (cf. *Hyndluljoth*, 11 and note) is a manifest error. Helgi, in the tradition as it came from Denmark, was undoubtedly an Ylfing, and the poet, in order to combine the two legends, has to treat the Ylfings and Volsungs as if they were the same family.

6. *Sigmund*: the chief link between the Helgi and Sigurth stories. He was

---

[1] The "Höðbrodd" part is indeed illegible in the manuscript, as Bellows says, only the *h* can be read; but the Völsunga Saga is not mentioned there.

the son of Volsung, great-grandson of Odin. His children by his first wife, Borghild, were Helgi and Hamund (belonging to the Helgi cycle); his son by his second wife, Hjordis, was Sigurth. An incestuous connection with his sister, Signy (cf. Wagner's Siegmund and Sieglinde) resulted in the birth of Sinfjotli (cf. *Fra Dautha Sinfjotla* and note).

7. *The king*: Sigmund, who gives his son a symbol of the lands which he bestows on him. Regarding the leek, cf. *Voluspo*, 4; *Guthrunarkvitha* I, 17, and *Sigrdrifumol*, 7.

8. *Hringstathir* ("Ring-Stead"): quite possibly the historical Ringsted, long a possession of the Danish kings, and thus a relic of the old Helgi tradition. *Hringstoth* may be another form of the same name. *Solfjoll* ("Sun-Mountain") and *Snæfjoll* ("Snow-Mountain") are fictitious names. Regarding *Sigarsvoll* cf. *Helgakvitha Hjorvarthssonar*, stanzas 8 and 35. Saxo mentions a Danish king named Sigar, and the frequency with which the name appears in the Helgi poems may be taken as a reminiscence of Denmark. *Hotun* ("High Place"): possibly the village of Tune in Seeland. *Himinvangar* ("Heaven's Field"): an imaginary place. *Blood-snake*: a sword. *Sinfjotli*: cf. note on stanza 6.

9. *Elm*: a not uncommon word for "man." *Blood-flecked*: i.e., won in battle.

10. *Fifteen*: until early in the eleventh century a Norwegian or Icelandic boy became "of age" at twelve, and Maurer cites this passage as added proof of the poem's lateness. *Hunding*: the annotator (introductory prose to *Helgakvitha Hundingsbana* II) calls him king of Hundland, which shows no great originality. Saxo mentions a Hunding who was a Saxon king ruling in Jutland, probably the origin of Helgi's traditional foe.

12. *Storm*, etc.: war.

13. *Logafjoll* ("Flame-Mountain"): a mythical name. *Frothi*: a traditional king of Denmark, whose peaceful reign was so famous that "Frothi's peace" became a by-word for peace of any kind. *Vithrir's hounds*: wolves; Vithrir is Odin, and his hounds are the wolves Freki and Geri.

14. In this poem Helgi kills all the sons of Hunding, but in the poems of the Sigurth cycle, and the prose notes attached thereto, Sigmund and his father-in-law, Eylimi, are killed by Hunding's sons, on whom Sigurth subsequently takes vengeance (cf. *Fra Dautha Sinfjotla* and *Reginsmol*).

15. No gap is indicated in the manuscript, but almost certainly something has been lost mentioning more specifically the coming of the Valkyries.

The lightning which accompanies them suggests again their identification with the clouds (cf. *Helgakvitha Hjorvarthssonar*, 28). Some editions fill out the first line: "He saw there mighty maidens riding." The manuscript indicates line 4 as the beginning of a new stanza.[2]

16. *Wolf-wood*: dark forest; the original word is not altogether clear. *Southern*: this variety of Valkyrie, like the swan maidens of the *Völundarkvitha*, was clearly regarded as of southern (i.e., German) origin. Here again there is a confusion of traditions; the Valkyries of the *Voluspo* were as essentially Norse as any part of the older mythology. I doubt if a poet much earlier than the author of the first Helgi Hundingsbane lay would have made his Sigrun, daughter of Hogni, a Valkyrie. It is to be noted that the same complication appears in the Sigurth story, where the undoubted Valkyrie, Brynhild-Sigrdrifa (the latter name is really only an epithet) is hopelessly mixed up with the quite human Brynhild, daughter of Buthli.

17. *Breaker of rings*: generous prince, because the breaking of rings was the customary form of distributing gold.

18. *Granmar*: the annotator gives an account of him and his family in the prose following stanza 12 of *Helgakvitha Hundingsbana II*.

19. No gap indicated in the manuscript; some editors combine the stanza with the fragmentary stanza 21, and others fill in with "And home will carry Hogni's daughter."

20. The manuscript has only lines 1 and 4 with the word "first" of line 2, and does not indicate Helgi as the speaker. The *Volsungasaga*, which follows this poem pretty closely, expands Helgi's speech, and lines 2–3 are conjectural versifications of the saga's prose. *Isung*: nothing is known of him beyond the fact, here indicated, that Hothbrodd killed him.

21. *Water's gleam*: gold.

22. *Brandey* ("Brand-Isle"): not mentioned elsewhere. *Hethinsey* ("Hethin's Isle"): possibly the island of Hiddensee, east of Rügen.

23. *Stafnsnes* ("Steersman's Cape"): an unidentifiable promontory. *Fair*: a guess, as the adjective in the manuscript is obscure. *Hjorleif* does not appear elsewhere, and seems to be simply one of Helgi's lieutenants.

24. *Tronueyr*: "Crane-Strand." *Long-stemmed*: literally "long-headed," as the high, curving stem of a Norse ship was often carved to represent a

---

[2] It is at this stanza that Bellows' numbering scheme deviates from that of the Old Norse used in this edition.

head and neck. *Orvasund*: almost certainly the Danish Öresund, off Seeland. Such bits of geography as this followed Helgi persistently.

25. No gap indicated in the manuscript. *Hotun*: cf. stanza 8 and note.

26. Line 3 seems to have been interpolated from line 4 of *Helgakvitha Hundingsbana* II, 42. *Ship's-tents*: the awnings spread over the deck to shelter the crews from sun and rain when the ships were at anchor. *Varinsfjord*: cf. *Helgakvitha Hjorvarthssonar*, 22 and note.

27. The manuscript indicates line 3 as the beginning of a new stanza, and some editions follow this arrangement, making lines 1-2 a separate stanza.

28. The manuscript indicates no gap, and some editions combine the stanza with lines 3-4 of stanza 27. *Sisters of Kolga*: the waves, Kolga ("The Gold") being one of the daughters of the sea-god, Ægir. As the *Volsungasaga* says, "Now there was a great storm."

29. Helgi demonstrates his courage, whatever one may think of his seamanship. *Ægir's daughters*: the waves; cf. stanza 28 and note.

30. Sigrun here appears again as a Valkyrie. *Rán*: Ægir's wife; cf. *Helgakvitha Hjorvarthssonar*, 18 and note. *Sea-beast*: ship. *Gnipalund*: "Crag-Wood." [Original Bellows translation has Ron for Ægir's wife; this has been corrected.]

31. *Unavagar*: "Friendly Waves." *Svarin's hill*: the hill where Granmar had his dwelling.

32. Here begins the long dialogue between *Gothmund*, one of Gramnar's sons, and *Sinfjotli*, Helgi's half-brother. Two lines (stanza 32, lines 3-4) are quoted by the annotator in the prose note following stanza 16 of the second Helgi Hundingsbane lay, and the dialogue, in much abbreviated form, together with Helgi's admonition to Sinfjotli to cease talking, is closely paralleled in stanzas 21-26 of that poem. It has been suggested that this whole passage (stanzas 32-47) is an interpolation, perhaps from "the Old Volsung lay." This may be, but it seems more probable that the poet used an older poem simply as the basis for this passage, borrowing a little but making up a great deal more. The manuscript indicates no gap in stanza 32.

33. *Sinfjotli*: cf. note on stanza 6. *Red*: raising a red shield was the signal for war.

34. *Ylfings*: cf. stanza 5 and note.

ENDNOTES 451

35. *Quern*: turning the hand mill was, throughout antiquity, the task of slaves.

36. The manuscript does not name the speakers in this dialogue. No gap indicated in the manuscript, and editors have attempted various combinations of stanzas 37 and 38 [37 and 38 in Bellows original transcription here they have been combined for consistency]. *Wolves*: the *Volsungasaga* tells that Sigmund and Sinfjotli lived in the woods for a time as *Ulfhethnar* (werewolves). *Brothers*: Sinfjotli killed the two sons of his mother, Signy, and her husband, Siggeir, as part of the vengeance wreaked on Siggeir for the treacherous murder of Sigmund's father, Volsung, and nine of his brothers (cf. *Fra Dautha Sinfjotla* and note). The manuscript marks line 3 as the beginning of a new stanza.

37. *Varin's isle*: cf. stanza 27 and note, and *Helgakvitha Hjorvarthssonar*, 22. Reproaching a man with having been a woman and borne children was not uncommon.

38. This stanza may be an interpolation in the dialogue passage. *Allfather*: Odin. We have no information regarding Gothmund's career, but it looks as though Sinfjotli were drawing solely on his imagination for his taunts, whereas Gothmund's insults have a basis in Sinfjotli's previous life.

39. No gap indicated in the manuscript; some editors combine the two lines with stanza 40, some regard them as the first instead of the last lines of a separate stanza, and some assume the lacuna here indicated. *Sogunes* ("Saga's Cape"): of the goddess Saga little is known; cf. *Grimnismol*, 7.

40. *Fenrir's-wolves*: wolves in general. *Thorsnes*: "Thor's Cape."

41. The phrase "under houses," which follows the manuscript, may be an error for "in wolf-caves." Line 3 (or 4) may be an interpolation. The manuscript indicates line 5 as the beginning of a new stanza. *Siggeir*: cf. stanza 38, note.

42. Several editions assign this stanza to Sinfjotli instead of to Gothmund. *Bravoll* ("Field of the Brow"): not elsewhere mentioned in the poems. *Grani*: Sigurth's horse (cf. *Völundarkvitha*, 16 and note); Gothmund means that Sinfjotli had turned into a mare, after the fashion of Loki (cf. *Grimnismol*, 44, note). The meaning of line 4 in the original is uncertain.

43. A few editions give this stanza to Gothmund. *Gollnir*: possibly a giant. *Imth*: nothing is known of him or his daughter.

44. A few editions give this stanza to Sinfjotli. *Frekastein*: cf. *Helgakvitha Hjorvarthssonar*, 39 and note. A stanza may have been lost after stanza 44, parallel to stanza 25 of the second Helgi Hundingsbane lay.

45. *Ring-breakers*: cf. stanza 17 and note.

46. *Moinsheimar*: a battlefield of which nothing is known, where, however, the sons of Granmar appear to have fought bravely.

47. Here the scene shifts to the shore among Hothbrodd's followers. *Sviputh* and *Sveggjuth* ("Swift" and "Lithe"): horses' names. *Mist's horse*: the Valkyrie's name is the same as the English word "mist," and the "horse" on which the mist rides is the earth. The two lines in parenthesis may be interpolated, or line 5 may begin a new stanza, as the manuscript indicates.

48. No gap indicated in the manuscript. *Hniflungs*: cf. introductory note [Appendix B].

49. Lines 2–3 may be interpolated, or a new stanza may begin, as the manuscript indicates, with line 5. Many editors combine lines 5–6 with all or part of stanza 50. Possibly Gothmund is not the speaker. *Mast-ring harts*: ships, so called from the ring attaching the yard to the mast. *Ylfings*: cf. stanza 5 and note. *Sogn*: this name, which actually belongs in western Norway, seems to have been used here with no particular significance.

50. The manuscript indicates line 3 as beginning a new stanza; some editors combine lines 3–4 with all or part of stanza 51, while others assume the loss of two lines following line 4. *Fire-beasts*: dragons, i.e., ships. The Norse ships of war, as distinguished from merchant vessels, were often called dragons because of their shape and the carving of their stems.

51. The manuscript does not indicate the speaker, and a few editors assume the loss of one or two lines embodying the phrase "Hothbrodd spake." In the manuscript line 3, which many editors have suspected of being spurious, stands before line 2. Possibly lines 4–5 are the remains of a separate stanza. *Reginthing* ("The Great Council"): apparently the council-place for the whole country, as distinct from the local council, or "herathsthing." *Melnir* ("Bit-Bearer"), *Mylnir* ("The Biter") and *Spornvitnir* ("Spur-Wolf"): horses' names. *Myrkwood*: a mythologed Hercynian Forest; cf. *Lokasenna*, 42, and *Atlakvitha*, 3. *Sparinsheith* ("Sparin's Heath"): nothing more is known of Sparin or his heath. *Flame of wounds*: sword.

ENDNOTES 453

52. *Hogni*: the father of Sigrun; cf. *Helgakvitha Hundingsbana* II, 18. Of *Hring* and his sons nothing further is known. *Volsungs*: here for the first time the poet gives Helgi and Sinfjotli the family name to which, as sons of Sigmund Volsungsson, they are entitled.

53. The manuscript indicates line 5 as the beginning of a new stanza, but many editors have rejected lines 5–6 as spurious, while others regard them as the first half of a stanza the last two lines of which have been lost.

54. *Wound-givers*: probably this means "Valkyries," but there is considerable doubt as to the original word. *Horse*, etc.: i.e., the wolf (because giantesses customarily had wolves for their steeds) ate corpses (the food of birds of prey).

55. *Yngvi*: one of the sons of Halfdan the Old, and traditional ancestor of the Ynglings, with whom the Ylfings seem to have been confused (cf. *Hynduljoth*, 11 and note). The confusion between the Ylfings (or Ynglings) and Volsungs was carried far enough so that Sigurth himself is once called a descendant of Yngvi (*Reginsmol*, 14). Gering identifies the name of Yngvi with the god Freyr, but the Volsungs certainly claimed descent from Odin, not Freyr, and there is nothing to indicate that Helgi in the Danish tradition was supposed to be descended from Freyr, whereas his descent from Yngvi Halfdansson fits well with the rest of his story. However, cf. *Sigurtharkvitha en skamma*, 24 and note.

56. This entire stanza may be an interpolation; nearly every edition has a different way of dealing with it. *Hringstathir*: as this place had been given to Helgi by his father (cf. stanza 8 and note), the poet has apparently made a mistake in naming it here as a conquest from Granmar's sons, unless, indeed, they had previously captured it from Helgi, which seems unlikely.

HELGAKVITHA HUNDINGSBANA II
THE SECOND LAY OF HELGI HUNDINGSBANE

INTRODUCTION

The *Second Lay of Helgi Hundingsbane* is, properly speaking, merely a collection of disparate poetic narratives regarding the life of the famous hero, with no criterion for chronological order or direct association with the previous lay other than the fact that they are clearly about the same set of characters. The work is a fine example of early poetic composition with extensive prose narrative setting up the events of each section, and most scholars assign the date of authorship to be somewhere between the late 9th and early 10th centuries. This makes the poems important and distinct for being wholly pre-Christian heroic material.

This impressive status is somewhat mitigated by the fact that the poems recorded are all separate works likely by different authors which have been haphazardly patched together into a longer narrative regarding the hero. Several of the prose sections allude to stories and lays which have not come down to us such as the *Old Volsung Lay* and the *Kara Lay*, of which the author has presumably only included small fragments within this poem. The tantalizing details and promise of a much larger poetic tradition right at our fingertips reminds us of that much of our knowledge of the material, while extensive by all accounts, is still just a small fraction of that available and known to our forefathers.

Despite the poems being fragmentary and disconnected narrative elements, they are widely known as some of the most vivid and technically proficient examples of Old Norse verse ever produced, and will surely be appreciated by anyone who sets about reading them.

A Viking Foray
(J. C. Dollman)

Sigmundr konungr Völsungsson átti Borghildi af Brálundi. Þau hétu son sinn Helga ok eftir Helga Hjörvarðssyni. Helga fóstraði Hagall. Hundingr hét ríkr konungr. Við hann er Hundland kennt. Hann var hermaðr mikill ok átti marga sonu, þá er í hernaði váru. Ófriðr ok dylgjur váru á milli þeira Hundings konungs ok Sigmundar konungs. Drápu hvárir annarra frændr. Sigmundr konungr ok hans ættmenn hétu Völsungar ok Ylfingar. Helgi fór ok njósnaði til hirðar Hundings konungs á laun. Hemingr, son Hundings konungs, var heima. En er Helgi fór í brott, þá hitti hann hjarðarsvein ok kvað:

"Segðu Hemingi   at Helgi man,   1
hvern í brynju   bragnar felldu;
ér ulf gráan   inni höfðuð,
þar er Hamal hugði   Hundingr konungr."

Hamall hét son Hagals. Hundingr konungr sendi menn til Hagals at leita Helga, en Helgi mátti eigi forðast annan veg en tók klæði ambáttar ok gekk at mala. Þeir leituðu ok fundu eigi Helga. Þá kvað Blindr inn bölvísi:

HELGAKVITHA HUNDINGSBANA II

King Sigmund, the son of Volsung, had as wife Borghild, from Bralund. They named their son Helgi, after Helgi Hjorvarthsson; Hagal was Helgi's foster-father. Hunding was the name of a powerful king, and Hundland is named from him. He was a mighty warrior, and had many sons with him on his campaigns. There was enmity and strife between these two, King Hunding and King Sigmund, and each slew the other's kinsmen. King Sigmund and his family were called Volsungs and Ylfings.

Helgi went as a spy to the home of King Hunding in disguise. Hæming, a son of King Hunding's, was at home. When Helgi went forth, then he met a young herdsman, and said:

1. "Say to Hæming that Helgi knows
Whom the heroes in armor hid;
A gray wolf had they within their hall,
Whom King Hunding Hamal thought."

Hamal was the name of Hagal's son. King Hunding sent men to Hagal to seek Helgi, and Helgi could not save himself in any other way, so he put on the clothes of a bond-woman and set to work at the mill. They sought Helgi but found him not.

"Hvöss eru augu   í Hagals þýju; 2
er-a þat karls ætt,   er á kvernum stendr;
steinar rifna   stökk lúðr fyrir.

Nú hefir hörð dæmi   hildingr þegit, 3
er vísi skal   valbygg mala;
heldr er sæmri   hendi þeiri
meðalkafli   en möndultré."

Hagall svaraði ok kvað:

"Þat er lítil vá,   þótt lúðr þrumi 4
er mær konungs   möndul hrærir;
hon skævaði   skýjum efri
ok vega þorði   sem víkingar,
áðr hana Helgi   höftu gerði;
systir er hon þeira   Sigars ok Högna;
því hefir ötul augu   Ylfinga man."

Undan komst Helgi ok fór á herskip. Hann felldi Hunding konung ok var síðan kallaðr Helgi Hundingsbani. Hann lá með her sinn í Brunavágum ok hafði þar strandhögg ok átu þar hrátt. Högni hét konungr. Hans dóttir var Sigrún. Hon var valkyrja ok reið loft ok lög. Hon var Sváfa endrborin. Sigrún reið at skipum Helga ok kvað:

"Hverir láta fljóta   fley við bakka? 5
Hvar, hermegir,   heima eiguð?
Hvers bíðið ér   í Brunavágum?
Hvert lystir yðr   leið at kanna?"

Helgi kvað: 6
"Hagall lætr fljóta   fley við bakka,
eigum heima   í Hléseyju,
bíðum byrjar   í Brunavágum,
austr lystir oss   leið at kanna."

Then Blind spake out, the evil-minded: 2
"Of Hagal's bond-woman bright are the eyes;
Yon comes not of churls who stands at the quern;
The millstones break, the boards are shattered."

"The hero has a doom full hard, 3
That barley now he needs must grind;
Better befits his hand to feel
The hilt of the sword than the millstone's handle."

Hagal answered and said:

"Small is the wonder if boards are splintered 4
By a monarch's daughter the mill is turned;
Once through clouds she was wont to ride,
And battles fought like fighting men,
Till Helgi a captive held her fast;
Sister she is of Sigar and Hogni,
Thus bright are the eyes of the Ylfings' maid."

Helgi escaped and went to a fighting ship. He slew King Hunding, and thenceforth was called Helgi Hundingsbane.

He lay with his host in Brunavagar, and they had there a strand-slaughtering, and ate the flesh raw. Hogni was the name of a king. His daughter was Sigrun; she was a Valkyrie and rode air and water; she was Svava reborn. Sigrun rode to Helgi's ship and said:

"Who rules the ship by the shore so steep? 5
Where is the home ye warriors have?
Why do ye bide in Brunavagar,
Or what the way that ye wish to try?"

Helgi spake: 6
"Hamal's the ship by the shore so steep,
Our home in Hlesey do we have;
For fair wind bide we in Brunavagar,
Eastward the way that we wish to try."

Sigrún kvað: 7
"Hvar hefir þú, hilmir,   hildi vakða
eða gögl alin   Gunnar systra?
Hví er brynja þín   blóði stokkin?
Hví skal und hjalmum   hrátt kjöt eta?"

Helgi kvað: 8
"Þat vann næst nýs   niðr Ylfinga
fyr vestan ver,   ef þik vita lystir,
er ek björnu tók   í Bragalundi
ok ætt ara   oddum saddak.

Nú er sagt, mær,   hvaðan sakar gerðusk, 9
því var á legi mér   lítt steikt etit."

Sigrún kvað: 10
"Víg lýsir þú,   varð fyr Helga
Hundingr konungr   hníga at velli;
bar sókn saman,   er sefa hefnduð
ok busti blóð   á brimis eggjar."

Helgi kvað: 11
"Hvat vissir þú,   at þeir séim,
snót svinnhuguð,   er sefa hefndum?
Margir ro hvassir   hildings synir
ok ámunir ossum   niðjum."

Sigrún kvað: 12
"Vark-a ek fjarri,   folks oddviti,
gær á morgun   grams aldrlokum,
þó tel ek slægjan   Sigmundar bur,
er í valrúnum   vígspjöll segir.

Leit ek þik um sinn   fyrr á langskipum, 13
þá er þú byggðir   blóðga stafna
ok úrsvalar   unnir léku;
nú vill dyljask   döglingr fyr mér,
en Högna mær   Helga kennir."

Granmarr hét ríkr konungr, er bjó at Svarinshaugi. Hann átti marga sonu: Höðbroddr, annarr Guðmundr, þriði Starkaðr. Höðbroddr var í konungastefnu. Hann fastnaði sér Sigrúnu Högnadóttur. En er hon spyrr þat, þá reið hon með valkyrjur um loft ok um lög at leita Helga. Helgi var þá at Logafjöllum ok hafði barizt við Hundings sonu. Þar felldi hann þá Álf ok Eyjólf, Hjörvarð ok Hervarð, ok var hann allvígmóðr ok sat undir Arasteini. Þar hitti Sigrún hann ok rann á háls honum ok kyssti hann ok sagði

Sigrun spake: 7
"Where hast thou, warrior, battle wakened,
Or gorged the birds of the sisters of Guth?
Why is thy byrnie spattered with blood,
Why helmed dost feast on food uncooked?"

Helgi spake: 8
"Latest of all, the Ylfings' son
On the western sea, if know thou wilt,
Captured bears in Bragalund,
And fed the eagles with edge of sword.

Now is it shown why our shirts are bloody, 9
And little our food with fire is cooked."

Sigrun spake: 10
"Of battle thou tellest, and there was bent
Hunding the king before Helgi down;
There was carnage when thou didst avenge thy kin,
And blood flowed fast on the blade of the sword."

Helgi spake: 11
"How didst thou know that now our kin,
Maiden wise, we have well avenged?
Many there are of the sons of the mighty
Who share alike our lofty race."

Sigrun spake: 12
"Not far was I from the lord of the folk,
Yester morn, when the monarch was slain;
Though crafty the son of Sigmund, methinks,
When he speaks of the fight in slaughter-runes."

"On the long-ship once I saw thee well, 13
When in the blood-stained bow thou wast,
And round thee icy waves were raging;
Now would the hero hide from me,
But to Hogni's daughter is Helgi known."

Granmar was the name of a mighty king, who dwelt at Svarin's hill. He had many sons; one was named Hothbrodd, another Gothmund, a third Starkath. Hothbrodd was in a kings' meeting, and he won the promise of having Sigrun, Hogni's daughter, for his wife. But when she heard this, she rode with the Valkyries over air and sea to seek Helgi. Helgi was then at Logafjoll, and had fought with Hunding's sons; there he killed Alf and Eyolf, Hjorvarth and Hervarth. He was all weary with battle, and sat un-

honum erindi sitt, svá sem segir í Völsungakviðu inni fornu:

Sótti Sigrún   sikling glaðan,   14
heim nam hon Helga   hönd at sækja,
kyssti ok kvaddi   konung und hjalmi;
þá varð hilmi   hugr á vífi.

Fyrr lézk hon unna   af öllum hug   15
syni Sigmundar   en hon sét hafði.

Sigrún kvað: 16
"Var ek Höðbroddi   í her föstnuð,
en jöfur annan   eiga vildak;
þó sjámk, fylkir,   frænda reiði,
hefi ek míns föður   munráð brotit."

Nam-a Högna mær   of hug mæla,   17
hafa kvaðsk hon Helga   hylli skyldu.

Helgi kvað: 18
"Hirð eigi þú   Högna reiði
né illan hug   ættar þinnar.
Þú skalt, mær ung,   at mér lifa;
ætt áttu, in góða,   er ek eigi sjámk."

Helgi samnaði þá miklum skipaher ok fór til Frekasteins, ok fengu í hafi ofviðri mannhætt. Þá kómu leiftr yfir þá, ok stóðu geislar í skipin. Þeir sá í loftinu, at valkyrjur níu riðu, ok kenndu þeir Sigrúnu. Þá lægði storminn, ok kómu þeir heilir til lands. Granmarssynir sátu á bjargi nokkuru, er skipin sigldu at landi. Guðmundr hljóp á hest ok reið á njósn á bergit við höfnina. Þá hlóðu Völsungar seglum. Þá kvað Guðmundr:

"Hver er skjöldungr,   sá er skipum stýrir,   19
lætr gunnfana   gullinn fyr stafni?
Þykkja mér fríð   í fararbroddi;
verpr vígroða   um víkinga."

Sinfjötli kvað: 20
"Hér má Höðbroddr   Helga kenna
flótta trauðan   í flota miðjum,
hann hefir eðli   ættar þinnar
arf Fjörsunga,   und sik þrungit."

der the eagle-stone. There Sigrun found him, and ran to throw her arms about his neck, and kissed him, and told him her tidings, as is set forth in the old Volsung lay:

Sigrun the joyful chieftain sought, Forthwith Helgi's hand she took; She greeted the hero helmed and kissed him, The warrior's heart to the woman turned.	14
From her heart the daughter of Hogni spake, Dear was Helgi, she said, to her.	15

Sigrun spake: 16
"At the meeting to Hothbrodd mated I was,
But another hero I fain would have;
Though, king, the wrath of my kin I fear,
Since I broke my father's fairest wish."

"Long with all my heart I loved   17
Sigmund's son ere ever I saw him."

Helgi spake: 18
"Fear not ever Hogni's anger,
Nor yet thy kinsmen's cruel wrath;
Maiden, thou with me shalt live,
Thy kindred, fair one, I shall not fear."

Helgi then assembled a great sea-host and went to Frekastein. On the sea he met a perilous storm; lightning flashed overhead and the bolts struck the ship. They saw in the air that nine Valkyries were riding, and recognized Sigrun among them. Then the storm abated, and they came safe and sound to land. Granmar's sons sat on a certain mountain as the ships sailed toward the land. Gothmund leaped on a horse and rode for news to a promontory near the harbor; the Volsungs were even then lowering their sails. Then Gothmund said, as is written before in the Helgi lay:

"Who is the king who captains the fleet,   19
And to the land the warriors leads?"

"Never shall Sigrun from Sevafjoll,   20
Hothbrodd king, be held in thine arms;
Granmar's sons full cold have grown,
And the giant-steeds gray on corpses gorge."

Guðmundr kvað: 21
"Því fyrr skulu   at Frekasteini
sáttir saman   um sakar dæma;
mál er, Höðbroddr,   hefnd at vinna
ef vér lægra hlut   lengi bárum."

Sinfjötli kvað: 22
"Fyrr mundu, Guðmundr,   geitr of halda
ok bergskorar   brattar klífa,
hafa þér í hendi   heslikylfu,
þat er þér blíðara   en brimis dómar."

Helgi kvað: 23
"Þér er, Sinfjötli,   sæmra miklu
gunni at heyja   ok glaða örnu
en ónýtum   orðum at bregða,
þótt hildingar   heiftir deili."

Þykkja-t mér góðir   Granmars synir, 24
þó dugir siklingum   satt at mæla;
þeir merkt hafa   á Móinsheimum,
at hug hafa   hjörum at bregða;
eru hildingar   hölzti snjallir."

Guðmundr reið heim með hersögu. Þá sömnuðu Granmarssynir her. Kómu þar margir konungar. Þar var Högni, faðir Sigrúnar, ok synir hans, Bragi ok Dagr. Þar var orrusta mikil, ok fellu allir Granmarssynir ok allir þeira höfðingjar nema Dagr Högnason fekk grið ok vann eiða Völsungum. Sigrún gekk í valinn ok hitti Höðbrodd at kominn dauða. Hon kvað:

"Mun-a þér, Sigrún   frá Sefafjöllum 25
Höðbroddr konungr,   hníga at armi;
liðin er ævi   oft náir hrævi
gránstóð gríðar,   Granmars sona."

Þá hitti hon Helga ok varð allfegin. Hann kvað:

"Er-at þér at öllu,   alvitr, gefit, 26
þó kveð ek nökkvi   nornir valda:
fellu í morgun   at Frekasteini
Bragi ok Högni,   varð ek bani þeira.

Gothmund spake: 21
"First shall swords at Frekastein
Prove our worth in place of words;
Time is it, Hothbrodd, vengeance to have,
If in battle worsted once we were."

Sinfjotli spake: 22
"Better, Gothmund, to tend the goats,
And climb the rocks of the mountain cliffs;
A hazel switch to hold in thy hand
More seemly were than the hilt of a sword."

Helgi spake: 23
"Better, Sinfjotli, thee 'twould beseem
Battles to give, and eagles to gladden,
Than vain and empty speech to utter,
Though warriors oft with words do strive."

"Good I find not the sons of Granmar, 24
But for heroes 'tis seemly the truth to speak;
At Moinsheimar proved the men
That hearts for the wielding of swords they had,
And ever brave the warriors are."

Then Granmar's sons summoned an army. Many kings came there; there were Hogni, Sigrun's father, and his sons Bragi and Dag. There was a great battle, and all Granmar's sons were slain and all their allies; only Dag, Hogni's son, was spared, and he swore loyalty to the Volsungs. Sigrun went among the dead and found Hothbrodd at the coming of death. She said:

"Never shall Sigrun from Sevafjoll, 25
Hothbrodd king, be held in thine arms;
Granmar's sons full cold have grown,
And the giant-steeds gray on corpses gorge."

Then she sought out Helgi, and was full of joy. He said:

"Maid, not fair is all thy fortune, 26
The Norns I blame that this should be;
This morn there fell at Frekastein
Bragi and Hogni beneath my hand.

En at Styrkleifum   Starkaðr konungr,   27
en at Hlébjörgum   Hrollaugs synir;
þann sá ek gylfa   grimmúðgastan,
er barðisk bolr,   var á brott höfuð.

Liggja at jörðu   allra flestir   28
niðjar þínir,   at náum orðnir;
vannt-at-tu vígi,   var þér þat skapat,
at þú at rógi   ríkmenni vart."

Þá grét Sigrún. Hann kvað: 29
"Huggastu, Sigrún!   Hildr hefr þú oss verið;
vinna-t skjöldungar sköpum."
Sigrún kvað:
"Lifna mynda ek nú kjósa,   er liðnir eru,
ok knætta ek þér þó í faðmi felask."

Helgi fekk Sigrúnar, ok áttu þau sonu. Var Helgi eigi gamall. Dagr Högnason blótaði Óðin til föðurhefnda. Óðinn léði Dag geirs síns. Dagr fann Helga, mág sinn, þar sem heitir at Fjöturlundi. Hann lagði í gögnum Helga með geirnum. Þar fell Helgi, en Dagr reið til Sefafjalla ok sagði Sigrúnu tíðindi.

"Trauðr em ek, systir,   trega þér at segja,   30
því at ek hefi nauðigr   nifti grætta;
fell í morgun   und Fjöturlundi
buðlungr, sá er var   beztr í heimi
ok hildingum á   halsi stóð."

Sigrún kvað   31
"Þik skyli allir   eiðar bíta,
þeir er Helga   hafðir unna
at inu ljósa   Leiftrar vatni
ok at úrsvölum   Unnarsteini.

Skríði-at þat skip,   er und þér skríði,   32
þótt óskabyrr   eftir leggisk;
renni-a sá marr,   er und þér renni,
þóttú fjándr þína   forðask eigir.

"At Hlebjorg fell the sons of Hrollaug, 27
Starkath the king at Styrkleifar;
Fighters more noble saw I never,
The body fought when the head had fallen."

"On the ground full low the slain are lying, 28
Most are there of the men of thy race;
Nought hast thou won, for thy fate it was
Brave men to bring to the battle-field."

Then Sigrun wept. Helgi said: 29
"Grieve not, Sigrun, the battle is gained,
The fighter can shun not his fate."

Sigrun spake:
"To life would I call them who slaughtered lie,
If safe on thy breast I might be."

Helgi took Sigrun to wife, and they had sons. Helgi did not reach old age. Dag, the son of Hogni, offered sacrifice to Odin to be avenged for his father's death; Odin gave Dag his spear. Dag found Helgi, his brother-in-law, at a place which is called Fjoturlund. He thrust the spear through Helgi's body. Then Helgi fell, and Dag rode to Sevafjoll and told Sigrun the tidings:

"Sad am I, sister, sorrow to tell thee, 30
Woe to my kin unwilling I worked;
In the morn there fell at Fjoturlund
The noblest prince the world has known,
And his heel he set on the heroes' necks."

Sigrun spake: 31
"Now may every oath thee bite
That with Helgi sworn thou hast,
By the water bright of Leipt,
And the ice-cold stone of Uth."

"The ship shall sail not in which thou sailest, 32
Though a favoring wind shall follow after;
The horse shall run not whereon thou ridest,
Though fain thou art thy foe to flee."

Bíti-a þér þat sverð,   er þú bregðir,   33
nema sjalfum þér   syngvi of höfði.
Þá væri þér hefnt   Helga dauða,
ef þú værir vargr   á viðum úti
auðs andvani   ok alls gamans,
hefðir eigi mat,   nema á hræjum spryngir."

Dagur kvað: 34
"Ær ertu, systir,   ok örvita,
er þú bræðr þínum   biðr forskapa;
einn veldr Óðinn   öllu bölvi,
því at með sifjungum   sakrúnar bar.

Þér býðr bróðir   bauga rauða,   35
öll Vandilsvé   ok Vígdali;
hafðu halfan heim   harms at gjöldum,
brúðr baugvarið,   ok burir þínir."

Sigrún kvað: 36
"Sitk-a ek svá sæl   at Sefafjöllum
ár né of nætr,   at ek una lífi,
nema at liði lofðungs   ljóma bregði,
renni und vísa   Vígblær þinig,
gullbitli vanr,   knega ek grami fagna.

Svá hafði Helgi   hrædda görva   37
fjándr sína alla   ok frændr þeira
sem fyr ulfi   óðar rynni
geitr af fjalli   geiskafullar.

Svá bar Helgi   af hildingum   38
sem ítrskapaðr   askr af þyrni
eða sá dýrkalfr   döggu slunginn
er efri ferr   öllum dýrum
ok horn glóa   við himin sjalfan."

Haugr var gjörr eftir Helga. En er hann kom til Valhallar, þá bauð Óðinn honum öllu at ráða með sér.

Helgi kvað: 39
"Þú skalt, Hundingr,   hverjum manni
fótlaug geta   ok funa kynda,
hunda binda,   hesta gæta,
gefa svínum soð,   áðr sofa gangir."

"The sword shall bite not which thou bearest, 33
Till thy head itself it sings about.
"Vengeance were mine for Helgi's murder,
Wert thou a wolf in the woods without,
Possessing nought and knowing no joy,
Having no food save corpses to feed on."

Dag spake: 34
"Mad art thou, sister, and wild of mind,
Such a curse on thy brother to cast;
Odin is ruler of every ill,
Who sunders kin with runes of spite."

"Thy brother rings so red will give thee, 35
All Vandilsve and Vigdalir;
Take half my land to pay the harm,
Ring-decked maid, and as meed for thy sons."

Sigrun spake: 36
"I shall sit not happy at Sevafjoll,
Early or late, my life to love,
If the light cannot show, in the leader's band,
Vigblær bearing him back to his home,
The golden-bitted; I shall greet him never."

"Such the fear that Helgi's foes 37
Ever felt, and all their kin,
As makes the goats with terror mad
Run from the wolf among the rocks."

"Helgi rose above heroes all 38
Like the lofty ash above lowly thorns,
Or the noble stag, with dew besprinkled,
Bearing his head above all beasts,
And his horns gleam bright to heaven itself."

A hill was made in Helgi's memory. And when he came to Valhall, then Odin bade him rule over every Thing with himself.

Helgi said: 39
"Thou shalt, Hunding, of every hero
Wash the feet, and kindle the fire,
Tie up dogs, and tend the horses,
And feed the swine ere to sleep thou goest."

Ambótt Sigrúnar gekk um aftan hjá haugi Helga ok sá, at Helgi reið til haugsins með marga menn. Ambótt kvað:

"Hvárt eru þat svik ein,   er ek sjá þykkjumk,   40
eða ragnarök,   ríða menn dauðir,
er jóa yðra   oddum keyrið
eða er hildingum   heimför gefin?"

Helgi kvað: 41
"Er-a þat svik ein,   er þú sjá þykkisk,
né aldar rof,   þóttú oss lítir,
þótt vér jóa óra   oddum keyrim,
né er hildingum   heimför gefin."

Heim gekk ambátt ok sagði Sigrúnu:

"Út gakk þú, Sigrún   frá Sefafjöllum,   42
ef þik folks jaðar   finna lystir;
upp er haugr lokinn,   kominn er Helgi,
dolgspor dreyra,   döglingr bað þik,
at þú sárdropa   svefja skyldir."

Sigrún gekk í hauginn til Helga ok kvað:

"Nú em ek svá fegin   fundi okkrum   43
sem átfrekir   Óðins haukar,
er val vitu,   varmar bráðir,
eða dögglitir   dagsbrún sjá.

Fyrr vil ek kyssa   konung ólifðan   44
en þú blóðugri   brynju kastir;
hár er þitt, Helgi,   hélu þrungit,
allr er vísi   valdögg sleginn,
hendr úrsvalar   Högna mági;
hvé skal ek þér, buðlungr,   þess bót of vinna?"

One of Sigrun's maidens went one evening to Helgi's hill, and saw that Helgi rode to the hill with many men, The maiden said:

"Is this a dream that methinks I see,   40
Or the doom of the gods, that dead men ride,
And hither spurring urge your steeds,
Or is home-coming now to the heroes granted?"

Helgi spake: 41
"No dream is this that thou thinkest to see,
Nor the end of the world, though us thou beholdest,
And hither spurring we urge our steeds,
Nor is home-coming now to the heroes granted."

The maiden went home and said to Sigrun:

"Go forth, Sigrun, from Sevafjoll,   42
If fain the lord of the folk wouldst find;
The hill is open, Helgi is come;
The sword-tracks bleed; the monarch bade
That thou his wounds shouldst now make well."

Sigrun went in the hill to Helgi, and said:

"Now am I glad of our meeting together,   43
As Odin's hawks, so eager for prey,
When slaughter and flesh all warm they scent,
Or dew-wet see the red of day."

"First will I kiss the lifeless king,   44
Ere off the bloody byrnie thou cast;
With frost thy hair is heavy, Helgi,
And damp thou art with the dew of death;
Ice-cold hands has Hogni's kinsman,
What, prince, can I to bring thee ease?"

Helgi kvað: 45
"Ein veldr þú, Sigrún   frá Sefafjöllum,
er Helgi er   harmdögg sleginn;
grætr þú, gullvarið,   grimmum tárum,
sólbjört, suðræn,   áðr þú sofa gangir;
hvert fellr blóðugt   á brjóst grami,
úrsvalt, innfjalgt,   ekka þrungit."

Helgi kvað: 46
Vel skulum drekka   dýrar veigar,
þótt misst hafim   munar ok landa;
skal engi maðr   angrljóð kveða,
þótt mér á brjósti   benjar líti;
nú eru brúðir   byrgðar í haugi,
lofða dísir,   hjá oss liðnum."

Sigrún bjó sæing í hauginum.

"Hér hefi ek þér, Helgi,   hvílu görva 47
angrlausa mjök,   Ylfinga niðr,
vil ek þér í faðmi,   fylkir, sofna
sem ek lofðungi   lifnum myndak."

Helgi kvað: 48
"Nú kveð ek enskis   örvænt vera
síð né snimma   at Sefafjöllum,
er þú á armi   ólifðum sefr,
hvít, í haugi,   Högna dóttir,
ok ertu kvik,   in konungborna.

Mál er mér at ríða   roðnar brautir, 49
láta fölvan jó   flugstíg troða;
skal ek fyr vestan   vindhjalms brúar,
áðr Salgófnir   sigrþjóð veki."

Þeir Helgi riðu leið sína, en þær fóru heim til bæjar. Annan aftan lét Sigrún ambótt halda vörð á hauginum. En at dagsetri, er Sigrún kom til haugsins, hon kvað:

Helgi spake: 45
"Thou alone, Sigrun of Sevafjoll,
Art cause that Helgi with dew is heavy;
Gold-decked maid, thy tears are grievous,
Sun-bright south-maid, ere thou sleepest;
Each falls like blood on the hero's breast,
Burned-out, cold, and crushed with care."

Helgi spake: 46
"Well shall we drink a noble draught,
Though love and lands are lost to me;
No man a song of sorrow shall sing,
Though bleeding wounds are on my breast;
Now in the hill our brides we hold,
The heroes' loves, by their husbands dead."

Sigrun made ready a bed in the hill.

"Here a bed I have made for thee, Helgi, 47
To rest thee from care, thou kin of the Ylfings;
I will make thee sink to sleep in my arms,
As once I lay with the living king."

Helgi spake: 48
"Now do I say that in Sevafjoll
Aught may happen, early or late,
Since thou sleepest clasped in a corpse's arms,
So fair in the hill, the daughter of Hogni!
Living thou comest, a daughter of kings."

"Now must I ride the reddened ways, 49
And my bay steed set to tread the sky;
Westward I go to wind-helm's bridges,
Ere Salgofnir wakes the warrior throng."

Then Helgi and his followers rode on their way, and the women went home to the dwelling. Another evening Sigrun bade the maiden keep watch at the hill. And at sunset when Sigrun came to the hill she said:

"Kominn væri nú,   ef koma hygði,   50
Sigmundar burr   frá sölum Óðins;
kveð ek grams þinig   grænask vánir,
er á asklimum   ernir sitja
ok drífr drótt öll   draumþinga til."

Ambótt kvað: 51
"Verðu eigi svá ær,   at ein farir,
dís skjöldunga,   draughúsa til;
verða öflgari   allir á nóttum
dauðir dolgar, mær,   en um daga ljósa."

Sigrún varð skammlíf af harmi ok trega. Þat var trúa í forneskju, at menn væri endrbornir, en þat er nú kölluð kerlingavilla. Helgi ok Sigrún, er kallat, at væri endrborin. Hét hann þá Helgi Haddingjaskati, en hon Kára Hálfdanardóttir, svá sem kveðit er í Káruljóðum, ok var hon valkyrja.

"Now were he come, if come he might, 50
Sigmund's son, from Odin's seat;
Hope grows dim of the hero's return
When eagles sit on the ash-tree boughs,
And men are seeking the meeting of dreams."

The Maiden said: 51
"Mad thou wouldst seem alone to seek,
Daughter of heroes, the house of the dead;
For mightier now at night are all
The ghosts of the dead than when day is bright."

Sigrun was early dead of sorrow and grief. It was believed in olden times that people were born again, but that is now called old wives' folly. Of Helgi and Sigrun it is said that they were born again; he became Helgi Haddingjaskati, and she Kara the daughter of Halfdan, as is told in the Lay of Kara, and she was a Valkyrie.

ENDNOTES

Prose. In the manuscript the poem is headed "Of the Volsungs," but most editions give it the title used here. *Sigmund*: cf. *Helgakvitha Hundingsbana I*, 6 and note, which also mentions *Volsung*. *Borghild* and *Bralund*: cf. *Helgakvitha Hundingsbana I*, 1 and note. *Helgi*: [the annotator's explanation that the child was named after Helgi Hjorvarthsson is a reference to the common Norse tradition of solidifying patrilineal reincarnation by naming one after the kin in question]. *Hagal*: not elsewhere mentioned; it was a common custom to have boys brought up by foster-parents. *Hunding* and *Hundland*: cf. *Helgakvitha Hundingsbana I*, 10 and note. *Volsungs* and *Ylfings*: regarding this confusion of family names cf. *Helgakvitha Hundingsbana I*, 5 and note. *Hæming*: his name does not appear in the list of Hunding's sons. It is quite possible that these opening stanzas (1–4) do not refer to Hunding at all.

1. Helgi appears to have stayed with Hunding under the name of Hamal, but now, thinking himself safe, he sends word of who he really is. *Hunding*: it has been suggested that the compiler may have inserted this name to fit what he thought the story ought to be, in place of Hæming, or even Hadding. If stanzas 1–4 are a fragment of the *Karuljoth* (Lay of Kara), this latter suggestion is quite reasonable, for in that poem, which we do not possess, but which supplied material for the compilers of the *Hromundar saga Greipssonar*, Helgi appears as Helgi Haddingjaskati (cf. final prose note). Nothing beyond this one name connects stanzas 1–4 with Hunding.

Prose. Hagal: Helgi's foster-father, who naturally protects him.

2. The manuscript indicates line 2 as the beginning of the stanza, the copyist evidently regarding line 1 as prose. This has caused various re-

arrangements in the different editions. *Blind*: leader of the band sent to capture Helgi.

3. The manuscript marks line 3 as the beginning of a stanza. *Barley*: the word literally means "foreign grain," and would afford an interesting study to students of early commerce.

4. Possibly two stanzas with one line lost, or perhaps the lines in parenthesis are spurious; each editor has his own guess. *Sigar* and *Hogni*: it seems unlikely that Hagal refers to the Hogni who was Sigrun's father, for this part of the story has nothing whatever to do with Sigrun. As Hagal is, of course, deliberately lying, it is useless to test any part of his speech for accuracy.

Prose. No division indicated in the manuscript. *Brunavagar* ("Bruni's Sea"): mentioned only in this section. *Strand-slaughtering*: a killing on the shore of cattle stolen in a raid. *Hogni* and *Sigrun*: cf. *Helgakvitha Hundingsbana I*, 17 and note; the annotator's notion of Sigrun as the reincarnated Svava (cf. *Helgakvitha Hjorvarthssonar*, concluding prose note) represents a naive form of scholarship. There is nothing in stanzas 5–12 which clearly identifies Sigrun as a Valkyrie, or which, except for the last line of stanza 12, identifies the speaker as Sigrun. Some editors, therefore, call her simply "the Valkyrie," while Vigfusson, who thinks this section is also a remnant of the *Karuljoth*, calls her Kara.

6. The manuscript does not indicate the speakers. *Hamal*: Helgi's assumption of this name seems to link this section (stanzas 5–12) with stanza 1. *Hlesey* ("Island of Hler"—i.e., Ægir, the sea-god): generally identified as the Danish island of Läsö; cf. *Harbarthsljoth*, 37 and note.

7. *Guth*: a Valkyrie (cf. *Voluspo*, 31) the birds of her sisters are the kites and ravens.

8. The manuscript indicates line 5 as the beginning of a new stanza; some editors reject lines 1–2, while others make lines 5–6 into a fragmentary stanza. *Ylfings*: cf. introductory prose and note. *Bragalund* ("Bragi's Wood"): a mythical place. *Bears*: presumably Berserkers, regarding whom cf. *Hyndluljoth*, 23.

9. [Has been separated from the Bellows original translation to conform with the Old Norse. The numbering between the original and this edition will diverge from this stanza on].

11. Helgi's meaning in lines 3–4 is that, although he has already declared himself an Ylfing (stanza 8, line 1), there are many heroes of that race,

and he does not understand how Sigrun knows him to be Helgi.

12. *Slaughter-runes*: equivocal or deceptive speech regarding the battle. The word "rune" had the meaning of "magic" or "mystery" long before it was applied to the signs or characters with which it was later identified.

13. Some editors reject line 3, others line 5. The manuscript omits Helgi's name in line 5, thereby destroying both the sense and the meter. Vigfusson, following his *Karuljoth* theory (cf. note on prose following stanza 4), changes Hogni to Halfdan, father of Kara.

Prose. The manuscript indicates no division. Most of this prose passage is evidently based on *Helgakvitha Hundingsbana I*; the only new features are the introduction of *Starkath* as a third son of Granmar, which is clearly an error based on a misunderstanding of stanza 19, and the reference to the *kings' meeting*, based on stanza 16. Kings' meetings, or councils, were by no means unusual; the North in early days was prolific in kings. For the remaining names, cf. *Helgakvitha Hundingsbana I*: *Granmar*, stanza 19; *Hothbrodd*, stanza 33; *Gothmund*, stanza 33; *Svarin's hill*, stanza 32; *Logafjoll*, stanza 13; *Alf, Eyjolf, Hjorvarth* and *Hervarth*, stanza 14. *The old Volsung lay*: cf. Introductory Note [Appendix B].

14. Some editions combine lines 3–4, Or line 4, with part of stanza 14.

15. The lines of stanzas 15 and 16 are here rearranged in accordance with Bugge's emendation; in the manuscript they stand as follows: lines 3–4 of stanza 15; stanza 16; lines 1–2 of stanza 15. This confusion has given rise to various editorial conjectures.[1]

> "Long with all | my heart I loved
> Sigmund's son | ere ever I saw him."

These lines were removed and inserted as Stanza 17 in the restructuring of the poem to conform to the Old Norse.

Prose. The manuscript indicates no division. Here again, the annotator has drawn practically all his information from *Helgakvitha Hundingsbana I*, which he specifically mentions and even quotes. The only new features are the names of Hogni's sons, *Bragi* and *Dag*. Bragi is mentioned in stanza 19, though it is not there stated that he is Hogni's son. Dag, who figures largely in stanzas 28–34, is a puzzle, for the verse never names him, and it is an open question where the annotator got his name.

---

1 The Old Norse does not reflect this change. Bellows has also changed one statement from indirect to direct speech, it is necessary to point this out, since Bellows did not.

482   POETIC EDDA

Frekastein: cf. *Helgakvitha Hjorvarthssonar*, 39 and note. *As is written*: the two lines are quoted, with a change of two words, from *Helgakvitha Hundingsbana* I, 33. *Sinfjotli*: cf. *Helgakvitha Hundingsbana* I, 6 and note, and stanzas 33–48, in which the whole dialogue is given. *Loyalty*: apparently the annotator got this bit of information out of stanza 29, in which Sigrun refers to the oaths which her brother had sworn to Helgi.

20. *Sevafjoll* ("Wet Mountain"): mentioned only in this poem. *Giant-steeds*: wolves, the usual steeds of giantesses; cf. *Helgakvitha Hundingsbana* I, 56.[2]

21. The word here translated *swords* is a conjectural emendation; the manuscript implies merely an invitation to continue the quarrel at Frekastein. *Hothbrodd*: apparently he is here considered as present during the dispute; some editors, in defiance of the meter, have emended the line to mean "Time is it for Hothbrodd vengeance to have."

23–24. Cf. *Helgakvitha Hundingsbana* I, 47–48, which are nearly identical. Stanza 27 in the manuscript is abbreviated to the first letters of the words, except for line 5, which does not appear in the other poem, and which looks like an interpolation.[3]

26. *Maid*: the word thus rendered is the same doubtful one which appears in *Völundarkvitha*, 1 and 5, and which may mean specifically a Valkyrie (Gering translates it "helmed" or "heroic") or simply "wise." Cf. *Völundarkvitha*, note on introductory prose. *Norns*: cf. *Voluspo*, 20 and note. In stanza 33 Dag similarly lays the blame for the murder he has committed on Odin. *Bragi*: probably Sigrun's brother.

27. This stanza looks like an interpolation, and there is little or nothing to connect it with the slaying of Gramnar's sons. In the manuscript line 2, indicated as the beginning of a stanza, precedes line 1. *Hlebjorg* ("Sea-Mountain") and *Styrkleifar* ("Battle-Cliffs"): place names not elsewhere mentioned. Of *Hrollaug's sons* nothing further is known. *Starkath*: this name gives a hint of the origin of this stanza, for Saxo Grammaticus tells of the slaying of the Swedish hero Starkath ("The Strong") the son of Storverk, and describes how his severed head bit the ground in anger (cf. line 4). In all probability this stanza is from an entirely different poem,

---

2 The structure of the original Bellows translation has been altered greatly to conform to the Old Norse; this alteration spans stanza 20 to 24 where the order resumes with the original Bellows translation at stanza 17.

3 There is still some conforming occurring within the Bellows translation; stanzas 26–29 are from the original manuscript that spans stanzas 17–20, stanza 30 is stanza 28 in the original. From stanza 30 to the end most of the conforming does not consist of major reworking of the structure.

dealing with the Starkath story, and the annotator's attempt to identify the Swedish hero as a third son of Granmar is quite without foundation.

29. The difference of meter would of itself be enough to indicate that this stanza comes from an entirely different poem. A few editions assign the whole stanza to Helgi, but lines 3–4. are almost certainly Sigrun's, and the manuscript begins line 3 with a large capital letter following a period.

Prose. Here begins a new section of the poem, dealing with Helgi's death at the hands of *Dag*, Sigrun's brother. The note is based wholly on stanzas 28–34 [Bellows original translation], except for the introduction of Dag's name (cf. note on prose following stanza 16), and the reference to *Odin's spear*, the weapon which made victory certain, and which the annotator brought in doubtless on the strength of Dag's statement that Odin was responsible for Helgi's death (stanza 34). *Fjoturlund* ("Fetter-Wood"): mentioned only here and in stanza 28.

30. Line 5 looks like an interpolation.

31. *Leipt*: this river is mentioned in *Grimnismol*, 29. *Uth*: a daughter of the sea-god Ægir; regarding her sacred stone we know nothing. According to the annotator, Dag's life had been spared because he swore loyalty to Helgi.

33. No gap indicated in the manuscript, but most editors have assumed that either the first or the last two lines have been lost. Bugge adds a line: "The shield shall not help thee which thou holdest."[4]

35. *Vandilsve* ("Vandil's Shrine"): who Vandil was we do not know; this and Vigdalir ("Battle-Dale") are purely mythical places.

36. Line 5 may be spurious. *Vigblær* ("Battle-Breather") Helgi's horse.

38. Line 5 (or possibly line 4) may be spurious. Cf. *Guthrunarkvitha I*, 17, and *Guthrunarkvitha II*, 2.

Prose. Valhall, etc.: there is no indication as to where the annotator got this notion of Helgi's sharing Odin's rule. It is most unlikely that such an idea ever found place in any of the Helgi poems, or at least in the earlier ones; probably it was a late development of the tradition in a period when Odin was no longer taken seriously.

39. This stanza apparently comes from an otherwise lost passage containing a contest of words between Helgi and Hunding; indeed the name of

---

[4] Stanzas 31 and 32 from the original Bellows translation were combined.

Hunding may have been substituted for another one beginning with "H," and the stanza originally have had no connection with Helgi at all. The annotator inserts it here through an obvious misunderstanding, taking it to be Helgi's application of the power conferred on him by Odin.

40. Here begins the final section, wherein Sigrun visits the dead Helgi in his burial hill. *Doom of the gods*: the phrase "ragna rök" has been rather unfortunately Anglicized into the work "ragnarok" (the Norse term is not a proper name), and *rök*, "doom," has been confused with *rökkr*, "darkness," and so translated "dusk of the Gods," or "Götterdämmerung."[5]

41. In the manuscript most of this stanza is abbreviated to the first letters of the words.

42. Line 3 (or possibly line 2) may be spurious. *Sword-tracks*: wounds. One edition places stanza 49 after stanza 43, and another does the same with stanza 51.

44. Possibly lines 5–6 are spurious, or part of a stanza the rest of which has been lost. It has also been suggested that two lines may have been lost after line 2, making a new stanza of lines 3–6. *Kinsman*: literally "son-in-law."

45. Lines 4 and 6 have been marked by various editors as probably spurious. Others regard lines 1–2 as the beginning of a stanza the rest of which has been lost, or combine lines 5–6 with lines 5–6 of stanza 45 to make a new stanza. *South-maid*: cf. *Helgakvitha Hundingsbana I*, 17 and note.

46. Both lines 3–4 and lines 5–6 have been suspected by editors of being interpolated, and the loss of two lines has also been suggested. *Brides*: the plural here is perplexing. Gering insists that only Sigrun is meant, and translates the word as singular, but both "brides" and "loves" are uncompromisingly plural in the text. Were the men of Helgi's ghostly following likewise visited by their wives? The annotator may have thought so, for in the prose he mentions the "women" returning to the house, although, of course, this may refer simply to Sigrun and the maid.

48. Line 5 (or possibly line 4) may be interpolated.

49. *Wind-helm*: the sky; the bridge is Bifrost, the rainbow (cf. *Grimnismol*, 29). *Salgofnir* ("Hall-Crower"): the cock Gollinkambi who awakes the gods and warriors for the last battle.

---

5 Bellows' bracketed reference to stanzas 39–50 have been removed here, owing to rearrangement of stanzas.

50. Many editors assign this speech to the maid. Line 5 (or 4) may be spurious. *Meeting of dreams* ("Dream-Thing"): sleep.

Prose. The attitude of the annotator is clearly revealed by his contempt for those who put any faith in such "old wives' folly" as the idea that men and women could be reborn. The *Lay of Kara* (*Karuljoth*) is lost, although, as has been pointed out, parts of the *Helgakvitha Hundingsbana II* may be remnants of it, but we find the main outlines of the story in the *Hromundar saga Greipssonar*, whose compilers appear to have known the *Karuljoth*. In the saga *Helgi Haddingjaskati* (Helgi the Haddings' Hero) is protected by the Valkyrie Kara, who flies over him in the form of a swan (note once more the Valkyrie swan-maiden confusion); but in his fight with Hromund he swings his sword so high that he accidentally gives Kara a mortal wound, whereupon Hromund cuts off his head. As this makes the third recorded death of Helgi (once at the hands of Alf, once at those of Dag, and finally in the fight with Hromund), the phenomenon of his rebirth is not surprising. The points of resemblance in all the Helgi stories, including the one told in the lost *Karuljoth*, are sufficiently striking so that it is impossible not to see in them a common origin, and not to believe that Helgi the son of Hjorvarth, Helgi the son of Sigmund and Helgi the Haddings'-Hero (not to mention various other Helgis who probably figured in songs and stories now lost) were all originally the same Helgi who appears in the early traditions of Denmark.

FRA DAUTHA SINFJOTLA
OF SINFJOTLI'S DEATH

INTRODUCTION

Fra Dautha Sinfjotla represents a curious artifact in the *Codex Regius*, filled as it is with poetic lays and ballads representing ancient traditions of old; and yet we find amid these a single, short prose narrative describing the events of Sinfjotli's death. Sinfjotli being of no small repute, it would make sense that any sort of description of his death would be considered noteworthy by our forebears, with him being the son of Sigmund and party to his original experience as sacred warriors of the *ulfhethnar*, those wolf warriors of Odin who "live in the woods and prey upon men", also recounted twice in the Helgi lays and thus representing the primary narrative connection between his half-brother and the *Volsungasaga* proper with his other half-brother Sigurth Fafnirsbane.

So it seems incongruous that we should be left with only a prose account of the narrative, especially one remarking upon otherwise unmentioned qualities, namely that Sigmund and his sons were resistant to poison due to their godly heritage, and that this quality was stronger in the father due to him having more godly blood than his children did.[1] Perhaps we are merely missing an attendant poetic lay of the narrative events which would follow, or perhaps the lay was so badly damaged that the original compiler chose to simply describe the events to us in his own

---

[1] Sinfjotli should actually have the same percentage of godly blood, as he is the son of Sigmund and his twin sister Signy, a fact which was well known to ancient poets and implies that perhaps the issue was not a "Blood Quantum" as we understand it today but literally the number of generations removed from godhood and a function of the soul, rather than biology.

hand in its place.

Bellows himself in his introduction to the narrative passage relates, rather confusingly, his position that the story might have been handed down in prose form itself along with many other poems, because we have a poetic section quoted from an older *Volsungasaga* narrative. This claim does not make sense because the original narrative tradition of the Germanic people was in poetic lays, which are much older than the prose narratives which start to occur with frequency only after the 10th century.

The Death of Sinfjolti
(Jenny Nystrom)

Sigmundr Völsungsson var konungr á Frakklandi. Sinfjötli var elztr hans sona, annarr Helgi, þriði Hámundr. Borghildr, kona Sigmundar, átti bróður, er hét ——. En Sinfjötli, stjúpson hennar, ok —— báðu einnar konu báðir, ok fyrir þá sök drap Sinfjötli hann.

En er hann kom heim, þá bað Borghildr hann fara á brott, en Sigmundr bauð henni fébætr, ok þat varð hon at þiggja. En at erfinu bar Borghildr öl. Hon tók eitr mikit, horn fullt, ok bar Sinfjötla.

En er hann sá í hornit, skilði hann, at eitr var í, ok mælti til Sigmundar: "Göróttr er drykkrinn, ái."

Sigmundr tók hornit ok drakk af. Svá er sagt at Sigmundr var harðgörr, at hvárki mátti hánum eitr granda útan né innan, en allir synir hans stóðust eitr á hörund útan.

Borghildr bar annat horn Sinfjötla ok bað drekka, ok fór allt sem fyrr. Ok enn it þriðja sinn bar hon hánum hornit ok þó ámælisorð með, ef hann drykki eigi af. Hann mælti enn sem fyrr við Sigmund.

Hann sagði: "Láttu grön sía þá, sonr."

Sinfjötli drakk ok varð þegar dauðr. Sigmundr bar hann langar leiðir í fangi sér ok kom at firði einum mjóvum ok löngum, ok var þar skip eitt lítit ok maðr einn á. Hann bauð Sigmundi far of fjörðinn. En er Sigmundr bar líkit út á skipit, þá var bátrinn hlaðinn. Karl mælti, at Sigmundr skyldi fara fyrir innan fjörðinn. Karl hratt út skipinu ok hvarf þegar.

Sigmundr konungr dvalðisk lengi í Danmörk í ríki Borghildar, síðan er hann fekk hennar. Fór Sigmundr þá suðr í Frakkland til þess ríkis, er hann átti þar. Þá fekk hann Hjördísar, dóttur Eylima konungs. Þeira son

FRA DAUTHA SINFJOTLA

Sigmund, the son of Volsung, was a king in the land of the Franks; Sinfjotli was his eldest son, the second was Helgi, and the third Hamund. Borghild, Sigmund's wife, had a brother who was named ——. Sinfjotli, her stepson, and —— both wooed the same woman, wherefore Sinfjotli slew him. And when he came home, Borghild bade him depart, but Sigmund offered her atonement-money, and this she had to accept. At the funeral feast Borghild brought in ale; she took poison, a great horn full, and brought it to Sinfjotli. But when he looked into the horn, he saw that it was poison, and said to Sigmund: "Muddy is the drink, Father!" Sigmund took the horn and drank therefrom. It is said that Sigmund was so hardy that poison might not harm him, either outside or in, but all his sons could withstand poison only without on their skin. Borghild bore another horn to Sinfjotli and bade him drink, and all happened as before. And yet a third time she brought him a horn, and spoke therewith scornful words of him if he should not drink from it. He spoke as before with Sigmund. The latter said: "Let it trickle through your beard, Son!" Sinfjotli drank, and straightway was dead. Sigmund bore him a long way in his arms, and came to a narrow and long fjord, and there was a little boat and a man in it. He offered to take Sigmund across the fjord. But when Sigmund had borne the corpse out into the boat, then the craft was full. The man told Sigmund to go round the inner end of the fjord. Then the man pushed the boat off, and disappeared.

King Sigmund dwelt long in Denmark in Borghild's kingdom after he had married her. Thereafter Sigmund went south into the land of the

var Sigurðr.

Sigmundr konungr fell í orrostu fyrir Hundingssonum, en Hjördís giftist þá Álfi, syni Hjálpreks konungs. Óx Sigurðr þar upp í barnæsku. Sigmundr ok allir synir hans váru langt um fram alla menn aðra um afl ok vöxt ok hug ok alla atgervi. Sigurðr var þó allra framastr, ok hann kalla allir menn í fornfræðum um alla menn fram ok göfgastan herkonunga.

Franks, to the kingdom which he had there. There he married Hjordis, the daughter of King Eylim; their son was Sigurth. King Sigmund fell in a battle with the sons of Hunding, and Hjordis then married Alf the son of King Hjalprek. There Sigurth grew up in his boyhood. Sigmund and all his sons were far above all other men in might and stature and courage and every kind of ability. Sigurth, however, was the foremost of all, and all men call him in the old tales the noblest of mankind and the mightiest leader.

ENDNOTES

Prose. Regarding *Sigmund*, *Sinfjotli*, and *Volsung* see Introductory Note [Appendix B]. *The Franks*: although the Sigurth story had reached the North as early as the sixth or seventh century, it never lost all the marks of its Frankish origin. *Helgi* and *Hamund*: sons of Sigmund and Borghild; Helgi is, of course Helgi Hundingsbane; of Hamund nothing further is recorded. *Borghild*: the manuscript leaves a blank for the name of her brother; evidently the compiler hoped some day to discover it and write it in, but never did. A few editions insert wholly unauthorized names from late paper manuscripts, such as Hroar, Gunnar, or Borgar. In the *Volsungasaga* Borghild bids Sinfjotli drink "if he has the courage of a Volsung." Sigmund gives his advice because "the king was very drunk, and that was why he spoke thus." Gering, on the other hand, gives Sigmund credit for having believed that the draught would deposit its poisonous contents in Sinfjotli's beard, and thus do him no harm. *Boat*: the man who thus carries off the dead Sinfjotli in his boat is presumably Odin. *Denmark*: Borghild belongs to the Danish Helgi part of the story. *The Franks*: with this the Danish and Norse stories of Helgi and Sinfjotli come to an end, and the Frankish story of Sigurth begins. Sigmund's two kingdoms are an echo of the blended traditions. *Hjordis*: just where this name came from is not clear, for in the German story Siegfried's mother is Sigelint, but the name of the father of Hjordis, *Eylimi*, gives a clue, for Eylimi is the father of Svava, wife of Helgi Hjorvarthsson. Doubtless the two men are not identical, but it seems likely that both Eylimi and Hjordis were introduced into the Sigmund-Sigurth story, the latter replacing Sigelint, from some version of the Helgi tradition. *Hunding*: in the Helgi lays the sons of Hunding are all killed, but they reappear here and in two of the poems (*Gripisspo*, 9, and *Reginsmol*, 15), and the *Volsungasaga* names Lyngvi as the son of Hunding who, as the rejected lover of Hjordis, kills

Sigmund and his father-in-law, Eylimi, as well. The episode of Hunding and his sons belongs entirely to the Danish (Helgi) part of the story; the German legend knows nothing of it, and permits the elderly Sigmund to outlive his son. There was doubtless a poem on this battle, for the Volsungasaga quotes two lines spoken by the dying Sigmund to Hjordis before he tells her to give the pieces of his broken sword to their unborn son.

Alf: after the battle, according to the *Volsungasaga*, Lyngvi Hundingsson tried to capture Hjordis, but she was rescued by the sea-rover Alf, son of King Hjalprek of Denmark, who subsequently married her. Here is another trace of the Danish Helgi tradition. The *Nornageststhattr* briefly tells the same story.

GRIPISSPO
GRIPIR'S PROPHECY

INTRODUCTION

Generally accepted as among the youngest—if not outright *the* youngest—of the stories in the *Poetic Edda*, *Gripir's Prophecy* or the *Gripisspo* (sometimes called *Sigurðarkviða Fáfnisbana I*) is a prophecy delivered by Sigurth's maternal uncle Gripir (of whom nothing else is known) regarding the full events of his life, and thereby functions as a sort of summary poem regarding his fame and adventures. Certainly, we can consider this narrative as wholly a fictional conceit intended to deliver information to the listeners, for it would be unintelligible to assume that Sigurth was aware of the various misunderstandings and tragic turns of fate that would characterize his saga tales. We can rest assured that he was not.

The narrative of the *Sigurth Lays* begins here, however, and we might do well to unpack some of the layers in its formation as we have done with the closely related Helgi Lays. Sigurth is the son of Sigmund Volsungsson through his wife, the Valkyrie Hjordis. This makes him the half-brother of the famous heroes Sinfjiotli and Helgi Hundingsbane, on whom other poems center. Sigurth is far and away the most famous of all heroes in the *Eddic* tradition and probably among the Germanic folk in general, with his name being known as Sivrit and Siegfried in Middle High German and modern High German respectively. In the *Eddas* and among the Norse peoples he is known by many different epithets with "Fafnirsbane" and "Dragonslayer" or simply "Sigurth the Volsung" being the most commonly used. The origin of the Sigurth narrative is intimately connected to that of his father Sigmund, a well-established hero in his own right with pan-Germanic credentials who also slays a dragon, leading many early scholars to question whether the son has simply become confused with his father over time and his heroic exploits split up, but this is generally rejected in modern scholarship due to the narrative purposes surrounding each dragon slaying, with Sigmund's being done near the end of his life as a generic heroic feat and Sigurth's being done as a young man as a sort of initiatic quest.

The narrative can be divided into two distinct parts. The first is largely agreed upon between Continental and Nordic sources, in which Sigurth slays the dragon Fafnir and gains wisdom from his blood, then acquires the Hoard of the Nibelungs whereupon he promises to marry his Valkyrie bride Brynhildr/Sigrdrifa. The latter part of his narrative is a more confusing, and likely later, romantic addition. The narrative here also starts to diverge wildly between *Eddic* and continental sources. In the *Eddic* structure, Sigurth promises to marry Brynhildr but drinks a love potion that turns his eye only to Guthrun, daughter of King Gjuki of Burgundy. He then swears a blood oath to his new brothers-in-law Gunnar and Hogni, and their mother Grimhildr convinces Gunnar to marry Brynhildr. Unfortunately, Brynhildr has barricaded herself behind a wall of flames and sealed it with magic so that only her true love might pass—Gunnar fails to do so. Grimhildr teaches the pair a magic spell that allows them to exchange shapes and Sigurth rides across the barrier in the form of Gunnar, wherein he wakes Brynhildr and sleeps with her, laying a sword between them so they do not have sex. She is then led back, and the pair of men retake their original forms and marry their respective wives. Sometime later the wives fall out in an argument over seniority and rank and Guthrun informs Brynhildr that Sigurth was the one to cross the barrier. Brynhildr is enraged and Sigurth talks to her, confessing his love and offering to marry her once more, but Brynhildr, out of pride, refuses this and demands that her husband Gunnar kill Sigurth in vengeance. Gunnar balks at this and maintains that he cannot slay his oath-brother and so convinces his younger brother Guthorm to do so. Guthorm stabs Sigurth in the back and kills him, and Brynhildr immolates herself on Sigurth's pyre afterwards.

In the continental source, Siegfried befriends Gunther, Gernot, and Giselher, brother-kings of the Bergundians, and aids them in Gunther's quest to woo the warrior queen of Iceland Brünhild (despite Iceland not having a monarch, female or male, nor having even been settled by this early time). Siegfried uses his cloak of invisibility to secretly aid Gunther in each of the tasks meted out by Brünhild, and eventually to overpower her and allow Gunther to sleep with her, with him having lied to Brünhild that he was merely a vassal of Gunther. For his efforts, Siegfried is then allowed to marry their sister Kriemhild. The two women have a falling out over the lie about Siegfried's vassalage, and Kriemhild falsely claims that Siegfried rather than Gunther took Brünhild's virginity. Kriemhild convinces Hagen, Gunther's maternal uncle, to help her kill Siegfried and he stabs him in the back and throws his corpse before Kriemhild, who mourns his loss. Certain aspects of the story show some connection with material history, with the Burgundian King Gundicarius (a Latin transliteration but one solidly connected to the *Eddic* Gunnar and German Gunther) being defeated by the Hunnic armies of Atilla (who becomes Etzel in Germany and Atli in the *Eddas*) in the year 437, and the Gothic King Ermanarich, hero of many unconnected continental tales being connected to the greater legend by marrying Sigurth's daughter Svanhild as Jormunrek (despite having died nearly 60 years before the battle between Gundicarius and the Huns). Sigurth himself is often taken to be a folk version of the Frankish king Sigebert, who was murdered following a feud between Brunhild of Austrasia and her sister-in-law Fredegund. Many early scholars have noted these connections and have come to the conclusion that the narrative of the Sigurth tale is likely a mishmash of various continental legends and quasi-historical sources and thus of originally broadly Frankish origin.

More recent scholarship in comparative Indo-European studies points to many foundational aspects of the Sigurth myth as having deep Proto Indo-European provenance, such as the slaying of the dragon Fafnir, his use of magical trickery and deceit to accomplish later tasks, and even the aspects of Sigurth bathing in the blood of Fafnir to gain impenetrable skin except for a small location on his back being reminiscent of the Achilles narrative. A further connection might be explained via the Merovingian line of Frankish kings and their mythic origins from the Quinotaur (a sea beast of some sort, extremely mysterious in its origins) being connected in some sense to the mother of Achilles being the Sea-Nymph Thetis. Regardless of the truth of the matter it can confidently be asserted that the foundational aspects of the Sigurth myth have much older provenance than the early medieval period as many early scholars once assumed.[1]

---

1 For more on this, including a dating of aspects of the Sigurth saga no later than 750 BCE, see the foreword to *Folktales in the Indo-European Tradition*, Imperium Press, 2022.

Grípir hét sonr Eylima, bróðir Hjördísar. Hann réð löndum ok var allra manna vitrastr ok framvíss. Sigurðr reið einn saman ok kom til hallar Grípis. Sigurðr var auðkenndr. Hann hitti mann at máli úti fyrir höllini. Sá nefndist Geitir. Þá kvaddi Sigurðr hann máls ok spyrr:

"Hverr byggir hér   borgir þessar?   1
Hvat þann þjóðkonung   þegnar nefna?"
Geitir kvað:
"Grípir heitir   gumna stóri,
sá er fastri ræðr   foldu ok þegnum."

Sigurðr kvað: 2
"Er horskr konungr   heima í landi?
Mun sá gramr við mik   ganga at mæla?
Máls er þarfi   maðr ókunnigr,
vil ek fljótliga   finna Grípi."

Geitir kvað: 3
"Þess mun glaðr konungr   Geiti spyrja,
hverr sá maðr sé,   er máls kveðr Grípi."
Sigurðr kvað:
"Sigurðr ek heiti,   borinn Sigmundi,
en Hjördís er   hilmis móðir."

GRIPISSPO

Gripir was the name of Eylimi's son, the brother of Hjordis; he ruled over lands and was of all men the wisest and most forward-seeing. Sigurth once was riding alone and came to Gripir's hall. Sigurth was easy to recognize; he found out in front of the hall a man whose name was Geitir. Then Sigurth questioned him and asked:

"Who is it has this dwelling here, 1
Or what do men call the people's king?"
Geitir spake:
"Gripir the name of the chieftain good
Who holds the folk and the firm-ruled land."

Sigurth spake: 2
"Is the king all-knowing now within,
Will the monarch come with me to speak?
A man unknown his counsel needs,
And Gripir fain I soon would find."

Geitir spake: 3
"The ruler glad of Geitir will ask
Who seeks with Gripir speech to have."
Sigurth spake:
"Sigurth am I, and Sigmund's son,
And Hjordis the name of the hero's mother."

Þá gekk Geitir   Grípi at segja;   4
"Hér er maðr úti   ókuðr kominn;
hann er ítarligr   at áliti;
sá vill, fylkir,   fund þinn hafa."

Gengr ór skála   skatna dróttinn   5
ok heilsar vel   hilmi komnum:
"þiggðu hér, Sigurðr,   væri sæmra fyrr,
en þú, Geitir, tak   við Grana sjalfum."

Mæla námu   ok margt hjala   6
þá er ráðspakir   rekkar fundusk.
Sigurðr kvað:
"Segðu mér, ef þú veizt,   móðurbróðir:
Hvé mun Sigurði   snúna ævi."

Grípir kvað: 7
"Þú munt maðr vera   mæztr und sólu
ok hæstr borinn   hverjum jöfri,
gjöfull af gulli,   en glöggr flugar,
ítr áliti   ok í orðum spakr."

Sigurðr kvað: 8
"Segðu, gegn konungr,   gerr en ek spyrja,
snotr, Sigurði,   ef þú sjá þykkisk:
Hvat mun fyrst gerask   til farnaðar,
þá er ór garði emk   genginn þínum?"

Grípir kvað: 9
"Fyrst muntu, fylkir,   föður of hefna,
ok Eylima   alls harms reka;
þú munt harða   Hundings sonu
snjalla fella,   muntu sigr hafa."

Sigurðr kvað: 10
"Segðu, ítr konungr,   ættingi, mér
heldr horskliga,   er vit hugat mælum:
Sér þú Sigurðar   snör brögð fyrir,
þau er hæst fara   und himinskautum?"

Grípir kvað: 11
"Muntu einn vega
orm inn frána,   þann er gráðugr liggr
á Gnitaheiði;   þú munt báðum
at bana verða   Regin ok Fáfni,
rétt segir Grípir."

Then Geitir went and to Gripir spake: | 4
"A stranger comes and stands without;
Lofty he is to look upon,
And, prince, thyself he fain would see."

From the hall the ruler of heroes went, | 5
And greeted well the warrior come:
"Sigurth, welcome long since had been thine;
Now, Geitir, shalt thou Grani take."

Then of many things they talked, | 6
When thus the men so wise had met.

Sigurth spake:
"To me, if thou knowest, my mother's brother,
Say what life will Sigurth's be."

Gripir spake: | 7
"Of men thou shalt be on earth the mightiest,
And higher famed than all the heroes;
Free of gold-giving, slow to flee,
Noble to see, and sage in speech."

Sigurth spake: | 8
"Monarch wise, now more I ask;
To Sigurth say, if thou thinkest to see,
What first will chance of my fortune fair,
When hence I go from out thy home?"

Gripir spake: | 9
"First shalt thou, prince, thy father avenge,
And Eylimi, their ills requiting;
The hardy sons of Hunding thou
Soon shalt fell, and victory find."

Sigurth spake: | 10
"Noble king, my kinsman, say
Thy meaning true, for our minds we speak:
For Sigurth mighty deeds dost see,
The highest beneath the heavens all?"

Gripir spake: | 11
"The fiery dragon alone thou shalt fight
That greedy lies at Gnitaheith;
Thou shalt be of Regin and Fafnir both
The slayer; truth doth Gripir tell thee."

Sigurðr kvað: 12
"Auðr mun ærinn,   ef ek eflik svá
víg með virðum,   sem víst segir;
leið at huga   ok lengra seg:
Hvat mun enn vera   ævi minnar?"

Grípir kvað: 13
"Þú munt finna   Fáfnis bæli
ok upp taka   auð inn fagra,
gulli hlæða   á Grana bógu;
ríðr þú til Gjúka,   gramr vígrisinn."

Sigurðr kvað: 14
"Enn skaltu hilmi   í hugaðsræðu,
framlyndr jöfurr,   fleira segja.
Gestr em ek Gjúka   ok ek geng þaðan,
hvat mun enn vera   ævi minnar?"

Grípir kvað: 15
"Sefr á fjalli   fylkis dóttir
björt í brynju   eftir bana Helga;
þú munt höggva   hvössu sverði,
brynju rísta   með bana Fáfnis."

Sigurðr kvað: 16
"Brotin er brynja,   brúðr mæla tekr,
er vaknaði   víf ór svefni.
Hvat mun snót at heldr   við Sigurð mæla,
þat er at farnaði   fylki verði?"

Grípir kvað: 17
"Hon mun ríkjum þér   rúnar kenna,
allar þær er aldir   eignask vildu,
ok á manns tungu   mæla hverja,
líf með lækning;   lifðu heill, konungr."

Sigurðr kvað: 18
"Nú er því lokit,   numin eru fræði
ok em braut þaðan   búinn at ríða,
leið at huga   ok lengra seg:
Hvat mun meir vera   minnar ævi?"

Sigurth spake: 12
"Rich shall I be if battles I win
With such as these, as now thou sayest;
Forward look, and further tell:
What the life that I shall lead?"

Gripir spake: 13
"Fafnir's den thou then shalt find,
And all his treasure fair shalt take;
Gold shalt heap on Grani's back,
And, proved in fight, to Gjuki fare."

Sigurth spake: 14
"To the warrior now in words so wise,
Monarch noble, more shalt tell;
I am Gjuki's guest, and thence I go:
What the life that I shall lead?"

Gripir spake: 15
"On the rocks there sleeps the ruler's daughter,
Fair in armor, since Helgi fell;
Thou shalt cut with keen-edged sword,
And cleave the byrnie with Fafnir's killer."

Sigurth spake: 16
"The mail-coat is broken, the maiden speaks,
The woman who from sleep has wakened;
What says the maid to Sigurth then
That happy fate to the hero brings?"

Gripir spake: 17
"Runes to the warrior will she tell,
All that men may ever seek,
And teach thee to speak in all men's tongues,
And life with health; thou'rt happy, king!"

Sigurth spake: 18
"Now is it ended, the knowledge is won,
And ready I am forth thence to ride;
Forward look and further tell:
What the life that I shall lead?"

Grípir kvað:

"Þú munt hitta   Heimis byggðir
ok glaðr vera   gestr þjóðkonungs;
farit er, Sigurðr,   þats ek fyrir vissak,
skal-a fremr en svá   fregna Grípi."

Sigurðr kvað:

"Nú fær mér ekka   orð þatstu mæltir,
því at þú fram of sér   fylkir, lengra;
veiztu ofmikit   angr Sigurði,
því þú, Grípir, þat   gerr-a segja."

Grípir kvað:

"Lá mér um æsku   ævi þinnar
ljósast fyrir   líta eftir;
rétt em ek   ráðspakr taliðr
né in heldr framvíss,   farit þats ek vissak."

Sigurðr kvað:

"Mann veit ek engi   fyr mold ofan,
þann er fleira sé   fram en þú, Grípir;
skal-at-tu leyna,   þótt ljót séi,
eða mein gerisk   á mínum hag."

Grípir kvað:

"Er-a með löstum   lögð ævi þér,
láttu, inn ítri, þat,   öðlingr, nemask,
því at uppi mun,   meðan öld lifir,
naddéls boði,   nafn þitt vera."

Sigurðr kvað:

"Verst hyggjum því,   verðr at skiljask
Sigurðr við fylki   at sógöru;
leið vísa þú,   —lagt er allt fyrir—
mærr, mér, ef þú vilt,   móðurbróðir."

Grípir kvað:

"Nú skal Sigurði   segja görva,
alls þengill mik   til þess neyðir;
muntu víst vita   at vætki lýgr;
dægr eitt er þér   dauði ætlaðr."

Gripir spake: 19
"Then to Heimir's home thou comest,
And glad shalt be the guest of the king;
Ended, Sigurth, is all I see,
No further aught of Gripir ask."

Sigurth spake: 20
"Sorrow brings me the word thou sayest,
For, monarch, forward further thou seest;
Sad the grief for Sigurth thou knowest,
Yet nought to me, Gripir, known wilt make."

Gripir spake: 21
"Before me lay in clearest light
All of thy youth for mine eyes to see;
Not rightly can I wise be called,
Nor forward-seeing; my wisdom is fled."

Sigurth spake: 22
"No man, Gripir, on earth I know
Who sees the future as far as thou;
Hide thou nought, though hard it be,
And base the deeds that I shall do."

Gripir spake: 23
"With baseness never thy life is burdened,
Hero noble, hold that sure;
Lofty as long as the world shall live,
Battle-bringer, thy name shall be."

Sigurth spake: 24
"Nought could seem worse, but now must part
The prince and Sigurth, since so it is,
My road I ask—the future lies open—
Mighty one, speak, my mother's brother."

Gripir spake: 25
"Now to Sigurth all shall I say,
For to this the warrior bends my will;
Thou knowest well that I will not lie,
A day there is when thy death is doomed."

Sigurðr kvað: 26
"Vilk-at ek reiði ríks þjóðkonungs,
góð ráð at heldr Grípis þiggja;
nú vill víst vita, þótt viltki sé,
hvat á sýnt Sigurðr sér fyr höndum."

Grípir kvað: 27
"Fljóð er at Heimis fagrt álitum,
hana Brynhildi bragnar nefna,
dóttir Buðla, en dýrr konungr
harðugðigt man Heimir fæðir."

Sigurðr kvað: 28
"Hvat er mik at því, þótt mær séi
fögr áliti fædd at Heimis?
Þat skaltu, Grípir, görva segja,
því at þú öll of sér örlög fyrir."

Grípri kvað: 29
"Hon firrir þik flestu gamni,
fögr áliti, fóstra Heimis,
svefn þú né sefr né of sakar dæmir,
gár-a þú manna nema þú mey séir."

Sigurðr kvað: 30
"Hvat mun til líkna lagt Sigurði?
Segðu, Grípir, þat, ef þú sjá þykkisk:
Mun ek mey ná mundi kaupa,
þá ina fögru fylkis dóttur?"

Grípir kvað: 31
"It munuð alla eiða vinna
fullfastliga, fá munuð halda;
verit hefr þú Gjúka gestr eina nótt,
mant-at-tu horska Heimis fóstru."

Sigurðr kvað: 32
"Hvat er þá, Grípir, get þú þess fyr mér,
sér þú geðleysi í grams skapi,
er ek skal við mey þá málum slíta,
er ek alls hugar unna þóttumk."

Sigurth spake: 26
"No scorn I know for the noble king,
But counsel good from Gripir I seek;
Well will I know, though evil awaits,
What Sigurth may before him see."

Gripir spake: 27
"A maid in Heimir's home there dwells,
Brynhild her name to men is known,
Daughter of Buthli, the doughty king,
And Heimir fosters the fearless maid."

Sigurth spake: 28
"What is it to me, though the maiden be
So fair, and of Heimir the fosterling is?
Gripir, truth to me shalt tell,
For all of fate before me thou seest."

Gripir spake: 29
"Of many a joy the maiden robs thee,
Fair to see, whom Heimir fosters;
Sleep thou shalt find not, feuds thou shalt end not,
Nor seek out men, if the maid thou seest not."

Sigurth spake: 30
"What may be had for Sigurth's healing?
Say now, Gripir, if see thou canst;
May I buy the maid with the marriage-price,
The daughter fair of the chieftain famed?"

Gripir spake: 31
"Ye twain shall all the oaths then swear
That bind full fast; few shall ye keep;
One night when Gjuki's guest thou hast been,
Will Heimir's fosterling fade from thy mind."

Sigurth spake: 32
"What sayst thou, Gripir? give me the truth,
Does fickleness hide in the hero's heart?
Can it be that troth I break with the maid,
With her I believed I loved so dear?"

Grípir kvað: 33
"Þú verðr, siklingr, fyr svikum annars,
muntu Grímhildar gjalda ráða,
mun bjóða þér bjarthaddat man
dóttur sína, dregr hon vél at gram."

Sigurðr kvað: 34
"Mun ek við þá Gunnar görva hleyti
ok Guðrúnu ganga at eiga?
Fullkvæni þá fylkir væri,
ef meintregar mér angraði-t."

Grípir kvað: 35
"Þik mun Grímhildr görva véla,
mun hon Brynhildar biðja fýsa
Gunnari til handa, Gotna dróttni,
heitr þú fjótliga för fylkis móður."

Sigurðr kvað: 36
"Mein eru fyr höndum, má ek líta þat;
ratar görliga ráð Sigurðar,
ef ek skal mærrar meyjar biðja
öðrum til handa, þeirar ek unna vel."

Grípir kvað: 37
"Ér munuð allir eiða vinna
Gunnar ok Högni, en þú, gramr, þriði;
þá it litum víxlið, er á leið eruð,
Gunnar ok þú; Grípir lýgr eigi."

Sigurðr kvað: 38
"Hví gegnir þat? Hví skulum skipta
litum ok látum, er á leið erum?
Þar mun fláræði fylgja annat
atalt með öllu; enn segðu, Grípir."

Grípir kvað: 39
"Lit hefir þú Gunnars ok læti hans,
mælsku þína ok meginhyggjur;
muntu fastna þér framlundaða
fóstru Heimis, sér vætr fyr því."

Gripir spake: 33
"Tricked by another, prince, thou art,
And the price of Grimhild's wiles thou must pay;
Fain of thee for the fair-haired maid,
Her daughter, she is, and she drags thee down."

Sigurth spake: 34
"Might I with Gunnar kinship make,
And Guthrun win to be my wife,
Well the hero wedded would be,
If my treacherous deed would trouble me not."

Gripir spake: 35
"Wholly Grimhild thy heart deceives,
She will bid thee go and Brynhild woo
For Gunnar's wife, the lord of the Goths;
And the prince's mother thy promise shall win."

Sigurth spake: 36
"Evil waits me, well I see it,
And gone is Sigurth's wisdom good,
If I shall woo for another to win
The maiden fair that so fondly I loved."

Gripir spake: 37
"Ye three shall all the oaths then take,
Gunnar and Hogni, and, hero, thou;
Your forms ye shall change, as forth ye fare,
Gunnar and thou; for Gripir lies not."

Sigurth spake: 38
"How meanest thou? Why make we the change
Of shape and form as forth we fare?
There must follow another falsehood
Grim in all ways; speak on, Gripir!"

Gripir spake: 39
"The form of Gunnar and shape thou gettest,
But mind and voice thine own remain;
The hand of the fosterling noble of Heimir
Now dost thou win, and none can prevent."

Sigurðr kvað: 40
"Verst hyggjum því,   vándr munk heitinn
Sigurðr með seggjum   at sógöru;
vilda ek eigi   vélum beita
jöfra brúði, er ek æðsta veitk."

Grípir kvað: 41
"Þú munt hvíla,   hers oddviti
mærr, hjá meyju   sem þín móðir sé;
því mun uppi,   meðan öld lifir,
þjóðar þengill,   þitt nafn vera."

Sigurðr kvað: 42
"Mun góða kván   Gunnarr eiga,
mærr með mönnum,   mér segðu, Grípir,
þótt hafi þrjár nætr   þegns brúðr hjá mér
snarlynd sofit?   Slíks eru-t dæmi."

Grípir kvað: 43
"Saman munu brullup   bæði drukkin
Sigurðar ok Gunnars   í sölum Gjúka;
þá hömum víxlið,   er it heim komið;
hefr hvárr fyr því   hyggju sína."

Sigurðr kvað: 44
"Hvé mun at yndi   eftir verða
mægð með mönnum?   Mér segðu, Grípir.
Mun Gunnari   til gamans ráðit
síðan verða   eða sjalfum mér?"

Grípir kvað: 45
"Minnir þik eiða,   máttu þegja þó,
anntu Guðrúnu   góðra ráða;
en Brynhildr þykkisk   brúðr vargefin,
snót fiðr vélar   sér at hefndum."

Sigurðr kvað: 46
"Hvat mun at bótum   brúðr sú taka,
er vélar vér   vífi gerðum?
Hefir snót af mér   svarna eiða
enga efnda,   en unað lítit."

Sigurth spake: 40
"Most evil it seems, and men will say
Base is Sigurth that so he did;
Not of my will shall I cheat with wiles
The heroes' maiden whom noblest I hold."

Gripir spake: 41
"Thou dwellest, leader lofty of men,
With the maid as if thy mother she were;
Lofty as long as the world shall live,
Ruler of men, thy name shall remain."

Sigurth spake: 42
"Shall Gunnar have a goodly wife,
Famed among men, speak forth now, Gripir!
Although at my side three nights she slept,
The warrior's bride? Such ne'er has been."

Gripir spake: 43
"The marriage draught will be drunk for both,
For Sigurth and Gunnar, in Gjuki's hall;
Your forms ye change, when home ye fare,
But the mind of each to himself remains."

Sigurth spake: 44
"Shall the kinship new thereafter come
To good among us? Tell me, Gripir!
To Gunnar joy shall it later give,
Or happiness send for me myself?"

Gripir spake: 45
"Thine oaths remembering, silent thou art,
And dwellest with Guthrun in wedlock good;
But Brynhild shall deem she is badly mated,
And wiles she seeks, herself to avenge."

Sigurth spake: 46
"What may for the bride requital be,
The wife we won with subtle wiles?
From me she has the oaths I made,
And kept not long; they gladdened her little."

Grípir kvað:　47
"Mun hon Gunnari　görva segja,
at þú eigi vel　eiðum þyrmðir,
þá er ítr konungr　af öllum hug,
Gjúka arfi,　á gram trúði."

Sigurðr kvað:　48
"Hvat er þá, Grípir,　get þú þess fyr mér,
mun ek saðr vera　at sögu þeiri,
eða lýgr á mik　lofsæl kona
ok á sjalfa sik?　Segðu, Grípir, þat."

Grípir kvað:　49
"Mun fyr reiði　rík brúðr við þik
né af oftrega　allvel skipa;
viðr þú góðri　grand aldrigi,
þó ér víf konungs　vélum beittuð."

Sigurðr kvað:　50
"Mun horskr Gunnarr　at hvötun hennar
Gutþormr ok Högni　ganga síðan?
Munu synir Gjúka　á sifjugum mér
eggjar rjóða?　Enn segðu, Grípir."

Grípir kvað:　51
"Þá er Guðrúnu　grimmt um hjarta;
bræðr hennar　þér til bana ráða,
ok at engu verðr　ynði síðan
vitru vífi;　veldr því Grímhildr."

Grípir kvað:　52
"Því skal hugga þik,　hers oddviti,
sú mun gift lagið　á grams ævi:
Mun-at mætri maðr　á mold koma
und sólar sjöt,　en þú, Sigurðr, þykkir."

Sigurðr kvað:　53
"Skiljumk heilir,　mun-at sköpum vinna.
Nú hefir þú, Grípir, vel　gört sem ek beiddak.
Fljótt myndir þú　fríðri segja
mína ævi,　ef þú mættir þat."

Gripir spake: 47
"To Gunnar soon his bride will say
That ill didst thou thine oath fulfill,
When the goodly king, the son of Gjuki,
With all his heart the hero trusted."

Sigurth spake: 48
"What sayst thou, Gripir? give me the truth!
Am I guilty so as now is said,
Or lies does the far-famed queen put forth
Of me and herself? Yet further speak."

Gripir spake: 49
"In wrath and grief full little good
The noble bride shall work thee now;
No shame thou gavest the goodly one,
Though the monarch's wife with wiles didst cheat."

Sigurth spake: 50
"Shall Gunnar the wise to the woman's words,
And Gotthorm and Hogni, then give heed?
Shall Gjuki's sons, now tell me, Gripir,
Redden their blades with their kinsman's blood?"

Gripir spake: 51
"Heavy it lies on Guthrun's heart,
When her brothers all shall bring thee death;
Never again shall she happiness know,
The woman so fair; 'tis Grimhild's work."

Sigurth spake: 52
"Now fare thee well! our fates we shun not;
And well has Gripir answered my wish;
More of joy to me wouldst tell
Of my life to come if so thou couldst."

Gripir spake: 53
"Ever remember, ruler of men,
That fortune lies in the hero's life;
A nobler man shall never live
Beneath the sun than Sigurth shall seem."

ENDNOTES

Prose. The manuscript gives the poem no title. *Gripir*: this uncle of Sigurth's was probably a pure invention of the poet's. The *Volsungasaga* mentions him, but presumably only because of his appearance here. On *Eylimi* and *Hjordis* see *Fra Dautha Sinfjotla* note. *Geitir*, the serving-man, is likewise apparently an invention of the poet's.

1. The manuscript does not indicate the speakers anywhere in the poem. Some editors have made separate stanzas out of the two-line speeches in stanzas 1, 3 and 6.

3. *Sigurth*: a few editions use in the verse the older form of this name, "Sigvorth," though the manuscript here keeps to the form used in this translation. The Old High German "Sigifrid" ("Peace-Bringer through Victory") became the Norse "Sigvorth" ("Victory-Guarder"), this, in turn, becoming "Sigurth."

4. Bugge thinks a stanza has been lost after stanza 4, in which Geitir tells Gripir who Sigurth is.

5. *Grani*. Sigurth's horse. According to the *Volsungasaga* his father was Sleipnir, Odin's eight-legged horse, and Odin himself gave him to Sigurth. The introductory note to the *Reginsmol* [Appendix B] tells a different story.

9. *Thy father*: on the death of Sigmund and Eylimi at the hands of *Hunding's sons* see *Fra Dautha Sinfjotla* and note.

11. *The dragon*: *Fafnir*, brother of the dwarf Regin, who turns himself into a dragon to guard Andvari's hoard; cf. *Reginsmol* and *Fafnismol*.

Gnitaheith: a relic of the German tradition; it has been identified as lying south of Paderborn.

13. *Gjuki*: the Norse form of the name Gibeche ("The Giver"). Gjuki is the father of Gunnar, Hogni, and Guthrun, the family which reflects most directly the Burgundian part of the tradition (cf. Introductory Note [Appendix B]). The statement that Sigurth is to go direct from the slaying of Fafnir to Gjuki's hall involves one of the confusions resulting from the dual personality of Brynhild. In the older (and the original South Germanic) story, Sigurth becomes a guest of the Gjukungs before he has ever heard of Brynhild, and first sees her when, having changed forms with Gunnar, he goes to woo her for the latter. In another version he finds Brynhild before he visits the Gjukungs, only to forget her as the result of the magic draught administered by Guthrun's mother. Both these versions are represented in the poems of which the author of the *Gripisspo* made use, and he tried, rather clumsily, to combine them, by having Sigurth go to Gjuki's house, then find the unnamed Valkyrie, and then return to Gjuki, the false wooing following this second visit.

15. Basing his story on the *Sigrdrifumol*, the poet here tells of Sigurth's finding of the Valkyrie, whom he does not identify with Brynhild, daughter of Buthli (stanza 27), at all. His error in this respect is not surprising, in view of Brynhild's dual identity (cf. Introductory Note [Appendix B], and *Fafnismol*, 44 and note). *Helgi*: according to *Helreith Brynhildar* (stanza 8), with which the author of the *Gripisspo* was almost certainly familiar, the hero for whose death Brynhild was punished was named Hjalmgunnar. Is Helgi here identical with Hjalmgunnar, or did the author make a mistake? Finnur Jonsson thinks the author regarded Sigurth's Valkyrie as a fourth incarnation of Svava-Sigrun-Kara, and wrote Helgi's name in deliberately. Many editors, following Bugge, have tried to reconstruct line 2 so as to get rid of Helgi's name.

19. *Heimir*: the *Volsungasaga* says that Heimir was the husband of Brynhild's sister, Bekkhild. Brynhild's family connections involve a queer mixture of northern and southern legend. Heimir and Bekkhild are purely of northern invention; neither of them is mentioned in any of the earlier poems, though Brynhild speaks of her "foster-father" in *Helreith Brynhildar*. In the older Norse poems Brynhild is a sister of Atli (Attila), a relationship wholly foreign to the southern stories, and the father of this strangely assorted pair is Buthli, who in the *Nibelungenlied* is apparently Etzel's grandfather. Add to this her role of Valkyrie, and it is small wonder that the annotator himself was puzzled.

27. *Brynhild* ("Armed Warrior"): on her and her family see introductory

note [Appendix B] and note to stanza 19.

33. Most editions have no comma after line 3, and change the meaning to "Fain of thee the fair-haired one / For her daughter is." *Grimhild*: in the northern form of the story Kriemhild, Gunther's sister and Siegfried's wife, becomes Grimhild, mother of Gunnar and Guthrun, the latter taking Kriemhild's place. The *Volsungasaga* tells how Grimhild gave Sigurth a magic draught which made him utterly forget Brynhild. Edzardi thinks two stanzas have been lost after stanza 33, their remains appearing in stanza 37.

35. In the *Volsungasaga* Grimhild merely advises Gunnar to seek Brynhild for his wife, and to have Sigurth ride with him. *Goths*: the historical Gunnar (Gundicarius, cf. Introductory Note [Appendix B]) was not a Goth, but a Burgundian, but the word "Goth" was applied in the North without much discrimination to the southern Germanic peoples.

REGINSMOL
THE BALLAD OF REGIN

INTRODUCTION

The *Reginsmol* is the first true poem of the *Sigurth Lays* and is found within the *Codex Regius* immediately before the *Gripisspo*. It is quoted within both the *Volsungasaga* and the *Nornageststhattr*, thus predating either of these two, and making it one of the earlier of the *Sigurth Lays* of which we have actual textual examples. It is also often referred to as the *The First Lay of Sigurth Fafnisbane* in reference to the fact that the *Codex Regius* copy has the faint words, generally agreed to read "Of Sigurth", at the top of its heading.

That the *Gripisspo* is a much younger inserted work within the tradition is further attested by the agreement of many scholars old and new that the end of the preceding work *Fra Dautha Sinfjotla* as well as *Reginsmol* and the following works of *Fafnismol* and *Sigrdrifumol* all appear to be a largely coterminous and singular work that tie into each other, and may not have even been intended as separate poems to begin with by the original authors.

This poem is notable for the personage and sayings of Hnikar, as he comes to be called, but who is quite obviously Odin if one but understands the meaning of his own introduction. Some scholars have questioned whether the lines of advice given by "Hnikar" in the ballad are meant to be taken from a better-known source of poetic wisdom, perhaps something akin to the *Hovamol*, and indeed many of them do seem to fit that mold.[1] We can say that speculation on this matter is unwarranted

---

1 These, along with wisdom literature from other Norse sources, have been collected in the Imperium Press edition of *Havamal* in the *Studies in Reaction* series.

without further evidence, and note that the style and manner of his advice is possibly meant to remind the audience of Odin and thus lead them to the natural conclusion about Hnikar's actual identity, rather than being something lifted deliberately from another well-known source.

We disagree here with Bellows' introduction, in which he speculates that the advice section and the resulting tale of Sigurth's triumph might be lifted from somewhere else, with the latter perhaps stemming from one of the tales of Helgi Hundingsbane. There is simply no evidence for this beyond a desire to collapse the separate traditions into mutually exclusive ones and a rejection of the connection between the *Helgi Lays*. Furthermore, the previous narration from Regin referring to Sigurth as Sigmund's son and Yngvi's heir can only be ascribed to Regin himself and not any other figure from the poems of Helgi Hundingsbane, given the description of him fostering the child and the use of the first person in contradistinction to the third person narrative of the Helgi Hundingsbane poem.

Sigurðr gekk til stóðs Hjálpreks ok kaus sér af hest einn, er Grani var kallaðr síðan. Þá var kominn Reginn til Hjálpreks, sonr Hreiðmars. Hann var hverjum manni hagari ok dvergr of vöxt. Hann var vitr, grimmr ok fjölkunnigr. Reginn veitti Sigurði fóstr ok kennslu ok elskaði hann mjök. Hann sagði Sigurði frá forellri sínu ok þeim atburðum, at Óðinn ok Hænir ok Loki höfðu komit til Andvarafors. Í þeim forsi var fjölði fiska. Einn dvergr hét Andvari. Hann var löngum í forsinum í geddu líki ok fekk sér þar matar. "Otr hét bróðir várr," kvað Reginn, " er oft fór í forsinn í otrs líki. Hann hafði tekit einn lax ok sat á árbakkanum ok át blundandi. Loki laust hann með steini til bana. Þóttust æsir mjök heppnir verit hafa ok flógu belg af otrinum. Þat sama kveld sóttu þeir gisting til Hreiðmars ok sýndu veiði sína. Þá tókum vér þá höndum ok lögðum þeim fjörlausn at fylla otrbelginn með gulli ok hylja útan með rauðu gulli. Þá sendu þeir Loka at afla gullsins. Hann kom til Ránar ok fekk net hennar ok fór þá til Andvarafors ok kastaði netinu fyrir gedduna, en hon hljóp í netit. Þá mælti Loki:

"Hvat er þat fiska,   er renn flóði í,   1
kann-at sér við víti varask?   Höfuð þitt
leystu helju ór,   finn mér lindar loga."

REGINSMOL

Sigurth went to Hjalprek's stud and chose for himself a horse, who thereafter was called Grani. At that time Regin, the son of Hreithmar, was come to Hjalprek's home; he was more ingenious than all other men, and a dwarf in stature; he was wise, fierce and skilled in magic. Regin undertook Sigurth's bringing up and teaching, and loved him much. He told Sigurth of his forefathers, and also of this: that once Odin and Hönir and Loki had come to Andvari's waterfall, and in the fall were many fish. Andvari was a dwarf, who had dwelt long in the waterfall in the shape of a pike, and there he got his food. "Otr was the name of a brother of ours," said Regin, "who often went into the fall in the shape of an otter; he had caught a salmon, and sat on the high bank eating it with his eyes shut. Loki threw a stone at him and killed him; the gods thought they had had great good luck, and stripped the skin off the otter. That same evening they sought a night's lodging at Hreithmar's house, and showed their booty. Then we seized them, and told them, as ransom for their lives, to fill the otter skin with gold, and completely cover it outside as well with red gold. Then they sent Loki to get the gold; he went to Ron and got her net, and went then to Andvari's fall and cast the net in front of the pike, and the pike leaped into the net." Then Loki said:

"What is the fish that runs in the flood, | 1
And itself from ill cannot save?
If thy head thou wouldst from hell redeem,
Find me the water's flame."

Geddan kvað: 2
"Andvari ek heiti, Óinn hét minn faðir,
margan hef ek fors of farit; aumlig norn
skóp oss í árdaga, at ek skylda í vatni vaða."

Loki kvað: 3
"Segðu þat, Andvari, ef þú eiga vill
líf í lýða sölum, hver gjöld fáa
gumna synir, ef þeir höggvask orðum á?"

Andvari kvað: 4
"Ofrgjöld fáa gumna synir,
þeir er Vaðgelmi vaða; ósaðra orða,
hverr er á annan lýgr, oflengi leiða limar."

Loki sá allt gull þat, er Andvari átti. En er hann hafði framreitt gullit, þá hafði hann eftir einn hring, ok tók Loki þann af hánum. Dvergrinn gekk inn í steininn ok mælti:

"Þat skal gull, er Gustr átti, 5
bræðrum tveim at bana verða
ok öðlingum átta at rógi;
mun míns féar manngi njóta."

Æsir reiddu Hreiðmari féit ok tráðu upp otrbelginn ok reistu á fætr. Þá skyldu æsirnir hlaða upp gullinu ok hylja. En er þat var gört, gekk Hreiðmarr fram ok sá eitt granahár ok bað hylja. Þá dró Óðinn fram hringinn Andvaranaut ok huldi hárit. Loki kvað:

"Gull er þér nú reitt, en þú gjöld hefir 6
mikil míns höfuðs; syni þínum
verðr-a sæla sköpuð; þat verðr ykkarr beggja bani."

Andvari spake: 2
"Andvari am I, and Oin my father,
In many a fall have I fared;
An evil Norn in olden days
Doomed me in waters to dwell."

Loki spake: 3
"Andvari, say, if thou seekest still
To live in the land of men,
What payment is set for the sons of men
Who war with lying words?"

Andvari spake: 4
"A mighty payment the men must make
Who in Valthgelmir's waters wade;
On a long road lead the lying words
That one to another utters."

Loki saw all the gold that Andvari had. But when he had brought forth all the gold, he held back one ring, and Loki took this from him. The dwarf went into his rocky hole and said:

"Now shall the gold that Gust once had 5
Bring their death to brothers twain,
And evil be for heroes eight;
joy of my wealth shall no man win."

The gods gave Hreithmar the gold, and filled up the otter-skin, and stood it on its feet. Then the gods had to heap up gold and hide it. And when that was done, Hreithmar came forward and saw a single whisker, and bade them cover it. Then Odin brought out the ring Andvaranaut and covered the hair.

Then Loki said: 6
"The gold is given, and great the price
Thou hast my head to save;
But fortune thy sons shall find not there,
The bane of ye both it is."

Hreiðmarr sagði: 7
"Gjafar þú gaft,   gaft-at-tu ástgjafar,
gaft-at-tu af heilum hug;   fjörvi yðru
skylduð ér firrðir vera,   ef ek vissa ek þat fár fyrir."

Loki kvað: 8
"Enn er verra   þat vita þykkjumk
niðja stríð of neppt;   jöfra óborna
hygg ek þá enn vera   er þat er til hatrs hugat."

Hreiðmarr kvað: 9
"Rauðu gulli   hygg ek mik ráða munu,
svá lengi sem ek lifi;   hót þín
hræðumk ekki lyf,   of haldið heim heðan."

Fáfnir ok Reginn kröfðu Hreiðmarr niðgjalda eftir Otr bróður sinn. Hann kvað nei við. En Fáfnir lagði sverði Hreiðmar, föður sinn, sofanda. Hreiðmarr kallaði á dætr sínar:

"Lyngheiðr ok Lofnheiðr,   vitið mínu lífi farit, 10
mart er þat, er þörf þéar.
Lyngheiðr sagði:
"Fá mun systir,   þótt föður missi,
hefna hlýra harms."

Hreiðmarr kvað: 11
"Al þú þó dóttur,   dís ulfhuguð,
ef þú getr-at son   við siklingi;
fá mey mann   í meginþarfar;
þá mun þeirar sonr   þíns harms reka."

Þá dó Hreiðmarr, en Fáfnir tók gullit allt. Þá beiddist Reginn at hafa föðurarf sinn, en Fáfnir galt þar nei við. Þá leitaði Reginn ráða við Lyngheiði, systur sína, hvernig hann skyldi heimta föðurarf sinn. Hon kvað:

Hreithmar spake: 7
"Gifts ye gave, but ye gave not kindly,
Gave not with hearts that were whole;
Your lives ere this should ye all have lost,
If sooner this fate I had seen."

Loki spake: 8
"Worse is this that methinks I see,
For a maid shall kinsmen clash;
Heroes unborn thereby shall be,
I deem, to hatred doomed."

Hreithmar spake: 9
"The gold so red shall I rule, methinks,
So long as I shall live;
Nought of fear for thy threats I feel,
So get ye hence to your homes."

Fafnir and Regin asked Hreithmar for a share of the wealth that was paid for the slaying of their brother, Otr. This he refused, and Fafnir thrust his sword through the body of his father, Hreithmar, while he was sleeping. Hreithmar called to his daughters:

"Lyngheith and Lofnheith, fled is my life, 10
And mighty now is my need!"

Lyngheith spake:
"Though a sister loses her father, seldom
Revenge on her brother she brings."

Hreithmar spake: 11
"A daughter, woman with wolf's heart, bear,
If thou hast no son with the hero brave;
If one weds the maid, for the need is mighty,
Their son for thy hurt may vengeance seek."

Then Hreithmar died, and Fafnir took all the gold. Thereupon Regin asked to have his inheritance from his father, but Fafnir refused this. Then Regin asked counsel of Lyngheith, his sister, how he should win his inheritance. She said:

"Bróður kveðja   skaltu blíðliga 12
arfs ok æðra hugar;   er-a þat hæft,
at þú hjörvi skylir   kveðju Fáfni féar."

Þessa hluti sagði Reginn Sigurði. Einn dag, er hann kom til húsa Regins, var hánum vel fagnat. Reginn kvað:

"Kominn er hingat   konr Sigmundar, 13
seggr inn snarráði,   til sala várra,
móð hefir meira   en maðr gamall,
ok er mér fangs ván   at frekum ulfi.

Ek mun fæða   folkdjarfan gram; 14
nú er Yngva konr   með oss kominn;
sjá mun ræsir   ríkstr und sólu;
þrymr um öll lönd   örlögsímu."

Sigurðr var þá jafnan með Regin, ok sagði hann Sigurði, at Fáfnir lá á Gnitaheiði ok var í orms líki. Hann átti ægishjalm, er öll kvikendi hræddust við. Reginn gerði Sigurði sverð, er Gramr hét. Þat var svá hvasst, at hann brá því ofan í Rín ok lét reka ullarlagð fyrir straumi ok tók í sundr lagðinn sem vatnit. Því sverði klauf Sigurðr í sundr steðja Regins. Eftir þat eggjaði Reginn Sigurð at vega Fáfni. Hann sagði:

"Hátt munu hlæja   Hundings synir, 15
þeir er Eylima   aldrs synjuðu,
ef meir tyggja   munar at sækja
hringa rauða   en hefnd föður."

Hjálprekr konungr fekk Sigurði skipalið til föðurhefnda. Þeir fengu storm mikinn ok beittu fyrir bergsnös nökkura. Maðr einn stóð á berginu ok kvað:

"In friendly wise the wealth shalt thou ask | 12
Of thy brother, and better will;
Not seemly is it to seek with the sword
Fafnir's treasure to take."

All these happenings did Regin tell to Sigurth.
    One day, when he came to Regin's house, he was gladly welcomed. Regin said:

"Hither the son of Sigmund is come, | 13
The hero eager, here to our hall;
His courage is more than an ancient man's,
And battle I hope from the hardy wolf."

"Here shall I foster the fearless prince, | 14
Now Yngvi's heir to us is come;
The noblest hero beneath the sun,
The threads of his fate all lands enfold."

Sigurth was there continually with Regin, who said to Sigurth that Fafnir lay at Gnitaheith, and was in the shape of a dragon. He had a fear-helm, of which all living creatures were terrified. Regin made Sigurth the sword which was called Gram; it was so sharp that when he thrust it down into the Rhine, and let a strand of wool drift against it with the stream, it cleft the strand asunder as if it were water. With this sword Sigurth cleft asunder Regin's anvil. After that Regin egged Sigurth on to slay Fafnir, but he said:

"Loud will the sons of Hunding laugh, | 15
Who low did Eylimi lay in death,
If the hero sooner seeks the red
Rings to find than his father's vengeance."

King Hjalprek gave Sigurth a fleet for the avenging of his father. They ran into a great storm, and were off a certain headland. A man stood on the mountain, and said:

"Hverir ríða þar   Ræfils hestum   16
hávar unnir,   haf glymjanda?
Seglvigg eru   sveita stokkin,
mun-at vágmarar   vind of standask."

Reginn svaraði: 17
"Hér ro vér Sigurðr   á sætréum;
er oss byrr gefinn   við bana sjalfan;
fellr brattr breki   bröndum hæri,
hlunnvigg hrapa.   Hverr spyrr at því?"

Maðr kvað: 18
"Hnikar hétu mik,   þá er hugin gladdak
Völsungr ungi,   ok vegit hafðak;
nú máttu kalla   karl af bergi
Fengi eða Fjölni;   far vil ek þiggja."

Þeir viku at landi, ok gekk karl á skip, ok lægði þá veðrit. Sigurðr kvað:

"Segðu mér þat, Hnikarr,   alls þá hvárttveggja veizt   19
goða heill ok guma: hver bözt eru,
ef berjask skal,   heill at sverða svipun."

Hnikarr kvað: 20
"Mörg eru góð,   ef gumar vissi,
heill at sverða svipun;   dyggva fylgju
hygg ek ins dökkva vera   hrottameiði hrafns.

Hnikarr kvað: 21
Þat er annat,   ef þú ert út of kominn
ok ert á braut búinn,   tvá þú lítr
á tái standa   hróðrfúsa hali.

Þat er it þriðja,   ef þú þjóta heyrir   22
ulf und asklimum;   heilla auðit
verðr þér af hjalmstöfum,   ef þú sér þá fyrri fara.

Engr skal gumna   í gögn vega   23
síð skínandi   systur Mána;
þeir sigr hafa,   er séa kunnu,
hjörleiks hvatir,   eða hamalt fylkja.

"Who yonder rides on Rævil's steeds, 16
O'er towering waves and waters wild?
The sail-horses all with sweat are dripping,
Nor can the sea-steeds the gale withstand."

Regin answered: 17
"On the sea-trees here are Sigurth and I,
The storm wind drives us on to our death;
The waves crash down on the forward deck,
And the roller-steeds sink; who seeks our names?"

The Man spake: 18
"Hnikar I was when Volsung once
Gladdened the ravens and battle gave;
Call me the Man from the Mountain now,
Feng or Fjolnir; with you will I fare."

They sailed to the land, and the man went on board the ship, and the storm subsided. Sigurth spake:

"Hnikar, say, for thou seest the fate 19
That to gods and men is given;
What sign is fairest for him who fights,
And best for the swinging of swords?"

Hnikar spake: 20
"Many the signs, if men but knew,
That are good for the swinging of swords;
It is well, methinks, if the warrior meets
A raven black on his road."

"Another it is if out thou art come, 21
And art ready forth to fare,
To behold on the path before thy house
Two fighters greedy of fame."

"Third it is well if a howling wolf 22
Thou hearest under the ash;
And fortune comes if thy foe thou seest
Ere thee the hero beholds."

"A man shall fight not when he must face 23
The moon's bright sister setting late;
Win he shall who well can see,
And wedge-like forms his men for the fray."

Þat er fár mikit, ef þú fæti drepr, 24
þars þú at vígi veðr; tálar dísir
standa þér á tvær hliðar ok vilja þik sáran sjá.

Kembðr ok þveginn skal kænna hverr 25
ok at morgni mettr, því at ósýnt er,
hvar at aftni kemr; illt er fyr heill at hrapa."

Sigurðr átti orrostu mikla við Lyngva Hundingsson ok bræðr hans. Þar fell Lyngvi ok þeir þrír bræðr. Eftir orrostu kvað Reginn:

"Nú er blóðugr örn bitrum hjörvi 26
bana Sigmundar á baki ristinn;
engr var fremri, sá er fold ryði,
hilmis arfi, ok hugin gladdi."

Heim fór Sigurðr til Hjálpreks. Þá eggjaði Reginn Sigurð til at vega Fáfni.

"Foul is the sign if thy foot shall stumble 24
As thou goest forth to fight;
Goddesses baneful at both thy sides
Will that wounds thou shalt get."

"Combed and washed shall the wise man go, 25
And a meal at morn shall take;
For unknown it is where at eve he may be;
It is ill thy luck to lose."

Sigurth had a great battle with Lyngvi, the son of Hunding, and his brothers; there Lyngvi fell, and his two brothers with him. After the battle Regin said:

"Now the bloody eagle with biting sword 26
Is carved on the back of Sigmund's killer;
Few were more fierce in fight than his son,
Who reddened the earth and gladdened the ravens."

Sigurth went home to Hjalprek's house; thereupon Regin egged him on to fight with Fafnir.

ENDNOTES

Prose. Hjalprek: father of Alf, Sigurth's step-father; cf. *Fra Dautha Sinfjotla*, and note. *Grani*: cf. *Gripisspo*, 5 and note. *Regin* ("Counsel-Giver"): undoubtedly he goes back to the smith of the German story; in the *Thithrekssaga* version he is called Mimir, while Regin is there the name of the dragon (here Regin's brother, Fafnir). The *Voluspo* (stanza 12) names a Regin among the dwarfs, and the name may have assisted in making Regin a dwarf here. *Hreithmar*: nothing is known of him outside of this story. *Andvari's fall*: according to Snorri, who tells this entire story in the *Skaldskaparmal*, Andvari's fall was in the world of the dark elves, while the one when Loki killed the otter was not; here, however, the two are considered identical. *With his eyes shut*: according to Snorri, Otr ate with his eyes shut because he was so greedy that he could not bear to see the food before him diminishing. *Ron*: wife of the sea-god Ægir, who draws down drowning men with her net; cf. *Helgakvitha Hjorvarthssonar*, 18 and note. Snorri says that Loki caught the pike with his hands.

1. Snorri quotes this stanza. *Water's game*: gold, so called because Ægir, the sea-god, was wont to light his hall with gold.

2. Snorri quotes this stanza. The name of the speaker is not given in the manuscripts. *Oin*: nothing further is known of Andvari's father. *Norn*: cf. *Voluspo*, 20.

3. Stanzas 3–4 may well be fragments of some other poem. Certainly Loki's question does not fit the situation, and the passage looks like an extract from some such poem as *Vafthruthnismol*. In *Regius* the phrase "Loki spake" stands in the middle of line 1.

4. The manuscript does not name the speaker. *Vathgelmir* ("Raging to

Wade"): a river not elsewhere mentioned, but cf. *Voluspo*, 39.

Prose. Snorri says Andvari's ring had the power to create new gold. In this it resembled Odin's ring, Draupnir; cf. *Skirnismol*, 21 and note.

5. This stanza apparently comes from a different source from stanzas 1–4 (or 1–2 if 3–4 are interpolated) and 6–10; cf. Introductory Note [Appendix B]. In the *Volsungasaga* Andvari lays his curse particularly on the ring. *Gust*: possibly a name for Andvari himself, or for an earlier possessor of the treasure. *Brothers twain*: Fafnir and Regin. *Heroes eight*: the word "eight" may easily have been substituted for something like "all" to make the stanza fit the case; the "eight" in question are presumably Sigurth, Gotthorm, Gunnar, Hogni, Atli, Erp, Sorli and Hamther, all of whom are slain in the course of the story. But the stanza may originally not have referred to Andvari's treasure at all.

Prose. Andvaranaut: "Andvari's Gem."

6. Snorri quotes this stanza, introducing it, as here, with "Then Loki said" in the prose. *Regius* omits this phrase, but inserts "said Loki" in line 1.

8. The word translated "maid" in line 2 is obscure, and "gold" may be meant. Apparently, however, the reference is to the fight between Sigurth and the sons of Gjuki over Brynhild. The manuscript does not name the speaker, and many editions assign this stanza to Hreithmar.

9. The manuscript includes "said Hreithmar" (abbreviated) in the middle of line 1, and some editors have followed this.

10. Hreithmar's daughters do not appear elsewhere. It has been suggested that originally stanza 10 was followed by one in which Lofnheith lamented her inability to avenge her father, as she was married and had no son.

11. Apparently an interpolation (cf. Introductory Note [Appendix B]). Vigfusson tries to reconstruct lines 2 and 4 to fit the Ljothahattr rhythm, but without much success. Hreithmar urges his daughter, as she has no sons, to bear a daughter who, in turn, will have a son to avenge his great-grandfather. Grundtvig worked out an ingenious theory to fit this stanza, making Sigurth's grand-father, Eylimi, the husband of Lyngheith's daughter, but there is absolutely no evidence to support this. The stanza may have nothing to do with Hreithmar.

13. This and the following stanza may be out of place here, really belonging, together with their introductory prose sentence, in the opening prose passage, following the first sentence describing Regin. Certainly they seem

to relate to Regin's first meeting with Sigurth. Stanzas 13–26, interspersed with prose, are quoted in the *Nornageststhattr*. Stanzas 13–18 may be the remnants of a lost poem belonging to the Helgi cycle (cf. Introductory Note [Appendix B]). *Hardy wolf*: warrior, i. e., Sigurth.

14. *Yngvi's heir*: Yngvi was one of the sons of the Danish king Halfdan the Old, and traditionally an ancestor of Helgi (cf. *Helgakvitha Hundingsbana I*, 57 and note). Calling Sigurth a descendant of Yngvi is, of course, absurd, and the use of this phrase is one of the many reasons for believing that stanzas 13–18 belonged originally to the Helgi cycle. *The threads*, etc.: another link with Helgi; cf. *Helgakvitha Hundingsbana I*, 3–4. As Helgi was likewise regarded as a son of Sigmund, stanzas 13–14 would fit him just as well as Sigurth.

Prose. *Gnitaheith*: cf. *Gripisspo*, 11 and note. *Fear-helm*: [the *Ægishjálmr* or the Helm of Awe, not to be confused with the later hermetic symbol used in syncretic late Icelandic witchcraft.] *Gram*: according to the *Volsungasaga* Regin forged this sword from the fragments of the sword given by Odin to Sigmund (cf. *Fra Dautha Sinfjotla* and note).

15. Regarding the *sons of Hunding* and *Eylimi*, father of Sigurth's mother, all of whom belong to the Helgi-tradition, cf. *Fra Dautha Sinfjotla* and note.

Prose. The fleet, and the subsequent storm, are also reminiscent of the Helgi cycle; cf. *Helgakvitha Hundingsbana I*, 29–31, and *II*, prose after stanza 16. *A man*: Odin.

16. *Rævil's steeds* (Rævil was a sea-king, possibly the grandson of Ragnar Lothbrok mentioned in the *Hervararsaga*), sail-horses and sea-steeds all mean "ships."

17. *Sea-trees* and *roller-steeds* (the latter because ships were pulled up on shore by means of rollers) both mean "ships."

18. The *Volsungasaga* quotes this stanza. *Hnikar* and *Fjolnir*: Odin gives himself both these names in *Grimnismol*, 47; *Feng* ("The Seizer") does not appear elsewhere. According to the *Volsungasaga*, no one knew Odin's name when he came to Volsung's house and left the sword there for Sigmund.

19. This and the following stanzas are strongly suggestive of the *Hovamol*, and probably came originally from some such collection.

23. This stanza is clearly an interpolation, drawn in by the common-sense

advice, as distinct from omens, given in the last lines of stanza 22. *Moon's sister*: the sun; cf. *Vafthruthnismol*, 23 and note. *Wedge-like*: the wedge formation (prescribed anew in 1920 for the United States Army under certain circumstances) was said to have been invented by Odin himself, and taught by him only to the most favored warriors.

24. *Goddesses*: Norse mythology included an almost limitless number of minor deities, the female ones, both kind and unkind, being generally classed among the lesser Norns.

25. This stanza almost certainly had nothing originally to do with the others in this passage; it may have been taken from a longer version of the *Hovamol* itself.

Prose. Lyngvi: the son of Hunding who killed Sigmund in jealousy of his marriage with Hjordis; cf. *Fra Dautha Sinfjotla* and note. The *Volsungasaga* names one brother who was with Lyngvi in the battle, Hjorvarth, and Sigurth kills him as readily as if he had not already been killed long before by Helgi. But, as has been seen, it was nothing for a man to be killed in two or three different ways.

26. *Bloody eagle*, etc.: the *Nornageststhattr* describes the manner in which the captured Lyngvi was put to death. "Regin advised that they should carve the bloody eagle on his back. So Regin took his sword and cleft Lyngvi's back so that he severed his back from his ribs, and then drew out his lungs. So died Lyngvi with great courage."

Prose. In *Regius* there is no break of any kind between this prose passage and the prose introduction to the *Fafnismol* (cf. Introductory Note [Appendix B]).

FAFNISMOL
THE BALLAD OF FAFNIR

INTRODUCTION

The *Fafnismol* follows the *Reginsmol* and is also found wholly intact within the *Codex Regius* and is quoted many times by Snorri in his *Prose Edda*, and also by the court scribe and author of *Sverris Saga*, the saga of King Sveris of Norway who ruled between 1177–1202 and is thought to have directed the creation of his own saga in a semi-autobiographical account, starting sometime around 1185. While the *Volsungasaga* does not directly quote the *Fafnismol*, large sections of the work are broadly compatible with the events portrayed and likely reflect a similar, if not identical, literary or oral tradition.

Fafnismol follows on from the *Reginsmol* without a formal break or title, and its narrative is so compatible with it that many scholars have joined them together, denying that they were ever originally intended as a separate work at all. Further discussion of this can be found in the *Reginsmol* introduction.

The poem is notable for featuring both the dramatic act of Sigurth slaying the dragon by piercing his heart from below, but also because Sigurth appears to engage in a sort of wisdom game with Fafnir in his dying words. Sigurth and Fafnir banter back and forth, exchanging pithy sayings and advice, with Fafnir insulting Sigurth and Sigurth responding with claims of his nobility and might. Sigurth also is particularly given to sage advice reminiscent of the *Hovamol*, sometimes almost directly paraphrasing Odin himself in response to Fafnir's barbed words. Sigurth's responses of:

> Few are keen when old age comes,
> Who timid in boyhood be.
>
> Oft one finds, when the foe he meets,
> That he is not the bravest of all.
>
> Some one the hoard shall ever hold,
> Till the destined day shall come;
> For a time there is when every man
> Shall journey hence to hell.

are highly reminiscent of the *Hovamol* lines 16 and 64, in which Odin advises man to show courage and bravery and disparages those who think avoiding manly pursuits might allow them to live to old age, but also cautions against being overbearing in force and effect since one is sure to eventually meet one's match among other men. This almost perfect recitation of Odinic wisdom is probably meant to stem from Sigurth's previous association with "Hnikar", the man who is quite clearly Odin in disguise, and thus further confirms the likelihood that the two poems were not originally distinct.

The Rainbow Bridge
(H. Hendrich)

Sigurðr ok Reginn fóru upp á Gnitaheiði ok hittu þar slóð Fáfnis, þá er hann skreið til vatns. Þar gerði Sigurðr gröf mikla á veginum, ok gekk Sigurðr þar í. En er Fáfnir skreið af gullinu, blés hann eitri, ok hraut þat fyrir ofan höfuð Sigurði. En er Fáfnir skreið yfir gröfina, þá lagði Sigurðr hann með sverði til hjarta. Fáfnir hristi sik ok barði höfði ok sporði. Sigurðr hljóp ór gröfinni, ok sá þá hvárr annan. Fáfnir kvað:

"Sveinn ok sveinn,   hverjum ertu svein of borinn?   1
Hverra ertu manna mögr,   er þú á Fáfni rautt
þinn inn frána mæki?   Stöndumk til hjarta hjörr."

Sigurðr duldi nafn síns, fyrir því at þat var trúa þeira í forneskju, at orð feigs manns mætti mikit, ef hann bölvaði óvin sínum með nafni. Hann kvað:

"Göfugt dýr ek heiti,   en ek gengit hefk   2
inn móðurlausi mögr,   föður ek ákk-a
sem fira synir;   æ geng ek einn saman."

FAFNISMOL

Sigurth and Regin went up to the Gnitaheith, and found there the track that Fafnir made when he crawled to water. Then Sigurth made a great trench across the path, and took his place therein. When Fafnir crawled from his gold, he blew out venom, and it ran down from above on Sigurth's head. But when Fafnir crawled over the trench, then Sigurth thrust his sword into his body to the heart. Fafnir writhed and struck out with his head and tail. Sigurth leaped from the trench, and each looked at the other. Fafnir said:

"Youth, oh, youth! of whom then, youth, art thou born? 1
Say whose son thou art,
Who in Fafnir's blood thy bright blade reddened,
And struck thy sword to my heart."

Sigurth concealed his name because it was believed in olden times that the word of a dying man might have great power if he cursed his foe by his name. He said:

"The Noble Hart my name, and I go 2
A motherless man abroad;
Father I had not, as others have,
And lonely ever I live."

Fáfnir kvað: 3
"Veiztu, ef föður né átt-at   sem fira synir,
af hverju vastu undri alinn?"

Sigurðr kvað: 4
"Ætterni mitt   kveð ek þér ókunnigt vera
ok mik sjalfan it sama;   Sigurðr ek heiti,
Sigmundr hét minn faðir,   er hefk þik vápnum vegit."

Fáfnir kvað: 5
"Hverr þik hvatti?   Hví hvetjask lézt
mínu fjörvi at fara?   Inn fráneygi sveinn,
þú áttir föður bitran;   óbornum skjór á skeið."

Sigurðr kvað: 6
"Hugr mik hvatti,   hendr mér fulltýðu
ok minn inn hvassi hjörr;
fár er hvatr,   er hröðask tekr,
ef í barnæsku er blauðr."

Fáfnir kvað: 7
"Veit ek, ef þú vaxa næðir   fyr þinna vina brjósti,
sæi maðr þik vreiðan vega;
nú ertu haftr   ok hernuminn;
æ kveða bandingja bifask."

Sigurðr kvað: 8
"Því bregðr þú mér,   Fáfnir, at til fjarri séak
mínum feðrmunum;
eigi em ek haftr,   þótt ek væra hernumi;
þú fannt, at ek laus lifi."

Fáfnir kvað: 9
"Heiftyrði ein   telr þú þér í hvívetna,
en ek þér satt eitt segik: It gjalla gull
ok it glóðrauða fé,   þér verða þeir baugar at bana."

Fafnir spake: | 3
"If father thou hadst not, as others have,
By what wonder wast thou born?
Though thy name on the day of my death thou hidest,
Thou knowest now thou dost lie."

Sigurth spake: | 4
"My race, methinks, is unknown to thee,
And so am I myself;
Sigurth my name, and Sigmund's son,
Who smote thee thus with the sword."

Fafnir spake: | 5
"Who drove thee on? why wert thou driven
My life to make me lose?
A father brave had the bright-eyed youth,
For bold in boyhood thou art."

Sigurth spake: | 6
"My heart did drive me, my hand fulfilled,
And my shining sword so sharp;
Few are keen when old age comes,
Who timid in boyhood be."

Fafnir spake: | 7
"If thou mightest grow thy friends among,
One might see thee fiercely fight;
But bound thou art, and in battle taken,
And to fear are prisoners prone."

Sigurth spake: | 8
"Thou blamest me, Fafnir, that I see from afar
The wealth that my father's was;
Not bound am I, though in battle taken,
Thou hast found that free I live."

Fafnir spake: | 9
"In all I say dost thou hatred see,
Yet truth alone do I tell;
The sounding gold, the glow-red wealth,
And the rings thy bane shall be."

Sigurðr kvað: 10
"Féi ráða   vill fyrða hverr
æ til ins eina dags;
því at einu sinni   skal alda hverr
fara til heljar heðan."

Fáfnir kvað: 11
"Norna dóm   þú munt fyr nesjum hafa
ok ósvinns apa;
í vatni þú drukknar,   ef í vindi rær;
allt er feigs forað."

Sigurðr kvað: 12
"Segðu mér, Fáfnir,   alls þik fróðan kveða
ok vel margt vita,   hverjar ro þær nornir,
er nauðgönglar ro   ok kjósa mæðr frá mögum."

Fáfnir kvað: 13
"Sundrbornar mjök   segi ek nornir vera,
eigu-t þær ætt saman;
sumar eru áskunngar,   sumar alfkunngar,
sumar dætr Dvalins."

Sigurðr kvað: 14
"Segðu mér þat, Fáfnir,   alls þik fróðan kveða
ok vel margt vita,   hvé sá holmr heitir,
er blanda hjörlegi   Surtr ok æsir saman."

Fáfnir kvað: 15
"Óskópnir hann heitir,   en þar öll skulu
geirum leika goð;
Bilröst brotnar,   er þeir á brú fara,
ok svima í móðu marir."

Fáfnir kvað: 16
Ægishjalm   bar ek of alda sonum,
meðan ek of menjum lák;
einn rammari   hugðumk öllum vera,
fannk-a ek svá marga mögu."

Sigurðr kvað: 17
"Ægishjalmr   bergr einungi,
hvar skulu vreiðir vega;
þá þat finnr,   er með fleirum kemr,
at engi er einna hvatastr."

Sigurth spake: 10
"Some one the hoard shall ever hold,
Till the destined day shall come;
For a time there is when every man
Shall journey hence to hell."

Fafnir spake: 11
"The fate of the Norns before the headland
Thou findest, and doom of a fool;
In the water shalt drown if thou row 'gainst the wind,
All danger is near to death."

Sigurth spake: 12
"Tell me then, Fafnir, for wise thou art famed,
And much thou knowest now:
Who are the Norns who are helpful in need,
And the babe from the mother bring?"

Fafnir spake: 13
"Of many births the Norns must be,
Nor one in race they were;
Some to gods, others to elves are kin,
And Dvalin's daughters some."

Sigurth spake: 14
"Tell me then, Fafnir, for wise thou art famed,
And much thou knowest now:
How call they the isle where all the gods
And Surt shall sword-sweat mingle?"

Fafnir spake: 15
"Oskopnir is it, where all the gods
Shall seek the play of swords;
Bilrost breaks when they cross the bridge,
And the steeds shall swim in the flood."

"The fear-helm I wore to afright mankind, 16
While guarding my gold I lay;
Mightier seemed I than any man,
For a fiercer never I found."

Sigurth spake: 17
"The fear-helm surely no man shields
When he faces a valiant foe;
Oft one finds, when the foe he meets,
That he is not the bravest of all."

Fáfnir kvað: 18
"Eitri ek fnæsta,   er ek á arfi lá
miklum míns föður."
[...]

Sigurðr kvað: 19
"Inn fráni ormr,   þú gerðir fræs mikla
ok galzt harðan hug;
heift at meiri   verðr hölða sonum,
at þann hjalm hafi."

Fáfnir kvað: 20
"Ræð ek þér nú, Sigurðr,   en þú ráð nemir,
ok ríð heim heðan;
it gjalla gull   ok it glóðrauða fé,
þér verða þeir baugar at bana."

Sigurðr kvað: 21
"Ráð er þér ráðit,   en ek ríða mun
til þess gulls, er í lyngvi liggr,
en þú, Fáfnir,   ligg í fjörbrotum,
þar er þik hel hafi."

Fáfnir kvað: 22
"Reginn mik réð,   hann þik ráða mun,
hann mun okkr verða báðum at bana;
fjör sitt láta,   hygg ek, at Fáfnir myni;
þitt varð nú meira megin."

Reginn var á brott horfinn, meðan Sigurðr vá Fáfni, ok kom þá aftr, er Sigurðr strauk blóð af sverðinu. Reginn kvað:

"Heill þú nú, Sigurðr,   nú hefir þú sigr vegit 23
ok Fáfni of farit;
manna þeira,   er mold troða,
þik kveð ek óblauðastan alinn."

Fafnir spake: 18
"Venom I breathed when bright I lay
By the hoard my father had;
There was none so mighty as dared to meet me,
And weapons nor wiles I feared."

Sigurth spake: 19
"Glittering worm, thy hissing was great,
And hard didst show thy heart;
But hatred more have the sons of men
For him who owns the helm."

Fafnir spake: 20
"I counsel thee, Sigurth, heed my speech,
And ride thou homeward hence,
The sounding gold, the glow-red wealth,
And the rings thy bane shall be."

Sigurth spake: 21
"Thy counsel is given, but go I shall
To the gold in the heather hidden;
And, Fafnir, thou with death dost fight,
Lying where Hel shall have thee."

Fafnir spake: 22
"Regin betrayed me, and thee will betray,
Us both to death will he bring;
His life, methinks, must Fafnir lose,
For the mightier man wast thou."

Regin had gone to a distance while Sigurth fought Fafnir, and came back while Sigurth was wiping the blood from his sword. Regin said:

"Hail to thee, Sigurth! Thou victory hast,   23
And Fafnir in fight hast slain;
Of all the men who tread the earth,
Most fearless art thou, methinks."

Sigurðr kvað: 24
"Þat er óvíst at vita,   þá er komum allir saman,
sigtíva synir,   hverr óblauðastr er alinn;
margr er sá hvatr,   er hjör né rýðr
annars brjóstum í."

Reginn kvað: 25
"Glaðr ertu nú, Sigurðr,   ok gagni feginn,
er þú þerrir Gram á grasi;
bróður minn   hefr þú benjaðan,
ok vald ek þó sjalfr sumu."

Sigurðr kvað: 26
"Þú því rétt,   er ek ríða skyldak
hélug fjöll hinig;
féi ok fjörvi   réði sá inn fráni ormr,
nema þú frýðir mér hvats hugar."

Þá gekk Reginn at Fáfni ok skar hjarta ór hánum með sverði, er Riðill heitir, ok þá drakk hann blóð ór undinni eftir. Reginn kvað:

"Sittu nú, Sigurðr,   en ek mun sofa ganga, 27
ok halt Fáfnis hjarta við funa;
eisköld ek vil   etin láta
eftir þenna dreyra drykk."

Sigurðr kvað: 28
"Fjarri þú gekkt,   meðan ek á Fáfni rauðk
minn inn hvassa hjör;
afli mínu   atta ek við orms megin,
meðan þú í lyngvi látt."

Reginn kvað: 29
"Lengi liggja   létir þú lyngvi í
þann inn aldna jötun,   ef þú sverðs né nytir,
þess er ek sjalfr gerða,   ok þíns ins hvassa hjörs."

Sigurðr kvað: 30
"Hugr er betri   en sé hjörs megin,
hvars vreiðir skulu vega,
því at hvatan mann   ek sé harðliga vega
með slævu sverði sigr."

Sigurth spake: 24
"Unknown it is, when all are together,
The sons of the glorious gods,
Who bravest born shall seem;
Some are valiant who redden no sword
In the blood of a foeman's breast."

Regin spake: 25
"Glad art thou, Sigurth, of battle gained,
As Gram with grass thou cleansest;
My brother fierce in fight hast slain,
And somewhat I did myself."

Sigurth spake: 26
"Afar didst thou go while Fafnir reddened
With his blood my blade so keen;
With the might of the dragon my strength I matched,
While thou in the heather didst hide."

Regin spake: 27
"Longer wouldst thou in the heather have let
Yon hoary giant hide,
Had the weapon availed not that once I forged,
The keen-edged blade thou didst bear."

Sigurth spake: 28
"Better is heart than a mighty blade
For him who shall fiercely fight;
The brave man well shall fight and win,
Though dull his blade may be."

"Brave men better than cowards be, 29
When the clash of battle comes;
And better the glad than the gloomy man
Shall face what before him lies."

"Thy rede it was that I should ride 30
Hither o'er mountains high;
The glittering worm would have wealth and life
If thou hadst not mocked at my might."

Then Regin went up to Fafnir and cut out his heart with his sword, that was named Rithil, and then he drank blood from the wounds. Regin said:

Sigurðr kvað: 31
"Hvötum er betra   en sé óhvötum
í hildileik hafask;
glöðum er betra   en sé glúpnanda,
hvat sem at hendi kemr."

Sigurðr tók Fáfnis hjarta ok steikði á teini. Er hann hugði, at fullsteikt væri ok freyddi sveitinn ór hjartanu, þá tók hann á fingri sínum ok skynjaði, hvárt fullsteikt væri. Hann brann ok brá fingrinum í munn sér. En er hjartablóð Fáfnis kom á tungu hánum, ok skilði hann fugls rödd. Hann heyrði, at igður klökuðu á hrísinu. Igðan kvað:

"Þar sitr Sigurðr   sveita stokkinn, 32
Fáfnis hjarta   við funa steikir;
spakr þætti mér   spillir bauga,
ef hann fjörsega   fránan æti."

Önnur kvað: 33
"Þar liggr Reginn,   ræðr um við sik,
vill tæla mög,   þann er trúir hánum,
berr af reiði   röng orð saman,
vill bölvasmiðr   bróður hefna."

In þriðja kvað: 34
"Höfði skemmra   láti hann inn hára þul
fara til heljar heðan;
öllu gulli   þá kná hann einn ráða,
fjölð því er und Fáfni lá."

In fjórða kvað: 35
Horskr þætti mér,   ef hafa kynni
ástráð mikit   yðvar systra,
hygði hann of sik   ok hugin gleddi;
þar er mér ulfs ván,   er ek eyru sék."

In fimmta kvað: 36
"Er-at svá horskr   hildimeiðr
sem ek hers jaðar   hyggja myndak,
ef hann bróður lætr   á brot komask,
en hann öðrum hefir   aldrs of synjat."

"Sit now, Sigurth, for sleep will I, 31
Hold Fafnir's heart to the fire;
For all his heart shall eaten be,
Since deep of blood I have drunk."

Sigurth took Fafnir's heart and cooked it on a spit. When he thought that it was fully cooked, and the blood foamed out of the heart, then he tried it with his finger to see whether it was fully cooked. He burned his finger, and put it in his mouth. But when Fafnir's heart's-blood came on his tongue, he understood the speech of birds. He heard nut-hatches chattering in the thickets. A nut hatch said:

"There sits Sigurth, sprinkled with blood, 32
And Fafnir's heart with fire he cooks;
Wise were the breaker of rings, I ween,
To eat the life-muscles all so bright."

A second spake: 33
"There Regin lies, and plans he lays
The youth to betray who trusts him well;
Lying words with wiles will he speak,
Till his brother the maker of mischief avenges."

A third spake: 34
"Less by a head let the chatterer hoary
Go from here to hell;
Then all of the wealth he alone can wield,
The gold that Fafnir guarded."

A fourth spake: 35
"Wise would he seem if so he would heed
The counsel good we sisters give;
Thought he would give, and the ravens gladden,
There is ever a wolf where his ears I spy."

A fifth spake: 36
"Less wise must be the tree of battle
Than to me would seem the leader of men,
If forth he lets one brother fare,
When he of the other the slayer is."

In sétta kvað: 37
"Mjök er ósviðr, ef hann enn sparir
fjánda inn folkskáa, þar er Reginn liggr,
er hann ráðinn hefr, kann-at hann við slíku at séa."

In sjaunda kvað: 38
"Höfði skemmra láti hann   þann inn hrímkalda jötun
ok af baugum búa;
þá mun hann fjár þess,   er Fáfnir réð,
einvaldi vera."

Sigurðr kvað: 39
"Verða-t svá rík sköp,   at Reginn skyli
mitt banorð bera;
því at þeir báðir bræðr   skulu bráðliga
fara til heljar heðan."

Sigurðr hjó höfuð af Regin, ok þá át han Fáfnis hjarta ok drakk blóð þeira beggja, Regins ok Fáfnis. Þá heyrði Sigurðr, hvar igður mæltu:

"Bitt þú, Sigurðr,   bauga rauða; 40
er-a konungligt   kvíða mörgu.
Mey veit ek eina   miklu fegrsta,
gulli gædda,   ef þú geta mættir."

"Liggja til Gjúka   grænar brautir, 41
fram vísa sköp   folklíðöndum;
þar hefir dýrr konungr   dóttur alna;
þá muntu, Sigurðr,   mundi kaupa."

"Salr er á háu   Hindarfjalli, 42
allr er hann útan   eldi sveipinn,
þann hafa horskir   halir of görvan
ór ódökkum   Ógnar ljóma."

"Veit ek á fjalli   folkvitr sofa 43
ok leikr yfir   lindar váði;
Yggr stakk þorni,   aðra felldi
hör-Gefn hali   en hafa vildi."

A sixth spake: 37
"Most foolish he seems if he shall spare
His foe, the bane of the folk,
There Regin lies, who hath wronged him so,
Yet falsehood knows he not."

A seventh spake: 38
"Let the head from the frost-cold giant be hewed,
And let him of rings be robbed;
Then all the wealth which Fafnir's was
Shall belong to thee alone."

Sigurth spake: 39
"Not so rich a fate shall Regin have
As the tale of my death to tell;
For soon the brothers both shall die,
And hence to hell shall go."

Sigurth hewed off Regin's head, and then he ate Fafnir's heart, and drank the blood of both Regin and Fafnir. Then Sigurth heard what the nuthatch said:

"Bind, Sigurth, the golden rings together, 40
Not kingly is it aught to fear;
I know a maid, there is none so fair,
Rich in gold, if thou mightest get her."

"Green the paths that to Gjuki lead, 41
And his fate the way to the wanderer shows;
The doughty king a daughter has,
That thou as a bride mayst, Sigurth, buy."

Another spake: 42
"A hall stands high on Hindarfjoll,
All with flame is it ringed without;
Warriors wise did make it once
Out of the flaming light of the flood."

"On the mountain sleeps a battle-maid, 43
And about her plays the bane of the wood;
Ygg with the thorn hath smitten her thus,
For she felled the fighter he fain would save."

"Knáttu, mögr, séa   mey und hjalmi, 44
þá er frá vígi   Vingskorni reið;
má-at Sigrdrífar   svefni bregða
skjöldunga niðr   fyr sköpum norna."

Sigurðr reið eftir slóð Fáfnis til bælis hans ok fann þat opit ok hurðir af járni ok gætti. Af járni váru ok allir timbrstokkar í húsinu, en grafit í jörð niðr. Þar fann Sigurðr stórmikit gull ok fylldi þar tvær kistur. Þar tók hann ægishjálm ok gullbrynju ok sverðit Hrotta ok marga dýrgripi ok klyfjaði þar með Grana, en hestrinn vildi eigi fram ganga, fyrr en Sigurðr steig á bak hánum.

"There mayst thou behold the maiden helmed, 44
Who forth on Vingskornir rode from the fight;
The victory-bringer her sleep shall break not,
Thou heroes' son, so the Norns have set."

Sigurth rode along Fafnir's trail to his lair, and found it open. The gate-posts were of iron, and the gates; of iron, too, were all the beams in the house, which was dug down into the earth. There Sigurth found a mighty store of gold, and he filled two chests full thereof; he took the fear-helm and a golden mail-coat and the sword Hrotti, and many other precious things, and loaded Grani with them, but the horse would not go forward until Sigurth mounted on his back.

ENDNOTES

Prose. The prose follows the concluding prose passage of the *Reginsmol* without any interruption; the heading "Of Fafnir's Death" is written in the manuscript very faintly just before stanza 1. *Gnitaheith*: cf. *Gripisspo*, 11 and note. *Fafnir*: Regin's brother: cf. *Reginsmol*, prose after stanza 14. *Venom*: in the *Volsungasaga* it was the blood, and not the venom, that poured down on Sigurth's head. Sigurth was much worried about this danger, and before he dug the trench asked Regin what would happen if the dragon's blood overcame him. Regin thereupon taunted him with cowardice (Sigurth refers to this taunt in stanza 30, but the stanza embodying it has disappeared). After Sigurth had dug his trench, an old man (Odin, of course) appeared and advised him to dig other trenches to carry off the blood, which he did, thereby escaping harm.

1. The first line in the original, as here, is unusually long, but dramatically very effective on that account.

3. The names of the speakers do not appear in the manuscript, though they seem originally to have been indicated in the margin for stanzas 3–30. The last two lines of stanza 3 are missing in the manuscript, with no gap indicated, but the *Volsungasaga* prose paraphrase indicates that something was omitted, and the lines here given are conjecturally reconstructed from this paraphrase.

4. The manuscript marks line 3 as the beginning of a stanza.

5. Line 4, utterly obscure in the manuscript, is guesswork.

7. Fafnir here refers to the fact that Hjordis, mother of the still unborn Sigurth, was captured by Alf after Sigmund's death; cf. *Fra Dautha Sin-*

fjotla, note.

11. Stanzas 11–15 are probably interpolated, and come from a poem similar to *Vafthruthnismol*. *The headland*: Fafnir is apparently quoting proverbs; this one seems to mean that disaster ("the fate of the Norns") awaits when one rounds the first headland (i.e., at the beginning of life's voyage, in youth). The third line is a commentary on obstinate rashness. The *Volsungasaga* paraphrases stanzas 11–15 throughout.

12. *Norns*: cf. stanza 13 and note. Sigurth has no possible interest in knowing what Norns are helpful in childbirth, but interpolations were seldom logical.

13. Snorri quotes this stanza. There were minor Norns, or fates, in addition to the three great Norns, regarding whom cf. *Voluspo*, 20. *Dvalin*: chief of the dwarfs; cf. *Voluspo*, 14.

14. *Surt*: ruler of the fire world; the reference is to the last great battle. *Sword-sweat*: blood.

15. *Oskopnir* ("Not-Made"): apparently another name for Vigrith, which is named in *Vafthruthnismol*, 18, as the final battle-ground. *Bilrost* (or Bifrost): the rainbow bridge which breaks beneath Surt's followers; cf. *Grimnismol*, 29 and note.

16. With this stanza Fafnir returns to the situation. *Fear-helm*: regarding the "ægis-hjalmr" cf. *Reginsmol*, prose after stanza 14 and note.

18. Lines 3–4 do not appear in the manuscript and no gap is indicated; they are here conjecturally paraphrased from the prose passage in the *Volsungasaga*.

20. It has been suggested that this stanza is spurious, and that stanza 21 ought to follow stanza 22. Lines 3–4, abbreviated in the manuscript, are identical with lines 3–4 of stanza 9. The *Volsungasaga* paraphrase in place of these two lines makes Fafnir say: "For it often happens that he who gets a deadly wound yet avenges himself." It is quite likely that two stanzas have been lost.

22. The *Volsungasaga* places its paraphrase of this stanza between those of stanzas 15 and 16.

24. Line 2 is probably spurious, but it is a phrase typical of such poems as *Grimnismol* or *Vafthruthnismol*.

25. *Gram*: Sigurth's sword; cf. *Reginsmol*, prose after 14.

ENDNOTES 563

26. In the manuscript stanzas 26–29 stand after stanza 31, which fails to make clear sense; they are here rearranged in accordance with the *Volsungasaga* paraphrase.

28–29. Almost certainly interpolated from some such poem as the *Hovamol*. Even the faithful *Volsungasaga* fails to paraphrase stanza 29.

30. Something has evidently been lost before this stanza. Sigurth clearly refers to Regin's reproach when he was digging the trench (cf. note on introductory prose), but the poem does not give such a passage.

Prose. Rithil ("Swift-Moving"): Snorri calls the sword Refil ("Serpent").

32. That the birds' stanzas come from more than one source is fairly apparent, but whether from two or from three or more is uncertain. It is also far from clear how many birds are speaking. The manuscript numbers II, III, and IV in the margin with numerals; the *Volsungasaga* makes a different bird speak each time. There are almost as many guesses as there are editions. I suspect that in the original poem there was one bird, speaking stanzas 34 and 37. Stanza 38 is little more than a repetition of stanza 34, and may well have been a later addition. As for the stanzas in Fornyrthislag (32–33 and 35–36), they apparently come from another poem, in which several birds speak (cf. "we sisters" in stanza 35). This may be the same poem from which stanzas 40–44 were taken, as well as some of the Fornyrthislag stanzas in the *Sigrdrifumol*.

34. Some editions turn this speech from the third person into the second, but the manuscript is clear enough.

35. *Wolf*, etc.: the phrase is nearly equivalent to "there must be fire where there is smoke." The proverb appears elsewhere in Old Norse.

36. *Tree of battle*: warrior.

37. Here, as in stanza 34, some editions turn the speech from the third person into the second.

38. *Giant*: Regin was certainly not a frost-giant, and the whole stanza looks like some copyist's blundering reproduction of stanza 34.

40. Neither the manuscript nor any of the editions suggest the existence of more than one bird in stanzas 40–44. It seems to me, however, that there are not only two birds, but two distinct stories. Stanzas 40–41 apply solely to Guthrun, and suggest that Sigurth will go straight to Gunnar's hall. Stanzas 42–44, on the other hand, apply solely to Brynhild, and indicate that Sigurth will find her before he visits the Gjukungs. The confusion

which existed between these two versions of the story, and which involved a fundamental difference in the final working out of Brynhild's revenge, is commented on in the note on *Gripisspo*, 13. In the present passage it is possible that two birds are speaking, each reflecting one version of the story; it seems even more likely that one speech or the other (40–41 or 42–44) reflects the original form of the narrative, the other having been added, either later or from another poem. In the *Volsungasaga* the whole passage is condensed into a few words by one bird: "Wiser were it if he should then ride up on Hindarfjoll, where Brynhild sleeps, and there would he get much wisdom." The Guthrun-bird does not appear at all.

41. *Gjuki*: father of Gunnar and Guthrun: cf. *Gripisspo*, 13 and note.

42. *Hindarfjoll*: "Mountain of the Hind." *Light of the flood*: gold; cf. *Reginsmol*, 1 and note.

43. *Battle-maid*: Brynhild, here clearly defined as a Valkyrie. *Bane of the wood*: fire. *Ygg*: Odin; cf. *Grimnismol*, 53. *The thorn*: a prose note in *Sigrdrifumol* calls it "sleep-thorn." *The fighter*: the story of the reason for Brynhild's punishment is told in the prose following stanza 4 of *Sigrdrifumol*.

44. *Vingskornir*: Brynhild's horse, not elsewhere mentioned. *Victory-bringer*: the word thus translated is in the original "sigrdrifa." The compiler of the collection, not being familiar with this word, assumed that it was a proper name, and in the prose following stanza 4 of the *Sigrdrifumol* he specifically states that this was the Valkyrie's name. Editors, until recently, have followed him in this error, failing to recognize that "sigrdrifa" was simply an epithet for Brynhild. It is from this blunder that the so-called *Sigrdrifumol* takes its name. Brynhild's dual personality as a Valkyrie and as the daughter of Buthli has made plenty of trouble, but the addition of a second Valkyrie in the person of the supposed "Sigrdrifa" has made still more.

Prose. There is no break in the manuscript between the end of this prose passage and the beginning of the one introducing the *Sigrdrifumol*; some editors include the entire prose passage with one poem or the other. *Hrotti*: "Thruster."

SIGRDRIFUMOL
THE BALLAD OF THE VICTORY-BRINGER

INTRODUCTION

The *Sigrdrifumol* follows on from the *Fafnismol* and is also found in the *Codex Regius*, though in a woefully fragmented state with entire portions lost, corrupted, or missing—including the ending, which has not been able to be recovered from other manuscripts. This has given rise to myriad disputes and interpretations in how the work is to be read and reconstructed, and likewise plagues the narrative itself with doubt as to authenticity that does not mar the more complete and ancient lays. Even the name is probably a scribal error by the hand that wrote the *Codex Regius*, with the title of *Sigrdrifa* (victory-bringer) being mistaken as a proper name and thus a different personage from Brynhildr, when assuredly the title merely refers to her nature as a Valkyrie.

All of that said, the *Sigrdrifumol* is also perhaps one of the more important of the heroic lays for the sheer amount of practical religious information it gives about the theological structure and behavior of our ancestors, a fact that has gone largely unremarked upon and unappreciated by many scholars, who prefer instead to see these lines as out of place insertions from some kind of wisdom lay, due to its similarity with works like the *Hovamol*. A more holistic and religious interpretation of the passages leaves us with a quite different view, and makes clear that Brynhildr is imparting a specific type of religious knowledge to Sigurth, primarily that of the magical art of *galdr* and runecraft, which can narratively be ascribed to her in her position as one of Odin's Valkyries, with the god being the accepted master and originator of these arts. Far from a pointless inclusion, Sigurth asks the Valkyrie to teach him such hidden wisdom if indeed Valkyrie she be, which is a quite reasonable turn of events should one stumble across such a distinguished figure and find them in debt to oneself.

The poem opens with an even more impressive and treasured find, in that Brynhildr recites a full metrical prayer to Dagr (Day), Nott (Night) and her daughter (who is almost certainly Nerthus, the twin sister of Njord and identical to the earth Goddess Jord). That such a prayer to the Gods would survive in full poetic form like this (and not just summarized in prose or vaguely alluded to) is, needless to say, almost wholly unique in the entire record of the Nordic peoples. For this reason alone the work merits close scrutiny and theological analysis.

Brynhildr then continues her chanting of wisdom by instructing Sigurth in the art of *galdr* and runecraft. It is not entirely certain if the verses describing this are mnemonic poems meant to preserve knowledge of specific spells and incantations to be performed, or if the verses themselves are the *galdr* and imbued with magical force. It is possible that the verses constitute a mix of these, with some bearing very clear and concise directions and others being incredibly esoteric and hard to follow in a practical sense, which we might ascribe to the latter category as being sacred metrical forms themselves. Without a clearer picture of how *galdr* actually works,[1] it is hard to definitively remark on what is going on here, aside from saying that it must be of tremendous importance and constitute sacred religious knowledge.

---

1 Few indications are present, mostly originating from the fact that the word itself describes a chant or song and stems from the root "to yell", with descriptions of the craft being sung in various works from the *Hovamol* itself to the *Grougaldr*.

The Road to Valhalla
(Severin Nilsson)

Sigurðr reið upp á Hindarfjall ok stefndi suðr til Frakklands. Á fjallinu sá hann ljós mikit, svá sem eldr brynni, ok ljómaði af til himins. En er hann kom at, þá stóð þar skjaldborg ok upp ór merki. Sigurðr gekk í skjaldborgina ok sá , at þar lá maðr ok svaf með öllum hervápnum. Hann tók fyrst hjálminn af höfði hánum. Þá sá hann, at þat var kona. Brynjan var föst sem hon væri holdgróin. Þá reist hann með Gram frá höfuðsmátt brynjuna í gögnum niðr ok svá út í gögnum báðar ermar. Þá tók hann brynju af henni, en hon vaknaði, ok settist hon upp ok sá Sigurð ok mælti:

"Hvat beit brynju? Hví brá ek svefni? 1
Hverr felldi af mér fölvar nauðir?"
Hann svaraði:
"Sigmundar burr, sleit fyr skömmu
hrafn hrælundir, hjörr Sigurðar!"

Hon kvað: 2
"Lengi ek svaf, lengi ek sofnuð var,
löng eru lýða læ;
Óðinn því veldr, er ek eigi máttak
bregða blundstöfum."

Sigurðr settist niðr ok spyrr hana nafns. Hon tók þá horn fullt mjaðar ok gaf honum minnisveig:

SIGRDRIFUMOL

Sigurth rode up on Hindarfjoll and turned southward toward the land of the Franks. On the mountain he saw a great light, as if fire were burning, and the glow reached up to heaven. And when he came thither, there stood a tower of shields, and above it was a banner. Sigurth went into the shield-tower, and saw that a man lay there sleeping with all his war-weapons. First he took the helm from his head, and then he saw that it was a woman. The mail-coat was as fast as if it had grown to the flesh. Then he cut the mail-coat from the head-opening downward, and out to both the arm-holes. Then he took the mail-coat from her, and she awoke, and sat up and saw Sigurth, and said:

"What bit through the byrnie? how was broken my sleep?   1
Who made me free of the fetters pale?"

He answered:
"Sigmund's son, with Sigurth's sword,
That late with flesh hath fed the ravens."

Sigurth sat beside her and asked her name. She took a horn full of mead and gave him a memory-draught.

"Hail, day! Hail, sons of day!   2
And night and her daughter now!
Look on us here with loving eyes,
That waiting we victory win."

"Heill dagr! 3
Heilir dags synir!
Heil nótt ok nift!
Óreiðum augum   lítið okkr þinig
ok gefið sitjöndum sigr!

Heilir æsir! 4
Heilar ásynjur!
Heil sjá in fjölnýta fold!
Mál ok mannvit   gefið okkr mærum tveim
ok læknishendr, meðan lifum."

Hon nefndist Sigrdrífa ok var valkyrja. Hon sagði, at tveir konungar börðust. Hét annarr Hjálmgunnarr. Hann var þá gamall ok inn mesti hermaðr, ok hafði Óðinn hánum sigri heitit en

"annarr hét Agnarr,   Auðu bróðir,
er vætr engi   vildi þiggja."

Sigrdrífa felldi Hjálmgunnarr í orrustunni, en Óðinn stakk hana svefnþorni í hefnd þess ok kvað hana aldri skyldu síðan sigr vega í orrustu ok kvað hana giftast skyldu—"en ek sagðak hánum, at ek strengðak heit þar í mót at giftast engum þeim manni, er hræðast kynni." Hann segir ok biðr hana kenna sér speki, ef hon vissi tíðindi ór öllum heimum. Sigrdrífa kvað:

"Bjór færi ek þér,   brynþings apaldr, 5
magni blandinn   ok megintíri;
fullr er hann ljóða   ok líknstafa,
góðra galdra   ok gamanrúna.

Sigrúnar skaltu kunna,   ef þú vilt sigr hafa, 6
ok rísta á hjalti hjörs,   sumar á véttrimum,
sumar á valböstum,   ok nefna tysvar Tý.

"Hail to the gods! Ye goddesses, hail,   3
And all the generous earth!
Give to us wisdom and goodly speech,
And healing hands, life-long."

"Long did I sleep, my slumber was long,   4
And long are the griefs of life;
Odin decreed that I could not break
The heavy spells of sleep."

Her name was Sigrdrifa, and she was a Valkyrie. She said that two kings fought in battle; one was called Hjalmgunnar, an old man but a mighty warrior, and Odin had promised him the victory, and

The other was Agnar, brother of Autha,
None he found who fain would shield him.

Sigrdrifa, slew Hjalmgunnar in the battle, and Odin pricked her with the sleep-thorn in punishment for this, and said that she should never thereafter win victory in battle, but that she should be wedded. "And I said to him that I had made a vow in my turn, that I would never marry a man who knew the meaning of fear." Sigurth answered and asked her to teach him wisdom, if she knew of what took place in all the worlds. Sigrdrifa said:

"Beer I bring thee, tree of battle,   5
Mingled of strength and mighty fame;
Charms it holds and healing signs,
Spells full good, and gladness-runes."

Winning-runes learn, if thou longest to win,   6
And the runes on thy sword-hilt write;
Some on the furrow, and some on the flat,
And twice shalt thou call on Tyr.

Ölrúnar skaltu kunna,   ef þú vill annars kvæn   7
véli-t þik í tryggð, ef þú trúir;
á horni skal þær rísta   ok á handar baki
ok merkja á nagli Nauð.

Full skal signa   ok við fári sjá   8
ok verpa lauki í lög;
þá ek þat veit,   at þér verðr aldri
meinblandinn mjöðr.

Bjargrúnar skaltu kunna,   ef þú bjarga vilt   9
ok leysa kind frá konum;
á lófum þær skal rísta   ok of liðu spenna
ok biðja þá dísir duga.

Brimrúnar skaltu rísta,   ef þú vilt borgit hafa   10
á sundi seglmörum;
á stafni skal rísta   ok á stjórnarblaði
ok leggja eld í ár,   er-a svá brattr breki
né svá bláar unnir,   þó kemstu heill af hafi.

Limrúnar skaltu kunna,   af þú vilt læknir vera,   11
ok kunna sár at sjá;
á berki skal þær rísta   ok á baðmi viðar,
þeim er lúta austr limar.

Málrúnar skaltu kunna,   ef þú vilt, at manngi þér   12
heiftum gjaldi harm:
þær of vindr, þær of vefr,   þær of setr allar saman
á því þingi,   er þjóðir skulu
í fulla dóma fara.

—◆—

Hugrúnar skaltu kunna,   ef þú vilt hverjum vera   13
geðsvinnari guma;
þær of réð,   þær of reist,
þær of hugði Hroftr   af þeim legi,
er lekit hafði   ór hausi Heiðdraupnis
ok ór horni Hoddrofnis.

Ale-runes learn, that with lies the wife 7
Of another betray not thy trust;
On the horn thou shalt write, and the backs of thy hands,
And Need shalt mark on thy nails.
Thou shalt bless the draught, and danger escape,
And cast a leek in the cup;
For so I know thou never shalt see
Thy mead with evil mixed.

Birth-runes learn, if help thou wilt lend, 8
The babe from the mother to bring;
On thy palms shalt write them, and round thy joints,
And ask the fates to aid.

Wave-runes learn, if well thou wouldst shelter 9
The sail-steeds out on the sea;
On the stem shalt thou write, and the steering blade,
And burn them into the oars;
Though high be the breakers, and black the waves,
Thou shalt safe the harbor seek.

Branch-runes learn, if a healer wouldst be, 10
And cure for wounds wouldst work;
On the bark shalt thou write, and on trees that be
With boughs to the eastward bent.

Speech-runes learn, that none may seek 11
To answer harm with hate;
Well he winds and weaves them all,
And sets them side by side,
At the judgment-place, when justice there
The folk shall fairly win.

Thought-runes learn, if all shall think 12
Thou art keenest minded of men.

Them Hropt arranged, and them he wrote, 13
And them in thought he made,
Out of the draught that down had dropped
From the head of Heithdraupnir,
And the horn of Hoddrofnir.

Á bjargi stóð   með Brimis eggjar,   14
hafði sér á höfði hjalm;
þá mælti Mímis   höfuð fróðligt it fyrsta orð
ok sagði sanna stafi.

Á skildi kvað ristnar,   15
þeim er stendr fyr skínandi goði,
á eyra Árvakrs   ok á Alsvinns hófi,
á því hvéli, er snýsk   undir reið Hrungnis,
á Sleipnis tönnum   ok á sleða fjötrum.

Á bjarnar hrammi   ok á Braga tungu,   16
á ulfs klóum   ok á arnar nefi,
á blóðgum vængjum   ok á brúar sporði,
á lausnar lófa   ok á líknar spori.

Á gleri ok á gulli   ok á gumna heillum,   17
í víni ok í virtri   ok vilisessi,
á Gugnis oddi   ok á Grana brjósti,
á nornar nagli   ok á nefi uglu.

Allar váru af skafnar,   þær er váru á ristnar,   18
ok hverfðar við inn helga mjöð
ok sendar á víða vega;
þær ro með ásum,   þær ro með alfum,
sumar með vísum vönum   sumar hafa mennskir menn.

Þat eru bókrúnar,   þat eru bjargrúnar   19
ok allar ölrúnar   ok mætar meginrúnar,
hveim er þær kná óvilltar
ok óspilltar   sér at heillum hafa;
njóttu, ef þú namst,   unz rjúfask regin.

On the mountain he stood with Brimir's sword, 14
On his head the helm he bore;
Then first the head of Mim spoke forth,
And words of truth it told.

He bade write on the shield before the shining goddess, 15
On Arvak's ear, and on Alsvith's hoof,
On the wheel of the car of Hrungnir's killer,
On Sleipnir's teeth, and the straps of the sledge.

On the paws of the bear, and on Bragi's tongue, 16
On the wolf's claws bared, and the eagle's beak,
On bloody wings, and bridge's end,
On freeing hands and helping foot-prints.

On glass and on gold, and on goodly charms, 17
In wine and in beer, and on well-loved seats,
On Gungnir's point, and on Grani's breast,
On the nails of Norns, and the night-owl's beak.

Shaved off were the runes that of old were written, 18
And mixed with the holy mead,
And sent on ways so wide;
So the gods had them, so the elves got them,
And some for the Wanes so wise,
And some for mortal men.

Beech-runes are there, birth-runes are there, 19
And all the runes of ale,
And the magic runes of might;
Who knows them rightly and reads them true,
Has them himself to help;
Ever they aid,
Till the gods are gone.

Nú skaltu kjósa, alls þér er kostr of boðinn, 20
hvassa vápna hlynr;
sögn eða þögn hafðu þér sjalfr í hug;
öll eru mein of metin."

Sigurðr kvað: 21
"Munk-a ek flæja, þótt mik feigan vitir,
emk-a ek með bleyði borinn;
ástráð þín ek vil öll hafa;
svá lengi sem ek lifi."

———⸻———

Sigrdrífa kvað: 22
"Þat ræð ek þér it fyrsta, at þú við frændr þína
vammalaust verir;
síðr þú hefnir, þótt þeir sakar geri;
þat kveða dauðum duga.

Þat ræð ek þér annat, at þú eið né sverir, 23
nema þann er saðr sé;
grimmar limar ganga at tryggðrofi;
armr er vára vargr.

Þat ræð ek þér þriðja, at þú þingi á 24
deili-t við heimska hali,
því að ósviðr maðr lætur oft kveðin
verri orð en viti.

Allt er vant, ef þú við þegir, 25
þá þykkir þú með bleyði borinn
eða sönnu sagðr;
hættr er heimis kviðr, nema sér góðan geti;
annars dags láttu hans öndu farit,
ok launa svá lýðum lygi.

Þat ræð ek þér it fjórða, 26
ef býr fordæða vammafull á vegi,
ganga er betra en giska sé,
þótt þik nótt of nemi.

Brynhild spake:
"Now shalt thou choose, for the choice is given,   20
Thou tree of the biting blade;
Speech or silence, 'tis thine to say,
Our evil is destined all."

Sigurth spake:
"I shall not flee, though my fate be near,   21
I was born not a coward to be;
Thy loving word for mine will I win,
As long as I shall live."

Then first I rede thee, that free of guilt   22
Toward kinsmen ever thou art;
No vengeance have, though they work thee harm,
Reward after death thou shalt win.

Then second I rede thee, to swear no oath   23
If true thou knowest it not;
Bitter the fate of the breaker of troth,
And poor is the wolf of his word.

Then third I rede thee, that thou at the Thing   24
Shalt fight not in words with fools;
For the man unwise a worser word
Than he thinks doth utter oft.

Ill it is if silent thou art,   25
A coward born men call thee,
And truth mayhap they tell;
Seldom safe is fame,
Unless wide renown be won;
On the day thereafter send him to death,
Let him pay the price of his lies.

Then fourth I rede thee, if thou shalt find   26
A wily witch on thy road,
It is better to go than her guest to be,
Though night enfold thee fast.

Fornjósnar augu   þurfu fira synir,   27
hvars skulu vreiðir vega;
oft bölvísar konur   sitja brautu nær,
þær er deyfa sverð ok sefa.

Þat ræð ek þér it fimmta,   28
þóttú fagrar séir   brúðir bekkjum á,
sifja silfr   lát-a-ðu þínum svefni ráða;
teygj-at-tu þér at kossi konur.

Þat ræð ek þér it sétta,   29
þótt með seggjum fari
ölðrmál til öfug,   drukkin deila
skal-at-tu við dolgviðu;
margan stelr vín viti.

Söngr ok öl   hefr seggjum verit   30
mörgum at móðtrega,   sumum at bana,
sumum at bölstöfum;
fjölð er, þat er fira tregr.

Þat ræð ek þér it sjaunda,   31
ef þú sakar deilir   við hugfulla hali,
berjask er betra   en brenna sé
inni auðstöfum.

Þat ræð ek þér it átta,   at þú skalt við illu sjá   32
ok firrask flærðarstafi;
mey þú teygj-at   né manns konu
né eggja ofgamans.

Þat ræð ek þér it níunda,   33
at þú náum bjargir,   hvars þú á foldu finnr,
hvárts eru sóttdauðir   eða eru sædauðir
eða eru vápndauðir verar.

Laug skal gera,   þeim er liðnir eru,   34
þváa hendr ok höfuð,   kemba ok þerra,
áðr í kistu fari,   ok biðja sælan sofa.

Þat ræð ek þér it tíunda,   35
at þú trúir aldregi   várum vargdropa,
hvárstu ert bróður bani
eða hafir þú felldan föður;
ulfr er í ungum syni,
þó sé hann gulli gladdr.

Eyes that see need the sons of men
Who fight in battle fierce;
Oft witches evil sit by the way,
Who blade and courage blunt.
27

Then fifth I rede thee, though maidens fair
Thou seest on benches sitting,
Let the silver of kinship not rob thee of sleep,
And the kissing of women beware.
28

Then sixth I rede thee, if men shall wrangle,
And ale-talk rise to wrath,
No words with a drunken warrior have,
For wine steals many men's wits.
29

Brawls and ale full oft have been
An ill to many a man,
Death for some, and sorrow for some;
Full many the woes of men.
30

Then seventh I rede thee, if battle thou seekest
With a foe that is full of might;
It is better to fight than to burn alive
In the hall of the hero rich.
31

Then eighth I rede thee, that evil thou shun,
And beware of lying words;
Take not a maid, nor the wife of a man,
Nor lure them on to lust.
32

Then ninth I rede thee: burial render
If thou findest a fallen corpse,
Of sickness dead, or dead in the sea,
Or dead of weapons' wounds.
33

A bath shalt thou give them who corpses be,
And hands and head shalt wash;
Wipe them and comb, ere they go in the coffin,
And pray that they sleep in peace.
34

Then tenth I rede thee, that never thou trust
The word of the race of wolves,
If his brother thou broughtest to death,
Or his father thou didst fell;
Often a wolf in a son there is,
Though gold he gladly takes.
35

Sakar ok heiftir　　hyggja-t svefngar vera　　　　　　　36
né harm in heldr;
vits ok vápna　　vant er jöfri at fá
þeim er skal fremstr með firum.

Þat ræð ek þér it ellifta,　　at þú við illu séir　　　　37
hvern veg at vini;
langt líf þykkjumk-a-k　　lofðungs vita;
römm eru róg of risin."

Battle and hate and harm, methinks, 36
Full seldom fall asleep;
Wits and weapons the warrior needs
If boldest of men he would be.

Then eleventh I rede thee, that wrath thou shun, 37
And treachery false with thy friends;
Not long the leader's life shall be,
For great are the foes he faces.

ENDNOTES

Prose. The introductory prose follows without break the prose concluding the *Fafnismol*, the point of division being arbitrary and not agreed upon by all editors. *Hindarfjoll*: cf. *Fafnismol*, 42 and note. *Franks*: this does not necessarily mean that Sigurth was on his way to the Gjukungs' home, for Sigmund had a kingdom in the land of the Franks (cf. *Fra Dautha Sinfjotla*). *Shields*: the annotator probably drew the notion of the shield-tower from the reference in *Helreith Brynhildar*, 9. The flame-girt tower was not uncommon; cf. Mengloth's hall in *Svipdagsmol*.

1. This stanza, and the two lines included in the prose after stanza 4, and possibly stanza 5 as well, evidently come from a different poem from stanzas 2–4. Lines 3–4 in the original are obscure, though the general meaning is clear.

Prose (after stanza 1). In the manuscript stanza 4 stands before this prose note and stanzas 2–3. The best arrangement of the stanzas seems to be the one here given, following Müllenhoff's suggestion, but the prose note is out of place anywhere. The first sentence of it ought to follow stanza 4 and immediately precede the next prose note; the second sentence ought to precede stanza 5.

2. *Sons of day*: most probably a reference to either the Vanir or the Alfar or perhaps both. *The daughter of night* (Not), according to Snorri, was Jorth (Earth).

Prose (after stanza 4). *Sigrdrifa*: on the error whereby this epithet, "victory-bringer," became a proper name cf. *Fafnismol*, 44 and note. *Hjalmgunnar*: in *Helreith Brynhildar* (stanza 8) he is called a king of the Goths, which means little; of him and his adversary, *Agnar*, we know, nothing beyond what is told here. The two lines quoted apparently come from the same poem as stanza 1; the two first lines of the stanza have been reconstructed from the prose thus: "Hjalmgunnar was one, the hoary king, / And triumph to him had Heerfather promised." A few editions insert in this prose passage stanzas 7–10 of *Helreith Brynhildar*, which may or may not have be longed originally to this poem.

5. This stanza is perhaps, but by no means surely, from the same poem as stanza 1. *Tree of battle*: warrior. *Runes*: the earliest runes were not letters, but simply signs supposed to possess magic power; out of them developed the "runic alphabet."

6. Stanzas 6–12 give a list of runes which probably had no original connection with the Brynhild-Sigurth story. *Tyr*: the sword-god (cf. *Hymiskvitha*, 4 and note); "tyr" is also the name of a rune which became "T."

7. *Regius* gives only lines 1–6; lines 7–8 are added from *Volsungasaga*. *Lies*, etc.: a guest on his arrival received a draught of ale from the hands of his host's wife, and it was to prevent this draught from bewitching him that the runes were recommended. *Need*: the word "nauth," meaning "need," is also the name of the rune which became "N." *Leek*: leeks were long supposed to have the power of counteracting poison or witchcraft.

9. *Sail-steeds*: ships.

10. *Branch-runes*: runes cut in the bark of trees. Such runes were believed to transfer sickness from the invalid to the tree. Some editors, however, have changed "limrunar" ("branch runes") to "lifrunar" ("life-runes").

11. Lines 3–6 look like an accidental addition, replacing two lines now lost. They mean, apparently, that the man who interweaves his speech with "speech-runes" when he pleads his case at the "Thing," or popular tribunal, will not unduly enrage his adversary in the argument of the case.

12. Here the list of runes breaks off, though the manuscript indicates no gap, and three short passages of a different type, though all dealing with runes, follow.

13. Stanzas 13–14 appear to have come from a passage regarding Odin's getting of the runes similar to *Hovamol*, 139–146. Editors have tried various combinations of the lines in stanzas 12–14. *Hropt*: Odin; cf. *Voluspo*, 62. *The draught*, etc.: apparently the reference is to the head of Mim, from which Odin derived his wisdom in magic (cf. *Voluspo*, 47 and note); *Heithdraupnir* ("Light-Dropper") and *Hoddrofnir* ("Treasure-Opener")

seem to be names for Mim.

14. This stanza is clearly in bad shape; perhaps, as the manuscript indicates, a new stanza, of which most has been lost, should begin with line 3. *Brimir*: a giant (cf. *Voluspo*, 9 and 37); why Odin should have his sword is unknown.

15. Stanzas 15-17 constitute a wholly distinct rune-chant. Line 1 is unusually long in the original, as here. *Shield*: the shield Svalin ("Cooling") that stands in front of the sun; cf. *Grimnismol*, 38. *Arvak* ("Early Waker") and *Alsvith* ("All Swift"): the horses that draw the sun's car; cf. *Grimnismol*, 37, *Hrungnir*: the slayer of the giant Hrungnir was Thor (cf. *Harbarthsljoth*, 14 and note), but the line is in bad shape; the name may not be Hrungnir, and "killer" is a conjectural addition. *Sleipnir*: Odin's eight-legged horse; cf. *Grimnismol*, 44 and note. *Sledge*: perhaps the one mentioned in *Grimnismol*, 49.

16. *Bragi*: the god of poetry; cf. *Grimnismol*, 44 and note.

17. *Charms*: the wearing of amulets was very common. *Gungnir*: Odin's spear, made by the dwarfs, which he occasionally lent to heroes to whom he granted victory. *Grani*: Sigurth's horse; the *Volsungasaga* has "giantesses'."

18. Stanzas 18-19, which editors have freely rearranged, apparently come from another source than any of the rest. *Shaved off*: the runes were shaved off by Odin from the wood on which they were carved, and the shavings bearing them were put into the magic mead. *Wanes*: cf. *Voluspo*, 21, note.

19. Lines 3, 6, and 7 look like spurious additions, but the whole stanza is chaotic. *Beech-runes*: runes carved on beech trees.

20. Stanzas 20-21 are all that remains of the dialogue between Brynhild and Sigurth from the poem to which stanzas 2-4 belong; cf. Introductory Note [Appendix B]. In the intervening lost stanzas Brynhild has evidently warned Sigurth of the perils that will follow if he swears loyalty to her; hence the choice to which she here refers. *Tree*, etc.: warrior. The manuscript does not indicate the speaker of either this or the following stanza; the *Volsungasaga* names Sigurth before stanza 21.

21. It is quite possible that the original poem concluded with two stanzas after this, paraphrased thus in the *Volsungasaga*: "Sigurth said: 'Nowhere is to be found any one wiser than thou, and this I swear, that I shall have thee for mine, and that thou art after my heart's desire.' She answered: 'I

would rather have thee though I might choose among all men.' And this they bound between them with oaths." Stanzas 22-37, which the *Volsungasaga* paraphrases, may have been introduced at a relatively early time, but can hardly have formed part of the original poem.

22. With this stanza begins the list of numbered counsels, closely resembling the *Loddfafnismol* (*Hovamol*, 111-138), here attributed to Brynhild. That the section originally had anything to do with Brynhild is more than improbable.

23. *Wolf of his word*: oath-destroyer, oath-breaker.

25. This chaotic and obscure jumble of lines has been unsuccessfully "improved" by various editors. It is clearly an interpolation, meaning, in substance: "It is dangerous to keep silent too long, as men may think you a coward; but if any one taunts you falsely because of your silence, do not argue with him, but the next morning kill him as proof that he is a liar."

27. Probably another interpolation.

28. *Silver of kinship*: the passage is doubtful, but apparently it means the "marriage-price" for which a bride was "bought."

29. Line 1 comes at the end of the thirty-second leaf of *Regius*, and whatever further was contained in that manuscript has vanished with the lost eight-leaf folio (cf. Introductory Note [Appendix B]). The rest of stanza 29, and stanzas 30-37, are added from later paper manuscripts, which were undoubtedly copied from an old parchment, though probably not from the complete *Regius*. The *Volsungasaga* paraphrases these additional stanzas.

31. The meaning is that it is better to go forth to battle than to stay at home and be burned to death. Many a Norse warrior met his death in this latter way; the burning of the house in the *Njalssaga* is the most famous instance.

34. Probably an interpolation.

35. Lines 3-4 are probably interpolated. *Race of wolves*: family of a slain foe.

36. Probably an interpolation.

37. Lines 3-4 may well have come from the old Sigurth-Brynhild poem, like stanzas 2-4 and 20-21, being inserted here, where they do not fit particularly well, in place of the two lines with which the eleventh coun-

sel originally ended. Perhaps they formed part of the stanza of warning which evidently preceded Brynhild's speech in stanza 20. In the *Volsungasaga* they are paraphrased at the end of Brynhild's long speech of advice (stanzas 20-37), and are immediately followed by the prose passage given in the note on stanza 21. It seems likely, therefore, that the paper manuscripts have preserved all of the so-called *Sigrdrifumol* which was contained in the lost section of *Regius*, with the possible exception of these two concluding stanzas, and these may very well have been given only in the form of a prose note, though it is practically certain that at one time they existed in verse form.

BROT AF SIGURTHARKVITHU
FRAGMENT OF A SIGURTH LAY

INTRODUCTION

Sigurtharkvitha in Meiri follows directly after *Sigrdrifumol* and is also found in the *Codex Regius*. It is notable for being made up of most of the missing eight leaves of the *Codex* that begin shortly before the ending of *Sigrdrifumol* and that continue until it is picked up by the fragment of the lay recorded here. As such, speculations regarding its content have been rife, with most scholars agreeing that all or almost all of the missing material belongs to the reported *Long Lay of Sigurth* in contrast to the *Short Lay of Sigurth* contained within the *Codex Regius* itself. Given that the *Short Lay* makes up seventy whole stanzas and is also one of the longest poems of the *Poetic Edda*, it stands to reason that the *Long Lay* must be significantly longer, assuming that we are indeed missing only the single poetic narrative and not several distinct poems.

The poem picks up very late in what must have been the narrative of Sigurth's life, immediately following his death at the hands of Hogni, who asks Gunnar why exactly he wished Sigurth slain; Gunnar responds that Sigurth has broken oaths to him. The matter is transparently connected to the selfish desires and pride of Bryndhildr, and Hogni accuses his brother Gunnar of this. As this occurs, a raven, surely representing the divine appearance of Odin himself, cries that both men shall be slain by Atli (the Sigurth tradition's version of the historical Atilla the Hun) as just deserts for their ill-fated slaying of the mighty hero. Also of interest here is that the men first consume the meat of a wolf before slaying Sigurth, a form of quasi-magical assimilation of the animal's wild, savage, and lawless nature which occurs infrequently but consistently across Old Norse literature, where it is assumed that the meat will impart strength and ferocity to the eater.

The narrative of the *Volsungasaga* offers a window into the likely prior events of the *Long Lay*, which summarizes the matter sometimes directly from the source, such as immediately prior to Sigurth's crossing of the flame barrier that surrounds the sleeping Brynhildr, illustrated here:

> The fire raged, the earth was rocked.
> The flames leaped high to heaven itself;
> Few were the hardy heroes would dare
> To ride or leap the raging flames.
> Sigurth urged Grani then with his sword,
> The fire slackened before the hero,
> The flames sank low for the greedy of fame,
> The armor flashed that Regin had fashioned.

A section of quoted verse follows during the fight between Gudrun and Brynhildr about their relative status, with Brynhildr insulting Gudrun and her brother's skills and fame relative to Sigurth. It is not entirely clear if this is actually from the *Long Lay of Sigurth*, but it seems very likely:

> Sigurth the dragon slew, and that
> Will men recall while the world remains;
> But little boldness thy brother had
> To ride or leap the raging flames.

A passage is again found in the *Volsungasaga* depicting the aftermath of Sigurth attempting to speak to Brynhildr after she has learned of his and Gunnar's deceit. This time we can be sure of the origin given that the saga itself prefaces the section with: "As is said in the Lay of Sigurth":

> Forth went Sigurth, and speech he sought not,
> The friend of heroes, his head bowed down;
> Such was his grief that asunder burst
> His mail-coat all of iron wrought.

It seems likely that after this point the narrative picks up from the beginning of the fragment that we have, and subsequently Brynhildr demands that Gunnar slay Sigurth for the insult rendered to her, and Gunnar, bound by his oath of friendship, entices his brother Hogni to perform the task for him.

The final prose epilogue of the poem notes that opinions differ as to how exactly the two brothers were supposed to have slain Sigurth, with the German tradition having it that Sigurth was slain outdoors in the forest, whereas the Nordic tradition has him slain inside as he slept. The author notes here that regardless of the matter, all are agreed that the two brothers utilized Sigurth's trust in them to slay him. This is a culturally relevant detail that may be missed by modern readers who are not used to thus distinguishing between types of killings, but among our ancestors it was accounted a deeply heinous religious crime ("Nith") to murder a man, by which they mean an assassination as opposed to a lawful killing where people know and understand that they are to be set upon by foes. The author is noting that Gunnar and Hogni's killing of Sigurth constituted the former, a murder as opposed to a decent and honorable Germanic killing, which is likely to be, or at least to have contributed to, what roused Odin's wrath in the matter.

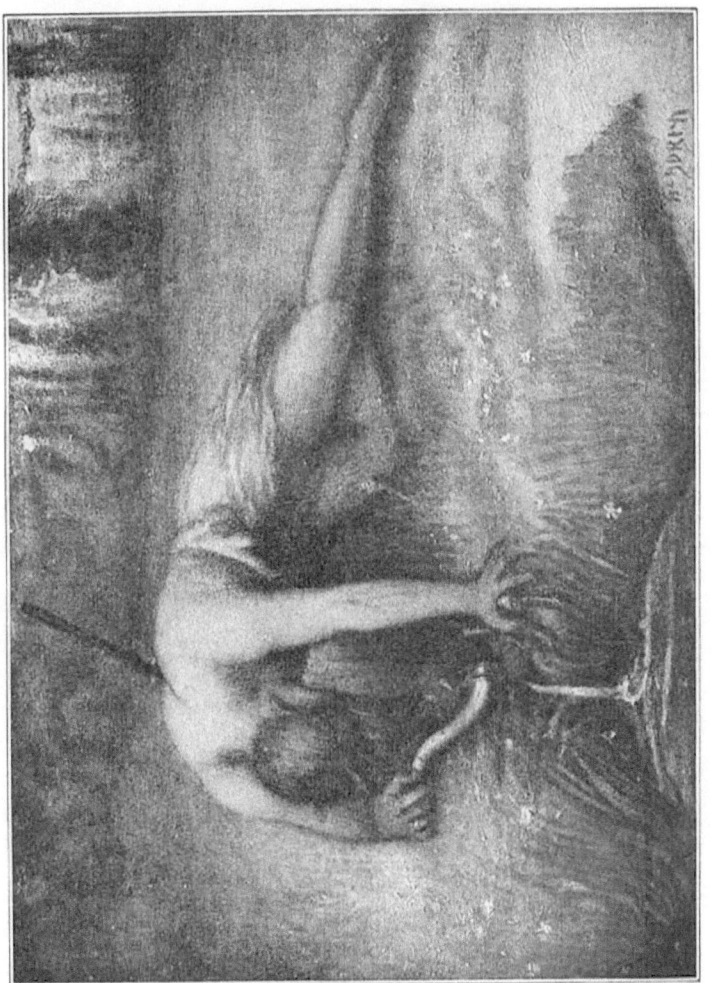

The Death of Siegfried
(H. Hendrich)

Eldr nam at æsask   en jörð at skjalfa   1
ok hár logi   við himni gnæfa;
fár treystisk þar   fylkis rekka
eld at ríða   né yfir stíga.

Sigurðr Grana   sverði keyrði;   2
eldr sloknaði   fyrir öðlingi,
logi allr lægðisk   fyrir lofgjörnum,
bliku reiði   er Reginn átti
[...]

Brynhildr kvað: 3
"Sigurðr vá at ormi,   en þat síðan mun
engum fyrnask,   meðan öld lifir;
en hlýri þinn   hvárki þorði
eld at ríða   né yfir stíga."
[...]

Út gekk Sigurðr   andspjalli frá,   4
hollvinr lofða,   ok hnipnaði,
svá at ganga nam   gunnarfúsum
sundr of síður   serkr járnofinn.
[...]

Högni kvað: 5
"[hvat hefir Sigurðr   til] saka unnit,
er þú fræknan vill   fjörvi næma?"

BROT AF SIGURTHARKVITHU

Hogni spake: 1
"What evil deed has Sigurth done,
That the hero's life thou fain wouldst have?"

Gunnar spake: 2
"Sigurth oaths to me hath sworn,
Oaths hath sworn, and all hath broken;
He betrayed me there where truest all
His oaths, methinks, he ought to have kept."

Hogni spake: 3
"Thy heart hath Brynhild whetted to hate,
Evil to work and harm to win;
She grudges the honor that Guthrun has,
And that joy of herself thou still dost have."

They cooked a wolf, they cut up a snake, 4
They gave to Gotthorm the greedy one's flesh,
Before the men, to murder minded,
Laid their hands on the hero bold.

Slain was Sigurth south of the Rhine; 5
From a limb a raven called full loud:
"Your blood shall redden Atli's blade,
And your oaths shall bind you both in chains."

Gunnar kvað: 6
"Mér hefir Sigurðr   selda eiða,
eiða selda,   alla logna;
þá vélti hann mik,   er hann vera skyldi
allra eiða   einn fulltrúi."

Högni kvað: 7
"Þik hefir Brynhildr   böl at gerva
heiftar hvattan   harm at vinna;
fyrman hon Guðrúnu   góðra ráða,
en síðan þér   sín at njóta."

Sumir ulf sviðu,   sumir orm sniðu, 8
sumir Gotþormi   af gera deildu;
áðr þeir mætti   meins of lystir
á horskum hal   hendr of leggja.

Soltinn varð Sigurðr   sunnan Rínar; 9
hrafn af meiði   hátt kallaði:
"Ykkr mun Atli   eggjar rjóða,
munu vígskáum   of viða eiðar."

Úti stóð Guðrún   Gjúka dóttir, 10
ok hon þat orða   alls fyrst of kvað:
"Hvar er nú Sigurðr,   seggja dróttinn,
er frændr mínir   fyrri ríða?"

Einn því Högni   andsvör veitti: 11
"Sundr höfum Sigurð   sverði höggvinn;
gnapir æ grár jór   yfir gram dauðum."

Þá kvað þat Brynhildr   Buðla dóttir: 12
"Vel skuluð njóta   vápna ok landa;
einn mundi Sigurðr   öllu ráða,
ef hann lengr litlu   lífi heldi.

Væri-a þat sæmt,   at hann svá réði 13
Gjúka arfi   ok Gota mengi,
er hann fimm sonu   at folkræði,
gunnarfúsa,   getna hafði."

Hló þá Brynhildr   14
bær allr dunði
einu sinni   af öllum hug:
"Lengi skuluð njóta   landa ok þegna,
er þér fræknan gram   falla létuð."

Without stood Guthrun, Gjuki's daughter, 6
Hear now the speech that first she spake:
"Where is Sigurth now, the noble king,
That my kinsmen riding before him come?"

Only this did Hogni answer: 7
"Sigurth we with our swords have slain;
The gray horse mourns by his master dead."

Then Brynhild spake, the daughter of Buthli: 8
"Well shall ye joy in weapons and lands;
Sigurth alone of all had been lord,
If a little longer his life had been."

"Right were it not that so he should rule 9
O'er Gjuki's wealth and the race of the Goths;
Five are the sons for ruling the folk,
And greedy of fight, that he hath fathered."

Then Brynhild laughed—and the building echoed— 10
Only once, with all her heart;
"Long shall ye joy in lands and men,
Now ye have slain the hero noble."

Then Guthrun spake, the daughter of Gjuki: 11
"Much thou speakest in evil speech;
Accursed be Gunnar, Sigurth's killer,
Vengeance shall come for his cruel heart."

Early came evening, and ale was drunk, 12
And among them long and loud they talked;
They slumbered all when their beds they sought,
But Gunnar alone was long awake.

His feet were tossing, he talked to himself, 13
And the slayer of hosts began to heed
What the twain from the tree had told him then,
The raven and eagle, as home they rode.

Brynhild awoke, the daughter of Buthli, 14
The warrior's daughter, ere dawn of day:
"Love me or hate me, the harm is done,
And my grief cries out, or else I die."

Þá kvað þat Guðrún   Gjúka dóttir: 15
"Mjök mælir þú   miklar firnar;
gramir hafi Gunnar,   götvað Sigurðar;
heiftgjarns hugar   hefnt skal verða."

Fram var kvelda,   fjölð var drukkit,   16
þá var hvívetna   vilmál talið,
sofnuðu allir,   er i sæing kómu,
einn vakði Gunnarr   öllum lengr.

Fót nam-at hræra,   fjölð nam-at spjalla,   17
hitt herglötuðr   hyggja téði,
hvat þeir í bölvi   báðir sögðu
hrafn ey ok örn,   er þeir heim riðu.

Vaknaði Brynhildr   Buðla dóttir,   18
dís skjöldunga,   fyr dag litlu:
"Hvetið mik eða letið mik
harmr er unninn
sorg at segja   eða svá láta."

Þögðu allir   við því orði,   19
fár kunni þeim   fljóða látum,
er hon grátandi   gerðisk at segja
þat er hlæjandi   hölða beiddi:

"Hugða ek mér, Gunnarr,   grimmt í svefni,   20
svalt allt í sal,   ætta sæing kalda;
enn þú, gramr, riðir   glaums andvani,
fjötri fatlaðr,   í fjánda lið;
svá mun öll yðvr   ætt Niflunga
afli gengin,   eruð eiðrofa.

Mant-at-tu, Gunnarr,   til görva þat,   21
er þit blóði í spor   báðir rennduð;
nú hefir þú hánum þat allt
illu launat, er hann fremstan
þik finna vildi.

Þá reyndi þat,   er riðit hafði   22
móðigr á vit   mín at biðja,
hvé herglötuðr   hafði fyrri
eiðum haldit   við inn unga gram.

Silent were all who heard her speak,   15
And nought of the heart of the queen they knew,
Who wept such tears the thing to tell
That laughing once of the men she had won.

Brynhild spake: 16
"Gunnar, I dreamed a dream full grim:
In the hall were corpses; cold was my bed;
And, ruler, thou didst joyless ride,
With fetters bound in the foemen's throng."

"[...]   17
[...]
Utterly now your Niflung race
All shall die; your oaths ye have broken."

"Thou hast, Gunnar, the deed forgot,   18
When blood in your footprints both ye mingled;
All to him hast repaid with ill
Who fain had made thee the foremost of kings."

"Well did he prove, when proud he rode   19
To win me then thy wife to be,
How true the host-slayer ever had held
The oaths he had made with the monarch young."

"The wound-staff then, all wound with gold,   20
The hero let between us lie;
With fire the edge was forged full keen,
And with drops of venom the blade was damp."

Here it is told in this poem about the death of Sigurth, and the story goes here that they slew him out of doors, but some say that they slew him in the house, on his bed while he was sleeping. But German men say that they killed him out of doors in the forest; and so it is told in the old Guthrun lay, that Sigurth and Gjuki's sons had ridden to the council-place, and that he was slain there. But in this they are all agreed, that they deceived him in his trust of them, and fell upon him when he was lying down and unprepared.

Benvönd of lét, brugðinn gulli, 23
margdýrr konungr á meðal okkar;
eldi váru eggjar útan görvar,
en eitrdropum innan fáðar."

Frá dauða Sigurðar

Hér er sagt í þessi kviðu frá dauða Sigurðar, ok víkr hér svá til sem þeir dræpi hann úti, en sumir segja svá, at þeir dræpi hann inni í rekkju sinni sofanda. En þýðverskir menn segja svá, at þeir dræpi hann úti í skógi, ok svá segir í Guðrúnarkviðu inni fornu, at Sigurðr ok Gjúkasynir hefði til þings riðit, þá er hann var drepinn. En þat segja allir einnig, at þeir sviku hann í tryggð ok vógu at hánum liggjanda ok óbúnum.

ENDNOTES

1. The fragment begins with the last words of line 1 (probably line 3 of the stanza). A few editors ascribe this speech to Gunnar and the next to Brynhild; one reconstruction of lines 1–2 on this probably false assumption runs: "Why art thou, Brynhild, daughter of Buthli, / Scheming ill with evil counsel?" *Hogni* (German Hagene): brother of Gunnar and Guthrun.[1]

2. A few editors ascribe this speech to Brynhild. Gunnar, if the stanza is his, has believed Brynhild's statement regarding Sigurth's disloyalty to his blood-brother.

4. The *Volsungasaga* quotes a somewhat different version of this stanza, in which the snake is called "wood-fish" and the third line adds "beer and many things." Eating snakes and the flesh of beasts of prey was commonly supposed to induce ferocity. *Gotthorm*: Grimhild's son, half-brother to Gunnar. He it is who, not having sworn brotherhood with Sigurth, does the killing.

5. In the manuscript this stanza stands between stanzas 11 and 12; most editions have made the change here indicated. *South of the Rhine*: the definite localization of the action shows how clearly all this part of the story was recognized in the North as of German origin. *Atli* (Attila; cf. introductory note to *Gripisspo* [Appendix B]): the Northern version of the story makes him Brynhild's brother. His marriage with Guthrun, and his slaying of hex brothers, are told in the Atli poems. Regarding the manner of Sigurth's death cf. concluding prose passage and note. Stanza 13

---

[1] Bellows' numbering scheme deviates from that of the Old Norse used in this edition immediately, due to the insertion of four stanzas at the beginning in the Old Norse edition.

indicates that after stanza 5 a stanza containing the words of an eagle has been lost.

7. One line of this stanza, but it is not clear which, seems to have been lost. *The gray horse*: Grani.

8. Some editions set stanzas 8 and 9 after stanza 11; Sijmons marks them as spurious. *Buthli*: cf. *Gripisspo*, 19, note.

9. *Goths*: a generic term for any German race; cf. *Gripisspo*, 35 and note. *Five sons*: according to the *Volsungasaga* Sigurth had only one son, named Sigmund, who was killed at Brynhild's behest. *Sigurtharkvitha en skamma* and *Guthrunarkvitha II* likewise mention only one son. The daughter of Sigurth and Guthrun, Svanhild, marries Jormunrek (Ermanarich).

12. The manuscript marks line 4 as the beginning of a new stanza, and a few editions combine it with stanza 13.

13. *Slayer of hosts*: warrior (Gunnar). *Raven and eagle*: cf. note on stanza 5.

16. Mogk regards stanzas 16 and 17 as interpolated, but on not very satisfactory grounds. On the death of Gunnar cf. *Drap Niflunga*.

17. No gap is indicated in the manuscript, and some editions attach these two lines to stanza 16. *Niflungs*: this name (German Nibelungen), meaning "sons of the mist," seems to have belonged originally to the race of supernatural beings to which the treasure belonged in the German version, [probably a reference to their dwarven ancestry and their race's home in Niflheim]. It was subsequently extended to include the Gjukungs and their Burgundians. This question, of minor importance in the Norse poems, has evoked an enormous amount of learned discussion in connection with the *Nibelungenlied*.

18. *Footprints*: the actual mingling of blood in one another's footprints was a part of the ceremony of swearing blood-brotherhood, the oath which Gunnar and Sigurth had taken. The fourth line refers to the fact that Sigurth had won many battles for Gunnar.

20. Regarding the sword episode cf. *Gripisspo*, 41 and note. *Wound-staff*: sword.

Prose. This prose passage has in the manuscript, written in red, the phrase "Of Sigurth's Death" as a heading; there is no break between it and the prose introducing *Guthrunarkvitha I*, the heading for that poem coming just before stanza 1. This note is of special interest as an effort at real criticism. The annotator, troubled by the two versions of the story of Sigurth's death, feels it incumbent on him not only to point the fact out, but to cite the authority of "German men" for the form which appears in this poem. The alternative version, wherein Sigurth is slain in bed, appears in *Sigurtharkvitha en skamma*, *Guthrunarhvot*, and *Hamthesmol*, and also in the *Volsungasaga*, which tells how Gotthorm tried twice to kill Sigurth but was terrified by the brightness of his eyes, and succeeded only after the hero had fallen asleep. That the annotator was correct in citing German authority for the slaying of Sigurth in the forest is shown by the *Nibelungenlied* and the *Thithrekssaga*. The "old" Guthrun lay is unquestionably *Guthrunarkvitha II*.

GUTHRUNARKVITHA I
THE FIRST LAY OF GUTHRUN

INTRODUCTION

The *First Lay of Guthrun*, found in the *Codex Regius*, immediately follows the remaining fragment of (what is likely) the *Long Lay of Sigurth* fragment that we have within the *Codex*. The work is considered to be wholly intact with no notable interpolations or foreign editing to be found, and is generally noted for its emotional depth and skilful poetry, owing to its subject matter as a mournful lamentation on the part of Sigurth's wife Guthrun following his death. It is quite probable that this lamentation was well known among the ancients, as Guthrun "mourning Sigurth" is mentioned in other poems. Unfortunately the poem is not actually quoted anywhere else, and the addition of several unique characters within it implies for many scholars that the work is a late addition to the *Sigurth Lays*, and is certainly older than its sister piece, come down to us as the *The Second Lay of Guthrun* and quoted by the annotator of the broken fragment as the *Old Lay of Guthrun*. It seems reasonable to conclude, then, that this piece is an Icelandic work that was probably not composed any earlier than the year 1000.

The work itself is notable for being almost wholly concerned with women and their tales of grief and mourning as they all attempt to comfort Guthrun over the death of her husband, recounting how they faced similar if not greater anguish with the men of their lives ripped from them by war, and yet still persevere. Such a focus on the topic and character of women's suffering is uncommon within the saga traditions of the Germanic peoples or the Icelandic people specifically.

Guthrun follows up her grief with an outpouring of righteous anger, cursing her brothers to suffer harm due to their slaying of Sigurth and their breaking of the oaths to him. This is likely related to the common folk belief mentioned in the *Fafnismol* that the dying words of a man held the power to curse those that slew him if he knew their name, a convention known across the Indo-European world and most famously in the *Odyssey*, where Odysseus arrogantly gives the Cyclops Polyphemus his name and from his death cry Odysseus suffers the curse of Polyphemus' father Poseidon. While Guthrun herself is not dying, it seems reasonable to conclude that our ancestors felt that the curse of one's lamenting wife held a similar power in some respect.

Interestingly, Brynhildr attempts to use this as evidence that Guthrun is guilty of witchcraft (a serious accusation even among our pagan forebears) and is roundly berated for being the cause of the issue herself. The subsequent narration in which she sacrifices herself on Sigurth's pyre afterward, traditionally taken to occur due to the love she has for him, might be interpreted here as an attempt at doing penance for her actions and in response to the vehement hate toward her held by all and sundry. However, it is worth noting that a wife immolating herself on the pyre of her husband out of love is a well-worn saga tradition with diverse Indo-European parallels such as the Indian Hindu practice of *Sati* or *Suttee*.

The Funeral Procession
(H. Hendrich)

Guðrún sat yfir Sigurði dauðum. Hon grét eigi sem aðrar konur, en hon var búinn til at springa af harmi. Til gengu bæði konur ok karlar at hugga hana, en þat var eigi auðvelt. Þat er sögn manna, at Guðrún hefði etit af Fáfnis hjarta ok hon skilði því fugls rödd. Þetta er enn kveðit um Guðrúnu:

Ár var, þats Guðrún   gerðisk at deyja,   1
er hon sat sorgfull   yfir Sigurði;
gerði-t hon hjúfra   né höndum slá,
né kveina um   sem konur aðrar.

Gengu jarlar   alsnotrir fram,   2
þeir er harðs hugar   hana löttu;
þeygi Guðrún   gráta mátti,
svá var hon móðug,   mundi hon springa.

Sátu ítrar   jarla brúðir,   3
gulli búnar,   fyr Guðrúnu;
hvar sagði þeira   sinn oftrega,
þann er bitrastan   of beðit hafði.

Þá kvað Gjaflaug,   Gjúka systir: 4
"Mik veit ek á moldu   munarlausasta;
hefi ek fimm vera   forspell beðit,
tveggja dætra,   þriggja systra,
átta bræðra,   þó ek ein lifi."

GUTHRUNARKVITHA I

Guthrun sat by the dead Sigurth; she did not weep as other women, but her heart was near to bursting with grief. The men and women came to her to console her, but that was not easy to do. It is told of men that Guthrun had eaten of Fafnir's heart, and that she understood the speech of birds. This is a poem about Guthrun.

Then did Guthrun think to die, 1
When she by Sigurth sorrowing sat;
Tears she had not, nor wrung her hands,
Nor ever wailed, as other women.

To her the warriors wise there came, 2
Longing her heavy woe to lighten;
Grieving could not Guthrun weep,
So sad her heart, it seemed, would break.

Then the wives of the warriors came, 3
Gold-adorned, and Guthrun sought;
Each one then of her own grief spoke,
The bitterest pain she had ever borne.

Then spake Gjaflaug, Gjuki's sister: 4
"Most joyless of all on earth am I;
Husbands five were from me taken,
Two daughters then, and sisters three,
Brothers eight, yet I have lived."

Þeygi Guðrún   gráta mátti, 5
svá var hon móðug   at mög dauðan
ok harðhuguð   of hrör fylkis.

Þá kvað þat Herborg,   Húnalands dróttning: 6
"Hefi ek harðara   harm at segja;
mínir sjau synir   sunnan lands,
verr inn átti,   í val fellu.

Faðir ok móðir,   fjórir bræðr, 7
þau á vági   vindr of lék,
barði bára   við borðþili.

Sjalf skylda ek göfga, 8
sjalf skylda ek götva,
sjalf skylda ek höndla
hrör þeira;
þat ek allt of beið   ein misseri,
svá at mér maðr engi   munar leitaði.

Þá varð ek hafta   ok hernuma 9
sams misseris   síðan verða;
skylda ek skreyta   ok skúa binda
hersis kván   hverjan morgin.

Hon ægði mér   af afbrýði 10
ok hörðum mik   höggum keyrði;
fann ek húsguma   hvergi in betra,
en húsfreyju   hvergi verri."

Þeygi Guðrún   gráta mátti, 11
svá var hon móðug   at mög dauðan
ok harðhuguð   of hrör fylkis.

Þá kvað þat Gullrönd   Gjúka dóttir: 12
"Fá kanntu, fóstra,   þótt þú fróð séir,
ungu vífi   andspjöll bera."
Varaði hon at hylja   um hrör fylkis.

Svipti hon blæju   af Sigurði 13
ok vatt vengi   fyr vífs knéum:
"Líttu á ljúfan,   leggðu munn við grön,
sem þú halsaðir   heilan stilli."

Grieving could not Guthrun weep, 5
Such grief she had for her husband dead,
And so grim her heart by the hero's body.

Then Herborg spake, the queen of the Huns: 6
"I have a greater grief to tell;
My seven sons in the southern land,
And my husband, fell in fight all eight."

"Father and mother and brothers four 7
Amid the waves the wind once smote,
And the seas crashed through the sides of the ship."

"The bodies all with my own hands then 8
I decked for the grave, and the dead I buried;
A half-year brought me this to bear;
And no one came to comfort me."

"Then bound I was, and taken in war, 9
A sorrow yet in the same half-year;
They bade me deck and bind the shoes
Of the wife of the monarch every morn."

"In jealous rage her wrath she spake, 10
And beat me oft with heavy blows;
Never a better lord I knew,
And never a woman worse I found."

Grieving could not Guthrun weep, 11
Such grief she had for her husband dead,
And so grim her heart by the hero's body.

Then spake Gollrond, Gjuki's daughter: 12
"Thy wisdom finds not, my foster-mother,
The way to comfort the wife so young."
She bade them uncover the warrior's corpse.

The shroud she lifted from Sigurth, laying 13
His well-loved head on the knees of his wife:
"Look on thy loved one, and lay thy lips
To his as if yet the hero lived."

Á leit Guðrún   einu sinni,   14
sá hon döglings skör   dreyra runna,
fránar sjónir   fylkis liðnar,
hugborg jöfurs   hjörvi skorna.

Þá hné Guðrún   höll við bolstri,   15
haddr losnaði,   hlýr roðnaði,
en regns dropi   rann niðr of kné.

Þá grét Guðrún   Gjúka dóttir,   16
svá at tár flugu   tresk í gögnum
ok gullu við   gæss í túni,
mærir fuglar,   er mær átti.

Þá kvað þat Gullrönd   Gjúka dóttir: 17
"Ykkrar vissa ek   ástir mestar
manna allra   fyr mold ofan;
unðir þá hvárki   úti né inni,
systir mín   nema hjá Sigurði."

Guðrún kvað: 18
"Svá var minn Sigurðr   hjá sonum Gjúka
sem væri geirlaukr   ór grasi vaxinn
eða væri bjartr steinn   á band dreginn,
jarknasteinn   yfir öðlingum.

Ek þótta ok   þjóðans rekkum   19
hverri hæri   Herjans dísi;
nú em ek svá lítil   sem lauf séi
oft í jölstrum   at jöfur dauðan.

Sakna ek í sessi   ok í sæingu   20
míns málvinar,   valda megir Gjúka;
valda megir Gjúka   mínu bölvi
ok systur sinnar   sárum gráti.

Svá ér of lýða   landi eyðið   21
sem ér of unnuð   eiða svarða;
mun-a þú, Gunnarr,   gulls of njóta;
þeir munu þér baugar   at bana verða,
er þú Sigurði   svarðir eiða.

Oft var í túni   teiti meiri,   22
þá er minn Sigurðr   söðlaði Grana
ok þeir Brynhildar   biðja fóru,
armar véttar,   illu heilli."

Once alone did Guthrun look; 14
His hair all clotted with blood beheld,
The blinded eyes that once shone bright,
The hero's breast that the blade had pierced.

Then Guthrun bent, on her pillow bowed, 15
Her hair was loosened, her cheek was hot,
And the tears like raindrops downward ran.

Then Guthrun, daughter of Gjuki, wept, 16
And through her tresses flowed the tears;
And from the court came the cry of geese,
The birds so fair of the hero's bride.

Then Gollrond spake, the daughter of Gjuki: 17
"Never a greater love I knew
Than yours among all men on earth;
Nowhere wast happy, at home or abroad,
Sister mine, with Sigurth away."

Guthrun spake: 18
"So was my Sigurth o'er Gjuki's sons
As the spear-leek grown above the grass,
Or the jewel bright borne on the band,
The precious stone that princes wear."

"To the leader of men I loftier seemed 19
And higher than all of Herjan's maids;
As little now as the leaf I am
On the willow hanging; my hero is dead."

"In his seat, in his bed, I see no more 20
My heart's true friend; the fault is theirs,
The sons of Gjuki, for all my grief,
That so their sister sorely weeps."

"So shall your land its people lose 21
As ye have kept your oaths of yore;
Gunnar, no joy the gold shall give thee,
The rings shall soon thy slayers be,
Who swarest oaths with Sigurth once."

"In the court was greater gladness then 22
The day my Sigurth Grani saddled,
And went forth Brynhild's hand to win,
That woman ill, in an evil hour."

Þá kvað þat Brynhildr   Buðla dóttir: 23
"Vön sé sú véttr   vers ok barna,
er þik, Guðrún,   gráts of beiddi
ok þér í morgun   málrúnar gaf."

Þá kvað þat Gullrönd   Gjúka dóttir: 24
"Þegi þú, þjóðleið,   þeira orða;
urðr öðlinga   hefir þú æ verit;
rekr þik alda hver   illrar skepnu,
sorg sára   sjau konunga
ok vinspell   vífa mest."

Þá kvað þat Brynhildr   Buðla dóttir: 25
"Veldr einn Atli   öllu bölvi
of borinn Buðla   bróðir minn."

Þá er vit í höll   húnskrar þjóðar   26
eld á jöfri   ormbeðs litum,
þess hefi ek gangs   goldit síðan,
þeirar sýnar,   sáumk ey."

Stóð hon und stoð,   strengði hon efli;   27
brann Brynhildi   Buðla dóttur
eldr ór augum,   eitri fnæsti,
er hon sár of leit   á Sigurði.

Guðrún gekk þaðan á braut til skógar á eyðimerkr ok fór allt til Danmarkar ok var þar með Þóru Hákonardóttur sjau misseri. Brynhildr vildi eigi lifa eftir Sigurð. Hon lét drepa þræla sína átta ok fimm ambóttir. Þá lagði hon sik sverði til bana, svá sem segir í Sigurðarkviðu inni skömmu.

Then Brynhild spake, the daughter of Buthli: 23
"May the witch now husband and children want
Who, Guthrun, loosed thy tears at last,
And with magic today hath made thee speak."

Then Gollrond, daughter of Gjuki, spake: 24
"Speak not such words, thou hated woman;
Bane of the noble thou e'er hast been,
Borne thou art on an evil wave,
Sorrow hast brought to seven kings,
And many a woman hast loveless made."

Then Brynhild, daughter of Buthli, spake: 25
"Atli is guilty of all the sorrow,
Son of Buthli and brother of mine."

"When we saw in the hall of the Hunnish race 26
The flame of the snake's bed flash round the hero;
For the journey since full sore have I paid,
And ever I seek the sight to forget."

By the pillars she stood, and gathered her strength, 27
From the eyes of Brynhild, Buthli's daughter,
Fire there burned, and venom she breathed,
When the wounds she saw on Sigurth then.

Guthrun went thence away to a forest in the waste, and journeyed all the way to Denmark, and was there seven half-years with Thora, daughter of Hokon. Brynhild would not live after Sigurth. She had eight of her thralls slain and five serving-women. Then she killed herself with a sword, as is told in the Short Lay of Sigurth.

ENDNOTES

Prose. The prose follows the concluding prose of the Brot without indication of a break, the heading standing immediately before stanza 1. Fafnir's heart: this bit of information is here quite without point, and it is nowhere else stated that Guthrun understood the speech of birds. In the Volsungasaga it is stated that Sigurth gave Guthrun some of Fafnir's heart to eat, "and thereafter she was much grimmer than before, and wiser."

1. This stanza seems to be based on Guthrunarkvitha II, 11–12.

4. Gjaflaug: nothing further is known of this aunt of Guthrun, or of the many relatives whom she has lost. Very likely she is an invention of the poet's, for it seems improbable that otherwise all further trace of her should have been lost. Line 4 has been marked by many editors as spurious.

5. Some editors assume the loss of a line, after either line 1 or line 3. I prefer to believe that here and in stanza 10 the poet knew exactly what he was doing, and that both stanzas are correct.

6. Herborg: neither she nor her sorrows are elsewhere mentioned, nor is it clear what a "queen of the Huns" is doing in Gunnar's home, but the word "Hun" has little definiteness of meaning in the poems, and is frequently applied to Sigurth himself (cf. note on stanza 24). Herborg appears from stanza 11 to have been the foster-mother of Gollrond, Guthrun's sister. Lines 5–7 may be interpolations, or may form a separate stanza.

7. Lines 1 and 2 stand in reversed order in the manuscript; I have followed Gering's conjectural transposition.[1]

---

[1] To conform to the Old Norse, stanzas 7–24 have been renumbered; in the Bellows translation at stanza 24 another renumbering occurs.

10. Herborg implies that the queen's jealousy was not altogether misplaced.

11. Cf. stanza 5 and note. The manuscript abbreviates to first letters.

12. Gollrond: not elsewhere mentioned. Line 4 looks like an interpolation replacing a line previously lost.

13. The manuscript indicates line 3 as the beginning of a stanza, and some editors have attempted to follow this arrangement. Many editors assume the loss of a line from this stanza.

16. The word here translated "tresses" is sheer guesswork. The detail of the geese is taken from Sigurtharkvitha en skamma, 29, line 3 here being identical with line 4 of that stanza.

17. Line 1, abbreviated in the manuscript, very likely should be simply "Gollrond spake."

18. Cf. Guthrunarkvitha II, 2. The manuscript does not name the speaker, and some editions have a first line, "Then Guthrun spake, the daughter of Gjuki."

19. Herjan: Odin; his maids are the Valkyries; cf. Voluspo, 31, where the same phrase is used.

21. Line 4 looks like an interpolation (cf. Fafnismol, 9, line 4), but some editors instead have queried line 5. How Guthrun's curse is fulfilled is told in the subsequent poems. That desire for Sigurth's treasure (the gold cursed by Andvari and Loki) was one of the motives for his murder is indicated in Sigurtharkvitha en skamma (stanza 16), and was clearly a part of the German tradition, as it appears in the Nibelungenlied.

22. Cf. Gripisspo, 35 and note.

23. Line 1 is abbreviated in the manuscript.

24. Editors are agreed that this stanza shows interpolations, but differ as to the lines to reject. Line 4 (literally "every wave of ill-doing drives thee") is substantially a proverb, and line 5, with its apparently meaningless reference to "seven" kings, may easily have come from some other source.

25. The stanza is obviously in bad shape; perhaps it represents two separate stanzas, or perhaps three of the lines are later additions. Atli: Brynhild here blames her brother, following the frequent custom of transferring the responsibility for a murder (cf. Helgakvitha Hundingsbana II,

33), because he compelled her to marry Gunnar against her will, an idea which the poet seems to have gained from Sigurtharkvitha en skamma, 32-39. These stanzas represent an entirely different version of the story, wherein Atli, attacked by Gunnar and Sigurth, buys them off by giving Gunnar his sister, Brynhild, as wife. He seems to have induced the latter to marry Gunnar by falsely telling her that Gunnar was Sigurth (a rationalistic explanation of the interchange of forms described in the Volsungasaga and Gripisspo, 37-39). In the present stanza Atli is made to do this out of desire for Sigurth's treasure. Hunnish race: this may be merely an error (neither Gunnar nor Sigurth could properly have been connected in any way with Atli and his Huns), based on Sigurtharkvitha en skamma, wherein Sigurth appears more than once as the "Hunnish king." The North was very much in the dark as to the differences between Germans, Burgundians, Franks, Goths, and Huns, and used the words without much discrimination. On the other hand, it may refer to Sigurth's appearance when, adorned with gold, he came with Gunnar to besiege Atli, in the alternative version of the story just cited (cf. Sigurtharkvitha en skamma, 36). Flame of the snake's bed: gold, so called because serpents and dragons were the traditional guardians of treasure, on which they lay.[2]

Prose. The manuscript has "Gunnar" in place of "Guthrun," but this is an obvious mistake; the entire prose passage is based on Guthrunarkvitha II, 14. The Volsungasaga likewise merely paraphrases Guthrunarkvitha II, and nothing further is known of Thora or her father, Hokon, though many inconclusive attempts have been made to identify the latter. Brynhild: the story of her death is told in great detail in the latter part of Sigurtharkvitha en skamma.

---

[2] Renumbering change occurs again, as half of the stanza is placed as stanza 26 to conform with the Old Norse.

SIGURTHARKVITHA EN SKAMMA
THE SHORT LAY OF SIGURTH

INTRODUCTION

The *Short Lay of Sigurth* follows immediately on from *Guthrunarkvitha I* in the *Codex Regius*, and is titled in the manuscript simply *Sigurtharkvitha* but is otherwise noted by the annotator as the *Short Lay of Sigurth*, implying the existence of a once well-known *Long Lay of Sigurth*, which most agree should be found within the missing eight pages of the *Codex Regius*. See the introduction to *Sigurtharkvitha in Meiri* for details.

The actual contents of the *Short Lay* lack a coherent narrative format and showcase many signs of a late origin, such that the specifics of the story are well known to the audience and can merely be alluded to or referenced primarily for evocative literary effect and poetic splendor, rather than to tell a structurally engaging tale. References to a glacier in stanza 8 have also led many scholars to conclude that a late Icelandic origin is most reasonable for the poem with suggestions ranging from the late 11th to the early 12th century. Several possible errors in the narrative structure of the work may testify to the author's remoteness from the wider continental and Scandinavian tradition and from a familiarity with its people and places.

Sigurth is repeatedly referred to in the poem as being of Hunnish extraction, which is a common error made in later times derived from the original Latin name of the Frankish tribe (the Hugones) being conflated with the historical tribe of the Huns, along with the origins and lands of the Goths in Reidgotaland. This can be seen in the sometimes shifting location of the saga-based Hunaland, whose origin can vary between modern Germany (representing the historical Frankish people), near Reidgotaland or north around Bjarmaland (representing the Nordic peoples' perception of the historical eastern-derived Hunnic peoples), or near to either side of the Gulf of Bothnia around Swedish Gästrikland and modern Finland (possibly representing a cultural or ethnic conflation between the Huns and the Sami/Finns/Lapplanders as vaguely eastern peoples). In any case, this is error stems from a case of mistaken identity and the distortion of the story over time, and is not a realistic supposition that the Franks and Huns share a common origin or peoplehood.

Another interesting passage to note here is the 45th stanza, wherein Hogni proclaims about Brynhildr:

> From the long road now shall ye hold her not,
> That born again she may never be!
> Foul she came from her mother forth,
> And born she was for wicked deeds,
> Sorrow to many a man to bring.

"That born again she may never be" is a clear but puzzling reference to the reincarnation beliefs of our ancestors, in which kinsmen are reborn within the same lineage anew (see the introduction to the *Helgakvida Hjorvarthssonar* for discussion on this point), yet Brynhildr is herself never shown to undergo such a reincarnation unless this is a reference to narrative elements now lost to us. It is, perhaps, a conflation between her and the heroine of the Helgi lays who is uniquely shown to be reincarnated multiple times, or perhaps it is a statement about the nature of these mortal Valkyries themselves which is simply occluded from us but would make sense in a fully realized religious context. A third possibility is that this represents a vague and generalized curse that is simply being too much read into. Without more information it is difficult to say whether the line is even intentional or simply an error on the part of the author, but given the late nature of the poem's likely origin, the latter must be considered as a possibility.

Sigurd and Gunnar
(J. C. Dollman)

Ár var, þats Sigurðr   sótti Gjúka,   1
Völsungr ungi,   er vegit hafði;
tók við tryggðum   tveggja bræðra,
seldusk eiða   eljunfræknir.

Mey buðu hánum   ok meiðma fjölð,   2
Guðrúnu ungu,   Gjúka dóttur;
drukku ok dæmðu   dægr margt saman
Sigurðr ungi   ok synir Gjúka.

Unz þeir Brynhildar   biðja fóru,   3
svá at þeim Sigurðr   reið í sinni
Völsungr ungi,   ok vega kunni;
hann of ætti,   ef hann eiga knætti.

Sigurðr inn suðræni   lagði sverð nökkvit,   4
mæki málfán,   á meðal þeirra;
né hann konu   kyssa gerði
né húnskr konungr   hefja sér at armi,
mey frumunga   fal hann megi Gjúka.

Hon sér at lífi   löst né vissi   5
ok at aldrlagi   ekki grand,
vamm þat er væri   eða vera hygði;
gengu þess á milli   grimmar urðir.

SIGURTHARKVITHA EN SKAMMA

1. Of old did Sigurth Gjuki seek,
The Volsung young, in battles victor;
Well he trusted the brothers twain,
With mighty oaths among them sworn.

2. A maid they gave him, and jewels many,
Guthrun the young, the daughter of Gjuki;
They drank and spake full many a day,
Sigurth the young and Gjuki's sons.

3. Thereafter went they Brynhild to woo,
And so with them did Sigurth ride,
The Volsung young, in battle valiant,
Himself would have had her if all he had seen.

4. The southern hero his naked sword,
Fair-flashing, let between them lie;
Nor would he come the maid to kiss;
The Hunnish king in his arms ne'er held
The maiden he gave to Gjuki's sons.

5. Ill she had known not in all her life,
And nought of the sorrows of men she knew;
Blame she had not, nor dreamed she should bear it,
But cruel the fates that among them came.

Ein sat hon úti   aftan dags,   6
nam hon svá margt   um at mælask:
"Hafa skal ek Sigurð,   eða þó svelta,
mög frumungan   mér á armi.

Orð mæltak nú,   iðrumk eftir þess: 7
kván er hans Guðrún,   en ek Gunnars;
ljótar nornir   skópu oss langa þrá."

Opt gengr hon innan   ills of fylld,   8
ísa ok jökla,   aftan hvern,
er þau Guðrún   ganga á beð
ok hana Sigurðr   sveipr í rifti,
konungr inn húnski   kván frjá sína.

"Vön geng ek vilja,   vers ok beggja,   9
verð ek mik gæla   af grimmum hug."

Nam af þeim heiftum   hvetjask at vígi: 10
"Þú skalt, Gunnarr,   gerst of láta
mínu landi   ok mér sjalfri;
mun ek una aldri   með öðlingi.

Mun ek aftr fara,   þars ek áðan vark   11
með nábornum   niðjum mínum;
þar mun ek sitja   ok sofa lífi,
nema þú Sigurð   svelta látir
ok jöfurr öðrum   æðri verðir.

Látum son fara   feðr í sinni,   12
skal-at ulf ala   ungan lengi.
Hveim verðr hölða   hefnd léttari
síðan til sátta,   at sonr lifi?"

Hryggr varð Gunnarr   ok hnipnaði,   13
sveip sínum hug,   sat of allan dag;
hann vissi þat   vilgi görla,
hvat hánum væri   vinna sæmst
eða hánum væri   vinna bezt,
alls sik Völsung   vissi firrðan
ok at Sigurð   söknuð mikinn.

By herself at the end of day she sat,   6
And in open words her heart she uttered:
"I shall Sigurth have, the hero young,
E'en though within my arms he die."

"The word I have spoken; soon shall I rue it,   7
His wife is Guthrun, and Gunnar's am I;
Ill Norns set for me long desire."

Oft did she go with grieving heart   8
On the glacier's ice at even-tide,
When Guthrun then to her bed was gone,
And the bedclothes Sigurth about her laid.
And the Hunnish king with his wife is happy;

"Now Gjuki's child to her lover goes,   9
Joyless I am and mateless ever,
Till cries from my heavy heart burst forth."

In her wrath to battle she roused herself: 10
"Gunnar, now thou needs must lose
Lands of mine and me myself,
No joy shall I have with the hero ever."

"Back shall I fare where first I dwelt,   11
Among the kin that come of my race,
To wait there, sleeping my life away,
If Sigurth's death thou shalt not dare,
And best of heroes thou shalt not be."

"The son shall fare with his father hence,   12
And let not long the wolf-cub live;
Lighter to pay is the vengeance-price
After the deed if the son is dead."

Sad was Gunnar, and bowed with grief,   13
Deep in thought the whole day through;
Yet from his heart it was ever hid
What deed most fitting he should find,
Or what thing best for him should be,
Or if he should seek the Volsung to slay,
For with mighty longing Sigurth he loved.

Ýmist hann hugði   jafnlanga stund: 14
þat var eigi   afartítt,
at frá konungdóm   kvánir gengi.
Nam hann sér Högna   heita at rúnum,
þar átti hann   alls fulltrúa:

"Ein er mér Brynhildr   öllum betri, 15
of borin Buðla,   hon er bragr kvenna;
fyrr skal ek mínu   fjörvi láta
en þeirar meyjar   meiðmum týna.

Vildu okkr fylki   til fjár véla? 16
Gótt er at ráða   Rínar malmi
ok unandi   auði stýra
ok sitjandi   sælu njóta."

Einu því Högni   andsvör veitti: 17
"Samir eigi okkr   slíkt at vinna,
sverði rofna   svarna eiða,
eiða svarna,   unnar tryggðir.

Vitum-a vit á moldu   menn in sælli, 18
meðan fjórir vér   folki ráðum
ok sá inn húnski   her-Baldr lifir,
né in mætri   mægð á foldu,
ef vér fimm sonu   fæðum lengi,
áttumgóða   æxla knættim.

Ek veit görla,   hvaðan vegir standa: 19
eru Brynhildar   brek ofmikil."

Gunnarr kvað: 20
"Vit skulum Guthorm   gerva at vígi,
yngra bróður,   ofróðara;
hann var fyr útan   eiða svarna,
eiða svarna,   unnar tryggðir."

Dælt var at eggja   óbilgjarnan, 21
stóð til hjarta   hjörr Sigurði.

Réð til hefnda   hergjarn í sal 22
ok eftir varp   óbilgjörnum;
fló til Guthorms   Grams ramliga
kynbirt járn   ór konungs hendi.

Much he pondered for many an hour;   14
Never before was the wonder known
That a queen should thus her kingdom leave;
In counsel then did he Hogni call,
For him in truest trust he held.

"More than all to me is Brynhild,   15
Buthli's child, the best of women;
My very life would I sooner lose
Than yield the love of yonder maid."

"Wilt thou the hero for wealth betray?   16
'Twere good to have the gold of the Rhine,
And all the hoard in peace to hold,
And waiting fortune thus to win."

Few the words of Hogni were: 17
"Us it beseems not so to do,
To cleave with swords the oaths we swore,
The oaths we swore and all our vows."

"We know no mightier men on earth   18
The while we four o'er the folk hold sway,
And while the Hunnish hero lives,
Nor higher kinship the world doth hold.
"If sons we five shall soon beget,
Great, methinks, our race shall grow;"

"Well I see whence lead the ways;   19
Too bitter far is Brynhild's hate."

Gunnar spake: 20
"Gotthorm to wrath we needs must rouse,
Our younger brother, in rashness blind;
He entered not in the oaths we swore,
The oaths we swore and all our vows."

It was easy to rouse the reckless one.   21
[...]
The sword in the heart of Sigurth stood.

In vengeance the hero rose in the hall,   22
And hurled his sword at the slayer bold;
At Gotthorm flew the glittering steel
Of Gram full hard from the hand of the king.

Hné hans of dolgr   til hluta tveggja,   23
hendr ok höfuð   hné á annan veg,
en fóta hlutr   féll aftr í stað.

Sofnuð var Guðrún   í sæingu   24
sorgalaus   hjá Sigurði,
en hon vaknaði   vilja firrð,
er hon Freys vinar   flaut í dreyra.

Svá sló hon svárar   sínar hendr,   25
at rammhugaðr   reis upp við beð:
"Grát-a-ðu, Guðrún,   svá grimmliga,
brúðr frumunga,   þér bræðr lifa.

Á ek til ungan   erfinytja,   26
kann-at hann firrask   ór fjándgarði;
þeir sér hafa   svárt ok dátt
enn nær numit   nýlig ráð.

Ríðr-a þeim síðan,   þótt sjau alir,   27
systursonr   slíkr at þingi.
Ek veit görla,   hví gegnir nú:
ein veldr Brynhildr   öllu bölvi.

Mér unni mær   fyr mann hvern,   28
en við Gunnar   grand ekki vannk;
þyrmða ek sifjum,   svörnum eiðum,
síðr værak heitinn   hans kvánar vinr."

Kona varp öndu,   en konungr fjörvi,   29
svá sló hon   svárar sínar hendr,
at kváðu við   kálkar í vá
ok gullu við   gæss í túni.

Hló þá Brynhildr   Buðla dóttir   30
einu sinni   af öllum hug,
er hon til hvílu   heyra knátti
gjallan grát   Gjúka dóttur.

Hitt kvað þá Gunnarr   gramr haukstalda: 31
"Hlær-a þú af því,   heiftgjörn kona,
glöð á gólfi,   at þér góðs viti.
Hví hafnar þú   inum hvíta lit,
feikna fæðir?   Hygg ek, at feig séir.

The foeman cleft asunder fell,   23
Forward hands and head did sink,
And legs and feet did backward fall.

Guthrun soft in her bed had slept,   24
Safe from care at Sigurth's side;
She woke to find her joy had fled,
In the blood of the friend of Freyr she lay.

So hard she smote her hands together   25
That the hero rose up, iron-hearted:
"Weep not, Guthrun, grievous tears,
Bride so young, for thy brothers live."

"Too young, methinks, is my son as yet,   26
He cannot flee from the home of his foes;
Fearful and deadly the plan they found,
The counsel new that now they have heeded."

"No son will ride, though seven thou hast,   27
To the Thing as the son of their sister rides;
Well I see who the ill has worked,
On Brynhild alone lies the blame for all."

"Above all men the maiden loved me,   28
Yet false to Gunnar I ne'er was found;
I kept the oaths and the kinship I swore;
Of his queen the lover none may call me."

In a swoon she sank when Sigurth died;   29
So hard she smote her hands together
That all the cups in the cupboard rang,
And loud in the courtyard cried the geese.

Then Brynhild, daughter of Buthli, laughed,   30
Only once, with all her heart,
When as she lay full loud she heard
The grievous wail of Gjuki's daughter.

Then Gunnar, monarch of men, spake forth: 31
"Thou dost not laugh, thou lover of hate,
In gladness there, or for aught of good;
Why has thy face so white a hue,
Mother of ill? Foredoomed thou art."

Þú værir þess   verðust kvenna,   32
at fyr augum þér   Atla hjöggim,
sæir bræðr þínum blóðugt sár,
undir dreyrgar   knættir yfir binda."

Brynhildr kvað: 33
"Frýr-a maðr þér engi,
hefir þú fullvegit;
lítt sésk Atli   ófu þína;
hann mun ykkar   önd síðari
ok æ bera   afl it meira.

Segja mun ek þér, Gunnarr,   34
sjalfr veiztu görla,
hvé er yðr snemma   til saka réðuð;
varð ek til ung   né ofþrungin,
fullgædd féi   á fleti bróður.

Né ek vilda þat,   at mik verr ætti,   35
áðr þér Gjúkungar   riðuð at garði,
þrír á hestum   þjóðkonungar,
en þeira för   þörfgi væri.

Þeim hétumk   þá þjóðkonungi,   36
er með gulli sat   á Grana bógum;
var-at hann í augu   yðr um líkr
né á engi hlut   at álitum,
þó þykkizk ér   þjóðkonungar.

Ok mér Atli þat   einni sagði,   37
at hvárki lézk   höfn of deila,
gull né jarðir,   nema ek gefask létak,
ok engi hlut   auðins féar,
þá er mér jóðungri   eigu seldi
ok mér jóðungri   aura talði.

Þá var á hvörfun   hugr minn um þat,   38
hvárt ek skylda vega   eða val fella
böll í brynju   um bróður sök;
þat myndi þá   þjóðkunnt vera
mörgum manni   at munar stríði.

Létum síga   sáttmál okkur   39
lék mér meir í mun   meiðmar þiggja,
bauga rauða   burar Sigmundar;
né ek annars manns   aura vildak.

"A worthier woman wouldst thou have been   32
If before thine eyes we had Atli slain;
If thy brother's bleeding body hadst seen
And the bloody wounds that thou shouldst bind."

Brynhild spake: 33
"None mock thee, Gunnar! thou hast mightily fought,
But thy hatred little doth Atli heed;
Longer than thou, methinks, shall he live,
And greater in might shall he ever remain."

"To thee I say, and thyself thou knowest,   34
That all these ills thou didst early shape;
No bonds I knew, nor sorrow bore,
And wealth I had in my brother's home."

"Never a husband sought I to have,   35
Before the Gjukungs fared to our land;
Three were the kings on steeds that came,
Need of their journey never there was."

"To the hero great my troth I gave   36
Who gold-decked sat on Grani's back;
Not like to thine was the light of his eyes,
Nor like in form and face are ye,
Though kingly both ye seemed to be."

"And so to me did Atli say   37
That share in our wealth I should not have,
Of gold or lands, if my hand I gave not;
More evil yet, the wealth I should yield,
The gold that he in my childhood gave me,
The wealth from him in my youth I had."

"Oft in my mind I pondered much   38
If still I should fight, and warriors fell,
Brave in my byrnie, my brother defying;
That would wide in the world be known,
And sorrow for many a man would make."

"But the bond at last I let be made,   39
For more the hoard I longed to have,
The rings that the son of Sigmund won;
No other's treasure e'er I sought."

Unnak einum   né ýmissum,   40
bjó-at of hverfan   hug men-Skögul;
allt mun þat Atli   eftir finna,
er hann mína spyrr   morðför görva,

At þeygi skal   þunngeð kona   41
annarrar ver   aldri leiða;
þá mun á hefndum   harma minna."

Upp reis Gunnarr   gramr verðungar,   42
ok um hals konu   hendr of lagði;
gengu allir   ok þó ýmissir
af heilum hug   hana at letja.

Hratt af halsi   hveim þar sér,   43
lét-a mann sik letja   langrar göngu.

Nam hann sér Högna   hvetja at rúnum: 44
"Seggi vil ek alla   í sal ganga
þína með mínum,
nú er þörf mikil,
vita, ef meini   morðför konu,
unz af méli   enn mein komi;
þá látum því   þarfar ráða.»

Einu því Högni   andsvör veitti: 45
"Leti-a maðr hana   langrar göngu,
þars hon aftrborin   aldri verði;
hon kröng of komsk   fyr kné móður,
hon æ borin   óvilja til,
mörgum manni   at móðtrega."

Hvarf sér óhróðugr   andspilli frá,   46
þar er mörk menja   meiðmum deildi.

Leit hon of alla   eigu sína,   47
soltnar þýjar   ok salkonur;
gullbrynju smó,   var-a gott í hug,
áðr sik miðlaði   mækis eggjum.

Hné við bollstri   hon á annan veg   48
ok hjörunduð   hugði at ráðum:

"Nú skulu ganga,   þeir er gull vili   49
ok minni því   at mér þiggja;
ek gef hverri   of hróðit sigli,
bók ok blæju,   bjartar váðir."

"One alone of all I loved, 40
Nor changing heart I ever had;
All in the end shall Atli know,
When he hears I have gone on the death-road hence."

"Never a wife of fickle will 41
Yet to another man should yield.
[...]
So vengeance for all my ills shall come."

Up rose Gunnar, the people's ruler, 42
And flung his arms round her neck so fair;
And all who came, of every kind,
Sought to hold her with all their hearts.

But back she cast all those who came, 43
Nor from the long road let them hold her.

In counsel then did he Hogni call: 44
"Of wisdom now full great is our need.
Let the warriors here in the hall come forth,
Thine and mine, for the need is mighty,
If haply the queen from death they may hold,
Till her fearful thoughts with time shall fade."

Few the words of Hogni were: 45
"From the long road now shall ye hold her not,
That born again she may never be!
Foul she came from her mother forth,
And born she was for wicked deeds,
Sorrow to many a man to bring."

From the speaker gloomily Gunnar turned, 46
For the jewel-bearer her gems was dividing.

On all her wealth her eyes were gazing, 47
On the bond-women slain and the slaughtered slaves.
Her byrnie of gold she donned, and grim.

Was her heart ere the point of her sword had pierced it; 48
On the pillow at last her head she laid,
And, wounded, her plan she pondered o'er.

"Hither I will that my women come 49
Who gold are fain from me to get;
Necklaces fashioned fair to each
Shall I give, and cloth, and garments bright."

Þögðu allir,   við því orði   50
ok allir senn   andsvör veittu:
"Ærnar soltnar,   munum enn lifa.
Verða salkonur   sæmð at vinna."

Unz af hyggjandi   hörskrýdd kona,   51
ung at aldri   orð viðr of kvað:
"Vilk-at ek mann trauðan   né torbænan
um óra sök   aldri týna.

Þó mun á beinum   brenna yðrum   52
færi eyrir,   þá er ér fram komið,
neitt Menju góð,   mín at vitja.

Sezktu niðr, Gunnarr,   mun ek segja þér   53
lífs örvæna   ljósa brúði;
mun-a yðvart far   allt í sundi,
þótt ek hafa   öndu látit.

Sátt munuð it Guðrún   snemr, en þú hyggir;   54
hefir kunn kona   við konungi
daprar minjar   at dauðan ver.

Þar er mær borin,   55
móðir fæðir,
sú mun hvítari   en inn heiði dagr
Svanhildr vera,   sólar geisla.

Gefa muntu Guðrúnu   góðra nökkurum   56
skeyti skæða   skatna mengi;
mun-at at vilja   versæl gefin;
hana mun Atli   eiga ganga,
of borinn Buðla,   bróðir minn.

Margs á ek minnask,   hvé við mik fóru,   57
þá er mik sára   svikna höfðuð,
vaðin at vilja   vark, meðan ek lifðak.

Muntu Oddrúnu   eiga vilja,   58
en þik Atli mun   eigi láta;
it munuð lúta   á laun saman,
hon mun þér unna   sem ek skyldak,
ef okkr góð of sköp   gerði verða.

Þik mun Atli   illu beita,   59
muntu í öngan   ormgarð lagiðr.

Silent were all as so she spake,   50
And all together answer made:
"Slain are enough; we seek to live,
Not thus thy women shall honor win."

Long the woman, linen-decked, pondered,   51
—Young she was—and weighed her words:
"For my sake now shall none unwilling
Or loath to die her life lay down."

"But little of gems to gleam on your limbs   52
Ye then shall find when forth ye fare
To follow me, or of Menja's wealth.
[...]"

"Sit now, Gunnar! for I shall speak   53
Of thy bride so fair and so fain to die;
Thy ship in harbor home thou hast not,
Although my life I now have lost."

"Thou shalt Guthrun requite   54
More quick than thou thinkest,
Though sadly mourns the maiden wise
Who dwells with the king, o'er her husband dead."

"A maid shall then the mother bear;   55
Brighter far than the fairest day
Svanhild shall be, or the beams of the sun."

"Guthrun a noble husband thou givest,   56
Yet to many a warrior woe will she bring,
Not happily wedded she holds herself;
Her shall Atli hither seek,
Buthli's son, and brother of mine."

"Well I remember how me ye treated   57
When ye betrayed me with treacherous wiles;
Lost was my joy as long as I lived."

"Oddrun as wife thou fain wouldst win,   58
But Atli this from thee withholds;
Yet in secret tryst ye twain shall love;
She shall hold thee dear, as I had done
If kindly fate to us had fallen."

"Ill to thee shall Atli bring,   59
When he casts thee down in the den of snakes."

Þat mun ok verða   þvígit lengra,   60
at Atli mun   öndu týna,
sælu sinni,   ok sona lífi,
því at hánum Guðrún   grýmir á beð
snörpum eggjum   af sárum hug.

Sæmri væri Guðrún,   systir ykkur,   61
frumver sínum   at fylgja dauðum,
ef henni gæfi   góðra ráða
eða ætti hon hug   ossum líkan.

Ört mæli ek nú,   en hon eigi mun   62
of óra sök   aldri týna;
hana munu hefja   hávar bárur
til Jónakrs   óðaltorfu.

Ala mun hún sér jóð,   erfivörðu,   63
erfivörðu,   Jónakrs sonum;
mun hon Svanhildi   senda af landi,
sína mey   ok Sigurðar.

Hana munu bíta   Bikka ráð,   64
því at Jörmunrekkr   óþarft lifir;
þá er öll farin   ætt Sigurðar;
eru Guðrúnar   græti at fleiri.

Biðja mun ek þik   bænar einnar,   65
sú mun í heimi   hinzt bæn vera:
Láttu svá breiða   borg á velli,
at undir oss öllum   jafnrúmt séi,
þeim er sultu   með Sigurði.

Tjaldi þar um þá borg   tjöldum ok skjöldum,   66
valarift vel fáð   ok Vala mengi;
brenni mér inn húnska   á hlið aðra.

Brenni inum húnska   á hlið aðra   67
mína þjóna   menjum göfga:
tveir at höfðum   ok tveir haukar;
þá er öllu skipt   til jafnaðar.

Liggi okkar enn í milli   68
malmr hringvariðr,   egghvast járn,
sem endr lagit,   þá er vit bæði
beð einn stigum   ok hétum þá
hjóna nafni.

"But soon thereafter Atli too
His life, methinks, as thou shalt lose,
His fortune lose and the lives of his sons;
Him shall Guthrun, grim of heart,
With the biting blade in his bed destroy."

60

"It would better beseem thy sister fair
To follow her husband first in death,
If counsel good to her were given,
Or a heart akin to mine she had."

61

"Slowly I speak, but for my sake
Her life, methinks, she shall not lose;
She shall wander over the tossing waves,
To where Jonak rules his father's realm."

62

"Sons to him she soon shall bear,
Heirs therewith of Jonak's wealth;
But Svanhild far away is sent,
The child she bore to Sigurth brave."

63

"Bikki's word her death shall be,
For dreadful the wrath of Jormunrek;
So slain is all of Sigurth's race,
And greater the woe of Guthrun grows."

64

"Yet one boon I beg of thee,
The last of boons in my life it is:
Let the pyre be built so broad in the field
That room for us all will ample be,
For us who slain with Sigurth are."

65

"With shields and carpets cover the pyre,
Shrouds full fair, and fallen slaves,
And besides the Hunnish hero burn me."

66

"Besides the Hunnish hero there
Slaves shall burn, full bravely decked,
Two at his head and two at his feet,
A brace of hounds and a pair of hawks,
For so shall all be seemly done."

67

"Let between us lie once more
The steel so keen, as so it lay
When both within one bed we were,
And wedded mates by men were called."

68

Hrynja hánum þá   á hæl þeygi   69
hlunnblik hallar   hringi litkuð,
ef hánum fylgir   ferð mín heðan;
þeygi mun ór för   aumlig vera.

Því at hánum fylgja   fimm ambáttir,   70
átta þjónar,   eðlum góðir,
fóstrman mitt   ok faðerni,
þat er Buðli gaf   barni sínu.

Margt sagða ek,   munda ek fleira,   71
er mér meir mjötuðr   málrúm gæfi;
ómum þverr,   undir svella,
satt eitt sagðak,   svá mun ek láta."

"The door of the hall shall strike not the heel 69
Of the hero fair with flashing rings,
If hence my following goes with him;
Not mean our faring forth shall be."

"Bond-women five shall follow him, 70
And eight of my thralls, well-born are they,
Children with me, and mine they were
As gifts that Buthli his daughter gave."

"Much have I told thee, and more would say 71
If fate more space for speech had given;
My voice grows weak, my wounds are swelling;
Truth I have said, and so I die."

ENDNOTES

1. *Gjuki*: father of *the brothers twain*, Gunnar and Hogni, and of *Guthrun*. In this version of the story Sigurth goes straight to the home of the Gjukungs after his victory over the dragon Fafnir, without meeting Brynhild on the way (cf. *Gripisspo*, 13 and note). *Volsung*: Sigurth's grandfather was Volsung; cf. *Fra Dautha Sinfjotla* and note. *Oaths*: regarding the blood-brotherhood sworn by Sigurth, Gunnar, and Hogni cf. *Brot*, 18 and note.

3. *Brynhild*: on the winning of Brynhild by Sigurth in Gunnar's shape cf. *Gripisspo*, 37 and note. The poet here omits details, and in stanzas 32–39 appears a quite different tradition regarding the winning of Brynhild, which I suspect he had in mind throughout the poem.

4. *Southern hero*: Sigurth, whose Frankish origin is seldom wholly lost sight of in the Norse versions of the story. On the episode of the sword cf. *Gripisspo*, 41 and note. Line 3 may well be an interpolation; both lines 4 and 5 have also been questioned, and some editions combine line 5 with lines 1–3 of stanza 5. *Hunnish king*: Sigurth, who was, of course, not a king of the Huns, but was occasionally so called in the later poems owing to the lack of ethnological distinction made by the Norse poets (cf. *Guthrunarkvitha I*, 24 and note).

5. This stanza may refer, as Gering thinks, merely to the fact that Brynhild lived happy and unsuspecting as Gunnar's wife until the fatal quarrel with Guthrun (cf. *Gripisspo*, 45 and note) revealed to her the deceit whereby she had been won, or it may refer to the version of the story which appears in stanzas 32–39, wherein Brynhild lived happily with Atli, her brother, until he was attacked by Gunnar and Sigurth, and was compelled to give his sister to Gunnar, winning her consent thereto by representing

Gunnar as Sigurth, her chosen hero (cf. *Guthrunarkvitha I*, 24 and note). The manuscript marks line 4 as the beginning of a new stanza, and many editors combine it with stanza 6.

6. Brynhild has now discovered the deceit that has been practised on her. That she had loved Sigurth from the outset (cf. stanza 40) fits well with the version of the story wherein Sigurth meets her before he comes to Gunnar's home (the version not used in this poem), or the one outlined in the note on stanza 5, but does not accord with the story of Sigurth's first meeting Brynhild in Gunnar's form—an added reason for believing that the poet in stanzas 5–6 had in mind the story represented by stanzas 32–39. *The hero*: the manuscript originally had the phrase thus, then corrected it to "though I die," and finally crossed out the correction. Many editions have "I."

7. Perhaps a line is missing after line 3.

8. *Glacier*: a bit of Icelandic (or Greenland) local color.[1]

9. Line 1 does not appear in the manuscript, and is based on a conjecture by Bugge. The manuscript indicates line 3 as the beginning of a stanza, and some editors assume a gap of two lines after line 4. *Hunnish king*: cf. stanza 4.

10. *Lands*: Brynhild's wealth again points to the story represented by stanzas 32–39; elsewhere she is not spoken of as bringing wealth to Gunnar.

11. Line 5, or perhaps line 3, may be interpolated.

12. *The son*: the three-year-old son of Sigurth and Guthrun, Sigmund, who was killed at Brynhild's behest.

13. This stanza has been the subject of many conjectural emendations. Some editions assume a gap after line 2, and make a separate stanza of lines 3–7; others mark lines 5–7 as spurious. The stanza seems to have been expanded by repetition. *Grief* (line 1): the manuscript has "wrath," involving a metrical error.

14. Bugge and Gering transfer lines 4–5 to the beginning of stanza 16, on the basis of the *Volsungasaga* paraphrase, and assume a gap of one line after line 3. Line 5, which is in the nature of a stereotyped clause, may well be interpolated.

---

1 "And the Hunnish king with his wife is happy;" has been added to the end of stanza 8 to conform with the Old Norse; in the Bellows original translation this line is line 2 of stanza 9.

15. After "Buthli" in line 2 the manuscript has "my brother," apparently a scribal error. In line 4 the manuscript has "wealth" instead of "love," apparently with stanza 10 in mind, but the *Volsungasaga* paraphrase has "love," and many editors have suspected an error.

16. Cf. note on stanza 14. After thus adding lines 4–5 of stanza 14 at the beginning of stanza 16, Gering marks line 4 as probably spurious; others reject both lines 3 and 4 as mere repetitions. *Rhine*: the Rhine, the sands of which traditionally contained gold, was apparently the original home of the treasure of the Nibelungs, converted in the North to Andvari's treasure (cf. *Reginsmol*, 1–9). That greed for Sigurth's wealth was one of the motives for his slaying is indicated likewise in *Guthrunarkvitha I*, 20, and in the German versions of the story.

18. *We four*: if line 5 of stanza 18 is spurious, or the reference therein to "five" is a blunder, as may well be the case, then the "four" are Sigurth and the three brothers, Gunnar, Hogni, and Gotthorm. But it may be that the poet had in mind a tradition which, as in the *Thithrekssaga*, gave Gjuki a fourth son, in which case the "four" refers only to the four Gjukungs. *Hunnish hero*: Sigurth; cf. stanza 4 and note. Some editions put line 2 Stanza 19 between lines 4 and 5 Stanza 18.[2]

19. *We five*: see note on preceding stanza. Some editors mark lines:

> If sons we five shall soon beget,
> Great, methinks, our race shall grow;

as spurious, and either assume a gap of two lines after:

> Too bitter far is Brynhild's hate.

or combine lines

> Well I see whence lead the ways;
> Too bitter far is Brynhild's hate.

with stanza 20. *Whence lead the ways*: a proverbial expression signifying "whence the trouble comes."[3]

20. The manuscript does not name the speaker. *Gotthorm* (the name is variously spelt): half-brother of Gunnar and Hogni (cf. *Hyndluljoth*, 27 and note, and *Brot*, 4 and note). The name is the northern form of Gun-

---

2 Lines 4 and 5 of stanza 18 are lines 1 and 2 in the original Bellows translation; they have been added to the end of stanza 18 to conform with the Old Norse. The references in footnote 18 have therefore been altered to reflect this.
3 The wording of footnote 19 has been altered to reflect changes made to the stanza.

domar; a prince of this name is mentioned in the *Lex Burgundionum*, apparently as a brother of Gundahari (Gundicarius). In the *Nibelungenlied* the third brother is called Gernot.

21. No gap is indicated in the manuscript, and many editors combine stanza 21 with stanza 22, but it seems likely that not only two lines, but one or more stanzas in addition, have been lost; cf. *Brot*, 4, and also the detailed account of the slaying of Sigurth in the *Volsungasaga*, wherein, as here, Sigurth is killed in his bed (cf. stanza 24) and not in the forest.

22. Some editions combine lines 3-4 with stanza 23. *Gram*: {Sigurth's sword (cf. *Reginsmol*, prose after stanza 14); the word here, however, may not be a proper name, but may mean "the hero."

23. A line may well have been lost from this stanza.

24. *Freyr*: if the phrase "the friend of Freyr" means anything more than "king" (cf. *Rigsthula*, 46 etc.), which I doubt, it has reference to the late tradition that Freyr, and not Odin, was the ancestor of the Volsungs (cf. *Helgakvitha Hundingsbana I*, 57).

25. Müllenhoff thinks this stanza, or at any rate lines 1-2, a later addition based on stanza 29.

26. *My son*: Sigmund; cf. stanza 12 and note, and also *Brot*, 9 and note.

27. Sigurth means that although Guthrun may have seven sons by a later marriage, none of them will equal Sigmund, "son of their (i.e., Gunnar's and Hogni's) sister." *Thing*: council.

28. Sigurth's protestation of guiltlessness fits perfectly with the story of his relations with Brynhild used in this poem, but not, of course, with the alternative version, used in the *Gripisspo* and elsewhere, wherein Sigurth meets Brynhild before he woos her for Gunnar, and they have a daughter, Aslaug.

29. Cf. *Guthrunarkvitha I*, 15.

30. Cf. *Brot*, 10.

31. Line 1 may well be a mere expansion of "Gunnar spake." The manuscript marks line 4 as the beginning of a new stanza, and some editions combine lines 4-5 with stanza 32.

32. This stanza, which all editors have accepted as an integral part of the poem, apparently refers to the same story represented by stanzas 37-39,

ENDNOTES 647

which most editors have (I believe mistakenly) marked as interpolated. As is pointed out in the notes on stanzas 3, 5, 6 and 10, the poet throughout seems to have accepted the version of the story wherein Gunnar and Sigurth besiege Atli, and are bought off by the gift of Atli's sister, Brynhild, to Gunnar as wife, her consent being won by Atli's representation that Gunnar is Sigurth (cf. also *Guthrunarkvitha I*, 24 and note).

33. The manuscript does not name the speaker, and some editions add a first line: "Then Brynhild, daughter of Buthli, spake."

34. Cf. stanza 5.

35. *Three kings*: Gunnar, Hogni, and Sigurth.

36. Some editions place this stanza after stanza 39, on the theory that stanzas 37–39 are interpolated. Line 4, as virtually a repetition of line 3, has generally been marked as spurious. In this version of the winning of Brynhild it appears that Atli pointed out Sigurth as Gunnar, and Brynhild promptly fell in love with the hero whom, as he rode on *Grani* and was decked with some of the spoils taken from Fafnir, she recognized as the dragon's slayer. Thus no change of form between Sigurth and Gunnar was necessary. The oath to marry Gunnar had to be carried out even after Brynhild had discovered the deception.

37. Most editors mark stanzas 37–39 as interpolated, but cf. note on stanza 32. Stanza 37 has been variously emended. Lines 4 and 6 look like interpolated repetitions, but many editors make two stanzas, following the manuscript in beginning a new stanza with line 4. After line 1 Grundtvig adds: "Son of Buthli, and brother of mine." After line 6 Bugge adds: "Not thou was it, Gunnar, who Grani rode, / Though thou my brother with rings didst buy." Regarding Brynhild's wealth cf. stanza 10 and note.

38. Brynhild here again appears as a Valkyrie. The manuscript marks line 4 as the beginning of a new stanza. Any one of the last three lines may be spurious.

39. Some editions combine this stanza with lines 4–5 of stanza 38, with lines 1–2 of stanza 40, or with the whole of stanza 40. *The bond*: Brynhild thought she was marrying Sigurth, owner of the treasure, whereas she was being tricked into marrying Gunnar.

41. At this point there seem to be several emissions. Brynhild's statement in lines 1–2 seems to refer to the episode, not here mentioned but told in detail in the *Volsungasaga*, of Sigurth's effort to repair the wrong that has been done her by himself giving up Guthrun in her favor, an offer which

648   POETIC EDDA

she refuses. The lacuna here suggested, which is not indicated in the manuscript, may be simply a single line (line 1) or a stanza or more. After line 2 there is almost certainly a gap of at least one stanza, and possibly more, in which Brynhild states her determination to die.

42. Hardly any two editions agree as to the arrangement of the lines in stanzas 42–44. I have followed the manuscript except in transposing line 4 of stanza 43 to this position from the place it holds in the manuscript after line 4 of stanza 44. All the other arrangements involve the rejection of two or more lines as spurious and the assumption of various gaps. Gering and Sijmons both arrange the lines thus: 42, 1–2; two-line gap; 43, 3 (marked probably spurious); 44, 1–4; 43–4 (marked probably spurious); 42, 3–4; 43, 1–2.[4]

44. Cf. note on stanza 42.[5]

45. Perhaps the remains of two stanzas; the manuscript marks line 4 as the beginning of a new stanza, and after line 4 an added line has been suggested: "She was ever known for evil thoughts." On the other hand, line 1, identical with line 1 of stanza 17, may well be a mere expansion of "Hogni spake," and line 6 may have been introduced, with a slight variation, from line 5 of stanza 38. *Born again*: [refers to the doctrine of reincarnation common to the Germanics, in which people were taken to be reborn into their own kin generations later.]

46. The manuscript marks line 3 as beginning a stanza; some editions treat lines 1–2 as a separate stanza, and combine lines 3–4 with lines 1–2 of stanza 47. *Jewel-bearer* (literally "land of jewels"): woman, here Brynhild. *Bond-women*, etc.: in stanza 69 we learn that five female slaves and eight [thralls] were killed to be burned on the funeral pyre, and thus to follow Sigurth in death. See note 47.

47. The manuscript marks line 3, and not line 1, as beginning a stanza, and some editions treat lines 3–4 as a separate stanza, or combine them with stanza 48.[6]

---

4 Footnote 43 has been removed, as explained in the next note.
5 The lines:

   In counsel then did he Hogni call:
   Of wisdom now full great is our need.

Were moved from the original position as lines 3 and 4 stanza 43 in Bellows original translation to lines 1 and 2 stanza 44 to conform with the Old Norse.
6 The lines:

   On all her wealth her eyes were gazing,
   On the bond-women slain and the slaughtered slaves.

49. Brynhild means, as stanzas 50–52 show, that those of her women who wish to win rewards must be ready to follow her in death. The word translated "women" in line 1 is conjectural, but the general meaning is clear enough.

50. In place of "as so she spake" in line 1 the manuscript has "of their plans they thought," which involves a metrical error.

52. No gap indicated in the manuscript; many editions place it between lines 3 and 4. *Menja's wealth*: gold; the story of the mill Grotti, whereby the giantesses Menja and Fenja ground gold for King Frothi, is told in the *Grottasongr*.

53. With this stanza begins Brynhild's prophesy of what is to befall Gunnar, Guthrun, Atli, and the many others involved in their fate. Line 3 is a proverbial expression meaning simply "your troubles are not at an end."

54. No gap is indicated in the manuscript; one suggestion for line 2 runs: "Grimhild shall make her to laugh once more." Gering suggests a loss of three lines, and joins lines 3–4 with stanza 55.

55. Probably a line has been lost from this stanza. Grundtvig adds as a new first line: "Her shalt thou find in the hall of Half." Some editions query line 3 as possibly spurious. *Svanhild*: the figure of Svanhild is exceedingly old. The name means "Swan-Maiden-Warrior," applying to just such mixtures of swan-maiden and Valkyrie as appear in the *Völundarkvitha*. Originally part of a separate tradition, Svanhild appears first to have been incorporated in the Jormunrek (Ermanarich) story as the unhappy wife of that monarch, and much later to have been identified as the daughter of Sigurth and Guthrun, thus linking the two sets of legends.

56. Line 2 in the original is almost totally obscure. Line 4 should very possibly precede line 2, while line 5 looks like an unwarranted addition.

57. This stanza probably ought to follow stanza 53, as it refers solely to) the winning of Brynhild by Gunnar and Sigurth. Müllenhoff regards stanzas 54–56 as interpolated. The manuscript indicates no gap after line 3.

Were moved to the beginning of stanza 47 to conform with the Old Norse. Whereas the lines:

> Was her heart ere the point of her sword had pierced it;
> On the pillow at last her head she laid,
> And, wounded, her plan she pondered o'er.

Were made into a separate stanza numbered 48 to conform to the Old Norse. Thus the Bellows translation stanza numbers are renumbered from stanzas 48–71.

58. Stanzas 58–59 seem to be the remains of two stanzas, but the *Volsungasaga* paraphrase follows closely the form here given. Line 3 may well be spurious; line 5 has likewise been questioned. *Oddrun*: this sister of Atli and Brynhild, known mainly through the *Oddrunargratr*, is a purely northern addition to the cycle, and apparently one of a relatively late date. She figures solely by reason of her love affair with Gunnar.

59. Possibly two lines have been lost; many editions combine the two remaining lines with lines 1–3 of stanza 60. Concerning the manner of Gunnar's death cf. *Drap Niflunga*.

60. Line 3 may well be spurious, as it is largely repetition. The manuscript has "sofa" ("sleep") in place of "sona" ("sons"), but the *Volsungasaga* paraphrase says clearly "sons." The slaying of Atli by Guthrun in revenge for his killing of her brothers is told in the two Atli lays. The manuscript marks line 4 as the beginning of a new stanza, and some editions make a separate stanza out of lines 4–5, or else combine them with stanza 61.

61. *To follow in death*: this phrase is not in *Regius*, but is included in late paper manuscripts, and has been added in most editions.

62. *Jonak*: this king, known only through the *Hamthesmol* and the stories which, like this one, are based thereon, is another purely northern addition to the legend. The name is apparently of Slavic origin. He appears solely as Guthrun's third husband and the father of Hamther, Sorli, and Erp (cf. introductory prose to *Guthrunarhvot*).

63. *Svanhild*: cf. stanza 55 and note.[7]

64. *Bikki*: Svanhild is married to the aged Jormunrek (Ermanarich), but Eikki, one of his followers, suggests that she is unduly intimate with Jormunrek's son, Randver. Thereupon Jormunrek has Randver hanged, and Svanhild torn to pieces by wild horses. Ermanarich's cruelty and his barbarous slaying of his wife and son were familiar traditions long before they became in any way connected with the Sigurth cycle (cf. introductory note to *Gripisspo* [Appendix B]).

65. Line 5 is very probably spurious.

66. The manuscript indicates no gap; a suggested addition runs "Gold let there be, and jewels bright." *Fallen slaves*: cf. stanzas 67 and 70. *Hunnish hero*: cf. stanza 4 and note.

---

[7] The text: "Ala mun hún sér jóð, erfivörðu" is reconstructed and amended based on Völsungasaga. The original text says "daughter of her and Sigurð", not "to Sigurth brave", as transcribed by Bellows.

67. In place of lines 3–4 the manuscript has one line "Two at his head, and a pair of hawks"; the addition is made from the *Volsungasaga* paraphrase. The burning or burying of slaves or beasts to accompany their masters in death was a general custom in the North. The number of slaves indicated in this stanza does not tally with the one given in stanza 70, wherefore Vigfusson rejects most of this stanza.

68. Cf. *Gripisspo*, 41 and note. After line 1 the manuscript adds the phrase "bright, ring-decked," referring to the sword, but it is metrically impossible, and many editions omit it.

69. *The door*: The gate of Hel's domain, like that of Mengloth's house (cf. *Svipdagsmol*, 26 and note), closes so fast as to catch anyone attempting to pass through. Apparently the poet here assumes that the gate of Valhall does likewise, but that it will be kept open for Sigurth's retinue.

70. Cf. stanza 67.

HELREITH BRYNHILDAR
BRYNHILD'S HELL-RIDE

INTRODUCTION

The *Helreith Brynhildar* follows from the *Short Lay of Sigurth* and, aside from a missing half a stanza, comes down to us complete and intact from the *Codex Regius*. It is a small work of only fourteen stanzas wherein Brynhildr defends herself against the accusations of a giantess for her role in Sigurth's death and the destruction of the house of the Nibelungs. The work is generally considered to be of late origin—in the 11th century—with its author basing it heavily upon readings of the older poetic and prose works of the *Sigurth Lays*.

The narrative is notable for two main occurrences within the text, wherein Brynhildr mentions that she used to be called Hild the Helmed and dwelt in in Hlymdalir, a place name not otherwise attested to but which means "Tumult-Dale", and likely refers to a mythical home of Valkyries within the heavens. Brynhildr maintains that she had her swan coat stolen by a mortal King (likely Agnar, brother of Autha) and was forced to swear an oath to him at 12 years old and marry him, for which she disobeyed Odin's command in battle. The narrative element of the swan coat is indicative of a late and popular origin, introducing folk tale elements with no legitimate mythological origin, but serves to explain to some degree how and why a Valkyrie of Odin is operating as a mortal woman in the first place. Although it cannot be considered religiously orthodox, it likely serves as a convenient cover for some narrative element that explained the issue in a theological sense. We would suggest that perhaps the narrative has the situation backwards, and rather than her marriage and fall to mortality causing her to break her oath to Odin, that the latter is the cause of her fall and demotion in a properly constructed theological context. Such a foreshadowing of Brynhild's treacherous nature and lack of fidelity to oaths would be narratively appropriate to her role in the *Sigurth Lay*.

Finally, the narrative structure of Brynhildr facing accusations from the giantess along the road to Hel is reminiscent of the function of the Helthing in which men will have to defend themselves in court among the Gods and answer for their crimes, which has likely been transferred to a confrontation with a giantess out of either legitimate ignorance or, more likely, deliberate concern for Christian teachings so as to not imply Pagan Gods as judging the dead.

Eftir dauða Brynhildar váru gör bál tvau, annat Sigurði, ok brann það fyrr, enn Brynhildr var á öðru brennd, ok var hon í reið þeiri, er guðvefjum var tjölduð. Svá er sagt, at Brynhildr ók með reiðinni á helveg ok fór um tún, þar er gýgr nökkur bjó. Gýgrin kvað:

"Skaltu í gögnum   ganga eigi 1
grjóti studda   garða mína,
betr semði þér   borða at rekja
heldr en vitja   vers annarrar.

Hvat skaltu vitja   af Vallandi, 2
hvarfúst höfuð,   húsa minna?
Þú hefir, Vár gulls,   ef þik vita lystir,
mild af höndum   manns blóð þvegit."

Brynhildr kvað: 3
"Bregðu eigi mér,   brúðr ór steini,
þótt ek værak   í víkingu;
ek mun okkur   æðri þykkja,
hvars menn eðli   okkart kunna."

Gýgrin kvað: 4
"Þú vart, Brynhildr   Buðla dóttir,
heilli verstu   í heim borin;
þú hefir Gjúka   of glatat börnum
ok búi þeira   brugðit góðu."

HELREITH BRYNHILDAR

After the death of Brynhild there were made two bale-fires, the one for Sigurth, and that burned first, and on the other was Brynhild burned, and she was on a wagon which was covered with a rich cloth. Thus it is told, that Brynhild went in the wagon on Hel-way, and passed by a house where dwelt a certain giantess. The giantess spake:

"Thou shalt not further forward fare,   1
My dwelling ribbed with rocks across;
More seemly it were at thy weaving to stay,
Than another's husband here to follow."

"What wouldst thou have from Valland here,   2
Fickle of heart, in this my house?
Gold-goddess, now, if thou wouldst know,
Heroes' blood from thy hands hast washed."

Brynhild spake: 3
"Chide me not, woman from rocky walls,
Though to battle once I was wont to go;
Better than thou I shall seem to be,
When men us two shall truly know."

The giantess spake: 4
"Thou wast, Brynhild, Buthli's daughter,
For the worst of evils born in the world;
To death thou hast given Gjuki's children,
And laid their lofty house full low."

Brynhildr kvað: 5
"Ek mun segja þér   svinn ór reiðu
vitlaussi mjök,   ef þik vita lystir,
hvé gerðu mik   Gjúka arfar
ástalausa   ok eiðrofa.

Brynhildr kvað: 6
Hétu mik allir   í Hlymdölum
Hildi undir hjalmi   hverr er kunni.

Lét hami vára   hugfullr konungr 7
átta systra   undir eik borit;
var ek vetra tolf,   ef þik vita lystir,
er ek ungum gram   eiða seldak.

Þá lét ek gamlan   á Goðþjóðu 8
Hjalmgunnar næst   heljar ganga;
gaf ek ungum sigr   Auðu bróður;
þar varð mér Óðinn   ofreiðr of þat.

Lauk hann mik skjöldum   í Skatalundi 9
rauðum ok hvítum,   randir snurtu;
þann bað hann slíta   svefni mínum,
er hvergi lands   hræðask kynni.

Lét hann um sal minn   sunnanverðan 10
hávan brenna   her alls viðar;
þar bað hann einn þegn   yfir at ríða,
þanns mér færði gull,   þats und Fáfni lá.

Brynhildr kvað: 11
Reið góðr Grana   gullmiðlandi,
þars fóstri minn   fletjum stýrði;
einn þótti hann þar   öllum betri
víkingr Dana   í verðungu.

Sváfu við ok unðum   í sæing einni, 12
sem hann minn bróðir   of borinn væri;
hvárki knátti   hönd yfir annat
átta nóttum   okkart leggja.

Því brá mér Guðrún   Gjúka dóttir, 13
at ek Sigurði   svæfak á armi,
þar varð ek þess vís,   er ek vildig-a-k,
at þau véltu mik   í verfangi.

Brynhild spake:

"Truth from the wagon here I tell thee, 5
Witless one, if know thou wilt
How the heirs of Gjuki gave me to be
joyless ever, a breaker of oaths."

"Hild the helmed in Hlymdalir 6
They named me of old, all they who knew me."
[...]
[...]

"The monarch bold the swan-robes bore 7
Of the sisters eight beneath an oak;
Twelve winters I was, if know thou wilt,
When oaths I yielded the king so young."

"Next I let the leader of Goths, 8
Hjalmgunnar the old, go down to hell,
And victory brought to Autha's brother;
For this was Odin's anger mighty."

"He beset me with shields in Skatalund, 9
Red and white, their rims o'erlapped;
He bade that my sleep should broken be
By him who fear had nowhere found."

"He let round my hall, that southward looked, 10
The branches' foe high-leaping burn;
Across it he bade the hero come
Who brought me the gold that Fafnir guarded."

"On Grani rode the giver of gold, 11
Where my foster-father ruled his folk;
Best of all he seemed to be,
The prince of the Danes, when the people met."

"Happy we slept, one bed we had, 12
As he my brother born had been;
Eight were the nights when neither there
Loving hand on the other laid."

"Yet Guthrun reproached me, Gjuki's daughter, 13
That I in Sigurth's arms had slept;
Then did I hear what I would were hid,
That they had betrayed me in taking a mate."

Munu við ofstríð   alls til lengi 14
konur ok karlar   kvikvir fæðask;
við skulum okkrum   aldri slíta
Sigurðr saman.   Sökkstu, gýgjar kyn."

"Ever with grief and all too long
Are men and women born in the world;
But yet we shall live our lives together,
Sigurth and I. Sink down, Giantess!"

ENDNOTES

Prose. The prose follows the last stanza of *Sigurtharkvitha en skamma* without break. *Two bale-fires*: this contradicts the statement made in the concluding stanzas of *Sigurtharkvitha en skamma*, that Sigurth and Brynhild were burned on the same pyre; there is no evidence that the annotator here had anything but his own mistaken imagination to go on.

2. *Valland*: this name ("Land of Slaughter") is used elsewhere of mythical places; cf. *Harbarthsljoth*, 24, and prose introduction to *Völundarkvitha*; it may here not be a proper name at all. *Gold-goddess*: poetic circumlocution for "woman."

6. In *Regius* these two lines stand after stanza 7, but most editions place them as here. They are not quoted in the *Nornagetsthattr*. Presumably two lines, and perhaps more, have been lost. It has frequently been argued that all or part of the passage from stanza 6 through stanza 10 (6-10, 7-10 or 8-10) comes originally from the so-called *Sigrdrifumol*, where it would undoubtedly fit exceedingly well. *Hild*: a Valkyrie name meaning "Fighter" (cf. *Voluspo*, 31). In such compound names as Brynhild ("Fighter in Armor") the first element was occasionally omitted. *Hlymdalir* ("Tumult-Dale"): a mythical name, merely signifying the place of battle as the home of Valkyries.

7. Regarding the identification of swan-maidens with Valkyries, and the manner in which men could get them in their power by stealing their swan-garments, cf. *Völundarkvitha*, introductory prose and note, where the same thing happens. *The monarch*: perhaps Agnar, brother of Autha, mentioned in *Sigrdrifumol* (prose and quoted verse following stanza 4) as the warrior for whose sake Brynhild defied Odin in slaying Hjalmgunnar. *Eight*: the *Nornagetsthattr* manuscripts have "sisters of Atli" instead of

"sisters eight."[1]

8. *Hjalmgunnar*: regarding this king of the Goths (the phrase means little) and his battle with Agnar, brother of *Autha* cf. *Sigrdrifumol*, prose after stanza 4. One *Nornageststhattr* manuscript has "brother of the giantess" in place of "leader of Goths."

9. Cf. *Sigrdrifumol*, prose introduction. *Skatalund* ("Warriors' Grove"): a mythical name; elsewhere the place where Brynhild lay is called Hindarfjoll.

10. *Branches' foe*: fire. Regarding the treasure cf. *Fafnismol*.

11. This stanza is presumably an interpolation, reflecting a different version of the story, wherein Sigurth meets Brynhild at the home of her brother-in-law and foster-father, Heimir (cf. *Gripisspo*, 19 and 27). *Grani*: Sigurth's horse. *Danes*: nowhere else does Sigurth appear in this capacity. Perhaps this is a curious relic of the Helgi tradition.

12. *Eight nights*: elsewhere (cf. *Gripisspo*, 42) the time is stated as three nights, not eight. There is a confusion of traditions here, as in *Gripisspo*. In the version of the story wherein Sigurth met Brynhild before he encountered the Gjukungs, Sigurth was bound by no oaths, and the union was completed; it is only in the alternative version that the episode of the sword laid between the two occurs.

---

[1] Stanza 7 was removed as it comes from the *Sigrdrifumol*; it is likely in error that this appears:

Annar hét Agnarr, Auðu bróðir,
er véttr engi vildi týja.

Stanza 8 has become Stanza 7.

DRAP NIFLUNGA
THE SLAYING OF THE NIFLUNGS

INTRODUCTION

The *Drap Niflunga* is a very short and wholly prose narrative annotation that follows immediately after the *Helreith Brynhildar*, meant to connect the narrative series between it and the following *Second Lay of Gudrun* regarding the death of her brothers at the hands of Atli. It was almost certainly written by the compiler of the *Codex Regius*, and thus originates in the 13th century and cannot be considered an authentic work of ancient lore.

The events of the prose narrative seem to be wholly informed by the contents of the two *Atli Lays* within the *Codex Regius* itself, so why the compiler of the manuscript did not simply place them after the *Helreith Brynhildar* with the *Second Lay of Gudrun* following thereafter is a mystery. As it stands, the work is largely extraneous unless one chooses to read the sagas in the precise order compiled.

Gunnarr ok Högni tóku þá gullit allt, Fáfnis arf. Ófriðr var þá í milli Gjúkunga ok Atla. Kenndi hann Gjúkungum völd um andlát Brynhildar. Þat var til sætta, at þeir skyldu gifta hánum Guðrúnu, ok gáfu henni óminnisveig at drekka, áðr hon játti at giftast Atla. Synir Atla váru þeir Erpr ok Eitill, en Svanhildr var Sigurðar dóttir ok Guðrúnar. Atli konungr bauð heim Gunnari ok Högna ok sendi Vinga eða Knéfröð. Guðrún vissi vélar ok sendi með rúnum orð, at þeir skyldu eigi koma, ok til jartegna sendi hon Högna hringinn Andvaranaut ok knýtti í vargshár. Gunnarr hafði beðit Oddrúnar, systur Atla, ok gat eigi. Þá fekk hann Glaumvarar, en Högni átti Kostberu. Þeira synir váru þeir Sólarr ok Snævarr ok Gjúki. En er Gjúkungar kómu til Atla, þá bað Guðrún sonu sína, at þeir bæði Gjúkungum lífs, en þeir vildu eigi. Hjarta var skorit ór Högna, en Gunnarr settr í ormgarð. Hann sló hörpu ok svæfði ormana, en naðra stakk hann til lifrar.

DRAP NIFLUNGA

Gunnar and Hogni then took all the gold that Fafnir had had. There was strife between the Gjukungs and Atli, for he held the Gjukungs guilty of Brynhild's death. It was agreed that they should give him Guthrun as wife, and they gave her a draught of forgetfulness to drink before she would consent to be wedded to Atli. The sons of Atli were Erp and Eitil, and Svanhild was the daughter of Sigurth and Guthrun. King Atli invited Gunnar and Hogni to come to him, and sent as messenger Vingi or Knefröth. Guthrun was aware of treachery, and sent with him a message in runes that they should not come, and as a token she sent to Hogni the ring Andvaranaut and tied a wolf's hair in it. Gunnar had sought Oddrun, Atli's sister, for his wife, but had her not; then he married Glaumvor, and Hogni's wife was Kostbera; their sons were Solar and Snævar and Gjuki. And when the Gjukungs came to Atli, then Guthrun besought her sons to plead for the lives of both the Gjukungs, but they would not do it. Hogni's heart was cut out, and Gunnar was cast into the serpent's den. He smote on the harp and put the serpents to sleep, but an adder stung him in the liver.

ENDNOTES

Prose. Niflungs: regarding the mistaken application of this name to the sons of Gjuki, who were Burgundians, cf. *Brot*, 17 and note. *Draught of forgetfulness*: according to the *Volsungasaga* Grimhild, Guthrun's mother, administered this, just as she did the similar draught which made Sigurth forget Brynhild. *Erp and Eitil*: Guthrun kills her two sons by Atli as part of her revenge; the annotator here explains her act further by saying that Guthrun asked her sons to intercede with their father in favor of Guthrun's brothers, but that they refused, a detail which he appears to have invented, as it is found nowhere else. *Svanhild*: cf. *Sigurtharkvitha en skamma*, 55 and note. *Vingi or Knefröth*: *Atlakvitha* (stanza 1) calls the messenger Knefröth; *Atlamol* (stanza 4) speaks of two messengers, but names only one of them, Vingi. The annotator has here tried, unsuccessfully, to combine the two accounts. *Andvaranaut*: regarding the origin of Andvari's ring cf. *Reginsmol*, prose after stanzas 4 and 5 and notes; Sigurth gave the ring to Guthrun. Here again the annotator is combining two stories; in *Atlakvitha* (stanza 8) Guthrun sends a ring (not Andvaranaut) with a wolf's hair; in *Atlamol* (stanza 4) she sends a message written in runes. The messenger obscures these runes, and Kostbera, Hogni's wife, who attempts to decipher them, is not clear as to their meaning, though she suspects danger. *Oddrun*: cf. *Sigurtharkvitha en skamma*, 57 and note. *Glaumvor*: almost nothing is told of Gunnar's second wife, though she appears frequently in the *Atlamol*. *Kostbera* (or Bera), Hogni's wife, is known only as skilled in runes. Her brother was Orkning. The sons of Hogni and Kostbera, according to the *Atlamol* (stanza 28), were *Solar* and *Snævar*; the third son, *Gjuki*, named after his grandfather, seems to be an invention of the annotator's. *Adder*: according to *Oddrunargratr* (stanza 30) Atli's mother assumed this form in order to complete her son's vengeance.

GUTHRUNARKVITHA EN FORNA
THE SECOND, OR OLD, LAY OF GUTHRUN

INTRODUCTION

The *Second Lay of Guthrun* is to be found within the *Codex Regius* where it is simply titled *Guthrunarkvitha*, but it has almost unanimously come to be referenced as either *Guthrunarkvitha II* or *The Old Lay of Guthrun*. The quality of the preservation of the work is variable, with a few missing lines in some stanzas, but without large chunks of narrative or entire sections of the poem missing. The work is generally regarded as the oldest of the *Sigurth Lays* to come down to us in complete form, with its origins somewhere in the 10th century.[1]

One notable element of the narrative is the death of Sigurth himself which is depicted in the forest, in contrast to the sister narrative in which he is ambushed in his sleep at home, in agreement with continental tradition, which the annotator of the *Codex Regius* mentions with the words "As German Men Say", implying that the latter narrative is the agreed upon Nordic custom at least by the 13th century. Another notable element is the wording of the response from Hogni to his sister Guthrun's curse that he should suffer a fate similar to her late husband. He responds, saying:

> Greater, Guthrun, thy grief shall be
> If the ravens so my heart shall rend.

The wording of this passage foregrounds a specifically Germanic way of

---

[1] The *Reginsmol*, *Fafnismol*, and *Sigrdrifumol* are all also of ancient repute, but quite clearly fragments of larger narratives rather than a whole and complete one.

understanding the world and its social relations that may strike many modern people as foreign or alien. The inability of the Germanic mind to countenance taking vengeance upon one's own kin or striving to cause them harm, and the abject horror when it finds such a situation forced upon someone by trickery, ignorance, or deceit, is a marked feature of saga works and folk stories from the continental Germans to the Scandinavians, ranging from the *Hildebrand Lay*,[2] in which the father Hildebrand is forced to slay his son Hadubrand in combat when his son does not recognize him upon the field, to the *Saga of Gisli Sursson* where Gisli slays his brother Thorkel's companion, with it being said to him, "you have done me no little wrong, I should say, in slaying Thorgrim, my brother-in-law and partner and close friend"—and yet Thorkel cannot even think of responding in kind to such an outrage.

The truth of Hogni's statement to Guthrun is verified in the course of her own story, with her husband Atli's slaying of her brothers leaving her miserable and aghast, she being limited to warning them of this despite the clear enmity modern man would assume that she feels.

---

[2] See the Imperium Press edition of *Beowulf*, which contains this Old High German poem.

Þjóðrekr konungr var með Atla ok hafði þar látit flesta alla menn sína. Þjóðrekr ok Guðrún kærðu harma sín á milli. Hon sagði hánum ok kvað:

Mær var ek meyja, móðir mik fæddi, 1
björt í búri, unna ek vel bræðrum,
unz mik Gjúki gulli reifði,
gulli reifði, gaf Sigurði.

Svá var Sigurðr of sonum Gjúka 2
sem væri grænn laukr ór grasi vaxinn
eða hjörtr hábeinn of hvössum dýrum
eða gull glóðrautt af gráu silfri.

Unz mér fyrmunðu mínir bræðr, 3
at ek ætta ver öllum fremra;
sofa þeir né máttu-t né of sakar dæma,
áðr þeir Sigurð svelta létu.

Grani rann at þingi, gnýr var at heyra, 4
en þá Sigurðr sjalfr eigi kom;
öll váru söðuldýr sveita stokkin
ok of vanið vási und vegöndum.

GUTHRUNARKVITHA EN FORNA

King Thjothrek was with Atli, and had lost most of his men. Thjothrek and Guthrun lamented their griefs together. She spoke to him, saying:

A maid of maids my mother bore me, 1
Bright in my bower, my brothers I loved,
Till Gjuki dowered me with gold,
Dowered with gold, and to Sigurth gave me.

So Sigurth rose o'er Gjuki's sons 2
As the leek grows green above the grass,
Or the stag o'er all the beasts doth stand,
Or as glow-red gold above silver gray.

Till my brothers let me no longer have 3
The best of heroes my husband to be;
Sleep they could not, or quarrels settle,
Till Sigurth they at last had slain.

From the Thing ran Grani with thundering feet, 4
But thence did Sigurth himself come never;
Covered with sweat was the saddle-bearer,
Wont the warrior's weight to bear.

Gekk ek grátandi   við Grana ræða,   5
úrughlýra   jó frá ek spjalla;
hnipnaði Grani þá,   drap í gras höfði,
jór þat vissi,   eigendr né lifðu-t.

Lengi hvarfaðak,   lengi hugir deildusk,   6
áðr ek of frægak   folkvörð at gram.

Hnipnaði Gunnarr,   sagði mér Högni   7
frá Sigurðar   sárum dauða:
"Liggr of höggvinn   fyr handan ver
Gothorms bani   of gefinn ulfum.

Líttu þar Sigurð   á suðrvega;   8
þá heyrir þú   hrafna gjalla,
örnu gjalla   æzli fegna,
varga þjóta   of veri þínum."

"Hví þú mér, Högni,   harma slíka   9
viljalaussi   vill of segja?
Þitt skyli hjarta   hrafnar slíta
við lönd yfir   en þú vitir manna!"

Svaraði Högni   sinni einu,   10
trauðr góðs hugar,   af trega stórum:
"Þess áttu, Guðrún,   græti at fleiri,
at hjarta mitt   hrafnar slíti."

Hvarf ek ein þaðan   annspilli frá   11
á við lesa   varga leifar;
gerðig-a ek hjúfra   né höndum slá
né kveina um   sem konur aðrar,
þá er sat soltin   of Sigurði.

Nótt þótti mér   niðmyrkr vera,   12
er ek sárla satk   yfir Sigurði;
ulfar þóttumk   öllu betri,
ef þeir léti mik   lífi týna
eða brenndi mik   sem birkinn við.

Fór ek af fjalli   fimm dægr talið,   13
unz ek höll Halfs   háva þekkðak.

Weeping I sought with Grani to speak,   5
With tear-wet cheeks for the tale I asked;
The head of Grani was bowed to the grass,
The steed knew well his master was slain.

Long I waited and pondered well   6
Ere ever the king for tidings I asked.
[...]

His head bowed Gunnar, but Hogni told   7
The news full sore of Sigurth slain:
"Hewed to death at our hands he lies,
Gotthorm's slayer, given to wolves.

"On the southern road thou shalt Sigurth see,   8
Where hear thou canst the ravens cry;
The eagles cry as food they crave,
And about thy husband wolves are howling."

"Why dost thou, Hogni, such a horror   9
Let me hear, all joyless left?
Ravens yet thy heart shall rend
In a land that never thou hast known."

Few the words of Hogni were,   10
Bitter his heart from heavy sorrow:
"Greater, Guthrun, thy grief shall be
If the ravens so my heart shall rend."

From him who spake I turned me soon,   11
In the woods to find what the wolves had left;
Tears I had not, nor wrung my hands,
Nor wailing went, as other women,
When by Sigurth slain I sat.

Never so black had seemed the night   12
As when in sorrow by Sigurth I sat;
The wolves [...]
[...]
Best of all methought 'twould be
If I my life could only lose,
Or like to birch-wood burned might be.

From the mountain forth five days I fared,   13
Till Hoalf's hall so high I saw;

678 POETIC EDDA

Sat ek með Þóru   sjau misseri,   14
dætr Hákonar   í Danmörku;
hon mér at gamni   gullbókaði
sali suðræna   ok svani danska.

Hafðu vit á skriftum   þat er skatar léku,   15
ok á hannyrðum   hilmis þegna,
randir rauðar,   rekka Húna,
hjördrótt, hjalmdrótt,   hilmis fylgju.

Skip Sigmundar   skriðu frá landi,   16
gylltar grímur,   grafnir stafnar;
byrðu vit á borða,   þat er þeir börðusk
Sigarr ok Siggeirr   suðr á Fjóni.

Þá frá Grimildr,   gotnesk kona,   17
hvat ek væra   hyggjuð [...];
hon brá borða   ok buri heimti
þrágjarnliga   þess at spyrja,
hverr vildi son   systur bæta
eða ver veginn   vildi gjalda.

Görr lézk Gunnarr   gull at bjóða   18
sakar at bæta,   ok it sama Högni.
Hon frétti at því,   hverr fara vildi
vigg at söðla   vagn at beita,
hesti ríða,   hauki fleygja,
öðrum at skjóta   af ýboga.

Valdarr Dönum   með Jarizleifi,   19
Eymóðr þriði   með Jarizskári
inn gengu þá,   jöfrum líkir,
Langbarðs liðar,   höfðu loða rauða,
stuttar brynjur,   steypða hjalma,
skalmum gyrðir,   höfðu skarar jarpar.

Hverr vildi mér   hnossir velja,   20
hnossir velja   ok hugat mæla,
ef þeir mætti mér   margra súta
tryggðir vinna,   né ek trúa gerða.

Færði mér Grímhildr   full at drekka   21
svalt ok sárligt,   né ek sakar munðak;
þat var of aukit   jarðar magni,
svalköldum sæ   ok sónum dreyra.

Seven half-years with Thora I stayed, 14
Hokon's daughter, in Denmark then.
With gold she broidered, to bring me joy,
Southern halls and Danish swans;

On the tapestry wove we warrior's deeds, 15
And the hero's thanes on our handiwork;
Flashing shields and fighters armed,
Sword-throng, helm-throng, the host of the king.

Sigmund's ship by the land was sailing, 16
Golden the figure-head, gay the beaks;
On board we wove the warriors faring,
Sigar and Siggeir, south to Fjon.

Then Grimhild asked, the Gothic queen, 17
Whether willingly would I [...]
[...]
Her needlework cast she aside, and called
Her sons to ask, with stern resolve,
Who amends to their sister would make for her son,
Or the wife requite for her husband killed.

Ready was Gunnar gold to give, 18
Amends for my hurt, and Hogni too;
Then would she know who now would go,
The horse to saddle, the wagon to harness,
The horse to ride, the hawk to fly,
And shafts from bows of yew to shoot.

Valdar, king of the Danes, was come, 19
With Jarizleif, Eymoth, and Jarizskar.
In like princes came they all,
The long-beard men, with mantles red,
Short their mail-coats, mighty their helms,
Swords at their belts, and brown their hair.

Each to give me gifts was fain, 20
Gifts to give, and goodly speech,
Comfort so for my sorrows great
To bring they tried, but I trusted them not.

A draught did Grimhild give me to drink, 21
Bitter and cold; I forgot my cares;
For mingled therein was magic earth,
Ice-cold sea, and the blood of swine.

Váru í horni   hvers kyns stafir   22
ristnir ok roðnir,   ráða ek né máttak,
lyngfiskr langr,   lands Haddingja
ax óskorit,   innleið dyra.

Váru þeim bjóri   böl mörg saman,   23
urt alls viðar   ok akarn brunnin,
umdögg arins,   iðrar blótnar,
svíns lifr soðin,   því at hon sakar deyfði.

En þá gleymðu,   er getit höfðu,   24
öll jöfurs   jórbjúg í sal;
kómu konungar   fyr kné þrennir,
áðr hon sjalfa mik   sótti at máli.

Grímhildr kvað: 25
"Gef ek þér, Guðrún,   gull at þiggja,
fjölð alls féar,   at þinn föður dauðan,
hringa rauða,   Hlöðvés sali,
ársal allan   at jöfur fallinn.

Grímhildr kvað: 26
Húnskar meyjar,   þær er hlaða spjöldum
ok gera gull fagrt,   svá at þér gaman þykki;
ein skaltu ráða   auði Buðla,
gulli göfguð   ok gefin Atla."

Guðrún kvað: 27
"Vilk eigi ek   með veri ganga
né Brynhildar   bróður eiga;
samir eigi mér   við son Buðla
ætt at auka   né una lífi."

Grímhildr kvað: 28
"Hirð-a-ðu höldum   heiftir gjalda,
því at vér höfum   valdit fyrri;
svá skaltu láta,   sem þeir lifi báðir
Sigurðr ok Sigmundr,   ef þú sonu fæðir."

Guðrún kvað: 29
"Mák-a ek, Grímhildr,   glaumi bella
né vígrisins   vánir telja,
siz Sigurðar   sárla drukku
hrægífr, huginn   hjartblóð saman."

In the cup were runes of every kind, 22
Written and reddened, I could not read them;
A heather-fish from the Haddings' land,
An ear uncut, and the entrails of beasts.

Much evil was brewed within the beer, 23
Blossoms of trees, and acorns burned,
Dew of the hearth, and holy entrails,
The liver of swine, all grief to allay.

Then I forgot, when the draught they gave me, 24
There in the hall, my husband's slaying;
On their knees the kings all three did kneel,
Ere she herself to speak began:

"Guthrun, gold to thee I give, 25
The wealth that once thy father's was,
Rings to have, and Hlothver's halls,
And the hangings all that the monarch had."

"Hunnish women, skilled in weaving, 26
Who gold make fair to give thee joy,
And the wealth of Buthli thine shall be,
Gold-decked one, as Atli's wife."

Guthrun spake: 27
"A husband now I will not have,
Nor wife of Brynhild's brother be;
It beseems me not with Buthli's son
Happy to be, and heirs to bear."

Grimhild spake: 28
"Seek not on men to avenge thy sorrows,
Though the blame at first with us hath been;
Happy shalt be as if both still lived,
Sigurth and Sigmund, if sons thou bearest."

Guthrun spake: 29
"Grimhild, I may not gladness find,
Nor hold forth hopes to heroes now,
Since once the raven and ravening wolf
Sigurth's heart's-blood hungrily lapped."

Grímhildr kvað: 30
"Þann hefi ek allra   ættgöfgastan
fylki fundit   ok framast nökkvi;
hann skaltu eiga   , unz þik aldr viðr,
verlaus vera,   nema þú vilir þenna."

Guðrún kvað: 31
"Hirð-a-ðu bjóða   bölvafullar
þrágjarnliga   þær kindir mér;
hann mun Gunnar   grandi beita
ok ór Högna   hjarta slíta;

Grátandi Grímhildr   greip við orði, 32
er burum sínum   bölva vætti
ok mögum sínum   meina stórra.

Grímhildr kvað: 33
"Lönd gef ek enn þér,   lýða sinni,
Vinbjörg, Valbjörg,   ef þú vill þiggja;
eigðu um aldr þat   ok uni, dóttir."

Guðrún kvað: 34
"Þann mun ek kjósa   af konungum
ok þó af niðjum   nauðig hafa;
verðr eigi mér   verr at yndi
né böl bræðra   at bura skjóli."

Hjarta slíta;   munk-at ek létta, 35
áðr lífshvatan   eggleiks hvötuð
aldri næmik."

Guðrún kvað: 36
Senn var á hesti   hverr drengr litinn,
en víf valnesk   hafið í vagna;
vér sjau daga   svalt land riðum,
en aðra sjau   unnir kníðum,
en ina þriðju sjau   þurrt land stigum.

Þar hliðverðir   hárar borgar 37
grind upp luku,   áðr í garð riðum.

Vakði mik Atli,   en ek vera þóttumk 38
full ills hugar   at frændr dauða.

Grimhild spake:
"Noblest of birth is the ruler now   30
I have found for thee, and foremost of all;
Him shalt thou have while life thou hast,
Or husbandless be if him thou wilt choose not."

Guthrun spake:
"Seek not so eagerly me to send   31
To be a bride of yon baneful race;
On Gunnar first his wrath shall fall,
And the heart will he tear from Hogni's breast."

Weeping Grimhild heard the words   32
That fate full sore for her sons foretold,
And mighty woe for them should work;

"Lands I give thee, with all that live there,   33
Vinbjorg is thine, and Valbjorg too,
Have them forever, but hear me, daughter."

So must I do as the kings besought,   34
And against my will for my kinsmen wed,
Ne'er with my husband joy I had,
And my sons by my brothers' fate were saved not.

[...]   35
I could not rest till of life I had robbed
The warrior bold, the maker of battles.

Soon on horseback each hero was,   36
And the foreign women in wagons faring;
A week through lands so cold we went,
And a second week the waves we smote,
And a third through lands that water lacked.

The warders now on the lofty walls   37
Opened the gates, and in we rode.

Atli woke me, for ever I seemed   38
Of bitterness full for my brothers' death.

684 POETIC EDDA

Atli kvað: 39
"Svá mik nýliga   nornir vekja,"
vílsinnis spá   vildi, at ek réða,
"hugða ek þik, Guðrún   Gjúka dóttir,
læblöndnum hjör   leggja mik í gögnum."

Guðrún kvað: 40
"Þat er fyr eldi,   er éarn dreyma,
fyr dul ok vil   drósar reiði;
mun ek þik við bölvi   brenna ganga,
líkna ok lækna,   þótt mér leiðir séir."

Atli kvað: 41
"Hugða ek hér í túni   teina fallna,
þá er ek vildak   vaxna láta,
rifnir með rótum,   roðnir í blóði,
bornir á bekki,   beðit mik at tyggva.

Hugða ek mér af   hendi hauka fljúga   42
bráðalausa   bölranna til;
hjörtu hugða ek þeira   við hunang tuggin,
sorgmóðs sefa,   sollin blóði.

Hugða ek mér af hendi   hvelpa losna,   43
glaums andvana,   gylli báðir;
hold hugða ek þeira   at hræum orðit,
nauðigr nái   nýta ek skyldak."

Guðrún kvað: 44
"Þar munu seggir   of sæing dæma
ok hvítinga   höfði næma;
þeir munu feigir   fára nátta
fyrir dag litlu,   drótt of bergja."

Atli kvað: 45
"Lægja ek síðan,   né ek sofa vildak,
þrágjarn í kör;   þat man ek görva."

Atli spake:
"Now from sleep the Norns have waked me
With visions of terror, to thee will I tell them;
Methought thou, Guthrun, Gjuki's daughter,
With poisoned blade didst pierce my body."

Guthrun spake:
"Fire a dream of steel shall follow
And willful pride one of woman's wrath;
A baneful sore I shall burn from thee,
And tend and heal thee, though hated thou art."

Atli spake:
"Of plants I dreamed, in the garden drooping,
That fain would I have full high to grow;
Plucked by the roots, and red with blood,
They brought them hither, and bade me eat."

"I dreamed my hawks from my hand had flown,
Eager for food, to an evil house;
I dreamed their hearts with honey I ate,
Soaked in blood, and heavy my sorrow."

"Hounds I dreamed from my hand I loosed,
Loud in hunger and pain they howled;
Their flesh methought was eagles' food,
And their bodies now I needs must eat."

Guthrun spake:
"Men shall soon of sacrifice speak,
And off the heads of beasts shall hew
Die they shall ere day has dawned,
A few nights hence, and the folk shall have them."

Atli spake:
"On my bed I sank, nor slumber sought,
Weary with woe, full well I remember.
[...]

ENDNOTES

Prose. Thjothrek: the famous Theoderich, king of the Ostrogoths, who became renowned in German story as Dietrich von Bern. The German tradition early accepted the anachronism of bringing together Attila (Etzel, Atli), who died in 453, and Theoderich who was born about 455, and adding thereto Ermanarich (Jormunrek), king of the Goths, who died about 376. Ermanarich, in German tradition, replaced Theoderich's actual enemy, Odovakar, and it was in battle with Jormunrek (i.e., Odovakar) that Thjothrek is here said to have lost most of his men. The annotator found the material for this note in *Guthrunarkvitha III*, in which Guthrun is accused of having Thjothrek as her lover. At the time when *Guthrunarkvitha II* was composed (early tenth century) it is probable that the story of Theoderich had not reached the North at all, and the annotator is consequently wrong in giving the poem its setting.

2. Cf. *Guthrunarkvitha I*, 17.

4. Regarding the varying accounts of the manner of Sigurth's death cf. *Brot*, concluding prose and note. *Grani*: cf. *Brot*, 7.

6. No gap indicated in the manuscript. Some editions combine these two lines with either stanza 5 or stanza 7.

7. *Gotthorm*: from this it appears that in both versions of the death of Sigurth the mortally wounded hero killed his murderer, the younger brother of Gunnar and Hogni. The story of how Gotthorm, was slain after killing Sigurth in his bed is told in *Sigurtharkvitha en skamma*, 22–23, and in the *Volsungasaga*.

11. On lines 3–4 cf. *Guthrunarkvitha I*, 1. Line 5 is probably spurious.

688   POETIC EDDA

12. Many editions make one stanza of stanzas 12 and 13, reconstructing line 3; the manuscript shows no gap. Bugge fills out the stanza thus: "The wolves were howling on all the ways, / The eagles cried as their food they craved."[1] [2]

13. & 14. The manuscript marks line 3 as beginning a stanza, and many editions combine lines 3-4 with lines 1-2 of stanza 15. *Hoalf* (or Half): Gering thinks this Danish king may be identical with Alf, son of King Hjalprek, and second husband of Hjordis, Sigurth's mother (cf. *Fra Dautha Sinfjotla* and note), but the name was a common one. *Thora* and *Hokon* have not been identified (cf. *Guthrunarkvitha I*, concluding prose, which is clearly based on this stanza). A Thora appears in *Hyndluljoth*, 18, as the wife of Dag, one of the sons of Halfdan the Old, the most famous of Denmark's mythical kings, and one of her sons is Alf (Hoalf?).

15. The manuscript marks line 3 as the beginning of a stanza. Some editors combine lines 5-6 with lines 1-2 of stanza 16, while others mark them as interpolated.

16. Some editions combine lines 3-4 with stanza 17. *Sigmund*: Sigurth's father, who here appears as a sea-rover in Guthrun's tapestry. *Sigar*: named in *Fornaldar sögur* II, 10, as the father of *Siggeir*, the latter being the husband of Sigmund's twin sister, Signy (cf. *Fra Dautha Sinfjotla*). *Fjon*: this name, referring to the Danish island of Fünen, is taken from the *Volsungasaga* paraphrase as better fitting the Danish setting of the stanza than the name in *Regius*, which is "Fife" (Scotland).

17. No gap is indicated in the manuscript, and most editions combine these two lines either with lines 3-4 of stanza 16, with lines 1-2 of stanza 18, or with the whole of stanza 18. Line 2 has been filled out in various ways. The *Volsungasaga* paraphrase indicates that these two lines are the remains of a full stanza, the prose passage running: "Now Guthrun was somewhat comforted of her sorrows. Then Grimhild learned where Guthrun was now dwelling." The first two lines may be the ones missing. *Gothic*: the term "Goth" was used in the North without much discrimination to apply to all south-Germanic peoples. In *Gripisspo*, 35, Gunnar, Grimhild's son, appears as "lord of the Goths." The manuscript marks line 6 as the beginning of a stanza. Grimhild is eager to have amends

---

[1] Grundtvig suggests as a first line: "Long did I bide, / my brothers awaiting." Many editors reject line 4.
[2] Stanzas 12-15 have been revised to conform to the Old Norse. Stanzas 12 and 13 have been combined, as Bugge noted was done with certain other editions. Footnotes 12 and 13 have therefore been combined, and the line "Cf. note on preceding stanza" has been omitted.

made to Guthrun for the slaying of Sigurth and their son, Sigmund, because Atli has threatened war if he cannot have Guthrun for his wife.[3]

18. Lines 5–6 are almost certainly interpolations, made by a scribe with a very vague understanding of the meaning of the stanza, which refers simply to the journey of the Gjukungs to bring their sister home from Denmark.

19. Lines 1–2 are probably interpolated, though the *Volsungasaga* includes the names. Someone apparently attempted to supply the names of Atli's messengers, the "long-beard men" of line 4, who have come to ask for Guthrun's hand. Some commentators assume, as the *Volsungasaga* does, that these messengers went with the Gjukungs to Denmark in search of Guthrun, but it seems more likely that a transitional stanza has dropped out after stanza 19, and that Guthrun received Atli's emissaries in her brothers' home. *Long-beards*: the word may actually mean Langobards or Lombards, but, if it does, it is presumably without any specific significance here. Certainly the names in the interpolated two lines do not fit either Lombards or Huns, for Valdar is identified as a Dane, and Jarizleif and Jarizskar are apparently Slavic. The manuscript indicates line 5 as beginning a new stanza.

20. *Each*: the reference is presumably to Gunnar and Hogni, and perhaps also Grimhild.[4] [5]

21. Stanzas 22–25 describe the draught of forgetfulness which Grimhild gives Guthrun, just as she gave one to Sigurth (in one version of the story) to make him forget Brynhild. The draught does not seem to work despite Guthrun's statement in stanza 24 (cf. stanza 29), for which reason Vigfusson, not unwisely, places stanzas 21–24 after stanza 33. *Blood of swine*: cf. *Hyndluljoth*, 39 and note.

22. The *Volsungasaga* quotes stanzas 22–23. *Heather-fish*: a snake. *Haddings' land*: the world of the dead, so called because, according to Saxo Grammaticus, the Danish king Hadingus once visited it. It is possible that the comma should follow "heather-fish," making the "ear uncut" (of grain) come from the world of the dead.

23. *Dew of the hearth*: soot.

---

3 Stanzas 17 and 18 have been combined to match the Old Norse, and thus footnotes 17 and 18 have been combined also.
4 This stanza probably belongs before stanza 19.
5 The original reference was to stanza 20, not stanza 19, but the reference has been amended to reflect the renumbering of the stanzas.

24. In the manuscript, and in some editions, the first line is in the third person plural: "Then they forgot, when the draught they had drunk." The second line in the original is manifestly in bad shape, and has been variously emended. *I forgot*: this emendation is doubtful, in view of stanza 30, but cf. note to stanza 21. *The kings all three*: probably Atli's emissaries, though the interpolated lines of stanza 20 name four of them. I suspect that line 4 is wrong, and should read: "Ere he himself (Atli) to speak began." Certainly stanzas 25–26 fit Atli much better than they do Grimhild, and there is nothing unreasonable in Atli's having come in person, along with his tributary kings, to seek Guthrun's hand. However, the "three kings" may not be Atli's followers at all, but Gunnar, Hogni, and the unnamed third brother possibly referred to in *Sigurtharkvitha en skamma*, 18.

25. *Thy father's*: So the manuscript, in which case the reference is obviously to Gjuki. But some editions omit the "thy," and if Atli, and not Grimhild, is speaking (cf. note on stanza 24), the reference may be, as in line 3 of stanza 26, to the wealth of Atli's father, Buthli. *Hlothver*: the northern form of the Frankish name Chlodowech (Ludwig), but who this Hlothver was, beyond the fact that he was evidently a Frankish king, is uncertain. If Atli is speaking, he is presumably a Frankish ruler whose land Atli and his Huns have conquered.

26. Cf. note on stanza 24 as to the probable speaker.

27. In stanzas 27–31 the dialogue, in alternate stanzas, is clearly between Guthrun and her mother, Grimhild, though the manuscript does not indicate the speakers.

28. *Sigmund*: son of Sigurth and Guthrun, killed at Brynhild's behest.

29. This stanza presents a strong argument for transposing the description of the draught of forgetfulness (stanzas 21–23 and lines 1–2 of stanza 24) to follow stanza 33. *Raven*, etc.: the original is somewhat obscure, and the line may refer simply to the "corpse-eating raven."

31. In the manuscript this stanza is immediately followed by the two lines which here, following Bugge's suggestion, appear as stanza 35. In lines 3–4 Guthrun foretells what will (and actually does) happen if she is forced to become Atli's wife. If stanza 35 really belongs here, it continues the prophesy to the effect that Guthrun will have no rest till she has avenged her brothers' death.

32. Very likely the remains of two stanzas; the manuscript marks line 4 as beginning a new stanza. On the other hand, lines 3 and 5 may be in-

terpolations.

33. *Vinbjorg and Valbjorg*: apparently imaginary place-names.[6]

34. *The kings*: presumably Gunnar and Hogni. *My sons*: regarding Guthrun's slaying of her two sons by Atli, Erp and Eitil, cf. *Drap Niflunga*, note.

35. In the manuscript this stanza follows stanza 31. The loss of two lines, to the effect that "Ill was that marriage for my brothers, and ill for Atli himself," and the transposition of the remaining two lines to this point, are indicated in a number of editions. *The warrior*, etc.: Atli, whom Guthrun kills.[7]

36. The stanza describes the journey to Atli's home, and sundry unsuccessful efforts have been made to follow the travellers through Germany and down the Danube. *Foreign women*: slaves. Line 5, which the manuscript marks as be ginning a stanza, is probably spurious.

37. After these two lines there appears to be a considerable gap, the lost stanzas giving Guthrun's story of the slaying of her brothers. It is possible that stanzas 38-45 came originally from another poem, dealing with Atli's dream, and were here substituted for the original conclusion of Guthrun's lament. Many editions combine stanzas 37 and 38, or combine stanza 38 (the manuscript marks line 1 as beginning a stanza) with lines 1-2 of stanza 39.

39. The manuscript indicates line 3 as the beginning of a stanza. The manuscript and most editions do not indicate the speakers in this and the following stanzas.

40. Guthrun, somewhat obscurely, interprets Atli's first dream (stanza 39) to mean that she will cure him of an abscess by cauterizing it. Her interpretation is, of course, intended merely to blind him to her purpose.

41. In stanzas 41-43 Atli's dreams forecast the death of his two sons, whose flesh Guthrun gives him to eat (cf. *Atlakvitha*, 39, and *Atlamol*, 78).

44. This stanza is evidently Guthrun's intentionally cryptic interpretation of Atli's dreams, but the meaning of the original is more than doubtful. The word here rendered "sacrifice" may mean "sea-catch," and the one

---

6 This stanza was created to conform Bellows' translation to the Old Norse.
7 The last four stanzas of stanza 31 are used to construct stanza 35. This has resulted in re-numbering of the Old Norse from stanza 35 in the original to the end.

rendered "beasts" may mean "whales." None of the attempted emendations have rendered the stanza really intelligible, but it appears to mean that Atli will soon make a sacrifice of beasts at night, and give their bodies to the people. Guthrun of course has in mind the slaying of his two sons.

45. With these two lines the poem abruptly ends; some editors assign the speech to Atli (I think rightly), others to Guthrun. Ettmüller combines the lines with stanza 38. Whether stanzas 38–45 originally belonged to Guthrun's lament, or were interpolated here in place of the lost conclusion of that poem from another one dealing with Atli's dreams (cf. note on stanza 37), it is clear that the end has been lost.

GUTHRUNARKVITHA III
THE THIRD LAY OF GUTHRUN

INTRODUCTION

Guthrunarkvitha III immediately follows the *Old Lay of Guthrun* in the *Codex Regius*, where it is found wholly intact. The narrative shows strong signs of being of very late provenance, probably from German lands. It is not mentioned or quoted in any of the other old *Sigurth Lays* even in fragments, and the invention of the ordeal by boiling water is a custom clearly derived from Christianity, only introduced to Norway in 1030 by St. Olaf Trygvasson.

The narrative of the unfaithful wife and the covetous former lover who conspires to undermine her is so cliché as to remove all doubt that the story is simply a common folk tale variant making use of otherwise famous characters.

The narrative inclusion of Thjothrek at the court of Atli is further evidence of a late origin, as it is agreed by both ancient and modern scholars that the man is the historical personage of Theoderich the Great, King of the Ostrogoths, through the vehicle of the German legend of Dietrich Von Bern. Theoderich the Great was not a contemporary of Attila and was born in the year 454, after Atilla's death in 453, with his childhood being well documented, as he was raised as a hostage in the court of Constantinople until the year 469. The inclusion of this king in the *Sigurth Lays* as a contemporary of the figures mentioned is a well-attested late addition to the saga narrative that serves to date this story as one of the older folk tales.

Guthrun and Her Sons
(Jenny Nystrom)

Herkja hét ambótt Atla. Hon hafði verit frilla hans. Hon sagði Atla, at hon hefði sét Þjóðrek ok Guðrúnu bæði saman. Atli var þá allókátr. Þá kvað Guðrún:

"Hvat er þér, Atli,   æ, Buðla sonr?   1
Er þér hryggt í hug?   Hví hlær þú æva?
Hitt mundi æðra   jörlum þykkja,
at við menn mæltir   ok mik sæir."

Atli kvað: 2
"Tregr mik þat, Guðrún   Gjúka dóttir,
mér í höllu   Herkja sagði,
at þit Þjóðrekr   und þaki svæfið
ok léttliga   líni verðið."

Guðrún kvað: 3
"Þér mun ek alls þess   eiða vinna
at inum hvíta   helga steini,
at ek við Þjóðrek   þatki áttak,
er vörðr né verr   vinna knátti.

Nema ek halsaða   herja stilli,   4
jöfur óneisinn,   einu sinni;
aðrar váru   okkrar spekjur,
er vit hörmug tvau   hnigum at rúnum.

GUTHRUNARKVITHA III

Herkja was the name of a serving-woman of Atli's; she had been his concubine. She told Atli that she had seen Thjothrek and Guthrun both together. Atli was greatly angered thereby. Then Guthrun said:

"What thy sorrow, Atli, Buthli's son? 1
Is thy heart heavy-laden? Why laughest thou never?
It would better befit the warrior far
To speak with men, and me to look on."

Atli spake: 2
"It troubles me, Guthrun, Gjuki's daughter,
What Herkja here in the hall hath told me,
That thou in the bed with Thjothrek liest,
Beneath the linen in lovers' guise."

Guthrun spake: 3
"This shall I with oaths now swear,
Swear by the sacred stone so white,
That nought was there with Thjothmar's son
That man or woman may not know."

"Nor ever once did my arms embrace 4
The hero brave, the leader of hosts;
In another manner our meeting was,
When our sorrows we in secret told."

Hér kom Þjóðrekr   með þría tegu,   5
lifa þeir né einir   þriggja tega manna;
hnöggt þú mik at bræðrum   ok at brynjuðum,
hnöggt þú mik at öllum   höfuðniðjum.

Sentu at Saxa,   Sunnmanna gram,   6
hann kann helga   hver vellanda."

Sjau hundruð manna   í sal gengu,   7
áðr kvæn konungs   í ketil tæki.

Guðrún kvað: 8
"Kemr-a nú Gunnarr,   kallig-a ek Högna,
sékk-a ek síðan   svása bræðr;
sverði mundi Högni   slíks harms reka,
nú verð ek sjalf fyrir mik   synja lýta."

Brá hon til botns   björtum lófa   9
ok hon upp of tók   jarknasteina:
"Sé nú, seggir,   sykn em ek orðin
heilagliga,   hvé sá hverr velli."

Hló þá Atla   hugr í brjósti,   10
er hann heilar sá   hendr Guðrúnar:
"Nú skal Herkja   til hvers ganga,
sú er Guðrúnu   grandi vændi."

Sá-at maðr armligt,   hverr er þat sá-at,   11
hvé þar á Herkju   hendr sviðnuðu;
leiddu þá mey   í mýri fúla.
Svá þá Guðrún   sinna harma.

"With thirty warriors Thjothrek came, 5
Nor of all his men doth one remain;
Thou hast murdered my brothers and mail-clad men,
Thou hast murdered all the men of my race."

"Summon Saxi, the southrons' king, 6
For he the boiling kettle can hallow."

Seven hundred there were in the hall, 7
Ere the queen her hand in the kettle thrust."

Guthrun spake: 8
"Gunnar comes not, Hogni I greet not,
No longer I see my brothers loved;
My sorrow would Hogni avenge with the sword,
Now myself for my woes I shall payment win."

To the bottom she reached with hand so bright, 9
And forth she brought the flashing stones:
"Behold, ye warriors, well am I cleared
Of sin by the kettle's sacred boiling."

Then Atli's heart in happiness laughed, 10
When Guthrun's hand unhurt he saw;
"Now Herkja shall come the kettle to try,
She who grief for Guthrun planned."

Ne'er saw man sight more sad than this, 11
How burned were the hands of Herkja then;
In a bog so foul the maid they flung,
And so was Guthrun's grief requited.

ENDNOTES

Prose. The annotator derived all the material for this note from the poem itself, except for the reference to Herkja as Atli's former concubine. *Herkja*: the historical Kreka and the Helche of the *Nibelungenlied*, who there appears as Etzel's (Attila's) first wife. *Thjothrek*: cf. Introductory Note [Appendix B].

2. The manuscript omits the names of the speakers throughout.

3. *Holy stone*: just what this refers to is uncertain; it may be identical with the "ice-cold stone of Uth" mentioned in an oath in *Helgakvitha Hundingsbana II*, 29. *Thjothmar's son*: the manuscript has simply "Thjothmar." Some editions change it as here, some assume that Thjothmar is another name or an error for Thjothrek, and Finnur Jonsson not only retains Thjothmar here but changes Thjothrek to Thjothmar in stanza 5 to conform to it. [This may be connected in some sense to the oath stones of Odin that lie scattered around the Hebrides and represent an ancient tradition.]

5. Regarding the death of Thjothrek's men cf. *Guthrunarkvitha II*, introductory prose, note. It was on these stanzas of *Guthrunarkvitha III* that the annotator based his introduction to *Guthrunarkvitha II*. The manuscript repeats the "thirty" in line 2, in defiance of metrical requirements.[1]

6. Who *Saxi* may be is not clear, but the stanza clearly points to the time when the ordeal by boiling water was still regarded as a foreign institution, and when a southern king (i.e., a Christian from some earlier-converted region) was necessary to consecrate the kettle used in the test.

---

1 Stanzas 6–11 are reordered to conform to the Old Norse.

7. The ordeal by boiling water followed closely the introduction of Christianity, which took place around the year 1000. Some editions make two stanzas out of [Bellows' original] stanza 7:

> Summon Saxi, the southrons' king,
> For be the boiling kettle can hallow."
> Seven hundred there were in the hall,
> Ere the queen her hand in the kettle thrust.

and Müllenhoff contends that lines 1-2 do not constitute part of Guthrun's speech.

11. The word "requited" in line 4 is omitted in the manuscript, but it is clear that some such word was intended.

ODDRUNARGRATR
THE LAMENT OF ODDRUN

INTRODUCTION

The *Oddrunargratr* follows in the *Codex Regius* from the *Third Lay of Gudrun* and precedes the *Atlakvitha*. The story follows the lament of Atli's (Atilla the Hun's) sister Oddrun and her apparent mourning for the death of her lover Gunnar, on whom Atli has taken vengeance and slain.

The origin of the character of Oddrun is something of a mystery, for she exists neither as a recorded historical figure nor as a narrative element of any of the old German lays, nor even of the earlier Norse ones. It seems reasonable to conclude that she is a later creation of Norse poets to further tie the sons of Gjuki to Atli and into the continuing narrative. An argument against this can be raised, however, on the basis that the compiler of the poems seems to be very familiar with the character and implies the existence of further stories surrounding her, and that it is not altogether clear what motivates Atli to slay the sons of Gjuki in such a hideous fashion without the justification of an inappropriate love affair with his sister. There is a slight indication in the *Atlakvitha* that the motive might have been for possession of the treasure of the Nibelungs, but this is interposed within a large number of missing passages. The circumstances surrounding it are likewise very unclear, and it is never remarked upon again in other works.

It is also worth noting here that the German tradition presents Kriemhild's (Guthrun's) motive as being solely for vengeance for the death of Sigurth, but this narrative element is incongruous with Hogni's response to Guthrun about the matter in the *Old Lay of Guthrun*, which is itself commensurate with what we would expect to see culturally in the Germanic tradition regarding the nature of kin. Regardless, it seems reasonable to conclude that there once existed a larger series of tales surrounding the occurrences in the poem, due to Atli's vague remarks to the effect that this is partially his wife's fault, and due to allusions to her enmity with his mother which are unknown to us as modern readers but appear to have been well understood by the ancient listeners familiar with his meanings.

Heiðrekr hét konungr. Dóttir hans hét Borgný. Vilmundr hét sá, er var friðill hennar. Hon mátti eigi fæða börn, áðr til kom Oddrún Atlasystir. Hon hafði verit unnusta Gunnars Gjúkasonar. Um þessa sögu er hér kveðit:

Heyrða ek segja   í sögum fornum,   1
hvé mær of kom   til Mornalands;
engi mátti   fyr jörð ofan
Heiðreks dóttur   hjalpir vinna.

Þat frá Oddrún   Atla systir,   2
at sú mær hafði   miklar sóttir;
brá hon af stalli   stjórnbitluðum
ok á svartan   söðul of lagði.

Lét hon mar fara   moldveg sléttan,   3
unz at hári kom   höll standandi;
svipti hon söðli   af svöngum jó,
ok hon inn of gekk   endlangan sal,
ok hon þat orða   alls fyrst of kvað:

"Hvat er frægst   hér á foldu,   4
eða hvat er hlézt   Húnalands?"
Ambótt kvað:
"Hér liggr Borgný   of borin verkjum,
vina þín, Oddrún,   vittu, ef þú hjalpir."

ODDRUNARGRATR

Heithrek was the name of a king, whose daughter was called Borgny. Vilmund was the name of the man who was her lover. She could not give birth to a child until Oddrun, Atli's sister, had come to her; Oddrun had been beloved of Gunnar, son of Gjuki. About this story is the following poem.

I have heard it told in olden tales 1
How a maiden came to Morningland;
No one of all on earth above
To Heithrek's daughter help could give.

This Oddrun learned, the sister of Atli, 2
That sore the maiden's sickness was;
The bit-bearer forth from his stall she brought,
And the saddle laid on the steed so black.

She let the horse go o'er the level ground, 3
Till she reached the hall that loftily rose,
And in she went from the end of the hall;
From the weary steed the saddle she took;
Hear now the speech that first she spake:

"What news on earth [...] 4
Or what has happened in Hunland now?"

A serving-maid spake:
"Here Borgny lies in bitter pain,
Thy friend, and, Oddrun, thy help would find."

Oddrún kvað: 5
"Hverr hefir vísir　　vamms of leitat?
Hví eru Borgnýjar　　bráðar sóttir?"

Ambótt kvað: 6
"Vilmundr heitir　　vinr haukstalda,
hann varði mey　　varmri blæju
fimm vetr alla,　　svá hon sinn föður leyndi."

Þær hykk mæltu　　þvígit fleira, 7
gekk mild fyr kné　　meyju at sitja;
ríkt gól Oddrún,　　rammt gól Oddrún,
bitra galdra　　at Borgnýju.

Knátti mær ok mögr　　moldveg sporna, 8
börn þau in blíðu　　við bana Högna;
þat nam at mæla　　mær fjörsjúka,
svá at hon ekki kvað　　orð it fyrra:

"Svá hjalpi þér　　hollar véttir, 9
Frigg ok Freyja　　ok fleiri goð,
sem þú feldir mér　　fár af höndum."

Oddrún kvað: 10
"Hnék-at ek af því　　til hjalpar þér,
at þú værir þess　　verð aldregi;
hét ek ok efndak,　　er ek hinig mælta,
at ek hvívetna　　hjalpa skyldak,
þá er öðlingar　　arfi skiptu."

Borgný kvað: 11
Ær ertu, Oddrún,　　ok örvita,
er þú mér af fári　　flest orð of kvatt,
en ek fylgðak þér　　á fjörgynju,
sem vit bræðrum tveim　　of bornar værim."

Oddrún kvað: 12
"Man ek, hvat þú　　mæltir enn um aftan,
þá er ek Gunnari　　gerðak drekku;
slíks dæmi kvað-at-tu　　síðan mundu
meyja verða　　nema mér einni."

Þá nam at setjask　　sorgmóð kona 13
at telja böl　　af trega stórum:

Oddrun spake: 5
"Who worked this woe for the woman thus,
Or why so sudden is Borgny sick?"

The serving-maid spake: 6
"Vilmund is he, the heroes' friend,
Who wrapped the woman in bedclothes warm,
For winters five, yet her father knew not."

Then no more they spake, methinks; 7
She went at the knees of the woman to sit;
With magic Oddrun and mightily Oddrun
Chanted for Borgny potent charms.

At last were born a boy and girl, 8
Son and daughter of Hogni's slayer;
Then speech the woman so weak began,
Nor said she aught ere this she spake:

"So may the holy ones thee help, 9
Frigg and Freyja and favoring gods,
As thou hast saved me from sorrow now."

Oddrun spake: 10
"I came not hither to help thee thus
Because thou ever my aid didst earn;
I fulfilled the oath that of old I swore,
That aid to all I should ever bring,
When they shared the wealth the warriors had."

Borgny spake: 11
"Wild art thou, Oddrun, and witless now,
That so in hatred to me thou speakest;
I followed thee where thou didst fare,
As we had been born of brothers twain."

Oddrun spake: 12
"I remember the evil one eve thou spakest,
When a draught I gave to Gunnar then;
Thou didst say that never such a deed
By maid was done save by me alone."

Then the sorrowing woman sat her down 13
To tell the grief of her troubles great.

"Var ek upp alin   í jöfra sal,   14
flestr fagnaði   at fira ráði;
unða ek aldri   ok eign föður
fimm vetr eina,   svá at minn faðir lifði.

Þat nam at mæla   mál ið efsta   15
sjá móðr konungr,   áðr hann sylti:
mik bað hann gæða   gulli rauðu
ok suðr gefa   syni Grímhildar.

Oddrún kvað: 16
En hann Brynhildi   bað hjalm geta,
hana kvað hann óskmey   verða skyldu;
kvað-a hann ina æðri   alna mundu
mey í heimi,   nema mjötuðr spillti.

Brynhildr í búri   borða rakði,   17
hafði hon lýði   ok lönd um sik;
jörð dúsaði   ok upphiminn,
þá er bani Fáfnis   borg of þátti.

Þá var víg vegit   völsku sverði   18
ok borg brotin,   sú er Brynhildr átti;
var-a langt af því   heldr válítit,
unz þær vélar   vissi allar.

Þess lét hon harðar   hefndir verða,   19
svá at vér öll höfum   ærnar raunir;
þat mun á hölða   hvert land fara,
er hon lét sveltask   at Sigurði.

En ek Gunnari   gatk at unna,   20
bauga deili,   sem Brynhildr skyldi.

Oddrún kvað: 21
Buðu þeir árla   bauga rauða
ok bræðrum mínum   bætr ósmáar;
bað hann enn við mér   bú fimmtían,
hliðfarm Grana,   ef hann hafa vildi.

En Atli kvaðsk   eigi vilja   22
mund aldrigi   at megi Gjúka;
þeygi vit máttum   við munum vinna,
nema ek helt höfði   við hringbrota.

"Happy I grew in the hero's hall 14
As the warriors wished, and they loved me well;
Glad I was of my father's gifts,
For winters five, while my father lived."

"These were the words the weary king, 15
Ere he died, spake last of all:
He bade me with red gold dowered to be,
And to Grimhild's son in the South be wedded."

Oddrun spake: 16
"But Brynhild the helm he bade to wear,
A wish-maid bright he said she should be;
For a nobler maid would never be born
On earth, he said, if death should spare her."

"At her weaving Brynhild sat in her bower, 17
Lands and folk alike she had;
The earth and heaven high resounded
When Fafnir's slayer the city saw."

"Then battle was fought with the foreign swords, 18
And the city was broken that Brynhild had;
Not long thereafter, but all too soon,
Their evil wiles full well she knew."

"Woeful for this her vengeance was, 19
As so we learned to our sorrow all;
In every land shall all men hear
How herself at Sigurth's side she slew."

"Love to Gunnar then I gave, 20
To the breaker of rings, as Brynhild might;"

Oddrun spake: 21
"To Atli rings so red they offered,
And mighty gifts to my brother would give.
Fifteen dwellings fain would he give
For me, and the burden that Grani bore;"

"But Atli said he would never receive 22
Marriage gold from Gjuki's son.
Yet could we not our love o'ercome,
And my head I laid on the hero's shoulder;"

Mæltu margir   mínir niðjar,   23
kváðusk okkr hafa   orðit bæði;
en mik Atli kvað   eigi mundu
lýti ráða   né löst gera.

En slíks skyli   synja aldri   24
maðr fyr annan,   þar er munúð deilir.

Sendi Atli   áru sína   25
um myrkvan við   mín at freista;
ok þeir kómu þar,   er þeir koma né skyldu-t,
þá er breiddum vit   blæju eina.

Oddrún kvað: 26
Buðum vit þegnum   bauga rauða,
at þeir eigi   til Atla segði,
en þeir hvatliga   heim skunduðu
ok óliga   Atla sögðu.

En þeir Guðrúnu   görla leyndu því,   27
at hon heldr vita   halfu skyldi.

Hlymr var at heyra   hófgullinna,   28
þá er í garð riðu   Gjúka arfar;
þeir ór Högna   hjarta skáru,
en i ormgarð   annan lögðu.

Var ek enn farin   einu sinni   29
til Geirmundar   gerva drykkju;
nam horskr konungr   hörpu sveigja,
því at hann hugði mik   til hjalpar sér
kynríkr konungr,   of koma mundu.

Nam ek at heyra   ór Hléseyju,   30
hvé þar af stríðum   strengir gullu;
bað ek ambáttir   búnar verða,
vilda ek fylkis   fjörvi bjarga.

Oddrún kvað: 31
Létum fljóta   far sund yfir,
unz ek alla sák   Atla garða.

"Many there were of kinsmen mine
Who said that together us they had seen.
Atli said that never I
Would evil plan, or ill deed do;" 23

"But none may this of another think, 24
Or surely speak, when love is shared."

"Soon his men did Atli send, 25
In the murky wood on me to spy;
Thither they came where they should not come,
Where beneath one cover close we lay."

Oddrun spake: 26
"To the warriors ruddy rings we offered,
That nought to Atli e'er they should say;
But swiftly home they hastened thence,
And eager all to Atli told."

"But close from Guthrun kept they hid 27
What first of all she ought to have known.
[...]
[...]"

"Great was the clatter of gilded hoofs 28
When Gjuki's sons through the gateway rode;
The heart they hewed from Hogni then,
And the other they cast in the serpents' cave."

"Alone was I gone to Geirmund then, 29
The draught to mix and ready to make;
The hero wise on his harp then smote,
[...]
For help from me in his heart yet hoped
The high-born king, might come to him."

"Sudden I heard from Hlesey clear 30
How in sorrow the strings of the harp resounded.
I bade the serving-maids ready to be,
For I longed the hero's life to save;"

Oddrun spake: 31
"Across the sound the boats we sailed,
Till we saw the whole of Atli's home."

Þá kom in arma　　út skævandi 32
móðir Atla,　　hon skyli morna,
ok Gunnari　　gróf til hjarta,
svá at ek máttig-a-k　　mærum bjarga.

Oft undrumk þat,　　hví ek eftir mák, 33
linnvengis Bil,　　lífi halda;
er ek ógnhvötum　　unna þóttumk
sverða deili,　　sem sjalfri mér.

Sattu ok hlýddir,　　meðan ek sagðak þér 34
mörg ill of sköp　　mín ok þeira;
maðr hverr lifir　　at munum sínum;
nú er of genginn　　grátr Oddrúnar."

"Then crawling the evil woman came,   32
Atli's mother—may she ever rot!
And hard she bit to Gunnar's heart,
So I could not help the hero brave."

"Oft have I wondered how after this,   33
Serpents'-bed goddess! I still might live,
For well I loved the warrior brave,
The giver of swords, as my very self."

"Thou didst see and listen, the while I said   34
The mighty grief that was mine and theirs;
Each man lives as his longing wills,
Oddrun's lament is ended now."

ENDNOTES

Prose. Nothing further is known of *Heithrek*, *Borgny* or *Vilmund*. The annotator has added the name of Borgny's father, but otherwise his material comes from the poem itself. *Oddrun*, sister of Atli and Brynhild, here appears as proficient in birth-runes (cf. *Sigrdrifumol*, 8). Regarding her love for *Gunnar*, Guthrun's brother, and husband of her sister, Brynhild, cf. *Sigurtharkvitha en skamma*, 57 and note.

1. *Olden tales*: this may be merely a stock phrase, or it may really mean that the poet found his story in oral prose tradition. *Morningland*: the poem's geography is utterly obscure. "Morningland" is apparently identical with "Hunland" (stanza 4), and yet Oddrun is herself sister of the king of the Huns. Vigfusson tries to make "Mornaland" into "Morva land" and explain it as Moravia. Probably it means little more than a country lying vaguely in the East. With stanza 28 the confusion grows worse.

3. Line 3 (cf. *Völundarkvitha*, 17) or line 5 (cf. *Thrymskvitha*, 2), both quoted from older poems, is probably spurious; the manuscript marks line 3 as the beginning of a new stanza.

4. Line 1 in the original appears to have lost its second half. In line 2 the word rendered "has happened" is doubtful. The manuscript does not indicate the speaker of lines 3–4, and a few editors assign them to Borgny herself.

5. The manuscript does not indicate the speakers. *For the woman*: conjectural; the manuscript has instead: "What warrior now hath worked this woe?" The manuscript indicates line 3 as beginning a new stanza. Line 5,

apparently modeled on line 4 of stanza 14, is probably spurious.[1]

7. *Charms*: cf. *Sigrdrifumol*, 8.

8. *Hogni's slayer*: obviously Vilmund, but unless he was the one of Atli's followers who actually cut out Hogni's heart (cf. *Drap Niflunga*), there is nothing else to connect him with Hogni's death. Sijmons emends the line to read "Born of the sister of Hogni's slayer."

9. Regarding *Frigg* as a goddess of healing cf. *Svipdagsmol*, 52, note. Regarding *Freyja* as the friend of lovers cf. *Grimnismol*, 14, note. A line is very possibly missing from this stanza.

10. The manuscript does not name the speaker. In line 2 the word rendered "earn" is omitted in the manuscript, but nearly all editions have supplied it. Line 5 is clearly either interpolated or out of place. It may be all that is left of a stanza which stood between stanzas 16 and 17, or it may belong in stanza 13.

11–21. In the manuscript the order is as follows: 13; 14; 15; 16, 3–4; 11; 12; 17; 18; 16; 20, 1–2; 20, 1–2; 20, 3–4; 21. The changes made here, following several of the editions, are: (a) the transposition of stanzas 11–12, which are clearly dialogue, out of the body of the lament to a position just before it; (b) the transposition of lines 1–2 of stanza 15 to their present position from the middle of stanza 19.

11. The manuscript does not name the speaker; cf. note on stanzas 11–21.

12. The manuscript does not name the speaker; cf. note on stanzas 11–21. The word rendered "evil" in line 1 is a conjectural addition. Apparently Borgny was present at Atli's court while the love affair between Oddrun and Gunnar was in progress, and criticised Oddrun for her part in it. *A draught*, etc.: apparently in reference to a secret meeting of the lovers.

13. In the manuscript this stanza follows stanza 10; cf. note on stanzas 11–21. No gap is indicated, but something has presumably been lost. Grundtvig supplies as a first line: "The maid her evil days remembered," and inserts as a second line line 5 of stanza 10.

14. The manuscript indicates line 3 as the beginning of a new stanza; many editions combine lines 1–2 with stanza 13 and lines 3–4 with lines 1–2 of stanza 15. *The hero*: Buthli, father of Oddrun, Atli, and Brynhild.

---

1 From stanza 5–32 in the Bellows original translation the numbering has been reordered to conform to the Old Norse. The reference in footnote 5 has been changed from stanza 13 to stanza 14.

15. The manuscript indicates line 3, but not line 1, as the beginning of a new stanza; some editions combine lines 3-4 with lines 3-4 of stanza 16. Making Buthli plan the marriage of Oddrun and Gunnar may be a sheer invention of the poet, or may point to an otherwise lost version of the legend.

16. Lines 1-2 have here been transposed from the middle of stanza 19; cf. note on stanzas 11-21. *Wish-maid*: a Valkyrie, so called because the Valkyries fullfilled Odin's wish in choosing the slain heroes for Valhall. The reference to Brynhild as a Valkyrie by no means fits with the version of the story used in stanzas 16-17, and the poet seems to have attempted to combine the two contradictory traditions, cf. *Fafnismol*, note on stanza 44. In the manuscript stanzas 11-12 follow line 4 of stanza 16.

17. In stanzas 16-17 the underlying story seems to be the one used in *Sigurtharkvitha en skamma* (particularly stanzas 32-39), and referred to in *Guthrunarkvitha I*, 24, wherein Gunnar and Sigurth lay siege to Atli's city (it here appears as Brynhild's) and are bought off only by Atli's giving Brynhild to Gunnar as wife, winning her consent thereto by falsely representing to her that Gunnar is Sigurth. This version is, of course, utterly at variance with the one in which Sigurth wins Brynhild for Gunnar by riding through the ring of flames, and is probably more closely akin to the early German traditions. In the *Nibelungenlied* Brynhild appears as a queen ruling over lands and peoples. *Fafnir's slayer*: Sigurth.

18. Cf. note on preceding stanza.

20. Cf. *Sigurtharkvitha en skamma*, stanzas 64-70.

20. In the manuscript lines 1-2 of stanza 15 follow line 2, resulting in various conjectural combinations. The manuscript marks line 3 as beginning a new stanza. *Rings*, etc.: possibly, as Gering maintains, payment offered by Gunnar and Hogni for Brynhild's death, but more probably, as in stanza 21, Gunnar's proffered "marriage gold" for the hand of Oddrun.

21. *Grani's burden*: the treasure won by Sigurth from Fafnir; cf. *Fafnismol*, concluding prose. The manuscript marks line 3 as beginning a new stanza, as also in stanzas 21 and 22.

25. *Murky wood*: the forest which divided Atli's realm from that of the Gjukungs is in *Atlakvitha*, 3, called Myrkwood. This hardly accords with the extraordinary geography of stanzas 29-30, or with the journey described in *Guthrunarkvitha II*, 36.

26. In the manuscript lines 3 and 4 stand in reversed order.

27. No gap is indicated in the manuscript; some editors assume the loss not only of two lines, but of an additional stanza. Evidently *Guthrun* has already become Atli's wife.

28. If a stanza has been lost after stanza 27, it may well have told of Atli's treacherous invitation to the Gjukungs to visit him; cf. *Drap Niflunga*, which likewise tells of the slaying of *Hogni* and Gunnar (*the other*).

27. In the manuscript these three lines follow line 2 of stanza 29. No gap is indicated in the manuscript, In the *Volsungasaga* Guthrun gives her brother the harp, with which he puts the serpents to sleep. The episode is undoubtedly related to the famous thirtieth Adventure of the *Nibelungenlied*, in which Volker plays the followers of Gunther to sleep before the final battle.

29. In the manuscript the three lines of stanza 28 follow line 2, and line 3 is marked as beginning a new stanza. *Geirmund*: nothing further is known of him, but he seems to be an ally or retainer of Atli, or possibly his brother. *Hlesey*: the poet's geography is here in very bad shape. Hlesey is (or may be) the Danish island of Läsö, in the Kattegat (cf. *Harbarthsljoth*, 37 and note), and thither he has suddenly transported not only Gunnar's death-place but Atli's whole dwelling (cf. stanza 30), despite his previous references to the ride to Hunland (stanzas 3–4) and the "murky wood" (stanza 25). Geirmund's home, where Oddrun has gone, is separated from Hlesey and Atli's dwelling by a sound (stanza 30). However, geographical accuracy is seldom to be looked for in heroic epic poetry.

30. Many editions combine this stanza with lines 3–4 of stanza 29. *The sound*: cf. note on stanza 29.

32. The manuscript marks line 3 as beginning a new stanza. *Atli's mother*: the *Volsungasaga* does not follow this version; Gunnar puts all the serpents but one to sleep with his harp playing, "but a mighty and evil adder crawled to him and drove his fangs into him till they reached his heart, and so he died." It is possible that "Atli" is a scribal error for a word meaning "of serpents."

33. *Serpents'-bed goddess*: woman (i.e., Borgny); "goddess of gold" was a frequent term for a woman, and gold was often called the "serpents' bed" (cf. *Guthrunarkvitha I*, 24 and note).

34. Some editions make line 4 a statement of the poet's, and not part of Oddrun's speech

ATLAKVITHA EN GRÖNLENZKA
THE GREENLAND LAY OF ATLI

INTRODUCTION

The *Atlakvitha* follows on from the *Oddrunargratr* in the *Codex Regius*, and is found in exceptionally bad state; whether this is the result of poor transmission over time or simply due to the incompetence of the original poet is not entirely clear, but it can probably be attributed to some degree to both.

The most famous contention over the poem is regarding its origins, with the manuscript copy referencing it as Greenlandic in origin. Other evidence of its origin lies in the frequent use of mythological references as normal poetic kennings (such as *Valhall* for a war hall in general) such as to imply that the author is ignorant of the original implications and associations beyond it simply being famous. Given that Greenland was a mostly Christian colony from almost its founding, it is reasonable to conclude that the authors might have had less contact with the traditions of their pagan forebears. Evidence against this, however, is the isolation of the Greenlandic settlement in light of the diverse and precise geographical depictions within the work that imply a solid working knowledge of the continent. Most modern scholars such as Ursula Dronke favor a Norwegian origin for the poem and posit that it predates the settlement of the Greenlandic colony, with it being thought due to stylistic and lexical similarities that the 9th century Skald Þorbjörn Hornklofi may have been the original author, or at least a strong influence on the work. We agree with Bellows' original introduction that the lack of mythological knowledge on the part of the author invalidates an origin of the poem prior to widespread Christianization, let alone an origin in the court of a pagan-era heathen king. Discrepancies noted here and by other scholars in its stylistic origins can probably be ascribed to the work being based on a continental traditional source that has simply not come down to us, and indeed some have suggested either a High German narrative tradition or possibly a lost Gothic transmission of the story to Scandinavia with little to no German involvement.

While it is quite possible that the work, and its Greenlandic brother, is based on a separate continental prose or poetic tradition, and while it tends towards inclusion of the German traditional works with no signs of Nordic-centric material, no hard evidence exists for this beyond this speculation of its content. Regardless of its origins, we can be assured that it is the older of the Greenlandic *Atli Lays*.

Old Houses with Carved Posts
(Photo of Hengist and Hors architecture)

Guðrún Gjúkadóttir hefndi bræðra sinna, svá sem frægt er orðit. Hon drap fyrst sonu Atla, en eftir drap hon Atla ok brenndi höllina ok hirðina alla. Um þetta er sjá kviða ort:

Atli sendi   ár til Gunnars 1
kunnan segg at ríða,   Knéfröðr var sá heitinn;
at görðum kom hann Gjúka   ok at Gunnars Höllu,
bekkjum aringreypum   ok at bjóri svásum.

Drukku þar dróttmegir,   en dyljendr þögðu, 2
vín í valhöllu,   vreiði sásk þeir Húna;
kallaði þá Knéfröðr   kaldri röddu,
seggr inn suðræni   sat hann á bekk háum:

"Atli mik hingat sendi   ríða erendi 3
mar inum mélgreypa   myrkvið inn ókunna,
at biðja yðr, Gunnarr,   at it á bekk kæmið
með hjalmum aringreypum   at sækja heim Atla.

Skjöldu kneguð þar velja   ok skafna aska, 4
hjalma gullroðna   ok Húna mengi,
silfrgyllt söðulklæði,   serki valrauða,
dafar darraðar,   drösla mélgreypa.

ATLAKVITHA EN GRÖNLENZKA

Guthrun, Gjuki's daughter, avenged her brothers, as has become well known. She slew first Atli's sons, and thereafter she slew Atli, and burned the hall with his whole company. Concerning this was the following poem made:

Atli sent of old to Gunnar
A keen-witted rider, Knefröth did men call him;
To Gjuki's home came he and to Gunnar's dwelling,
With benches round the hearth, and to the beer so sweet.
    1

Then the followers, hiding their falseness, all drank
Their wine in the war-hall, of the Huns' wrath wary;
And Knefröth spake loudly, his words were crafty,
The hero from the south, on the high bench sitting:
    2

"Now Atli has sent me his errand to ride,
On my bit-champing steed through Myrkwood the secret,
To bid you, Gunnar, to his benches to come,
With helms round the hearth, and Atli's home seek."
    3

"Shields shall ye choose there, and shafts made of ash-wood,
Gold-adorned helmets, and slaves out of Hunland,
Silver-gilt saddle-cloths, shirts of bright scarlet,
With lances and spears too, and bit-champing steeds."
    4

Völl lézk ykkr ok mundu   gefa víðrar Gnitaheiðar,   5
af geiri gjallanda   ok af gylltum stöfnum,
stórar meiðmar   ok staði Danpar,
hrís þat it mæra,   er meðr Myrkvið kalla."

Höfði vatt þá Gunnarr   ok Högna til sagði: 6
"Hvat ræðr þú okkr, seggr inn æri,
alls vit slíkt heyrum?
Gull vissa ek ekki   á Gnitaheiði,
þat er vit ættim-a   annat slíkt.

Sjau eigum vit salhús   sverða full,   7
hverju eru þeira   hjölt ór gulli;
minn veit ek mar beztan,   en mæki hvassastan,
boga bekksæma,   en brynjur ór gulli,
hjalm ok skjöld hvítastan   kominn ór höll Kíars,
einn er minn betri   en sé allra Húna."

Högni kvað: 8
"Hvat hyggr þú brúði bendu,   þá er hon okkr baug sendi,
varinn váðum heiðingja?   Hygg ek, at hon vörnuð byði.
Hár fann ek heiðingja   riðit í hring rauðum,
ylfskr er vegr okkarr   at ríða erendi."

Niðjar hvöttu Gunnar   né náungr annarr,   9
rýnendr né ráðendr   né þeir er ríkir váru;
kvaddi þá Gunnarr,   sem konungr skyldi,
mærr í mjöðranni   af móði stórum:

"Rístu nú, Fjörnir,   láttu á flet vaða   10
greppa gullskálir   með gumna höndum.

Ulfr mun ráða   arfi Niflunga,   11
gamlir, gránvarðir,   ef Gunnars missir,
birnir blakkfjallir   bíta þreftönnum,
gamna greystóði,   ef Gunnarr né kemr-at."

Leiddu landrögni   lýðar óneisir,   12
grátendr gunnhvata   ór garði húna.
Þá kvað þat inn æri   erfivörþr Högna:
"Heilir farið nú ok horskir,
hvars ykkr hugr teygir!"

"The field shall be given you of wide Gnitaheith, 5
With loud-ringing lances, and stems gold-o'er-laid,
Treasures full huge, and the home of Danp,
And the mighty forest that Myrkwood is called."

His head turned Gunnar, and to Hogni he said: 6
"What thy counsel, young hero, when such things we hear?
No gold do I know on Gnitaheith lying
So fair that other its equal we have not."

"We have seven halls, each of swords is full, 7
And all of gold is the hilt of each;
My steed is the swiftest, my sword is sharpest,
My bows adorn benches, my byrnies are golden,
My helm is the brightest that came from Kjar's hall,
Mine own is better than all the Huns' treasure."

Hogni spake: 8
"What seeks she to say, that she sends us a ring,
Woven with a wolf's hair? methinks it gives warning;
In the red ring a hair of the heath-dweller found I,
Wolf-like shall our road be if we ride on this journey."

Not eager were his comrades, nor the men of his kin, 9
The wise nor the wary, nor the warriors bold.
But Gunnar spake forth as befitted a king,
Noble in the beer-hall, and bitter his scorn:

"Stand forth now, Fjornir! and hither on the floor 10
The beakers all golden shalt thou bring to the warriors."
[...]
[...]

"The wolves then shall rule the wealth of the Niflungs, 11
Wolves aged and grey-hued, if Gunnar is lost,
And black-coated bears with rending teeth bite,
And make glad the dogs, if Gunnar returns not."

A following gallant fared forth with the ruler, 12
Yet they wept as their home with the hero they left;
And the little heir of Hogni called loudly:
"Go safe now, ye wise ones, wherever ye will!"

Fetum létu fræknir   um fjöll at þyrja   13
mari ina mélgreypu   Myrkvið inn ókunna;
hristisk öll Húnmörk   þar er harðmóðgir fóru,
ráku þeir vandstyggva   völlu algræna.

Land sáu þeir Atla   ok liðskjalfar djúpa,   14
Bikka greppar standa   á borg inni háu,
sal of suðrþjóðum   sleginn sessmeiðum,
bundnum röndum,   bleikum skjöldum,
dafar darraðar;   en þar drakk Atli
vín í valhöllu,   verðir sátu úti
at varða þeim Gunnari,   af þeir hér vitja kvæmi
með geiri gjallanda   at vekja gram hildi.

Systir fann þeira snemst,   at þeir í sal kómu   15
bræðr hennar báðir,   bjóri var hon lítt drukkin:
"Ráðinn ertu nú, Gunnarr.   Hvat muntu, ríkr, vinna
við Húna harmbrögðum?   Höll gakk þú ór snemma.

Betr hefðir þú, bróðir,   at þú í brynju færir,   16
sem hjalmum aringreypum   at séa heim Atla,
sætir þú í söðlum   sólheiða daga,
nái nauðfölva   létir nornir gráta,
Húna skjaldmeyjar   herfi kanna,
en Atla sjalfan   létir þú í ormgarð koma,
nú er sá ormgarðr   ykkr of folginn."

Gunnarr kvað: 17
"Seinat er nú, systir,   at samna Niflungum;
langt er at leita   lýða sinnis til,
ef rosmufjöll Rínar   rekka óneissa."

Fengu þeir Gunnar   ok í fjötur settu   18
vin Borgunda   ok bundu fastla.

Sjau hjó Högni   sverði hvössu,   19
en inum átta   hratt hann í eld heitan;
svá skal frækn   fjándum verjask
sem Högni varði   hendr sínar.

ATLAKVITHA EN GRÖNLENZKA

Then let the bold heroes their bit-champing horses 13
On the mountains gallop, and through Myrkwood the secret;
All Hunland was shaken where the hard-souled ones rode,
On the whip-fearers fared they through fields that were green.

Then they saw Atli's halls, and his watch-towers high, 14
On the walls so lofty stood the warriors of Buthli;
The hall of the southrons with seats was surrounded,
With targets bound and shields full bright.

Mid weapons and lances did Atli his wine 15
In the war-hall drink, without were his watchmen,
For Gunnar they waited, if forth he should go,
With their ringing spears they would fight with the ruler.

This their sister saw, as soon as her brothers 16
Had entered the hall, little ale had she drunk:
"Betrayed art thou, Gunnar! what guard hast thou, hero,
'Gainst the plots of the Huns? from the hall flee swiftly!
Brother, 'twere far better to have come in byrnie,
With thy household helmed, to see Atli's home,
And to sit in the saddle all day 'neath the sun,
That the sword-norns might weep for the death-pale warriors,
And the Hunnish shield-maids might shun not the sword,
And send Atli himself to the den of the snakes;
Now the den of the snakes for thee is destined."

Gunnar spake: 17
[...]
"Too late is it, sister, to summon the Niflungs,
Long is it to come to the throng of our comrades,
The heroes gallant, from the hills of the Rhine."

Then Gunnar they seized, and they set him in chains, 18
The Burgundians' king, and fast they bound him.

Hogni slew seven with sword so keen, 19
And an eighth he flung in the fire hot;
A hero should fight with his foemen thus,
As Hogni strove in Gunnar's behalf.

[...] Gunnars; 20
frágu fræknan,   ef fjör vildi,
gotna þjóðann,   gulli kaupa.

Gunnarr kvað: 21
"Hjarta skal mér   Högna í hendi liggja
blóðugt, ór brjósti   skorit baldriða
saxi slíðrbeitu,   syni þjóðans."

Skáru þeir hjarta   Hjalla ór brjósti 22
blóðugt ok á bjóð lögðu   ok báru þat fyr Gunnar.

Þá kvað þat Gunnarr,   gumna dróttinn: 23
"Hér hefi ek hjarta   Hjalla ins blauða,
ólíkt hjarta   Högna ins frækna,
er mjök bifask,   er á bjóði liggr,
bifðisk halfu meir,   er í brjósti lá."

Hló þá Högni,   er til hjarta skáru 24
kvikvan kumblasmið,   klökkva hann sízt hugði;
blóðugt þat á bjóð lögðu   ok báru fyr Gunnar.

Mærr kvað þat Gunnarr   geirniflungr: 25
"Hér hefi ek hjarta   Högna ins frækna,
ólíkt hjarta   Hjalla ins blauða,
er lítt bifask,   er á bjóði liggr,
bifðisk svági mjök,   þá er í brjósti lá.

Svá skaltu, Atli,   augum fjarri, 26
sem munt   menjum verða;
er und einum mér   öll of folgin
hodd Niflunga,   lifir-a nú Högni.

Ey var mér týja,   meðan vit tveir lifðum, 27
nú er mér engi,   er ek einn lifik.
Rín skal ráða   rógmalmi skatna,
svinn, áskunna   arfi Niflunga,
í veltanda vatni   lýsask valbaugar,
heldr en á höndum gull   skíni Húna börnum."

ATLAKVITHA EN GRÖNLENZKA

[...] 20
[...]
The leader they asked if his life he fain
With gold would buy, the king of the Goths.

Gunnar spake: 21
"First the heart of Hogni shall ye lay in my hands,
All bloody from the breast of the bold one cut
With keen-biting sword, from the son of the king."

[...] 22
They cut out the heart from the breast of Hjalli,
On a platter they bore it, and brought it to Gunnar.

Then Gunnar spake forth, the lord of the folk: 23
"Here have I the heart of Hjalli the craven,
Unlike to the heart of Hogni the valiant,
For it trembles still as it stands on the platter;
Twice more did it tremble in the breast of the man."

Then Hogni laughed when they cut out the heart 24
Of the living helm-hammerer; tears he had not.
[...]
On a platter they bore it, and brought it to Gunnar.

Then Gunnar spake forth, the spear of the Niflungs: 25
"Here have I the heart of Hogni the valiant,
Unlike to the heart of Hjalli the craven,
Little it trembles as it lies on the platter,
Still less did it tremble when it lay in his breast.

"So distant, Atli, from all men's eyes, 26
Shalt thou be as thou [...] from the gold.
[...]
[...]
"To no one save me is the secret known
Of the Niflungs' hoard, now Hogni is dead;"

"Of old there were two, while we twain were alive, 27
Now is none but I, for I only am living.
The swift Rhine shall hold the strife-gold of heroes,
That once was the gods', the wealth of the Niflungs,
In the depths of the waters the death-rings shall glitter,
And not shine on the hands of the Hunnish men."

Atli kvað: 28
"Ýkvið ér hvélvögnum, haftr er nú í böndum."

Atli inn ríki reið Glaum mönum, 29
sleginn rógþornum, sifjungr þeira.
[...]
Guðrún sigtífa, varnaði við tárum,
vaðin í þyshöllu.

Guðrún kvað: 30
"Svá gangi þér, Atli, sem þú við Gunnar áttir
eiða oft of svarða ok ár of nefnda,
at sól inni suðrhöllu ok at Sigtýs bergi,
hölkvi hvílbeðjar ok at hringi Ullar."
Ok meir þaðan menvörð bituls
dolgrögni dró til dauðs skokkr.

Lifanda gram lagði í garð, 31
þan er skriðinn var, skatna mengi,
innan ormum, en einn Gunnarr
heiftmóðr hörpu hendi kníði,
glumðu strengir; svá skal gulli
frækn hringdrifi við fira halda.

Atli lét lands síns á vit 32
jó eyrskáan aftr frá morði;
dynr var í garði, dröslum of þrungit,
vápnsöngr virða, váru af heiði komnir.

Út gekk þá Guðrún Atla í gögn 33
með gylltum kálki at reifa gjöld rögnis:
"Þiggja knáttu, þengill, í þinni höllu
glaðr at Guðrúnu gnadda niflfarna."

Umðu ölskálir Atla vínhöfgar, 34
þá er í höll saman Húnar tölðusk,
gumar gransíðir, gengu inn hvatir.

Skævaði þá in skírleita 35
[...]
veigar þeim at bera, afkár dís jöfrum
ok ölkrásir valði nauðug neffölum,
en níð sagði Atla:

Atli spake: 28
"Ye shall bring the wagon, for now is he bound."

———⦅⦆———

On the long-maned Glaum rode Atli the great, 29
About him were warriors [...]
But Guthrun, akin to the gods of slaughter,
Yielded not to her tears in the hall of tumult.

Guthrun spake: 30
"It shall go with thee, Atli, as with Gunnar thou heldest
The oaths ofttimes sworn, and of old made firm,
By the sun in the south, by Sigtyr's mountain,
By the horse of the rest-bed, and the ring of Ull."
Then the champer of bits drew the chieftain great,
The gold-guarder, down to the place of death.
[...]

By the warriors' host was the living hero 31
Cast in the den where crawling about
Within were serpents, but soon did Gunnar
With his hand in wrath on the harp-strings smite;
The strings resounded, so shall a hero,
A ring-breaker, gold from his enemies guard.

Then Atli rode on his earth-treading steed, 32
Seeking his home, from the slaughter-place;
There was clatter of hoofs of the steeds in the court,
And the clashing of arms as they came from the field.

Out then came Guthrun to meeting with Atli, 33
With a golden beaker as gift to the monarch:
"Thou mayst eat now, chieftain, within thy dwelling,
Blithely with Guthrun young beasts fresh slaughtered."

The wine-heavy ale-cups of Atli resounded, 34
When there in the hall the Hunnish youths clamored,
And the warriors bearded, the brave ones, entered.

Then in came the shining one, [...] 35
[...] and drink she bore them;
Unwilling and bitter brought she food to the warrior,
Till in scorn to the white-faced Atli did she speak:

"Sona hefir þinna,   sverða deilir,   36
hjörtu hrædreyrug   við hunang of tuggin;
melta knáttu, móðugr,   manna valbráðir,
eta at ölkrásum   ok í öndugi at senda.

Kallar-a þú síðan   til knéa þinna   37
Erp né Eitil,   ölreifa tvá;
sér-a-ðu síðan   í seti miðju
gulls miðlendr   geira skefta,
manar meita   né mara keyra."

Ymr varð á bekkjum,   afkárr söngr virða,   38
gnýr und guðvefjum,   grétu börn Húna;
nema ein Guðrún,   er hon æva grét
bræðr sína berharða   ok buri svása,
unga, ófróða,   þá er hon við Atla gat.

Gulli söri   in gaglbjarta,   39
hringum rauðum   reifði hon húskarla;
sköp lét hon vaxa,   en skíran malm vaða,
æva fljóð ekki   gáði fjarghúsa.

Óvarr Atli   óðan hafði hann sik drukkit,   40
vápn hafði hann ekki,   varnaði-t hann við Gudrúnu,
oft var sá leikr betri,   þá er þau lint skyldu
oftar um faðmask   fyr öðlingum.

Hon beð broddi   gaf blóð at drekka   41
hendi helfússi   ok hvelpa leysti,
hratt fyr hallar dyrr   ok húskarla vakði
brandi brúðr heitum,   þau lét hon gjöld bræðra.

Eldi gaf hon þá alla,   er inni váru   42
ok frá morði þeira Gunnars   komnir váru ór Myrkheimi;
forn timbr fellu,   fjarghús ruku,
bær Buðlunga,   brunnu ok skjaldmeyjar
inni aldrstamar,   hnigu í eld heitan.

Fullrætt er um þetta,   ferr engi svá síðan   43
brúðr í brynju   bræðra at hefna;
hon hefir þriggja   þjóðkonunga
banorð borit,   björt, áðr sylti.
Enn segir gleggra í Atlamálum inum grænlenzkum.

"Thou giver of swords, of thy sons the hearts   36
All heavy with blood in honey thou hast eaten;
Thou shalt stomach, thou hero, the flesh of the slain,
To eat at thy feast, and to send to thy followers."

"Thou shalt never call to thy knees again   37
Erp or Eitil, when merry with ale;
Thou shalt never see in their seats again
The sharers of gold their lances shaping,
Clipping the manes or minding their steeds."

There was clamor on the benches, and the cry of men,   38
The clashing of weapons, and weeping of the Huns,
Save for Guthrun only, she wept not ever
For her bear-fierce brothers, or the boys so dear,
So young and so unhappy, whom with Atli she had.

Gold did she scatter, the swan-white one,   39
And rings of red gold to the followers gave she;
The fate she let grow, and the shining wealth go,
Nor spared she the treasure of the temple itself.

Unwise then was Atli, he had drunk to wildness,   40
No weapon did he have, and of Guthrun bewared not;
Oft their play was better when both in gladness
Each other embraced among princes all.

With her sword she gave blood for the bed to drink,   41
With her death-dealing hand, and the hounds she loosed,
The thralls she awakened, and a firebrand threw
In the door of the hall; so vengeance she had.

To the flames she gave all who yet were within,   42
And from Myrkheim had come from the murder of Gunnar;
The timbers old fell, the temple was in flames,
The dwelling of the Buthlungs, and the shield-maids burned,
They were slain in the house, in the hot flames they sank.

Now the tale is all told, nor in later time   43
Will a woman in byrnie avenge so her brothers;
The fair one to three of the kings of the folk
Brought the doom of death ere herself she died.
Still more is told in the Greenland ballad of Atli.

ENDNOTES

Prose. On the marriage of *Guthrun* to *Atli* at the instigation of her brothers, Gunnar and Hogni, and on the slaying of Atli and his two sons, Erp and Eitil, cf. *Drap Niflunga* and note.

1. Line 1 apparently is in Fornyrthislag. *Knefröth* (the name is spelt in various ways, and its meaning is uncertain): in the *Atlamol* (stanza 4) there are two messengers, one named Vingi and the other unnamed; the annotator combines the two versions in the *Drap Niflunga*. *Benches*, etc.: the adjective rendered "round the hearth," which etymologically it ought to mean, is made obscure by its application to "helmets" in stanzas 3 and 17.

2. *Falseness*: i.e., Gunnar's followers concealed their fear and hatred of the Huns at the feast; but the word may mean "fear of treachery." *Warhall*: the word used is "Valhall," the name of Odin's hall of slain warriors.

3. *Myrkwood the secret* (the adjective is literally "unknown") the which divided Atli's realm from that of the Gjukungs; cf. *Oddrunargratr*, 23 and note. *Around the hearth*: the adjective is the same one which is applied to "benches" in stanza 1 (cf. note); it may be an error here, or it may possibly have the force of "of your followers," i.e., Gunnar is to arm the men of his household (those who are round his hearth) for the journey.

4. *Slaves*, etc.: some editions have "swords in plenty." *Scarlet*: the word apparently means "slaughter-red," "blood-red," but it may mean something entirely different.

5. *Gnitaheith*: here the dragon Fafnir had his lair (cf. *Gripisspo*, 11). Sigurth doubtless owned it after Fafnir's death, and the Gjukungs after they

had killed Sigurth. Possibly they had given it to Atli in recompense for the death of his sister, Brynhild, and he now offered to restore it to them, or—as seems more likely—the poet was not very clear about its ownership himself. *Stems*: i.e., the gilded stems of ships, carved like dragons—an evident northern touch, if the word is correct, which is by no means certain. *Danp*: this name was early applied to a mythical Danish king (cf. *Rigsthula*, 49 and note) but it may have been fabricated by error out of the word "Danparstaþir" (the phrase here used is "staþi Danpar"), used in the *Hervararsaga* of a field of battle between the Goths and the Huns, and quite possibly referring to the region of the Dnieper. The name seems to have clung to the Atli tradition long after it had lost all definite significance. *Myrkwood*: cf. note on stanza 3.

7. The stanza is clearly in bad shape; the manuscript indicates line 5 as beginning a new stanza. In line 5 the manuscript has "and shield" after "helm." *Kjar*: Gering ingeniously identifies this Kjar with Kjar the father of Olrun, mentioned in the *Völundarkvitha*, introductory prose and stanza 2, on the basis of a genealogy in the *Flateyjarbok*, in which Authi, the grandfather of Kjar (by no means certainly the same man) and Buthli, father of Atli, are mentioned as making a raiding voyage together. This identification, however, rests on slight evidence.

8. The manuscript does not name the speaker. One editor gives the first sentence to Gunnar. *She*, etc.: Guthrun, seeking to warn her brothers of Atli's treachery, sends them a ring with a wolf's hair as a sign of danger; in the *Atlamol* (stanza 4) she sends a message written in runes; cf. *Drap Niflunga*. *Heath-dweller*: wolf.

9. In line 1 the manuscript has "His comrades did not urge Gunnar," but the name, involving a metrical error, seems to have been inserted through a scribal blunder.

10. The manuscript indicates no lacuna, but probably two lines have dropped out, for the *Volsungasaga* paraphrase runs: "Give us to drink in great cups, for it may well be that this shall be our last feast." *Fjornir*: Gunnar's cup-bearer.

11. Bugge thinks this stanza is spoken by Gunnar's terrified followers; Grundtvig assigns it to Hogni. Apparently, however, Gunnar means that if he and his men are not valiant enough to make the journey and return safely, it matters little what may happen to them. *Niflungs*: regarding the application of this name to Gunnar's Burgundians cf. *Brot*, 17 and note. *Bears*: these "black" bears have been used as arguments against the Greenland origin of the poem. *And make glad the dogs*: i.e., by giving

them corpses to eat, but the phrase in the original is more than doubtful.

12. Some editions in line 2 read "home of the Niflungs" instead of "their home," and others "home of the Huns," the manuscript reading being "home of the men." *Heir*: the *Atlamol* (stanza 28) names two sons of Hogni, Snævar and Solar, both of whom make the journey with their father and are killed. The *Volsungasaga*, combining the two versions, says that Snævar and Solar went with their father, and implies that it was a third and still younger son who said: "Farewell, and have a good time" (thus literally).

13. *Myrkwood*: cf. stanza 3 and note; the journey is here made by land, whereas in the *Atlamol* it is made partly by boat; cf. *Atlamol*, 37 and note. *Whip-fearers*: horses, but there is some uncertainty as to the word.

14. In line 1 the manuscript has "land" instead of "halls," which involves a metrical error. *Watch-towers*: the word used is identical with the name of Odin's throne, Hlithskjolf (cf. *Grimnismol*, introductory prose). *Buthli*: the manuscript has "Bikki," which has. led some editors to transfer this stanza to the *Hamthesmol*, placing it between stanzas 16 and 17; it seems more likely, however, that "Bikki" was a scribal error for "Buthli." Regarding Bikki cf. *Sigurtharkvitha en skamma*, 63 and note. Line 4 is apparently in Fornyrthislag.

15. Line 1 in the manuscript is apparently incorrectly copied, and some editions omit "Mid weapons and lances" and assume a gap in either line 1 or line 3.

16. This may be the remains of two stanzas, the manuscript marks line 5 as beginning a new stanza. Editorial conjectures are numerous and varied. *Household*: the phrase is the same "helms round the hearth" commented on in stanza 3. Some editions insert a conjectural line after line 3. *Sword-norns*, etc.: the line is exceedingly obscure, and the phrase rendered "sword-norns" may mean "corpse-norns." Apparently it refers to the warrior-women of the Huns, the "shield-maids" of line 5 and of stanza 45. *Den of snakes*: concerning the manner of Gunnar's death cf. *Drap Niflunga*.[1]

17. The manuscript indicates no lacuna and does not name the speaker; perhaps a line similar to line 1 of stanza 23 (or 25) should be inserted here. *Rhine*: Gunnar's Burgundian home is here clearly localized. After

---

[1] Stanza 17 in Bellows' original translation is combined with stanza 16 to conform to the Old Norse. This has resulted in a re-numbering of the stanzas from 16 to 26, where the next restructuring occurs.

this stanza it is probable that a passage describing the battle has been lost.

18. These two lines, apparently the remains of a full stanza, may belong after stanza 19. *Burgundians' king*: the phrase may mean "Burgundians' men," i.e., they bound all the Burgundians who were left alive after the battle. This is the only place in the poems in which the name "Burgundian" appears; that the poet had no very clear conception of its meaning is indicated by the fact that in stanza 20 he calls Gunnar "king of the Goths."

19. Apparently a Fornyrthislag stanza, though most editions have attempted to expand the lines into Malahattr. The exploits of Hogni (Hagene), with the names of many of his victims, are told in the *Nibelungenlied*. *The fire*: in the *Nibelungenlied* Kriemhild has the hall set on fire, and the Burgundians fight amid the flames. Line 4 is clearly defective, and some editors regard the name "Gunnar" as all that is left of the first two lines of stanza 20.

20. Again apparently the remains of a Fornyrthislag stanza. Editors have attempted various combinations of the lines. *Gold*: presumably Sigurth's treasure.

21. The manuscript does not indicate the speaker; perhaps a first line similar to line 1 of stanza 24 should appear here. Some editors, however, assume that a line is missing after line 3. Gunnar demands proof that Hogni is dead because, as stanza 27 shows, he is unwilling to die himself until he is assured that the secret of the treasure will perish with him. He did not, of course, intend that the heart should be cut from the living Hogni.

22. Most editions assume a gap (lines 1-2, 2-3 or 3-4). *Hjalli*: Atli's cook, killed to deceive Gunnar, as Atli hoped to wring the secret of the hoard from Hogni if Gunnar remained silent. In the *Atlamol* (stanzas 59-60) Atli's men prepare to kill Hjalli, but he is spared at Hogni's intercession.

24. *Helm-hammerer* (literally "helmet-smith"): warrior, i.e., Hogni. No gap indicated in the manuscript.

25. Line 1 may belong elsewhere (stanzas 17 or 21).[2]

---

[2] In the Bellows original translation stanzas 27 and lines 1 & 2 of stanza 28 are used to conform the new stanza 26 to the Old Norse. Stanzas 28 lines 3 & 4 and stanza 29 from the original Bellows translation is used to create the new stanza 27 that conforms to the Old Norse. Stanzas 32 and 33 in the Bellows original translation are used to create the new stanza 30 that conforms to the Old Norse.

ENDNOTES 741

26. Apparently the remains of two Fornyrthislag lines; the manuscript combines them with lines 1-2 of stanza 28. Gunnar foretells Atli's speedy death. Apparently in Fornyrthislag. The manuscript indicates line 3 as the beginning of a stanza, and many editions combine lines 3-4 with stanza 29 [in original Bellows translation]. This stanza explains Gunnar's demand for Hogni's heart in stanza 21.[3]

27. The manuscript marks line 3, and not line 1, as the beginning of a stanza. *Rhine*, etc.: the stanza shows the blending of three different traditions with regard to the treasure: the German tradition of the gold of the Rhine (cf. *Völundarkvitha*, 16, and *Sigurtharkvitha en skamma*, 16), the tradition, likewise German, of the hoard of the Nibelungen (Niflungs), early blended with the first one, and finally the northern tradition of the theft of Andvari's treasure by Odin, Hönir, and Loki (cf. *Reginsmol*, 1-9).

28. Apparently all that is left of a full stanza. The manuscript does not name Atli as the speaker, and Grundtvig inserts:

"Then Atli called, the king of the Huns,"

as a first line. Some editors combine this line with the two lines of stanza 29. *Wagon*: in *Brot*, 16, Gunnar is led to his death in the serpents' den on horseback, not in a wagon.

29. The stanza in the original is hopelessly confused. *Glaum*: this horse of Atli's is mentioned by name elsewhere. *Long-maned*: uncertain. The manuscript indicates no gap, but something has evidently been lost. *Gods of slaughter*: perhaps the phrase, usually applied to Odin and the other gods, is here used simply to mean "heroes," i.e., Atli, Gunnar, and Hogni. Line 4 suggests Guthrun's tearlessness after Sigurth's death (cf. *Guthrunarkvitha II*, 11).

30. The manuscript does not indicate the speaker. *Sigtyr* ("Victory-God"): Odin; what particular mountain (if any) is meant is unknown. *Horse of the rest-bed*: probably this means "bedpost," i.e., the support of the marriage-bed. *Ull*: the archer god, cf. *Grimnismol*, 5 and note. Nothing is known of his ring. Apparently the remains of a Fornyrthislag stanza. Some editors combine the two lines with the line here indicated as stanza 30. *Champer of bits*: horse. The manuscript indicates no gap.[4]

31. Six Fornyrthislag lines which editors have tried to reconstruct in all

---

3 Endnote 26 has been edited to reflect changes in the structure of the poem. The references to stanzas 28 and 29 reflect the original verses in Bellows' version. Stanza 21 refers to what was originally stanza 22.
4 Original endnotes 32 and 33 combined to reflect combination of stanzas.

sorts of ways. The manuscript marks line 5 as the beginning of a new stanza, Regarding the serpents' den, Gunnar's harp-playing, and the manner of his death, cf. *Drap Niflunga* and *Oddrunargratr*, 27-30, and notes. In *Atlamol*, 62, Gunnar plays the harp with his feet, his hands being bound, and some editors change hand in line 4 to "foot." Lines 5-6 may be interpolated, or, as Bugge maintains, lines 1-4 may have been expanded out of two lines.

32. The manuscript marks line 3 as beginning a new stanza. Two (possibly three) of the lines appear to, be in Fornyrthislag. *Field*: so the manuscript, involving a metrical error; many editions have "wood."

33. *Young beasts*: Guthrun means Atli's sons, Erp and Eitil, but of course he thinks she refers to newly slaughtered beasts; cf. *Guthrunarkvitha II*, 41-45.

34. *Youths*: a conjectural addition. *The brave ones* is also conjectural, the manuscript having "each." No gap indicated in the manuscript; some editions insert as line 3 or line 4 a slightly altered version of line 2 of stanza 42.

35. No gap indicated in the manuscript, but the two fragments cannot be fitted together as one line. *The shining one*: Guthrun.

36. *Giver of swords*: generous prince, i.e., Atli. *Honey*: cf. *Guthrunarkvitha II*, 42. *To send to thy followers*: literally, "to send from thy high seat."

37. Apparently a Fornyrthislag stanza. *Merry with ale*: presumably this refers to Atli, but the manuscript reading makes it apply to the two boys. *Sharers of gold*: princes. Line 5 is either interpolated or all that is left of a separate stanza.

38. The text of the whole stanza has required a considerable amount of emendation. Lines 3-5 may have been expanded out of two lines, or line 5 may be an interpolation, possibly from stanza 12 of the *Guthrunarhvot*. *Weapons*: the word literally means "good-weaving," and may refer to silken garments, but this hardly fits the noun here rendered "clashing." *Wept not*: cf. stanza 29 and note.

39. Line 1 appears to be in Fornyrthislag. Guthrun distributes Atli's treasures among his followers apparently to prevent their wrath at the slaying of Erp and Eitil from turning against her; Atli, as stanza 43 shows, is too drunk to realize or prevent what she is doing.

40. The second half of line 4 is apparently an error, but none of the editorial suggestions have improved it.

41. Guthrun allows the dogs and the house-thralls, who had no part in Gunnar's death, to escape before she burns the dwelling with all who are left therein. In *Atlamol*, stanzas 83–84, Atli is slain by a son of Hogni (Hniflung?) with Guthrun's help.

42. Some editions transfer line 2 to stanza 34; others reject line 3 as interpolated. *Myrkheim* ("Dark-Home"): probably identical with Myrkwood; cf. stanza 3. *Temple*: probably both here and in stanza 42 the word means little more than the place where Atli's treasures were kept; the poet was by no means literal in his use of terms connected with the heathen religion. *Buthlungs*: sons of Buthli, i.e., Atli and his family. *Shield-maids*: cf. stanza 16 and note.

43. The entire stanza is very likely a later addition. *Three kings*: Atli and his two sons, Erp and Eitil.

ATLAMOL EN GRÖNLENZKU
THE GREENLAND BALLAD OF ATLI

INTRODUCTION

The *Atlamol* immediately follows the *Atlakvitha* in the *Codex Regius*, and comes down to us, barring a few missing lines, in relatively good shape with few additions or interpolations. The work is the longest of the heroic lays at 103 stanzas, and is clearly derivative of the older *Atlakvitha* work, with the main body of its poetic text consisting of lengthy and descriptive elements broadening out a story already familiar to its audience through the usage of evocative and emotional descriptions. Certainly, the work is technically skilled in its composition, and despite its younger origin, it will probably be the more well regarded of the two among modern readers.

The *Atlamol* is annotated within the poem as being of Greenlandic origin, and despite the likely much older brother being thus annotated, this is generally regarded as true of this poem. Scholars from the 19th century on have noted elements lending great credibility to a Greenlandic origin, such as the vivid and realistic description of a polar bear in Stanza 17—though it must be noted that such beasts were not uncommon in Iceland during the same period; the *Auðunar þáttr vestfirska* ("The Tale of Auðun of the West Fjords") follows the story of the main protagonist gifting the King of Denmark with just such a creature, implying that both Icelanders and the noble Scandinavian courts would likely be familiar with them. The grim and evocative nature of the violence in the story, the interpolation of a sea journey rather than a land journey, and the rather mean and comparatively impoverished description of the Niflung's court (they only arrive with three companions and their entire family's court appears to consist of at most ten retainers) imply a likely Greenlandic origin out of touch with the realities of the more wealthy, cultured, and connected continent, or Scandinavia proper.

The Dises
(Dorothy Hardy)

Frétt hefir öld óvu,   þá er endr of gerðu   1
seggir samkundu,   sú var nýt fæstum,
æxtu einmæli,   yggr var þeim síðan
ok it sama sonum Gjúka,   er váru sannráðnir.

Sköp æxtu skjöldunga,   skyldu-at feigir,   2
illa réðsk Atla,   átti hann þó hyggju;
felldi stoð stóra,   stríddi sér harðla,
af bragði boð sendi,   at kvæmi brátt mágar.

Horsk var húsfreyja,   hugði at mannviti;   3
lag heyrði hon orða,   hvat þeir á laun mæltu;
þá var vant vitri,   vildi hon þeim hjalpa,
skyldi of sæ sigla,   en sjalf né komsk-at.

Rúnar nam at rísta,   rengdi þær Vingi   4
fárs var hann flýtandi,   áðr hann fram seldi;
fóru þá síðan   sendimenn Atla
um fjörð Lima,   þar er fræknir bjuggu.

Ölværir urðu   ok elda kyndu,   5
hugðu vætr véla,   er þeir váru komnir;
tóku þeir fórnir,   er þeim fríðr sendi,
hengðu á súlu,   hugðu-t þat varða.

ATLAMOL
EN GRÖNLENZKU

There are many who know how of old did men 1
In counsel gather; little good did they get;
In secret they plotted, it was sore for them later,
And for Gjuki's sons, whose trust they deceived.

Fate grew for the princes, to death they were given; 2
Ill counsel was Atli's, though keenness he had;
He felled his staunch bulwark, his own sorrow fashioned,
Soon a message he sent that his kinsmen should seek him.

Wise was the woman, she fain would use wisdom, 3
She saw well what meant all they said in secret;
From her heart it was hid how help she might render,
The sea they should sail, while herself she should go not.

Runes did she fashion, but false Vingi made them, 4
The speeder of hatred, ere to give them he sought;
Then soon fared the warriors whom Atli had sent,
And to Limafjord came, to the home of the kings.

They were kindly with ale, and fires they kindled, 5
They thought not of craft from the guests who had come;
The gifts did they take that the noble one gave them,
On the pillars they hung them, no fear did they harbor.

Kom þá Kostbera,   kvæn var hon Högna,   6
kona kapps gálig,   ok kvaddi þá báða;
glöð var ok Glaumvör,   er Gunnarr átti,
fellsk-at saðr sviðri,   sýsti of þörf gesta.

Buðu þeir heim Högna,   ef hann þá heldr færi,   7
sýn var svipvísi,   ef þeir sín gæði;
hét þá för Gunnarr,   ef Högni vildi,
Högni því nítti-t,   er hinn of réði.

Báru mjöð mærar,   margs var alls beini;   8
fór þar fjölð horna,   unz þótti fulldrukkit.

Hjú gerðu hvílu   sem þeim hægst þótti;   9
kennd var Kostbera,   kunni hon skil rúna,
innti orðstafi   at eldi ljósum;
gæta varð hon tungu   í góma báða,
váru svá villtar,   at var vant at ráða.

Sæing fóru síðan   sína þau Högni;   10
dreymði dróttláta,   dulði þess vætki,
sagði horsk hilmi,   þegars hon réð vakna:

"Heiman gerisk þú, Högni,   hyggðu at ráðum,   11
fár er fullrýninn,   far þú í sinn annat;
réð ek þér rúnar,   er reist þín systir,
björt hefir þér eigi   boðit í sinn þetta.

Eitt ek mest undrumk,   mák-at ek enn hyggja,   12
hvat þá varð vitri,   er skyldi villt rísta;
því at svá var á vísat,   sem undir væri
bani ykkarr beggja,   ef it bráðla kvæmið;
vant er stafs vífi,   eða valda aðrir."

Högni kvað: 13
"Allar ro illúðgar,   ákk-a ek þess kynni
vilk-a ek þess leita,   nema launa eigim;
okkr mun gramr gulli   reifa glóðrauðu;
óumk ek aldregi,   þótt vér ógn fregnim."

Forth did Kostbera, wife of Hogni, then come, 6
Full kindly she was, and she welcomed them both;
And glad too was Glaumvor, the wife of Gunnar,
She knew well to care for the needs of the guests.

Then Hogni they asked if more eager he were, 7
Full clear was the guile, if on guard they had been;
Then Gunnar made promise, if Hogni would go,
And Hogni made answer as the other counseled.

Then the famed ones brought mead, and fair was the feast, 8
Full many were the horns, till the men had drunk deep;
[...]
Then the mates made ready their beds for resting.

Wise was Kostbera, and cunning in rune-craft, 9
The letters would she read by the light of the fire;
But full quickly her tongue to her palate clave,
So strange did they seem that their meaning she saw not.

Full soon then his bed came Hogni to seek, 10
[...]
The clear-souled one dreamed, and her dream she kept not,
To the warrior the wise one spake when she wakened:

"Thou wouldst go hence, Hogni, but heed my counsel, 11
Known to few are the runes, and put off thy faring;
I have read now the runes that thy sister wrote,
And this time the bright one did not bid thee to come."

"Full much do I wonder, nor well can I see, 12
Why the woman wise so wildly hath written;
But to me it seems that the meaning beneath
Is that both shall be slain if soon ye shall go.
But one rune she missed, or else others have marred it."

Hogni spake: 13
"All women are fearful; not so do I feel,
Ill I seek not to find till I soon must avenge it;
The king now will give us the glow-ruddy gold;
I never shall fear, though of dangers I know."

Kostbera kvað: 14
"Stopalt munuð ganga, ef it stundið þangat;
ykkr mun ástkynni eigi í sinn þetta;
dreymdi mik, Högni, dyljumk þat eigi;
ganga mun ykkr andæris, eða ella hræðumk.

Blæju hugða ek þína brenna í eldi, 15
hryti hár logi hús mín í gögnum."

Högni kvað: 16
"Liggja hér línklæði, þau er lítt rækið,
þau munu brátt brenna, þau er þú blæju sátt."

Kostbera kvað: 17
"Björn hugða ek hér inn kominn, bryti upp stokka,
hristi svá hramma, at vér hrædd yrðim;
munn oss mörg hefði, svá at vér mættim ekki;
þar var ok þrömmun þeygi svá lítil."

Högni kvað: 18
"Veðr mun þar vaxa, verða ótt snemma,
hvítabjörn hugðir, þar mun hregg austan."

Kostbera kvað: 19
"Örn hugða ek hér inn fljúga at endlöngu húsi,
þat mun oss drjúgt deilask, dreifði hann oss öll blóði,
hugða ek af heitum at væri hamr Atla."

Högni kvað: 20
"Slátrum sýsliga, séum þá roðru,
oft er þat fyr öxnum, er örnu dreymir;
heill er hugr Atla, hvatki er þik dreymir."
Lokit því létu, líðr hver ræða.

Vöknuðu vel borin, var þar sams dæmi, 21
gettisk þess Glaumvör, at væri grand svefna
[...] við Gunnarr at fáa tvær leiðir.

Glaumvör kvað: 22
"Görvan hugða ek þér galga, gengir þú at hanga,
æti þik ormar, yrða ek þik kvikvan,
gerðisk rök ragna; ráð þú, hvat þat væri."

Gunnarr kvað: 23
[...]

Kostbera spake: 14
"In danger ye fare, if forth ye go thither,
No welcoming friendly this time shall ye find;
For I dreamed now, Hogni, and nought will I hide,
Full evil thy faring, if rightly I fear."

"Thy bed-covering saw I in the flames burning, 15
And the fire burst high through the walls of my home."

Hogni spake: 16
"Yon garment of linen lies little of worth,
It will soon be burned, so thou sawest the bed-cover."

Kostbera spake: 17
"A bear saw I enter, the pillars he broke,
And he brandished his claws so that craven we were;
With his mouth seized he many, and nought was our might,
And loud was the tumult, not little it was."

Hogni spake: 18
"Now a storm is brewing, and wild it grows swiftly,
A dream of an ice-bear means a gale from the east."

Kostbera spake: 19
"An eagle I saw flying from the end through the house,
Our fate must be bad, for with blood he sprinkled us;
[...]
From the evil I fear that 'twas Atli's spirit."

Hogni spake: 20
"They will slaughter soon, and so blood do we see,
Oft oxen it means when of eagles one dreams;
True is Atli's heart, whatever thou dreamest."
Then silent they were, and nought further they said.

The high-born ones wakened, and like speech they had, 21
Then did Glaumvor tell how in terror she dreamed,
[...] Gunnar two roads they should go.

Glaumvor spake: 22
"A gallows saw I ready, thou didst go to thy hanging,
Thy flesh serpents ate, and yet living I found thee;
[...]
The gods' doom descended; now say what it boded."

Gunnar spake: 23
[...]

Glaumvör kvað: 24
"Blóðgan hugða ek mæki   borinn ór serk þínum
illt er svefn slíkan   at segja nauðmanni,
geir hugða ek standa   í gögnum þik miðjan,
emjuðu ulfar   á endum báðum."

Gunnarr kvað: 25
"Rakkar þar renna,   ráðask mjök geyja,
oft verðr glaumr hunda   fyr geira flaugun."

Glaumvör kvað: 26
"Á hugða ek hér inn renna   at endlöngu húsi,
þyti af þjósti,   þeystisk of bekki,
bryti fætr ykra   bræðra hér tveggja,
gerði-t vatn vægja;   vera mun þat fyr nökkvi."

Gunnarr kvað: 27
[...]

Glaumvör kvað: 28
"Konur hugðak dauðar   koma í nótt hingat,
væri-t vart búnar,   vildi þik kjósa,
byði þér bráðliga   til bekkja sinna;
ek kveð aflima   orðnar þér dísir."

Gunnarr kvað: 29
"Seinat er at segja,   svá er nú ráðit;
forumk-a för þó,   alls þó ar fara ætlat;
margt er mjök glíkligt,   at mynim skammæir."

Litu er lýsti,   létusk þeir fúsir, 30
allir upp rísa,   önnur þau löttu,
fóru fimm saman,   fleiri til váru
halfu húskarlar,   hugat var því illa.
Snævarr ok Sólarr,   synir váru þeir Högna,
Orkning þann hétu,   er þeim enn fylgði,
blíðr var börr skjaldar   bróðir hans kvánar.

Fóru fagrbúnar,   unz þau fjörðr skilði; 31
löttu ávallt ljósar,   létu-at heldr segjask.

Glaumvör kvað at orði,   er Gunnarr átti, 32
mælti hon við Vinga,   sem henni vert þótti:
"Veitk-at ek, hvárt verðlaunið   at vilja ossum;
glæpr er gests kváma,   ef í gerisk nakkvat."

"A sword drawn bloody from thy garments I saw, 24
Such a dream is hard to a husband to tell,
A spear stood, methought, through thy body thrust,
And at head and feet the wolves were howling."

Gunnar spake: 25
"The hounds are running, loud their barking is heard,
Oft hounds' clamor follows the flying of spears."

Glaumvor spake: 26
"A river the length of the hall saw I run,
Full swiftly it roared, o'er the benches it swept;
O'er the feet did it break of ye brothers twain,
The water would yield not; some meaning there was."

Gunnar spake: 27
[...]

Glaumvor spake: 28
"I dreamed that by night came dead women hither,
Sad were their garments, and thee were they seeking;
They bade thee come swiftly forth to their benches,
And nothing, methinks, could the Norns avail thee. "

Gunnar spake: 29
"Too late is thy speaking, for so is it settled
From the faring I turn not, the going is fixed,
Though likely it is that our lives shall be short."

Then bright shone the morning, the men all were ready, 30
They said, and yet each would the other hold back;
Five were the warriors, and their followers all
But twice as many, their minds knew not wisdom.
Snævar and Solar, they were sons of Hogni,
Orkning was he called who came with the others,
Blithe was the shield-tree, the brother of Kostbera.

The fair-decked ones followed, till the fjord divided them, 31
Full hard did they plead, but the others would hear not.

Then did Glaumvor speak forth, the wife of Gunnar, 32
To Vingi she said that which wise to her seemed:
"I know not if well thou requitest our welcome,
Full ill was thy coming if evil shall follow."

Sór þá Vingi, sér réð hann lítt eira: 33
"Eigi hann jötnar, ef hann at yðr lygi,
galgi görvallan, ef hann á grið hygði."

Bera kvað at orði, blíð í hug sínum: 34
"Sigli þér sælir ok sigr árnið;
fari sem ek fyr mælik, fæst eigi því níta."

Högni svaraði, hugði gótt nánum: 35
"Huggizk it, horskar, hvégi er þat gervisk;
mæla þat margir, missir þó stórum,
mörgum ræðr litlu, hvé verðr leiddr heiman."

Sásk til síðan, áðr í sundr hyrfi, 36
þá hygg ek sköp skiptu, skilðusk vegir þeira.

Róa námu ríki, rifu kjöl halfan, 37
beystu bakföllum, brugðusk heldr reiðir,
hömlur slitnuðu, háir brotnuðu,
gerðu-t far festa, áðr þeir frá hyrfi.

Litlu ok lengra, lok mun ek þess segja, 38
bæ sá þeir standa, er Buðli átti;
hátt hriktu grindr, er Högni kníði.

Orð kvað þá Vingi, þats án væri: 39
"Farið firr húsi, flátt er til sækja,
brátt hefi ek ykkr brennda, bragðs skuluð höggnir,
fagrt bað ek ykkr kvámu, flátt var þó undir
ella heðan bíðið, meðan ek hegg yðr galga."

Orð kvað hitt Högni, hugði lítt vægja, 40
varr at véttugi, er varð at reyna:
"Hirða þú oss hræða, hafðu þat fram sjaldan,
ef þú eykr orði, illt muntu þér lengja."

Hrundu þeir Vinga ok í hel drápu, 41
öxar at lögðu, meðan í önd hixti.

Flykkðusk þeir Atli ok fóru í brynjur, 42
gengu svá görvir, at var garðr milli;
urpusk á orðum allir senn reiðir:
"Fyrr várum fullráða at firra yðr lífi."

Then did Vingi swear, and full glib was his speech,   33
[...]
"May giants now take me if lies I have told ye,
And the gallows if hostile thought did I have."

Then did Bera speak forth, and fair was her thought,   34
[...]
"May ye sail now happy, and victory have,
To fare as I bid ye, may nought your way bar."

Then Hogni made answer, dear held he his kin,   35
"Take courage, ye wise ones, whatsoever may come;
Though many may speak, yet is evil oft mighty,
And words avail little to lead one homeward."

They tenderly looked till each turned on his way,   36
Then with changing fate were their farings divided.

Full stoutly they rowed, and the keel clove asunder,   37
Their backs strained at the oars, and their strength was
    fierce;
The oar-loops were burst, the thole-pins, were broken,
Nor the ship made they fast ere from her they fared.

Not long was it after—the end must I tell—   38
That the home they beheld that Buthli once had;
Loud the gates resounded when Hogni smote them;

Vingi spake then a word that were better unsaid: 39
"Go ye far from the house, for false is its entrance,
Soon shall I burn you, ye are swiftly smitten;
I bade ye come fairly, but falseness was under,
Now bide ye afar while your gallows I fashion."

Then Hogni made answer, his heart yielded little,   40
And nought did he fear that his fate held in store:
"Seek not to affright us, thou shalt seldom succeed;
If thy words are more, then the worse grows thy fate."

Then Vingi did they smite, and they sent him to hell,   41
With their axes they clove him while the death rattle came.

Atli summoned his men, in mail-coats they hastened,   42
All ready they came, and between was the courtyard.
Then came they to words, and full wrathful they were:
"Long since did we plan how soon we might slay you."

Högni kvað: 43
"Á sér þat illa,   ef höfðuð áðr ráðit,
en eruð óbúnir,   ok höfum einn felldan,
lamðan til heljar,   lids var sá yðvars."

Óðir þá urðu,   er þat orð heyrðu, 44
forðuðu fingrum   ok fengu í snæri,
skutu skarpliga   ok skjöldum hlífðusk.

Inn kom þá andspilli,   hvat úti drýgðu, 45
halir fyr höllu,   heyrðu þræl segja.

Ötul var þá Guðrún,   er hon ekka heyrði, 46
hlaðin halsmenjum,   hreytti hon þeim gervöllum,
slöngði svá silfri,   at í sundr hrutu baugar.

Út gekk hon síðan,   yppði-t lítt hurðum, 47
fór-a fælt þeygi   ok fagnaði komnum,
hvarf til Niflunga,   sú var hinzt kveðja,
fylgði saðr slíku,   sagði hon mun fleira:

"Leitaða ek í líkna   at letja ykkr heiman, 48
sköpum viðr manngi,   ok skuluð þó hér komnir."
Mælti af mannviti,   ef mundu sættask;
ekki at reðusk,   allir ní kváðu.

Sá þá sælborin,   at þeir sárt léku, 49
hugði á harðræði   ok hrauzk ór skikkju;
nökðan tók hon mæki   ok niðja fjör varði,
hæg var-at hjaldri,   hvars hon hendr festi.

Dóttir lét Gjúka   drengi tvá hníga, 50
bróður hjó hon Atla,   bera varð þann síðan,
skapði hon svá skæru,   skelldi fót undan.

Annan réð hon höggva,   svá at sá upp reis-at, 51
í helju hon þann hafði,   þeygi henni hendr skulfu.

Þjörku þar gerðu,   þeiri var við brugðit, 52
þat brá of allt annat,   er unnu börn Gjúka;
svá kváðu Niflunga,   meðan sjalfir lifðu,
skapa sókn sverðum,   slítask af brynjur,
höggva svá hjalma   sem þeim hugr dygði.

Hogni spake: 43
"Little it matters if long ye have planned it;
For unarmed do ye wait, and one have we felled,
We smote him to hell, of your host was he once."

Then wild was their anger when all heard his words; 44
Their fingers were swift on their bowstrings to seize,
Full sharply they shot, by their shields were they guarded.

In the house came the word how the heroes without 45
Fought in front of the hall; they heard a thrall tell it.

Grim then was Guthrun, the grief when she heard, 46
With necklaces fair, and she flung them all from her,
The silver she hurled so the rings burst asunder.

Then out did she go, she flung open the doors, 47
All fearless she went, and the guests did she welcome;
To the Niflungs she went—her last greeting it was—
In her speech truth was clear, and much would she speak.

"For your safety I sought that at home ye should stay; 48
None escapes his fate, so ye hither must fare."
Full wisely she spake, if yet peace they might win,
But to nought would they hearken, and "No" said they all.

Then the high-born one saw that hard was their battle, 49
In fierceness of heart she flung off her mantle;
Her naked sword grasped she her kin's lives to guard,
Not gentle her hands in the hewing of battle.

Then the daughter of Gjuki two warriors smote down, 50
Atli's brother she slew, and forth then they bore him;
So fiercely she fought that his feet she clove off;

Another she smote so that never he stood, 51
To hell did she send him, her hands trembled never.

Full wide was the fame of the battle they fought, 52
'Twas the greatest of deeds of the sons of Gjuki;
Men say that the Niflungs, while themselves they were
    living,
With their swords fought mightily, mail-coats they sundered,
And helms did they hew, as their hearts were fearless.

Morgin mest vágu, unz miðjan dag líddi, 53
óttu alla ok öndurðan dag;
fyrr var fullvegit, flóði völlr blóði,
átján áðr fellu, efri þeir urðu.
Beru tveir sveinar ok bróðir hennar.

Röskr tók at ræða, þótt hann reiðr væri: 54
"Illt er um litask, yðr er þat kenna;
várum þrír tigir, þegnar vígligir,
eftir lifum ellifu, ór er þar brunnit.

Bæðr várum fimm, er Buðla misstum; 55
hefir nú Hel halfa, en höggnir tveir liggja."

Högni kvað: 56
"Mægð gat ek mikla, mák-a-k því leyna,
kona váliga, knák-a ek þess njóta;
hljótt áttum sjaldan, síz komt í hendr ossar,
firrðan mik frændum, féi oft svikinn,
senduð systur helju, slíks ek mest kennumk."

Guðrún kvað: 57
"Getr þú þess, Atli, gerðir svá fyrri,
móður tókt mína ok myrðir til hnossa,
svinna systrungu sveltir þú í helli,
hlægligt mér þat þykkir, er þú þinn harm tínir;
goðum ek þat þakka, er þér gengsk illa."

Atli kvað: 58
"Eggja ek yðr, jarlar, auka harm stóran
vífs ins vegliga, vilja ek þat líta;
kostið svá keppa, at klökkvi Guðrún,
séa ek þat mætta, at hon sér né ynði-t.

Takið ér Högna ok hyldið með knífi, 59
skerið ór hjarta, skuluð þess görvir,
Gunnar grimmúðgan á galga festið,
bellið því bragði, bjóðið til ormum."

Högni kvað: 60
"Ger, sem til lystir, glaðr munk þess bíða,
röskr munk þér reynask, reynt hefi ek fyrr brattara;
höfuð hnekking, meðan heilir várum,
nú erum svá sárir, at þá mátt sjalfr valda."

All the morning they fought until midday shone,   53
All the dusk as well and the dawning of day,
When the battle was ended, the field flowed with blood;
Ere they fell, eighteen of their foemen were slain,
By the two sons of Bera and her brother as well.

Then the warrior spake, and wild was his anger: 54
"This is evil to see, and thy doing is all;
Once we were thirty, we thanes, keen for battle,
Now eleven are left, and great is our lack.

"There were five of us brothers when Buthli we lost,   55
Now Hel has the half, and two smitten lie here."

Hogni spake: 56
"A great kinship had I, the truth may I hide not,
From a wife bringing slaughter small joy could I win.
We lay seldom together since to me thou wast given,
Now my kin all are gone, of my gold am I robbed;
Nay, and worst, thou didst send my sister to hell."

Guthrun spake: 57
"Hear me now, Atli! the first evil was thine;
My mother didst thou take, and for gold didst murder her,
My sister's daughter thou didst starve in a prison.
A jest does it seem that thy sorrow thou tellest,
And good do I find it that grief to thee comes."

Atli spake: 58
"Go now, ye warriors, and make greater the grief
Of the woman so fair, for fain would I see it;
So fierce be thy warring that Guthrun shall weep,
I would gladly behold her happiness lost."

"Seize ye now Hogni, and with knives shall ye hew him,   59
His heart shall ye cut out, this haste ye to do;
And grim-hearted Gunnar shall ye bind on the gallows,
Swift shall ye do it, to serpents now cast him."

Hogni spake: 60
"Do now as thou wilt, for glad I await it,
Brave shalt thou find me, I have faced worse before;
We held thee at bay while whole we were fighting,
Now with wounds are we spent, so thy will canst thou
    work."

Beiti þat mælti,   bryti var hann Atla: 61
"Tökum vér Hjalla,   en Högna forðum,
högum vér halft yrkjum,   hann er skapdauði,
lifir-a svá lengi,   löskr mun hann æ heitinn."

Hræddr var hvergætir,   helt-a in lengr rúmi,   62
kunni klökkr verða,   kleif í rá hverja;
vesall lézk vígs þeira,   er skyldi váss gjalda,
ok sinn dag dapran   at deyja frá svínum,
allri örkostu,   er hann áðr hafði.

Tóku þeir brás Buðla   ok brugðu til knífi,   63
æpði illþræli,   áðr odds kenndi,
tóm lézk at eiga   teðja vel garða,
vinna it vergasta,   ef hann við rétti,
feginn lézk þó Hjalli,   at hann fjör þægi.

Gættisk þess Högni   —gerva svá færi—   64
at árna ánauðgum,   at undan gengi:
"Fyrir kveð ek mér minna   at fremja leik þenna.
Hví mynim hér vilja   heyra á þá skræktun?"

Þrifu þeir þjóðgóðan,   þá var kostr engi   65
rekkum rakklátum   ráð enn lengr dvelja;
hló þá Högni,   heyrðu dagmegir,
keppa hann svá kunni,   kvöl hann vel þolði.

Harpu tók Gunnarr,   hrærði ilkvistum,   66
sláa hann svá kunni,   at snótir grétu,
klukku þeir karlar,   er kunnu görst heyra;
ríkri ráð sagði;   raftar sundr brustu.

Dó þá dýrir,   dags var heldr snemma,   67
létu þeir á lesti   lifa íþróttir.

Stórr þóttisk Atli,   sté hann of þá báða,   68
horskri harm sagði   ok réð heldr at bregða:
"Morginn er nú, Guðrún,   misst hefir þú þér hollra;
sums ertu sjalfskapa,   at hafi svá gengit."

Guðrún kvað: 69
"Feginn ertu, Atli,   ferr þú víg lýsa,
á munu þér iðrar,   ef þú allt reynir;
sú mun erfð eftir,   ek kann þér segja:
Ills gengsk þér aldri,   nema ek ok deyja."

Then did Beiti speak, he was Atli's steward: 61
"Let us seize now Hjalli, and Hogni spare we!
Let us fell the sluggard, he is fit for death,
He has lived too long, and lazy men call him."

Afraid was the pot-watcher, he fled here and yon, 62
And crazed with his terror he climbed in the corners:
"Ill for me is this fighting, if I pay for your fierceness,
And sad is the day to die leaving my swine
And all the fair victuals that of old did I have."

They seized Buthli's cook, and they came with the knife, 63
The frightened thrall howled ere the edge did he feel;
He was willing, he cried, to dung well the court yard,
Do the basest of work, if spare him they would;
Full happy were Hjalli if his life he might have.

Then fain was Hogni—there are few would do thus— 64
To beg for the slave that safe hence he should go;
"I would find it far better this knife-play to feel,
Why must we all hark to this howling longer?"

Then the brave one they seized; to the warriors bold 65
No chance was there left to delay his fate longer;
Loud did Hogni laugh, all the sons of day heard him,
So valiant he was that well he could suffer.

A harp Gunnar seized, with his toes he smote it 66
So well did he strike that the women all wept,
And the men, when clear they heard it, lamented;
Full noble was his song, the rafters burst asunder.

Then the heroes died ere the day was yet come; 67
Their fame did they leave ever lofty to live.
[...]

Full mighty seemed Atli as o'er them he stood, 68
The wise one he blamed, and his words reproached her:
"It is morning, Guthrun; now thy dear ones dost miss,
But the blame is part thine that thus it has chanced."

Guthrun spake: 69
"Thou art joyous, Atli, for of evil thou tellest,
But sorrow is thine if thou mightest all see;
Thy heritage heavy here can I tell thee,
Sorrow never thou losest unless I shall die."

Atli kvað: 70
"Kann ek slíks synja,   sé ek til ráð annat
halfu hógligra,   —höfnum oft góðu—
mani mun ek þik hugga,   mætum ágætum,
silfri snæhvítu,   sem þú sjalf vilir."

Guðrún kvað: 71
"Ón er þess engi,   ek vil því níta;
sleit ek þá sáttir,   er váru sakar minni;
afkár ek áðr þótta,   á mun nú gæða,
hræfða ek um hotvetna,   meðan Högni lifði.

Alin vit upp várum   í einu húsi, 72
lékum leik margan   ok í lundi óxum,
gæddi okkr Grímhildr   gulli ok halsmenjum;
bana muntu mér bræðra   bæta aldrigi
né vinna þess ekki,   at mér vel þykki.

Kostum drepr kvenna   karla ofríki; 73
í kné gengr hnefi,   ef kvistir þverra;
tré tekr at hníga,   ef höggr tág undan;
nú máttu einn, Atli,   öllu hér ráða."

Gnótt var grunnýðgi,   er gramr því trúði, 74
sýn var sveipvísi,   ef hann sín gæði;
kröpp var þá Guðrún,   kunni of hug mæla,
létt hon sér gerði,   lék hon tveim skjöldum.

Æxti hon öldrykkjur   at erfa bræðr sína,
samr lézk ok Atli   at sína gerva. 75

Lokit því létu,   lagat var drykkju, 76
sú var samkunda   við svörfun ofmikla;
ströng var stórhuguð,   strídði hon ætt Buðla,
vildi hon ver sínum   vinna ofrhefndir.

Lokkaði hon litla   ok lagði við stokki, 77
glúpnuðu grimmir   ok grétu þeygi,
fóru í faðm móður,   fréttu, hvat þá skyldi.

Atli spake: | 70
"Not free of guilt am I; a way shall I find
That is better by far—oft the fairest we shunned—
With slaves I console thee, with gems fair to see,
And with silver snow-white, as thyself thou shalt choose."

Guthrun spake: | 71
"No hope shall this give thee, thy gifts I shall take not,
Requital I spurned when my sorrows were smaller;
Once grim did I seem, but now greater my grimness,
There was nought seemed too hard while Hogni was living."

"Our childhood did we have in a single house, | 72
We played many a game, in the grove did we grow;
Then did Grimhild give us gold and necklaces,
Thou shalt ne'er make amends for my brother's murder,
Nor ever shalt win me to think it was well."

"But the fierceness of men rules the fate of women, | 73
The tree-top bows low if bereft of its leaves,
The tree bends over if the roots are cleft under it;
Now mayest thou, Atli, o'er all things here rule."

Full heedless the warrior was that he trusted her, | 74
So clear was her guile if on guard he had been;
But crafty was Guthrun, with cunning she spake,
Her glance she made pleasant, with two shields she played.

The beer then she brought for her brothers' death feast, | 75
And a feast Atli made for his followers dead.

No more did they speak, the mead was made ready, | 76
Soon the men were gathered with mighty uproar.
Thus bitterly planned she, and Buthli's race threatened,
And terrible vengeance on her husband would take;

The little ones called she, on a block she laid them; | 77
Afraid were the proud ones, but their tears did not fall;
To their mother's arms went they, and asked what she would.

Guðrún kvað: 78
"Spyrið lítt eftir,　　spilla ætla ek báðum,
lyst várumk þess lengi　　at lyfja ykkr elli."

Sveinarnir kváðu:
"Blótt, sem vill, börnum,　　bannar þat manngi,
skömm mun ró reiði,　　ef þú reynir görva."

Brá þá barnæsku　　bræðra in kappsvinna, 79
skipti-t skapliga,　　skar hon á hals báða.
Enn frétti Atli,　　hvert farnir væri
sveinar hans leika,　　er hann sá þá hvergi.

Guðrún kvað: 80
"Yfir ráðumk ganga　　Atla til segja;
dylja munk þik eigi,　　dóttir Grímhildar;
glaða mun þik minnst, Atli,　　ef þú görva reynir;
vakðir vá mikla,　　er þú vátt bræðr mína.

Svaf ek mjök sjaldan,　　síðans þeir fellu, 81
hét ek þér hörðu,　　hefi ek þik nú minntan;
morgin mér sagðir,　　man ek enn þann görva,
nú er ok aftann,　　átt þú slíkt at frétta.

Maga hefir þú þinna　　misst, sem þú sízt skyldir, 82
hausa veizt þú þeira　　hafða at ölskálum,
drýgða ek þér svá drykkju,　　dreyra blett ek þeira.

Tók ek þeira hjörtu,　　ok á teini steikðak, 83
selda ek þér síðan,　　sagðak, at kalfs væri:
einn þú því ollir,　　ekki réttu leifa,
töggtu tíðliga,　　trúðir vel jöxlum.

Barna veiztu þinna,　　biðr sér fár verra; 84
hlut veld ek mínum,　　hælumk þó ekki."

Atli kvað: 85
"Grimm vartu, Guðrún,　　er þú gera svá máttir,
barna þinna blóði　　at blanda mér drykkju;
snýtt hefir þú sifjungum,　　sem þú sizt skyldir,
mér lætr þú ok sjalfum　　millum ills lítit."

Guthrun spake: 78
"Nay, ask me no more! You both shall I murder,
For long have I wished your lives to steal from you."

The boys spake:
"Slay thy boys as thou wilt, for no one may bar it,
Short the angry one's peace if all thou shalt do."

Then the grim one slew both of the brothers young, 79
Full hard was her deed when their heads she smote off;
Fain was Atli to know whither now they were gone,
The boys from their sport, for nowhere he spied them.

Guthrun spake: 80
"My fate shall I seek, all to Atli saying,
The daughter of Grimhild the deed from thee hides not;
No joy thou hast, Atli, if all thou shalt hear,
Great sorrow didst wake when my brothers thou slewest."

"I have seldom slept since the hour they were slain, 81
Baleful were my threats, now I bid thee recall them;
Thou didst say it was morning—too well I remember—

Now is evening come, and this question thou askest." 82
"Now both of thy sons thou hast lost [...]
[...] as thou never shouldst do;
The skulls of thy boys thou as beer-cups didst have,
And the draught that I made thee was mixed with their
   blood."

"I cut out their hearts, on a spit I cooked them, 83
I came to thee with them, and calf's flesh I called them;
Alone didst thou eat them, nor any didst leave,
Thou didst greedily bite, and thy teeth were busy."

"Of thy sons now thou knowest; few suffer more sorrow; 84
My guilt have I told, fame it never shall give me."

Atli spake: 85
"Grim wast thou, Guthrun, in so grievous a deed,
My draught with the blood of thy boys to mingle;
Thou hast slain thine own kin, most ill it be seemed thee,
And little for me twixt my sorrows thou leavest."

Guðrún kvað: 86
"Vili mér enn væri   at vega þik sjalfan,
fátt er fullilla   farit við gram slíkan;
drýgt þú fyrr hafðir   þat, er menn dæmi vissu-t til,
heimsku, harðræðis   í heimi þessum;
nú hefir þú enn aukit,   þat er áðan frágum;
greipt glæp stóran,   gört hefir þú þitt erfi."

Atli kvað: 87
"Brennd muntu á báli   ok barið grjóti áðr,
þá hefir þú árnat   þatstu æ beiðisk."

Guðrún kvað:
"Seg þér slíkar   sorgir ár morgin,
fríðra vil ek dauða   fara í ljós annat."

Sátu samtýnis,   sendusk fárhugi, 88
hendusk heiftyrði,   hvártki sér unði;
heift óx Hniflungi,   hugði á stórræði,
gat fyr Guðrúnu,   at hann væri grimmr Atla.

Kómu í hug henni   Högna viðfarar, 89
talði happ hánum,   ef hann hefnt ynni.
Veginn var þá Atli,   var þess skammt bíða,
sonr vá Högna   ok sjalf Guðrún.

Röskr tók at ræða,   rakðisk ór svefni, 90
kenndi brátt benja,   bands kvað hann þörf enga:
"Segið it sannasta,   hverr vá son Buðla,
emk-a ek lítt leikinn,   lífs tel ek ván enga."

Guðrún kvað: 91
"Dylja mun þik eigi   dóttir Grímhildar,
látumk því valda,   er líðr þína æfi,
en sumu sonr Högna,   er þik sár mæða."

Atli kvað: 92
"Vaðit hefir þú at vígi,   þótt væri-t skaplikt,
illt er vin véla,   þanns þér vel trúir;
beiddr fór ek heiman   at biðja þín, Guðrún.

Leyfð vartu ekkja,   létu stórráða, 93
varð-a ván lygi,   er vér of reyndum;
fórtu heim hingat,   fylgði oss herr manna,
allt var ítarligt   um órar ferðir.

Guthrun spake: 86
"Still more would I seek to slay thee thyself,
Enough ill comes seldom to such as thou art;
Thou didst folly of old, such that no one shall find
In the whole world of men a match for such madness.
Now this that of late we learned hast thou added,
Great evil hast grasped, and thine own death feast made."

Atli spake: 87
"With fire shall they burn thee, and first shall they stone thee,
So then hast thou earned what thou ever hast sought for."

Guthrun spake:
"Such woes for thyself shalt thou say in the morning,
From a finer death I to another light fare."

Together they sat and full grim were their thoughts, 88
Unfriendly their words, and no joy either found;
In Hniflung grew hatred, great plans did he have,
To Guthrun his anger against Atli was told.

To her heart came ever the fate of Hogni, 89
She told him 'twere well if he vengeance should win;
So was Atli slain, 'twas not slow to await,
Hogni's son slew him, and Guthrun herself.

Then the warrior spake, as from slumber he wakened, 90
Soon he knew for his wounds would the bandage do nought:
"Now the truth shalt thou say: who has slain Buthli's son?
Full sore am I smitten, nor hope can I see."

Guthrun spake: 91
"Ne'er her deed from thee hides the daughter of Grimhild,
I own to the guilt that is ending thy life,
And the son of Hogni; 'tis so thy wounds bleed."

Atli spake: 92
"To murder hast thou fared, though foul it must seem;
I'll thy friend to betray who trusted thee well.
Not glad went I hence thy hand to seek, Guthrun."

"In thy widowhood famed, but haughty men found thee; 93
My belief did not lie, as now we have learned;
I brought thee home hither, and a host of men with us.
Most noble was all when of old we journeyed."

Margs var alls sómi   manna tíginna, 94
naut váru ærin,   nutum af stórum,
þar var fjölð féar,   fengu til margir.

Mund galt ek mærri   meiðma fjölð þiggja, 95
þræla þría tigu,   þýjar sjau góðar,
sæmð var at slíku,   silfr var þó meira.

Atli kvað: 96
Léztu þér allt þykkja,   sem ekki væri,
meðan lönd þau lágu,   er mér leifði Buðli,
gróftu svá undir,   gerði-t hlut þiggja;
sværu léztu þína   sitja oft grátna,
fann ek í hug heilum   hjóna vætr síðan."

Guðrún kvað: 97
"Lýgr þú nú, Atli,   þótt ek þat lítt rekja;
heldr var ek hæg sjaldan,   hóftu þó stórum;
börðuzk ér bræðr ungir,   báruzk róg milli;
halft gekk til heljar   ór húsi þínu;
hrolldi hotvetna   þat er til hags skyldi.

Þrjú várum systkin,   þóttum óvægin, 98
fórum af landi,   fylgðum Sigurði,
skæva vér létum,   skipi hvert várt stýrði,
örkuðum at auðnu,   unz vér austr kómum.

Konung drápum fyrstan,   kurum land þaðra, 99
hersar oss á hönd gengu,   hræðslu þat vissi;
vágum ór skógi   þanns vildum syknan,
settum þann sælan,   er sér né átti-t.

Dauðr varð inn húnski,   drap þá brátt kosti, 100
strangt var angr ungri   ekkju nafn hljóta;
kvöl þótti kvikri   at koma í hús Atla,
átti áðr kappi,   illr var sá missir.

Guðrún kvað: 101
"Komt-a-ðu af því þingi,   er vér þat frægim,
at þú sök sættir   né slekðir aðra;
vildir ávallt vægja   en vætki halda,
kyrrt of því láta,   [...]"

"Great honor did we have of heroes full worthy; 94
Of cattle had we plenty, and greatly we prospered,
Mighty was our wealth, and many received it."

"To the famed one as bride-gift I gave jewels fair, 95
I gave thirty slaves, and handmaidens seven;
There was honor in such gifts, yet the silver was greater."

Atli spake: 96
"But all to thee was as if nought it were worth,
While the land lay before thee that Buthli had left me;
Thou in secret didst work so the treasure I won not;
My mother full oft to sit weeping didst make,
No wedded joy found I in fullness of heart."

Guthrun spake: 97
"Thou liest now, Atli, though little I heed it;
If I seldom was kindly, full cruel wast thou;
Ye brothers fought young, quarrels brought you to battle,
And half went to hell of the sons of thy house,
And all was destroyed that should e'er have done good.

"My two brothers and I were bold in our thoughts, 98
From the land we went forth, with Sigurth we fared;
Full swiftly we sailed, each one steering his ship,
So our fate sought we e'er till we came to the East."

"First the king did we slay, and the land we seized, 99
The princes did us service, for such was their fear;
From the forest we called them we fain would have guiltless,
And rich made we many who of all were bereft."

"Slain was the Hun-king, soon happiness vanished, 100
In her grief the widow so young sat weeping;
Yet worse seemed the sorrow to seek Atli's house,
A hero was my husband, and hard was his loss."

Guthrun spake: 101
"From the Thing thou camst never,
for thus have we heard,
Having won in thy quarrels, or warriors smitten;
Full yielding thou wast, never firm was thy will,
In silence didst suffer […]"

Atli kvað: 102
"Lýgr þú nú, Guðrún,   lítt mun við bætask
hluti hvárigra,   höfum öll skarðan.
Gerðu nú, Guðrún,   af gæzku þinni
okkr til ágætis,   er mik út hefja."

Guðrún kvað: 103
"Knörr mun ek kaupa   ok kistu steinda,
vexa vel blæju   at verja þitt líki,
hyggja á þörf hverja,   sem vit holl værim."

Nár varð þá Atli,   niðjum stríð æxti, 104
efndi ítrborin   allt þats réð heita;
fróð vildi Gudrún   fara sér at spilla,
urðu dvöl dægra,   dó hon í sinn annat.

Sæll er hverr síðan,   er slíkt getr fæða 105
jóð at afreki,   sems ól Gjúki;
lifa mun þat eftir   á landi hverju
þeira þrámæli,   hvargi er þjóð heyrir.

Atli spake: 102
"Thou liest now, Guthrun, but little of good
Will it bring to either, for all have we lost;
But, Guthrun, yet once be thou kindly of will,
For the honor of both, when forth I am home."

Guthrun spake: 103
"A ship will I buy, and a bright-hued coffin,
I will wax well the shroud to wind round thy body,
For all will I care as if dear were we ever."

Then did Atli die, and his heirs' grief doubled; 104
The high-born one did as to him she had promised;
Then sought Guthrun the wise to go to her death,
But for days did she wait, and 'twas long ere she died.

Full happy shall he be who such offspring has, 105
Or children so gallant, as Gjuki begot;
Forever shall live, and in lands far and wide,
Their valor heroic wherever men hear it.

ENDNOTES

1. *Men*: Atli and his advisers, with whom he planned the death of the sons of *Gjuki*, Gunnar and Hogni. The poet's reference to the story as well known explains the abruptness of his introduction, without the mention of Atli's name, and his reference to Guthrun in stanza 3 simply as "the woman" ("husfreyja," goddess of the house).

2. *Princes*: Atli, Gunnar, and Hogni. *Bulwark*: Atli's slaying of his wife's brothers, who were ready to support and defend him in his greatness, was the cause of his own death.

3. *The woman*: Guthrun, concerning whose marriage to Atli cf. *Guthrunarkvitha II*. *The sea*: a late and essentially Greenland variation of the geography of the Atli story. Even the *Atlakvitha*, perhaps half a century earlier, separates Atli's land from that of the Gjukungs only by a forest.

4. *Runes*: on the two versions of Guthrun's warning, and also on the name of the messenger (here Vingi), cf. *Drap Niflunga* and note. *Limafjord*: probably the Limfjord of northern Jutland, an important point in the wars of the eleventh century. The name was derived from "Eylimafjorþ," i.e., Eylimi's fjord. The poet may really have thought that the kingdom of the Burgundians was in Jutland, or he may simply have taken a well-known name for the sake of vividness.

5. Some editors assume a gap after this stanza.

6. Some editions place this stanza between stanzas 7 and 8. *Kostbera* ("The Giver of Food") and *Glaumvor* ("The Merry"): presumably creations of the poet. *Both*: Atli's two emissaries, Vingi and the one here unnamed (Knefröth?).

7. It is altogether probable that a stanza has been lost between stanzas 6 and 7, in which Gunnar is first invited, and replies doubtfully. *Made promise*: many editions emend the text to read "promised the journey." The text of line 4 is obscure; the manuscript reads "nitti" ("refused"), which many editors have changed to "hlitti," which means exactly the opposite.

8. No gap is indicated in the manuscript; Bugge adds (line 3): "Then the warriors rose, and to slumber made ready." The manuscript indicates line 4 as beginning a new stanza, and some editions make a separate stanza out of lines 1–2. Others suggest the loss of a line after line 4.

9. The manuscript does not indicate line 1 as the beginning of a stanza; cf. note on stanza 8.

10. Some editions combine this stanza with lines 1–2 of stanza 11. The manuscript indicates no gap. Grundtvig adds (line 2) "But sleep to the woman so wise came little."

11. Some editions make a separate stanza out of lines 1–2, or combine them with stanza 10, and combine lines 3–4 with stanza 12 (either lines 1–4 or 1–2). The manuscript marks line 3 as beginning a new stanza.

12. Line 5 may be spurious, or else all that is left of a lost stanza. The manuscript marks it as the beginning of a new stanza, which, as the text stands, is clearly impossible.

13. The manuscript, followed by some editions, has "Hogni spake" in the middle of line 1. *Ill*: the manuscript and many editions have "this." *The king*: Atli.

14. The manuscript does not indicate the speakers in this dialogue between Kostbera and Hogni (stanzas 14–19). Two lines may possibly have been lost after line 2, filling out stanza 14 and making stanza 15 (then consisting of lines 3–4 of stanza 14 and lines 1–2 of stanza 15) the account of Kostbera's first dream. The manuscript marks line 3 as beginning a new stanza. In any case, the lost lines cannot materially have altered the meaning.

15. *Saw I*: the manuscript here, as also in stanzas 16, 18, 21, 22, and 24, has "methought," which involves a metrical error. Some editors regard lines 3–4 as the remains of a four-line stanza. Regarding Kostbera's warning dreams, and Hogni's matter-of-fact interpretations of them, cf. *Guth-*

runarkvitha II, 39-44.[1]

18. Two lines may have been lost after line 2, but the *Volsungasaga* paraphrase gives no clue. *Ice-bear*: polar bears, common in Greenland, are very rarely found in Iceland, and never in Norway, a fact which substantiates the manuscript's reference to Greenland as the home of the poem.

19. The manuscript indicates no gap, but most editors assume the loss of a line after line 1 or 2; Grundtvig adds, after line 1: "Black were his feathers, with blood was he covered." *Atli's spirit*: the poet's folk-lore seems here a bit weak. Presumably he means such a female following-spirit ("fylgja") as appears in *Helgakvitha Hjorvarthssonar*, prose following stanza 34 (cf. note thereon), but the word he uses, "hamr" (masculine) means "skin," "shape." He may, however, imply that Atli had assumed the shape of an eagle for this occasion.

20. The manuscript indicates line 4 as beginning a new stanza.

21. The manuscript indicates no gap, but none of the many attempted emendations have made sense out of the words as they stand. The proper location for the missing words is sheer guesswork. *Two roads*: probably the meaning is that their way (i.e., their success) would be doubtful.

22. The manuscript does not indicate the speakers in this dialogue (stanzas 22-29). No gap is indicated after line 2. Most editors assume the loss of two lines or of a full stanza after stanza 22 giving Gunnar's interpretation of Glaumvor's dream, but the *Volsungasaga* gives no clue, as it does not mention this first dream at all. Grundtvig suggests as Gunnar's answer: "Banners are gleaming, since of gallows didst dream, / And wealth it must mean that thou serpents didst watch." *Gods' doom*: an odd, and apparently mistaken, use of the phrase "ragna rök" (cf. *Voluspo*, introductory note [Appendix B]).

26. Again Gunnar's interpretation is missing, and most editors either assume a gap or construct two Malahattr lines out of the *Volsungasaga* prose paraphrase, which runs: "The grain shall flow, since thou hast dreamed of rivers, and when we go to the fields, often the chaff rises above our feet."

28. The meaning of line 4 is uncertain, but apparently it refers to the guardian spirits or lesser Norns (cf. *Fafnismol*, 12-13 and notes).

---

[1] The last three lines of Bellows' original stanza 15 have been moved to form a new stanza 16 to conform with the Old Norse. The numbering of the rest of the poem has therefore been altered accordingly.

29. Possibly a line has been lost from this stanza.

30. *Five*: Gunnar, Hogni, and the three mentioned in Stanza 31. Perhaps a line has been lost before line 1; Grundtvig supplies: "Gunnar and Hogni, the heirs twain of Gjuki." *Snævar* (the manuscript here has "Snevar"), *Solar* and *Orkning* appear only in this poem and in the prose narratives based on it. Lines 2–3 may have been expanded out of one line, or possibly line 3 is spurious. The manuscript indicates line 4 as beginning a new stanza, and many editions make a separate stanza out of lines 4–5, many of them assuming the loss of two lines. *Shield-tree*: warrior (Orkning), here identified as Kostbera's brother. *Fair-decked ones*: women, i.e., Glaumvor and Kostbera. *Fjord*: perhaps specifically the *Limafjord* mentioned in stanza 4.[2]

31. [This stanza is conformed from Bellows' original stanza 28 lines 4–5 to match the Old Norse].

33. The manuscript indicates no gap. Grundtvig inserts (line 2): "The evil was clear when his words he uttered."

34. *Bera*: Kostbera; the first element in compound feminine proper names was not infrequently omitted; cf. Hild for Brynhild (*Helreith Brynhildar*, 6). The manuscript indicates no gap; Grundtvig inserts (line 2): "And clear was her cry to her kinsmen dear."

35. Hogni's method of cheering his wife and sister-in-law is somewhat unusual, for the meaning of lines 3–4 is that good wishes and blessings are of little use in warding off danger.

36. Perhaps two lines have been lost after line 2; Grundtvig supplies: "Then weeping did Glaumvor go to her rest-bed, / And sadly did Bera her spinning wheel seek."

37. *Keel*, etc.: in the *Nibelungenlied*, and presumably in the older German tradition, Hagene breaks his oar steering the Burgundians across the Danube (stanza 1564), and, after all have landed, splinters the boat (stanza 1581) in order that there may be no retreating. The poet here seems to have confused the story, connecting the breaking of the ship's keel with the violence of the rowing, but echoing the older legend in the last line, wherein the ship is allowed to drift away after the travellers have landed. *Oar-loops*: the thongs by which the oars in a Norse boat were made fast to the *thole-pins*, the combination taking the place of the modern oar-

---

[2] This stanza has been conformed from Bellows' original stanza 27 and stanza 28 lines 1–3 to match the Old Norse.

lock.³

38. The manuscript indicates line 4 as beginning a new stanza, and many editions combine it with stanza 36, some of them assuming the loss of a line from stanza 35. In the *Volsungasaga* paraphrase the second half of line 4 is made a part of Vingi's speech: "Better had ye left this undone."

39. Cf. note on preceding stanza; the manuscript does not indicate line 1 as beginning a stanza. Line 3 may be spurious.

40. In the *Volsungasaga* paraphrase the second half of line 1 and the first half of line 2 are included in Hogni's speech.

41. Possibly two lines have been lost after line 2.

42. [Stanza is conformed from Bellows' original stanza 39 and stanza 40.] It is probable that a considerable passage has been lost between stanzas 39 and 40 [Bellows original stanzas], for the *Volsungasaga* paraphrase includes a dialogue at this point. The manuscript indicates no gap, and most editions combine stanzas [Bellows' original stanzas] 39 and 40 as a single stanza. The prose passage, indicating the substance of what, if anything, is lost, runs as follows: "'Be welcome among us, and give me that store of gold which is ours by right, the gold that Sigurth had, and that now belongs to Guthrun.' Gunnar said: 'Never shalt thou get that gold, and men of might shalt thou find here, ere we give up our lives, if it is battle thou dost offer us; in truth it seems that thou hast prepared this feast in kingly fashion, and with little grudging toward eagle and wolf.'" The demand for the treasure likewise appears in the *Nibelungenlied*. These two lines, which most editions combine with stanza 39, may be the first or last two of a four-line stanza. The *Volsungasaga* gives Atli's speech very much as it appears here.

43. The manuscript does not indicate the speaker; Grundtvig adds as a first line: "Then Hogni laughed loud where the slain Vingi lay." Many editors assume the loss of a line somewhere in the stanza. *Unarmed*: Hogni does not see Atli's armed followers, who are on the other side of the courtyard (stanza 42). *One*: Vingi.

44. Most editors assume the loss of one line, after either line 1 or line 3.

45. [This stanza is conformed from Bellows' original stanza 43 lines 1-2 to match the Old Norse].

---

3 Stanza 38 is conformed from Bellows' original 35 lines 1-3. Stanza 39 is conformed from Bellows' original stanza 35 line 4 and stanza 36.

46. [This stanza is conformed from Bellows original stanza 43 lines 3-5.][4]

47. *Niflungs*: regarding the application of this term to the Burgundians cf. *Atlakvitha*, 11, and *Brot*, 17, and notes. The manuscript here spells the name with an initial N, as elsewhere, but in stanza 83 the son of Hogni appears with the name "Hniflung." In consequence, some editors change the form in this stanza to "Hniflungs," while others omit the initial H in both cases. I have followed the manuscript, though admittedly its spelling is illogical.

49. The warlike deeds of Guthrun represent an odd transformation of the German tradition. Kriemhild, although she did no actual fighting in the *Nibelungenlied*, was famed from early times for her cruelty and fierceness of heart, and this seems to have inspired the poet of the *Atlamol* to make his Guthrun into a warrior outdoing Brynhild herself. Kriemhild's ferocity, of course, was directed against Gunther and especially Hagene, for whose slaying she rather than Etzel was responsible; here, on the other hand, Guthrun's is devoted to the defense of her brothers.

50. Line 3 is very likely an interpolation. The manuscript marks line 4 as the beginning of a new stanza, and some editions make a separate stanza of lines 4-5. *Atli's brother*: doubtless a reminiscence of the early tradition represented in the *Nibelungenlied* by the slaying of Etzel's brother, Blœdelin (the historical Bleda), by Dancwart.[5]

51. This stanza is conformed from Bellows original stanza 47 lines 4-5.

52. Line 3 may well be spurious, for it implies that Gunnar and Hogni were killed in battle, whereas they were taken prisoners. Some editors, in an effort to smooth out the inconsistency, change "themselves" in this line to "sound." Line 5 has also been questioned as possibly interpolated. *Niflungs*: on the spelling of this name in the manuscript and the various editions cf. note on stanza 44.

53. Line 2 is probably an interpolation, and the original apparently lacks a word. There is some obscurity as to the exact meaning of lines 4-5. *The two sons of Bera*: Snævar and Solar; her brother is Orkning; cf. stanza 31.

54. *The warrior*: Atli. Thirty: perhaps an echo of the "thirty warriors" of Thjothrek (cf. *Guthrunarkvitha III*, 5). Subtracting the eighteen killed by Snævar, Solar and Orkning (stanza 53), and Vingi, killed by the whole company (stanza 41), we have eleven left, as Atli says, but this does not

---

[4] The original footnote 43 in Bellows' edition has been removed.
[5] This stanza has been conformed consisting of Bellows original stanza 47 lines 1-3 to match the Old Norse.

allow much for the exploits of Gunnar and Hogni, who, by this reckoning, seem to have killed nobody. The explanation probably is that lines 4–5 of stanza 53 are in bad shape.

55. *Five brothers*: the *Volsungasaga* speaks of four (not five) sons of Buthli, but names only Atli. Regarding the death of the first two brothers cf. stanza 97 and note. The manuscript marks line 3 as beginning a stanza, and many editions combine lines 3–4 with stanza 56. Some insert lines 2–3 of stanza 56 ahead of lines 3–4 of stanza 55.[6]

56. Possibly a line has been lost from this stanza. The manuscript marks line 3 as beginning a new stanza, which is impossible unless something has been lost. *Gold*: the meaning of this half line is somewhat doubtful, but apparently Atli refers to Sigurth's treasure, which should have been his as Brynhild's brother. *Sister*: Brynhild; regarding Guthrun's indirect responsibility for Brynhild's death cf. *Gripisspo*, 45 and note.

[Editor's Note]: This stanza has been conformed from Bellows original 51 lines 3–4 and Bellows' original stanza 52.

57. The manuscript does not name the speaker. The *Volsungasaga* gives the speech, in somewhat altered form, to Hogni. "Why speakest thou so? Thou wast the first to break peace; thou didst take my kinswoman and starved her in a prison, and murdered her and took her wealth; that was not kinglike; and laughable does it seem to me that thou talkest of thy sorrow, and good shall I find it that all goes ill with thee." This presumably represents the correct form of the stanza, for nowhere else is it intimated that Atli killed Guthrun's mother, Grimhild, nor is the niece elsewhere mentioned. Some editions make a separate stanza of lines 4–5, Grundtvig adding a line after line 3 and two more after line 5. Other editors are doubtful about the authenticity of either line 3 or line 5.

58. The manuscript does not indicate the speaker.

60. The text of the first half of line 3 is somewhat uncertain, but the general meaning of it is clear enough.

61. *Beiti*: not elsewhere mentioned. The *Atlakvitha* version of this episode (stanzas 25–28) does not mention Beiti, and in the *Volsungasaga* the advice to cut out Hjalli's heart instead of Hogni's is given by an unnamed "counsellor of Atli." In the *Atlakvitha* Hjalli is actually killed; the *Volsungasaga* combines the two versions by having Hjalli first let off at Hogni's

---

[6] This stanza was conformed from Bellows' original stanza 51 lines 1–2 to match the Old Norse.

intercession and then seized a second time and killed, thus introducing the *Atlakvitha* episode of the quaking heart (stanza 26). The text of the first half of line 3 is obscure, and there are many and widely varying suggestions as to the word here rendered "sluggard."[7]

63. *Cook*: the original word is doubtful. The *Volsungasaga* does not paraphrase lines 3–5; the passage may be a later addition, and line 5 is almost certainly so.

65. It is probable that a stanza describing the casting of Gunnar into the serpents' den has been lost after this stanza. *Sons of day*: the phrase means no more than "men."

66. Regarding Gunnar's harp-playing, and his death, cf. *Oddrunargratr*, 27–30 and notes, and *Atlakvitha*, 34. *Toes* (literally "sole-twigs"): the *Volsungasaga* explains that Gunnar's hands were bound. *Rafters*: thus literally, and probably correctly; Gering has an ingenious but unlikely theory that the word means "harp."

67. There is some doubt as to the exact meaning of line 2. After this line two lines may have! been lost; Grundtvig adds: "Few braver shall ever be found on the earth, / Or loftier men in the world ever give."

68. *Wise one*: Guthrun. The manuscript marks line 3 as beginning a new stanza.

69. The manuscript does not indicate the speaker.

70. The manuscript does not name the speaker. The negative in the first half of line 1 is uncertain, and most editions make the clause read "Of this guilt I can free myself." *The fairest*, etc.: i. e., I have often failed to do the wise thing.

71. The manuscript does not indicate the speaker. *Requital*, etc.: it is not clear just to what Guthrun refers; perhaps she is thinking of Sigurth's death, or possibly the poet had in mind his reference to the slaying of her mother in stanza 57.

72. Line 5 is very probably a later addition, though some editors question line 3 instead.

73. Guthrun suddenly changes her tone in order to make Atli believe that she is submissive to his will, and thus to gain time for her vengeance. Line 2 in the original is thoroughly obscure; it runs literally: "On the knee goes

---

7 Footnote 58 in Bellows' original edition has been removed.

the fist if the twigs are taken off." Perhaps the word meaning "fist" may also have meant "tree-top," as Gering suggests, or perhaps the line is an illogical blending of the ideas contained in lines 1 and 3.

74. The manuscript indicates line 3 as the beginning of a new stanza. *Two shields*, etc.: i.e., Guthrun concealed her hostility (symbolized by a red shield, cf. *Helgakvitha Hundingsbana* I, 34) by a show of friendliness (a white shield).

75. Many editions make a separate stanza of lines 1–2, some of them suggesting the loss of two lines, and combine lines 3–4 with lines 1–2 of stanza 72. The manuscript marks both lines 1 and 3 as beginning stanzas. [8]

76. The manuscript marks line 3 as beginning a new stanza; some editions make a separate stanza of lines 3–5, while others combine them with lines 1–2 of stanza 73. Line 2 in the original is clearly defective, the verb being omitted. The meaning of line 3 is uncertain; the *Volsungasaga* paraphrase has: "At evening she took the sons of King Atli (Erp and Eitil) where they were playing with a block of wood." Probably the text of the line as we have it is faulty. Lines 4–5 may possibly have been expanded out of a single line, or line 5 may be spurious.[9]

78. The manuscript does not name the speakers. It indicates line 3 as beginning a new stanza, in which it is followed by many editions. The *Volsungasaga* paraphrases line 4 thus: "But it is shameful for thee to do this." Either the text of the line has been changed or the *Volsungasaga* compilers misunderstood it. *The angry one*: Atli.[10]

79. The manuscript indicates line 3 as beginning a new stanza.

80. The manuscript does not name the speaker.

81. *Morning*: Guthrun refers to Atli's taunt in stanza 64.

82. The manuscript indicates no gap (lines 1–2), and most editions make a single line, despite the defective meter: "Thy sons hast thou lost as thou never shouldst lose them." The second part of line 2 is in the original identical with the second half of line 3 of stanza 80, and may perhaps have been inserted here by mistake. *Skulls*: it is possible that line 3 was borrowed from a poem belonging to the Völund tradition (cf. *Völundark-*

---

[8] This stanza has been conformed from Bellows' original stanza 71 lines 1–2.
[9] This stanza has been conformed from Bellows' original stanza 71 lines 3–4 and stanza 72 lines 1–2 to match the Old Norse.
[10] This stanza has been conformed from Bellows' original stanza 72 lines 3–5 to match the Old Norse.

vitha, 25 and 37), and the idea doubtless came from some such source, but probably the poet inserted it in a line of his own composition to give an added touch of horror. The *Volsungasaga* follows the *Atlamol* in including this incident.

83. Some editions add lines 3-4 to stanza 84; Finnur Jonsson marks them as probably spurious.

84. Perhaps these two lines should form part of stanza 83, or perhaps they, rather than lines 3-4 of stanza 83, are a later addition. A gap of two lines after line 1 has also been conjectured.

85. The manuscript does not indicate the speaker.

86. The manuscript does not indicate the speaker. Lines 1-2 may be the remains of a separate stanza; Grundtvig adds: "Thou wast foolish, Atli, when wise thou didst feel, / Ever the whole of thy race did I hate." The *Volsungasaga* paraphrase, however, indicates no gap. Many editions make a separate stanza of lines 3-6, which, in the *Volsungasaga*, are paraphrased as a speech of Atli's. Lines 5-6 may be spurious.

87. The manuscript does not indicate the speakers. Many editions make two separate stanzas of the four lines.

88. The manuscript marks line 3 as the beginning of a new stanza. *Hniflung*: the *Volsungasaga* says that "Hogni had a son who was called Hniflung," but the name appears to be nothing more than the familiar "Niflung" applied in general to the sons of Gjuki and their people. On the spelling cf. note on stanza 47. This son of Hogni appears in later versions of the story. In the *Thithrekssaga* he is called Aldrian, and is begotten by Hogni the night before his death. Aldrian grows up and finally shuts Attila in a cave where he starves to death. The poet here has incorporated the idea, which finds no parallel in the *Atlakvitha*, without troubling himself to straighten out the chronology.

89. Line 4 may be in Fornyrthislag, and from another poem.

90. The manuscript marks line 3 as beginning a new stanza. The *Volsungasaga* makes line 2 part of Atli's speech.

91. The manuscript does not name the speakers. It marks line 4 as the beginning of a new stanza, and many editions follow this arrangement, in most cases making a stanza of lines 4-5 and line 1 of stanza 93. However, line 1 may well have been interpolated here from stanza 80. Grundtvig adds after line 3: "His father he avenged, and his kinsmen fully." Some

editors assume the loss of one or two lines after line 5.[11]

92. [Stanza conformed from Bellows' original stanza 86 lines 4–5 and stanza 87 line 1 to match the Old Norse.]

93. The manuscript marks line 2 as beginning a new stanza, and some editions make a stanza out of lines 2–4 and line 1 of stanza 94.[12]

94. The manuscript marks line 2 as the beginning of a stanza, and many editions make a stanza out of lines 2–4, or combine them with stanza 89. Some question the genuineness of line 4.

95. Many editions assume a gap of one line after line 3; Grundtvig adds: "Bit-champing horses and wheel-wagons bright." Line 4 may be spurious. *Greater*: i. e., the silver which Atli gave Guthrun was of greater value even than the honor of receiving such royal gifts. Line 4 may be spurious.[13]

95. [Line 4 may be in Fornyrthislag, and from another poem.]

96. Some editions mark line 3 as spurious or defective. The manuscript marks line 4 as the beginning of a new stanza. *The land*, etc.: there is much obscurity as to the significance of this line. Some editors omit or question "me," in which case Atli is apparently reproaching Guthrun for having incited him to fight with his brothers to win for himself the whole of Buthli's land. In stanza 97 Guthrun denies that she was to blame for Atli's quarrels with his brothers. The *Volsungasaga* reading supports this interpretation. The historical Attila did actually have his brother, Bleda, killed in order to have the sole rule. *The treasure*: Sigurth's hoard, which Atli claimed as the brother of Brynhild and husband of Guthrun, Sigurth's widow, but which Gunnar and Hogni kept for themselves, with, as Atli here charges, Guthrun's connivance. *My mother*: the only other reference to Atli's mother is in *Oddrunargratr*, 30, wherein she appears as the adder who stings Gunnar to death, and in the prose passages based on that stanza.

97. The manuscript does not indicate the speaker. It marks both lines 4 and 5 as beginning new stanzas, but line 5 is presumably an interpolation. The text of the second half of line 2 is obscure, and many emendations have been suggested. *Ye brothers*: cf. note on stanza 96. *Half*: i. e., two of Atli's brothers were killed, the other two dying in the battle with Gunnar

---

11 Stanza conformed from Bellows' original stanza 86 lines 1–3 to match the Old Norse.
12 Stanza conformed from Bellows' original stanza 87 lines 2–4 and stanza 88 line 1 to match the Old Norse.
13 Stanza conformed from Bellows' original stanza 88 lines 2–4 to match the Old Norse.

and Hogni; cf. stanza 55 & 56.

98. *From the land*: this maritime expedition of Guthrun and her two brothers, Gunnar and Hogni (the poet seems to know nothing of her half-brother, Gotthorm), with Sigurth seems to have been a pure. invention of the poet's, inserted for the benefit of his Greenland hearers. Nothing further is reported concerning it.

99. *The forest*: i. e., men who were outlawed in the conquered land were restored to their rights—another purely Norse touch.

100. *Hun-king*: Sigurth, though most illogically so called; cf. *Sigurtharkvitha en skamma*, 4 and note. The *Volsungasaga* paraphrase of line 2 is so remote as to be puzzling: "It was little to bear the name of widow." Perhaps, however, the word "not" fell out between "was" and "little."

101. *Thing*, etc.: here the poet makes Atli into a typical Norse land-owner, going to the "Thing," or general law council, to settle his disputes. Even the compilers of the *Volsungasaga* could not accept this, and in their paraphrase changed "Thing" to "battle." The text of the second half of line 2 is uncertain. The manuscript leaves a blank to indicate the gap in- line 4; Grundtvig adds: "as beseems not a king."

103. The manuscript does not indicate the speaker. Many editors assume a gap either before or after line 1. *A ship*: the burial of Norse chiefs in ships was of frequent occurrence, but the Greenland poet's application of the custom to Atli is somewhat grotesque.

104. *Heirs*, etc.: merely a stock phrase, here quite meaningless, as Atli's heirs had all been killed. *Long*: cf. *Guthrunarhvot*, introductory prose.

GUTHRUNARHVOT
GUTHRUN'S INCITING

INTRODUCTION

The *Guthrunarhvot* is the penultimate of the heroic lays within the *Codex Regius* and comes down to us in remarkably bad shape with a large number of suspected interpolations, required interpretations, and missing stanzas. Nonetheless, this appears to be a long-standing situation regarding the poem as its contents as we have them are quoted so thoroughly and exactly by other narratives such as the *Volsungasaga* that we can infer that the text was, during the same period, in the state in which we find it in the *Codex*.

The narrative of the poem consists of Guthrun inciting her sons Hamdir and Sorli and her stepson Erpr to violence to avenge the death of their sister Svanhild, who was slain by her own husband Jormunrek after the discovery of her infidelity with his own son. Guthrun's three sons and the King Jormunrek actually existed as real historical personages, attested in classical histories, specifically that of the Gothic historian Jordanes, writing in his capacity within the Byzantine Empire. It is universally acknowledged that the legendary personage of Jormunrek originates in the historical Gothic King Ermanaric, as do his slayers in the historical personages of Hamdir (Ammius) and Sorli (Sarus), who are recorded by Jordanes in his *Getica*. By the 10th century, we also find within the *Annals of Quedlinburg* the addition of a historical Addacar in the form of the legendary Erpr, though this may be an interpolation of the historical Odoacer, the military leader of the late Western Roman Empire, likely of east Germanic descent, who deposed the boy king Romulus Augustulus and became king of Italy.

The narrative, depicting the inciting to violence of close kin by a female relation, is so common a theme within saga stories and Germanic lore in general, that we may consider it a trope or simple cliché. This represents the social power women wielded in Viking age Scandinavia and the influence of honor and shame upon men during this time. A narrative element that might be lost on modern readers is that the women's condemnations of their kin for cowardice and dishonor, should they not rightly avenge themselves, is an instance of a religious institution known as "scolding". To simplify the principle, one's spoken words have metaphysical power and act as an assault upon the soul such that speaking the words "you coward, you dishonorable cur" and the like would *ipso facto* make them true and taint the spirit with their force unless rebuked by action. Although it may appear to modern readers that Guthrun is merely cajoling her sons to action, she is actually manipulating the situation to force their hand, lest they be harmed and tainted by her words, knowing that they cannot take action against her and thus their only recourse is to perform the vengeance.

Guðrún gekk þá til sævar, er hon hafði drepit Atla. Gekk hon út á sæinn ok vildi fara sér. Hon mátti eigi sökkva. Rak hana yfir fjörðinn á land Jónakrs konungs. Hann fekk hennar. Þeira synir váru þeir Sörli ok Erpr ok Hamðir. Þar fæddist upp Svanhildr Sigurðardóttir. Hon var gift Jörmunrekk inum ríkja. Með honom var Bikki. Hann réð þat, at Randvér konungs son skyldi taka hana. Þat sagði Bikki konungi. Konungr lét hengja Randvé, en troða Svanhildi undir hrossa fótum. En er þat spurði Guðrún, þá kvaddi hon sonu sína.

Þá frá ek sennu	slíðrfengligsta,	1
trauð mál, talið	af trega stórum,	
er harðhuguð	hvatti at vígi	
grimmum orðum	Guðrún sonu:	

"Hví sitið ér,	hví sofið lífi,	2
hví tregr-at ykkr	teiti at mæla,	
er Jörmunrekkr	yðra systur,	
unga at aldri,	jóm of traddi,	
hvítum ok svörtum,	á hervegi,	
grám, gangtömum	Gotna hrossum?	

GUTHRUNARHVOT

Guthrun went forth to the sea after she had slain Atli. She went out into the sea and fain would drown herself, but she could not sink. The waves bore her across the fjord to the land of King Jonak; he took her as wife; their sons were Sorli and Erp and Hamther. There was brought up Svanhild, Sigurth's daughter; she was married to the mighty Jormunrek. With him was Bikki, who counselled that Randver, the king's son, should have her. This Bikki told to the king. The king had Randver hanged, and Svanhild trodden to death under horses' feet. And when Guthrun learned this, she spake with her sons.

A word-strife I learned, most woeful of all, 1
A speech from the fullness of sorrow spoken,
When fierce of heart her sons to the fight
Did Guthrun whet with words full grim.

"Why sit ye idle, why sleep out your lives, 2
Why grieve ye not in gladness to speak?
Since Jormunrek your sister young
Beneath the hoofs of horses hath trodden,
White and black on the battle-way,
Gray, road-wonted, the steeds of the Goths."

Urðu-a it glíkir   þeim Gunnari   3
né in heldr hugðir   sem var Högni;
hennar munduð it   hefna leita,
ef móð ættið   minna bræðra
eða harðan hug   Húnkonunga."

Þá kvað þat Hamðir   inn hugumstóri: 4
"Lítt myndir þú   leyfa dáð Högna,
þá er Sigurð vökðu   svefni ór;
bækr váru þínar   enar bláhvítu
roðnar í vers dreyra,   folgnar í valblóði.

Urðu þér beggja   bræðra hefndir   5
slíðrar ok sárar,   er þú sonu myrðir;
knættim allir   Jörmunrekki
samhyggjendr   systur hefna.

Berið hnossir fram   Húnkonunga;   6
hefir þú okkr hvatta   at hjörþingi."

Hlæjandi Guðrún   hvarf til skemmu,   7
kumbl konunga   ór kerum valði,
síðar brynjur,   ok sonum færði,
hlóðusk móðgir   á mara bógu.

Þá kvað þat Hamðir   inn hugumstóri: 8
"Svá kemsk meir aftr   móður at vitja
geir-Njörðr hniginn   á Goðþjóðu,
at þú erfi   at öll oss drykkir,
at Svanhildi   ok sonu þína."

Guðrún grátandi,   Gjúka dóttir,   9
gekk hon tregliga   á tái sitja
ok at telja   tárughlýra
móðug spjöll   á margan veg:

"Þrjá vissa ek elda,   þrjá vissa ek arna,   10
var ek þrimr verum   vegin at húsi;
einn var mér Sigurðr   öllum betri,
er bræðr mínir   at bana urðu.

Svárra sára   sák-at ek né kunna,   11
[...]
meir þóttusk   mér of stríða,
er mik öðlingar   Atla gáfu.

"Not like are ye to Gunnar of yore, 3
Nor have ye hearts such as Hogni's was;
Vengeance for her ye soon would have
If brave ye were as my brothers of old,
Or hard your hearts as the Hunnish kings'."

Then Hamther spake, the high of heart: 4
"Little the deed of Hogni didst love,
When Sigurth they wakened from his sleep;
Thy bed-covers white were red with blood
Of thy husband, drenched with gore from his heart.

"Bloody revenge didst have for thy brothers, 5
Evil and sore, when thy sons didst slay;
Else yet might we all on Jormunrek
Together our sister's slaying avenge."

"[...] 6
The gear of the Hunnish kings now give us!
Thou hast whetted us so to the battle of swords."

Laughing did Guthrun go to her chamber, 7
The helms of the kings from the cupboards she took,
And mail-coats broad, to her sons she bore them;
On their horses' backs the heroes leaped.

Then Hamther spake, the high of heart: 8
"Homeward no more his mother to see
Comes the spear-god, fallen mid Gothic folk;
One death-draught thou for us all shalt drink,
For Svanhild then and thy sons as well."

Weeping Guthrun, Gjuki's daughter, 9
Went sadly before the gate to sit,
And with tear-stained cheeks to tell the tale
Of her mighty griefs, so many in kind.

"Three home-fires knew I, three hearths I knew, 10
Home was I brought by husbands three;
But Sigurth only of all was dear,
He whom my brothers brought to his death."

"A greater sorrow I saw not nor knew, 11
Yet more it seemed I must suffer yet
When the princes great to Atli gave me."

Húna hvassa   hét ek mér at rúnum;   12
máttig-a-k bölva   betr of vinna,
áðr ek hnóf höfuð   af Hniflungum.

Gekk ek til strandar,   gröm vark nornum,   13
vilda ek hrinda   stríð grið þeira;
hófu mik, né drekkðu,   hávar bárur,
því ek land of sték,   at lifa skyldak.

Gekk ek á beð,   hugðak mér fyr betra,   14
þriðja sinni   þjóðkonungi;
ól ek mér jóð,   erfivörðu,
erfivörðu,   Jónakrs sonum.

En um Svanhildi   sátu þýjar,   15
er ek minna   barna bazt fullhugðak;
svá var Svanhildr   í sal mínum
sem væri sæmleitr   sólar geisli.

Gædda ek gulli   ok guðvefjum,   16
áðr ek gæfak   Goðþjóðar til;
þat er mér harðast   harma minna
of þann inn hvíta   hadd Svanhildar,
auri tröddu   und jóa fótum.

En sá sárastr,   er þeir Sigurð minn,   17
sigri ræntan,   í sæing vágu,
en sá grimmastr,   er þeir Gunnari
fránir ormar   til fjörs skriðu,
en sá hvassastr,   er til hjarta
konung óblauðan   kvikvan skáru.

Fjölð man ek bölva,   18
[...]
Beittu, Siguðr,   inn blakka mar,
hest inn hraðfæra   láttu hinig renna;
sitr eigi hér   snör né dóttir,
sú er Guðrúnu   gæfi hnossir.

Minnsktu, Sigurðr,   hvat vit mæltum,   19
þá er vit á beð   bæði sátum,
at þú myndir mín,   móðugr, vitja,
halr, ór helju,   en ek þín ór heimi.

"The brave boys I summoned to secret speech; 12
For my woes requital I might not win
Till off the heads of the Hniflungs I hewed."

"To the sea I went, my heart full sore 13
For the Norns, whose wrath I would now escape;
But the lofty billows bore me undrowned,
Till to land I came, so I longer must live."

"Then to the bed—of old was it better!— 14
Of a king of the folk a third time I came;
Boys I bore his heirs to be,
Heirs so young, the sons of Jonak."

"But round Svanhild handmaidens sat, 15
She was dearest ever of all my children;
So did Svanhild seem in my hall
As the ray of the sun is fair to see."

"Gold I gave her and garments bright, 16
Ere I let her go to the Gothic folk;
Of my heavy woes the hardest it was
When Svanhild's tresses fair were trodden
In the mire by hoofs of horses wild."

"The sorest it was when Sigurth mine 17
On his couch, of victory robbed, they killed;
And grimmest of all when to Gunnar's heart
There crept the bright-hued crawling snakes.
And keenest of all when they cut the heart
From the living breast of the king so brave;"

"Many woes I remember, [...] 18
[...]
Bridle, Sigurth, thy steed so black,
Hither let run thy swift-faring horse;
Here there sits not son or daughter
Who yet to Guthrun gifts shall give."

"Remember, Sigurth, what once we said, 19
When together both on the bed we sat,
That mightily thou to me wouldst come
From hell and I from earth to thee."

Hlaðið ér, jarlar, eikiköstinn, 20
látið þann und hilmi hæstan verða;
megi brenna brjóst bölvafullt eldr,
þrungit um hjarta þiðni sorgir."

Jörlum öllum óðal batni, 21
snótum öllum sorg at minni,
at þetta tregróf of talit væri.

"Pile ye up, jarls, the pyre of oak, 20
Make it the highest a hero e'er had;
Let the fire burn my grief-filled breast,
My sore-pressed heart, till my sorrows melt."

May nobles all less sorrow know, 21
And less the woes of women become,
Since the tale of this lament is told.

ENDNOTES

Prose. In the manuscript the prose is headed "Of Guthrun," the title "Guthrunarhvot" preceding stanza 1. The prose introduction is used both by Snorri (*Skaldskaparmal*, chapter 42) and in the *Volsungasaga*. It would be interesting to know on what the annotator based this note, for neither Bikki nor Randver is mentioned by name in either the *Guthrunarhvot* or the *Hamthesmol*. On the prose notes in general, cf. *Reginsmol*, introductory note [Appendix B]. *Guthrun*: on the slaying of Atli by his wife, Guthrun, Sigurth's widow, cf. *Atlamol*, 83–86 and notes. *Jonak*: a Northern addition to the legend, introduced to account for Svanhild's half-brothers; the name is apparently of Slavic origin. *Sorli, Erp,* and *Hamther*: Sorli and Hamther are the Sarus and Ammius of the Jordanes story (cf. introductory note [Appendix B]). The *Volsungasaga* follows this note in making Erp likewise a son of Guthrun, but in the *Hamthesmol* he is a son of Jonak by another wife. *Svanhild*: cf. *Sigurtharkvitha en skamma*, 54 and note. *Jormunrek* (Ermanarich): cf. introductory note [Appendix B]. *Bikki*: the Sifka or Sibicho of the Gothic legends of Ermanarich, whose evil counsel always brings trouble. *Randver*: in the *Volsungasaga* Jormunrek sends his son Randver with Bikki to seek Svanhild's hand. On the voyage home Bikki says to Randver: "It were right for you to have so fair a wife, and not such an old man." Randver was much pleased with this advice, "and he spake to her with gladness, and she to him." Thus the story becomes near of kin to those of Tristan and Iseult and Paolo and Francesca. According to the *Volsungasaga*, Bikki told Ermanarich that a guilty love existed between his son and his young wife, and presumably the annotator here meant as much by his vague "this."

1. The poet's introduction of himself in this stanza is a fairly certain indication of the relative lateness of the poem.

2. *Idle*: a guess; a word is obviously missing in the original. The manuscript marks line 5 as beginning a new stanza, and lines 5–6 may well have been inserted from another part of the "old" *Hamthesmol* (cf. *Hamthesmol*, 3).

3. *Gunnar* and *Hogni*: cf. *Drap Niflunga*. Line 5 may be interpolated. *Hunnish*: here used, as often, merely as a generic term for all South Germanic peoples; the reference is to the Burgundian Gunnar and Hogni.

4. *Hamther*: some editions spell the name "Hamthir." *Sigurth*, etc.: cf. *Sigurtharkvitha en skamma*, 21–24, and *Brot*, concluding prose. This stanza has been subjected to many conjectural re-arrangements, some editors adding two or three lines from the *Hamthesmol*.

5. *Bloody*: a guess; a word in the original is clearly missing, and the same is true of *all* in line 3. *Thy sons*: i.e., by killing her sons Erp and Eitil (cf. *Atlamol*, 72–74) Guthrun deprived Hamther, Sorli, and the second Erp of valuable allies in avenging Svanhild's death.

6. The manuscript indicates no gap, but most editors assume the loss of one, two or even more lines before the two here given.

7. The manuscript indicates line 4 as beginning a new stanza.

8. Line 1, identical with line 1 of stanza 4, may be interpolated here. *Spear-god*: warrior, i.e., Hamther himself. With this stanza the introductory *hvot* ("inciting") ends, and stanza 9 introduces the lament which forms the real body of the poem.

11. Line 1 in the original is of uncertain meaning. Many editors assume the loss of a line after line 1, and some completely reconstruct line 1 on the basis of a hypothetical second line. *Princes*: Gunnar and Hogni.

12. Some editors assume the loss of one line, or more, before line 1. *Hniflungs*: Erp and Eitil, the sons of Guthrun and Atli. On the application of the name Niflung (or, as later spelt, Hniflung) to the descendants of Gjuki, Guthrun's father, cf. *Brot*, 17, note.

13. *Norns*: the fates; cf. *Voluspo*, 8 and note.

14. The manuscript omits the first half of line 4.

16. Some editors assume a gap of two lines after line 2, and make a separate stanza of lines 3–5; Gering adds a sixth line of his own coining, while Grundtvig inserts one between lines 3 and 4. The manuscript indicates line 5 as beginning a new stanza.

17. The manuscript does not indicate line 1 as beginning a stanza (cf. note on stanza 16). Stanzas 17 and 18 are very likely later interpolations, although the compilers of the *Volsungasaga* knew them as they stand here. The whole passage depends on the shades of difference in the meanings of the various superlatives: *harþastr*, "hardest"; *sárastr*, "sorest"; *grimmastr*, "grimmest," and *hvassastr*, "keenest." *Snakes*: cf. *Drap Niflunga*. *The king*: Hogni; cf. *Atlakvitha*, 25.[1]

18. The manuscript marks line 3 as beginning a new stanza. Most editors agree that there is a more or less extensive gap after stanza 19, and some of them contend that the original ending of the poem is lost, stanzas 19–21 coming from a different poem, probably a lament closely following Sigurth's death. The manuscript does not indicate line 1 as beginning a stanza, and it immediately follows the fragmentary line 3 of stanza 18. The resemblance between stanzas 18–21 and stanzas 64–69 of *Sigurtharkvitha en skamma* suggests that, in some other wise lost version of the story, Guthrun, like Brynhild, sought to die soon after Sigurth's death. *Thy steed*: Guthrun's appeal to the dead Sigurth to ride back to earth to meet her is reminiscent of the episode related in *Helgakvitha Hundingsbana II*, 39–48 The promise mentioned in stanza 20 is spoken of elsewhere only in the *Volsungasaga* paraphrase of this passage.

20. Perhaps something has been lost between stanzas 20 and 21, or possibly stanza 21, while belonging originally to the same poem as stanzas 19 and 20, did not directly follow them. *Sore-pressed*: a guess; a word seems to have been omitted in the original.

21. Words of the poet's, like stanza 1, and perhaps constituting a later addition. Many editors assume the loss of a line after line 3. The meaning, of course, is that the poet hopes the story of Guthrun's woes will make all other troubles seem light by comparison.

---

[1] Stanzas 17, 18 and 19 have been restructured to conform with the Old Norse, resulting in re-numbering from stanzas 17–21.

HAMTHESMOL
THE BALLAD OF HAMTHER

INTRODUCTION

The *Hamthesmol*, or the *Ballad of Hamther*, is the final poem of the heroic lays and is traditionally accounted as the end of the *Poetic Edda* itself. It is the final poem in the *Codex Regius*, where it is found in remarkably bad shape—it appears to have never originally been a single coherent poem at all if we take the position of the older scholars such as Bellows as gospel on the matter.

The history of the argument regarding the *Hamthesmol* is really the history of the argument of the metrical forms outlined originally by Sievers, which account for strict rules of syllable counting and metrical schemes for all Norse prosody. On this view we would struggle to make sense at all of the *Hamthesmol's* metrical formulae, for as Bellows writes: "Some of the stanzas are in Fornyrthislag, some are in Malahattr, one (stanza 29) appears to be in Ljothahattr, and in many cases the words can be adapted to any known metrical form only by liberal emendation." However as early as 1893 Sievers himself notes the possible existence of a "free verse Malahattr" to explain the discrepancies of formulaic poetry which present themselves. The prevailing view of the modern academic community is that the strict adherence to the verse forms described by Sievers is a late skaldic construction, with only haphazard adherence found in the older works, and sometimes almost none at all in the oldest works of Germanic legend and myth.

In 1939, some ten years after the original publication of Bellows' translation of the *Poetic Edda*, Caroline Brady argues in her work "*The Date and Metre of the 'Hamðismál'*" that the discrepancies found among the contemporary scholarly tradition arose from an overreliance upon self-constructed and biased interpretations of what a given verse form should be like, rather than an academic analysis of what they actually are in firsthand sources. She notes also that many of these scholars cannot even agree among themselves as to the prosody of various passages, writing:

> Precisely the same strophes which Bugge regards as revised remnants of the original poem (12–17, 31) Jonsson and Siemons condemn as late interpolations; Three of the four strophes which Mogk regards as composed in pure fornyrðislag (3, 6, 7) Jonsson and Siemons regard as Málaháttr.

The modern academic consensus generally agrees that, just as the *Codex Regius* states, the *Hamthesmol* is in fact a very old poem whose metrical schema simply does not easily align with what was expected by late Scandinavian skaldic society, but which is a whole and complete, and generally regarded as quite powerful and evocative work.

The Three Norns
(Arthur Rackham)

Spruttu á tái   tregnar íðir,   1
græti alfa   in glýstömu;
ár of morgin   manna bölva
sútir hverjar   sorg of kveykva.

Var-a þat nú   né í gær,   2
þat hefir langt liðit síðan,
er fátt fornara, fremr var þat halfu,
er hvatti Guðrún Gjúka borin,
sonu sína unga   at hefna Svanhildar:

"Systir var ykkur   Svanhildr of heitin,   3
sú er Jörmunrekkr   jóm of traddi,
hvítum ok svörtum   á hervegi,
grám, gangtömum   Gotna hrossum.

Eftir er ykkr þrungit   þjóðkonunga;   4
lifið einir ér   þátta ættar minnar.

Einstæð em ek orðin,   sem ösp í holti,   5
fallin at frændum   sem fura at kvisti,
vaðin at vilja,   sem viðr at laufi,
þá er in kvistskæða kemr um dag varman."

HAMTHESMOL

Great the evils once that grew, 1
With the dawning sad of the sorrow of elves;
In early morn awake for men
The evils that grief to each shall bring.

Not now, nor yet of yesterday was it, 2
Long the time that since hath lapsed,
So that little there is that is half as old,
Since Guthrun, daughter of Gjuki, whetted
Her sons so young to Svanhild's vengeance.

"The sister ye had was Svanhild called, 3
And her did Jormunrek trample with horses,
White and black on the battle-way,
Gray, road-wonted, the steeds of the Goths."

"Little the kings of the folk are ye like, 4
For now ye are living alone of my race."

"Lonely am I as the forest aspen, 5
Of kindred bare as the fir of its boughs,
My joys are all lost as the leaves of the tree
When the scather of twigs from the warm day turns."

Hitt kvað þá Hamðir   inn hugumstóri: 6
"Lítt myndir þú þá, Guðrún,
leyfa dáð Högna,   er þeir Sigurð vökðu
svefni ór,   saztu á beð,
en banar hlógu.

Bækr váru þínar   inar bláhvítu   7
ofnar völundum,   flutu í vers dreyra;
svalt þá Sigurðr,   saztu yfir dauðum,
glýja þú né gáðir,   Gunnarr þér svá vildi.

Atla þóttisk þú stríða   at Erps morði   8
ok at Eitils aldrlagi,   þat var þér enn verra;
svá skyldi hverr öðrum   verja til aldrlaga
sverði sárbeitu,   at sér né stríddi-t."

Hitt kvað þá Sörli,   9
svinna hafði hann hyggju:
"Vilk-at ek við móður   málum skipta;
orðs þykkir enn vant   ykkru hváru.
Hvers biðr þú nú, Guðrún,
er þú at gráti né fær-at?

Bræðr grát þú þína   ok buri svása,   10
niðja náborna   leidda nær rógi;
okkr skaltu ok, Guðrún,   gráta báða,
er hér sitjum feigir á mörum,
fjarri munum deyja."

Gengu ór garði   görvir at eiskra,   11
liðu þá yfir ungir   úrig fjöll
mörum húnlenzkum   morðs at hefna.

Fundu á stræti   stórbrögðóttan: 12
"Hvé mun jarpskammr   okkr fulltingja?"

Svaraði inn sundrmæðri,   svá kvaðsk veita mundu   13
fullting frændum,   sem fótr öðrum.
"Hvat megi fótr   fæti veita
né holdgróin   hönd annarri?"

Þá kvað þat Erpr   einu sinni,   14
mærr of lék   á mars baki:
"Illt er blauðum hal   brautir kenna."
Kóðu harðan mjök   hornung vera.

Then Hamther spake forth, the high of heart: 6
"Small praise didst thou, Guthrun, to Hogni's deed give
When they wakened thy Sigurth from out of his sleep,
Thou didst sit on the bed while his slayers laughed."

"Thy bed-covers white with blood were red 7
From his wounds, and with gore of thy husband were wet;
So Sigurth was slain, by his corpse didst thou sit,
And of gladness didst think not: 'twas Gunnar's doing."

"Thou wouldst strike at Atli by the slaying of Erp 8
And the killing of Eitil; thine own grief was worse;
So should each one wield the wound-biting sword
That another it slays but smites not himself."

Then did Sorli speak out, for wise was he ever: 9
"With my mother I never a quarrel will make;
Full little in speaking methinks ye both lack;
What askest thou, Guthrun, that will give thee no tears?"

"For thy brothers dost weep, and thy boys so sweet, 10
Thy kinsmen in birth on the battlefield slain;
Now, Guthrun, as well for us both shalt thou weep,
We sit doomed on our steeds, and far hence shall we die."

Then the fame-glad one—on the steps she was— 11
The slender-fingered, spake with her son:
"Ye shall danger have if counsel ye heed not;
[...]
By two heroes alone shall two hundred of Goths
Be bound or be slain in the lofty-walled burg."

From the courtyard they fared, and fury they breathed; 12
The youths swiftly went o'er the mountain wet,
On their Hunnish steeds, death's vengeance to have.

On the way they found the man so wise; 13
[...]
"What help from the weakling brown may we have?"

So answered them their half-brother then: 14
"So well may I my kinsmen aid
As help one foot from the other has."

Drógu þeir ór skíði   skíðiéarn,   15
mækis eggjar,   at mun flagði;
þverrðu þeir þrótt sinn   at þriðjungi,
létu mög ungan   til moldar hníga.

Skóku loða,   skalmir festu,   16
ok góðbornir   smugu í guðvefi.

Fram lágu brautir,   fundu vástigu   17
ok systurson   sáran á meiði,
vargtré vindköld   vestan bæjar,
trýtti æ trönu hvöt,   titt var-at bíða.

Glamr var í höllu,   halir ölreifir,   18
ok til gota ekki   gerðu at heyra,
áðr halr hugfullr   í horn of þaut.

Segja fóru ærir   Jörmunrekki,   19
at sénir váru   seggir und hjalmum:
"Ræðið ér um ráð,   ríkir eru komnir,
fyr máttkum hafið ér mönnum   mey of tradda."

Hló þá Jörmunrekkr,   hendi drap á kampa,   20
beiddisk-at bröngu,   böðvaðisk at víni;
skók hann skör jarpa,   sá á skjöld hvítan,
lét hann sér í hendi   hvarfa ker gullit.

"Sæll ek þá þóttumk,   ef ek sjá knætta   21
Hamði ok Sörla   í höllu minni,
buri mynda ek þá binda   með boga strengjum,
góð börn Gjúka   festa á galga."

Hitt kvað þá Hróðrglöð,   stóð of hleðum,   22
mæfingr mælti   við mög þenna:
[...]
"Því at þat heita,   at hlýðigi myni;
megu tveir menn einir   tíu hundruð Gotna
binda eða berja   í borg inni háu."

Styrr varð í ranni,   stukku ölskálir,   23
í blóði bragnar lágu,   komit ór brjósti Gotna.

Hitt kvað þá Hamðir   inn hugumstóri: 24
"Æstir, Jörmunrekkr,   okkarrar kvámu
bræðra sammæðra   innan borgar þinnar;
fætr sér þína,   höndum sér þú þínum,
Jörmunrekkr, orpit   í eld heitan."

"How may afoot its fellow aid, 15
Or a flesh-grown hand another help?"

Then Erp spake forth, his words were few, 16
As haughty he sat on his horse's back:
"To the timid 'tis ill the way to tell."
A bastard they the bold one called.

From their sheaths they drew their shining swords, 17
Their blades, to the giantess joy to give;
By a third they lessened the might that was theirs,
The fighter young to earth they felled.

Their cloaks they shook, their swords they sheathed, 18
The high-born men wrapped their mantles close.

On their road they fared and an ill way found, 19
And their sister's son on a tree they saw,
On the wind-cold wolf-tree west of the hall,
And cranes'-bait crawled; none would care to linger.

In the hall was din, the men drank deep, 20
And the horses' hoofs could no one hear,
Till the warrior hardy sounded his horn.

Men came and the tale to Jormunrek told 21
How warriors helmed without they beheld:
"Take counsel wise, for brave ones are come,
Of mighty men thou the sister didst murder."

Then Jormunrek laughed, his hand laid on his beard, 22
His arms, for with wine he was warlike, he called for;
He shook his brown locks, on his white shield he looked,
And raised high the cup of gold in his hand.

"Happy, methinks, were I to behold 23
Hamther and Sorli here in my hall;
The men would I bind with strings of bows,
And Gjuki's heirs on the gallows hang."

In the hall was clamor, the cups were shattered, 24
Men stood in blood from the breasts of the Goths.

Þá hraut við   inn reginkunngi   25
baldr í hrynju,   sem björn hryti:
"Grýtið ér á gumna,   alls geirar né bíta,
eggjar né éarn   Jónakrs sonu."

Hitt kvað þá Hamðir   inn hugumstóri: 26
"Böl vanntu, bróðir,   er þú þann belg leystir;
oft ór þeim belg   böll ráð koma."

Sörli Kvað: 27
"Hug hefðir þú, Hamðir,   ef þú hefðir hyggjandi;
mikils er á mann hvern vant,   er mannvits er!"

Hamðir kvað: 28
"Af væri nú höfuð,   ef Erpr lifði,
bróðir okkarr inn böðfrækni,
er vit á braut vágum,   verr inn vígfrækni,
—hvöttumk at dísir—
gumi inn gunnhelgi,   gerðumk at vígi."

Sörli kvað: 29
"Ekki hygg ek okkr   vera ulfa dæmi,
at vit mynim sjalfir   of sakask
sem grey norna,   þá er gráðug eru
í auðn of alin.

Vel höfum vit vegit,   stöndum á val Gotna,   30
ofan eggmóðum,   sem ernir á kvisti;
góðs höfum tírar fengit,
þótt skylim nú eða í gær deyja;
kveld lifir maðr ekki   eftir kvið norna."

Þar fell Sörli   at salar gafli,   31
enn Hamðir hné   at húsbaki.

Þetta eru kölluð Hamðissmál in fornu.

Then did Hamther speak forth, the haughty of heart: 25
"Thou soughtest, Jormunrek, us to see,
Sons of one mother seeking thy dwelling;
Thou seest thy hands, thy feet thou beholdest,
Jormunrek, flung in the fire so hot."

Then roared the king, of the race of the gods,   26
Bold in his armor, as roars a bear:
"Stone ye the men that steel will bite not,
Sword nor spear, the sons of Jonak."

Sorli spake: 27
"Ill didst win, brother, when the bag thou didst open,
Oft from that bag came baleful counsel;
Heart hast thou, Hamther, if knowledge thou hadst!
A man without wisdom is lacking in much."

Hamther spake: 28
"His head were now off if Erp were living,
The brother so keen whom we killed on our road,
The warrior noble—'twas the Norns that drove me
The hero to slay who in fight should be holy."

"In fashion of wolves it befits us not   29
Amongst ourselves to strive,
Like the hounds of the Norns, that nourished were
In greed mid wastes so grim."

"We have greatly fought, o'er the Goths do we stand   30
By our blades laid low, like eagles on branches;
Great our fame though we die today or tomorrow;
None outlives the night when the Norns have spoken."

Then Sorli beside the gable sank,   31
And Hamther fell at the back of the house.

This is called the old ballad of Hamther.

ENDNOTES

1. This stanza looks like a later interpolation from a totally unrelated source. *Sorrow of elves*: the sun; cf. *Alvissmol*, 16 and note.

2. Some editors regard lines 1-2 as interpolated, while others question line 3. *Guthrun*, etc.: regarding the marriage of Jonak and Guthrun (daughter of Gjuki, sister of Gunnar and Hogni, and widow first of Sigurth and then of Atli), and the sons of this marriage, Hamther and Sorli (but not Erp), cf. *Guthrunarhvot*, introductory prose and note.

3. *Svanhild* and *Jormunrek*: regarding the manner in which Jormunrek (Ermanarich) married Svanhild, daughter of Sigurth and Guthrun, and afterwards had her trodden to death by horses, cf. *Guthrunarhvot*, introductory note [Appendix B]. Lines 3-4 are identical with lines 5-6 of *Guthrunarhvot*, 2.

4. These two lines may be all that is left of a four-line stanza. The manuscript and many editions combine them with stanza 5, while a few place them after stanza 5 as a separate stanza, reversing the order of the two lines. *Kings of the folk*: Guthrun's brothers, Gunnar and Hogni, slain by Atli.

5. Cf. note on stanza 4; the manuscript does not indicate line 1 as beginning a stanza. *Scather of twigs*: poetic circumlocution for the wind (cf. *Skaldskaparmal*, chapter 27), though some editors think the phrase here means the sun. Some editors assume a more or less extensive gap between stanzas 5 and 6.

6. Lines 1-3 are nearly identical with lines 1-3 of *Guthrunarhvot*, 4. On the death of *Sigurth* cf. *Sigurtharkvitha en skamma*, 21-24, and *Brot*,

concluding prose. The word *thy* in line 3 is omitted in the original.

7. Lines 1-2 are nearly identical with lines 4-5 of *Guthrunarhvot*, 4. The manuscript, followed by many editions, indicates line 3 and not line 1 as beginning a stanza.

8. Some editors regard this stanza as interpolated. *Erp* and *Eitil*: regarding Guthrun's slaying of her sons by Atli, cf. *Atlamol*, 72-75. The Erp here referred to is not to be confused with the Erp, son of Jonak, who appears in stanza 13. The whole of stanza 8 is in doubtful shape, and many emendations have been suggested.

10. Some editors assign this speech to Hamther. *Brothers*: Gunnar and Hogni. *Boys*: Erp and Eitil.

11. In the manuscript this stanza follows stanza 21, and some editors take the word here rendered "fame-glad one" (hróþrgoþ) to be a proper name (Jormunrek's mother or his concubine). The *Volsungasaga*, however, indicates that Guthrun at this point "had so fashioned their war-gear that iron would not bite into it, and she bade them to have nought to do with stones or other heavy things, and told them that it would be ill for them if they did not do as she said." The substance of this counsel may well have been conveyed in a passage lost after line 3, though the manuscript indicates no gap. It is by being stoned that Hamther and Sorli are killed (stanza 26). On the other hand, the second part of line 3 may possibly mean "if silent ye are not," in which case the advice relates to Hamther's speech to Jormunrek and Sorli's reproach to him thereupon (stanzas 25 and 27). *Steps*: the word in the original is doubtful. Line 3 is thoroughly obscure. Some editors make a separate stanza of lines 3-5, while others question line 5.

12. Many editors assume the loss of a line after line 1. In several editions lines 2-3 are placed after line 2 of stanza 18. *Hunnish*: the word meant little more than "German"; cf. *Guthrunarhvot*, 3 and note.

13. In the manuscript these two lines follow stanza 16; some editors insert them in place of lines 2-3 of stanza 11. The manuscript indicates no gap. *The man so wise*: Erp, here represented as a son of Jonak but not of Guthrun, and hence a half-brother of Hamther and Sorli. There is nothing further to indicate whether or not he was born out of wedlock, as intimated in stanza 16. Some editors assign line 3 to Hamther, and some to Sorli.

14. The stanza is obviously defective. Many editors add Erp's name in line 1, and insert between lines 2 and 1 a line based on stanza 15 and the *Volsungasaga* paraphrase: "As a flesh grown hand | another helps." In

the *Volsungasaga*, after Erp's death, Hamther stumbles and saves himself from falling with his hand, whereupon he says: "Erp spake truly; I had fallen had I not braced myself with my hand." Soon thereafter Sorli has a like experience, one foot slipping but the other saving him from a fall. "Then they said that they had done ill to Erp, their brother."

15. Many editions attach these two lines to stanza 14, while a few assume the loss of two lines.

16. In the manuscript this stanza stands between stanzas 12 and 13. Some editors make line 4 a part of Erp's speech.

17. The manuscript does not indicate line 1 as beginning a stanza. *The giantess*: presumably the reference is to Hel, goddess of the dead, but the phrase is doubtful.

18. In the manuscript these two lines are followed by stanza 19 with no indication of a break. Some editions insert here lines 2–3 of stanza 12, while others assume the loss of two or more lines.

19. Cf. note on stanza 18. *Ill way*: very likely the road leading through the gate of Jormunrek's town at which Svanhild was trampled to death. *Sister's son*: many editors change the text to read "stepson," for the reference is certainly to Randver, son of Jormunrek, hanged by his father on Bikki's advice (cf. *Guthrunarhvot*, introductory note [Appendix B]). *Wolf-tree*: the gallows, the wolf being symbolical of outlaws. *Cranes'-bait*: presumably either snakes or worms, but the passage is doubtful.

20. Many editors assume the loss of a line after line 3. *The warrior*: presumably a warder or watchman, but the reference may be to Hamther himself.

21. The word here rendered *men* (line 1) is missing in the original, involving a metrical error, and various words have been suggested.

22. Line 2 in the original is thoroughly obscure; some editors directly reverse the meaning here indicated by giving the line a negative force, while others completely alter the phrase rendered "his arms he called for" into one meaning "he stroked his cheeks."

23. *Gjuki's heirs*: the original has "the well-born of Gjuki," and some editors have changed the proper name to Guthrun, but the phrase apparently refers to Hamther and Sorli as Gjuki's grandsons. In the manuscript this stanza is followed by stanza 11, and such editors as have retained this arrangement have had to resort to varied and complex explanations

to account for it.

24. Editors have made various efforts to reconstruct a four-line stanza out of these two lines, in some cases with the help of lines borrowed from the puzzling stanza 11 (cf. note on stanza 23). Line 2 in the original is doubtful.

25. Some editors mark line 1 as an interpolation. The manuscript marks line 4 as beginning a new stanza. As in the story told by Jordanes, Hamther and Sorli succeed in wounding Jormunrek (here they cut off his hands and feet), but do not kill him.

26. The manuscript marks line 3, and not line 1, as beginning a stanza. *Of the race of the gods*: the reference here is apparently to Jormunrek, but in the *Volsungasaga* the advice to kill Hamther and Sorli with stones, since iron will not wound them (cf. note on stanza 11), comes from Odin, who enters the hall as an old man with one eye.

27. in the manuscript this stanza is introduced by the same line as stanza 25: "Then did Hamther speak forth, the haughty of heart," but the speaker in this case must be Sorli and not Hamther. Some editors, however, give lines 1–2 to Hamther and lines 3–4 to Sorli. *Bag*: i.e., Hamther's mouth; cf. note on stanza 11. The manuscript indicates line 3 as beginning a new stanza.

28. Most editors regard stanzas 28–30 as a speech by Hamther, but the manuscript does not indicate the speaker, and some editors assign one or two of the stanzas to Sorli. Lines 1–2 are quoted in the *Volsungasaga*. The manuscript does not indicate line 1 as beginning a stanza. *Erp*: Hamther means that while the two brothers had succeeded only in wounding Jormunrek, Erp, if he had been with them, would have killed him. Lines 3–4 may be a later interpolation. *Norns*: the fates; the word used in the original means the goddesses of ill fortune."

29. This is almost certainly an interpolated Ljothahattr stanza, though some editors have tried to expand it into the Fornyrthislag form. *Hounds of the Norns*: wolves.

30, Some editors assume a gap after this stanza.

31. Apparently a fragment of a stanza from the "old" *Hamthesmol* to which the annotator's concluding prose note refers. Some editors assume the loss of two lines after line 2.

Prose. Regarding the "old" *Hamthesmol*, cf. *Guthrunarhvot*, introductory note [Appendix B].

The Ride of the Valkyrs
(J. C. Dollman)

GENEALOGIES

Aegir — Sea giant

Aurboda — Giant sorceress

Baldr — God of light and beauty

Bestla — Giantess

Bolthorn — Giant

Bor — First God to be born

Bragi — God of song and poetry

Buri — Born from a block of ice

Dagr — God of the day

Dellingr — God, possibly "the shining one"

Farbauti — Giant

Fenris wolf — Slayer of Odin

Forseti — God of justice and law

Freya — Goddess of the sun, war, and magic, Freyr's twin

Gerd — Giantess

Gridr — Giantess

Gymir — Giant

Heimdall — God of protection and watcher of Bifrost

Hel — Ruler of the underworld

Hodr — Blind God

Jarl caste — Caste of nobles

Jarl — Scion of Heimdall

Jarnsaxa — A daughter of the waves

Jord/Nerthus — Goddess of the earth

Jormungandr — The Midgard serpent

Karl caste — Caste of freemen

Karl — Scion of Heimdall

Kon the Kingly — Son of Jarl

Laufey — Goddess

Loki — Giant

Magni — God

Many kings — Kingly lineages descended from Odin

Mothi — God

Nine Daughters — Daughters of the waves

Njord — God of the sea

Nott — Goddess of night

Odin — God of war, magic, and knowledge

Ran — Sea giantess

Sif — Goddess of fertility

Skadi — Goddess of mountains, winter, and archery

Thiazi — Giant

Thor — God of Thunder

Thrall caste — Caste of slaves

Thrall — Scion of Heimdall

Thrudr — God

Tyr — God of war and justice

Ullr — God of the hunt and archery

Unknown Aesir — Parents of Laufey

Unknown Vanir — Parents of Sif and Nanna

Vali — God and slayer of Fenris

Ve — Odin's brother

Vili — Odin's brother

Vithar — God of vengeance of dueling

Ymir — Primordial ice giant

Yngling kings — Kingly lineage descended from Yngvi-Freyr

Yngvi-Freyr — God of the sun, Freya's twin

GENEALOGIES

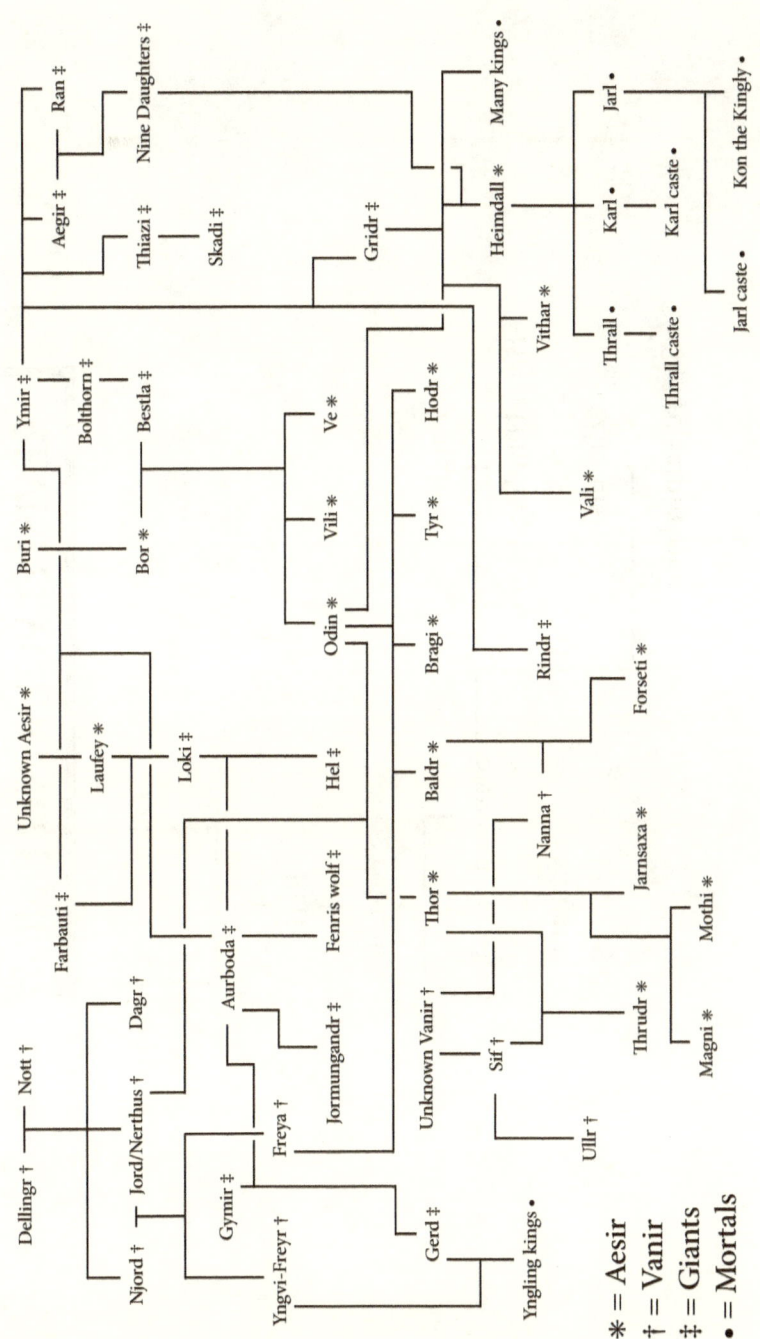

∗ = Aesir
† = Vanir
‡ = Giants
• = Mortals

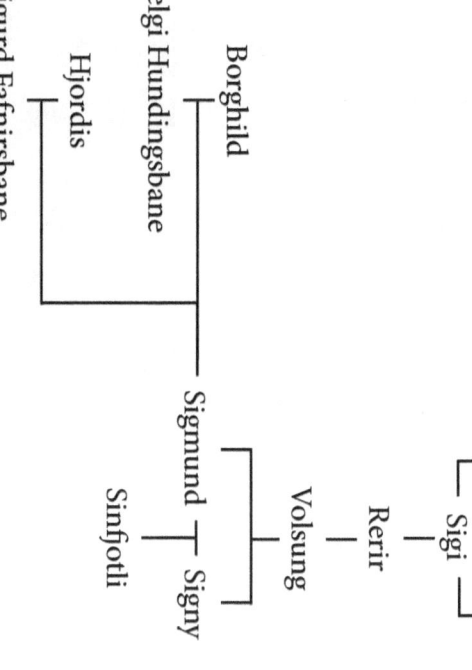

GENEALOGIES 827

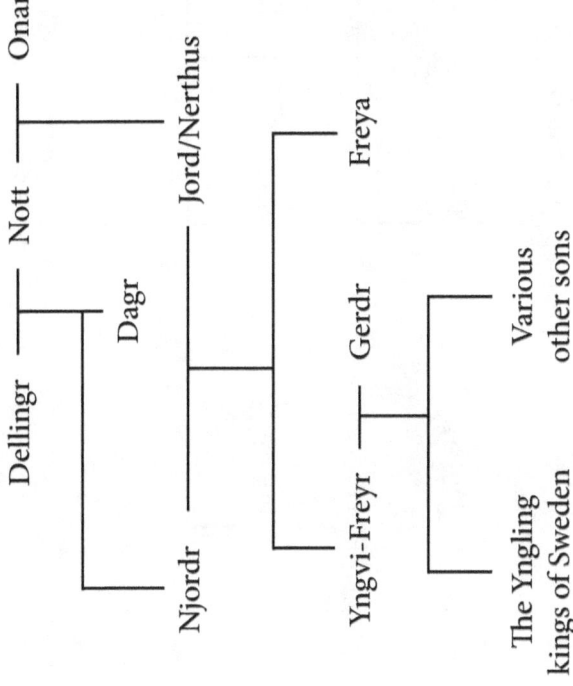

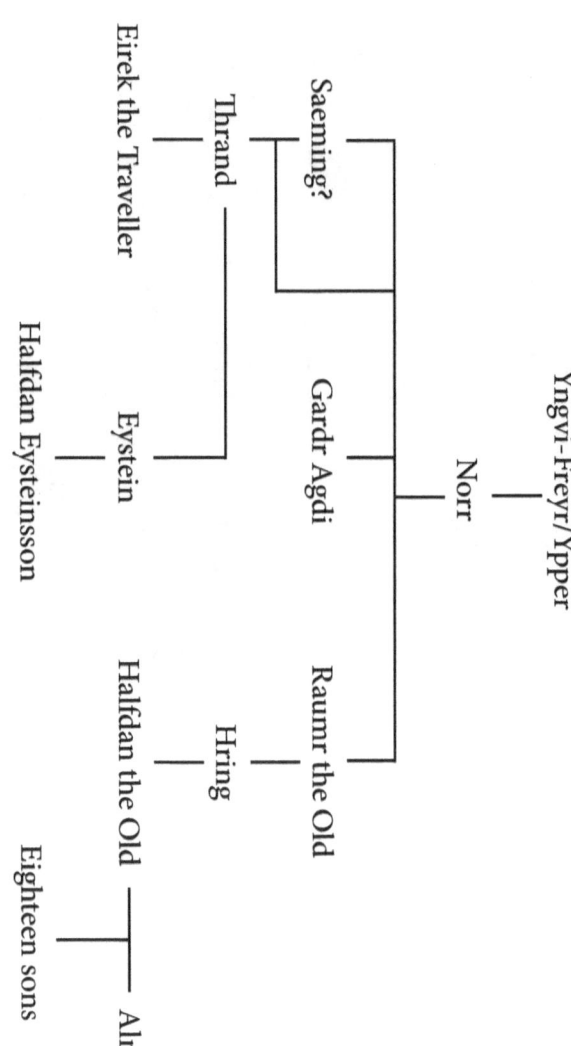

THE MANY SONS
OF YNGVI-FREYR

The first lay of Helgi Hundsingsbane is connected to the previous story of Helgi, son of Hjorvarth, and as such we shall not simply restate the various difficulties of this connected narrative. Suffice it to say that this poem in particular is accounted as being very late in origination based on the plethora of skaldic motifs and kennings and the extensive use of narrative poetry, which was not native to the Germanic epic tradition and can thus be used to safely date the poem to sometime after the year 1000. Although the author appears to have compiled it fairly late, the poem's story is probably far older; we have simply received a newly written version of a very old and popular tale.

There is substantial scholarly dispute concerning the poem's origins, intentions, and character, with one school of thought holding that it originated in Denmark, with Helgi thus being a member of the Royal house of the Ylfings, and another school holding that the characters and locations are centered in Sweden and descended variously from either the line of the Völsungs or the Ynglings, which is a matter of much broader scholarly dispute.

At the end of the poem, Helgi's beloved Valkyrie-wife Sigrun says to him:

> Hail to thee, hero! full happy with men,
> Offspring of Yngvi, shalt ever live,
> For thou the fearless foe hast slain
> Who to many the dread of death had brought.

This would seemingly and somewhat inaccurately depict Helgi as a scion of Yngvi (that is, the god Ingvi-Freyr) and a member of the Yngling royal lineage of Sweden. Such a lineage conflicts even with the general narrative of the poem itself that portrays Helgi as the son of Sigmund Völsungsson, whose dynastic lineage is straightforwardly obvious. To further confuse matters, this cannot be taken as a simple scribal error, nor as a carelessly interpolated passage from some other poem or story, because the *Hyndluljoth* features a similar error, if not precisely the same, in depicting the hero Ottar as the scion of both the Ylfings and Ynglings simultaneously. This is further supported by Snorri's account in *Skaldskaparmal* confirming the narrative of *Hyndluljoth* in prose form, where he recounts that King Halfdan the Old fathered eighteen sons, nine of whom gave rise to famous houses ranging from the Hildings to the Ylfings.

Snorri reckons Yngvi as a son of Halfdan and giving rise to the Ynglings but follows this by saying that a few other unconnected but equally prestigious houses exist, and he titles them confusingly as the Ynglings (again), the Skjöldungs (conflicting with *Hyndluljoth* which explicitly titles Halfdan as the foremost of the Skjöldungs), and the Völsungs, the house of Sigmund, Sigurth, and reportedly our hero Helgi Hundingsbane. Further complicating matters, and perhaps giving rise to some of this confusion, is the narrative of the *Völsungasaga* which records Sigurth's mother as remarrying Alf, a son of King Hjálprek of Denmark and thus ostensibly a Skjöldung.

While we might be tempted to chalk this up to a series of scribal errors across many different works, such a continuity of seeming errors of transmission can be attributed to what was originally a wholly connected narrative tradition—the Skjöldungs, Ylfings, and Völsungs (and perhaps others) originated as ancient cadet dynasties of the Yngling house. Evidence for this can be seen in the continual connection of the Völsung and Ylfing lineage with the House of Yngling, and similar connections can be seen within the narrative of the Skjöldung lineage across multiple distinct works, time periods, and authors. The Skjöldungs are recorded as the Royal house of Denmark descended ultimately from Odin through his son Skjöldr, who in Anglo-Saxon tradition is recorded in *Beowulf* as Scyld, son of Sceafa, a quasi-divine heroic king in his own right. We have a tradition parallel to that recorded by the *Yngling Saga* and the *Rigsthula* which maintains that Denmark is named after King Dan, whose daughter married Kon Ungr, the Son of Jarl Rigsson. This narrative is also supported by the *Lejre Chronicle*, a Danish work of history composed around 1170, and the sadly lost *Skjöldungasaga*, surviving only in the summary written by Arngrímur Jónsson, with the following said about this lineage:

THE MANY SONS OF YNGVI-FREYR

Dygvi's mother was Drótt, a daughter of King Danp, the son of Ríg, who was first called *konungr* in the Danish tongue. His descendants always afterwards considered the title of *konungr* the title of highest dignity. Dygvi was the first of his family to be called *konungr*, for his predecessors had been called *dróttinn*, and their wives *dróttning*, and their court *drótt*. Each of their race was called Yngvi, or Ynguni, and the whole race together Ynglingar. Queen Drótt was a sister of King Dan Mikilláti, from whom Denmark took its name.

Ynglinga Saga

Ríg (Rigus) was a man not the least among the great ones of his time. He married the daughter of a certain Danp [Old Norse Danpr], lord of Danpsted, whose name was Dana; and later, having won the royal title for his province, left as his heir his son by Dana, called Dan or Danum, all of whose subjects were called Danes.

Skjöldungasaga summary by Arngrímur Jónsson

The *Chronicle of Lejre* (Chronicon Lethrense) written about 1170 introduces a primeval King Ypper of Uppsala whose three sons were Dan, who afterwards ruled Denmark, Nori, who afterwards ruled Norway, and Østen, who afterwards ruled the Swedes. Dan apparently first ruled in Zealand, for the Chronicle states that it was when Dan had saved his people from an attack by the Emperor Augustus that the Jutes and the men of Fyn and Scania also accepted him as king, whence the resultant expanded country of Denmark was named after him. Dan's wife was named Dana and his son was named Ro.

Summary of the *Lejre Chronicle*

King Ypper of Uppsala, this primeval king, can be taken very clearly as a variant name of Yngvi-Freyr. This still leaves unexplained King Skjöldr/Scyld, the son of Sceafa, however we can piece together that these two narratives may not be as dissimilar as they seem. Scyld is presented to us in *Beowulf* as a foundling child who arrived on a boat (named *sig*, suggested by Anatoly Liberman to mean etymologically, "shining") set adrift in the ocean, with a sheaf of grain about his head. Upon landing on the shore he is taken in and raised by the people there who recognize him as special and who then choose him as their king. Various accounts of the basic tale run as follows:

> Scyld the Sheaf-Child from scourging foemen,
> From raiders a-many their mead-halls wrested.
> He lives to be feared, the first has a waif,
> Puny and frail he was found on the shore.
> He grew to be great, and was girt with power
> Till the border-tribes all obeyed his rule,

And sea-folk hardy that sit by the whale-path
Gave him tribute, a good king was he.

Beowulf

This Scef came in a light boat to an island of the ocean which is called Scani, arms around about him, and he was a very young boy, unknown to the dwellers in the land. But he was accepted by them and cared for like one of their own kind, and afterwards they chose him as king, from whose family descended King Æthelwulf.

Æthelweard, *Chronica*

Sceaf; who, as some affirm, was driven on a certain island in Germany, called Scandza, (of which Jornandes, the historian of the Goths, speaks), a little boy in a skiff, without any attendant, asleep, with a handful of corn at his head, whence he was called Sceaf; and, on account of his singular appearance, being well received by the men of that country.

William of Malmesbury, *Gesta Regum Anglorum*

The story of Scyld continues in *Beowulf*, depicting his funeral and the ritual method employed, sending off the foundling child who had ruled over them in the exact manner in which he had arrived: by bundling him into a small skiff with only a sheaf of corn about his head to carry him back across the waves:

They decked his body no less bountifully
With offerings than those first ones did
Who cast him away when he was a child
And launched him alone out over the waves.

Beowulf

This narrative of a special, quasi-divine heroic king bears a striking resemblance to a narrative recorded by the *Old English Rune Poem*, saying:

Ing was first amidst the East Danes
So seen, until he went eastward:
Over the sea. His wagon ran after.
Thus the Heardings named that hero.

This Ing can surely be none other than the Yngvi-Freyr of Norse myth, and taken together, the narrative all but demands an equivalence between him and Scyld. A child arrives from the sea (Freyr's father being Njord, God thereof) bundled only with a sheaf of corn (Freyr being a God intimately associated with prosperity and agriculture), whose boat likely bears a name meaning "Shining" (Freyr being God of the Sun) and who grows to become a great king.

The actual recorded kings of the House of Skjöldungs, or that of Denmark in general, also bear a marked tendency towards naming conventions honoring Freyr, their scions having names with clear variants of Yngvi, Freyr, or connected associations like Alf (Freyr being prince of the Alfar) or Dagr (meaning "Day", named after the God who is Freyr's paternal uncle). Some of these include: Fróði Mikilláti, Svipdagr (Lit: "Shining Day"), Frotho II–VI, Fridleif I–II, Ingellus, Yngwin and others. *Beowulf* also notably refers to King Hrothgar, and thus the Danes themselves, as "Lord of the Ingwines". It is commonly accepted that Ingwine is a derivation of a term used as early as the first century by Tacitus in his *Germania*, when he records the entirety of the North Sea coast (today's Denmark and the areas originally populated by the Angles and Saxons) as belonging to the tribal group of the "Ingaevones" or "The Friends of Ing".

If we take it as given that the original King Skjöldr of the Danish line must be either a byname of Freyr himself or the name of his son or a lineal descendent who came to rule Denmark, the confusions that these authors must have been trying to rectify in their narratives become quite clear. The House of Skjöldungs should rightfully be considered agnatic kin, if not outright a cadet branch, of the Yngling lineage, which accounts for all the various discrepancies. Due to the extreme historical tension between Danes and Swedes, the Danish line fabricated an alternative narrative that saw them as sons of Odin instead, in an attempt to differentiate and create a separate legitimizing narrative for their origin and rule.

To connect these matters with the Ylfings and Völsungs, we need only refer to the narrative of the *Hyndluljoth* and *Skaldskaparmal*, with the personage of Halfdan the Old said to have fathered many of these lineages himself. The Icelandic *Ættartolur* records Halfdan as the son of King Hring, son of Raum the Old, Son of Nórr for whom the nation of Norway is named. If we then cast our eye back to the aforementioned *Chronicle of Lejre*, we find Nórr as a son of "the primordial king Ypper of Uppsala" who can be none other than Yngvi-Freyr. Supporting this connection is the chronicle's traditional genealogy in which Nórr also sires Thránd who gives his name to Þrándheimr, the ancient name for the modern county of Trøndelag. Trøndelag was well known as home to a thriving cultic center devoted to Freyr and Njord, which makes sense if the area's kingly tradition could be traced back ultimately to this father and son pair. While the traditional account of the origins of the Völsung line, as depicted in the *Völsungasaga* itself, would feature Völsung as the son of Rerir, son of Sigi, son of Odin, in light of the information within the poems and the clear narrative structure connecting all of these families in the minds of our forefathers, we must consider an alternative hypothesis that sees the lineage originally reckoned from Yngvi-Freyr, with the lineage reckoned from Odin as a late incorporation, perhaps with political motivations to distance themselves from the Swedish throne and to establish a more amenable descent from Odin. Certainly the early origins of the Franks (the generally accepted origin for the kingly Völsungs) are accepted by modern historians as being found further north and east than what is today France, in the area of modern Frisia and Schleswig-Holstein. This area is well within the historical borders constituting the "Ingaevonic tribes" or the "Friends of Ing" documented by Tacitus. This origin also makes sense of the poetic stanza quoted at the beginning of this article by the Valkyrie Sigrun said to Helgi Hundingsbane, whom the poem explicitly denotes as both an Ylfing and the son of Sigmund Völsungsson.

> Hail to thee, hero! full happy with men,
> Offspring of Yngvi, shalt ever live,
> For thou the fearless foe hast slain
> Who to many the dread of death had brought.

It also makes sense of the *Reginsmol*, in which the eponymous dwarf Regin comes to the home of Sigurth Fafnirsbane to foster him, saying:

> Here shall I foster the fearless prince,
> Now Yngvi's heir to us is come;
> The noblest hero beneath the sun,
> The threads of his fate all lands enfold.

TRISTAN POWERS.

MAY 2022.

BELLOWS INTRODUCTIONS

VOLUSPO

At the beginning of the collection in the *Codex Regius* stands the *Voluspo*, the most famous and important, as it is likewise the most debated, of all the *Eddic* poems. Another version of it is found in a huge miscellaneous compilation of about the year 1300, the *Hauksbok*, and many stanzas are included in the *Prose Edda* of Snorri Sturluson. The order of the stanzas in the *Hauksbok* version differs materially from that in the *Codex Regius*, and in the published editions many experiments have been attempted in further rearrangements. On the whole, however, and allowing for certain interpolations, the order of the stanzas in the *Codex Regius* seems more logical than any of the wholesale "improvements" which have been undertaken.

The general plan of the *Voluspo* is fairly clear. Odin, chief of the gods, always conscious of impending disaster and eager for knowledge, calls on a certain "Volva," or wise-woman, presumably bidding her rise from the grave. She first tells him of the past, of the creation of the world, the beginning of years, the origin of the dwarfs (at this point there is a clearly interpolated catalogue of dwarfs' names, stanzas 10–16), of the first man and woman, of the world-ash Yggdrasil, and of the first war, between the gods and the Vanir, or, in Anglicized form, the Wanes. Then, in stanzas 27–29, as a further proof of her wisdom, she discloses some of Odin's own secrets and the details of his search for knowledge. Rewarded by Odin for what she has thus far told (stanza 30), she then turns to the real prophesy, the disclosure of the final destruction of the gods. This final battle, in which fire and flood overwhelm heaven and earth as the gods fight with their enemies, is the great fact in Norse mythology; the phrase describing it, ragna rök, "the fate of the gods," has become familiar, by confusion with the word rökkr, "twilight," in the German Götterdämmerung. The wise-woman tells of the Valkyries who bring the slain warriors to support Odin and the other gods in the battle, of the slaying of Baldr, best and fairest of the gods, through the wiles of Loki, of the enemies of the gods, of the summons to battle on both sides, and of the mighty struggle, till Odin is slain, and "fire leaps high about heaven itself" (stanzas 31–58). But this is not all. A new and beautiful world is to rise on the ruins of the old; Baldr comes back, and "fields unsowed bear ripened fruit" (stanzas 59–66).

This final passage, in particular, has caused wide differences of opinion as to the date and character of the poem. That the poet was heathen and not Christian seems almost beyond dispute; there is an intensity and vividness in almost every stanza which no archaizing Christian could possibly have achieved. On the other hand, the evidences of Christian influence are sufficiently striking to outweigh the arguments of Finnur Jonsson, Müllenhoff and others who maintain that the *Voluspo* is purely a product of heathendom. The roving Norsemen of the tenth century, very few of whom had as yet accepted Christianity, were nevertheless in close contact with Celtic races which had already been converted, and in many ways the Celtic influence was strongly felt. It seems likely, then, that the *Voluspo* was the work of a poet living chiefly in Iceland, though possibly in the "Western Isles," in the middle of the tenth century, a vigorous believer in the old gods, and yet with an imagination active enough to be touched by the vague tales of a different religion emanating from his neighbor Celts.

How much the poem was altered during the two hundred years between its composition and its first being committed to writing is largely a matter of guesswork, but, allowing for such an obvious interpolation as the catalogue of dwarfs, and for occasional lesser errors, it seems quite needless to assume such great changes as many editors do. The poem was certainly not composed to tell a story with which its early hearers were quite familiar; the lack of continuity which baffles modern readers presumably did not trouble them in the least. It is, in effect, a series of gigantic pictures, put into words with a directness and sureness which bespeak the poet of genius. It is only after the reader, with the help of the many notes, has familiarized himself with the names and incidents involved that he can begin to understand the effect which this magnificent poem must have produced on those who not only understood but believed it.

HOVAMOL

This poem follows the *Voluspo* in the *Codex Regius*, but is preserved in no other manuscript. The first stanza is quoted by Snorri, and two lines of stanza 84 appear in one of the sagas.

In its present shape it involves the critic of the text in more puzzles than any other of the *Eddic* poems. Without going in detail into the various theories, what happened seems to have been somewhat as follows. There existed from very early times a collection of proverbs and wise counsels, which were attributed to Odin just as the Biblical proverbs were to Solomon. This collection, which presumably was always elastic in extent, was known as "The High One's Words," and forms the basis of the present poem. To it, however, were added other poems and fragments dealing with wisdom which seemed by their nature to imply that the speaker was Odin. Thus a catalogue of runes, or charms, was tacked on, and also a set of proverbs, differing essentially in form from those comprising the main collection. Here and there bits of verse more nearly narrative crept in; and of course the loose structure of the poem made it easy for any reciter to insert new stanzas almost at will. This curious miscellany is what we now have as the *Hovamol*.

Five separate elements are pretty clearly recognizable: (1) the *Hovamol* proper (stanzas 1-80), a collection of proverbs and counsels for the conduct of life; (2) the *Loddfafnismol* (stanzas 111-138), a collection somewhat similar to the first, but specifically addressed to a certain Loddfafnir; (3) the *Ljothatal* (stanzas 147-165), a collection of charms; (4) the love-story of Odin and Billing's daughter (stanzas 96-102), with an introductory dissertation on the faithlessness of women in general (stanzas 81-95), which probably crept into the poem first, and then pulled the story, as an apt illustration, after it; (5) the story of how Odin got the mead of poetry-the draught which gave him the gift of tongues-from the maiden Gunnloth (stanzas 103-110). There is also a brief passage (stanzas 139-146) telling how Odin won the runes, this passage being a natural introduction to the *Ljothatal*, and doubtless brought into the poem for that reason.

It is idle to discuss the authorship or date of such a series of accretions as this. Parts of it are doubtless among the oldest relics of ancient Germanic poetry; parts of it may have originated at a relatively late period. Probably, however, most of its component elements go pretty far back, although we have no way of telling how or when they first became associated.

It seems all but meaningless to talk about "interpolations" in a poem which has developed almost solely through the process of piecing together originally unrelated odds and ends. The notes, therefore, make only such suggestions as are needed to keep the main divisions of the poem distinct.

Few gnomic collections in the world's literary history present sounder wisdom more tersely expressed than the *Hovamol*. Like the Book of Proverbs it occasionally rises to lofty heights of poetry. If it presents the worldly wisdom of a violent race, it also shows noble ideals of loyalty, truth, and unfaltering courage.

VAFTHRUTHNISMOL

The *Vafthruthnismol* follows the Hovamol in the *Codex Regius*. From stanza 20 on it is also included in the *Arnamagnæn Codex*, the first part evidently having appeared on a leaf now lost. Snorri quotes eight stanzas of it in the *Prose Edda*, and in his prose text closely paraphrases many others.

The poem is wholly in dialogue form except for a single narrative stanza (stanza 5). After a brief introductory discussion between Odin and his wife, Frigg, concerning the reputed wisdom of the giant Vafthruthnir, Odin, always in quest of wisdom, seeks out the giant, calling himself Gagnrath. The giant immediately insists that they shall demonstrate which is the wiser of the two, and propounds four questions (stanzas 11, 13, 15, and 17), each of which Odin answers. It is then the god's turn to ask, and he begins with a series of twelve numbered questions regarding the origins and past history of life. These Vafthruthnir answers, and Odin asks five more questions, this time referring to what is to follow the destruction of the gods, the last one asking the name of his own slayer. Again Vafthruthnir answers, and Odin finally propounds the unanswerable question: "What spake Odin himself in the ears of his son, ere in the bale-fire he burned?" Vafthruthnir, recognizing his questioner as Odin himself, admits his inferiority in wisdom, and so the contest ends.

The whole poem is essentially encyclopaedic in character, and thus was particularly useful to Snorri in his preparation of the *Prose Edda*. The encyclopaedic poem with a slight narrative outline seems to have been exceedingly popular; the *Grimnismol* and the much later *Alvissmol* represent different phases of the same type. The *Vafthruthnismol* and *Grimnismol* together, indeed, constitute a fairly complete dictionary of Norse mythology. There has been much discussion as to the probable date of the *Vafthruthnismol*, but it appears to belong to about the same period as the *Voluspo*: in other words, the middle of the tenth century. While there may be a few interpolated passages in the poem as we now have it, it is clearly a united whole, and evidently in relatively good condition.

GRIMNISMOL

The *Grimnismol* follows the *Vafthruthnismol* in the *Codex Regius* and is also found complete in the *Arnamagnæn Codex*, where also it follows the *Vafthruthnismol*. Snorri quotes over twenty of its stanzas.

Like the preceding poem, the *Grimnismol* is largely encyclopedic in nature, and consists chiefly of proper names, the last forty-seven stanzas containing no less than two hundred and twenty-five of these. It is not, however, in dialogue form. As Müllenhoff pointed out, there is underneath the catalogue of mythological names a consecutive and thoroughly dramatic story. Odin, concealed under the name of Grimnir, is through an error tortured by King Geirröth. Bound between two blazing fires, he begins to display his wisdom for the benefit of the king's little son, Agnar, who has been kind to him. Gradually he works up to the great final moment, when he declares his true name, or rather names, to the terrified Geirröth, and the latter falls on his sword and is killed.

For much of this story we do not have to depend on guesswork, for in both manuscripts the poem itself is preceded by a prose narrative of considerable length, and concluded by a brief prose statement of the manner of Geirröth's death. These prose notes, of which there are many in the *Eddic* manuscripts, are of considerable interest to the student of early literary forms. Presumably they were written by the compiler to whom we owe the *Eddic* collection, who felt that the poems needed such annotation in order to be clear. Linguistic evidence shows that they were written in the twelfth or thirteenth century, for they preserve none of the older word-forms which help us to date many of the poems two or three hundred years earlier.

Without discussing in detail the problems suggested by these prose passages, it is worth noting, first, that the *Eddic* poems contain relatively few stanzas of truly narrative verse; and second, that all of them are based on narratives which must have been more or less familiar to the hearers of the poems. In other words, the poems seldom aimed to tell stories, although most of them followed a narrative sequence of ideas. The stories themselves appear to have lived in oral prose tradition, just as in the case of the sagas; and the prose notes of the manuscripts, in so far as they contain material not simply drawn from the poems themselves, are relics of this tradition. The early Norse poets rarely conceived verse as a suitable means for direct storytelling, and in some of the poems even the simplest action is told in prose "links" between dialogue stanzas.

The applications of this fact, which has been too often overlooked, are almost limitless, for it suggests a still unwritten chapter in the history of ballad poetry and the so-called "popular" epic. It implies that narrative among early peoples may frequently have had a period of prose existence before it was made into verse, and thus puts, for example, a long series of transitional stages before such a poem as the *Iliad*. In any case, the prose notes accompanying the *Eddic* poems prove that in addition to the poems themselves there existed in the twelfth century a considerable amount of narrative tradition, presumably in prose form, on which these notes were based by the compiler.

Interpolations in such a poem as the *Grimnismol* could have been made easily enough, and many stanzas have undoubtedly crept in from other poems, but the beginning and end of the poem are clearly marked, and presumably it has come down to us with the same essential outline it had when it was composed, probably in the first half of the tenth century.

SKIRNISMOL

The *Skirnismol* is found complete in the *Codex Regius*, and through stanza 27 in the *Arnamagnæn Codex*. Snorri quotes the concluding stanza. In *Regius* the poem is entitled "For Scirnis" ("Skirnir's Journey").

The *Skirnismol* differs sharply from the poems preceding it, in that it has a distinctly ballad quality. As a matter of fact, however, its verse is altogether dialogue, the narrative being supplied in the prose "links," concerning which cf. introductory note to the *Grimnismol*. The dramatic effectiveness and vivid characterization of the poem seem to connect it with the *Thrymskvitha*, and the two may possibly have been put into their present form by the same man. Bugge's guess that the *Skirnismol* was the work of the author of the *Lokasenna* is also possible, though it has less to support it.

Critics have generally agreed in dating the poem as we now have it as early as the first half of the tenth century; Finnur Jonsson puts it as early as 900, and claims it, as usual, for Norway. Doubtless it was current in Norway, in one form or another, before the first Icelandic settlements, but his argument that the thistle (stanza 31) is not an Icelandic plant has little weight, for such curse-formulas must have traveled freely from place to place. In view of the evidence pointing to a western origin for many or all of the *Eddic* poems, Jonsson's reiterated "Digtet er sikkert norsk og ikke islandsk" is somewhat exasperating. Wherever the *Skirnismol* was composed, it has been preserved in exceptionally good condition, and seems to be practically devoid of interpolations or lacunæ.

HARBARTHSLJOTH

The *Harbarthsljoth* is found complete in the *Codex Regius*, where it follows the *Skirnismol*, and from the fourth line of Stanza 19 to the end of the poem in the *Arnamagnæn Codex*, of which it occupies the first page and a half.

The poem differs sharply from those which precede it in the *Codex Regius*, both in metrical form and in spirit. It is, indeed, the most nearly formless of all the *Eddic* poems. The normal metre is the Malahattr (cf. Introduction, where an example is given). The name of this verse-form means "in the manner of conversation," and the *Harbarthsljoth's* verse fully justifies the term. The Atli poems exemplify the conventional use of Malahattr, but in the *Harbarthsljoth* the form is used with extraordinary freedom, and other metrical forms are frequently employed. A few of the speeches of which the poem is composed cannot be twisted into any known Old Norse metre, and appear to be simply prose.

How far this confusion is due to interpolations and faulty transmission of the original poem is uncertain. Finnur Jonsson has attempted a wholesale purification of the poem, but his arbitrary condemnation of words, lines, and entire stanzas as spurious is quite unjustified by any positive evidence. I have accepted Mogk's theory that the author was "a first-rate psychologist, but a poor poet," and have translated the poem as it stands in the manuscripts. I have preserved the metrical confusion of the original by keeping throughout so far as possible to the metres found in the poem; if the rhythm of the translation is often hard to catch, the difficulty is no less with the original Norse.

The poem is simply a contest of abuse, such as the early Norwegian and Icelander delighted in, the opposing figures being Thor and Odin, the latter appearing in the disguise of the ferryman Harbarth. Such billingsgate lent itself readily to changes, interpolations and omissions, and it is little wonder that the poem is chaotic. It consists mainly of boasting and of references, often luckily obscure, to disreputable events in the life of one or the other of the disputants. Some editors have sought to read a complex symbolism into it, particularly by representing it as a contest between the noble or warrior class (Odin) and the peasant (Thor). But it seems a pity to take such a vigorous piece of broad farce too seriously.

Verse-form, substance, and certain linguistic peculiarities, notably the suffixed articles, point to a relatively late date (eleventh century) for the poem in its present form. Probably it had its origin in the early days, but its colloquial nature and its vulgarity made it readily susceptible to changes.

Owing to the chaotic state of the text, and the fact that none of the editors or commentators have succeeded in improving it much, I have not in this case attempted to give all the important emendations and suggestions. The stanza-divisions are largely arbitrary.

HYMISKVITHA

The *Hymiskvitha* is found complete in both manuscripts; in *Regius* it follows the *Harbarthsljoth*, while in the *Arnamagnæn Codex* it comes after the *Grimnismol*. Snorri does not quote it, although he tells the main story involved.

The poem is a distinctly inferior piece of work, obviously based on various narrative fragments, awkwardly pieced together. Some critics, Jessen and Edzardi for instance, have maintained that the compiler had before him three distinct poems, which he simply put together; others, like Finnur Jonsson and Mogk, think that the author made a new poem of his own on the basis of earlier poems, now lost. It seems probable that he took a lot of odds and ends of material concerning Thor, whether in prose or in verse, and worked them together in a perfunctory way, without much caring how well they fitted. His chief aim was probably to impress the credulous imaginations of hearers greedy for wonders.

The poem is almost certainly one of the latest of those dealing with the gods, though Finnur Jonsson, in order to support his theory of a Norwegian origin, has to date it relatively early. If, as seems probable, it was produced in Iceland, the chances are that it was composed in the first half of the eleventh century. Jessen, rather recklessly, goes so far as to put it two hundred years later. In any case, it belongs to a period of literary decadence,—the great days of *Eddic* poetry would never have permitted the nine hundred headed person found in Hymir's home—and to one in which the usual forms of diction in mythological poetry had yielded somewhat to the verbal subtleties of skaldic verse.

While the skaldic poetry properly falls outside the limits of this book, it is necessary here to say a word about it. There is preserved, in the sagas and elsewhere, a very considerable body of lyric poetry, the authorship of each poem being nearly always definitely stated, whether correctly or otherwise. This type of poetry is marked by an extraordinary complexity of diction, with a peculiarly difficult vocabulary of its own. It was to explain some of the "kennings" which composed this special vocabulary that Snorri wrote one of the sections of the *Prose Edda*. As an illustration, in a single stanza of one poem in the *Egilssaga*, a sword is called "the halo of the helm," "the wound-hoe," "the blood-snake" (possibly; no one is sure what the compound word means) and "the ice of the girdle," while men appear in the same stanza as "Odin's ash-trees," and battle is spoken of as "the iron game." One of the eight lines has defied translation completely.

Skaldic diction made relatively few inroads into the earlier *Eddic* poems, but in the *Hymiskvitha* these circumlocutions are fairly numerous. This sets the poem somewhat apart from the rest of the mythological collection. Only the vigor of the two main stories—Thor's expedition after

Hymir's kettle and the fishing trip in which he caught Mithgarthsorm—saves it from complete mediocrity.

LOKASENNA

The *Lokasenna* is found only in *Regius*, where it follows the *Hymiskvitha*; Snorri quotes four lines of it, grouped together as a single stanza.

The poem is one of the most vigorous of the entire collection, and seems to have been preserved in exceptionally good condition. The exchange or contest of insults was dear to the Norse heart, and the *Lokasenna* consists chiefly of Loki's taunts to the assembled gods and goddesses, and their largely ineffectual attempts to talk back to him. The author was evidently well versed in mythological lore, and the poem is full of references to incidents not elsewhere recorded. As to its date and origin there is the usual dispute, but the latter part of the tenth century and Iceland seem the best guesses.

The prose notes are long and of unusual interest. The introductory one links the poem closely to the *Hymiskvitha*, much as the *Reginsmol*, *Fafnismol* and *Sigrdrifumol* are linked together; the others fill in the narrative gaps in the dialogue—very like stage directions,—and provide a conclusion by relating Loki's punishment, which, presumably, is here connected with the wrong incident. It is likely that often when the poem was recited during the two centuries or so before it was committed to writing, the speaker inserted some such explanatory comments, and the compiler of the collection followed this example by adding such explanations as he thought necessary. The *Lokasenna* is certainly much older than the *Hymiskvitha*, the connection between them being purely one of subject-matter; and the twelfth-century compiler evidently knew a good deal less about mythology than the author whose work he was annotating.

THRYMSKVITHA

The *Thrymskvitha* is found only in the *Codex Regius*, where it follows the *Lokasenna*. Snorri does not quote from it, nor, rather oddly, does the story occur in the *Prose Edda*.

Artistically the *Thrymskvitha* is one of the best, as it is, next to the *Voluspo*, the most famous, of the entire collection. It has, indeed, been called "the finest ballad in the world," and not without some reason. Its swift, vigorous action, the sharpness of its characterization and the humor of the central situation combine to make it one of the most vivid short narrative poems ever composed. Of course we know nothing specific of its author, but there can be no question that he was a poet of extraordinary ability. The poem assumed its present form, most critics agree, somewhere about 900, and thus it is one of the oldest in the collection. It has been suggested, on the basis of stylistic similarity, that its author may also have composed the *Skirnismol*, and possibly *Baldrs Draumar*. There is also some resemblance between the *Thrymskvitha* and the *Lokasenna* (note, in this connection, Bugge's suggestion that the *Skirnismol* and the *Lokasenna* may have been by the same man), and it is not impossible that all four poems have a single authorship.

The *Thrymskvitha* has been preserved in excellent condition, without any serious gaps or interpolations. In striking contrast to many of the poems, it contains no prose narrative links, the story being told in narrative verse—a rare phenomenon in the poems of the *Edda*.

ALVISSMOL

No better summary of the Alvissmol can be given than Gering's statement that "it is a versified chapter from the skaldic Poetics." The narrative skeleton, contained solely in stanzas 1-8 and in 35, is of the slightest; the dwarf Alvis, desirous of marrying Thor's daughter, is compelled by the god to answer a number of questions to test his knowledge. That all his answers are quite satisfactory makes no difference whatever to the outcome. The questions and answers differ radically from those of the *Vafthruthnismol*. Instead of being essentially mythological, they all concern synonyms. Thor asks what the earth, the sky, the moon, and so on, are called "in each of all the worlds," but there is no apparent significance in the fact that the gods call the earth one thing and the giants call it another; the answers are simply strings of poetic circumlocutions, or "kennings." Concerning the use of these "kennings" in skaldic poetry, cf. introductory note to the *Hymiskvitha*.

Mogk is presumably right in dating the poem as late as the twelfth century, assigning it to the period of "the Icelandic renaissance of skaldic poetry." It appears to have been the work of a man skilled in poetic construction—Thor's questions, for instance, are neatly balanced in pairs—and fully familiar with the intricacies of skaldic diction, but distinctly weak in his mythology. In other words, it is learned rather than spontaneous poetry. Finnur Jonsson's attempt to make it a tenth century Norwegian poem baffles logic. Vigfusson is pretty sure the poem shows marked traces of Celtic influence, which is by no means incompatible with Mogk's theory (cf. introductory note to the *Rigsthula*).

The poem is found only in *Regius*, where it follows the *Thrymskvitha*. Snorri quotes stanzas 20 and 30, the manuscripts of the *Prose Edda* giving the name of the poem as *Alvissmol, Alsvinnsmol* or *Olvismol*. It is apparently in excellent condition, without serious errors of transmission, although interpolations or omissions in such a poem might have been made so easily as to defy detection.

The translation of the many synonyms presents, of course, unusual difficulties, particularly as many of the Norse words can be properly rendered in English only by more or less extended phrases. I have kept to the original meanings as closely as I could without utterly destroying the metrical structure.

BALDRS DRAUMAR

Baldrs Draumar is found only in the *Arnamagnæn Codex*, where it follows the *Harbarthsljoth* fragment. It is preserved in various late paper manuscripts, with the title *Vegtamskvitha* (The Lay of Vegtam), which has been used by some editors.

The poem, which contains but fourteen stanzas, has apparently been preserved in excellent condition. Its subject-matter and style link it closely with the *Voluspo*. Four of the five lines of stanza 11 appear, almost without change, in the *Voluspo*, 32-33, and the entire poem is simply an elaboration of the episode outlined in those and the preceding stanzas. It has been suggested that *Baldrs Draumar* and the *Voluspo* may have been by the same author. There is also enough similarity in style between *Baldrs Draumar* and the *Thrymskvitha* (note especially the opening stanza) to give color to Vigfusson's guess that these two poems had a common authorship. In any case, *Baldrs Draumar* presumably assumed its present form not later than the first half of the tenth century.

Whether the Volva (wise-woman) of the poem is identical with the speaker in the *Voluspo* is purely a matter for conjecture. Nothing definitely opposes such a supposition. As in the longer poem she foretells the fall of the gods, so in this case she prophesies the first incident of that fall, the death of Baldr. Here she is called up from the dead by Odin, anxious to know the meaning of Baldr's evil dreams; in the *Voluspo* it is likewise intimated that the Volva has risen from the grave.

The poem, like most of the others in the collection, is essentially dramatic rather than narrative, summarizing a story which was doubtless familiar to everyone who heard the poem recited.

RIGSTHULA

The *Rigsthula* is found in neither of the principal codices. The only manuscript containing it is the so-called *Codex Wormanius*, a manuscript of Snorri's *Prose Edda*. The poem appears on the last sheet of this manuscript, which unluckily is incomplete, and thus the end of the poem is lacking. In the *Codex Wormanius* itself the poem has no title, but a fragmentary parchment included with it calls the poem the *Rigsthula*. Some late paper manuscripts give it the title of *Rigsmol*.

The *Rigsthula* is essentially unlike anything else which editors have agreed to include in the so-called *Edda*. It is a definitely cultural poem, explaining, on a mythological basis, the origin of the different castes of early society: the thralls, the peasants, and the warriors. From the warriors, finally, springs one who is destined to become a king, and thus the whole poem is a song in praise of the royal estate. This fact in itself would suffice to indicate that the *Rigsthula* was not composed in Iceland, where for centuries kings were regarded with profound disapproval.

Not only does the *Rigsthula* praise royalty, but it has many of the earmarks of a poem composed in praise of a particular king. The manuscript breaks off at a most exasperating point, just as the connection between the mythical "Young Kon" (Konr ungr, konungr, "king"; but cf. stanza 44, note) and the monarch in question is about to be established. Owing to the character of the Norse settlements in Iceland, Ireland, and the western islands generally, search for a specific king leads back to either Norway or Denmark; despite the arguments advanced by Edzardi, Vigfusson, Powell, and others, it seems most improbable that such a poem should have been produced elsewhere than on the Continent, the region where Scandinavian royalty most flourished. Finnur Jonsson's claim for Norway, with Harald the Fair-Haired as the probable king in question, is much less impressive than Mogk's ingenious demonstration that the poem was in all probability composed in Denmark, in honor of either Gorm the Old or Harald Blue-Tooth. His proof is based chiefly on the evidence provided by stanza 49, and is summarized in the note to that stanza.

The poet, however, was certainly not a Dane, but probably a wandering Norse singer, who may have had a dozen homes, and who clearly had spent much time in some part of the western island world chiefly inhabited by Celts. The extent of Celtic influence on the *Eddic* poems in general is a matter of sharp dispute. Powell, for example, claims almost all the poems for the "Western Isles," and attributes nearly all their good qualities to Celtic influence. Without here attempting to enter into the details of the argument, it may be said that the weight of authoritative opinion, while clearly recognizing the marks of Celtic influence in the poems, is against this view; contact between the roving Norsemen of Norway and

Iceland and the Celts of Ireland and the "Western Isles," and particularly the Orkneys, was so extensive as to make the presumption of an actual Celtic home for the poems seem quite unnecessary.

In the case of the *Rigsthula* the poet unquestionably had not only picked up bits of the Celtic speech (the name Rig itself is almost certainly of Celtic origin, and there are various other Celtic words employed), but also had caught something of the Celtic literary spirit. This explains the cultural nature of the poem, quite foreign to Norse poetry in general. On the other hand, the style as a whole is vigorously Norse, and thus the explanation that the poem was composed by an itinerant Norse poet who had lived for some time in the Celtic islands, and who was on a visit to the court of a Danish king, fits the ascertainable facts exceedingly well. As Christianity was introduced into Denmark around 960, the *Rigsthula* is not likely to have been composed much after that date, and probably belongs to the first half of the tenth century. Gorm the Old died about the year 935, and was succeeded by Harald Blue-Tooth, who died about 985.

The fourteenth (or late thirteenth) century annotator identifies Rig with Heimdall, but there is nothing in the poem itself, and very little anywhere else, to warrant this, and it seems likely that the poet had Odin, and not Heimdall, in mind, his purpose being to trace the origin of the royal estate to the chief of the gods. The evidence bearing on this identification is briefly summed up in the note on the introductory prose passage, but the question involves complex and baffling problems in mythology, and from very early times the status of Heimdall was unquestionably confusing to the Norse mind.

HYNDLULJOTH

The *Hyndluljoth* is found in neither of the great manuscripts of the *Poetic Edda*, but is included in the so-called *Flateyjarbok* (Book of the Flat Island), an enormous compilation made somewhere about 1400. The lateness of this manuscript would of itself be enough to cast a doubt upon the condition in which the poem has been preserved, and there can be no question that what we have of it is in very poor shape. It is, in fact, two separate poems, or parts of them, clumsily put together. The longer one, the *Poem of Hyndla* proper, is chiefly a collection of names, not strictly mythological but belonging to the semi-historical hero-sagas of Norse tradition. The wise-woman, Hyndla, being asked by Freyja to trace the ancestry of her favorite, Ottar, for the purpose of deciding a wager, gives a complex genealogy including many of the heroes who appear in the popular sagas handed down from days long before the Icelandic settlements. The poet was learned, but without enthusiasm; it is not likely that he composed the *Hyndluljoth* much before the twelfth century, though the material of which it is compounded must have been very much older. Although the genealogies are essentially continental, the poem seems rather like a product of the archaeological period of Iceland.

Inserted bodily in the *Hyndluljoth* proper is a fragment of fifty-one lines, taken from a poem of which, by a curious chance, we know the name. Snorri quotes one stanza of it, calling it "the short *Voluspo*." The fragment preserved gives, of course, no indication of the length of the original poem, but it shows that it was a late and very inferior imitation of the great *Voluspo*. Like the *Hyndluljoth* proper, it apparently comes from the twelfth century; but there is nothing whatever to indicate that the two poems were the work of the same man, or were ever connected in any way until some blundering copyist mixed them up. Certainly the connection did not exist in the middle of the thirteenth century, when Snorri quoted "the short *Voluspo*."

Neither poem is of any great value, either as mythology or as poetry. The author of "the short *Voluspo*" seems, indeed, to have been more or less confused as to his facts; and both poets were too late to feel anything of the enthusiasm of the earlier school. The names of Hyndla's heroes, of course, suggest an unlimited number of stories, but as most of these have no direct relation to the poems of the *Edda*, I have limited the notes to a mere record of who the persons mentioned were, and the saga-groups in which they appeared.

SVIPDAGSMOL

The two poems, *Grougaldr* (Groa's Spell) and *Fjolsvinnsmol* (the *Ballad of Fjolsvith*), which many editors have, very wisely, united under the single title of *Svipdagsmol*, are found only in paper manuscripts, none of them antedating the seventeenth century. Everything points to a relatively late origin for the poems: their extensive use of "kennings" or poetical circumlocutions, their romantic spirit, quite foreign to the character of the unquestionably older poems, the absence of any reference to them in the earlier documents, the frequent errors in mythology, and, finally, the fact that the poems appear to have been preserved in unusually good condition. Whether or not a connecting link of narrative verse joining the two parts has been lost is an open question; on the whole it seems likely that the story was sufficiently well known so that the reciter of the poem (or poems) merely filled in the gap with a brief prose summary in pretty much his own words. The general relationship between dialogue and narrative in the *Eddic* poems is discussed in the introductory note to the *Grimnismol*, in connection with the use of prose links.

The love story of Svipdag and Mengloth is not referred to elsewhere in the *Poetic Edda*, nor does Snorri mention it; however, Groa, who here appears as Svipdag's mother, is spoken of by Snorri as a wise woman, the wife of Orvandil, who helps Thor with her magic charms. On the other hand, the essence of the story, the hero's winning of a bride ringed about by flames, is strongly suggestive of parts of the Sigurth-Brynhild traditions. Whether or not it is to be regarded as a nature or solar myth depends entirely on one's view of the whole "solar myth" school of criticism, not so highly esteemed today as formerly; such an interpretation is certainly not necessary to explain what is, under any circumstances, a very charming romance told, in the main, with dramatic effectiveness.

In later years the story of Svipdag and Mengloth became popular throughout the North, and was made the subject of many Danish and Swedish as well as Norwegian ballads. These have greatly assisted in the reconstruction of the outlines of the narrative surrounding the dialogue poems here given.

VOLUNDARKVITHA

Between the *Thrymskvitha* and the *Alvissmol* in the *Codex Regius* stands the *Völundarkvitha*. It was also included in the *Arnamagnæan Codex*, but unluckily it begins at the very end of the fragment which has been preserved, and thus only a few lines of the opening prose remain. This is doubly regrettable because the text in *Regius* is unquestionably in very bad shape, and the other manuscript would doubtless have been of great assistance in the reconstruction of the poem.

There has been a vast amount written regarding the Weland tradition as a whole, discussing particularly the relations between the *Völundarkvitha* and the Weland passage in Deor's Lament. There can be little question that the story came to the North from Saxon regions, along with many of the other early hero tales. In stanza 16 the Rhine is specifically mentioned as the home of treasure; and the presence of the story in Anglo-Saxon poetry probably as early as the first part of the eighth century proves beyond a doubt that the legend cannot have been a native product of Scandinavia. In one form or another, however, the legend of the smith persisted for centuries throughout all the Teutonic lands, and the name of Wayland Smith is familiar to all readers of Walter Scott, and even of Rudyard Kipling's tales of England.

In what form this story reached the North is uncertain. Sundry striking parallels between the diction of the *völundarkvitha* and that of the Weland passage in Deor's Lament make it distinctly probable that a Saxon song on this subject had found its way to Scandinavia or Iceland. But the prose introduction to the poem mentions the "old sagas" in which Völund was celebrated, and in the *Thithrekssaga* we have definite evidence of the existence of such prose narrative in the form of the *Velentssaga* (Velent, Völund, Weland, and Wayland all being, of course, identical), which gives a long story for which the *Völundarkvitha* can have supplied relatively little, if any, of the material. It is probable, then, that Weland stories were current in both prose and verse in Scandinavia as early as the latter part of the ninth century.

Once let a figure become popular in oral tradition, and the number and variety of the incidents connected with his name will increase very rapidly. Doubtless there were scores of Weland stories current in the eighth, ninth, and tenth centuries, many of them with very little if any traditional authority. The main one, however, the story of the laming of the smith by King Nithuth (or by some other enemy) and of Weland's terrible revenge, forms the basis of the *Völundarkvitha*. To this, by way of introduction, has been added the story of Völund and the swan-maiden, who, to make things even more complex, is likewise said to be a Valkyrie. Some critics maintain that these two sections were originally two distinct poems, merely strung together by the compiler with the help of narrative prose links; but the poem as a whole has a kind of dramatic unity which suggests rather that an early poet—for linguistically the poem belongs among the oldest of the *Eddic* collection—used two distinct legends, whether in prose or verse, as the basis for the composition of a new and homogeneous poem.

The swan-maiden story appears, of course, in many places quite distinct from the Weland tradition, and, in another form, became one of the most popular of German folk tales. Like the story of Weland, however, it is of German rather than Scandinavian origin, and the identification of the swan-maidens as Valkyries, which may have taken place before the legend reached the North, may, on the other hand, have been simply an attempt to connect southern tradition with figures well-known in northern mythology.

The *Völundarkvitha* is full of prose narrative links, including an introduction. The nature of such prose links has already been discussed in the introductory note to the *Grimnismol*; the *Völundarkvitha* is a striking illustration of the way in which the function of the earlier *Eddic* verse was limited chiefly to dialogue or description, the narrative outline being provided, if at all, in prose. This prose was put in by each reciter according to his fancy and knowledge, and his estimate of his hearers' need for such explanations; some of it, as in this instance, eventually found its way into the written record.

The manuscript of the *Völundarkvitha* is in such bad shape, and the conjectural emendations have been so numerous, that in the notes I have attempted to record only the most important of them.

HELGAKVITHA HJORVARTHSSONAR

The three Helgi lays, all found in the *Codex Regius*, have been the subjects of a vast amount of discussion, in spite of which many of the facts regarding them are still very far from settled. It is, indeed, scarcely possible to make any unqualified statement regarding these three poems for which a flat contradiction cannot be found in the writings of some scholar of distinction. The origin of the Helgi tradition, its connection with that of Sigurth, the authorship, date and home of the poems, the degree to which they have been altered from their original forms, the status of the composer of the copious prose notes: these and many other allied questions have been and probably always will be matters of dispute among students of the *Edda's* history.

Without attempting to enter into the discussion in detail, certain theories should be noted. Helgi appears originally to have been a Danish popular hero, the son of King Halfdan. Saxo Grammaticus has a good deal to say about him in that capacity, and it has been pointed out that many of the place names in the Helgi lays can be pretty clearly identified with parts of Denmark and neighboring stretches of the Baltic. The Danish Helgi, according to Saxo, was famed as the conqueror of Hunding and Hothbrodd, the latter as the result of a naval expedition at the head of a considerable fleet.

From Denmark the story appears to have spread northward into Norway and westward into the Norse settlements among the islands. Not many of its original features remained, and new ones were added here and there, particularly with regard to Helgi's love affair with Sigrun. The victories over Hunding and Hothbrodd, however, were generally retained, and out of material relating to these two fights, and to the Helgi-Sigrun story, were fashioned the two lays of Helgi Hundingsbane.

How the Helgi legend became involved with that of the Volsungs is an open question. Both stories travelled from the South, and presumably about the same time, so it is not unnatural that some confusion should have arisen. At no time, however, was the connection particularly close so far as the actual episodes of the two stories were concerned. In the two lays of Helgi Hundingsbane the relationship is established only by the statement that Helgi was the son of Sigmund and Borghild; Sigurth is not mentioned, and in the lay of Helgi the son of Hjorvarth there is no connection at all. On the other hand, Helgi does not appear in any of the *Eddic* poems dealing directly with the Volsung stories, although in one passage of doubtful authenticity (cf. *Reginsmol*, introductory note) his traditional enemy, Hunding, does, represented by his sons. In the *Volsungasaga* the story of Helgi, including the fights with Hunding and Hothbrodd and the love affair with Sigrun, is told in chapters 8 and 9 without otherwise affecting the course of the narrative. Here, as in the Helgi lays, Helgi is the son of Sigmund Volsungsson and Borghild; Sigurth, on the other hand, is the son of Sigmund and Hjordis, the latter being the daughter of King Eylimi. Still another son, who complicates both stories somewhat, is Sinfjotli, son of Sigmund and his own sister, Signy. Sinfjotli appears in both of the Helgi Hundingsbane lays and in the *Volsungasaga*, but not in any of the *Eddic* poems belonging to the Volsung cycle (cf. *Fra Dautha Sinfjotla* and note).

There is a certain amount of resemblance between the story of Helgi and Sigrun and that of Sigurth and Brynhild, particularly as the annotator responsible for the prose notes insists that Sigrun was a Valkyrie. Whether this resemblance was the cause of bringing the two stories together, or whether the identification of Helgi as Sigmund's son resulted in alterations of the love story in the Helgi poems, cannot be determined.

The first of the three Helgi poems, the lay of Helgi the son of Hjorvarth, is a somewhat distant cousin of the other two. The Helgi in question is apparently the same traditional figure, and he leads a naval expedition, but he is not the son of Sigmund, there is no connection with the Volsung cycle, and his wife is Svava, not Sigrun. At the same time, the points of general resemblance with the two Helgi Hundingsbane lays are such as to indicate a common origin, provided one goes far enough back. The annotator brings the stories together by the naive expedient of having Helgi "born again," and not once only, but twice.

The first Helgi lay is manifestly in bad shape, and includes at least two distinct poems, differentiated not only by subject-matter but by metrical form. Although the question is debatable, the longer of these poems (stanzas 1–11 and 31–43) seems in turn to have been compounded out of fragments of two or more Helgi poems. The first five stanzas are a dialogue between a bird and Atli, one of Hjorvarth's followers, concerning the winning of Sigrlin, who is destined to be Hjorvarth's wife and Helgi's mother. Stanzas 6–11 are a dialogue between Helgi and a Valkyrie (the accompanying prose so calls her, and identifies her as Svava, but there is nothing in the verse to prove this). Stanzas 12–30 form a fairly consecutive unit, in which Atli, on guard over Helgi's ship, has a vigorous argument with a giantess, Hrimgerth, whence this section has sometimes been called the *Hrimgertharmol* (*Lay of Hrimgerth*). The last section, stanzas 31–43, is again fairly consecutive, and tells of the death of Helgi following the rash oath of his brother, Hethin, to win Svava for himself.

Parts I, II, and IV may all have come from the same poem or they may not; it is quite impossible to tell surely. All of them are generally dated by commentators not later than the first half of the tenth century, whereas the *Hrimgertharmol* (section III) is placed considerably later. When and by whom these fragments were pieced together is another vexed question, and this involves a consideration of the prose notes and links, of which the *Helgakvitha Hjorvarthssonar* has a larger amount than any other poem in the *Edda*. These prose links contain practically all the narrative, the verse being almost exclusively dialogue. Whoever composed them seems to have been consciously trying to bring his chaotic verse material into some semblance of unity, but he did his work pretty clumsily, with manifest blunders and contradictions. Bugge has advanced the theory that these prose passages are to be regarded as an original and necessary part of the work, but this hardly squares with the evidence.

It seems probable, rather, that as the Helgi tradition spread from its native Denmark through the Norse regions of the North and West, and became gradually interwoven, although not in essentials, with the other great hero cycle from the South, that of the Volsungs, a considerable number of poems dealing with Helgi were composed, at different times and in different places, reflecting varied forms of the story. Many generations afterwards, when Iceland's literary period had arrived, some zealous scribe committed to writing such poems or fragments of poems as he knew, piecing them together and annotating them on the basis of information which had reached him through other channels. The prose notes to *Helgakvitha Hundingsbana II* frankly admit this patchwork process: a section of four stanzas (13–16) is introduced with the phrase, "as is said in the Old Volsung Lay"; the final prose note cites an incident "told in the *Karuljoth (Lay of Kara)*" and a two-line speech is quoted "as it was written before in the *Helgakvitha*."

The whole problem of the origin, character and home of the Helgi poems has been discussed in great detail by Bugge in his *Helge-Digtene i den Ældre Edda, Deres Hjem og Forbindelser*, which, as translated by W. H. Schofield under the title *The Home of the Eddic Poems*, is available for readers of English. This study is exceedingly valuable, if not in all respects convincing. The whole matter is so complex and so important in the history of Old Norse literature, and any intelligent reading of the Helgi poems is so dependent on an understanding of the conditions under which they have come down to us, that I have here discussed the question more extensively than the scope of a mere introductory note to a single poem would warrant.

HELGAKVITHA HUNDINGSBANA I

The general subject of the Helgi lays is considered in the introduction to

Helgakvitha Hjorvarthssonar, and it is needless here to repeat the statements there made. The first lay of Helgi Hundingsbane is unquestionably one of the latest of the *Eddic* poems, and was composed probably not earlier than the second quarter of the eleventh century. It presents several unusual characteristics. For one thing, it is among the few essentially narrative poems in the whole collection, telling a consecutive story in verse, and, except for the abusive dialogue between Sinfjotli and Gothmund, which clearly was based on another and older poem, it does so with relatively little use of dialogue. It is, in fact, a ballad, and in the main an exceedingly vigorous one. The annotator, who added his prose narrative notes so freely in the other Helgi poems, here found nothing to do. The available evidence indicates that narrative verse was a relatively late development in Old Norse poetry, and it is significant that most of the poems which consist chiefly, not of dialogue, but of narrative stanzas, such as the first Helgi Hundingsbane lay and the two Atli lays, can safely be dated, on the basis of other evidence, after the year 1000.

The first Helgi Hundingsbane lay is again differentiated from most of the *Eddic* poems by the character of its language. It is full of those verbal intricacies which were the delight of the Norse skalds, and which made Snorri's dictionary of poetic phrases an absolute necessity. Many of these I have paraphrased in the translation; some I have simplified or wholly avoided. A single line will serve to indicate the character of this form of complex diction (stanza 56, line 4): "And the horse of the giantess raven's-food had." This means simply that wolves (giantesses habitually rode on wolves) ate the bodies of the dead.

Except for its intricacies of diction, and the possible loss of a stanza here and there, the poem is comparatively simple. The story belongs in all its essentials to the Helgi tradition, with the Volsung cycle brought in only to the extent of making Helgi the son of Sigmund, and in the introduction of Sinfjotli, son of Sigmund and his sister Signy, in a passage which has little or nothing to do with the course of the narrative, and which looks like an expansion of a passage from some older poem, perhaps from the "old Volsung lay" to which the annotator of the second Helgi Hundingsbane lay refers (prose after stanza 12). There are many proper names, some of which betray the confusion caused by the blending of the two sets of traditions; for example, Helgi appears indiscriminately as an Ylfing (which presumably he was before the Volsung story became involved) and as a Volsung. Granmar and his sons are called Hniflungs (Nibelungen) in stanza 50, though they seem to have had no connection with this race. The place names have aroused much debate as to the localization of the action, but while some of them probably reflect actual places, there is so much geographical confusion, and such a profusion of names which are almost certainly mythical, that it is hard to believe that the poet had any definite locations in mind.

HELGAKVITHA HUNDINGSBANA II

As the general nature of the Helgi tradition has been considered in the introductory note to *Helgakvitha Hjorvarthssonar*, it is necessary here to discuss only the characteristics of this particular poem. The second Helgi Hundingsbane lay is in most respects the exact opposite of the first one: it is in no sense consecutive; it is not a narrative poem, and all or most of it gives evidence of relatively early composition, its origin probably going well back into the tenth century.

It is frankly nothing but a piece of, in the main, very clumsy patchwork, made up of eight distinct fragments, pieced together awkwardly by the annotator with copious prose notes. One of these fragments (stanzas 13–16) is specifically identified as coming from "the old Volsung lay." What was that poem, and how much more of the extant Helgi-lay compilation was taken from it, and did the annotator know more of it than he included in his patchwork? Conclusive answers to these questions have baffled scholarship, and probably always will do so. My own guess is that the annotator knew little or nothing more than he wrote down; having got the first Helgi Hundingsbane lay, which was obviously in fairly good shape, out of the way, he proceeded to assemble all the odds and ends of verse about Helgi which he could get hold of, putting them together on the basis of the narrative told in the first Helgi lay and of such stories as his knowledge of prose sagas may have yielded.

Section I (stanzas 1–4) deals with an early adventure of Helgi's, in which he narrowly escapes capture when he ventures into Hunding's home in disguise. Section II (stanzas 5–12) is a dialogue between Helgi and Sigrun at their first meeting. Section III (stanzas 13–16, the "old Volsung lay" group) is another dialogue between Helgi and Sigrun when she invokes his aid to save her from Hothbrodd. Section IV (stanzas 17–21), which may well be from the same poem as Section III, is made up of speeches by Helgi and Sigrun after the battle in which Hothbrodd is killed; stanza 21, however, is certainly an interpolation from another poem, as it is in a different meter. Section V (stanzas 22–27) is the dispute between Sinfjotli and Gothmund, evidently in an older form than the one included in the first Helgi Hundingsbane lay. Section VI (stanzas 28–37) gives Dag's speech to his sister, Sigrun, telling of Helgi's death, her curse on her brother and her lament for her slain husband. Section VII (stanza 38) is the remnant of a dispute between Helgi and Hunding, here inserted absurdly out of place. Section VIII (stanzas 39–50) deals with the return of the dead Helgi and Sigrun's visit to him in the burial hill.

Sljmons maintains that sections I and II are fragments of the Kara lay mentioned by the annotator in his concluding prose note, and that sections IV, VI, and VIII are from a lost Helgi-Sigrun poem, while Section III comes, of course, from the "old Volsung lay." This seems as good a guess as any other, conclusive proof being quite out of the question.

Were it not for sections VI and VIII the poem would be little more than a battle-ground for scholars, but those two sections are in many ways as fine as anything in Old Norse poetry. Sigrun's curse of her brother for the slaying of Helgi and her lament for her dead husband, and the extraordinary vividness of the final scene in the burial hill, have a quality which fully offsets the baffling confusion of the rest of the poem.

FRA DAUTHA SINFJOTLA

It has been pointed out that the Helgi tradition, coming originally from Denmark, was early associated with that of the Volsungs, which was of German, or rather of Frankish, origin (cf. Introductory Note to *Helgakvitha Hjorvarthssonar*). The connecting links between these two sets of stories were few in number, the main point being the identification of Helgi as a son of Sigmund Volsungsson. Another son of Sigmund, however, appears in the Helgi poems, though not in any of the poems dealing with the Volsung cycle proper. This is Sinfjotli, whose sole function in the extant Helgi lays is to have a wordy dispute with Gothmund Granmarsson.

Sinfjotli's history is told in detail in the early chapters of the *Volsungasaga*. The twin sister of Sigmund Volsungsson, Signy, had married Siggeir, who hated his brother-in-law by reason of his desire to possess a sword which had belonged to Odin and been won by Sigmund. Having treacherously invited Volsung and his ten sons to visit him, Siggeir slew Volsung and captured his sons, who were set in the stocks. Each night a wolf ("some men say that she was Siggeir's mother") came out of the woods and ate up one of the brothers, till on the tenth night Sigmund alone was left. Then, however, Signy aided him to escape, and incidentally to kill the wolf. He vowed vengeance on Siggeir, and Signy, who hated her husband, was determined to help him. Convinced that Sigmund must have a helper of his own race, Signy changed forms with a witch, and in this guise sought out Sigmund, who, not knowing who she was, spent three nights with her. Thereafter she gave birth to a boy, whom she named Sinfjotli ("The Yellow-Spotted"?), whom she sent to Sigmund. For a time they lived in the woods, occasionally turning into wolves (whence perhaps Sinfjotli's name). When Sinfjotli was full grown, he and his father came to Siggeir's house, but were seen and betrayed by the two young sons of Signy and Siggeir, whereupon Sinfjotli slew them. Siggeir promptly had Sigmund and Sinfjotli buried alive, but Signy managed to smuggle Sigmund's famous sword into the grave, and with this the father and son dug themselves out. The next night they burned Siggeir's house, their enemy dying in the flames, and Signy, who had at the last refused to leave her husband, from a sense of somewhat belated loyalty, perishing with him.

Was this story, which the *Volsungasaga* relates in considerable detail, the basis of an old poem which has been lost? Almost certainly it was, although, as I have pointed out, many if not most of the old stories appear to have been handed down rather in prose than in verse, for the *Volsungasaga* quotes two lines of verse regarding the escape from the grave. At any rate, Sinfjotli early became a part of the Volsung tradition, which, in turn, formed the basis for no less than fifteen poems generally included in the *Eddic* collection. Of this tradition we may recognize three distinct parts: the Volsung-Sigmund-Sinfjotli story; the Helgi story, and the Sigurth story, the last of these three being by far the most extensive, and suggesting an almost limitless amount of further subdivision. With the Volsung-Sigmund-Sinfjotli story the Sigurth legend is connected only by the fact that Sigurth appears as Sigmund's son by his last wife, Hjordis; with the Helgi legend it is not connected directly at all. Aside from the fact that Helgi appears as Sigmund's son by his first wife, Borghild, the only link between the Volsung story proper and that of Helgi is the appearance of Sinfjotli in two of the Helgi poems. Originally it is altogether probable that the three stories, or sets of stories, were entirely distinct, and that Sigurth (the familiar Siegfried) had little or nothing more to do with the Volsungs of northern mythological-heroic tradition than he had with Helgi.

The annotator or compiler of the collection of poems preserved in the *Codex Regius*, having finished with the Helgi lays, had before him the task of setting down the fifteen complete or fragmentary poems dealing with the Sigurth story. Before doing this, however, he felt it incumbent on him to dispose of both Sigmund and Sinfjotli, the sole links with the two other sets of stories. He apparently knew of no poem or poems concerning the deaths of these two; perhaps there were none, though this is unlikely. Certainly the story of how Sinfjotli and Sigmund died was current in oral prose tradition, and this story the compiler set forth in the short prose passage entitled *Of Sinfjotli's Death* which, in *Regius*, immediately follows the second lay of Helgi Hundingsbane. The relation of this passage to the prose of the *Reginsmol* is discussed in the introductory note to that poem.

GRIPISSPO

The *Gripisspo* immediately follows the prose *Fra Dautha Sinfjotla* in the *Codex Regius*, and is contained in no other early manuscript. It is unquestionably one of the latest of the poems in the *Eddic* collection; most critics agree in calling it the latest of all, dating it not much before the year 1200. Its author (for in this instance the word may be correctly used) was not only familiar with the other poems of the Sigurth cycle, but seems to have had actual written copies of them before him; it has, indeed, been suggested, and not without plausibility, that the *Gripisspo* may have been written by the very man who compiled and annotated the collection of poems preserved in the *Codex Regius*.

In form the poem is a dialogue between the youthful Sigurth and his uncle, Gripir, but in substance it is a condensed outline of Sigurth's whole career as told piecemeal in the older poems. The writer was sufficiently skillful in the handling of verse, but he was utterly without inspiration; his characters are devoid of vitality, and their speeches are full of conventional phrases, with little force or incisiveness. At the same time, the poem is of considerable interest as giving, in brief form, a summary of the story of Sigurth as it existed in Iceland (for the *Gripisspo* is almost certainly Icelandic) in the latter half of the twelfth century.

It is not desirable here to go in detail into the immensely complex question of the origin, growth, and spread of the story of Sigurth (Siegfried). The volume of critical literature on the subject is enormous, and although some of the more patently absurd theories have been eliminated, there are still wide divergencies of opinion regarding many important points. At the same time, a brief review of the chief facts is necessary in order to promote a clearer understanding of the poems which follow, and which make up more than a third of the *Eddic* collection.

That the story of Sigurth reached the North from Germany, having previously developed among the Franks of the Rhine country, is now universally recognized. How and when it spread from northwestern Germany into Scandinavia are less certainly known. It spread, indeed, in every direction, so that traces of it are found wherever Frankish influence was extensively felt; but it was clearly better known and more popular in Norway, and in the settlements established by Norwegians, than anywhere else. We have historical proof that there was considerable contact, commercial and otherwise, between the Franks of northwestern Germany and the Norwegians (but not the Swedes or the Danes) throughout the period from 600 to 800; coins of Charlemagne have been found in Norway, and there is other evidence showing a fairly extensive interchange of ideas as well as of goods. Presumably, then, the story of the Frankish hero found its way into Norway in the seventh century. While, at this stage of its development, it may conceivably have included a certain amount of verse, it is altogether probable that the story as it came into Norway in the seventh century was told largely in prose, and that, even after the poets had got hold of it, the legend continued to live among the people in the form of oral prose saga.

The complete lack of contemporary material makes it impossible for us to speak with certainty regarding the character and content of the Sigurth legend as it existed in the Rhine country in the seventh century. It is, however, important to remember the often overlooked fact that any popular traditional hero became a magnet for originally unrelated stories of every kind. It must also be remembered that in the early Middle Ages there existed no such distinction between fiction and history as we now make; a saga, for instance, might be anything from the most meticulously accurate history to the wildest of fairy tales, and a single saga might (and sometimes did) combine both elements. This was equally true of the Frankish traditions, and the two principles just stated account for most of the puzzling phenomena in the growth of the Sigurth story.

Of the origin of Sigurth himself we know absolutely nothing. No historical analogy can be made to fit in the slightest degree. If one believes in the possibility of resolving hero stories into nature myths, he may be explained in that fashion, but such a solution is not necessary. The fact remains that from very early days Sigurth (Sifrit) was a great traditional hero among the Franks. The tales of his strength and valor, of his winning of a great treasure, of his wooing a more or less supernatural bride, and of his death at the hands of his kinsmen, probably were early features of this legend.

The next step was the blending of this story with one which had a clear basis in history. In the year 437 the Burgundians, under their king, Gundicarius (so the Latin histories call him), were practically annihilated by the Huns. The story of this great battle soon became one of the foremost of Rhineland traditions; and though Attila was presumably not present in person, he was quite naturally introduced as the famous ruler of the invading hordes. The dramatic story of Attila's death in the year 453 was likewise added to the tradition, and during the sixth century the chain was completed by linking together the stories of Sigurth and those of the Burgundian slaughter. Gundicarius becomes the Gunther of the *Nibelungenlied* and the Gunnar of the *Eddic* poems; Attila becomes Etzel and Atli. A still further development came through the addition of another, and totally unrelated, set of historical traditions based on the career of Ermanarich, king of the Goths, who died about the year 376. Ermanarich figures largely in many stories unconnected with the Sigurth cycle, but, with the zeal of the medieval story-tellers for connecting their heroes, he was introduced as the husband of Sigurth's daughter, Svanhild, herself originally part of a separate narrative group, and as Jormunrek he plays a considerable part in a few of the *Eddic* poems.

Such, briefly, appears to have been the development of the legend before it came into Norway. Here it underwent many changes, though the clear marks of its southern origin were never obliterated. The names were given Scandinavian forms, and in some cases were completely changed (e.g., Kriemhild becomes Guthrun). New figures, mostly of secondary importance, were introduced, and a large amount of purely Northern local color was added. Above all, the earlier part of the story was linked with Northern mythology in a way which seems to have had no counterpart among the southern Germanic peoples. The Volsungs become direct descendants of Odin; the gods are closely concerned with Fafnir's treasure, and so on. Above all, the Norse story-tellers and poets changed the figure of Brynhild. In making her a Valkyrie, sleeping on the flame-girt rock, they were never completely successful, as she persisted in remaining, to a considerable extent, the entirely human daughter of Buthli whom Sigurth woos for Gunnar. This confusion, intensified by a mixing of names (cf. *Sigrdrifumol*, introductory note), and much resembling that which existed in the parallel cases of Svava and Sigrun in the Helgi tradition, created difficulties which the Norse poets and story-tellers were never able to smooth out, and which have perplexed commentators ever since.

Those who read the Sigurth poems in the *Edda*, or the story told in the *Volsungasaga*, expecting to find a critically accurate biography of the hero, will, of course, be disappointed. If, however, they will constantly keep in mind the general manner in which the legend grew, its accretions ranging all the way from the Danube to Iceland, they will find that most of the difficulties are simply the natural results of conflicting traditions. Just as the Danish Helgi had to be "reborn" twice in order to enable three different men to kill him, so the story of Sigurth, as told in the *Eddic* poems, involves here and there inconsistencies explicable only when the historical development of the story is taken into consideration.

REGINSMOL

The *Reginsmol* immediately follows the *Gripisspo* in the *Codex Regius*, and in addition stanzas 1, 2, 6, and 18 are quoted in the *Volsungasaga*, and stanzas 13–26 in the *Nornageststhattr*. In no instance is the title of the poem stated, and in *Regius* there stands before the introductory prose, very faintly written, what appears to be "Of Sigurth." As a result, various titles have been affixed to it, the two most often used being "the Ballad of Regin" and "the First Lay of Sigurth Fafnisbane."

As a matter of fact, it is by no means clear that the compiler of the *Ed-*

dic collection regarded this or either of the two following poems, the *Fafnismol* and the *Sigrdrifumol*, as separate and distinct poems at all. There are no specific titles given, and the prose notes link the three poems in a fairly consecutive whole. Furthermore, the prose passage introducing the *Reginsmol* connects directly with *Fra Dautha Sinfjotla*, and only the insertion of the *Gripisspo* at this point, which may well have been done by some stupid copyist, breaks the continuity of the story.

For convenience I have here followed the usual plan of dividing this material into distinct parts, or poems, but I greatly doubt if this division is logically sound. The compiler seems, rather, to have undertaken to set down the story of Sigurth in consecutive form, making use of all the verse with which he was familiar, and which, by any stretch of the imagination, could be made to fit, filling up the gaps with prose narrative notes based on the living oral tradition.

This view is supported by the fact that not one of the three poems in question, and least of all the *Reginsmol*, can possibly be regarded as a unit. For one thing, each of them includes both types of stanza commonly used in the *Eddic* poems, and this, notwithstanding the efforts of Grundtvig and Müllenhoff to prove the contrary, is almost if not quite conclusive proof that each poem consists of material taken from more than one source. Furthermore, there is nowhere continuity within the verse itself for more than a very few stanzas. An analysis of the *Reginsmol* shows that stanzas 1-4, 6-10, and 12, all in Ljothahattr stanza form, seem to belong together as fragments of a poem dealing with Loki's (not Andvari's) curse on the gold taken by the gods from Andvari and paid to Hreithmar, together with Hreithmar's death at the hands of his son, Fafnir, as the first result of this curse. Stanza 5, in Fornyrthislag, is a curse on the gold, here ascribed to Andvari, but the only proper name in the stanza, *Gust*, is quite unidentifiable, and the stanza may originally have had to do with a totally different story. Stanza 11, likewise in Fornyrthislag, is merely a father's demand that his daughter rear a family to avenge his death; there is nothing in it to link it necessarily with the dying Hreithmar. Stanzas 13-18, all in Fornyrthislag, give Regin's welcome to Sigurth (stanzas 13-14), Sigurth's announcement that he will avenge his father's death on the sons of Hunding before he seeks any treasure (stanza 15), and a dialogue between a certain Hnikar, who is really Odin, and Regin, as the latter and Sigurth are on the point of being shipwrecked. This section (stanzas 13-18) bears a striking resemblance to the Helgi lays, and may well have come originally from that cycle. Next follows a passage in Ljothahattr form (stanzas 19-22 and 24-25) in which Hnikar-Odin gives some general advice as to lucky omens and good conduct in battle; the entire passage might equally well stand in the *Hovamol*, and I suspect that it originally came from just such a collection of wise saws. Inserted in this passage is stanza 23, in Fornyrthislag, likewise on the conduct of battle, with a bit of tactical advice included. The "poem" ends with a single stanza, in Fornyrthislag, simply stating that the bloody fight is over and that Sigurth fought well—a statement equally applicable to any part of the hero's career.

Finnur Jonsson has divided the *Reginsmol* into two poems, or rather into two sets of fragments, but this, as the foregoing analysis has indicated, does not appear to go nearly far enough. It accords much better with the facts to assume that the compiler of the collection represented by the *Codex Regius*, having set out to tell the story of Sigurth, took his verse fragments pretty much wherever he happened to find them. In this connection, it should be remembered that in the fluid state of oral tradition poems, fragments, and stanzas passed readily and frequently from one story to another. Tradition, never critical, doubtless connected with the Sigurth story much verse that never originated there.

If the entire passage beginning with the prose *Fra Dautha Sinfjotla*, and, except for the *Gripisspo*, including the *Reginsmol*, *Fafnismol*, and *Sigrdrifumol*, be regarded as a highly uncritical piece of compilation, rendered consecutive by the compiler's prose narrative, its difficulties are largely smoothed away; any other way of looking at it results in utterly inconclusive attempts to reconstruct poems some of which quite possibly never existed.

The twenty-six stanzas and accompanying prose notes included under the heading of *Reginsmol* belong almost wholly to the northern part of the Sigurth legend; the mythological features have no counterpart in the southern stories, and only here and there is there any betrayal of the tradition's Frankish home. The story of Andvari, Loki, and Hreithmar is purely Norse, as is the concluding section containing Odin's counsels. If we assume that the passage dealing with the victory over Hunding's sons belongs to the Helgi cycle (cf. introductory notes to *Helgakvitha Hjorvarthssonar* and *Helgakvitha Hundingsbana I*), there is very little left to reflect the Sigurth tradition proper.

Regarding the general development of the story of Sigurth in the North, see the introductory note to the *Gripisspo*.

FAFNISMOL

The so-called *Fafnismol*, contained in full in the *Codex Regius*, where it immediately follows the *Reginsmol* without any indication of a break, is quoted by Snorri in the *Gylfaginning* (stanza 13) and the *Skaldskaparmal* (stanzas 32 and 33), and stanzas 6, 3, and 4 appear in the *Sverrissaga*. Although the *Volsungasaga* does not actually quote any of the stanzas, it gives a very close prose parallel to the whole poem in chapters 18 and 19.

The general character of the *Fafnismol*, and its probable relation to the *Reginsmol* and the *Sigrdrifumol*, have been discussed in the introductory note to the *Reginsmol*. While it is far more nearly a unit than the *Reginsmol*, it shows many of the same characteristics. It has the same mixture of stanza forms, although in this case only nine stanzas (32–33, 35–36 and 40–44) vary from the normal Ljothahattr measure. It shows, though to a much less marked extent, the same tendency to introduce passages from extraneous sources, such as the question-and-answer passage in stanzas 11–15. At the same time, in this instance it is quite clear that one distinct poem, including probably stanzas 1–10, 16–23, 25–31, and 34–39, underlay the compilation which we here have. This may, perhaps, have been a long poem (not, however, the "Long" Sigurth Lay; see introductory note to *Brot af Sigurtharkvithu*) dealing with the Regin-Fafnir-Sigurth-Brynhild story, and including, besides most of the *Fafnismol*, stanzas 1–4 and 6–11 of the *Reginsmol* and part of the so-called *Sigrdrifumol*, together with much that has been lost. The original poem may, on the other hand, have confined itself to the Fafnir episode.

In any case, and while the extant *Fafnismol* can be spoken of as a distinct poem far more justly than the *Reginsmol*, there is still no indication that the compiler regarded it as a poem by itself. His prose notes run on without a break, and the verses simply cover a dramatic episode in Sigurth's early life. The fact that the work of compilation has been done more intelligently than in the case of the *Reginsmol* seems to have resulted chiefly from the compiler's having been familiar with longer consecutive verse passages dealing with the Fafnir episode.

The *Reginsmol* is little more than a clumsy mosaic, but in the *Fafnismol* it is possible to distinguish between the main substance of the poem and the interpolations.

Here, as in the *Reginsmol*, there is very little that bespeaks the German origin of the Sigurth story. Sigurth's winning of the treasure is in itself undoubtedly a part of the earlier southern legend, but the manner in which he does it is thoroughly Norse. Moreover, the concluding section, which points toward the finding of the sleeping Brynhild, relates entirely to the northern Valkyrie, the warrior-maiden punished by Odin, and not at all to the southern Brynhild the daughter of Buthli. The *Fafnismol* is, however, sharply distinguished from the *Reginsmol* by showing no clear traces of the Helgi tradition, although a part of the bird song (stanzas 40–44, in Fornyrthislag form, as distinct from the body of the poem) sounds suspiciously like the bird passage in the beginning of the *Helgakvitha Hjorvarthssonar*. Regarding the general relations of the various sets of traditions in shaping the story of Sigurth, see the introductory note to *Gripisspo*.

The *Fafnismol*, together with a part of the *Sigrdrifumol*, has indirectly become the best known of all the *Eddic* poems, for the reason that Wagner used it, with remarkably little change of outline, as the basis for his "Siegfried."

SIGRDRIFUMOL

The so-called *Sigrdrifumol*, which immediately follows the *Fafnismol* in the *Codex Regius* without any indication of a break, and without separate title, is unquestionably the most chaotic of all the poems in the *Eddic* collection. The end of it has been entirely lost, for the fifth folio of eight sheets is missing from *Regius*, the gap coming after the first line of stanza 29 of this poem. That stanza has been completed, and eight more have been added, from much later paper manuscripts, but even so the conclusion of the poem is in obscurity.

Properly speaking, however, the strange conglomeration of stanzas which the compiler of the collection has left for us, and which, in much the same general form, seems to have lain before the authors of the *Volsungasaga*, in which eighteen of its stanzas are quoted, is not a poem at all. Even its customary title is an absurd error. The mistake made by the annotator in thinking that the epithet "sigrdrifa," rightly applied to Brynhild as a "bringer of victory," was a proper name has already been explained and commented on (note on *Fafnismol*, 44). Even if the collection of stanzas were in any real sense a poem, which it emphatically is not, it is certainly not the "Ballad of Sigrdrifa" which it is commonly called. "Ballad of Brynhild" would be a sufficiently suitable title, and I have here brought the established name "Sigrdrifumol" into accord with this by translating the epithet instead of treating it as a proper name.

Even apart from the title, however, the *Sigrdrifumol* has little claim to be regarded as a distinct poem, nor is there any indication that the compiler did so regard it. Handicapped as we are by the loss of the concluding section, and of the material which followed it on those missing pages, we can yet see that the process which began with the prose *Fra Dautha Sinfjotla*, and which, interrupted by the insertion of the *Gripisspo*, went on through the *Reginsmol* and the *Fafnismol*, continued through as much of the *Sigrdrifumol* as is left to us. In other words, the compiler told the story of Sigurth in mixed prose and verse, using whatever verse he could find without much questioning as to its origin, and filling in the gaps with his own prose. *Fra Dautha Sinfjotla*, *Reginsmol*, *Fafnismol*, and *Sigrdrifumol* are essentially a coherent unit, but one of the compiler's making only; they represent neither one poem nor three distinct poems, and the divisions and titles which have been almost universally adopted by editors are both arbitrary and misleading.

The *Sigrdrifumol* section as we now have it is an extraordinary piece of patchwork. It is most unlikely that the compiler himself brought all these fragments together for the first time; little by little, through a process of accretion and also, unluckily, through one of elimination, the material grew into its present shape. Certainly the basis of it is a poem dealing with the finding of Brynhild by Sigurth, but of this original poem only five stanzas (2–4 and 20–21) can be identified with any degree of confidence. To these five stanzas should probably, however, be added some, if not all, of the passage (stanzas 6–12) in which Brynhild teaches Sigurth the magic runes. These stanzas of rune-lore attracted sundry similar passages from other sources, including stanza 5, in which a magic draught is administered (not necessarily by Brynhild or to Sigurth), the curious rune-chant in stanzas 15–17, and stanzas 13–14 and 18–19. Beginning with stanza 22, and running to the end of the fragment (stanza 37), is a set of numbered counsels closely resembling the *Loddfafnismol* (*Hovamol*, stanzas 111–138), which manifestly has nothing whatever to do with Brynhild. Even in this passage there are probably interpolations (stanzas 25, 27, 30, 34, and 36). Finally, and bespeaking the existence at some earlier time of another Sigurth-Brynhild poem, is stanza 1, sharply distinguished by its metrical form from stanzas 2–4 and 20–21. Many critics argue that stanzas 6–10 of *Helreith Brynildar* belonged originally to the same poem as stanza 1 of the *Sigrdrifumol*.

The *Sigrdrifumol*, then, must be regarded simply as a collection of fragments, most of them originally having no relation to the main subject. All of the story, the dialogue and the characterization are embodied in stanzas 1–4 and 20–21 and in the prose notes accompanying the first four stanzas; all of the rest might equally well (or better) be transferred to the *Hovamol*, where its character entitles it to a place. Yet stanzas 2–4 are as fine as anything in Old Norse poetry, and it is out of the scanty material of these three stanzas that Wagner constructed much of the third act of "Siegfried."

The *Sigrdrifumol* represents almost exclusively the contributions of the North to the Sigurth tradition (cf. introductory note to the *Gripisspo*). Brynhild, here disguised by the annotator as "Sigrdrifa," appears simply as a battle-maid and supernatural dispenser of wisdom; there is no trace of the daughter of Buthli and the rival of Guthrun. There is, however, so little of the "poem" which can definitely be assigned to the Sigurth cycle that it is impossible to trace back any of the underlying narrative substance.

The nature and condition of the material have made editorial conjectures and emendations very numerous, and as most of the guesses are neither conclusive nor particularly important, only a few of them are mentioned in the notes.

BROT AF SIGURTHARKVITHU

The gap of eight leaves in the *Codex Regius* (cf. introductory note to the *Sigrdrifumol*) is followed by a passage of twenty stanzas which is evidently the end of a longer poem, the greater part of it having been contained in the lost section of the manuscript. There is here little question of such a compilation as made up the so-called *Reginsmol*, *Fafnismol*, and *Sigrdrifumol*; the extant fragment shows every sign of being part of a poem which, as it stood in the manuscript, was a complete and definite unit. The end is clearly marked; the following poem, *Guthrunarkvitha I*, carries a specific heading in the manuscript, so that there is no uncertainty as to where the fragment closes.

It seems altogether likely that the twenty stanzas thus remaining are the end of a poem entitled *Sigurtharkvitha* (Lay of Sigurth), and, more specifically, the "Long" Lay of Sigurth. The extant and complete Sigurth lay, a relatively late work, is referred to by the annotator as the "Short" Lay of Sigurth, which, of course, presupposes the existence of a longer poem with the same title. As the "short" lay is one of the longest poems in the whole collection (seventy stanzas), it follows that the other one must have been considerably more extensive in order to have been thus distinguished by its length. It may be guessed, then, that not less than eighty or a hundred stanzas, and possibly more, of the "Long" Lay of Sigurth have been lost with the missing pages of *Regius*.

The narrative, from the point at which the so-called *Sigrdrifumol* breaks off to that at which the *Brot* takes it up, is given with considerable detail in the *Volsungasaga*. In this prose narrative four stanzas are quoted, and one of them is specifically introduced with the phrase: "as is told in the Lay of Sigurth." It is possible, but most unlikely, that the entire passage paraphrases this poem alone; such an assumption would give the Lay of Sigurth not less than two hundred and fifty stanzas (allowing about fifteen stanzas to each of the missing pages), and moreover there are inconsistencies in the *Volsungasaga* narrative suggesting that different and more or less conflicting poems were used as sources. The chances are that the "Long" Lay of Sigurth filled approximately the latter half of the lost section of the manuscript, the first half including poems of which the only trace is to be found in the *Volsungasaga* prose paraphrase and in two of the stanzas therein quoted.

The course of the *Volsungasaga's* story from the *Sigrdrifumol* to the *Brot* is, briefly, as follows. After leaving the Valkyrie, Sigurth comes to the dwelling of Heimir, Brynhild's brother-in-law, where he meets Brynhild and they swear oaths of fidelity anew (the *Volsungasaga* is no more lucid with regard to the Brynhild-Sigrdrifa confusion than was the annotator of the poems). Then the scene shifts to the home of the Gjukungs. Guthrun, Gjuki's daughter, has a terrifying dream, and visits Brynhild to have it explained, which the latter does by foretelling pretty much everything that is going to happen; this episode was presumably the subject of a separate poem in the lost section of the manuscript. Guthrun returns home, and Sigurth soon arrives, to be made enthusiastically welcome. Grimhild, mother of Gunnar and Guthrun, gives him a magic draught which makes him forget all about Brynhild, and shortly thereafter he marries Guthrun.

Then follows the episode of the winning of Brynhild for Gunnar (cf. *Gripisspo*, 37 and note). This was certainly the subject of a poem, possibly of the first part of the "Long" Lay of Sigurth, although it seems more likely that the episode was dealt with in a separate poem. The *Volsungasaga* quotes two stanzas describing Sigurth's triumphant passing through the flames after Gunnar has failed and the two have changed forms. They run thus:

> The fire raged, the earth was rocked.
> The flames leaped high to heaven itself;
> Few were the hardy heroes would dare
> To ride or leap the raging flames.
>
> Sigurth urged Grani then with his sword,
> The fire slackened before the hero,
> The flames sank low for the greedy of fame,
> The armor flashed that Regin had fashioned.

After Sigurth has spent three nights with Brynhild, laying his sword between them (cf. *Gripisspo*, 41 and note), he and Gunnar return home, while Brynhild goes to the dwelling of her brother-in-law, Heimir, and makes ready for her marriage with Gunnar, directing Heimir to care for her daughter by Sigurth, Aslaug. The wedding takes place, to be followed soon after by the quarrel between Guthrun and Brynhild, in which the former betrays the fact that it was Sigurth, and not Gunnar, who rode through the flames. Brynhild speaks with contempt of Guthrun and her whole family, and the following stanza, which presumably belongs to the same Sigurth lay as the *Brot*, is quoted at this point:

> Sigurth the dragon slew, and that
> Will men recall while the world remains;
> But little boldness thy brother had
> To ride or leap the raging flames.

Gunnar and Sigurth alike try to appease the angry Brynhild, but in vain. After Sigurth has talked with her, his leaving her hall is described in the following stanza, introduced by the specific phrase: "as is said in the Lay of Sigurth":

> Forth went Sigurth, and speech he sought not,
> The friend of heroes, his head bowed down;
> Such was his grief that asunder burst
> His mail-coat all of iron wrought.

Brynhild then tells Gunnar that she had given herself wholly to Sigurth before she had become Gunnar's wife (the confusion between the two stories is commented on in the note to Gripisspo, 47), and Gunnar discusses plans of vengance with his brother, Hogni. It is at this point that the action of the Brot begins.

Beginning with this poem, and thence to the end of the cycle, the German features of the narrative predominate (cf. introductory note to Gripisspo).

GUTHRUNARKVITHA I

The *First Lay of Guthrun*, entitled in the *Codex Regius* simply *Guthrunarkvitha*, immediately follows the remaining fragment of the "long" Sigurth lay in that manuscript. Unlike the poems dealing with the earlier part of the Sigurth cycle, the so-called *Reginsmol*, *Fafnismol*, and *Sigrdrifumol*, it is a clear and distinct unit, apparently complete and with few and minor interpolations. It is also one of the finest poems in the entire collection, with an extraordinary emotional intensity and dramatic force. None of its stanzas are quoted elsewhere, and It is altogether probable that the compilers of the *Volsungasaga* were unfamiliar with It, for they do not mention the sister and daughter of Gjuki who appear in this poem, or Herborg, "queen of the Huns" (stanza 6).

The lament of Guthrun (Kriemhild) is almost certainly among the oldest parts of the story. The lament was one of the earliest forms of poetry to develop among the Germanic peoples, and I suspect, though the matter is not susceptible of proof, that the lament of Sigurth's wife had assumed lyric form as early as the seventh century, and reached the North in that shape rather than in prose tradition (cf. *Guthrunarkvitha II*, introductory note). We find traces of it in the seventeenth Aventiure of the *Nibelungenlied*, and in the poems of the *Edda* it dominates every appearance of Guthrun. The two first Guthrun lays (I and II) are both laments, one for Sigurth's death and the other including both that and the lament over the slaying of her brothers; the lament theme is apparent in the third Guthrun lay and in the *Guthrunarhvot*.

In their present forms the second Guthrun lay is undoubtedly older than the first; in the prose following the *Brot* the annotator refers to the "old" Guthrun lay in terms which can apply only to the second one in the collection. The shorter and "first" lay, therefore, can scarcely have been composed much before the year 1000, and may be somewhat later. The poet appears to have known and made use of the older lament; stanza 17, for example, is a close parallel to stanza 2 of the earlier poem; but whatever material he used he fitted into a definite poetic scheme of his own. And while this particular poem is, as critics have generally agreed, one of the latest of the collection, it probably represents one of the earliest parts of the entire Sigurth cycle to take on verse form.

Guthrunarkvitha I, so far as the narrative underlying it is concerned, shows very little northern addition to the basic German tradition. Brynhild appears only as Guthrun's enemy and the cause of Sigurth's death; the three women who attempt to comfort Guthrun, though unknown to the southern stories, seem to have been rather distinct creations of the poet's than traditional additions to the legend. Regarding the relations of the various elements in the Sigurth cycle, cf. introductory note to *Gripisspo*.

SIGURTHARKVITHA EN SKAMMA

Guthrunarkvitha I is immediately followed in the *Codex Regius* by a long poem which in the manuscript bears the heading "Sigurtharkvitha," but which is clearly referred to in the prose link between it and *Guthrunarkvitha I* as the "short" Lay of Sigurth. The discrepancy between this reference and the obvious length of the poem has led to many conjectures, but the explanation seems to be that the "long" Sigurth lay, of which the *Brot* is presumably a part, was materially longer even than this poem. The efforts to reduce the "short" Sigurth lay to dimensions which would justify the appellation in comparison with other poems in the collection, either by separating it into two poems or by the rejection of many stanzas as interpolations, have been utterly inconclusive.

Although there are probably several interpolated passages, and indications of omissions are not lacking, the poem as we now have it seems to be a distinct and coherent unit. From the narrative point of view it leaves a good deal to be desired, for the reason that the poet's object was by no means to tell a story, with which his hearers were quite familiar, but to use the narrative simply as the background for vivid and powerful characterization. The lyric element, as Mogk points out, overshadows the epic throughout, and the fact that there are frequent confusions of narrative tradition does not trouble the poet at all.

The material on which the poem was based seems to have existed in both prose and verse form; the poet was almost certainly familiar with some of the other poems in the *Eddic* collection, with poems which have since been lost, and with the narrative prose traditions which never fully assumed verse form. The fact that he seems to have known and used the *Oddrunargratr*, which can hardly have been composed before 1050, and that in any case he introduces the figure of Oddrun, a relatively late addition to the story, dates the poem as late as the end of the eleventh century, or even the first half of the twelfth. There has been much discussion as to where it was composed, the debate centering chiefly on the reference to glaciers (stanza 8). There is something to be said in favor of Greenland as the original home of the poem (cf. introductory note to *Atlakvitha*), but the arguments for Iceland are even stronger; Norway in this case is practically out of the question.

The narrative features of the poem are based on the German rather than the Norse elements of the story (cf. introductory note to *Gripisspo*), but the poet has taken whatever material he wanted without much discrimination as to its source. By the year 1100 the story of Sigurth, with its allied legends, existed throughout the North in many and varied forms, and the poem shows traces of variants of the main story which do not appear elsewhere.

HELREITH BRYNHILDAR

The little *Helreith Brynhildar* immediately follows the "short" Sigurth lay in the *Codex Regius*, being linked to it by the brief prose note; the heading, "Brynhild's Ride on Hel-Way," stands just before the first stanza. The entire poem, with the exception of stanza 6, is likewise quoted in the *Nornageststhattr*. Outside of one stanza (No. 11), which is a fairly obvious interpolation, the poem possesses an extraordinary degree of dramatic unity, and, certain pedantic commentators notwithstanding, it is one of the most vivid and powerful in the whole collection. None the less, it has been extensively argued that parts of it belonged originally to the so-called *Sigrdrifumol*. That it stands in close relation to this poem is evident enough, but it is difficult to believe that such a masterpiece of dramatic poetry was ever the result of mere compilation. It seems more reasonable to regard the *Helreith*, with the exception of stanza 11 and allowing for the loss of two lines from stanza 6, as a complete and carefully constructed unit, based undoubtedly on older poems, but none the less an artistic creation in itself.

The poem is generally dated as late as the eleventh century, and the concluding stanza betrays Christian influence almost unmistakably. It shows the confusion of traditions manifest in all the later poems; for example, Brynhild is here not only a Valkyrie but also a swan-maiden. Only three stanzas have any reference to the Guthrun-Gunnar part of the story; otherwise the poem is concerned solely with the episode of Sigurth's finding the sleeping Valkyrie. Late as it is, therefore, it is essentially a Norse creation, involving very few of the details of the German cycle (cf. introductory note to *Gripisspo*).

DRAP NIFLUNGA

It has been already pointed out (introductory note to *Reginsmol*) that the compiler of the *Eddic* collection had clearly undertaken to formulate a coherent narrative of the entire Sigurth cycle, piecing together the various poems by means of prose narrative links. To some extent these links were based on traditions existing outside of the lays themselves, but in the main the material was gathered from the contents of the poems. The short prose passage entitled *Drap Niflunga*, which in the *Codex Regius* immediately follows the *Helreith Brynhildar*, is just such a narrative link, and scarcely deserves a special heading, but as nearly all editions separate it from the preceding and following poems, I have followed their example.

With Sigurth and Brynhild both dead, the story turns to the slaying of the sons of Gjuki by Atli, Guthrun's second husband, and to a few subsequent incidents, mostly late incorporations from other narrative cycles, including the tragic death of Svanhild, daughter of Sigurth and Guthrun and wife of Jormunrek (Ermanarich), and the exploits of Hamther, son of Guthrun and her third husband, Jonak. These stories are told, or outlined, in the two Atli lays, the second and third Guthrun lays, the *Oddrunargratr*, the *Guthrunarhvot*, and the *Hamthesmol*. Had the compiler seen fit to put the Atli lays immediately after the *Helreith Brynhildar*, he would have needed only a very brief transitional note to make the course of the story clear, but as the second Guthrun lay, the next poem in the collection, is a lament following the death of Guthrun's brothers, some sort of a narrative bridge was manifestly needed.

Drap Niflunga is based entirely on the poems which follow it in the collection, with no use of extraneous material. The part of the story which it summarizes belongs to the semi-historical Burgundian tradition (cf. introductory note to *Gripisspo*), in many respects parallel to the familiar narrative of the *Nibelungenlied*, and, except in minor details, showing few essentially Northern additions. Sigurth is scarcely mentioned, and the outstanding episode is the slaying of Gunnar and Hogni, following their journey to Atli's home.

GUTHRUNARKVITHA EN FORNA

It has already been pointed out (introductory note to *Guthrunarkvitha I*) that the tradition of Guthrun's lament was known wherever the Sigurth story existed, and that this lament was probably one of the earliest parts of the legend to assume verse form. Whether it reached the North as verse cannot, of course, be determined, but it is at least possible that this was the case, and in any event it is clear that by the tenth and eleventh centuries there were a number of Norse poems with Guthrun's lament as the central theme. Two of these are included in the *Eddic* collection, the second one being unquestionably much the older. It is evidently the poem referred to by the annotator in the prose note following the *Brot* as "the old Guthrun lay," and its character and state of preservation have combined to lead most commentators to date it as early as the first half of the tenth century, whereas *Guthrunarkvitha I* belongs a hundred years later.

The poem has evidently been preserved in rather bad shape, with a number of serious omissions and some interpolations, but in just this form it lay before the compilers of the *Volsungasaga*, who paraphrased it faithfully, and quoted five of its stanzas. The interpolations are on the whole unimportant; the omissions, while they obscure the sense of certain passages, do not destroy the essential continuity of the poem, in which Guthrun reviews her sorrows from the death of Sigurth through the slaying of her brothers to Atli's dreams foretelling the death of their sons. It is, indeed, the only Norse poem of the Sigurth cycle antedating the year 1000 which has come down to us in anything approaching complete form; the *Reginsmol*, *Fafnismol*, and *Sigrdrifumol* are all collections of fragments, only a short bit of the "long" Sigurth lay remains, and the others—*Gripisspo*, *Guthrunarkvitha I* and *III*, *Sigurtharkvitha en skamma*, *Helreith Brynhildar*, *Oddrunargratr*, *Guthrunarhvot*, *Hamthesmol*, and the two Atli lays—are all generally dated from the eleventh and even the twelfth centuries.

An added reason for believing that *Guthrunarkvitha II* traces its origin back to a lament which reached the North from Germany in verse form is the absence of most of the characteristic Norse additions to the narrative, except in minor details. Sigurth is slain in the forest, as "German men say" (cf. *Brot*, concluding prose); the urging of Guthrun by her mother and brothers to become Atli's wife, the slaying of the Gjukungs (here only intimated, for at that point something seems to have been lost), and Guthrun's prospective revenge on Atli, all belong directly to the German tradition (cf. introductory note to *Gripisspo*).

In the *Codex Regius* the poem is entitled simply *Guthrunarkvitha*; the numeral has been added in nearly all editions to distinguish this poem from the other two Guthrun lays, and the phrase "the old" is borrowed from the annotator's comment in the prose note at the end of the *Brot*.

GUTHRUNARKVITHA III

The short *Guthrunarkvitha III*, entitled in the manuscript simply *Guthrunarkvitha*, but so numbered in most editions to distinguish it from the first and second Guthrun lays, appears only in the *Codex Regius*. It is neither quoted nor paraphrased in the *Volsungasaga*, the compilers of which appear not to have known the story with which it deals. The poem as we have it is evidently complete and free from serious interpolations. It can safely be dated from the first half of the eleventh century, for the ordeal by boiling water, with which it is chiefly concerned, was first introduced into Norway by St. Olaf, who died in 1030, and the poem speaks of it in stanza 7 as still of foreign origin.

The material for the poem evidently came from North Germany, but there is little indication that the poet was working on the basis of a narrative legend already fully formed. The story of the wife accused of faithlessness who proves her innocence by the test of boiling water had long been current in Germany, as elsewhere, and had attached itself to various women of legendary fame, but not except in this poem, so far as we can judge, to Guthrun (Kriemhild). The introduction of Thjothrek (Theoderich, Dietrich, Thithrek) is another indication of relative lateness, for the legends of Theoderich do not appear to have reached the North materially before the year 1000. On the anachronism of bringing Thjothrek to Atli's court cf. *Guthrunarkvitha II*, introductory prose note, in which the development of the Theoderich tradition in its relation to that of Atli is briefly outlined.

Guthrunarkvitha III is, then, little more than a dramatic German story made into a narrative lay by a Norse poet, with the names of Guthrun, Atli, Thjothrek, and Herkja incorporated for the sake of greater effectiveness. Its story probably nowhere formed a part of the living tradition of Sigurth and Atli, but the poem has so little distinctively Norse coloring that it may possibly have been based on a story or even a poem which its composer heard in Germany or from the lips of a German narrator.

ODDRUNARGRATR

The *Oddrunargratr* follows *Guthrunarkvitha III* in the *Codex Regius*; it is not quoted or mentioned elsewhere, except that the composer of the "short" Sigurth lay seems to have been familiar with it. The *Volsungasaga* says nothing of the story on which it is based, and mentions Oddrun only once, in the course of its paraphrase of Brynhild's prophecy from the "short" Sigurth lay. That the poem comes from the eleventh century is generally agreed; prior to the year 1000 there is no trace of the figure of Oddrun, Atli's sister, and yet the *Oddrunargratr* is almost certainly older than the "short" Sigurth lay, so that the last half of the eleventh century seems to be a fairly safe guess.

Where or how the figure of Oddrun entered the Sigurth-Atli cycle is uncertain. She does not appear in any of the extant German versions, and it is generally assumed that she was a creation of the North, though the poet refers to "old tales" concerning her. She does not directly affect the course of the story at all, though the poet has used effectively the episode of Gunnar's death, with the implication that Atli's vengeance on Gunnar and Hogni was due, at least in part, to his discovery of Gunnar's love affair with Oddrun. The material which forms the background of Oddrun's story belongs wholly to the German part of the legend (cf. introductory note to *Gripisspo*), and is paralleled with considerable closeness in the *Nibelungenlied*; only Oddrun herself and the subsidiary figures of Borgny and Vilmund are Northern additions. The geography, on the other hand, is so utterly chaotic as to indicate that the original localization of the Atli story had lost all trace of significance by the time this poem was composed.

In the manuscript the poem, or rather the brief introductory prose note, bears the heading "Of Borgny and Oddrun," but nearly all editions, following late paper manuscripts, have given the poem the title it bears here. Outside of a few apparently defective stanzas, and some confusing transpositions, the poem has clearly been preserved in good condition, and the beginning and end are definitely marked.

ATLAKVITHA EN GRÖNLENZKA

There are two Atli poems in the *Codex Regius*, the *Atlakvitha* (*Lay of Atli*) and the *Atlamol* (*Ballad of Atli*). The poems are not preserved or quoted in any other old manuscript, but they were extensively used by the compilers of the *Volsungasaga*. In the manuscript superscription to each of these poems appears the word "Greenland," which has given rise to a large amount of argument. The scribe was by no means infallible, and in this case his statement proves no more than that in the period round 1300 there was a tradition that these two poems originated in the Greenland settlement.

The two Atli poems deal with substantially the same material: the visit of the sons of Gjuki to Atli's court, their deaths, and the subsequent revenge of their sister, Guthrun, Atli's wife, on her husband. The shorter of the two, the *Atlakvitha*, tells the story with little elaboration; the *Atlamol*, with about the same narrative basis, adds many details, some of them apparently of the poet's invention, and with a romantic, not to say sentimental, quality quite lacking in the *Atlakvitha*. Both poems are sharply distinguished from the rest of the collection by their metrical form, which is the Malahattr (used irregularly also in the *Harbarthsljoth*), employed consistently and smoothly in the *Atlamol*, and with a considerable mixture of what appear to be Fornyrthislag lines (cf. Introduction) in the *Atlakvitha*.

It is altogether probable that both poems belong to the eleventh century, the shorter *Atlakvitha* being generally dated from the first quarter thereof, and the longer *Atlamol* some fifty years or more later. In each case the poet was apparently a Christian; in the *Atlamol* (stanza 82) Guthrun expresses her readiness to die and "go into another light," and in the *Atlakvitha* there is frequent use of mythological names (e.g., Valhall, Hlithskjolf) with an evident lack of understanding of their relation to the older gods. These facts fit the theory of a Greenland origin exceedingly well, for the Greenland settlement grew rapidly after the first explorations of Eirik the Red, which were in 982–985, and its most flourishing period was in the eleventh century. The internal evidence, particularly in the case of the *Atlamol*, points likewise to an origin remote from Iceland, Norway, and the "Western Isles"; and the two poems are sufficiently alike so that, despite the efforts of Finnur Jonsson and others to separate them, assigning one to Greenland and the other to Norway or elsewhere, it seems probable that the manuscript statement is correct in both instances, and that the two Atli poems did actually originate in Greenland. An interesting account of this Greenland settlement is given in William Hovgaard's *Voyages of the Norsemen to America*, published by the American-Scandinavian Foundation in 1914, and an extraordinarily vivid picture of the sufferings of the early settlers appears in Maurice Hewlett's *Thorgils*, taken from the *Floamannasaga*.

From the standpoint of narrative material there is little that is distinctively Norse in either the *Atlakvitha* or the *Atlamol*. The story is the one outlined in the prose *Drap Niflunga* (largely based on these two poems), representing almost exclusively the southern blending of the Attila and Burgundian legends (cf. introductory note to *Gripisspo*). In the *Atlakvitha*, indeed, the word "Burgundians" is actually used. Brynhild is not mentioned in either poem; Sigurth's name appears but once, in the *Atlamol*. Thus the material goes directly back to its South-Germanic origins, with little of the Northern making-over which resulted in such extensive changes in most parts of the Sigurth story. The general atmosphere, on the other hand, particularly in the *Atlamol*, is essentially Norse.

As has been said, the *Atlakvitha* is metrically in a chaotic state, the normal Malahattr lines being frequently interspersed with lines and even stanzas which apparently are of the older Fornyrthislag type. How much of this confusion is due to faulty transmission is uncertain, but it has been suggested that the composer of the *Atlakvitha* made over in Malahattr an older Atli poem in Fornyrthislag, and this suggestion has much to recommend it. That he worked on the basis of an older poem is, indeed, almost certain, for in oral prose tradition a far larger number of distinctively Norse traits would unquestionably have crept in than are found in the material of the *Atlakvitha*. As for the *Atlamol*, here again the poet seems to have used an older poem as his basis, possibly the *Atlakvitha* itself, although in that case he must have had other material as well, for there are frequent divergences in such matters as proper names.

The translation of the *Atlakvitha* is rendered peculiarly difficult by the irregularity of the metre, by the evident faultiness of the transmission, and above all by the exceptionally large number of words found nowhere else in Old Norse, involving much guesswork as to their meanings. The notes do not attempt to indicate all the varying suggestions made by editors and commentators as to the reconstruction of defective stanzas and the probable meanings of obscure passages; in cases which are purely or largely guesswork the notes merely point out the uncertainty without cataloguing the proposed solutions.

ATLAMOL EN GRÖNLENZKU

Many of the chief facts regarding the *Atlamol*, which follows the *Atlakvitha* in the *Codex Regius*, are outlined in the introductory note to the earlier Atli lay. That the superscription in the manuscript is correct, and that the poem was actually composed in Greenland, is generally accepted; the specific reference to polar bears (stanza 17), and the general color of the entire poem make this origin exceedingly likely. Most critics, again, agree in dating the poem nearer 1100 than 1050. As to its state of preservation there is some dispute, but, barring one or two possible gaps of some importance, and the usual number of passages in which the interpolation or omission of one or two lines may be suspected, the *Atlamol* has clearly come down to us in fairly good shape.

Throughout the poem the epic quality of the story itself is overshadowed by the romantically sentimental tendencies of the poet, and by his desire to adapt the narrative to the understanding of his fellow-Greenlanders. The substance of the poem is the same as that of the *Atlakvitha*; it tells of Atli's message to the sons of Gjuki, their journey to Atli's home, the slaying of Hogni and Gunnar, Guthrun's bitterness over the death of her brothers, and her bloody revenge on Atli. Thus in its bare outline the *Atlamol* represents simply the Frankish blending of the legends of the slaughter of the Burgundians and the death of Attila (cf. *Gripisspo*, introductory note). But here the resemblance ends. The poet has added characters, apparently of his own creation, for the sake of episodes which would appeal to both the men and the women of the Greenland settlement. Sea voyages take the place of journeys by land; Atli is reproached, not for cowardice in battle, but for weakness at the Thing or great council. The additions made by the poet are responsible for the *Atlamol's* being the longest of all the heroic poems in the *Eddic* collection, and they give it a kind of emotional vividness, but it has little of the compressed intensity of the older poems. Its greatest interest lies in its demonstration of the manner in which a story brought to the North from the South Germanic lands could be adapted to the understanding and tastes of its eleventh century hearers without any material change of the basic narrative.

In what form or forms the story of the Gjukungs and Atli reached the Greenland poet cannot be determined, but it seems likely that he was familiar with older poems on the subject, and possibly with the *Atlakvitha* itself. That the details which are peculiar to the *Atlamol*, such as the figures of Kostbera and Glaumvor, existed in earlier tradition seems doubtful, but the son of Hogni, who aids Guthrun in the slaying of Atli, appears, though under another name, in other late versions of the story, and it is impossible to say just how much the poet relied on his own imagination and how far he found suggestions and hints in the prose or verse stories of Atli with which he was familiar.

The poem is in Malahattr (cf. Introduction) throughout, the verse being far more regular than in the *Atlakvitha*. The compilers of the *Volsungasaga* evidently knew it in very much the form in which we now have it, for in the main it is paraphrased with great fidelity.

GUTHRUNARHVOT

The two concluding poems in the *Codex Regius*, the *Guthrunarhvot* (Guthrun's Inciting) and the *Hamthesmol* (*The Ballad of Hamther*), belong to a narrative cycle connected with those of Sigurth, the Burgundians, and Atli (cf. *Gripisspo*, introductory note) by only the slenderest of threads. Of the three early historical kings who gradually assumed a dominant place in Germanic legend, Ermanarich, king of the East Goths in the middle of the fourth century, was actually the least important, even though Jordanes, the sixth century author of *De Rebus Getecis*, compared him to Alexander the Great. Memories of his cruelty and of his tragic death, however, persisted along with the real glories of Theoderich, a century and a half later, and of the conquests of Attila, whose lifetime approximately bridged the gap between Ermanarich's death and Theoderich's birth.

Chief among the popular tales of Ermanarich's cruelty was one concerning the death of a certain Sunilda or Sanielh, whom, according to Jordanes, he caused to be torn asunder by wild horses because of her husband's treachery. Her brothers, Sarus and Ammius, seeking to avenge her, wounded but failed to kill Ermanarich. In this story is the root of the two Norse poems included in the *Codex Regius*. Sunilda easily became the wife as well as the victim of the tyrant, and, by the process of legend-blending so frequently observed, the story was connected with the more famous one of the Nibelungs by making her the daughter of Sigurth and Guthrun. To account for her brothers, a third husband had to be found for Guthrun; the Sarus and Ammius of Jordanes are obviously the Sorli and Hamther, sons of Guthrun and Jonak, of the Norse poems. The blending of the Sigurth and Ermanarich legends probably, though not certainly, took place before the story reached the North, in other words before the end of the eighth century.

Regarding the exact status of the *Guthrunarhvot* and the *Hamthesmol* there has been a great deal of discussion. That they are closely related is obvious; indeed the first parts of the two poems are nearly identical in content and occasionally so in actual diction. The annotator, in his concluding prose note, refers to the second poem as the "old" ballad of Hamther, wherefore it has been assumed by some critics that the composer of the *Guthrunarhvot* used the *Hamthesmol*, approximately as it now stands, as the source of part of his material. The extant *Hamthesmol*, however, is almost certainly a patchwork; part of it is in Fornyrthislag (cf. Introduction), including most of the stanzas paralleled in the *Guthrunarhvot*, and likewise the stanza followed directly by the reference to the "old" ballad, while the rest is in Malahattr. The most reasonable theory, therefore, is that there existed an old ballad of Hamther, all in Fornyrthislag, from which the composer of the *Guthrunarhvot* borrowed a few stanzas as the introduction for his poem, and which the composer of the extant, or "new," *Hamthesmol* likewise used, though far more clumsily.

The title "Guthrunarhvot," which appears in the *Codex Regius*, really applies only to stanzas 1–8, all presumably borrowed from the "old" ballad of Hamther. The rest of the poem is simply another Guthrun lament, following the tradition exemplified by the first and second Guthrun lays; it is possible, indeed, that it is made up of fragments of two separate laments, one (stanzas 9–18) involving the story of Svanhild's death, and the other (stanzas 19–21) coming from an otherwise lost version of the story in which Guthrun closely follows Sigurth and Brynhild in death. In any event the present title is really a misnomer; the poet, who presumably was an eleventh century Icelander, used the episode of Guthrun's inciting her sons to vengeance for the slaying of Svanhild simply as an introduction to his main subject, the last lament of the unhappy queen.

The text of the poem in *Regius* is by no means in good shape, and editorial emendations have been many and varied, particularly in interchanging lines between the *Guthrunarhvot* and the *Hamthesmol*. The *Volsungasaga* paraphrases the poem with such fidelity as to prove that it lay before the compilers of the saga approximately in its present form.

HAMTHESMOL

The *Hamthesmol*, the concluding poem in the *Codex Regius*, is on the whole the worst preserved of all the poems in the collection. The origin of the story, the relation of the *Hamthesmol* to the *Guthrunarhvot*, and of both poems to the hypothetical "old" *Hamthesmol*, are outlined in the introductory note to the *Guthrunarhvot*. The *Hamthesmol* as we have it is certainly not the "old" poem of that name; indeed it is so pronounced a patchwork that it can hardly be regarded as a coherent poem at all. Some of the stanzas are in Fornyrthislag, some are in Malahattr, one (stanza 29) appears to be in Ljothahattr, and in many cases the words can be adapted to any known metrical form only by liberal emendation. That anyone should have deliberately composed such a poem seems quite incredible, and it is far more likely that some eleventh century narrator constructed a poem about the death of Hamther and Sorli by piecing together various fragments, and possibly adding a number of Malahattr stanzas of his own.

It has been argued, and with apparently sound logic, that our extant *Hamthesmol* originated in Greenland, along with the *Atlamol*. In any case, it can hardly have been put together before the latter part of the eleventh century, although the "old" *Hamthesmol* undoubtedly long antedates this period. Many editors have attempted to pick out the parts of the extant poem which were borrowed from this older lay, but the condition of the text is such that it is by no means clear even what stanzas are in Fornyrthislag and what in Malahattr. Many editors, likewise, indicate gaps and omissions, but it seems doubtful whether the extant *Hamthesmol* ever had a really consecutive quality, its component fragments having apparently been strung together with little regard for continuity. The notes indicate some of the more important editorial suggestions, but make no attempt to cover all of them, and the metrical form of the translation is often based on mere guesswork as to the character of the original lines and stanzas. Despite the chaotic state of the text, however, the underlying narrative is reasonably clear, and the story can be followed with no great difficulty.

GLOSSARY OF OBSCURE AND ARCHAIC TERMS

Bale — Great evil, sorrow (*n.*)

Bale-fire — Funeral pyre, open-air fire (*n.*)

Bane — Killer (*n.*)

Bast rope — Rope made from the inner barnk of the lime tree (*n.*)

Blithe — Happy, carefree (*adj.*)

Bower — A lady's private apartment in a hall or castle (*n.*)

Byrnie — Coat of mail (*n.*)

Churl — The lowest rank of freeman (*n.*)

Doom — Fate, destiny (*n.*)

Ere — Before (*adv.*)

Fain — Gladly (*adv.*); willing, compelled (*adj.*)

Fane — Temple, shrine (*n.*)

Fosterling — Foster child (*n.*)

Geld — Castrate, neuter (*v.*)

Haft — Handle of a weapon (*n.*)

Hale — Strong, healthy (*adj.*)

Hart — Stag, buck; male deer (*n.*)

Hoary — Gray or white with age, ancient (*adj.*)

Jarl — Earl, nobleman (*n.*)

Leek — Spear, as in a weapon but also a "spear" of grass (n.)

Meed — Reward, recompense (*n.*)

Prithee — If you please, I pray you (*interj.*)

Quern — Hand-operated mill (*n.*)

Rede — Counsel, advise (*v.*)

Restive — Stubborn, restless (*adj.*)

Skald — Nordic poet (*n.*)

Southron — Southerner, man of the south (*n.*)

Switch — Branch, often a whip or lash (*n.*)

Tawny — Tan, yellow- or orange-brown (*adj.*)

Thane — Variously defined noble rank—chief of a clan; feudal lord; retainer to a king (*n.*)

Thing — The governing assembly in Germanic societies; parliament (*n.*)

Thrall — Slave (n.)

Tint — Paint (*v.*)

Troth — Faith, loyalty; pledge (*n.*)

Twain — Two (*n/adj.*)

Wanes — Vanir (*n.*)

Warder — Guardian; watchman (*n.*)

Ween — Think, suppose; believe (*v.*)

Wend — Go, travel (*v.*)

Wert — Were (*subjunctive past tense of "to be"*)

Wight — Creature; spirit, elf, or ancestor (*v.*)

PRONUNCIATION INDEX

The pronunciations indicated in the following index are in many cases, at best, mere approximations, and in some cases the pronunciation of the Old Norse is itself more or less conjectural. For the sake of clarity it has seemed advisable to keep the number of phonetic symbols as small as possible, even though the result is occasional failure to distinguish between closely related sounds. In every instance the object has been to provide the reader with a clearly comprehensible and approximately correct pronunciation, for which reason, particularly in such matters as division of syllables, etymology has frequently been disregarded for the sake of phonetic clearness. For example, when a root syllable ends in a long (double) consonant, the division has arbitrarily been made so as to indicate the sounding of both elements (e.g., Am-ma, not Amm-a).

As many proper names occur in the notes but not in the text, and as frequently the more important incidents connected with the names are outlined in notes which would not be indicated by textual references alone, the page numbers include all appearances of proper names in the notes as well as in the text.

The following general rules govern the application of the phonetic symbols used in the index, and also indicate the approximate pronunciation of the unmarked vowels and consonants.

VOWELS. The vowels are pronounced approximately as follows:

a - as in "alone"
ā - as in "father"
e - as in "men"
ē - as a in "fate"
i - as in "is"
ī - as in "machine"
o - as in "on"
ō - as in "old"
ö - as in German "öffnen"
ő - as in German "schön"
ǫ - as in in "law"

u - as *ou* in "would"
ū - as *ou* in "wound"
y - as *i* in "is"
ȳ - as *ee* in "free"
æ - as *e* in "men"
ǽ - as *a* in "fate"
ei - as *ey* in "they"
ey - as in "they"
au - as *ou* in "out"
ai - as *i* in "fine"

No attempt has been made to differentiate between the short open "o" and the short closed "o," which for speakers of English closely resemble one another.

CONSONANTS. The consonants are pronounced approximately as in English, with the following special points to be noted:

G is always hard, as in "get," never soft, as in "gem;" following "n" it has the same sound as in "sing."

J is pronounced as y in "young."

Th following a vowel is soft, as in "with;" at the beginning of a word or following a consonant it is hard, as in "thin."

The long (doubled) consonants should be pronounced as in Italian, both elements being distinctly sounded; e.g., "Am-ma."

S is always hard, as in "so," "this," never soft, as in "as."

H enters into combinations with various following consonants; with "v" the sound is approximately that of wh in "what"; with "l," "r" and "n" it produces sounds which have no exact English equivalents, but which can be approximated by pronouncing the consonants with a marked initial breathing.

ACCENTS. The accented syllable in each name is indicated by the acute accent ('). In many names, however, and particularly in compounds, there is both a primary and a secondary accent, and where this is the case the primary stress is indicated by a double acute accent (") and the secondary one by a single acute accent ('). To avoid possible confusion with the long vowel marks used in Old Norse texts, the accents are placed, not over the vowels, but after the accented syllables.

PRONUNCIATION INDEX 885

Æg'-ir, *the sea-God*, 133, 143, 190, 195–197, 207–210, 218–227, 238–242, 296, 423, 437, 450, 480, 483, 537

Æk'-in, *a river*, 129

Af'-i, *Grandfather*, 304–305, 313–315

Ag'-nar, *a warrior*, 571, 583, 653, 663–664, 839

Ag'-nar, *brother of Geirroth*, 120–123

Ag'-nar, *son of Geirroth*, 117, 120–123, 135–137

Āi, *a dwarf*, Ai, 11, 13

Āi, *Great-Grandfather*, 301

Alf, *a dwarf*, 13

Alf, *husband of Hjordis*, 493, 496, 537, 561, 688

Alf, *slayer of Helgi*, 417, 425

Alf, *son of Dag*, 325–327, 688

Alf, *son of Hring*, 443

Alf, *son of Hunding*, 435, 463, 481

Alf, *son of Ulf*, 325

Alf'-heim, *home of the elves*, 27, 122–123, 137, 284

Alf'-hild, *wife of Hjorvarth*, 403, 421

Alf'-roth-ul, *the sun*, 109, 116

Al'-grön, *an island*, 177

Al'-i, *a warrior*, 327

Alm'-veig, *wife of Halfdan*, 326–327, 339

Ā'-lof, *daughter of Franmar*, 403–407, 421–422

Al'-svith, *a giant*, 79

Al'-svith, *a horse*, 131, 575

Al'-thjof, *a dwarf*, 11, 29

Al'-vald-i, *a giant*, 177, 189

Al'-vis, *a dwarf*, 267, 271–284, 844

Al"-viss-mǫl, *the Ballad of Alvis*, 165, 267–282, 424, 815, 838, 844–849

Ām, *son of Dag*, 327

Am'-bott, *daughter of Thrall*, 303, 314

Am'-ma, *Grandmother*, 304–305, 313–315

Ān, *a dwarf*, 11

And'-hrim-nir, *a cook*, 127, 139

And"-var-a-naut, *a ring*, 167, 526–527, 538, 666–669

And'-var-i, *a dwarf*, 12–13, 29, 166, 393, 517, 524–527, 537–538, 618, 645, 669, 741, 861–862

An'-gan-tȳr, *a berserker*, 329

An'-gan-tȳr, *a warrior*, 337, 342

Ang'-eyj-a, *mother of Heimdall*, 330–331

Angr'-both-a, *a giantess*, 34–36, 211, 295, 333, 342

Arf'-i, *son of Jarl*, 310–311

Ar"-in-nef'-ja, *daughter of Thrall*, 302, 314

Arn'-grīm, *father of the berserkers*, 329, 339

Ār'-vak, *a horse*, 131, 142, 575, 585

Ās"-a-thor', *Thor*, 183, 190, 191

Ās'-garth, *home of the Gods*, 27, 31, 199, 257, 284

Ask, *Ash*, 12–13, 29, 284, 405

Ās'-laug, *daughter of Brynhild*, 646, 867

Ās'-mund, *a giant (?)*, 135, 144

Ath'-al, *son of Jarl*, 311, 317

At'-la, *mother of Heimdall*, 331

At"-la-kvith'-a, *the Lay of Atli,* 245, 391, 452, 669, 691, 703, 719, 721–736, 745, 775, 780–784, 801, 870, 874–877

At"-la-mǫl, *the Ballad of Atli,* 669, 691, 737–774, 780, 784, 799–800, 816, 874–879

At'-li, *Attila,* xx, xxiv, 29, 443, 499, 518, 538, 589, 595–601, 614–619, 632–639, 643, 647–650, 663–675, 681–809, 815–816, 841, 852–854, 859, 871–877

At'-li, *son of Hring,* 445

At'-li, *son of Ithmund,* 398–415, 421–424

At'-rith, *Odin,* 133, 144

Aur'-both-a, *a giantess,* 165, 337

Aur'-both-a, *Mengloth's handmaid,* 363

Aur'-gelm-ir, *Ymir,* 104–105, 114

Aur'-vang, *a dwarf,* 11

Austr'-i, *a dwarf,* 10–11, 29

Auth, *mother of Harald Battle-Tooth,* 329, 341

Auth'-a, *sister of Agnar,* 571, 653, 659, 663, 664

Auth'-i, *son of Halfdan the Old,* 338, 738

Baldr, *a God,* xxix, 17, 22–23, 33, 36–37, 116, 124–125, 138–139, 166, 215, 226–227, 244, 247, 267, 287, 289–291, 295–296, 330–331, 337, 341, 369–371, 628, 836, 845

Baldrs Draumar, *Baldr's Dreams,* xxi, 33–35, 166, 264, 288–294, 369, 844–845

Bāl'-eyg, *Odin,* 133, 144

Bar'-i, *a dwarf,* 363

Barn, *son of Jarl,* 310–311, 317

Bar'-ri, *a berserker,* 329

Bar'-ri, *a forest,* 161–163, 168

Beit'-i, *Atli's steward,* 762–763, 781

Bekk'-hild, *sister of Brynhild,* 518

Bel'-i, *a giant,* 21, 36, 166

Ber'-a, *Kostbera,* 669, 756–757, 761, 778, 780

Ber'-gel-mir, *a giant,* 104–107, 114–115

Best'-la, *Odin's mother,* 28, 77, 90, 244

Beyl'-a, *servant of Freyr,* 218–219, 234–237, 241, 246

Bif'-lind-i, *Odin,* 134–135, 144

Bif'-rost, *the rainbow bridge,* 36, 133, 138–143, 191, 484, 562

Bi'-fur, *a dwarf,* 11

Bik'-ki, *follower of Jormunrek,* 639, 650, 739, 790–791, 799, 817

Bīl'-eyg, *Odin,* 133, 144

Bil'-ling, *a giant,* 65, 87, 837

Bil'-rost, *the rainbow bridge,* 143, 549, 562

Bil'-skirn-ir, *Thor's dwelling,* 127, 137–139

Bjort, *Mengloth's handmaid,* 363

Blāin, *Ymir (?),* 11, 28, 29

Bleik, *Mengloth's handmaid,* 363

Blind, *follower of Hunding,* 461

Blith, *Mengloth's handmaid,* 363

Bod'-di, *son of Karl,* 306–307, 315

Bǫ'-fur, *a dwarf,* 11

Bolm, *an island,* 328–329, 340

Bol'-thorn, *Odin's grandfather,* 28,

PRONUNCIATION INDEX 887

77, 90

Bol'-verk, *Odin*, 67, 88, 118, 133, 144

Bom'-bur, *a dwarf*, 11

Bōnd'-i, *son of Karl*, 307, 315

Borg'-ar, *brother of Borghild (?)*, 495

Borg'-hild, *mother of Helgi*, 431, 447–448, 459, 479, 491, 495, 851–852, 857

Borg'-nȳ, *daughter of Heithrek*, 707–709, 717–720, 874

Both'-vild, *daughter of Nithuth*, 377, 381, 383, 385, 387, 389, 391, 393, 396

Brag'-a-lund, *a forest*, 463, 480

Brag'-i, *a God*, 132–133, 143, 218–225, 241–242, 341, 480–482, 575, 585

Brag'-i, *brother of Sigrun*, 467

Brā'-lund, *birthplace of Helgi*, 431, 447, 459, 479

Brām'-i, *a berserker*, 329

Brand'-ey, *an island*, 437, 449

Bratt'-skegg, *son of Karl*, 307, 315

Brā'-voll, *a field*, 441, 451

Breith, *son of Karl*, 307, 315

Breith'-a-blik, *Baldr's home*, 125, 138

Brim'-ir, *a giant*, 11, 16, 17, 28, 29, 34, 575, 585

Brim'-ir, *a sword*, 143

Brīs'-ings, *the dwarfs*, 243, 255–257, 264, 369

Brodd, *follower of Hrolf*, 326, 328, 329

Brot af Sig"-urth-ar-kvith'-u, *Fragment of a Sigurth Lay*, 242, 594–600, 863

Brun"-a-vāg'-ar, *a harbor*, 461, 480

Brūth, *daughter of Karl*, 307, 315

Bryn'-hild, *wife of Gunnar*, xx, xxiv, 32, 340, 449, 509–519, 538, 563–564, 577, 584–587, 595–602, 613–619, 625, 629, 631–633, 643–659, 663–669, 681, 689–690, 711, 717–719, 738, 778–785, 801, 849–852, 860–878

Bū'-i, *a berserker*, 329

Bū'-i, *son of Karl*, 307

Bund"-in-skeg'-gi, *son of Karl*, 306–307, 315

Bur, *father of Odin*, 3, 9, 28, 244, 311, 331, 341

Bur, *son of Jarl*, 317

Buth'-li, *father of Atli*, 449, 509, 518, 564, 597, 601–602, 615, 629, 631, 637, 641, 645–647, 657, 681, 690, 697, 718–719, 729, 738–739, 743, 757, 761–771, 781, 785, 860, 863–865

Buth'-lungs, *descendants of Buthli*, 735, 743

Bygg'-vir, *Freyr's servant*, 218–219, 232–233, 237, 241, 245–246

Bȳ'-leist (or Bȳ'-leipt), *brother of Loki*, 21, 36, 333, 342

Dag, *a God (Day)*, 91, 114, 285

Dag, *brother of Sigrun*, 467–471, 481–485

Dag, *husband of Thora*, 339, 688

Dāin, *a dwarf*, 11, 325

Dāin, *a hart*, 131

Dāin, *an elf*, 79

Dan, *a king*, 311, 317–318, 830–831

Dan'-a, *daughter of Danp*, 200,

317–318, 658, 831

Danp, *a king*, 311, 317, 727, 738, 831

Del'-ling, *father of Day*, 83, 91, 103, 114, 363, 372

Digr'-ald-i, *son of Thrall*, 302–303, 314

Dog'-ling, *Delling*, 114

Dög'-lings, *descendants of Dag*, 339

Dolg'-thras-ir, *a dwarf*, 13

Dōr'-i, *a dwarf*, 12, 13, 363, 372

Drāp Nifl'-ung-a, *the Slaying of the Niflungs*, 602, 650, 665–668, 691, 718–720, 737–742, 775, 800–801, 871, 875

Draup'-nir, *a dwarf*, 12–13

Draup'-nir, *a ring*, 166, 538

Dreng, *son of Karl*, 307, 315

Drott, *son of Thrall*, 303, 314

Drumb, *son of Thrall*, 303, 314

Drumb'-a, *daughter of Thrall*, 302–303, 314

Dūf, *a dwarf*, 13

Dun'-eyr, *a hart*, 131

Dur'-in, *a dwarf*, 11, 29

Dval'-in, *a dwarf*, 11, 13, 29, 79, 90, 131, 275, 284, 549, 562

Dval'-in, *a hart*,

Dyr'-a-thrōr, *a hart*, 131

Ed'-da, *Great-Grandmother*, 300–303

Egg'-thēr, *the giants' watchman*, 19, 34

Eg'-il, *brother of Folund*, 199, 210, 377–379, 391, 395–396, 428

Eg'-il, *father of Thjalfi (?)*, 199

Eg"-ils-sag'-a, *the Saga of Egil*, 842

Eik"-in-skjald'-i, *a dwarf*, 10–13, 29

Eik"-in-tjas'-na, *daughter of Thrall*, 302–303, 314

Eik'-thyrn-ir, *a hart*, 129, 140

Eir, *Mengloth's handmaid*, 362–363, 372

Eist'-la, *mother of Heimdall*, 330–331

Eit'-il, *son of Atli*, 667–669, 691, 734–737, 742–743, 783, 800, 809, 816

Eld'-hrim-nir, *a kettle*, 127, 139

Eld'-ir, *Ægir's servant*, 218–221, 242

Ēl"-i-vag'-ar, *the Milky Way (?)*, 105, 115, 197, 209

Emb'-la, *Elm*, 13, 29

Ern'-a, *wife of Jarl*, 308–309, 317

Erp, *son of Atli*, 667, 691, 735–737, 783, 800, 816

Erp, *son of Jonak*, 538, 650, 799, 809–816

Ey'-fur-a, *mother of the berserkers*, 329, 339

Eyj'-olf, *son of Hunding*, 435, 481

Ey'-lim-i, *father of Hjordis*, 329, 340, 398, 406, 422, 424, 448, 496, 501, 503, 517, 531, 538, 539, 775, 852

Ey'-lim-i, *father of Svava*, 407, 415–417, 495

Ey'-mōth, *Atli's emissary*, 679

Ey'-mund, *king of Holmgarth*, 326–327, 339

Eyr'-gjaf-a, *mother of Heimdall*, 330–331

Fāf'-nir, *brother of Regin*, 329, 340, 393, 421, 498–499, 503–505, 517–

PRONUNCIATION INDEX

518, 529–531, 535–541, 545–562, 609, 617, 643–647, 659, 667, 711, 719, 737, 860–863

Fāf'-nis-mǫl', *the Ballad of Fafnir*, 28–29, 188, 284, 317, 340, 421, 517–518, 521, 540–541, 544–560, 565, 583, 606, 618, 664, 671, 719, 777, 843, 861–864–866, 868, 872

Fal'-hōfn-ir, *a horse*, 129, 141

Far'-baut-i, *father of Loki*, 243, 246

Farm'-a-tȳr, *Odin*, 133, 144

Fath'-ir, *Father*, 307, 313, 316

Feim'-a, *daughter of Karl*, 306–307, 315

Feng, *Odin*, 533, 539

Fen'-ja, *a giantess*, 649

Fenr'-ir, *a wolf*, 19, 34–36, 109, 116, 139, 142, 203, 209–211, 219, 230–231, 241, 245–246, 295, 342, 441, 451

Fen'-sal-ir, *Frigg's hall*, 17, 33

Fīl'-i, *a dwarf*, 10–11

Fim'-a-feng, *Ægir's servant*, 218–219, 242

Fim'-bul-thul, *a river*, 129

Fith, *a dwarf*, 13

Fit'-jung, *Earth*, 59, 86

Fjal'-ar, *a cock*, 13, 34, 35, 85, 190, 371

Fjal'-ar, *a dwarf*, 18–19

Fjal'-ar, *Suttung (?)*, 45

Fjal'-ar, *Utgartha-Loki (?)*, 179

Fjol'-kald, *Svipdag's grandfather*, 355, 370

Fjol'-nir, *Odin*, 133, 144, 533, 539

Fjol"-svinns-mǫl', *the Ballad of Fjolsvith*, xxi, 345, 370, 848

Fjol'-svith, *Mengloth's watchman*, 133, 144, 345–346, 370

Fjol'-svith, *Odin*, 848, 353–367

Fjol'-var, *a giant (?)*, 177

Fjōn, *an island*, 679, 688

Fjorg'-yn, *Jorth*, 23, 37, 185, 191, 244

Fjorg'-yn, *Odin*, 37, 227

Fjorm, *a river*, 129

Fjorn'-ir, *Gunnar's cupbearer*, 727, 738

Fjōsn'-ir, *son of Thrall*, 303, 314

Fjot'-ur-lund, *a forest*, 469, 483

Fljōth, *daughter of Karl*, 307, 315

Folk'-vang, *Freyja's home*, 125, 138, 263

For'-set-i, *a God*, 124–125, 139, 341

Fōst"-brœth-ra-sag'-a, *the Saga of the Foster-Brothers*, 87

Frā Dauth'-a Sinf'-jotl-a, *Of Sinfjotli's Death*, 448, 451, 487, 490–494, 517, 521, 537–540, 561, 583, 643, 688, 852, 858, 861–864

Frǣg, *a dwarf*, 11

Frān'-ang, *a waterfall*, 239, 247

Frān'-mar, *Sigrlin's foster-father*, 403–405, 422

Frār, *a dwarf*, 11

Frath'-mar, *son of Dag*, 327

Frek'-a-stein, *a battlefield*, 417, 425, 441, 445, 452, 465–467, 482

Frek'-i, *a wolf*, 127, 139, 346, 448

Frek'-i, *son of Dag*, 327

Frey'-ja, *a Goddess*, 30–31, 36, 124–125, 138, 143, 165, 189, 218–219, 228–229, 241–244, 252–259, 263–265, 322–338, 342–343, 369, 708–709, 718, 847

Freyr, *a God,* 30, 36, 123, 133, 137–138, 143, 147–167, 216–219, 230–233, 241, 244–246, 263, 287, 330–331, 338, 341, 346, 424, 453, 631, 646, 829–834

Frī'-aut, *daughter of Hildigun,* 327, 338, 339

Frigg, *a Goddess,* 16–17, 21, 33, 36, 93, 96–97, 113, 117, 120–121, 137–138, 218–219, 226–229, 241–244, 265, 295, 369, 372, 708–709, 718, 838

Frīth, *Mengloth's handmaid,* 363

Frost'-i, *a dwarf,* 12–13

Frōth'-i, *a Danish king,* 433, 448, 649

Frōth'-i, *father of Hledis,* 327

Froth'-i, *father of Kari (?),* 327

Ful'-la, *Frigg's handmaid,* 121

Ful'-nir, *son of Thrœll,* 303, 314

Fund'-in, *a dwarf,* 11

Gagn'-rāth, *Odin,* 99, 101, 113, 838

Gand'-alf, *a dwarf,* 11, 29

Gang, *brother of Thjazi,*

Gang'-ler-i, *King Gylfi,* 132, 140, 144

Gang'-ler-i, *Odin,* 133

Garm, *a hound,* 19, 21, 23, 35, 133, 143, 209, 295

Gast'-ropn-ir, *Mengloth's dwelling,* 357, 371

Gaut, *Odin,* 135, 145

Gef-jun, *a Goddess,* 224–225, 242–243

Geir'-mund, *kinsman of Atli,* 713, 720

Geir'-on-ul, *a Valkyrie,* 131, 142

Geir'-rōth, *a king,* 117–118, 121–123, 135

Geir'-skog-ul, *a Valkyrie,* 17

Geir'-vim-ul, *a river,* 128–129

Geit'-ir, *Gripir's servant,* 500–503, 517

Ger'-i, *a hound,* 346, 356–357, 371

Ger'-i, *a wolf,* 127, 139, 448

Gerth, *daughter of Gymir,* 148, 153–157, 161–167, 241, 245, 331, 341

Gīf, *a hound,* 357, 371

Gim'-lē, *a mountain,* 23, 38

Gin'-nar, *a dwarf,* 13

Gin"-nung-a-gap', *Yawning Gap,* 3

Gip'-ul, *a river,* 128–129

Gīsl, *a horse,* 129, 141

Gjaf'-laug, *Gjuki's sister,* 608–609, 617

Gjal"-lar-horn', *Heimdall's horn,* 19, 31, 35

Gjol, *a river,* 129

Gjolp, *mother of Heimdall,* 331

Gjūk'-i, *father of Gunnar,* xxiv, 329, 340, 498, 505, 509, 513–515, 518, 538, 557, 564, 597, 599, 609, 611–618, 625–627, 631, 643–645, 657, 659, 668–669, 675, 685, 690, 697, 703, 707, 711–713, 725, 749, 759, 773–778, 784, 793, 800, 807, 811, 815–817, 867–876

Gjūk'-i, *son of Hogni,* 667

Gjūk'-ungs, *Gjuki's sons,* 518, 563, 583, 602, 633, 643–645, 664, 667, 689, 719–720, 737, 775, 867, 872, 877

Glap'-svith, *Odin,* 133

Glas'-ir, *a forest,* 405, 421

PRONUNCIATION INDEX

Glath, *a horse*, 129, 141
Glaths'-heim, *Odin's dwelling*, 125, 138
Glaum, *Atli's horse*, 732–733, 741
Glaum'-vor, *wife of Gunnar*, 667–669, 751–778, 877
Gleip'-nir, *a chain*, 34
Gler, *a horse*, 129, 141
Glit'-nir, *Forseti's dwelling*, 124–125, 139
Glō'-in, *a dwarf*, 13
Gnip"-a-hel'-lir, *a cave*, 19–23
Gnip'-a-lund, *a forest*, 437, 439, 441, 443, 450
Gnit'-a-heith, *Fafnir's mountain*, 503, 518, 531, 539, 545, 561, 727, 737
Gō'-in, *a serpent*, 131, 141
Gol, *a Valkyrie*, 131, 142
Gol"-lin-kamb'-i, *a cock*, 19, 35, 371, 484
Goll'-nir, *a giant (?)*, 441, 451
Goll'-rond, *daughter of Gjuki*, 611–618
Goll'-topp, *a horse*, 129, 141
Goll'-veig, *a Wane*, 13, 30
Gom'-ul, *a river*, 129
Gond'-lir, *Odin*, 135, 144
Gond'-ul, *a Valkyrie*, 17
Gop'-ul, *a river*, 129
Gorm (the Old), *King of Denmark*, 846–847
Goth'-mund, *son of Granmar*, 439–443, 450–452, 463–467, 481, 854–856
Got'-thorm, *slayer of Sigurth*, 329, 340, 515, 538, 595, 601–603, 629, 645, 677, 687, 786
Grā'-bak, *a serpent*, 131, 141
Graf'-vit-nir, *a serpent*, 131, 141
Graf'-vol-luth, *a serpent*, 131, 141
Gram, *Sigurth's sword*, 531, 539, 552–553, 562, 568, 629, 646
Gran'-i, *Sigurth's horse*, 381, 393, 441, 451, 503, 505, 517, 524, 525, 537, 559, 575, 585, 590, 602, 613, 633, 647, 659, 664, 674, 675, 676, 677, 687, 711, 719, 867
Gran'-mar, *father of Hothbrodd*, 435, 443, 449–453, 463–467, 481–483, 854
Greip, *mother of Heimdall*, 330–331
Gret'-tir, *a hero*, 91
Gret"-tis-sag'-a, *the Saga of Grettir*, 189
Grīm, *follower of Hrolf*, 329
Grīm, *Odin*, 133
Grīm'-hild, *wife of Gjuki*, 340, 511, 515, 519, 601, 649, 669, 679, 681–683, 688–690, 711, 765–769, 781, 867
Grim'-nir, *Odin*, 117, 123, 133, 135, 137, 144
Grim"-nis-mǫl, *the Ballad of Grimnir*, xxviii, 27–35, 90, 114, 117, 120–136, 165, 170, 187–191, 209, 241, 263–264, 295, 313, 338, 342, 346, 369, 451, 483–484, 539, 562–564, 585, 718, 739, 741, 838, 839–842, 848–850
Grīp'-ir, *Sigurth's uncle*, 497, 501–517, 858
Grīp"-is-spǫ', *Gripir's Prophecy*, 32, 137, 340, 495–518, 521, 537–539, 561, 564, 601–602, 618, 619, 643, 646, 650–651, 664, 688, 737, 781, 858–877

Grō'-a, *mother of Svipdag*, 345, 349, 351, 370, 848, 849

Grǫth, *a river*, 129

Grot"-ta-songr', *the Song of Grotti*, xxi, 649

Grot'-ti, *a mill*, 649

Grō"-u-galdr', *Groa's Spell*, xxi, 345, 349–353, 370, 566, 848

Gull'-fax-i, *a horse*, 188

Gull"-in-tan'-ni, *Heimdall*, 141

Gung'-nir, *a spear*, 143, 575, 585

Gun'-nar, *brother of Borghild (?)*, 495

Gun'-nar, *follower of Hrolf*, 329

Gun'-nar, *son of Gjuki*, 29, 340, 462, 498–499, 510–519, 538, 563–564, 589–591, 595–602, 609, 615–619, 627–637, 643–650, 667–669, 677–679, 682–683, 687–691, 699, 703, 707–711, 715–720, 725–755, 760–763, 775–786, 793–795, 800, 809, 815–816, 859–860, 867–871, 874–876

Gunn'-loth, *daughter of Suttung*, 45, 67, 85, 88, 837

Gunn'-thor-in, *a river*, 129

Gunn'-thro, *a river*, 129

Gust, *Andvari (?)*, 527, 538, 861

Guth, *a Valkyrie*, 17, 463, 480

Guth'-rūn, *wife of Sigurth*, 329, 340, 498, 511–519, 563–619, 625–627, 631, 637–639, 643–650, 659, 667–693, 697–703, 713, 717, 720, 725, 733–743, 759–801, 807–809, 815–817, 860, 865–878

Guth"-rūn-ar-hvot', *Guthrun's Inciting*, 340, 603, 650, 742, 786–787, 791, 799, 815–818, 869, 871–872, 877–879

Guth"-rūn-ar-kvith'-a I (en Fyrst'-a), *the First Lay of Guthrun*, 448, 483, 602, 605, 608–616, 621, 643–647, 687–688, 719–720, 866, 869, 872

Guth"-rūn-ar-kvith'-a II (On'-nur, en Forn'-a), *the Second (Old) Lay of Guthrun*, 342, 391, 483, 602–603, 617–619, 671, 687, 701, 719, 741–742, 775–776, 868, 872–873

Guth"-rūn-ar-kvith'- a III (Thrith'-ja), *the Third Lay of Guthrun*, 687, 693, 696–701, 780, 873

Gylf"-a-gin'-ning, *the Deceiving of Gylfi*, 3, 168, 193, 215, 283, 341–342, 372, 862

Gyl'-lir, *a horse*, 128–129, 141

Gym'-ir, *Ægir*, 218–219

Gym'-ir, *a giant*, 148, 153–157, 165, 231, 241, 245, 331, 341

Gyrth, *son of Dag*, 327

Had'-ding, *a Danish king*, 479, 689

Had"-ding-ja-skat'-i, *Haddings'-Hero (Helgi)*, 398, 476–479, 485

Had'-dings, *berserkers*, 329, 398, 485, 681, 689

Hæm'-ing, *son of Hunding*, 459, 479

Hag'-al, *Helgi's foster-father*, 459–461, 479–480

Hak'-i, *son of Hvethna*, 329–331

Hal, *son of Karl*, 307, 315

Hālf, *King of Horthaland*, 338–339

Half-dan, *father of Kara*, 477, 481

Half-dan (the Old), *a Danish king*, 326–327, 338–340, 398, 453, 539, 688, 830, 833, 851

Hālfs'-sag-a, *the Saga of Half*, 338–339

Ham'-al, *son of Hagal*, 458–461,

PRONUNCIATION INDEX

479–480

Ham-thēr, *son of Jonak*, 538, 650, 791–793, 799–800, 803, 809, 811–818, 871, 877–879

Ham"-thēs-mǫl, *the Ballad of Hamther*, 340, 603, 650, 739, 799–800, 803–804, 807, 818, 871–872, 877–879

Hā'-mund, *son of Sigmund*, 448, 491, 495

Han'-nar, *a dwarf*, 11

Hār, *Odin*, 140, 144

Har'-ald (Battle-Tooth), *son of Hrorek*, 329

Har'-ald (Blue-Tooth), *King of Denmark*, 846–847

Hār'-barth, *Odin*, 135, 144, 169, 170, 175–191, 841

Hār"-barths-ljōth', *the Poem of Harbarth*, 31, 37, 144, 169, 172–186, 209–210, 241, 246–247, 263, 283, 341, 480, 585, 663, 720, 840–842, 845, 875

Hat'-a-fjord, *a fjord*, 409, 423

Hat'-i, *a giant*, 34, 130–131, 142

Hat'-i, *a wolf*, 409–413, 423

Haug'-spor-i, *a dwarf*, 12, 13

Heer'-fath-er, *Odin*, 15, 32, 97, 113, 127–129, 139, 323, 337, 584

Heim'-dall, *a God*, 9, 15, 19, 27, 31, 34–35, 124–125, 138, 141, 167, 233, 245, 257, 264, 298, 301, 313, 316, 341, 342, 847

Heim'-ir, *Brynhild's foster-father*, 507–511, 518, 664, 866–867

Heith, *daughter of Hrimnir*, 331, 341

Heith, *Gollweg (?)*, 15, 30

Heith'-draup-nir, *Mimir (?)*, 573, 584

Heith'-rek, *father of Borgny*, 707, 717

Heith'-run, *a goat*, 127, 140, 333, 342

Hel, *Goddess of the dead*, 19, 21, 33–36, 128–129, 139, 144, 159, 161, 211, 289, 295, 337, 342, 351, 361, 551, 651, 654, 657, 760, 761, 817, 870

Hel'-blind-i, *Odin*, 133, 144

Helg"-a-kvith'-a Hjor"-varthsson'-ar, *the Lay of Helgi the Son of Hjorvarth*, 32, 268, 284, 397, 402–420, 447–452, 480–482, 537, 777, 853–856, 862–863

Helg"-a-kvith'-a Hund"-ingsban'-a I (en Fyr'-ri), *the First Lay of Helgi Hundingsbane*, 243, 421–425, 430–446, 479–484, 539, 646, 783, 862

Helg"-a-kvith'-a Hund"-ingsban'-a II (On'-nur), *the Second Lay of Helgi Hundingsbane*, 140, 425, 448–450, 453, 458–478, 485, 618, 701, 801, 853

Helg'-i (Had"-ding-ja-skat'-i), *Helgi the Haddings-Hero*, 477–479, 485

Helg'-i, *Hjalmgunnar (?)*, 505, 518

Helg'-i, *son of Hjorvarth*, 397–426, 851–853

Helg'-i, *son of Sigmund*, xxiii, 338, 455–485, 495–496, 497, 522, 539, 853, 854–857

Hel'-reith Bryn'-hild-ar, *Brynhild's Hell-Ride*, 189, 391, 518, 583–584, 653, 656–672, 665, 778, 870–872

Hept"-i-fil-i, *a dwarf*, 11

Her'-borg, *queen of the Huns*, 610–611, 617–618, 868

Her'-fjot-ur, *a Valkyrie*, 131, 142

Her'-jan, *Odin*, 17, 32, 133, 144, 613, 618

Herk'-ja, *Atli's servant*, 696–701, 873

Her'-mōth, *son of Odin*, 323, 337

Hers'-ir, *father of Erna*, 308–309, 317

Her'-teit, *Odin*, 133, 144

Her"-var-ar-sag'-a, *the Saga of Hervor*, 339, 539, 738

Her'-varth, *a berserker*, 329

Her'-varth, *son of Hunding*, 463, 481

Her'-vor, *a swan-maiden*, 377, 379, 391, 393

Heth'-in, *brother of Helgi*, 403, 415–421, 424–425, 449, 852

Heth'-ins-ey, *an island*, 437, 449

Hild, *a Valkyrie*, 32, 131, 663

Hild, *Brynhild*, 653, 659, 778

Hild, *mother of King Half*, 327, 339

Hild'-i-gun, *daughter of Sækonung*, 327, 339

Hild"-i-svin'-i, *a boar*, 325, 338

Hild'-olf, *a warrior*, 175, 187

Him'-in-bjorg, *Heimdall's duelling*, 125, 138

Him"-in-vang'-ar, *Heaven's-Field*, 433, 448

Hind'-ar-fjoll, *Brynhild's mountain*, 557, 564, 569, 583, 664

Hjalm'-ar, *a warrior*, 339

Hjalm'-ber-i, *Odin*, 132–133, 144

Hjalm'-gun-nar, *a Gothic king*, 518, 571, 583–584, 658–659, 663–664

Hjalp'-rek, *father of Alf*, 493, 496, 525, 531, 535–537, 688

Hjor'-dīs, *mother of Sigurth*, 329, 340, 398, 422, 448, 493–497, 501, 517, 540, 561, 688, 852, 857

Hjor'-leif, *father of King Half*, 339

Hjor'-leif, *follower of Helgi*, 437, 449

Hjor'-varth, *a berserker*, 329

Hjor'-varth, *father of Helgi*, 331, 397–398, 405–409, 415–419, 422, 427, 485, 829, 851–852

Hjor'-varth, *father of Hvethna*, 329

Hjor'-varth, *son of Hunding*, 403, 421, 435, 463, 481, 540

Hlath'-guth, *a swan-maiden*, 377–379, 391

Hlē'-barth, *a giant*, 177

Hlē'-bjorg, *a mountain*, 469, 482

Hlē'-dis, *mother of Ottar*, 327

Hlēr, *Ægir*, 190, 241, 480

Hlēs'-ey, *an island*, 181, 190, 209, 461, 480, 713, 720

Hlē'-vang, *a dwarf*, 13

Hlíf, *Mengloth's handmaid*, 363

Hlíf'-thras-a, *Mengloth's handmaid*, 363

Hlīn, *Frigg*, 21, 36

Hlith'-skjolf, *Odin's seat*, 121, 137–138, 151, 165, 739, 875

Hlokk, *a Valkyrie*, 131

Hlōr'-rith-i, *Thor*, 191, 197, 201–205, 209, 235, 246, 255, 259, 263

Hloth'-varth, *follower of Helgi*, 411, 423

Hloth'-vēr, *a Frankish king*, 377–379, 381, 391–393, 690

Hloth'-vēr, *father of Hervor*, 681

Hlōth'-yn, *Jorth*, 21, 36

Hlym'-dal-ir, *Brynhild's home*, 653, 659, 663

Hnifl'-ung, *son of Hogni*, 743, 769–780, 784, 800

Hnifl'-ungs, *the people of Gjuki (Nibelungs),* 443, 452, 780, 795, 800, 854

Hnik'-ar, *Odin,* 133, 144, 521–522, 532–533, 539, 542, 861

Hnik'-uth, *Odin,* 133, 144

Hǫ'-alf, *a Danish king,* 677, 688

Hǫ'-alf, *King Half of Horthaland,* 327, 339

Hǫ'-brōk, *a hawk,* 133, 143

Hodd'-mim-ir, *Mimir,* 109, 116

Hodd'-rof-nir, *Mimir (?),* 573, 584

Hog'-ni, *brother of Sigar,* 461, 480

Hog'-ni, *father of Sigrun,* 445, 449, 453, 463, 465–469, 473–475, 480–481

Hog'-ni, *son of Gjuki,* 329, 340, 398, 435, 443, 498, 511, 515, 518, 538, 589–601, 622, 629, 635, 643–648, 667–672, 677–679, 683, 687–691, 699, 703, 709, 713, 718–720, 727–731, 737–743, 751–769, 775–786, 793, 800, 801, 809, 815–816, 868, 871, 874–877

Hǫk'-on, *father of Thora,* 615, 619, 679, 688, 893

Hol, *a river,* 129

Holm'-garth, *Russia,* 339

Holth, *son of Karl,* 307, 315

Hön'-ir, *a God,* 29

Hǫr, *a dwarf,* 13

Hǫr, *Odin,* 30, 67–69, 83, 88–89, 133, 144

Horn, *a river,* 351, 369

Horn'-bor-i, *a dwarf,* 10, 11

Horth'-a-land, *Half's kingdom,* 338–339

Hörv'-ir, *follower of Hrolf,* 329

Hos'-vir, *son of Thrall,* 303, 314

Hoth, *slayer of Baldr,* 17, 23, 33, 37, 244, 291, 296, 341

Hoth'-brodd, *son of Granmar,* 435, 439, 443, 447–449, 452, 463–467, 481–482, 851–852, 855

Hǫ'-tun, *Helgi's home,* 433, 437, 448–450

Hǫv"-a-mǫl, *the Ballad of the High One,* xx, 28–29, 39, 42–84, 90, 113–114, 144, 166–168, 190, 284, 285, 314, 317, 369, 372, 521, 539–542, 563–566, 584–586, 837–838, 861, 865

Hǫ'-varth, *son of Hunding,* 435

Hræ'-svelg, *an eagle,* 36, 107, 115, 167

Hran'-i, *a berserker,* 328–329

Hrauth'-ung, *ancestor of Hjordis,* 329

Hrauth'-ung, *father of Geirroth,* 121, 137

Hreim, *son of Thrall,* 303, 314

Hreith'-mar, *father of Regin,* 29, 525–529, 537–538, 861–862

Hrīm'-fax-i, *a horse,* 101, 113

Hrīm'-gerth, *a giantess,* 284, 409–415, 423–424, 852

Hrīm"-gerth-a-mol, *the Ballad of Hrimgerth,* 423–424, 852–853

Hrīm'-grim-nir, *a giant,* 161, 168

Hrim'-nir, *a giant,* 159, 167, 331, 341

Hring, *a warrior,* 443, 453, 833

Hring'-stath-ir, *Ringsted,* 433, 445, 448, 453

Hring'-stoth, *Ringsted (?),* 433, 448

Hrist, *a Valkyrie,* 130–131, 142

Hrīth, *a river,* 129, 369

Hrō'-ar, *brother of Borghild (?)*, 495

Hrolf (the Old), *King of Gautland*, xxv, 329, 339

Hrol'-laug, *a warrior*, 469, 482

Hrō'-mund, *a warrior*, 485

Hrō'-mund-ar Sag'-a Greips'-son-ar, *the Saga of Hromund Greipsson*, 479, 485

Hron, *a river*, 129, 369

Hrōpt, *Odin*, 23, 37, 233, 245, 573, 584

Hrōpt'-a-tŷr, *Odin*, 83, 91, 135, 145

Hrö'-rek, *King of Denmark*, 329, 340–341

Hross'-thjōf, *son of Hrimnir*, 331, 341

Hrōth, *a giant*, 199, 210

Hrōth'-mar, *lover of Sigrlin*, 405, 409, 417, 422, 425

Hrōth'-vit-nir, *Fenrir*, 131, 142, 231, 245

Hrot'-ti, *a sword*, 559, 564

Hrung'-nir, *a giant*, 176–177, 188, 201, 210, 237–239, 246, 575, 585

Hrym, *a giant*, 21, 36

Hug'-in, *a raven*, xiv, 127, 139

Hum'-lung, *son of Hjorvarth*, 403, 421

Hund'-ing, *enemy of Sigmund*, 421, 432–435, 445, 448, 459, 460–463, 471, 479, 483–484, 493–496, 503, 517, 531, 535, 539, 540, 851–852, 855, 861–862

Hund'-land, *Hunding's kingdom*, 448, 458–459, 479

Hver'-gel-mir, *a spring*, 129, 140

Hveth'-na, *mother of Haki*, 329–331, 340

Hym'-ir, *a giant*, 115, 193–215, 229, 244, 842, 843

Hym"-is-kvith'-a, *the Lay of Hymir*, 36, 115, 167, 187, 193, 196–208, 215, 241, 244–246, 263–265, 584, 842–844

Hym'-ling, *son of Hjorvarth*, 403, 421

Hynd'-la, *a giantess*, 319, 322–328, 332–338, 342, 847, 848

Hynd"-lu-ljōth', *the Poem of Hyndla*, xxi, 167, 190, 242–245, 313, 319, 323, 421, 447, 480, 645, 688–689, 830, 833, 847–848

If'-ing, *a river*, 101, 113, 190

Im, *son of Vafthruthnir*, 99, 113

Imth, *a giant*, 441, 451

Imth, *mother of Heimdall*, 331

Ing'-un, *sister of Njorth (?)*, 245

Ing'-un-ar=Freyr, *Freyr*, 232–233, 245

In'-stein, *father of Ottar*, 325, 338–339

Īr'-i, *a dwarf*, 363

Īs'-olf, *son of Olmoth*, 329

Īs'-ung, *a warrior*, 435, 449

Ith'-a-voll, *meeting-place of the Gods*, 11, 23, 28, 37

Īth'-i, *brother of Thjazi*, Ithi

Ith'-mund, *follower of Hjorvarth*, 403–405

Īth'-un, *a Goddess*, 143, 166, 189, 219, 225, 241–242, 243, 263

Ī'-vald-i, *a dwarf*, 133, 143

Ī'-var, *King of Sweden*, 329, 341

Jafn'-họr, *Odin*, 135, 144

Jalk, *Odin,* 134–135, 144
Jar'-i, *a dwarf,* 10, 11, 363, 372
Jar'-iz-leif, *Atli's emissary,* 679, 689
Jar'-iz-skar, *Atli's emissary,* 679, 689
Jarl, *son of Rig,* 309–311
Jarn'-sax-a, *a giantess,* 188
Jarn'-sax-a, *mother of Heimdall,* 331
Jof'-ur-mar, *son of Dag,* 327
Jōn'-ak, *father of Hamther,* 639, 650, 791, 795, 799, 813–816, 871, 878
Jor'-mun-rek, *Ermanarich,* xxiv, 329, 340, 499, 602, 639, 649–650, 687, 787, 791–793, 799, 807, 811–818, 860, 871
Jorth, *Earth,* xxviii, 31, 37, 187, 191, 246, 253, 263, 583
Jōth, *son of Jarl,* 311, 317
Jot'-un-heim, *the world of the giants,* 4, 11, 21, 27–28, 36, 151–153, 189, 257–259, 264, 284

Kār'-a, *daughter of Halfdan,* 398, 455, 477–481, 485, 518, 853, 856
Kār'-i, *ancestor of Ketil,* 327, 339
Karl, *son of Rig,* 305
Kār"-u-ljōth', *the Poem of Kara,* 479–481, 485, 853
Kef-sir, *son of Thrall,* 302–303, 314
Ker'-laug, *a river,* 129
Ket'-il Horth'-a=Kar'-i, *husband of Hildigun,* 327, 339
Kīl'-i, *a dwarf,* 10–11
Kjal'-ar, *Odin,* 134, 135, 144
Kjār, *father of Olrun,* 377–379, 391–392, 727, 738
Kleg'-gi, *son of Thrall,* 302–303, 314

Klūr, *son of Thrall,* 303, 314
Klypp, *father of Ketil,* 327
Knē'-fröth, *Atli's messenger,* 667–669, 725, 737, 775
Kolg'-a, *daughter of Ægir,* 437, 450
Kon, *son of Rig,* 311, 315–317, 830, 846
Kormt, *a river,* 129
Kost'-ber-a, *wife of Hogni,* 667–669, 750–755, 775–778, 877
Kumb'-a, *daughter of Thrall,* 302–303, 314
Kund, *son of Jarl,* 311, 317

Læ'-gjarn, *Loki,* 361, 371
Læ'-rāth, *Yggdrasil,* 127–129, 140
Læv'-a-tein, *a sword,* 361
Lauf'-ey, *mother of Loki,* 235, 243, 246, 257, 263–264
Leg'-gjald-i, *son of Thrall,* 302–303, 314
Leipt, *a river,* 129, 140, 469, 483
Leir'-brim-ir, *Ymir (?),* 357, 371
Lētt'-fet-i, *a horse,* 129, 141
Līf, *mother of the new race,* 109, 116
Līf'-thras-ir, *father of the new race,* 109, 116
Lim'-a-fjord, *a fjord,* 749, 775, 778
Lit, *a dwarf,* 11
Ljōth'-a-tal, *the List of Charms,* 39, 87, 90, 91, 369, 837
Lodd'-fāf-nir, *a singer,* 39, 69, 71–77, 83, 88–89, 837
Lodd"-fāf-nis-mǫl, *the Ballad of Loddfafnir,* 39, 88, 586, 837, 865

Lof'-ar, *a dwarf*, 13, 29

Lofn'-heith, *daughter of Hreithmar*, 529, 538

Log'-a-fjoll, *a mountain*, 433, 435, 448, 463, 481

Lok"-a-sen'-na, *Loki's Wrangling*, xx, 28, 33, 37, 143, 147, 170, 190, 193, 209, 215, 281–241, 244–246, 249, 263–264, 283, 287, 295, 337, 341–342, 369, 392, 452, 840, 843–844

Lok'-i, *a God*, 17, 20–21, 29–37, 143, 170, 187–190, 194, 204–205, 211–257, 263–264, 292–296, 332–333, 341–342, 362–363, 371–372, 451, 524–529, 537–538, 618, 741, 836, 843, 861–862

Lōn'-i, *a dwarf*, 11

Lopt, *Loki*, 221, 242, 333, 342, 361, 371

Loth'-in, *a giant*, 413, 423

Lōth'-ur, *Loki*, 13, 29–30

Lūt, *son of Thrall*, 303, 314

Lyf'-ja-berg, *a mountain*, 362–363, 367, 372

Lyng'-heith, *daughter of Hreithmar*, 529, 538

Lyng'-vi, *son of Hunding*, 495–496, 534–535, 540

Lȳr, *Mengloth's hall*, 363, 372

Mag'-ni, *son of Thor*, 110–111, 116, 175, 185, 188, 191

Mān'-i, *Moon*, 114, 142

Meil'-i, *brother of Thor*, 175, 188

Mēln'-ir, *a horse*, 443, 452

Men'-gloth, *beloved of Svipdag*, 346, 349, 355, 363–372, 583, 651, 849

Men'-ja, *a giantess*, 637, 649

Mīm (or Mim'-ir), *a water-spirit*, 15, 19, 21, 31–32, 35, 90, 116, 371, 575, 584–585

Mīm'-a-meith, *Yggdrasil*, 359, 371

Mīm'-ir, *brother of Regin*, 537

Mist, *a Valkyrie*, 131, 142, 443, 452

Mith'-garth, *the world of men*, 9, 27–28, 127, 133, 139, 142, 179, 284, 325–327

Mith"-garths-orm', *a serpent*, 34–37, 187, 211, 246, 295, 342, 843

Mith'-vit-nir, *a giant*, 135, 144

Mjoll'-nir, *Thor's hammer*, 111, 116, 188, 205, 237–239, 246, 259, 263

Mjoth'-vit-nir, *a dwarf*, 11, 29

Mog, *son of Jarl*, 311, 317

Mog'-thras-ir, *a giant (?)*, 111, 116

Mō'-in, *a serpent*, 131, 141

Mō"-ins-heim'-ar, *a battlefield*, 443, 452, 467

Morn'-a-land, *an eastern country*, 717

Mōth'-i, *son of Thor*, 111, 116, 188, 205, 212

Mōth'-ir, *mother of Jarl*, 307–309, 313, 316

Mōt'-sog-nir, *a dwarf*, 11

Mund"-il-fer'-i, *father of Sol*, 28, 103, 114

Mun'-in, *a raven*, 126–127, 139

Mū'-spell, *father of the fire-dwellers*, 21, 36, 231, 245

Mū'-spells-heim, *home of the fire-dwellers*, 27, 35, 113, 142, 245

Mȳln'-ir, *a horse*, 443, 452

Myrk'-heim, *Myrkwood (Atli's land)*, 735, 743

Myrk'-wood, *a forest in Atli's land*,

719, 725–729, 737–739, 743

Myrk'-wood, *a forest in Hothbrodd's land,* 443, 452

Myrk'-wood, *a forest in Muspellsheim,* 231, 245

Myrk'-wood, *a forest in Nithuth's land,* 377, 392

Nab'-bi, *a dwarf,* 324–325, 338

Nagl'-far, *a ship,* 20–21, 36

Nāin, *a dwarf,* 11

Nal, *Laufey,* 246

Nāl'-i, *a dwarf,* 10–11

Nan'-na, *daughter of Nokkvi,* 326–327, 339

Nan'-na, *wife of Baldr,* 139

Nār, *a dwarf,* 11

Narf'-i, *Nor,* 33, 238–239, 246–247

Narf'-i, *son of Loki,* 114, 285

Nā'-strond, *Corpse-Strand,* 17, 34

Nep, *father of Nanna,* 139

Ner'-i, *a giant (?),* 431, 447

Nifl'-heim, *the world of the dead,* 27, 140, 602

Nifl'-hel, *land of the dead,* 108–109, 115, 289, 295

Nifl'-ungs, *the people of Gjuki (Nibelungs),* 602, 665, 669, 727, 729, 731, 738–741, 759, 780

Nīp'-ing, *a dwarf,* 11

Nith, *son of Jarl,* 311, 317, 591

Nith'-a-fjoll, *a mountain,* 5, 25, 33, 38

Nith"-a-ver-lir, *home of the dwarfs,* Nithaverlir

Nīth'-hogg, *a dragon,* 5, 19, 25, 34, 38, 129, 131, 141

Nith'-i, *a dwarf,* 11

Nith'-jung, *son of Jarl,* 311, 317

Nith'-uth, *king of the Njars,* 373, 377–396

Njāls'-sag-a, *the Saga of Njal,* 586

Njars, *the people of Nithuth,* 379–396

Njorth, *a Wane,* 30, 107, 115, 125, 133, 138–139, 151, 161–165, 189, 219, 229, 231, 241, 244–245, 257, 263–264, 341

Nō'-a-tūn, *home of Njorth,* 125, 138, 139, 165, 257, 264

Nokk'-vi, *father of Nanna,* 327, 339

Non, *a river,* 129

Nor (or **Norv'-i**), *father of Not,* 114, 285

Nōr'-i, *a dwarf,* Nori 10, 11, 831

Norn"-a-gests-thāttr', *the Story of Nornagest,* 496, 521, 539–540, 663–664, 860, 870

North'-ri, *a dwarf,* 11, 29

Not, *a river,* 129

Nǫt, *Night,* 91, 114, 285, 583

Nȳ'-i, *a dwarf,* 11

Nȳr, *a dwarf,* 11

Nȳ'-rath, *a dwarf,* 11

Nyt, *a river,* 128–129

Ō-din, *chief of the Gods,* xiv, xxix, 3–5, 13–39, 65–67, 77–79, 85–127, 133–148, 157–159, 165–166, 170, 175, 179, 185–193, 203–205, 209, 215–216, 219, 223–227, 241–246, 257, 261–263, 284, 287, 289–298, 313, 316, 333, 337–342, 346, 369, 398, 421, 433, 448–453, 469–473, 477, 482–487, 495, 517, 521–522, 525–527, 538–542, 561, 564–565,

571, 584–585, 589–591, 618, 646, 653, 659, 663, 701, 719, 737–741, 818, 830, 833–834

Odd'-rūn, *sister of Atli,* 637, 650, 667–669, 703, 707–720, 870, 873–874

Odd"-rūn-ar-gratr', *the Lament of Oddrun,* 190, 650, 669, 703, 707, 721, 737, 742, 782, 785, 870–874

Ofn'-ir, *a serpent,* 131, 135

Ofn'-ir, *Odin,* 141, 145

O'-in, *father of Andvari,* 527, 537

Ökk"-vin-kalf'-a, *daughter of Thrall,* 303, 315

Ō'-kōl-nir, *a volcano (?),* 17, 34

Ol'-mōth, *father of Isolf,* 329, 339

Ol'-rūn, *a swan-maiden,* 377–379, 391, 738

Ōm'-i, *Odin,* 135, 144

Ōn'-ar, *a dwarf,* 11

Ōr'-i, *a dwarf,* 12–13, 363, 372

Ork'-ning, *brother of Kostbera,* 669, 754–755, 778–780

Ormt, *a river,* 129

Orv'-and-il, *husband of Groa,* 849

Orv'-ar=Odd, *a warrior,* 339

Orv'-ar=Odds'-sag-a, *the Saga of Orvar-Odd,* 339–340

Orv'-a-sund, *a bay,* 437, 450

Ōsk'-i, *Odin,* 135, 144

Ō'-skōp-nir, *an island,* 549, 562

Ōs'-olf, *son of Olmoth,* 329

Ōth, *husband of Freyja,* 15, 31, 244, 333, 338, 342

Oth'-lings, *a mythical race,* 325–329, 338, 340

Ōth'-ror-ir, *a goblet,* 67, 77, 88, 90

Ōtr, *brother of Regin,* 524, 525, 528, 529, 537

Ōt'-tar, *a warrior,* 319, 325–329, 333–342, 830, 847

Ræv'-il, *a sea-king,* 533, 539

Rag'-nar Loth'-brōk, *a Danish king,* 539

Rand'-grīth, *a Valkyrie,* 131, 142

Rand'-vēr, *son of Jormunrek,* 650, 791, 799, 817

Rand'-vēr, *son of Rathbarth,* 329, 341

Ran'-i, *Odin,* 350, 351, 369

Rat'-a-tosk, *a squirrel,* 129, 141

Rāth'-barth, *a Russian king,* 329, 341

Rāth'-grīth, *a Valkyrie,* 131, 142

Rāths'-ey, *an island,* 175, 188

Rāth'-svith, *a dwarf,* 11, 29

Rat'-i, *a gimlet,* 67, 88

Reg'-in, *a dwarf,* 11, 29, 537

Reg'-in, *son of Hreithmar,* 502, 503, 517, 521–522, 525, 529–540, 545, 551–557, 561–563, 590, 834, 860–863, 867

Reg'-in-leif, *a Valkyrie,* 130, 131, 142

Reg"-ins-mǫl, *the Ballad of Regin,* 29, 167, 448, 453, 495, 517, 521, 524–536, 541, 561–564, 645–646, 669–671, 741, 799, 834, 843, 851, 857, 860–868, 871, 872

Reif'-nir, *a berserker,* 328–329

Rīg, *Heimdall (?),* 27, 297–317, 847

Rīgs'-thul-a, *the Song of Rig,* xxi, xxii, xxiv, 27, 138, 245, 297–301, 313, 317, 342, 646, 738, 830, 844–847

Rīn, *a river,* 129, 140

PRONUNCIATION INDEX 901

Rind, *mother of Vali*, 291, 296, 351, 369

Rin'-nand-i, *a river*, 129

Rist'-il, *daughter of Karl*, 307, 315

Rith'-il, *a sword*, 553, 563

Rog'-a-land, *Norway*, 423

Rog'-heim, *Home of Battle*, 419, 425

Rǫn, *wife of Ægir*, 411, 423, 450, 525, 537

Rosk'-va, *sister of Thjalfi*, 210

Roth'-uls-fjoll, *a mountain*, 419, 425

Roth'-uls-voll, *a field*, 422

Ruth, *a river*, 351, 369

Sæ'-far-i, *father of Ulf*, 324–325

Sæ'-hrim-nir, *a boar*, 127, 139

Sæk'-in, *a river*, 128–129

Sæ'-kon-ung, *father of Hildigun*, 327

Sæ'-morn, *a river*, 404–405, 422

Sæ'-reith, *wife of Hjorvarth*, 403, 421

Sæ'-var-stath, *an island*, 383, 394

Sāg'-a, *a Goddess*, 123, 138, 451

Sal'-gof-nir, *a cock*, 475, 484

Sāms'-ey, *an island*, 227, 243

Sann'-get-al, *Odin*, 133, 144

Sath, *Odin*, 133, 144

Sax'-i, *a southern king*, 699–702

Segg, *son of Karl*, 307, 315

Sess'-ryra-nir, *Freyja's hall*, 138, 263

Sev'-a-fjoll, *Sigrun's home*, 465–475, 482

Sif, *Thor's wife*, 137, 143, 182–183, 190, 197, 201, 205, 209, 212, 218–219, 234–235, 241–242, 246, 259, 264, 283

Sig'-ar, *a Danish king*, 448

Sig'-ar, *brother of Hogni*, 461, 480,

Sig'-ar, *father of Siggeir*, 679, 688

Sig'-ar, *Helgi's messenger*, 416–417, 422, 425

Sig'-ars-holm, *an island*, 407, 422

Sig'-ars-voll, *a battlefield*, 417, 422, 425, 433, 448

Sig'-fath-er, *Odin*, 21, 36, 133, 144, 237, 246

Sig-geir, *husband of Signy*, 441, 451, 679, 688, 856–857

Sig'-mund, *son of Sigurth*, 602, 633, 644–646, 679–681, 688–690

Sig'-mund, *son of Volsung*, 323, 337, 340, 398, 422, 433, 447–453, 459, 463–465, 477–481, 485–487, 490, 491–501, 517, 522, 531, 535, 539–540, 547, 561, 569, 583, 830, 834, 851–857

Sig'-nȳ, *sister of Sigmund*, 448, 451, 487, 688, 852–857

Sigr'-drif-a, *Brynhild*, 449, 498, 564–565, 571, 583, 864–867

Sigr"-drif-u-mǫl, *the Ballad of the Victory-Bringer*, 28, 142, 168, 448, 518, 521, 563–582, 587–589, 663–664, 671, 717–718, 843, 860–872

Sigr'-lin, *wife of Hjorvarth*, 403–407, 417, 421–422, 852

Sig'-rūn, *wife of Helgi*, 32, 398, 425, 437, 445, 449–450, 453, 461–484, 518, 829, 834, 851–856, 860

Sig'-trygg, *a king*, 326–327, 339

Sig'-tȳr, *Odin*, 733, 741

Sig'-urth, *son of Sigmund*, xx, xxiv, 29, 329, 340–341, 393, 397–398, 421–422, 447–453, 487, 493–522,

525, 531–566, 569, 571, 577, 583–591, 595,–606, 609, 611–639, 643–671, 675, 677, 681, 687–690, 693, 703, 711, 719, 737–741, 771, 779–782, 785–786, 791–795, 799–801, 809, 815, 830, 834, 849, 851–852, 857–878

Sig"-urth-ar-kvith'-a en Skam'-ma, *the Short Lay of Sigurth*, 621, 624–642

Sig'-urth Ring, *son of Randver*, 341

Sig'-yn, *wife of Loki*, 16–17, 33, 238–239, 246–247

Silf'-rin-topp, *a horse*, 129, 141

Sind'-ri, *a dwarf*, 17, 33

Sin'-fjot-li, *son of Sigmund*, 433, 439–441, 448, 450–453, 467, 482, 487, 491, 495, 852–857

Sin'-ir, *a horse*, 128–129, 141

Sin'-mor-a, *a giantess*, 359–361, 371–372

Sin'-rjōth, *wife of Hjorvarth*, 403, 421

Sīth, *a river*, 129

Sīth'-gran-i, *Odin*, 273, 284

Sīth'-hott, *Odin*, 133, 144

Sīth'-skegg, *Odin*, 133, 144

Skāf'-ith, *a dwarf*, 13

Skāld"-skap-ar-māl, *the Treatise on Poetics*, 141, 284, 285, 338, 421, 537, 799, 815, 830, 833, 862

Skat'-a-lund, *a forest*, 659, 664

Skath'-i, *a Goddess*, 125, 138, 165, 189, 219, 233–235, 239–246, 264, 331, 341

Skegg'-jold, *a Valkyrie*, 131, 142

Skeith'-brim-ir, *a horse*, 129, 141

Skek'-kil, *father of Skurhild*, 329

Skelf'-ir, *a king*, 338

Skilf'-ing, *Odin*, 135, 145, 338

Skilf'-ings, *descendants of Skelfir*, 325, 327, 338

Skin'-fax-i, *a horse*, 98–99, 113, 141

Skirf'-ir, *a dwarf*, 12, 13

Skirn'-ir, *Freyr's servant*, 147–167, 241, 840

Skirn"-is-mǫl, *the Ballad of Skirnir*, xxviii, 36, 115, 137, 143, 147, 150–166, 189, 212, 241–245, 249, 263, 285, 337, 341, 423, 538, 840–841, 844

Skīth'-blath-nir, *a ship*, 133, 143

Skjöld, *a Danish king*, 338

Skjold"-ung-a-sag'-a, *the Saga of the Skjoldungs*, 317

Skjold'-ungs, *descendants of Skjold*, 325–327, 338

Skog'-ul, *a Valkyrie*, 17, 131, 142

Skoll, *a wolf*, 34, 116, 131, 139, 142

Skor'-u-strond, *home of Varin*, 423

Skrȳm'-ir, *a giant*, 187–190, 239, 246–247

Skuld, *a Norn*, 12–13, 30

Skuld, *a Valkyrie*, 16–17

Skūr'-hild, *daughter of Skekkil*, 329

Slag'-fith, *brother of Volund*, 377–379, 391–392

Sleip'-nir, *Odin's horse*, 132–133, 141–143, 188, 243, 289, 295, 333, 342, 517, 575, 585

Slīth, *a river*, 17, 33, 129, 140

Smith, *son of Karl*, 307

Snæ'-fjoll, *a mountain*, 433, 448

Snæv'-ar, *son of Hogni*, 667–669, 739, 755, 778–780

Snör, *wife of Karl*, 305, 315

Snōt, *daughter of Karl*, 307, 315

Sogn, *a bay*, 442-443, 452

Sǫg'-u-nes, *a cape*, 441, 451

Sokk'-mim-ir, *a giant*, 135, 144

Sökk'-va-bekk, *Saga's dwelling*, 123, 138

Sōl, *Sun*, 114, 142

Sōl'-ar, *son of Hogni*, 667-669, 739, 755, 778-780

Sōl'-bjart, *father of Svipdag*, 367, 372

Sōl'-blind-i, *a dwarf*, 355, 370

Sōl'-fjoll, *a mountain*, 433, 448

Sōl'-heim-ar, *Hothbrodd's home*, 443

Sorl'-i, *son of Jonak*, 538, 650, 787, 791, 799-800, 809-818, 878-879

Spar'-ins-heith, *Sparin's Heath*, 443, 452

Spor'-vit-nir, *a horse*, 442-443

Sprak'-ki, *daughter of Karl*, 306-307, 315

Sprund, *daughter of Karl*, 306-307, 315

Stafns'-nes, *a cape*, 437, 449

Stark'-ath, *son of Granmar*, 463, 469, 481-483

Stor'-verk, *father of Starkath*, 482

Strond, *a river*, 129

Styr'-kleif-ar, *a battlefield*, 469, 482

Sun, *son of Jarl*, 311

Surt, *a giant*, 21, 34-36, 101, 111-113, 116, 166, 245, 359, 371, 549, 562

Suth'-ri, *a dwarf*, 11, 29

Sut'-tung, *a giant*, 66-67, 85, 88, 159, 168, 281, 284-285

Svaf'-nir, *a king*, 403-405, 421-422

Svaf'-nir, *a serpent*, 131, 141

Svaf'-nir, *Odin*, 135, 145

Svafr'-thor-in, *Mengloth's grandfather*, 355, 370

Sval'-in, *a shield*, 131, 142, 585

Svan, *father of Sæfari*, 324-325

Svan'-hild, *daughter of Sigurth*, 340, 499, 602, 637-639, 649-650, 667-669, 787, 791-795, 799-800, 807, 815-817, 859, 871, 878

Svan'-ni, *daughter of Karl*, 306-307, 315

Svār'-ang, *a giant*, 179, 190

Svar'-in, *a hill*, 439, 450, 463, 481

Svar'-ri, *daughter of Karl*, 306-307, 315

Svart"-alf-a-heim', *the world of the dark elves*, 27, 284

Svart'-hofth-i, *a magician*, 331

Svath"-il-far'-i, *a stallion*, 143, 243, 295, 333, 342

Svāv'-a, *daughter of Eylimi*, 32, 398, 407-409, 415-425, 461, 480, 495, 518, 852, 860

Svāv'-a, *wife of Sækonung*, 327

Svāv'-a-land, *Svafnir's country*, 405-407, 421-422

Svegg'-juth, *a horse*, 443, 452

Svein, *son of Jarl*, 308, 311, 317

Sver"-ris-sag'-a, *the Saga of Sverrir*, 862

Svip'-al, *Odin*, 133, 144

Svip'-dag, *son of Solbjart*, 345, 349, 351-370, 849

Svip"-dags-mǫl', *the Ballad of Svipdag*, xxi, 31, 90, 116, 242, 345,

348–368, 583, 651, 718, 848
Svip'-uth, *a horse*, 443, 452
Svith'-rir, *Odin*, 135, 144
Svith'-ur, *Odin*, 135, 144
Svi'-ur, *a dwarf*, 11
Svol, *a river*, 129
Svǫs'-uth, *father of Summer*, 103, 114
Sylg, *a river*, 129

Thakk'-rāth, *Nithuth's thrall*, 389, 396
Thegn, *son of Karl*, 307, 315
Thekk, *a dwarf*, 11
Thekk, *Odin*, 133, 144
Thīr, *wife of Thrall*, 303, 314
Thith"-reks-sag'-a, *the Saga of Theoderich*, 391, 394–396, 537, 603, 645, 784, 850
Thjalf'-i, *Thor's servant*, 181, 188–190, 210, 213
Thjaz'-i, *a giant*, 125, 138, 177, 189, 235, 241, 245, 263, 331, 341
Thjōth'-mar, *father of Thjothrek*, 697
Thjōth'-num-a, *a river*, 129
Thjōth'-rek, *Theoderich*, 675, 687, 693, 697–701, 780, 873
Thjōth'-rör-ir, *a dwarf*, Thjothrorir
Thjōth'-var-a, *Mengloth's handmaid*, 363
Thjōth'-vit-nir, *Skoll*, 127, 139
Thol, *a river*, 129
Tholl'-ey, *an island*, 413, 423
Thōr, *a God*, xiv, 15, 31, 36–37, 116, 123, 129, 137–140, 143, 147, 169–170, 173–194, 199, 203, 209–215, 219, 237–241, 246–250, 255–259, 263–284, 323, 341, 451, 585, 824, 841–844, 849
Thōr'-a, *daughter of Hokon*, 615, 619, 679, 688
Thōr'-a, *wife of Dag*, 327, 688
Thōr'-in, *a dwarf*, 11
Thōr'-ir, *follower of Hrolf*, 329, 339
Thōrs'-nes, *a cape*, 441, 451
Thrǣll, *son of Rig*, 303, 314
Thrāin, *a dwarf*, 11
Thrith'-i, *Odin*, 133, 144
Thrōr, *a dwarf*, 11
Thror, *Odin*, 135, 144
Thrūth, *a Valkyrie*, 131, 142
Thrūth, *daughter of Thor*, 283
Thrūth'-gel-mir, *a giant*, 105, 114, 115
Thrūth'-heim, *Thor's home*, 123, 137
Thrym, *a giant*,
Thrym'-gjol, *a gate*, 355, 370
Thrym'-heim, *Thjazi's home*, 125, 138
Thryms'-kvith-a, *the Lay of Thrym*, xx, xxviii, 31, 116, 147, 187–189, 210, 243–249, 252–262, 284, 287, 295, 316, 422, 717, 840, 843–845
Thund, *a river*, 79, 91, 135, 144
Thund, *Odin*, 127, 139
Thuth, *Odin*, 133, 144
Thyn, *a river*, 129
Tind, *a berserker*, 329
Tot"-rug-hyp'-ja, *daughter of Thrall*, 303, 314
Tron"-u-bein'-a, *daughter of Thrall*, 303, 314

PRONUNCIATION INDEX

Tron'-u-eyr, *Crane-Strand*, 437, 449

Tveg'-gi, *Odin*, 23, 37

Tȳr, *a God*, 34, 193, 197–199, 205, 209–219, 231, 241, 244–245, 341, 571, 584, 824

Tyrf'-ing, *a berserker*, 329

Ulf, *follower of Hrolf*, 329

Ulf, *son of Sæfari*, 325

Ulf'-dal-ir, *Volund's home*, 377–381, 391

Ulf'-rūn, *mother of Heimdall*, 331

Ulf'-sjār, *a lake*, 377, 391, 392

Ull, *a God*, 123, 133, 137, 143, 341, 733, 741

Un"-a-vāg'-ar, *a harbor*, 439, 450

Un'-i, *a dwarf*, 362–363

Urth, *a Norn*, 13, 30, 69, 88, 140, 351, 367, 369, 372

Ut'-garth-a=Lok'-i, *a giant*, 187, 190

Uth, *daughter of Ægir*, 469, 483, 701

Uth, *Odin*, 133, 144

Vaf'-thrūth-nir, *a giant*, 93, 97–116, 838

Vaf"-thrūth-nis-mǫl, *the Ballad of Vafthruthnir*, 28, 36, 93, 96–112, 141–142, 167, 190, 209, 212, 241, 263, 285, 371–372, 537, 540, 562, 838–839, 844

Vak, *Odin*, 135, 145

Vāl'-a-skjolf, *Odin's home*, 123, 137

Val'-bjorg, *Grimhild's land*, 683, 691

Vald'-ar, *a Danish king*, 679, 689

Val'-fath-er, *Odin*, 9, 15, 27, 31, 133, 144

Val'-grind, *a gate*, 126, 127, 139

Val'-hall, *Odin's hall*, 17, 27, 32, 37, 115, 125–127, 138–140, 323, 338, 342, 471, 483, 651, 719–721, 737, 875

Vāl'-i, *a God*, 111, 116, 291, 296, 331, 341, 369, 824

Vāl'-i, *son of Loki*, 33, 239, 246, 247

Val'-land, *Slaughter-Land*, 179, 189, 191, 377, 391–392, 657, 663

Val'-tam, *father of Vegtam*, 291, 295

Vam, *a river*, 245

Van'-a-heim, *home of the Wanes*, 27, 284

Vand'-ils-vē, *a shrine*, 471, 483

Van'-ir, *the Wanes*, 148, 216, 267, 583, 824, 835

Var, *a dwarf*, 363

Var'-in, *a Norwegian king (?)*, 411, 423, 439, 451

Var'-ins-fjord, *a bay*, 437, 450

Vār'-kald, *father of Vindkald*, 355, 370

Vath'-gel-mir, *a river*, 537

Vē, *brother of Odin*, 28, 37, 227, 244, 824

Veg'-dras-il, *a dwarf*, 363

Veg'-svin, *a river*, 129

Veg'-tara, *Odin*, Vegtara

Veg"-tams-kvith'-a, *the Lay of Vegtam*, 287, 845

Vel"-ents-sag'-a, *the Saga of Velent*, 850

Ver'-a-tȳr, *Odin*, 123, 137

Ver'-land, *Land of Men*, 184–185, 191

Verth'-and-i, *a Norn*, 13, 30

Vestr'-i, *a dwarf,* 10–11, 29

Vestr'-sal-ir, *Rind's home,* 291, 296

Vethr'-fol-nir, *a hawk,* 141

Vē'-ur, *Thor,* 199, 201–203, 210

Vif, *daughter of Karl,* 307, 315

Vig'-blær, *Helgi's horse,* 471, 483

Vig'-dal-ir, *Battle-Dale,* 471, 483

Vigg, *a dwarf,* 11

Vīg'-rīth, *a field,* 101, 113, 562

Vil'-i, *brother of Odin,* 10, 28–30, 37, 227, 244, 768, 824

Vil'-meith, *a dwarf (?),* 331, 341

Vil'-mund, *lover of Borgny,* 707–709, 717–718, 874

Vin, *a river,* 52, 129

Vin'-bjorg, *Grimhild's land,* 683, 691

Vind'-alf, *a dwarf,* 11, 29

Vind'-heim, *Wind-Home,* 23, 37

Vind'-kald, *Svipdag,* 355, 370

Vind'-ljōn-i, *Vindsval,* 114

Vind'-sval, *father of Winter,* 103, 114

Ving'-i, *Atli's messenger,* 667–669, 737, 748–749, 755–757, 775, 779–780

Ving'-nir, *Thor,* 111, 116, 191, 263

Ving'-skorn-ir, *a horse,* 559, 564

Ving'-thōr, *Thor,* xxviii, 190, 253, 263, 273, 284

Vin'-ǫ, *a river,* 129

Virf'-ir, *a dwarf,* 12–13

Vit, *a dwarf,* 11, 628

Vith, *a river,* 129

Vīth'-ar, *a God,* 21, 36, 37, 111, 116, 127, 139, 219, 223, 241, 242, 245, 246, 341, 824

Vith'-ga, *son of Volund,* 396

Vith'-i, *Fithar's land,* 127, 139

Vith'-of-nir, *a cock,* 359, 361, 371–372

Vith'-olf, *a dwarf (?),* 331, 341

Vith'-rir, *Odin,* 227, 244, 433, 448

Vith'-ur, *Odin,* 135, 144

Vǫf'-uth, *Odin,* 135, 145

Vols'-ung, *father of Sigmund,* 329, 337, 340, 398, 448, 450–451, 455, 459, 465, 479, 481, 491, 495–497, 533, 539, 625–627, 643, 851–857

Vols"-ung-a-sag'-a, *the Saga of the Volsungs,* 337, 340, 422, 449–451, 487–488, 495–496, 517–521, 538–541, 561–564, 584–587, 590, 601–603, 617–619, 644–647, 650–651, 669, 687–689, 720, 738–739, 777–787, 799–801, 816–818, 852, 856–857, 860–868, 872–874, 877–879

Vols'-ungs, *descendants of Volsung,* 427, 443, 447, 453, 459, 465–467, 479, 646, 851–853, 856–857, 860

Völ'-und, *a smith,* 373–374

Völ"-und-ar-kvith'-a, *the Lay of Volund,* 373, 376–390, 849

Vol"-u-spǫ', *the Wise-Woman's Prophecy,* xx, xxix, 3–4, 8–26, 38, 88–90, 113–116, 138–143, 165–167, 189–191, 209–211, 241–247, 263–264, 284, 287, 295–298, 313, 319, 331, 337–342, 369–372, 391, 422, 447–482, 537–538, 562, 584–585, 618, 663, 777, 800, 835–838, 843–845, 848

Vǫn, *a river,* 129, 693

Vond, *a river,* 129

Vǫr, *a Goddess,* 259, 265

Y'-dal-ir, *Ull's home,* 123, 137

Ygg, *Odin,* 99, 113, 118, 135, 144, 197, 209, 557, 564

Ygg'-dras-il, *the world-ash,* 13, 21, 27, 30–31, 34–35, 38, 90, 116, 129, 131–133, 140–143, 371, 835, 895–896

Ylf'-ings, *a Danish race,* 325, 338, 427, 433, 439, 443, 447, 450–453, 459–463, 475, 479–480, 829–830, 833

Ylg, *a river,* 129

Ym'-ir, *a giant,* 3, 9, 28–29, 34, 103–105, 114–115, 131, 142–143, 331, 341, 371, 824

Yng (or Yng'-vi), *son of Halfdan the Old,* 338, 445, 453, 531, 539

Yng"-ling-a-sag'-a, *the Saga of the Ynglings,* 244

Yng'-lings, *descendants of Yng,* 327, 338, 427, 453, 829, 830

Yng'-vi, *a dwarf,* 13

Yng'-vi, *son of Hring,* 453

Yng'-vi, *Yng,* 12, 147, 443, 522, 824, 829–834

Ys'-ja, *daughter of Thræll,* 302, 303, 314

www.ingramcontent.com/pod-product-compliance
Lightning Source LLC
Chambersburg PA
CBHW030251100526
44590CB00012B/361